D1627466

A History of
INTERIOR DESIGN

A History of INTERIOR DESIGN

John Pile

 Laurence King

Contents

Published in 2000 by
Laurence King Publishing
an imprint of
Calmann & King Ltd
71 Great Russell Street
London WC1B 3BN
Tel: + 44 20 7831 6351
Fax: +44 20 7831 8356
email: enquiries@calmann-king.co.uk
www.laurence-king.com

Copyright © 2000
Calmann & King Ltd

A catalogue record for this book is available from the British Library.

ISBN 1 85669 200 0

Design by Thomas Manss
& Company and
Richard Foenander
Picture research by
Susan Bolsom
Printed in Hong Kong

Frontispiece: Gentile
Mansueti, *The Miraculous
Healing of the Daughter of
Ser Benvegnudo of San
Polo, c. 1502-6.*

Contents

Preface

In the modern world, human life experience is largely played out in interior spaces. We may love the out-of-doors for the sense of open air and sky, for the escape it offers from life inside enclosure, but the very joy of being outside reflects the reality that so much of life is spent inside. Most of the time, most of us live inside a house, a flat, or a room. We sleep, eat, cook, bathe, and spend free time "at home"—that is, inside. Work takes place in an office, a factory, a specialized work space such as a hospital, concert hall, museum, school, or college . . . the list is endless. Agriculture still involves work in the open air, but even the modern farmer is likely to spend time inside the cab of a tractor, truck, or other piece of agricultural machinery and to go home to a house to eat, watch television, and sleep. Modern work activities such as driving a bus or truck, piloting an airplane, or being a member of the crew of a submarine, aircraft carrier, or spacecraft lead to a work life that takes place within a vehicle, a cockpit, or some other enclosure.

There have been human beings on earth, scientists now estimate, for about 1.7 million years. The detailed record of events and developments that we call "history" stretches back for only about 6000 or 7000 years. Before the beginning of history we have only myths, legends, and guesswork to tell us what events occurred in what order. There have been many speculations about when and where people first learned to use shelters and what the earliest habitations were like. Early shelters existed to provide the interior spaces that offered comfort to their inhabitants. Those interior spaces influenced the lives of their occupants in significant ways.

Interior design, whether professional or not, is an aspect of life that is impossible to escape. In addition to the domain of one's own home, the interiors of the homes of friends and relatives, of offices, stores, restaurants, schools, hospitals, transport vehicles, and every other sort of place where modern life is lived, make up the modern world as we know it. It is obvious that people in bygone times had a different life experience in large measure because they occupied interiors that were different from those that are now commonplace. To consider for a moment the life of a medieval serf living in a farm dwelling, a knight in a castle, a monk in a monastery, the lord and lady in an eighteenth-century mansion, a Victorian family in a city row house brings to mind a life pattern based on the spaces created in such past times. Social,

economic, and political realities also influenced life in the past and these forces have had major impact on built environments. Buildings and their interiors are planned to serve the purposes and styles of the times of their origins, but they exert their influence on the activities and lives that they house as long as they continue in use.

The study of interior design, its development and change through history is a useful way both to explore the past and to make sense of the spaces in which modern life is lived. Professional interior designers are expected to study design history, to know the practices of the past in terms of "styles," and to know the names and the nature of the contributions of those individuals who generated the most interesting and influential approaches to design.

Since the interiors that one might wish to visit are scattered across the globe and often difficult to access, it becomes necessary to turn to photographs, descriptions, and, increasingly, film, television, and the internet to gain an insight into the history of humanly constructed interior space. The sheer number of books on the subject and the variety of emphasis can make a coherent history of interior design difficult to extract and understand.

The purpose of this book is to deliver in one volume of reasonable size a basic survey of 6000 years of personal and public space. Development of such a book is inevitably beset by a number of complications. Interiors do not exist in isolation in the way that a painting or a sculpture does, but within some kind of shell—a hut, a building, even a ship or airplane. They are also crammed with a great range of objects and artifacts: furniture, lighting, textiles, sometimes art. This means that interior design is a field with unclear boundaries, overlapping as it does the realms of construction, architecture, art, the crafts, the technologies of heating, cooling, ventilation, lighting, water and drainage equipment, and what is now called "product design," in the forms of appliances, plumbing fixtures, and other kinds of equipment. The number of interiors that have been created over time, even the number currently in existence, is staggering. The author of one compact history is thus faced with a vast range of choices about what to include and what to exclude. No two writers in this field will make the same choices and the decisions made in writing this book are those of the writer and are based on the following assumptions:

1. Interiors are an integral part of the structures

that contain them—in most cases, buildings. This means that interior design is inextricably linked to architecture and can only be studied within an architectural context.

2. Owing to the vast geographical spread of human design activity, coverage is necessarily limited to a restricted part of the global totality. The choice made here is to examine Western, that is European and American, design practice and its prehistoric origins. This is not because non-Western work is in any way inferior or less interesting than Western achievement, but rather because the aim in writing history is to discover threads of connectedness that can be woven into an intelligible narrative. In this book, we follow the thread that runs through time from ancient Egypt, Greece, and Rome, through medieval and Renaissance Europe, the eighteenth and nineteenth centuries, and eventually culminates in the twentieth and twenty-first centuries. Coverage of the nineteenth and twentieth centuries is given emphasis to reflect the greater interest felt in the developments of recent times.

3. Making a selection of interiors for discussion and illustration requires the acceptance of certain criteria. The examples chosen in this book are either aesthetically outstanding in their own right or epitomize a certain time and place in history. Some examples are so well-known that they require inclusion (the Pantheon in Rome and the cathedral of Chartres, for example); other examples are chosen because they are unusually well preserved or because they illustrate the work of a particularly interesting or important designer. Along with discussion of well-known "important" examples, there is also attention to the "everyday," vernacular design of historic periods.

4. Enclosed spaces such as ruins, ancient sites, and open courtyards are given due consideration even though the sky may be their only ceiling and they are therefore not strictly interiors.

5. Related fields such as furniture, textiles, lighting, and product design are discussed since they have major impact on the history of interior design. However, demands on space mean that this coverage is limited to edited highlights.

6. Quotations from primary sources are included in "Insights" boxes within a number of chapters. These offer some sense of the contemporary view of the work of particular periods.

The reader is encouraged to seek further discussion of periods, examples, personages, and related subjects to whatever extent curiosity and interest allow. The bibliography provided will serve as a guide to books that offer extended coverage of innumerable aspects of interior design.

Best of all, of course, is visiting the spaces that are of interest. While time and expense will limit such visits for most readers, seeing examples that are closer to hand will fill out the limits of any book and offer a richer experience of the realities of interior space.

Acknowledgments

Many people have contributed to the development and production of this book. The following list names those who have had a particularly important role. To all of them I wish to extend my thanks for their efforts and patience.

For acceptance of the manuscript and decision to publish: Lee Ripley Greenfield, Editorial Director at Calmann & King Ltd and Amanda Miller, Executive Editor at John Wiley & Sons, Inc. For their diligent and skillful efforts at Calmann & King Ltd: Damian Thompson, Senior Developmental Editor; Nell Webb, Senior Editor; Susan Bolsom, Picture Manager; Richard Foenander, Designer; Kim Richardson, Copyeditor; and Felicity Awdry, Production Manager. For additional editorial work: Lydia Darbyshire, Jan Graffius, and Sharon Goldstein. For advice and commentary: Linda Keene at the Art School, Art Institute of Chicago.

1 Prehistory to Early Civilizations

Living in the modern, technologically advanced world, we take it for granted that a major portion of our time is spent inside, or "indoors." We live in houses or apartments, we work in offices, shops, or factories, we study in schools and colleges, we eat in restaurants, we stay in hotels, and we travel inside automobiles, buses, trains, ships, and airplanes. To be outside is most often a temporary situation while traveling from one inside space to another. Human beings differ from other living creatures in this acceptance of inside space as the most usual environment for living.

Prehistoric Interiors

There have been human beings on earth for about 1.7 million years. The detailed record of events and developments that we call "history" stretches back for only about six or seven thousand years. Before the beginning of history we have only myths, legends, and guesswork to tell us what events occurred and in what order. Thus the questions of when and where people first learned to use shelters, and what the earliest shelters were like, have been the subject of much speculation.

Guesswork is aided in some measure by information that comes from two lines of inquiry. These deal with, on one hand, prehistoric remains of various kinds known to archeologists and, on the other hand, with the current or recent practices of the "primitive" peoples usually studied by anthropologists. Prehistoric materials are physical objects, artifacts, or structures, that date from times before

the beginning of the recorded history of the regions where they exist. The term "primitive," as used here, does not signify simple, crude, or inferior, but refers to peoples, cultures, or civilizations untouched by the modern technological world as it has developed during the few thousands of years for which we have detailed history.

Archeological Evidence

The First Shelters

It is reasonable to assume that the first shelters were either found—caves for example—or were made with materials that were easy to work with bare hands or with very simple tools. Although the term "cave men" is often used to describe early human beings, and while there is certainly evidence that ancient people made use of caves, it is unlikely that caves were the most widely used of early human living places. Caves exist only in certain places and their number is limited, nor are they particularly comfortable or attractive places to live. While the famous cave paintings at Chauvet (**fig. 1.1**), Lascaux, and Altamira clearly prove that early peoples used these caves, there is no certainty that they were dwelling places. Perhaps they were emergency shelters, places for special rites or ceremonies, or they may have been used for the works of art that we admire because they preserved them from the weather.

Constructed shelters from prehistory have survived only where they were made from durable materials. The most available and easy to work

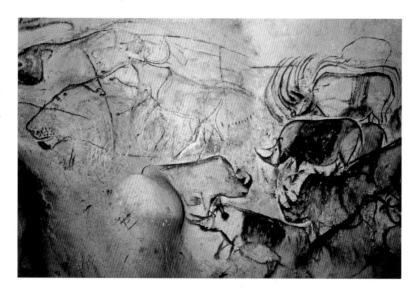

1.1 "Lion Panel," Chauvet cave, Ardèche, France. 15,000–10,000 B.C.E.

Evidence of human occupancy of caves comes from paintings that were made with only fire light as illumination. The intention of the paintings was probably not to ornament or decorate the natural spaces of the caves, but rather to provide images that might grant mystical power over hunted animals. To the modern viewer, the paintings have the effect of making the natural caves into spaces under some degree of human control.

1.2 (opposite) Paintings of Anubis, Tomb of Pa-schedu, Thebes, c. 1500 B.C.E.

Images of Anubis, the jackal-headed god of the dead, stand guard on simulated doors on either side of the passage leading to the inner chamber where the sarcophagus stood. The ceiling is covered with hieroglyphic inscriptions. While the intentions are mystical, the form and color generate spaces with richly decorative character typical of ancient Egyptian art.

materials—twigs and branches, leaves, rush and similar plant materials, and animal materials such as skins or hides—are all short-lived, subject to decay and disappearance within relatively brief time spans. Inorganic materials such as mud or (in cold climates) snow have limited lasting qualities, while stone, although very durable, is so difficult to work as to have very limited possibilities for shelter building. These realities mean that the materials surviving from prehistoric times are largely small objects of stone such as arrowheads and spear points, or large arrangements of stones set up in patterns or assembled into structures.

Dolmens and Barrows

The arrangements of stones (called ALIGNMENTS) and the DOLMENS of Brittany and other European locations are thoughtfully designed structures dating from prehistoric times. Most speculations assume that the larger sites, such as Stonehenge on Salisbury Plain in Britain, were used for ceremonies or rituals connected with observation of astronomical movements; dolmens are more often linked to burial rites. The arrangement of a large stone placed on top of two or three upright stones that makes up the many dolmens seems to have created the inner chamber of a tomb that took the form of an artificial hill. Where the earth has eroded away, the stone dolmen remains. Where the earth is still in place, it forms the kind of tomb called a BARROW in England. It is possible to go into the interior chambers of some of these surviving tombs. They are dark, mysterious, and

often impressive, if only for their evocation of unimaginably ancient origins. In some of these structures, it is possible to see carved or incised patterns cut into the stones with patterns of beauty, although their meanings are unknown.

Estimating dates for prehistoric sites was a matter of guesswork until the fairly recent development of the technique of radio-carbon dating in which measurements of the radioactivity of organic materials (such as bones or shells) gives a measure of their age. Stonehenge (**fig. 1.3**) is now dated with some confidence at about 2750–1500 B.C.E. All such structures date from the era now designated as the stone age in reference to the fact that the most advanced technologies of those times involved the working of stone as the best, most lasting, and most effective of available materials. The stone age is divided into the paleolithic period ("old stone age," extending to *c.* 5000 B.C.E.) and the neolithic period ("new stone age," extending to *c.* 1000 B.C.E.). The famous cave paintings are paleolithic; the prehistoric stone structures known to us date from the neolithic period.

It is virtually certain that the lack of houses surviving from these times can be explained by the use of less lasting materials, but that can in turn be explained in part by the reality that such ancient human life patterns were generally migratory or at least unattached to fixed locations. Early human life depended on water sources, hunting, and food gathering for sustenance and therefore required populations to move in pursuit of game and other food supply. Whatever shelter was used needed to

1.3 Stonehenge, Salisbury, England, *c.* 2750–1500 B.C.E.

Huge stones were carefully placed to create interior spaces with a strong aesthetic impact, whether they were originally open to the sky (as now) or roofed with materials that have since disappeared. The purpose seems to have been connected with rituals relating to the movements of the sun, moon, and stars. The circular form is characteristic of many ancient human constructions.

be easily portable and so made of light materials—wood sticks, leaves, and rush rather than stone. Ease of working and mobility worked together to favor shelter of modest scale, light materials, and easy mobility.

Evidence from Tribal Cultures

The oldest known traces of built human shelter found at Terra Amata in southern France are believed to be 400,000 years old, but only the most minimal remains suggest the form of these huts made from tree branches. Although there are few ancient relics to support assumptions about the nature of the earliest built structures, there is evidence to be found by turning to the other source of clues to early human shelter, the practices of "primitive" societies. Although now in retreat as modern societies press in upon them, "primitive" peoples survive in many inaccessible geographical regions and many others were extant as recently as one or two centuries ago. "Primitive" societies are characterized by a powerful conservatism, a devotion to traditional ways (often reinforced by a system of taboos that discourage change), and a mistrust of the concept of "progress" that dominates modern "developed" societies. As a result, "primitive" ways can be regarded as exemplifying more ancient ways—ways that can be traced back to the stone age. Most "primitive" societies depend on hunting, fishing, and food gathering for sustenance. They are therefore generally to some degree migratory and must build shelter that is readily portable.

Peoples in tribal Africa, in the islands of the Pacific, in the Arctic, and in the North and South American continents before the coming of Europeans are now or were recently living in ways that had not changed in many generations. Villages in tropical Africa, settlements in the Sahara and Mongolian deserts, native American (American Indian), Inuit (Eskimo), and Australian aborigine communities are all "primitive" living systems that provide examples of shelter types that can be assumed to be evidence of how human shelter may have developed.

In his 1876 book *The Habitations of Man in All Ages*, the French architectural theorist and historian Eugène-Emmanuel Viollet-le-Duc (1814–79) tried to show how shelter making began. In an illustration titled "The First House" (**fig. 1.4**) he shows us a "primitive" group of people building a structure made up of tree branches tied together at the top, with enclosing surfaces being built up by weaving more flexible twigs and branches through the main structure. This is clearly an early form of shelter of the kind that appears in many "primitive" cultures—a WIGWAM, or if covered with skins, a tepee. It might receive an exterior plastering with mud or, in the Arctic, a similar structure may be built up of blocks of snow in the dome-like form we call an igloo. In other locations where trees and branches are scarce, a similar form may be built of mud brick with a topping like a hat of straw or thatch.

Many such "primitive" shelters share certain characteristics. They are generally quite small and are almost invariably round. The small size reflects

1.4 (*far left*) Viollet-le-Duc, "The First House" from *The Habitations of Man in all Ages*, 1876.

The author has imagined a group of ancient people building an enclosure or hut from the available materials in their forest habitat. Such a structure might have been covered with leaves, skins, or even a plaster of mud.

1.5 (*left*) William Henry Jackson, photograph of a Bannock family camped near Medice Lodge Creek, Idaho, 1871.

The native American tepee was a round, portable structure with a frame of wooden poles and a covering of skin. Its interior was simply the inside of its structure without added treatment or furniture.

1.6 An engraving of a Mongolian yurt.

The yurt was a portable structure with an enclosing wall of lattice strips supporting a roof structure of poles. The exterior was covered with skins or mats. Inside, boxes to hold possessions, rugs, and stools created spaces with considerable aesthetic character.

1.7 Plan and sectional elevation of a Matakam homestead or tribal village in the Cameroon, Africa.

The circular form of the mud or stone hut creates a room, and several similar structures are grouped together to make a house complex, including work spaces (kitchens) and food storage areas, that would be occupied by an extended family and their animals. The walls are built up to head-height while a hat-like roof of straw or thatch completes the enclosure. The simple interiors held storage containers and sleeping pads on the dirt floors.

the limited availability of materials and the need to conserve effort, while the round form can be explained as a reflection of several realities that reinforce one another. The forms of nature are rarely straight-lined and square-cornered. Observation of trees and rocks, of the shelters built by birds and insects, would suggest circular forms; in the materials available the making of square corners might be difficult and create weak points in a fragile structure. A circle is also the geometric figure that will enclose most area with least perimeter, a concept that might not be understood in theoretical terms but could still be grasped intuitively in the process of building.

The TEPEE (**fig. 1.5**) of the American plains had a frame of long poles tied together at the top. Its outer walls were skins arranged to permit a flap doorway and a top flap that could be adjusted to control air circulation, allow penetration of daylight, and act as a smoke outlet. The whole tepee was easy to take down, pack, and transport when the migratory hunting users needed to follow the herds that were their food supply. The YURT (**fig. 1.6**) or GER of the Buryar peoples of Mongolia uses a vertical wall frame of lattice strips that collapse for transport but are expanded (like a modern elevator gate) and tied to form a circle. Willow strips form a roof structure and layers of felt are applied to form the wall and roof enclosure. The portable yurt, still in use, is an interesting example of a design developed to fit a particular way of life in a particular geographical location.

The round, portable structures built by migratory peoples generally stand alone; each house is a single unit, usually enclosing a single space. More complex houses of several rooms appear in villages in locations where climate, water, and food sources were sufficiently consistent to make constant relocation unnecessary. In the Cameroon in Africa, there are villages of multiroom houses where each room is actually a separate round hut with a special

function (living space, kitchen, store room, or stable, for example), with covered doorway links between related hut-rooms. Walls are constructed of mud, with roofs of thatch resting like hats on the walls (**fig. 1.7**).

Other "primitive" house types are not round. It is probably the use of strip materials, wood poles, or branches that suggests straight-line walls and so leads to more or less rectangular box forms (**figs. 1.8 and 1.9**). The A-frame form of the Dawi ceremonial chief's house and the dwellings of the people of New Guinea, packed mud houses in Yemen, Pueblo building in the American southwest, some wigwams (known to us from drawings made by early European settlers), and many house types built by South American natives have rectangular plans. In Apulia in southern Italy, an ancient house type still in regular use is built of dry field stones to form a roughly square room. This is topped by a round dome built by laying rings of stone in gradually diminishing circles until a single stone can cover the topmost opening. Such TRULLI houses have been built for thousands of years in the region.

Other types of "primitive" house forms are determined in part by the powerful environmental realities of topography, weather, availability of materials, and particularly climate. The snow-built igloo is well known but the underground houses of

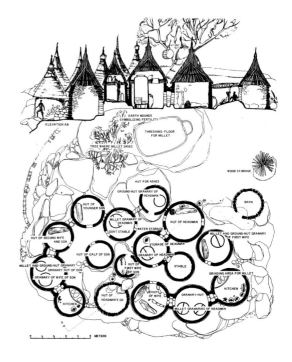

the Matmata in the Sahara are less familiar. A Matmata house is made up of a central court, a deep open-topped pit dug into the desert which gives access to surrounding rooms that are totally underground. A long, sloping entrance tunnel gives access to the court. This underground scheme requires no added material and provides insulation against desert heat by day and extreme cold at night.

Whether round or rectangular, on the surface of the earth, raised up on posts, or dug into the ground, it is the interior space of such houses that is their reason for existence. Such interiors are not "designed" with the sophistication of concept that we associate with modern interior design; the interior is simply a hollow space created by the technique of building the outside. Into the inside of all such houses must go the equipment used in daily life—cooking and eating utensils, weapons, stored clothing, blankets, and whatever there may be in the way of furniture. Tables and chairs are rarely used. Most "primitive" peoples sit on the ground and use the earth surface as the only table. Sleeping arrangements use portable materials laid on the ground rather than on a constructed bedstead. Rudimentary furniture appears in some "primitive" house types—shelf-like platforms or benches constructed as part of the built structure of mud huts, underground dug chambers, and snow-built igloos. Storage devices, bags, baskets, and, where they have been developed, pottery bowls, pots, and jugs are the most ubiquitous of artifacts.

Pattern and Design

The technique of weaving is an ancient invention that has appeared in many locations, making possible baskets, blankets, and rugs (and, of course, clothing) of a manufactured membrane as an alternative to animal skins. The weaving of fibers that are of varied colors either from natural sources or through dying leads to the discovery that patterns too can be woven. Such simple patterns as stripes and checks lead to the invention of more complex geometric patterns that appear in basketry, pottery, and woven blankets and rugs. The human urge

toward the introduction of designed pattern is in clear contrast to the hives and nests made by other creatures where pattern only appears (as in the webs of spiders) where it is a structural or other functional necessity. Painted decorative elements appear as fired pottery comes into use, with both geometric pattern and more or less representational imagery.

The patterns and images that enliven clothing, blankets, baskets, pots, and other objects of the interiors of these shelters allow them to be compared with more modern interiors where rugs, wall treatments, furniture, and other objects are the elements that make an interior space a designed entity. In "primitive" practice, pattern and imagery are rarely strictly ornamental, however they may appear to modern viewers. There are purposeful meanings in color, pattern, and design that serve to designate identity within a society, tribal loyalties, religious or mythic references, or magical significance. The designs of an African woven cloth (**fig. 1.10**) or a Navajo blanket, for example, follow customs that make the visible designs significant in reinforcing tribal traditions and taboos. Entering a house where a few utilitarian objects each offers some visible expression of a particular way of life confronts the occupant with reassurances that offers comfort and a kind of aesthetic experience. To the modern viewer, even if the significance is unknown, the aesthetic value can remain powerful.

1.8 (above left) John Webber, engraving of the interior of a house in Nootka Sound, Canada.

A structure of wooden logs creates an enclosure in which a fire generates heat. Fish are hung to dry, while blankets and mats serve as both clothing and minimal furnishings. Totem-like carvings have both mystical and aesthetic value.

1.9 (above right) The interior of a traditional house in Fiji.

A rectangular space is created by a wooden frame, while woven materials cover the floor and wall surfaces. Although there is no furniture, the patterns and colors of the floor mats and wall hangings create an interior of considerable complexity and richness.

1.10 Kente cloth, West Africa, c. 1975.

This African weaving uses bright colors in contrasting bands. The weaving is done in narrow strips that are sewn together to make wider areas for use in robes, blankets, or hangings.

The First Permanent Settlements

The key inventions or discoveries on which civilization is built are the controlled use of fire, the invention of language, and the development of agriculture. Of these three it is agriculture—fixed-base agriculture as it is often called—that has most directly influenced the design of built shelter. As long as food supply was dependent on hunting and gathering of growing plant products, the human population was forced to travel to locations where food was available and remain within those limited geographical regions. Human population, like the populations of other animal species, was controlled by the availability of food and so remained, by modern standards, very small. The discovery that it was possible to plant crops and harvest a larger and more reliable food supply was the basis for a chain of developments. Once crops are planted, it is necessary to remain close by to harvest the results. When staying in one place, it is no longer necessary to use only portable housing so that more lasting house types can be developed. Further improvement in food supply also makes the growth of population possible.

With more people and with techniques for building more lasting structures, villages and towns become more permanent settlements. The making of necessities (clothing, utensils, weapons) becomes more specialized with systems of barter and trade emerging to make it possible for a farmer, a shepherd, or a fisherman to make exchanges with a weaver, a potter, or a builder to the benefit of both. Around 4000 B.C.E., larger towns—even cities— began to appear, and, with the resulting complexities, systems for recording numbers and language were invented. It is the invention of writing that underlies the emergence of history, "recorded history" as it is called—the set of records of specific events, names, and dates that make it possible to say what happened in past times with a considerable degree of certainty. With food and shelter adequately assured, human energies over and above the needs of subsistence make possible the development of increasingly complex inventions and the arts.

All of these developments occurred at different rates in different places and all took thousands of years. The two areas where early western civilization first developed to high levels of complexity are the Nile valley of Egypt and the region in the Near East between the Tigris and Euphrates rivers called Mesopotamia.

Mesopotamia: Sumeria

The beginnings of a settled Sumerian civilization based on agriculture and making use of irrigation can be dated around 3500 B.C.E. when a system of picture writing came into use. Surviving traces of this and other subsequent societies in the Mesopotamian region include pottery, clay tablets (**fig. 1.11**), various other artifacts, and traces of buildings and cities. Unfortunately for the study of interior design, the available building materials were limited, with sun-baked MUD BRICK the primary material of construction. While large cities and many major buildings were built in mud brick, the poor lasting quality of this material has left only ruins as survivals. Excavations by archeologists in this region find layer after layer of remains of successive cities built in sequence, as older cities were destroyed or allowed to crumble with subsequent cities built on top.

It has, however, been possible to reconstruct in part plans of houses, temples, and palaces from these ruins. Excavations at the site of the ancient Sumerian city of Ur have uncovered traces of 4000-year-old closely packed neighborhoods of houses, each having several rectangular rooms around an open central court. This house type has continued to be used in many warm-climate regions up to the present time. ARCHED or VAULTED roofs of mud or clay brick may have been used. Mud-brick houses

1.11 A clay tablet with an inscribed map of Nippur, Sumeria, c. 1500 B.C.E.

The oldest known city map show the positions of important buildings such as temples, rivers and canals, and walls and gates. Although no records of the interiors of buildings exist, the sophistication of the map suggests that this was a highly developed civilization with a comparable level of design activity.

with DOMED roofs (similar to those of the Italian trulli described earlier) are still in use in regions of Iraq and Syria, suggesting that this house form may also be of very ancient origin.

The ancient temple, viewed by its builders as a house of a deity, tended to be an enlarged and elaborated version of the local house type. The White Temple at Uruk, so-called because of the traces that indicate that its walls were whitewashed, was built before 3000 B.C.E. It is a rectangular block with a number of rooms surrounding a central space that may have been covered or an open court. Deep walls have thickened vertical bands to aid in strengthening the inherently weak mud brick. Even earlier construction at Uruk includes fragments of walls surfaced with an elaborately patterned studding of small cones of clay painted in black, white, and red; the mosaic-like designs suggest the zig-zag and diamond forms of woven textile patterns.

Much later, Assyrian cities included vast and complex palaces with plans that can be studied as they survive in excavated remains. Large rooms in the palace of Sargon at Khorsabad (c. 700 B.C.E.) are thought to have had vaulted roofs and possibly made use of half domes. Glazed tile in rich colors was used as a surface material, and enough examples of these decorations survive to give some basis for imagined reconstructions.

Ancient Egypt

The civilization of ancient Egypt has left far more complete evidence for study so that, although no complete interiors survive intact, it is possible to gain a clear idea of what those spaces must have been like. Several circumstances have worked together to preserve Egyptian design. Stone of good lasting quality was available in the Nile valley, and the Egyptians learned to use it for important buildings although the everyday architecture of houses and even palaces continued to rely on mud brick. Many Egyptian structures of stone have survived, some ruined to a degree, but some, like the famous PYRAMIDS, in quite good condition. The pyramids were built as tombs and they call attention to the religious beliefs that were central to ancient Egyptian society.

Egyptian religion, like many other religions, included belief in a life after death, but it put extraordinary emphasis on the preservation of the bodies of dead persons. The afterlife would last as long as the body survived—hence the development

of techniques of embalmment and the concern for the building of tombs of maximal lasting qualities. Moreover, it was believed that objects placed in a tomb along with the carefully protected mummified body could be taken into the afterlife. Objects too large to be placed in a tomb—a house or a boat, for example—could be represented by a model. On the walls of tombs and temples (**fig. 1.2**), texts spelled out in hieroglyphic writing were combined with visual images, incised and painted in plaster or directly in stone. Taken together, the stone buildings, the objects found in tombs, and the surviving written and illustrated texts have made it possible for archeologists to develop a clear picture of ancient Egyptian ways and to place this knowledge in an accurate chronological history.

Geometry and Proportion

The largest and best-known of ancient Egyptian structures, the pyramids (**fig. 1.12**) are among the oldest surviving works (the oldest dating from *c.* 2800 B.C.E.) but their small interior passages and chambers are of less interest than their demonstrations of Egyptian conceptual thinking. Ancient Egypt developed great knowledge of and skill in geometric planning. The pyramids at Giza are positioned with a north–south axial orientation of great precision (particularly impressive as the spherical form of the earth with its north and south poles was unknown). It might seem that the slope of the pyramid sides (51 degrees 50 minutes 35 seconds) was an arbitrary choice until it is noted that this is the base angle of a triangle having a base and hypotenuse that are respectively the short and long sides of a "golden" rectangle, a figure in which the ratio of the short side to the long side is the

1.12 Cross-section of the Great Pyramid at Giza, Egypt, 2570–2500 B.C.E.

Although the internal spaces are tiny in comparison with the huge mass of the pyramid, their forms and relationships are complex and significant. A passage leads to a false tomb chamber, while the entrances to the passages leading to the actual tomb were carefully concealed in hope of defeating any efforts to break into the actual tomb of Khufu (Cheops), the pharaoh for whom the pyramid was built.

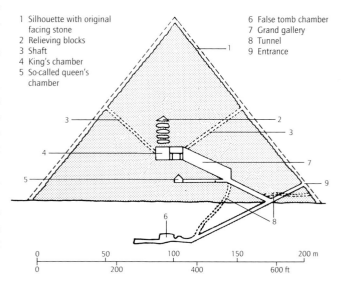

1 Silhouette with original facing stone
2 Relieving blocks
3 Shaft
4 King's chamber
5 So-called queen's chamber
6 False tomb chamber
7 Grand gallery
8 Tunnel
9 Entrance

0   50   100   150   200 m
0   200   400   600 ft

same as the ratio of the long side to the sum of the two; that is, calling the short side A and the long side B:

$$\frac{A}{B} = \frac{B}{A+B}$$

In numerical terms, the only values that satisfy this relationship are the ratios of 0.6180:1, which is equal to the ratio 1:1.6180. This relationship, often called the GOLDEN MEAN, has been discovered and rediscovered at various times in history as a unique proportion believed to have both aesthetic and mystic significance. That the Egyptians knew of it and used it seems certain. Without mathematical techniques a golden ratio can be constructed with straight-edges and a compass by laying out a right triangle with an altitude equal to one half the base (**fig. 1.13**).

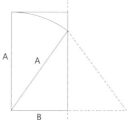

Another arc transfers the long side to make it the hypotenuse of the triangle that represents a half elevation view of the pyramid (**fig. 1.14**).

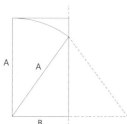

Egyptian art and design make regular use of this subtle relationship and many other simpler geometric concepts in architecture, in art, and in the design of everyday objects. This leads to the conviction that the striking aesthetic success of so many Egyptian works derives from such "harmonic" controls—so-called because of their relationship to the parallel mathematical bases of musical harmony. The musical chords that offer a pleasant ("harmonious") sound are made of tones with vibration frequencies in simple ratios such as 2:3, 3:4, and 3:5. Irregular ratios such as 17:19 produce harsh, discordant sounds. The proportions used in Egyptian design are "harmonic" in the same sense as the harmonious musical chords.

1.13 Geometric construction of a golden rectangle.

CDE is a right triangle with DE equal to one half CE. With D as a center and DE as a radius, an arc is swung to the hypotenuse CD marking point X. With C as a center, an arc is swung from point X to the baseline CE. The base is now divided in golden ratio, A:B. With B as its length and A as its width, a golden rectangle can be drawn.

1.14 Derivation of pyramid angle from golden rectangle.

Using a golden rectangle, the long side A is swung to make contact with the opposite long side. The resulting triangle has B as its base and A as its hypotenuse; it can be called a golden triangle.

1.15 (*right*) Temple of Amon, Karnak, Egypt, c. 1530 B.C.E.

The hypostyle hall is a vast space almost filled by the columns that supported a stone roof. Incised hieroglyphics covered the columns. Originally, the surfaces were painted in bright colors (still partially visible), which would have glowed in the dim light admitted by roof-level clerestories.

Egyptian Temples and Houses

The plans of Egyptian temples are expanded and elaborated versions of Egyptian house plans, with an innermost chamber—home of the god—surrounded by layers of walled spaces and reached only through a succession of outer walls, gateways, and courtyards. The mud-brick material of house building (probably retained in early, now vanished temples) was translated into construction using carefully cut and polished stone. The design of the typical stone column, with its suggestion of a binding of cord at the base and below the CAPITAL, was derived from the mud columns strengthened with bundled reeds of houses and palaces. The inward slope (called BATTER) of walls that had been used to improve stability in mud construction was retained in stone and is a common characteristic of ancient Egyptian building. Flat stones used as a roofing material can only span short distances and so compel plans that stick to small rooms and narrow passages, or, when a larger space was required, fill the space with columns spaced closely enough to make it possible for stones to span from one column to the next. Such spanning stones are called LINTELS; building that is based on columns and lintels is called POST AND LINTEL or TRABEATED construction.

A large space filled with many columns is called a HYPOSTYLE HALL. The enormous (170 × 338 feet) hypostyle hall of the Temple of Amon at Karnak (begun c. 1530 B.C.E.) contains 134 columns with surfaces covered with incised and painted hiero-glyphic inscriptions (**fig. 1.15**). The columns are built up of stone drums topped with capitals carved in papyrus bud or flower forms. The center portion of the hall is higher than the sides so that high, unglazed CLERESTORY windows could admit light. Access to the hall is through two gateways centered between huge masonry elements called PYLONS with a large open courtyard between. Beyond the hypostyle hall three more gates between pylons protect the vast complex of smaller chambers and passages, now partly in ruins, which led to the most sacred interior space, the chamber of the god.

Temple plans can be analyzed to demonstrate their use of complex systems of geometry that set the relationships and proportions of spaces, walls, and columns in a way that must have had mystic, symbolic significance as well as aesthetic impact. Simple bilateral symmetry is an almost invariable controlling concept. Only traces of mud-built palaces remain, but restoration drawings give some idea of what their interiors might have been like. There are surviving traces of whole towns of houses built as "suburbs" to house workers employed on vast royal building projects. Surviving traces have formed a basis for suggested reconstructions of houses built at one end of an enclosed garden used for food production as well as amenity. In some tombs, wooden models of houses, shops, and other facilities of everyday life have survived, giving addi-tional information about the pleasant and colorful character of these aspects of ancient Egyptian life.

Egyptian use of color was both strong and effec-tive. Pigments in clear primaries (red, yellow, and blue) as well as green were used, along with white and black, the latter generally only for linear forms that edged and defined areas of strong color. In interiors, ceilings were often painted in a strong blue, representative of the night sky. Floors were sometimes green, possibly symbolic of the Nile.

Egyptian Furniture and Other Interior Furnishings

Knowledge of Egyptian furniture comes from two sources: images in wall paintings that show scenes of everyday life in royal or other aristocratic houses, and actual examples that were placed in tombs and that have survived. The latter include

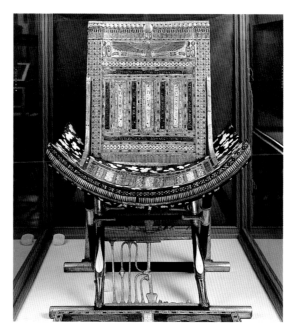

1.16 A ceremonial throne from the tomb of Tutankhamen, c. 1340 B.C.E..

The basic structure of ebony wood can only be glimpsed in the legs of the chair, which is encrusted with inlays of gold and ivory with panels of painted, symbolic imagery. The seating function is clearly subordinated to the display of wealth, grandeur, and power conveyed by the rich-ness of material and sublime craftsmanship with which they have been assembled.

chairs, tables, and cabinets, many of them richly decorated for use and display in the homes of the wealthy and powerful. The typical preserved chair has a simple wood frame with a low seat webbed with bands of rush or leather. Legs usually end at their base with carved, clawed animal foot forms. Simple folding stools of an X-form of great elegance also survive. The elaborate objects from the tomb of the pharaoh Tutankhamen (c. 1340 B.C.E.) are well-known examples of the colorful and ornate phases of Egyptian design (**fig. 1.16**). Many smaller objects, pieces of pottery, and glassware have also survived. Small wooden boxes, sometimes inlaid with ivory, were fitted out to contain cosmetics and tools for personal adornment. Such objects are often designed with attention to systems of geometric proportions, including the golden section. Surviving bits of woven textiles suggest that the Egyptians were also highly skilled weavers and colorists of woven cloths.

Ancient Egyptian civilization survived, in grad-ually diminishing strength, up until Roman times. Its influence on later European development is a matter for debate. Certainly, other peoples around the Mediterranean visited Egypt, but the extent to which the design of ancient Greece may have been influenced by knowledge of Egypt can only be guessed. Whether or not there is a direct path of progressive development, the design of ancient Egypt was clearly demonstrative of the power of strong conceptual thinking in the generation of a powerful aesthetic expression.

Classical Civilizations: Greece and Rome

Several clusters of habitation developed on the northern edge of the Mediterranean, generating the bases on which later European civilization grew. The term "prehistoric" is applied to these cultures since they have left no detailed written history. The first of these in chronological sequence overlaps the middle portion of ancient Egyptian history.

Minoan and Mycenaean Cultures

Minoan and Mycenaean communities developed on small islands in the Aegean Sea, on the larger island of Crete, and on the mainland of Greece beginning around 2200 B.C.E. The term Minoan, derived from the name of the legendary king Minos, is used to refer to the society, presumed to have come from Asia Minor (now Turkey), that built up a scattering of settlements on Crete—some twenty towns or small cities, each with its own palace and a population estimated at about 80,000 supported by agriculture and fishing. Some contact with the contemporary society of Egypt is assumed, although there is no clear evidence of its influence.

Knossos

Excavation has uncovered layer after layer of Minoan cities, each destroyed as the next level was built, leaving only traces of the mud-brick structures but more extensive remains of some of the palaces where stone was the primary building material. The best known and most complete of

these palaces is that at Knossos, thought to have been the palace of King Minos and his successors in 1450–1370 B.C.E. Its ruins are complex and confusing as a result of many rebuildings. Recent efforts at restoration have created portions that give some idea of what the building may have been like when it was inhabited. The plan is a loose agglomeration around a large central open area. On one side there is a lower level of narrow chambers—perhaps the basis for the legendary labyrinth where the fearsome Minotaur was supposed to have been kept. Stairs lead to an upper level of larger chambers thought to be the ceremonial rooms of the palace. Many of the rooms are narrow or small, but there are larger rooms with traces of free-standing columns spaced in a way that suggests that they supported the wooden beams of a roof structure. On the other side of the court there is a complex of smaller rooms, including a three-level grouping that seems to have been the royal residence. There are stairs and light courts leading to rooms that contain traces of wall paintings. The restored stair halls and "throne room" (**fig. 2.1**) give some idea of the surprisingly informal and colorful character of these spaces.

Mycenae and Tiryns

The term Mycenaean is used to identify the ruined palaces at Mycenae and Tiryns on the Greek mainland which date to the Late Bronze Age period (1400–1250 B.C.E.). These were placed on high ground and planned with fortification walls for

2.1 (*below*) Throne room at the palace at Knossos, Crete, *c.* 1450–1370 B.C.E.

The elaborate wall painting, with its images of animals and plants, contrasts with the simplicity of the stone floor, benches, and the high-backed throne of carved stone.

2.2 (*opposite*) Interior of the Pantheon, Rome as painted by G. P. Pannini, *c.* 1750.

The Roman temple to all the gods, built 118–28 C.E., is a domed structure containing a spectacular interior. The diameter of 142 feet and the matching height give the interior a geometric order, while daylight pouring in from the oculus (round opening) at the top of the dome illuminates the space. The niches (originally altars to the various gods), the tall Corinthian columns, and the wall surfaces are colored with marbles and gilded bronze.

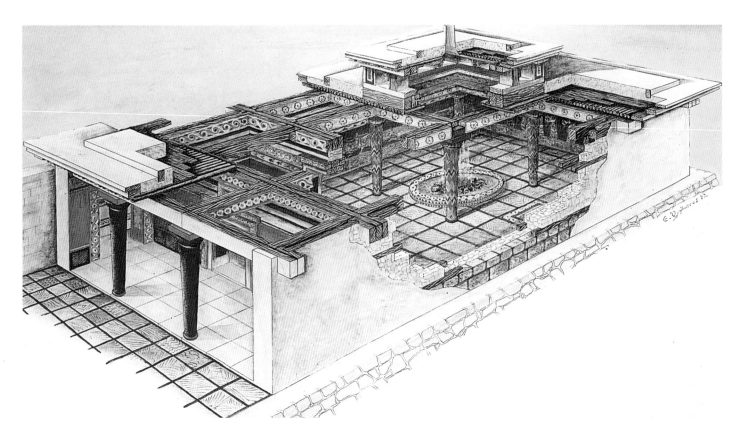

2.3 Reconstruction drawing of the megaron of the palace at Mycenae, Greece, second millennium B.C.E.

The megaron was a large rectangular or square room, with a central hearth below a raised roof with an opening through which the smoke could escape. The entrance was from a porch with two columns, which, like the interior columns, tapered from a larger capital to a smaller base. Although the style of roof is unknown, the artist's impression shows that it may have been decorated with complex, abstract, painted patterns.

defense. Giant rough-cut stones are laid up without mortar to form complex galleries and chambers, topped in places with stones tilted inward which meet to form a stone roofing. Enough stonework survives for plans to be reconstructed which exhibit the same complex and labyrinthine planning encountered in the Cretan palaces. At Tiryns a gateway leads to a courtyard with a columned surround on three sides and, on the fourth side, the facade of the major hall of the palace, a large room called a MEGARON (**fig. 2.3**) with an outer vestibule and PORTICO. Internally, there was a round central hearth, four columns supporting a wood roof structure, and a raised throne placed at the center of one side wall. The floor was paved with decorated tiles and surviving traces suggest walls with colorful painted decorative patterning. The symmetrical plan and placement of the megaron in relation to the forecourt suggest the beginnings of a formal and monumental approach to planning.

Excavation of town sites has revealed compact clusters of houses, usually of four or five rooms, grouped along narrow streets or alleys winding about without formal plan. Painted tiles, pottery, and wall paintings give some idea of the design vocabulary of the Aegean cultures, but there are no

intact pieces of everyday furniture or other artifacts to suggest a more complete sense of the interior vernacular of houses. The cities on Crete were all destroyed around 1400 B.C.E., probably by an earthquake. Mycenaean civilization lasted until sometime between 1200 and 1000 B.C.E., when it was displaced by the migration of Dorian invaders from northern Greece.

Greece

The migrating and invading Dorians and Ionians brought into Greece their own systems of wood building, but also seem to have absorbed aspects of the earlier Aegean architecture and even to display traces of Egyptian design. The development of the Greek alphabet and the related system of writing around 900 B.C.E. made it possible for the Homeric stories and others to be preserved, along with an increasingly complete historical record.

The Temple

The Greek temple developed from the Aegean megaron, the main room of the palace—it was thus the palace-house of a god, the only palace this increasingly democratic society required. No wooden temples have survived, but their nature can be deduced from later stone temples. The closely spaced columns support short stone lintels with a GABLED roof above. The band of lintels forms an ENTABLATURE carved with details that suggest the ends of wooden rafters and that even include the simulated ends of pegs of the sort that must have been used in the joinery of wood construction.

The functions of the Greek temple were minimal (strictly ceremonial or symbolic), its construction simple, and its design limited to a narrow range of variations on a formula. The enclosed space of the temple, the CELLA, was usually only one or two rooms dedicated to a god or goddess as a symbolic home. The striking visible form of the building comes from the surrounding PERISTYLE of columns, usually six or eight at the gabled front and rear with additional rows of columns along each side, making up a total surround of rhythmic repetition. This simple formula was made effective by a combination of devices, some so subtle as to have escaped discovery for many centuries.

The best-known and most obvious characteristic is the use of an ORDER, a systematic means of organizing elements according to a carefully integrated plan (**fig. 2.4**). The oldest and most admired order, called DORIC, uses a column with no base that rises from a three-stepped platform (the SYLOBATE) to a simple capital made up of a round ECHINUS with a square block or ABACUS above. The column is slightly tapered from bottom to top with a very slight curvature or ENTASIS. The entablature band above is made up of three parts: a plain ARCHITRAVE; a FRIEZE made up of alternating panels—the TRIGLYPHS that recall wood rafter ends, and the blank or sculptured METOPES between; and above, a projecting CORNICE or crowning element. All of these parts are given dimensions that relate through a MODULE or unit based on the diameter of the column. In the early (c. 550 B.C.E.) Doric temples, such as at Paestum, a Greek colony on the Italian peninsula, the column height is only about four and a half times its diameter. This proportion tended to be gradually altered in later work at different sites, with the height of the Parthenon column reaching eight times the diameter. The spacing of columns, the bands of the entablature, and even the smallest elements are

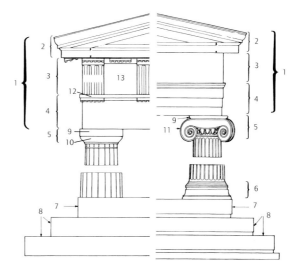

worked out as multiples or submultiples of the governing module.

Greek architecture also shows knowledge of the theories of proportion so significant in Egyptian architecture—the golden section proportion, for example. The Parthenon at Athens (**fig. 2.5**), usually considered the most perfect of Greek temples (c. 440 B.C.E.), is planned with its two interior spaces each of the golden 1:1.6180 ratio. Its front elevation fits into a rectangle of the same golden proportion, while the column spacing makes it possible to discover a series of related harmonious relationships. The Parthenon also displays many of the more subtle departures from strict regularity, called REFINEMENTS, that are characteristic of the most successful Greek temples. Corner columns are spaced closer to their neighbors than the regular spacing based on the governing module. In addition, the horizontal lines of the stylobate base platform are found to be bent upward in a slight curvature, columns lean slightly inward, and the lines of the entablature are also curved. These slight shifts from total regularity serve to correct the optical or perspective distortions that can make straight lines seem to curve or verticals to lean. They also introduce an aesthetic

2.4 Greek orders of architecture.
1 Entablature
2 Cornice
3 Frieze
4 Architrave
5 Capital
6 Base
7 Stylobate
8 Stereobate
9 Abacus
10 Echinus
11 Volute
12 Triglyph
13 Metope

The Doric order (left), which is the style used at the Parthenon, Athens, is austere and simple, its columns having no base and a simple capital. The column typical of the Ionic order (right) is characterized by a capital with two spiral volutes.

2.5 Plan of the Parthenon, Athens, Greece, 447–436 B.C.E.
1 Naos
2 Pronaos
3 Opisthodomos
4 Treasury
5 Base of Athena's statue
6 Peristyle columns
7 Solid wall
8 Steps (stereobate and stylobate)

Eight columns at front and back form, with the columns at each side, a peristyle surround. At front and back an additional row of six columns stands in front of the doorways which lead to the naos or main chamber at one end and the smaller chamber, or treasury, at the other end. Within the naos, columns support an upper balcony where additional columns support the roof. The statue of the goddess Athena dominates the naos.

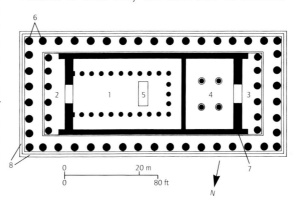

0   20 m
0   80 ft

N

2.7 Greek ornamental detail.

The patterns called a Greek key and the more complex variant, known as a Greek fret, were executed in mosaic tiles and are a frequent feature of Greek interiors.

quality that might be called "humane" in its delicate shifting of forms away from strictly mechanical precision.

Internally, many Greek temples contain only the simple single room of the megaron house, but some larger temples have internal rows of columns supporting a MEZZANINE or balcony with an upper range of columns supporting the roof above. Although no complete interior of any Greek temple has survived, the ruins of the temple of Poseidon at Paestum (**fig. 2.6**), for example, give an idea of the aesthetic success of this arrangement. The white ruins mislead modern viewers; the original buildings used strong color, as we know from traces discovered in the stones. Such POLYCHROMY (use of color) must have made these buildings quite different from the pristine image so often imagined.

Following the Doric order, two other orders came into use in Greek architecture. The IONIC order uses a column taller and thinner in proportion than the Doric, adds a base detail, and is most clearly identified by its capital with its twin scroll-form VOLUTES. The small temple called the Erectheum and the Temple of Athena Nike on the acropolis in Athens both used the Ionic order, which also appears in the interior of the Doric Temple of Apollo at Bassae. The Ionic order is usually viewed as more gentle, perhaps more "feminine" than the austerity of the Doric. The third order, called Corinthian, came into use much later.

It is the most ornate of the three orders, using both small volutes at the corners of the column capital and carved forms of acanthus leaves ringing the lower part of the capital. The Corinthian order was widely used in Roman times and has been a favorite of later users of classical architectural detail.

Even the smallest details of Greek design have become elements in our understanding of the concept of classicism. The moldings that are part of the orders and the ornamental details that were used—including moldings given names such as BEAD AND REEL or EGG AND DART, bands of carved DENTILS or GREEK KEY ornament (**fig. 2.7**)—continue to be used in classical design.

The influence that the design of Greek temples has had on western architecture and design is remarkable considering their small number, modest size, and specialized purpose. Ancient Roman design borrowed heavily from the admired work of the Greeks. Roman architecture was rediscovered in the RENAISSANCE, bringing back the romanized version of Greek design as the ideal of classical beauty. In the latter part of the eighteenth century, when travel to Greece became easier, knowledge of actual Greek sites through printed illustrations and detailed drawings became the basis for a revival of design based on Greek precedents. Imitation of Greek orders, of temple buildings, and of Greek ornament was a frequent theme of nineteenth-century design. In more recent times, interest in the conceptual aspects of Greek design has overshadowed literal imitation. Le Corbusier, the influential French modernist, in his manifesto *Towards a New Architecture*, praised the aesthetic logic of Greek design and illustrated details of Greek temples in direct comparison to images of automobiles and aircraft that he viewed as having parallel merit.

Secular Interiors

Aside from temples, the major building types of ancient Greece do not emphasize enclosed, interior spaces. The Greek theater was open to the sky and nature with its tiers of seats arranged in a semicircle about the circular *orchestra* that served as its stage. Towns included a central open square, the AGORA, which was both a market and a general public

2.6 The Temple of Poseidon, Paestum, Italy, *c.* 460 B.C.E.

This view of the Doric temple, which originally had a roof, looks down into the naos (principal room). The lower tier of columns supported a balcony, where another series of columns would have supported the wooden roof.

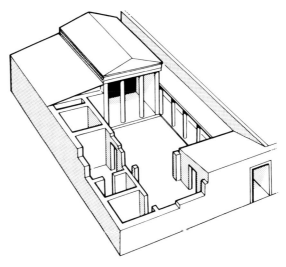

2.8 Reconstruction drawing of a typical Greek house at Priene, Asia Minor, fourth century B.C.E.

A central courtyard, open to the sky, is flanked by a portico on one side, various rooms on the opposite side, and by a columned megaron (large room) at the end. The street front is blank, apart from an unobtrusive entrance door. All the living quarters face into the interior court.

INSIGHTS

The Growth of Athens

Thucydides chronicled the long Peloponnesian War writing between 433 and 404 B.C.E. He comments on how the situation caused an unplanned and haphazard expansion of the city of Athens:

The Athenians took the advice he [Pericles] gave them and brought in from the country their wives and children and all their household goods, taking down even the woodwork on the houses themselves. But the move was a difficult experience for them since most of them had always been used to living in the country . . . . So they were far from pleased at having to move with their entire households. It was sadly and reluctantly that they now abandoned their homes and the temples time honoured from their patriotic past, that they prepared to change their whole way of life, leaving behind what each man regarded as his own city.

When they arrived in Athens, a few had houses of their own to go to, and a few were able to find shelter with friends or relations; but most of them had to settle down in those parts of the city that had not been built over, and in the temples and shrines of the heroes—except in the Acropolis. [1]

1. Thucydides, *The Peloponnesian War*, trs. Rex Warner (Penguin, 1972), pp. 133–5

bedrooms all forming the area primarily used by women and children. Larger houses occasionally had a second floor; a second courtyard is rare. A room with a bathtub of terracotta is not unusual. Only excavated foundations survive so that knowledge of interior detail is limited; evidence suggests that rooms were generally plain with white-painted walls and floors of TAMPED EARTH or, sometimes, of tile.

No furniture survives, but images in Greek painting, particularly the paintings on vases and other ceramics, give an idea of its design. A recurring image shows a chair of great elegance—probably of a kind only possessed by the wealthy (**fig. 2.9**). It has a slightly curved back supported by

2.9 The stele of Hegisto *c.* 410 B.C.E.

The bas-relief shows an elegantly dressed lady seated in a chair of the unique Greek type called a klismos. The outward curving legs of wood support a square frame, which has a surface of leather straps. The rear legs continue up to a backrest panel. There is a small footrest in front of the chair.

meeting place. The STOA at the edges of the agora provided shelter for commerce within long colonnades with small rooms at the back serving as shops, for storage, or as work spaces. The stoa of Attalos (**fig. 2.10**) in the Athenian agora (*c.* 150 B.C.E.) has been extensively restored, giving a convincing impression of what such places must have been. An outer row of Doric and an inner row of Ionic columns support the roof of wood and tile.

Greek houses were typically simple groupings of rooms around an open court (**fig. 2.8**). In cities the houses were packed together along streets with largely blank exteriors except for the entrance doorway. Material was sun-baked brick or, sometimes, rough stone with surfaces plastered or stuccoed and whitewashed. Plans vary in response to the preferences of individual families, but there is rarely any concern for symmetry or other formalities. The ANDRON, a kind of vestibuled parlor suggesting the form of the earlier megaron, is usually close to the entrance and is for the use of men—the owner and his friends. Beyond, the open court is surrounded by the OECUS, an all-purpose living and work space, a kitchen and, beyond that, by

2.10 The interior of the stoa of Attalos in the agora of Athens, Greece, *c.* 150 B.C.E.

The agora (civic center or market place) in Athens, now restored, was partly surrounded by a covered colonnade, called a stoa. A line of Doric columns on the left and a row of Ionic columns at the center supported a wooden roof. The doors at the right led to rooms that were used for dining and storage by the merchants, whose wares were displayed in the open portico.

2.11 The theater at Epidaurus, Greece, *c.* 350 B.C.E.

The Greek theater was open to the sky, with semicircular tiers of seating facing down toward the circular floor or orchestra, where a chorus might dance or sing. Actors played on a temporary raised platform or stage behind the orchestra. The theater was usually sited in a spectacular landscape that formed a natural backdrop.

corner uprights that continue the rear legs. The seat is an open square of round wooden members webbed with some material, probably leather. Both front and back legs take a strong outward curve, the characteristic of the KLISMOS chair type. The form suggests curved animal parts that may have been used in early versions of the klismos. It is not a structurally logical form and raises questions about how such chairs were made to have adequate strength. The legs could have been bent from straight strips if the technique of steam-bending had been discovered, or they may have been made from tree branches selected for providing the desired curve. Modern efforts to reproduce ancient Greek chairs and other furniture types have met with uncertain success.

From about 300 B.C.E. onward, during the Hellenistic age, Greek theaters, temples, and monuments became larger, richer, and more complex, with elaborate ornamental details (**fig. 2.11**). In the second century B.C.E. the loosely connected Greek city states came under the domination of Rome.

Rome

Ancient Roman design drew extensively on Greek precedents. The links were the Etruscan civilization on the Italian peninsula that had in turn been influenced by the Greek colonies in Italy, and the direct contact that occurred as the Romans invaded Greece, finally making it a part of the Roman empire. Etruscan houses and temples from before 300 B.C.E. are only known from surviving traces and from the verbal desciptions provided by the Roman writings of Vitruvius. Houses followed the Greek megaron type with mud brick and wood as primary materials. In temple building, a columned front portico with gabled pediment above suggests Greek temple architecture. An order based on Greek practice was used, having a simplified Doric column with a base similar to that of the Ionic order. As taken over and executed in stone later by the Romans, this became known as the TUSCAN ORDER, the first of the five orders identified as Roman. Pottery and wall paintings from Etruscan tombs often show details of everyday life, and give a limited idea of furniture and other artifacts predating Roman times.

Rome was founded, according to tradition, in 753 B.C.E. By 300 B.C.E. Rome expanded its power to control all of Italy until, from about 150 B.C.E. to 400 C.E., its empire controlled most of the known western civilized world. In design, the Romans were content to borrow the aesthetic concepts of the Greeks, expanding, elaborating, and ornamenting as they chose, usually to the detriment of quality. Roman skills were organizational and technical. It is in the great engineering works—roads, bridges, and AQUEDUCTS—and in the creation of vast interior spaces that Roman achievement is most striking.

Arches, Vaults, and Domes

The use of arches in spanning over wide openings with permanent materials was known to the Egyptians and to the Greeks, but arched construction was used in limited, generally utilitarian ways by these civilizations. It remained for the Romans to explore the full possibilities of the arch and to apply its potentialities in the creation of interior spaces within major buildings. An arch is an arrangement of wedge-shaped stones put together so that each stone, or VOUSSOIR, is held trapped between its neighbors on either side. Many small stones can thus be made to reach across wide openings that no one stone lintel could span. Arches are most often made in the familiar curved form (although they can be slightly curved or flat); its semicircular form is often called a ROMAN ARCH (**fig. 2.12**).

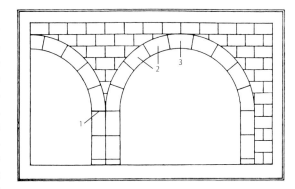

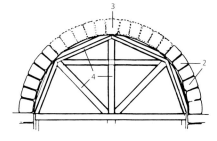

2.12 A typical Roman arch and an arch under construction with centering.
1 Springing
2 Voussoir
3 Keystone
4 Centering

Ancient Roman architects and builders made extensive use of various forms of arch in the construction of doors, windows, and interior spaces. The typical arch was semicircular, and its construction required the use of a temporary wooden support structure known as centering.

Arches pose two technical problems. The first involves technique of construction: all of the stones of an arch must be in place before it will stand. This means that a temporary scaffolding structure, usually of wood, called CENTERING must be built to support the stones as they are put in place until the arch is complete. The Romans understood how to support centering from projecting stones near the base of an arch, which avoided the need to build the wooden structure from the ground up, and they reused centering for the successive arches of an ARCADE, removing the centering from under a complete arch so that it could support the next one under construction.

The second problem of arch construction results from the fact that the wedging action of the voussoirs transmits pressure sideways through the arch, generating an outward force or THRUST that must be resisted in some way. In a series of arches making up an arcade, the thrust of each arch is absorbed by the balancing thrust of the neighboring arches on either side. In a bridge or aqueduct (**fig. 2.13**), the last arches of the series press against a hillside or a massive abutment heavy enough to absorb the thrust. In building construction, thick and heavy walls take over the function of the hill or abutment. Arches can span wide openings, but masonry roofing of an interior space requires the extension of an arch to form a vault. The simple extended arch vault, called a BARREL VAULT (or sometimes a tunnel vault) must rest on massive walls on either side to absorb its thrust. A more complex vault results from the form generated by the right-angle intersection of two barrel vaults. Such a GROIN VAULT requires support only at its four corners as it exerts outward thrust in two directions at those points.

In addition to their skilled exploitation of these constructional techniques, the Romans also developed the dome, a kind of round vault having the form of a half, or smaller segment of a sphere. A dome can only cover a circular space and requires support around its perimeter. In addition to arch, vault, and dome building in neatly cut stone called ASHLAR, the Romans added the use of a strong and lasting fired brick. Roman bricks, unlike their modern equivalent, were thin, flat squares. The Romans also developed concrete, a mix of cement or mortar (the Romans used a volcanic ash called *pozzolana*) with stones or gravel and water to make a substance that would flow into place in any desired form and subsequently harden into an artificial stone. Stone was the material most used for visible exterior and interior surfaces, but the structure behind the surface often made use of the easily handled (and inexpensive) brick or concrete in whatever combination was most practical and efficient.

Amphitheaters and Baths

Roman engineering was put to use in the building of huge stadium amphitheaters such as the famous Colosseum in Rome (72–80 C.E.) and theaters with similar tiers of seating in a semicircle facing an elaborate stage structure. Since they were open to the sky, the only enclosed spaces of theaters and amphitheaters were the complex systems of passages and stairs that gave access to the seating. Arches and barrel vaults were ideal structural devices for these elements. The great amphitheaters were provided with temporary roofing through awnings or a tent-like covering, although it is not certain whether this was arranged through CANTILEVERS from the perimeter or through cables spanning the space in the manner of modern tension structures.

The great public baths—another public service building type developed by the Romans—called for vast clusters of enclosed spaces in varied sizes and shapes, making full use of vault and dome construction. Furnace heat was passed through under-floor spaces (HYPOCAUSTS) and through flues in walls which, along with the generous flow of water, produced steam and heated air at the varied temperatures that the Roman bathing

2.13 The Pont du Gard, Nîmes, France, late first century B.C.E.

This Roman aqueduct bridge uses three tiers of arches to support a large water channel (at the top), carrying water from sources high in the mountains down to the coastal city of Nîmes. In bridge and aqueduct structures, each arch transfers its thrust to its neighbors while the end arches thrust against the adjacent hills.

2.14 Reconstruction drawing of the Baths of Caracalla, Rome, 211–17 C.E.

Enormous Corinthian columns supported the overhead vaulting, while openings and clerestory windows high in the walls flooded the interior with light. The floors, walls, and vaulting were covered with richly colored marble as an expression of the greatness of the Roman empire and its emperor.

2.16 Plan and section of the Pantheon, Rome, *c.* 118–128 C.E.
1 Rotunda
2 Niche
3 Portico
4 Oculus

The circle that forms the basis of the plan also controls the section. The dome is a half sphere, while the walls below form a cylinder with a height just half its diameter. The circle drawn on the section thus fits the interior of the dome and touches the floor at its center.

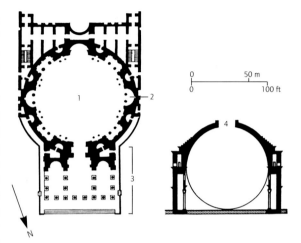

system required. The sequence of TEPIDARIUM (warm), CALDARIUM (hot), and LACONICUM (very hot) led to the FRIGIDARIUM, a large pool open to the sky. Areas were provided for gymnastic exercises and sports, for social relaxation, and even for a library. Arched openings permitted daylight to enter the halls of the bath; the *tepidaria* of the great Roman baths are the first large interior spaces to be fully lighted by daylight. Although the enclosing roof structures are in ruins, the surviving portions of the Baths of Caracalla (211–17 C.E.; **fig. 2.14**) and of Diocletian (298–306 C.E.) make it possible to study their elaborate, totally symmetrical plans and have encouraged efforts to recreate the interior spaces for modern functions. The main concourse of New York's old Pennsylvania Railroad Station (demolished 1963), for example, was designed to recreate the vast, Corinthian columned and vaulted *tepidarium* of the Baths of Caracalla.

Temples

The practical and secular Romans were less interested in temples than in amphitheaters, baths, and aqueducts, but they did build temples to their gods. The Roman temple used the Greek concept of a single room (cella) housing a statue of the god with a columned portico in front using a Roman version of one of the Greek orders. The Roman preference was for their own versions of the more elaborate Ionic and Corinthian orders and the hybrid COMPOSITE ORDER (combining Ionic and Corinthian elements) rather than the more austere Doric. Along the sides and rear of temples, freestanding columns were not used—either plain walls or attached ("engaged") PILASTERS were the norm. Some smaller Roman temples, such as the

so-called Maison Carré at Nîmes (**fig. 2.15**; now in France, but a Roman colony in *c.* 20 B.C.E. when the temple was built), have survived in excellent condition thanks to their sturdy construction with a barrel-vaulted roof enclosing the cella. The interior of such smaller Roman temples was a simple, smooth-walled room with a COFFERED vault above and a statue of the god to whom the temple was dedicated as its only contents.

Larger Roman temples, now in ruins, show evidence of more elaborate interiors. The Temple of Venus and Rome in Rome (135 C.E.), for example, had two interior chambers facing toward the two ends of the building, each with side walls covered by a columned order with niches between columns and at the back-to-back ends of the rooms, APSES with half-dome tops—obviously the locations of the obligatory statues.

The best known of Roman temples, fortunately well preserved, is the huge and impressive Pantheon in Rome (*c.* 118–28 C.E.), a temple to all the gods (**figs. 2.2** and **2.16**). Its interior is a single round room 142 feet in diameter topped by a half-spherical dome. On the plaza there is an entrance portico with eight Corinthian columns. Across its width is a triangular PEDIMENT. Two additional rows of four columns each make the portico a deep space leading to the great bronze entrance doors (still in place and working on their original hinges). The main body of the building has walls 14 feet thick hollowed out with spaced columned recesses each dedicated to a particular god. The total height of the space matches its diameter, making the lower half a cylinder matching the height of the dome above. The walls below the dome are in the Corinthian order with a simulated ATTIC, or upper story, above. The dome is coffered with five tiers of

2.15 Maison Carré, Nîmes, France, first century B.C.E.

Corinthian columns and half columns surround the enclosed cella of this Roman temple. It is a simple chamber with a barrel-vaulted roof of stone. Its fine construction has kept the building in nearly original condition. It has been the inspiration for many later works—such as the American eighteenth-century Virginia State House by Thomas Jefferson.

coffers of decreasing size; a smooth ring at the top below the open OCULUS ("eye") is the only source of internal lighting. The dome is of concrete, 4 feet thick at the top and becoming thicker at its lower levels to carry the increasing load and add weight to aid in resisting outward thrust. The walls are of concrete and brick with stone facing inside and out. The vast size of the ROTUNDA interior, its rich surface ornamentation, the dramatic effect of the beams of sunlight which stream in through the oculus to be reflected from the polished marble floor, and the special acoustical quality generated in a round room make the Pantheon interior one of the most remarkable spaces surviving from ancient times.

With the spread of the Roman empire over a major part of the European and Near Eastern civilized world, variations on the basic Roman themes developed with a tendency toward more complex and more elaborate—often over-elaborate—design. Roman temple structures such as those at Baalbek, Lebanon, and at Pergamum, Turkey, had complex and richly ornamented interiors. The Temple of Venus at Baalbek, for example, included a kind of small temple within the large temple cella.

Secular Buildings

The Roman BASILICA (**fig. 2.17**) was a major secular building type that was destined to have a huge impact on later building. The basilica, a large hall built for use as a courtroom, had a central space (called a NAVE through its supposed similarity to an inverted ship hull) to accommodate a public involved in the litigation or trials; the judge sat on a raised level in an apse at the end of the building. On either side, separated by an arcade, aisles provided space for circulation adjacent to the nave proper. The nave was made higher than the aisles so that windows could be introduced high up in the nave walls, forming a clerestory. Walls of masonry supported a wooden roof. This arrangement of nave and aisles with a focal apse turned out to be highly suitable to conversion into a Christian church after Christianity became an accepted Roman religion under the emperor Constantine around (306–37 C.E.).

Other secular Roman building types included markets with vaulted covered halls (**fig. 2.18**) suggestive of the modern shopping mall, warehouses to service commerce at port cities such as Ostia, and multi-storied apartment houses or tene-

ments surprisingly similar to their modern counterparts. Knowledge of the settings and character of everyday residential life in Roman times has been vastly aided through the extraordinary way in which whole towns were preserved when the eruption of Mount Vesuvius in 79 C.E. buried the cities of Pompeii and Herculaneum in lava and ash. These were resort towns where the well-to-do had houses of considerable luxury, but they can be taken to be quite typical examples of the Roman approach to domestic architecture. Excavations at

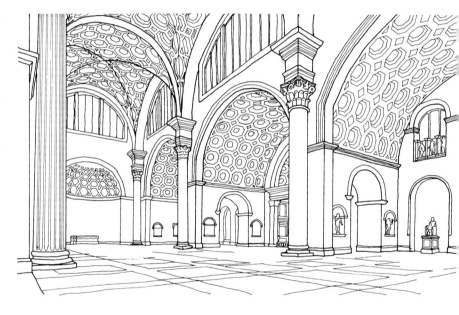

2.17 Reconstruction drawing of the basilica of Maxentius, Rome, 307–312 C.E.

Only three bays survive of this massive public assembly hall, but they reveal the scale and richness of this exercise in concrete vaulted construction. High clerestory windows admitted light to illuminate the rich decoration.

2.18 The markets of Trajan, Rome, 100–112 C.E.

A large, enclosed, vaulted hall had openings on both sides giving access to the various shops, and an upper gallery giving access to additional shops. This hall was part of a complex of commercial buildings built under the Emperor Trajan as part of an urban renewal project. It included a basilica, forums, and other public buildings.

2.19 Plan of the House of the Vettii, Pompeii, Italy, 63–79 C.E.
1 Entrance
2 Atrium
3 Kitchen
4 Dining room
5 Parlor
6 Main room

The House of the Vettii was typical of the comfortable houses inhabited by the residents of Pompeii. The rooms were arranged around the atrium, while the exterior front of the house was simply a blank wall with an unobtrusive entrance door. Other houses were built near by, the layouts of which interlock with the House of the Vettii.

the sites of the disaster have uncovered streets, houses, shops, even people caught in the eruption. An astonishing variety of small objects, paintings, and MOSAICS make it possible to understand ancient Roman design in great detail. Although quite varied in plan in response to the size and shape of its lot and to the needs and means of its owner, the Pompeiian house follows patterns that had become norms in Roman Mediterranean regions.

The house was usually a one- or two-story building fronting on a street with a blank wall or, often, with shops on the street and an unobtrusive entrance through a passage leading to a courtyard

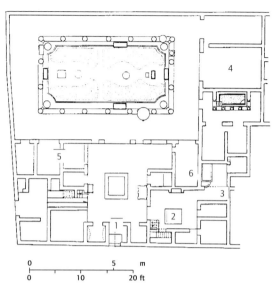

open to the sky. In the center of this open ATRIUM there would be a pool (IMPLUVIUM) with surrounding columns supporting a wood and tile roof that covered the colonnaded passage that gave access to most of the rooms of the house. On axis with the entrance, there was usually a sort of formal parlor or TABLINUM with an adjacent TRICLINIUM or dining room furnished with three couches on three sides of an open square. Here a table could be placed, the whole arrangement suiting the Roman preference for eating in a semi-reclining posture. Windows were rare since the light admitted by the door openings facing the atrium were considered ample. Smaller special purpose rooms such as a kitchen, bakery, and baths were fitted in where they served their purposes most conveniently.

Pompeiian houses varied in size from a few rooms off an atrium to large mansions occupied by wealthy families. Larger houses often had two courtyards, an atrium in front surrounded by rooms making up a formal outer zone linked by a transitional room to a larger court or peristyle surrounded by another set of rooms forming a private living realm. The House of the Vettii (**figs. 2.19–2.22**) at Pompeii has a very large peristyle court but a small number of rooms, although there is a kitchen and service zone with its own small open court. The very large House of Pansa is arranged around two courtyards and has a large garden at the rear. The planning of such Roman houses is developed from the interior outward, so that the outermost perimeter is often surrounded by smaller houses and shops fronting on the public streets. Thus the house can be described as having no visible exterior unless there is a garden with a

2.20 The atrium, House of the Vettii.

The luxurious house was partially preserved by being buried by the eruption of Mount Vesuvius. The atrium has a central pool, open to the sky, and is surrounded by a symmetrical arrangement of rooms. Beyond, there is a garden surrounded by a peristyle of columns supporting a roof. Pieces of the original mosaic wall decoration survived and are now preserved under glass.

2.21 Wall paintings in the House of the Vettii.

The walls of the rooms of the houses in Pompeii often included paintings of simulated architectural detail. The painting was of considerable artistic merit, and other paintings with architectural themes, such as those in the corner of this room, may give clues to the design of local buildings no longer extant.

2.22 Wall paintings in the House of the Vettii.

A wall painting in another room of the house of the Vettii includes a band of amusing cupids, which may illustrate a story no longer known. The cupids appear to be at work in a pharmacy, mixing up potions in great vats. The details of cabinets and cauldrons provide information about the design of the furniture and equipment that might have been found in Roman houses of the time. The wall surfaces above and below are painted in the orange-red generally known as Pompeiian red.

LOGGIA facing toward it. Plans are quite varied according to the size and shape of the lot: often there was an upper story with rooms having secondary functions, perhaps rooms for children, servants, or storage.

Furniture and Other Interior Furnishings

The hot volcanic lava and ash that buried Pompeii and Herculaneum destroyed the wooden structural parts of houses and objects of wood, but elements that were not of inflammable materials survived— stone couches and tables, iron and bronze artifacts, oil lamps and charcoal braziers, and decorative fresco paintings and mosaics. Taken together, the ruins, the surviving objects, and the images in paintings and mosaics have made it possible to reconstruct Pompeiian, and therefore ancient Roman, design in considerable detail. Walls of rooms, uncluttered by windows, were generally painted with simulated architectural detail of moldings and pilasters forming a plain WAINSCOT below; the PANELS above might be painted in solid color or with naturalistic painting of exterior scenes or imagery from mythology or scenes of daily life. Perspective was partially understood and used to heighten realistic, TROMPE L'OEIL effects— framed paintings seemingly hung on walls, false decorative details, and, in mosaic, objects that appear to lie on floors. Favorite colors were black and a vermilion red that has come to be called "Pompeiian." Roman furniture was developed from Greek prototypes with a tendency toward greater elaboration of ornamental detail and the use of fine woods and inlays of ivory or metal. Folding stools and certain types of chairs developed a role as symbols of rank or status rather than as devices solely for seating comfort. A wall painting

from the House of the Vettii illustrates a fanciful scene of cupids at work (**fig. 2.22**) in what appears to be a pharmacy, which is shown furnished with work tables, stools, and cabinets that give an idea of what the varied and rich furniture of Rome must have been.

The Legacy of Rome: Technology

Technological skills of the Romans can be traced in the surviving evidence of their well-planned water supply systems, using aqueducts and tanks to feed efficient plumbing, their sanitary sewage disposal arrangements, and even a central heating system of considerable sophistication. While the Mediterranean climate hardly required any heating beyond that provided by portable charcoal burners, as the Romans pushed northward they faced colder weather. As far north as the great wall built by Hadrian across the British Isles at the limit of Roman colonization, houses (or VILLAS) were built where surviving ruins make it possible to inspect a radiant heating system. This involved a stone floor supported a short distance above the ground on brick or stone posts. The hollow space below the floor was connected with a furnace on one side of the building and a chimney on the opposite side. When a fire was built in the furnace, combustion gases were drawn through the under-floor chamber, the same technique used to heat the great baths in Rome. The warmed floor surface reached a mild but comfortable temperature. This approach to heating was not rediscovered until modern times when it appeared with the name "radiant heating."

Knowledge of Roman design is considerably aided by the oldest extant text on architecture, *De*

A Entablature
B Column
C Cornice
D Frieze
E Architrave
F Capital
G Shaft
H Base
I Plinth

1 Abacus
2 Volute
3 Dentils
4 Fascia

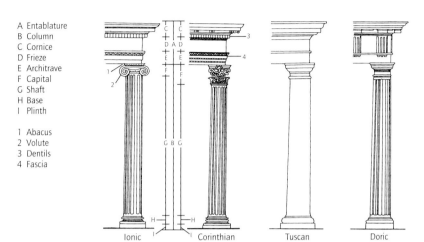

Ionic   Corinthian   Tuscan   Doric   Composite

2.23 Roman orders of architecture.

From left to right: Ionic (similar to the earlier Greek Ionic); Corinthian (the most elaborate of Roman orders, hardly differing from the Greek Corinthian); Tuscan (a simplified Doric); Doric (unlike Greek Doric, it has a base and more ornate capital); and Composite (a Roman attempt to combine Corinthian and Ionic forms—the last of the Roman developments).

Architectura, written sometime between 90 and 20 B.C.E. by the Roman architect and engineer Marcus Vitruvius Pollio, now generally known simply as Vitruvius. Ten books dealt with many technical matters, fortification building, the making of bricks and concrete, machinery, clocks, and water supply systems, and the education of the architect. It also included chapters on the design of temples, public buildings, and houses, discussion of aesthetic issues, and a full account of the Roman Doric, Ionic, and Corinthian orders (**fig. 2.23**). It sets forth the analysis of design goals as made up of the three phases—*utilitas*, *firmitas*, and *venustas*. Translated by Sir Henry Wotton in 1624 as "commodity, firmness, and delight," and often rendered today as function, structure, and aesthetics, Vitruvius's analysis is still viewed as a useful basis for understanding the complexities that all design involves. In the Renaissance, study of surviving Roman remains was supported by study of significant portions of Vitruvius's text. It is still valued as the oldest surviving written work to present a thorough study of architectural practice.

From a modern point of view, Roman design seems technically advanced, orderly, systematic, and aesthetically impressive, although often ostentatious, overly decorative, and lacking in subtlety. Influence of Roman design can be traced through subsequent periods, recessive in the Middle Ages, but reemergent in the Renaissance as the dominant theme of European architecture and design. The gradual decline of Roman civilization and its eventual collapse form the background for the complex developments that followed.

3

Early Christian, Byzantine, and Romanesque

By 400 C.E., Roman world domination had declined significantly. The empire split into separate eastern and western empires, each with its own capital and emperor. The western empire was destined to collapse under the pressure of northern European invaders whom the Romans called Vandals. From several competing religions, Christianity took a dominant role, with its center moving eastward to Constantinople (now Istanbul). In design history, a time of conflicting trends begins with the growth of the European direction usually called Early Christian design, the work centering in the eastern empire called Byzantine, and the emergence of the ROMANESQUE style that came to dominate the design of medieval Europe. These aspects of design history overlap, interrelate, and to a degree conflict so that the years from the "fall" of Rome, usually dated at 410, until 1000 or 1100 can seem disordered and confusing.

Early Christian Design

When Christianity was made an officially accepted religion by the Roman emperor Constantine in 313 C.E., it became possible for Christians to abandon secret meetings and catacomb burial places in favor of a public and visible presence. The rituals of

Christianity such as baptism and, in particular, the celebration of the mass called for new building types. Earlier temples had not been intended to accommodate a public gathering, but a Christian church was primarily an auditorium where a congregation could assemble to watch and participate in religious rites. To serve this need, the Christians turned to the earlier Roman building type that came closest to serving their needs; this was the basilica, a public meeting hall used by the Romans as a courtroom.

The Early Christian basilican church had a high central nave suited to processions and the gathering of a congregation. At one end, in an apse, was the altar and other arrangements for the clergy conducting a mass or other service. On either side of the naves, AISLES, in larger churches sometimes twin aisles, provided space for the public and for various shrines and secondary functions. The nave, higher than the aisles, was lighted by high clerestory windows. Walls were constructed of masonry, the roofs spanned by large wooden members. The upper walls of the nave were supported by rows of closely spaced columns carrying lintels or arches. The change in height and the line of columns made a clear separation between nave and aisles. This simple configuration was the basis on which most subsequent church building developed. In the Early Christian era, elaboration developed in several ways. Columns were generally based on one of the Roman orders, sometimes Ionic, most often Corinthian. Their material was stone, frequently marble of rich color. The walls above the columns were often painted, the half dome over the apse painted or lined with mosaic illustrating religious themes. Floors were often paved with colored stones in geometric patterns and strong colors. Materials, even complete columns with their capitals, were often taken from earlier Roman temples and other buildings, thereby transferring Roman design into basilican churches in a most direct manner.

The large Roman basilican churches of S. Paul Outside the Walls (386 C.E.) and S. Maria Maggiore (432) are examples of the type although much altered by later elaboration. The smaller churches of S. Maria in Cosmedin (**fig. 3.1**) in Rome (772–95) or of S. Apollinare in Classe (*c.* 500) in Ravenna are less modified by later reconstruction. At S. Maria in Cosmedin, there is a partially enclosed area at the front of the nave, almost a building within the building, that provided a

3.1 (*below*) S. Maria in Cosmedin, Rome, 772–95.

The basic scheme of the Roman basilica—a long nave with aisles on either side and an apse at the end—has been converted to serve as a Christian church. The ancient Roman columns have been reused to support a wall with a high clerestory. The roof is of wood. A choir has been built that extends into the nave. The largely red and green floor mosaic adds color.

3.2 (*opposite*) S. Marco, Venice, Italy, *c.* 1063–73 and after.

Five domes on pendentives—three for the nave, one for each transept—create the space of this famous church. The mosaics that cover the surface of every wall and dome introduce spectacular color into an otherwise dim interior. The building represents a link between the earlier work in Constantinople and other Asian locations and the Romanesque style that was developing in Europe.

3.3 S. Costanza, Rome, c. 350.

Built as a mausoleum for the daughter of the Emperor Constantine, the building was later converted to a Christian church. The central domed space is surrounded by an aisle or ambulatory with a mosaic-covered barrel vault overhead. Clerestory windows light the central space, while marble wall surfaces and the mosaic introduce varied color.

forward extension of the apse to make a CHANCEL or CHOIR, an element that gradually became an important part of church buildings.

An alternative type of religious building used a round or octagonal plan to focus on a centrally placed baptismal font, altar or tomb. S. Costanza (**fig. 3.3**; 350 C.E.) and S. Stefano Rotondo (468–83 C.E.), both in Rome, are of this type. Such central planning with its RADIAL SYMMETRY has been used for many Christian churches, but the basilican model with its BILATERAL SYMMETRY and its strong orientation toward an altar, usually placed at the east end to establish an eastward-facing direction for its symbolic significance (facing toward the Holy Land), tended to become the favored plan

type. In both designs, painted and mosaic decoration in rich color contributed to internal richness while also serving as a teaching tool through the illustration of events of religious historical significance to a generally illiterate public.

Byzantine Design

With the relocation of the Roman capital to Byzantium (330 C.E.), renamed Constantinople by the emperor Constantine, and with the eventual break into separate eastern and western Roman empires, a new center of development was created. The influence of Byzantine architecture and design developed in the east, flowed back to Italy to

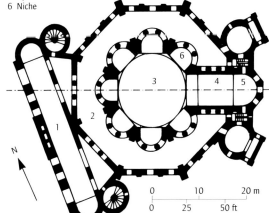

1 Narthex
2 Ambulatory
3 Nave
4 Sanctuary
5 Apse
6 Niche

The Ravenna Mosaics

And I saw light in river form with tide
Of fulgent fire between two margins teeming
Which wondrously with flowers of spring were dyed
Out of that current, living sparks were teeming
And flashing from the flowers with hues intense
Like very rubies from gold patinas gleaming.[1]

The great Italian poet Dante Alighieri wrote these lines from the *Divine Comedy* in Ravenna. He was inspired by the glowing mosaics which had been created in a series of churches and chapels there in the sixth century to reflect the glory of God and the Byzantine court.

The lines of another, unknown, poet were transcribed into the mosaics in the Archiepiscopal Chapel:

Aut lux nata est, aut capta hic libera regnat (Either light was born or imprisoned here, it reigns supreme)[2]

The Emperor Justinian and his wife Theodora had their own portraits set into mosaic in the church of S. Vitale, next to Archbishop Maximian, the founder of the church. The forceful portrait of the latter prompted the following comment by Andreas Agnellus, a sixth-century chronicler of the work at the church:

tall in stature, slender in body, lean in face, bald headed but for a few hairs, grey eyed and saintly in character . . . . In architecture and in technical execution there is nothing similar to it in Italy.[3]

All the figures in the mosaics wear Byzantine official court robes, presenting images so powerful and impressive that even at the height of the Renaissance, the early fifteenth-century humanist Antonio Traversari remarked:

never have we gazed upon a finer or more elegant wall decoration.[4]

1. Dante Alighieri, *The Divine Comedy*, trs. Melville Anderson; 2. Quoted in Guiseppe Bovini, *Ravenna Mosaics* (London, 1957), p. 6; 3. *Ibid*, p. 474; 4. *Ibid*, p. 9

mingle with the Early Christian work evolving there at the same time. At Ravenna, the western outpost of Constantine's eastern empire, the two styles can be seen developing side by side. In Byzantine work, the classical detail of Roman architecture faded in favor of limited and freer use of such basics as the column and its capital. The engineering skills of ancient Rome were, however, retained and developed with skillful use of vaulting and domed construction.

Ravenna

At Ravenna, S. Apollinare in Classe (mentioned above) is of basilican type and uses extraordinary mosaic art that serves both as decoration and as didactic illustration of religious subjects. The church of S. Vitale (**figs. 3.4** and **3.5**; c. 532–48) made use of an octagonal central plan with a domed roof built from hollow pottery units that reduced the weight of the structure. There is a chancel extending from one face of the octagon making the building ambiguously both radial and bilateral in its symmetry. It can be regarded both as an example of Early Christian work relating to churches in Rome, and as Byzantine. The latter stylistic attribution can be supported by the richly decorated interior, with wall surfaces covered in colored marbles in complex patterns together with mosaic images representing figures from religious texts. The central space is surrounded by an

3.4 (*above left*)
S. Vitale, Ravenna, Italy, c. 532–48.

A church built to an octagonal central plan with a short apse extending to the east. The domed central space is surrounded by an aisle with an upper gallery. Light enters from clerestory windows high above, while the column capitals are of the simplified carved block type, typical of Byzantine design. Colorful marbles and mosaics and the complexity of the plan generate an extraordinary internal space within a simple, almost barren exterior.

3.5 (*above right*)
Section and plan of S. Vitale.

The circular central area is surrounded by niches and then by an outer aisle, or ambulatory, which converts the exterior of the building to an octagon. The entrance narthex (vestibule) is angled to relate to two adjacent faces of the octagon.

AMBULATORY passage with a gallery above, its columned niches forming links between the central space and its surround. The columns suggest Roman precedent, but the capitals are now carved in abstract forms closer to Near Eastern origins. Daylight, entering from the high, clerestory windows, aided in creating an atmosphere suggestive of mystical religious belief.

Hagia Sophia

By far the most important of Byzantine works is the great church of Hagia Sophia (S. Sophia; 532–7) in Constantinople (**figs. 3.6** and **3.7**). The vast, striking interior space of this building is dependent on its daringly engineered structure. The problem of placing a domed roof on a space of any shape other than round had been studied by the Romans but never fully solved. The PENDENTIVE, a curving triangular wedge shaped to fill the space between two adjacent arches built at right angles to one another and curved so as to become a quarter circle at its top, is a device developed by Byzantine builders and used at Hagia Sophia to support the central, 107 foot diameter brick dome. The arches on either side of the central space are filled in; the walls are penetrated at floor and gallery levels by columned arcades. Those at front and back are open to half domes that open in turn to smaller domed EXEDRAE (niches). The geometry of the great central dome on pendentives can be understood as being a half-spherical dome from which four segments have been cut away to convert it to a square needing support only at its four corners. The corners are BUTTRESSED at Hagia Sophia by the half domes at front and rear and by external solid masonry masses at either side. Just above the pendentives, there is a ring of forty small windows that light the interior and lend the dome a sense of weightlessness.

The mosaic images that lined Hagia Sophia were obliterated when the building became a mosque, in accordance with the Islamic prohibition of realistic representation in art. The much later (tenth to eleventh century) church of S. Marco in Venice (**fig. 3.2**), built with five domes on pendentives that cover the four arms of a GREEK CROSS plan and its central crossing, has retained its elaborately carved choir screen, chancel fittings, and rich interior lining of mosaics. It is probably the most complete and best example of Byzantine church interior treatment.

3.6 Hagia Sophia, Istanbul, Turkey, 532–7.

The largest and most spectacular of Byzantine churches, Hagia Sophia has a vast central space that is surmounted by a dome on pendentives with a circle of windows at its base. The windows appear to make the dome float. Some of the original mosaics covering the wall and dome have been preserved. Columns with typically Byzantine capitals support arches that open to aisles and galleries above the aisles.

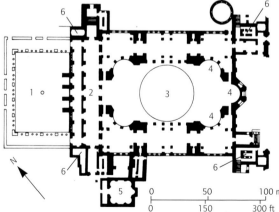

3.7 Plan of Hagia Sophia.
1 Atrium
2 Narthex
3 Nave
4 Apse
5 Baptistry
6 Minaret

The central domed space is extended by half domes at the front and back to give the exterior a strong lengthways axis, which extends from the entrance narthex toward the apse facing the southeast.

Secular Buildings

Secular building contemporary with the Early Christian and Byzantine churches survives in such limited fragments and ruins that study of the interiors is difficult. Great baths and palaces were built by the eastern Roman empire following earlier Roman practice, but almost nothing remains intact. Residential building and the buildings of early monasteries have also largely disappeared or have been extensively reconstructed. Some houses in Venice date from the era of Byzantine influence. They are typically several stories in height; each floor is laid out with a broad central hall space lighted from front and back with smaller rooms opening from both sides. Byzantine influence can also be traced in the architecture of medieval Greece, Italy, and in the domed churches of Russia.

Early Medieval: The "Dark Ages"

In Europe, after the collapse of Roman authority—the sack of Rome by the Visigoths in 410 C.E. is a convenient date to mark its ending— a period of confusion followed, often referred to as the "Dark Ages." Historians dislike this term, feeling that it suggests a time totally lacking civilized culture. Certainly the period from about 400 to about 1200 suffered from the absence of any centralized government or authority and from the disappearance of the organized systems of Roman law, roads, and economy. In this anarchic period, what order there was came from the authority exercised by local strong men who were themselves a threat to order as they fought one another for territory and exploited the general population in any way they chose.

A feudal system gradually emerged in which power was established by force and apportioned, along with control of land, by a hierarchical, authoritarian system. Control passed downward from a royal or imperial top level to layers of titled aristocrats to, at the bottom, the serfs or peasants who farmed land and paid taxes to support the feudal structure. In this situation, with chaos only restrained to a degree by the exercise of armed force, military authority became dominant.

With offensive warfare constantly waged between feudal strong men, conduct of normal life became dependent on defensive techniques. The weapons of the strong were only swords, spears, and bows and arrows. A man dressed in armor had

a decisive advantage over any attacker. The building of a sturdy wall around a house, making it a castle, or around a town or city made the occupants relatively secure. The feudal lord occupying a castle could offer protection to a walled town, establishing a relationship of mutual advantage between the often brutal leader and the exploited population that lived under his protection. The development of this pattern in the early Middle Ages (before 1000) established the context for design, art, and architecture usually identified by the stylistic designation Romanesque.

The Romanesque Style

It was not until Charlemagne (771–814) established a new center of authority and power that the "darkness" of the Dark Ages began to give way to the appearance of a new strain of enlightenment in

3.8 Odo von Metz, Palatine chapel, Aachen (Aix-la-Chapelle), Germany, 798.

A space built as a chapel for the palace of Charlemagne is the only remaining part of the proposed building. The octagonal interior, based on S. Vitale, Ravenna, has an eight-sided vault roof; two galleries surround the space, with a clerestory above. Mosaic decoration was used in the surrounding passages at ground level, and colorful marbles cover the surfaces of the central space. Semicircular arches use voussoirs of light and dark stone.

3.9 Plan of the monastery of S. Gall, Switzerland, c. 820.
1 Church
2 Cloister
3 Infirmary
4 Chapel
5 Novitiate
6 Orchard/Cemetery
7 Garden
8 Barn
9 Workshops
10 Brewery and bakery
11 Stables
12 Animal pens
13 Hostel
14 Guesthouse
15 School
16 Abbot's house
17 Scriptorium and library
18 Dormitory
19 Refectory
20 Kitchens
21 Cellars
22 Hospice for the poor
23 Baths and latrines

The early medieval Benedictine monastery, now replaced by a later building, is known only from a plan that shows its extensive elements. Such a monastery was conceived as a closed, self-sustaining community, able to provide for all of its residents' needs. The church's double-ended design—it has an apse at each end—was intended to be the ideal scheme for other churches and cathedrals of Germany and adjacent regions in the ninth century.

the arts to parallel developments in other aspects of life. The term Carolingian (which derives from the name Charles) is used to describe the work of this era, which can be viewed as an early phase of Romanesque architecture and art. The term Romanesque derives from the continued use of aspects of Roman design, the semicircular arch in particular, and versions of the detail of Roman interiors. It is somewhat misleading in its implication of a strong connection with Rome. The Roman empire, its culture, and its art had been largely lost and forgotten in the early Middle Ages.

At Charlemagne's capital at Aachen (Aix-la-Chapelle) a great palace, built with regard for concepts of order and symmetry, is the epitome of Romanesque style. Only the chapel survives (**fig. 3.8**), a centrally planned octagon topped by an eight-sided vault with surrounding passages at floor level and at the two levels of galleries above. Semicircular arches and barrel vaults recall the techniques of ancient Rome. The building is now embedded in later construction, but the interior survives much as built.

The visual element most readily identified with Romanesque design is the semicircular arch. It was the most advanced structural technique remaining in use—clearly a primary device of Roman architecture remembered or, perhaps, rediscovered for use in stone building. Wood was the usual material for everyday structures—no longer surviving—and was the most common material for floor and roof construction of stone buildings. Vaults eventually came into use where the desire for permanence

justified their use. The early Romanesque vault was a simple barrel vault, invariably semicircular in form. Eventually more complex vaulting systems developed and groin vaulting appeared, but always with semicircular form.

Barrel vaults were often used in placing a stone roof over a long church nave, a problem that was approached in a variety of ways during the Romanesque era. In general, continuity of space was best served by a continuous barrel vault which made provision of windows difficult and so led to a dark interior. Other solutions tended to break the nave up into a series of separate units, each topped with its own vault, or regressed to the acceptance of a wooden roof with limited lasting qualities. At Tournus in France, the abbey church of S. Philibert (960–1120) has a nave higher than the adjacent groin-vaulted aisles. The roof is a series of transverse barrel vaults, each thus buttressed by its neighbor leaving the clerestory wall available for large windows. The interior effect of the many vaults breaks up the unity of the nave in a way that left this approach an experiment not repeated. There is also at S. Philibert a Narthex or vestibule on two levels, approaching the concept of the German Westwork (see below). The chancel end with an apse surrounded by a curving aisle or ambulatory with radiating small chapels was to become a characteristic element of later French church building.

Churches

Germany

At Corvey-on-the-Weser in Germany, the abbey church of S. Michael (873–85) is a basilican church with an aisled nave. To its eastward-facing main body, a massive unit, almost a complete building in itself, was added at the west (front) end. This element, called a "westwork," became a frequent part of German Carolingian and early Romanesque churches. The development of major spaces at the west end of churches can be observed in the surviving plan drawing of the monastery of S. Gall (**fig. 3.9**; *c.* 820). It shows an orderly but intricate layout for all the parts of this vast institution, with the large church laid out with an apse at each end making the building almost symmetrical length-wise as well as transversely. This double-ended church plan survived in varying forms in Germany, in the building of westworks and in the plans of later German churches. At S. Michael at

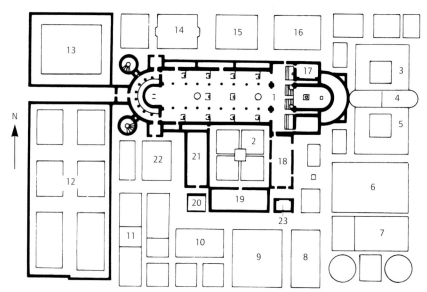

3.12 (*left*) Cathedral, Speyer, Germany, from 1024–33.

This massive cathedral, built as a symbol of the power of the Frankish emperors, has semicircular arches and, originally, a wooden roof. Later modifications, including the thickening of the piers, made possible the substitution of a groin-vaulted stone roof.

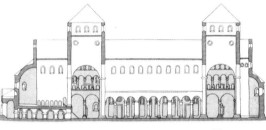

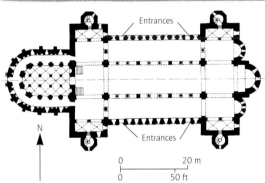

3.10 (*above left*) S. Michael's, Hildesheim, Germany, 1010–33 (reconstructed after World War II).

The Romanesque interior is of basilican type with a center nave and aisles on either side connected to the nave by arcades. There are small windows high up on the nave walls forming a clerestory. The roof is of wood and a square tower rises at each end of the nave supported by arches.

3.11 (*left*) Plan of S. Michael's.

At each end of the church, transepts on either side were topped by towers. The aisles on either side of the nave are almost double its width. A small apse on the east was later outmatched by a large, vaulted chancel extending to the west.

3.13 (*right*) S. Miniato al Monte, Florence, Italy, 1018–62.

The nave is divided into three sections, each of which is roofed in wood. At each end is a crypt that opens to the nave. Above, a choir rises above eye-level. Contrasting black and white marble covers the walls. The windows are of thin, translucent marble.

Hildesheim (**figs. 3.10** and **3.11**; 1010–33) TRANSEPTS and tower are placed symmetrically at each end of the basilican nave with aisles.

The cathedrals of Speyer (**fig. 3.12**; begun *c.* 1024), Mainz (after 1009), and Worms (begun 1170) indicate the spread of Romanesque concepts eastward from Germany into that part of Europe.

Italy

The church of S. Miniato in Florence (**fig. 3.13**; 1018–62) is wood roofed but its interior is elaborately decorated with black and white marble in geometric pattern. The chancel is raised to open up a view into a lower CRYPT level below the chancel. S. Ambrogio, Milan (1080–1128), has a plan based on the Early Christian basilica with an open atrium in front. The nave is in four BAYS (units), three

3.14 Church of S. Foy, Conques, France, 1050–1120.

The pilgrimage church is built to a cruciform plan, with tall, narrow proportions. An octagonal tower tops the crossing. The barrel-vaulted nave has arches defining each bay, and the arched openings into aisles and galleries above permit only limited light to reach the nave from small windows in the outer walls. At the east end, in contrast, larger windows admit light to the ambulatory choir. The church was originally richly decorated with carvings, paintings, and tapestries, but all have been removed. The reliquary statue of the saint (see p. 50) gives an idea of the nature of the original ornamental richness.

roofed with a square groin vault, having the diagonal lines of the groins emphasized as stone ribs. The fourth bay is the chancel, now topped by an octagonal stubby tower or LANTERN. The two-level aisles are topped by square groin vaults.

France

The church of S. Foy at Conques in France (**fig. 3.14**; 1050–1120) is a station on one of the great pilgrimage routes of the Middle Ages. The relic of the martyred saint, housed in a gilded and jeweled statue, attracted hordes of worshipers on the traditional route to Santiago de Compostela in Spain. Its nave, high and narrow in relation to width, is topped by a barrel vault with aisles two levels in height on either side. The upper aisles are covered with half barrel vaults rising to the top of the nave side walls so that there is no clerestory level. Windows here are large enough to light the aisles so that they are brighter than the nave; the octagonal, domed tower above the crossing where transepts and nave meet is also windowed. Except for carved column capitals, the interior is simple and austere, although the "treasure" that attracted the pilgrims' attention would have been displayed in the chancel in mountings of gold and jewels.

3.15 Abbey Church of La Madeleine, Vézelay, France, 1104–32.

This is a high, light church, with an uninterrupted view from the narthex to the apse. A stone roof of groin vaulting is defined at each of the three bays by arches that use voussoirs of contrasting light and dark stone, as do the arches of the nave arcades that open into the aisles. The wall above the nave arcades has clerestory windows. The column capitals retain their elaborate and fanciful carving. The distant choir is a later, Gothic addition.

In the Madeleine at Vézelay (**fig. 3.15**; 1104–32), another French pilgrimage church, the roof vaulting has become more complex. The arches that separate the nave from the aisles define bays marked by an arch that spans the nave and supports a groin vault. The voussoirs of the arches are of alternating light and dark stone. The chancel end at Vézelay is of later date and GOTHIC in design.

A number of structural systems for the building of large churches developed in parallel during the Romanesque era. S. Front at Périgueux (twelfth century) is made up of five domed units arranged in a Greek cross similar to the design of S. Marco in

Venice, but the interior effect is strikingly different because the simplicity of bare stone has replaced the richness of Venetian mosaic. In Normandy, a step toward the cathedral type was taken with the building of the Abbaye-aux-Hommes (S. Etienne, 1060–81), built at Caen by William the Conqueror to celebrate his successful conquest of England in 1066. The plan is CRUCIFORM (having the shape of a LATIN CROSS), with a long, groin-vaulted nave, transepts, and a deep chancel. There are aisles, an upper level above the aisles called a TRIFORIUM, and a clerestory level above at the level of the main vaulting. The vaults are square, but each is divided by a cross arch at its center to match the spacing of the supporting columns, two bays to each main vault. With its two diagonal groin ribs, such a vault is divided into six triangular panels and is therefore called SEXPARTITE. This scheme comes very close to the design that would become typical for the Gothic cathedrals that were to follow.

With an island location off the Normandy coast, the monastic grouping of Mont S. Michel (**fig. 3.16**; eleventh century) includes a number of spaces dating from the Romanesque era, long before the building of the church and other Gothic structures

that top the Mont. There are chapels from the tenth century with unornamented stone arches and vaults, and a groin-vaulted crypt with stubby columns centered in the space to support the vaults. The only decoration is simple, abstract carving of the column capitals. The nave of the church is also typically Romanesque, with semicircular arches at the aisle and triforium levels and for the clerestory windows above. The roof is constructed of wood. The walls and houses of the town built on the lower edges of the Mont contribute to the remarkable historic cross-section of French medieval architecture, built and rebuilt from Carolingian times to the fifteenth century, all available for study in this single complex.

England

The Romanesque way of building was brought into England by the Norman conquest of 1066. The term NORMAN is used in England to denote the work that would be called Romanesque elsewhere in Europe. Many English cathedrals began as Norman buildings—some, reconstructed or altered in the Gothic era, retain only fragments of Norman parts; others are largely of Norman construction. The naves of Durham (**fig. 3.17**) and

3.16 (*left*) Abbey of Mont S. Michel, France, from 1017.

The vast Salle des Chevaliers (Knights' Hall) is one of the rooms in the abbey complex. It may be named from the fact that it housed the knights who defended the abbey or from the military order of St. Michael, established by Louis XI. The stone vaulting marks the beginning of the transition from the use of semicircular arches, which form the diagonal of each bay, into pointed arches, which form the four sides of each bay. The openness of the space results from the way in which the vault arches are supported on relatively slim piers.

3.17 Durham Cathedral, County Durham, England, 1110-33.

The semicircular arches of the nave arcades indicate the Norman (Romanesque) date of this fine cathedral. The groin vaulting above, with its slightly pointed transverse arches points to the Gothic developments that follow. The grey stone was probably originally painted in bright colors, while the carved patterning of the round piers, which alternate with the compound piers, introduces a striking element of visual activity. The cathedral, unusually, still has its original clerestory windows.

3.18 St. Andrew's Church, Borgund, Sogne Fjord, Norway, *c.* 1150.

In the construction of the Norwegian buildings known as stave churches, the stone vocabulary of Romanesque building is translated into wood. The arch forms are not structural but exist to offer a simulation of the stone-built monasteries of France. This church is nearly 50 feet high, and tiny windows high up provide the only light. Many stave churches house wall and ceiling painting, reminiscent of the illumination of medieval manuscripts.

of Gloucester with their massive arcade columns date from the end of the eleventh century. At Durham, alternate columns are of simple cylindrical form, but carry carved abstract, geometric patterning. Almost all of Peterborough (begun 1118)'is Norman, as is all but the chancel of Ely. Richly painted wood ceilings hide the trusses of the wooden roof structure.

Scandinavia

In Denmark, Sweden, Finland, and Norway, in particular, a number of wooden churches and other buildings have survived from around the years 1000 to 1200. The most striking of these are the Finnish wood churches, called STAVE CHURCHES with reference to the great wooden poles—virtually whole tree trunks—that form their main structure. The typical stave church is small, usually about 30 × 50 feet in ground plan, but tall—often as much as 100 feet high. The central body of these churches is a tall space formed by the great vertical timbers that suggest the masts of ships. Around the central space there is a lower aisle with an outside wall of wide boards. The resulting building can be read as a small wooden version of the typical nave and aisle Romanesque church type. It seems probable that both the general concept and many details were brought to Scandinavia by missionary monks who came north to make Christian converts of the Norse Vikings and who taught church building with verbal descriptions of the monastic churches of the south. The semicircular arches of stone arcades are reproduced in wood, and details carved in wood suggest memory of comparable work in stone. Hundreds of such churches were standing in the nineteenth century but there are now only about twenty-four. Borgund church (**fig. 3.18**; *c.* 1150) is a fine example. The church at Torpo (*c.* 1190) is remarkable for its colorful interior paintings that line an arched partial ceiling, which suggests an intention to simulate a stone barrel vault. The painted figures acting out events of religious legends suggest the style of medieval manuscript illumination.

Fortresses and Castles

Early castles were simply houses built on a raised mound, a natural hill, or in some other place easy to defend and to surround with a wall—at first merely a fence or palisade of wood. Before long, wood was replaced by stone as a more lasting and more resistant material. The house or KEEP of the castle might stand free within the wall, or be built up against it sharing part of its stone structure. The castle keep was usually of several stories, forming a compact mass easy to defend from its upper levels and roof.

Some early castles, called TOWER HOUSES, were simply towers with rooms stacked up vertically inside, often with corner projections to make defense of the walls easier. Gradually, as military techniques for attack improved, castles were improved with defensive towers along the walls, elaborate gates, and multiple systems of walls. The castle garrison grew larger and living accommodations had to become more elaborate. The rooms of a castle were generally as bare and simple as those of an ordinary house. An all-purpose main room, the hall, served as living and dining room for the owner, his family, and for whatever servants and garrison the castle might house. Private rooms for the family, service spaces, and other conveniences were added

very slowly as medieval life became increasingly settled and orderly with the passage of time.

Since castles were usually stone built (although with most floors and roofs of wood) a number of examples survive or have been restored which give us an idea of what interiors were like. A feudal lord would often hold several castles, each intended to enforce his authority over a particular area. Exercise of that authority meant appearing periodically at each castle in sequence to conduct audiences, settle legal disputes, and simply be visible in a context where there was no organized system of communication. The castle family and garrison were, accordingly, transient, setting up housekeeping for a time in a particular castle before moving on. Most furniture and other possessions of value were portable so that they could move with the family.

The rooms of a castle usually had walls of bare stone (sometimes whitewashed), floors of bare stone or bare wood boards, a structural wooden ceiling, and tiny, slit windows for protection and because there was no glass available to keep out the weather. The hall might have a hearth for a fire at its center with a smoke-hole in the roof. A fireplace and chimney were late innovations. At one end, a raised portion of floor, the dais, made a separate space for the table where the family and honored guests would sit. In the body of the hall, boards set up on trestles served as tables and serving stands. Seating was on benches or stools—if there was a chair at all it was an honorary seat for the lord at the head table. Eventually hangings appeared as a way to cover bare walls and make them less cold and forbidding. Tapestries developed as an art form that provided portable wall covering along with decoration. The main fire and burning torches placed on stands or in wall brackets were the light sources at night.

In England there are a number of castles with intact halls dating from around 1100 or 1200. The hall of Hedingham Castle (**fig. 3.19**; *c.* 1140) in Essex is two stories high with doors, windows, and overlooking balconies topped with Norman (Romanesque semicircular) arches. There is a great stone arch across the center of the room to support the ends of the wooden beams of the roof overhead. An arched fireplace is an indication of unusual luxury.

3.19 Hedingham Castle, Essex, England, *c.* 1140.

The hall of this English castle has a great, central stone arch to support the wooden timbers that carry the smaller beams of the roof construction. The semicircular arches identify the construction as Norman (Romanesque), while ornament is limited to simple moldings at the spring of the arches. An arched fireplace connects to a flue within the wall leading to a chimney. The furniture and small objects here are not original, but most are of a sort that might have been present during the Middle Ages.

Monasteries and Abbeys

While the castle provided protection to make a settled life possible for knights whose lives were oriented toward warfare, the Middle Ages developed another institution to provide a different means of protection to those inclined toward religion, learning, and the arts. This was the institution of monasticism, the development of religious communities whose members gave up the life of the secular world in exchange for the protected isolation of the monastery. The protection came not from defensive structure, but from remote location, the vows of poverty that meant the absence of treasure that might tempt attack, and from the respect granted to those who devoted themselves to good works and religious pursuits. The monastic orders—Benedictine, Cistercian, Cluniac, and others—gathered member monks and built monasteries that included a church, housing, and all the services needed to make a closed, self-sustaining community. In the Pyrenees in France, the monastery of S. Martin du Canigou (**fig. 3.22**; 1007–26) is still today a small cluster of buildings built in a virtually inaccessible location high in the mountains. The church is a basilican structure with nave and side aisles roofed in stone with simple barrel vaults. The outward thrust of the nave vault is restrained by the vaults of the aisles whose vaults are in turn buttressed by thick

3.20 Monastery of S. Martin du Canigou, France, 1007–26.

The monastery's church has a barrel-vaulted interior, with the vault resting on walls that are, in turn, supported by a simple arcade of arches resting on simple columns, the capitals of which are only a faint shadow of their Roman prototypes. Tiny windows at the distant apse end and in side walls admit limited light, and the only color is that of the natural stone.

The Abbey at Cluny

The great Abbey at Cluny was modeled on the rule of St. Benedict. The saint, who died in 547, was renowned for his ascetic and hermit-like ways and the austerity of his rule, as his first community of monks at Vicovaro witnessed:

It soon became evident that his strict notions of monastic discipline did not suit them, for all that they lived in rock-hewn cells; and in order to get rid of him they went so far as to mingle poison in his wine. When, as was his wont, he made the sign of the cross over the jug, it broke in pieces as if a stone had fallen upon it. "God forgive you, brothers," the abbot said without anger, "Why have you plotted this wicked thing against me? Did I not tell you that my customs would not accord with yours? Go and find an abbot to your taste." [1]

Benedictine communities became renowned for their simple life, devotion to prayer, and music. The Abbey at Cluny was the most famous example in terms of architecture and music. The security and beauty of life there attracted many rich benefactors, prompting the reforming St. Bernard to thunder in 1115 against the richness and grandeur found in the abbey, which,

while they attract the eye of the worshipper, hinder the soul's devotion. However, let that pass; we suppose it is done, as we are told, for the glory of God. But as a monk, I say, Tell me, O ye professor of poverty, what does gold do in a holy place . . . by the sight of wonderful and costly vanities, men are prompted to give rather than to pray [2]

1. *Discourses of St. Gregory,* quoted in Butler, *Lives of the Saints,* ed. Herbert Thurston SJ (London, 1956), p. 652; 2. St. Bernard, *Apologia,* quoted in Olive Cook, *English Abbeys and Priories* (London, 1960), p. 67

walls. Only tiny windows penetrate the thick walls leading to a dark interior. The columns that support arches opening between nave and aisles are simple drums with capitals that carry a slight suggestion of the Roman Corinthian type. The adjacent CLOISTER with arcaded passages around an open central court, an important element of the monastery plan, led to the dormitory, refectory (dining hall), and other rooms serving the various functions of the community.

The Cistercian abbeys of Le Thoronet (**fig. 3.21**), Senanque, and Silvacane, built in southern France around 1130, have austere vaulted churches with aisles and projecting transepts generating a cross-shaped plan with obvious symbolic significance. A barrel vault covers the nave and half barrel

vaults the side aisles. The outward thrust of the nave vault is resisted by the half barrel vaults of the aisles which act as continuous buttresses; their thrust is absorbed by massive masonry side walls. Only tiny windows were possible, except in the end wall where larger windows could be placed. There was originally no furniture in the church except for stone benches at the sides and stone altars in the center apse and in the secondary apses—two on each side, making up the five required by the typical Cistercian monastic plan. The church had only a small door at one side of the front, indicating its closure to the outside world: primary access was from the adjacent cloister and by a stair that led directly from the dormitory to be used by the monks coming in to nightly services.

Stone vaulting was used to roof the other principal rooms and the passages surrounding the cloisters. The carefully cut and fitted stonework is of great beauty although there is almost no decoration. In the communal dormitory, each monk would have had a curtained area for his bed, but the design of such elements can only be studied in painted illustrations that appear in some illuminated manuscripts of the time.

Houses

Serfs working the land lived in a simple, wooden box-like houses of one room topped with a gable roof. Few examples survive. In the Scandinavian countries where wood was often tarred according to the practice of shipbuilders, there are examples of simple farm buildings of the sort that must have been common in the Middle Ages (**fig. 3.22**). With

no glass for windows, interiors were generally dark with a fireplace of some masonry material used for both heat and cooking. The house was often a barn as well as a residence, with people and animals sharing a common space or with minimal separation. Where field stone was readily available, house walls were often of stone with roofing of wood poles carrying thatch (bundled straw). Such houses survive, some still in use, in remote rural locations in Europe.

As towns developed, farm families often preferred to give up a house on the land in exchange for one in town where a town wall and gates offered protection and where a church and market square provided centers for communal life. The house in town might consist of several levels of rooms with wooden floors and stairs of stone or wood. Such houses were crowded together along narrow streets since space within the town wall was at a premium. When wood was the building material, upper floors of houses often projected out over the street to gain extra interior space.

Simple house types emerged within the towns. Surviving examples are those built with stone walls; the wooden floor and roof structure has generally been replaced with periodic rebuilding. A number of houses in the French city of Cluny built in the twelfth century are good examples (**fig. 3.23**). The houses are built with shared side walls (Row HOUSES) and fill their lots completely. A small courtyard near the rear gives some light and ventilation to the back room. The ground-floor front room can be opened to the street; it was usually a shop, a workshop, or a storage space rather than a

3.21 Dormitory, Abbey of Le Thoronet, France, c. 1130.

The dormitory was in a barrel-vaulted room in which each window corresponded to the area allotted to one monk, whose bed would have been surrounded by a screen of wood and cloth. The floor tiles are banded to define each cell. The metal tie-rods are a modern attempt to brace the ancient stone structure.

3.22 Farmhouse, Finland, Middle Ages; now preserved in the Norsk Folkmuseum.

The kitchen was the most important room of the farmhouse. The natural wood used for the floor, walls, and roof establishes a color tonality interrupted only by the white plaster of the fireplace and the black iron of the wood stove. A bench and the hanging cradle are the only pieces of furniture.

3.23 Viollet-le-Duc, engraving from *The Habitations of Man in all Ages*, 1875.

A reconstruction of the exterior of a house in the French city of Cluny shown as it would have looked c. 1200. It was the home and shop of a bourgeois merchant or craftsman who lived with his family above the place of business.

living space. A narrow stair at one side leads to an upper level with one large, all-purpose living room. Behind the courtyard, smaller spaces served as kitchen and bedroom. A third level above was an attic or loft used by children, servants, or workmen and for storage. A well in the courtyard was the source of water.

Inside, the house in town was no different from the farm cottage except that, when wood was used for multistoried building, a heavy wood frame with diagonal bracing was visible inside as well as outside. The familiar look of HALF-TIMBER construction results from a frame of heavy wood members with infilling between the wood members of plaster and rubble. The luxury of a wood-lined or plastered interior was unknown in early medieval times. Water came from dug wells or fountains used communally. Waste water and sewage ran in open gutters, making town sanitation dangerously inadequate. Life expectancy was short (averaging as little as twenty-nine years), with epidemics and plagues commonplace.

Bathing, where it occurred, might take place in a communal bath house, a luxury that disappeared as Roman customs were forgotten, but that was reintroduced into Europe at the time of the Crusades when word of Islamic bath methods was brought back by returning crusaders. Bath houses were often places for social gathering and tended to be viewed dimly by church authorities because of their association with nudity and possible (often actual) sexual freedom. Private bathing was occasionally introduced into aristocratic homes where a

wooden tub—simply a half barrel—might be filled with warm water for washing. Plumbing in the modern sense was unknown. In castles there were sometimes small chambers in the thickness of walls or projecting out from the walls that served as latrines, with the waste simply discharging through openings or chutes into the moat or adjacent stream or gutter.

Furniture and Other Interior Furnishings

Our evidence for early medieval interiors comes mainly from illuminated manuscripts and books. With few possessions to store, storage furniture was slow to develop. The chest, generally a simple lift-top box, was a place to hold folded articles of clothing. In churches, chests held precious relics and stored ritual accouterments that were often of gold and jeweled. Carved surface ornamentation was added to these objects and, at their most elaborate, surface treatment with gold and jewels might make the chest as valuable as the materials it contained. The richly ornamental RELIQUARY at S. Foy in Conques (**fig. 3.24**) is a well-preserved example of this type. A simple box chest was a standard feature of every church as a money collection

3.24 The reliquary statue, Church of S. Foy, Conques, France, 983–1013.

The carved wooden statue of the saint seated in a chair is encrusted with gold and jewels. It is a symbol of the veneration felt by those who visited this church, which was sited on the pilgrimage route to Santiago de Compostela. (See also p. 44.)

container. For the powerful feudal family that moved from one castle to another, the chest served as baggage as well as storage equipment. The development of locks, hinges, and corner reinforcements of iron gradually advanced as means of making chests secure in a time when there were no banks with vaults to hold coin and other valuables. Chests might be placed beside or at the foot of a bed or up against a wall and, possibly with a cushion on top, they became useful for seating as an alternative to the stool or bench. Chests were sometimes lined up along the walls of a room to form an all-purpose storage and seating facility.

Early chair designs were often the result of modification of chest construction. A box chest of a size that made a seat for one person could be modified by the addition of a upward extension to form a back, and possible other extensions to form arms, to create a rather massive chair of the sort that could serve as a throne. A chair was primarily a symbolic object, a throne used by royalty, bishops, and perhaps by the lord of a castle. Even stools existed as status emblems denoting the importance of the user. A manuscript illustration showing the meeting of the English Parliament under Edward I shows the king seated on the only chair, his elaborate throne (**fig. 3.25**). His vassals, rulers of Scotland and Wales, are seated on a bench which is covered with an embroidered textile. Judges are seated on sacks of wool, four to a large sack, while bishops and barons sit on long bare benches without backs. It can be assumed that the walls of the chamber were of bare stone; the floor, however, is shown as paved with diamond-shaped slabs or tiles of alternate white and bright green.

Color came most often from textiles as the ability to produce many dyes developed. Clear, bright colors were used for apparel while, in pictures of interiors, they appear in bench or table covers, in wall hangings, and in curtains (**fig. 3.26**). Windows were not treated with drapery, but curtains were used to give some privacy to beds, to provide some limited space division, and probably to control drafts. Curtains were simply panels of cloth with cloth loops or metal rings to permit hanging from rods in the manner of the modern shower curtain. Even these limited luxuries were probably only available to aristocrats. Common people had to make do with bare walls, peg-legged benches, boards on trestles as tables, slabs of bread for plates, and earthenware mugs or crocks for drinking and storing liquids. The greys and browns

of undyed textiles, the colors of unpainted wood and stone walls, and the earth, stones, or tiles of bare floors established the most usual color range of neutrals, relieved by the occasional bright dyed colors of clothing. Artificial lighting was generally confined to the candles used in churches and in the dwellings of the rich. Candles were usually of tallow; those made from beeswax were a great luxury. Lamps were simply wicks of cord floating in a bowl of fish or vegetable oil. In the houses of common people, light was generally daylight or whatever light might come from an open fire. Water came from a jug, pitcher, or bucket filled at a well and poured into a basin for washing or into a cook pot as needed.

3.25 (above) Wriothesley manuscript, c. 1250. (Royal Collection, Windsor Castle)

King Edward I is seated on a throne between the kings of Scotland and Wales. Churchmen, barons, and others form a parliament, while judges are seated on woolsacks in the center. The minimal furniture is typical of even this most important scene of power.

3.26 (left) Manuscript illustration of Christine of Pisan presenting her poems to Isabel of Bavaria, c.1300.

The elaborate costume and hair arrangements of the ladies seem appropriate to the room with its embroidered wall hangings, the rich red of the bed and seat coverings, and the colorfully painted ceiling structure overhead. A chair can be seen between the bed and the open shutters of the window. A woven rug with abstract pattern covers the floor.

3.27 Great Mosque, Córdoba, Spain, 785–987.

In the extensive hall regularly spaced columns support arches with contrasting white and red voussoirs. The column capitals are decorated with carvings of abstract forms, and these and the pattern of the repeating striped arches, with their suggestion of infinite distance, are the only decorative elements.

Islamic Influence

While the Crusades (1095–1144) brought some awareness of Near Eastern culture into central Europe, another connection developed as a result of the earlier spread of Islamic religion and related customs across northern Africa and eventually, through military invasion, along the north edge of the Mediterranean into Italy, France, and Spain. Cordoba in Spain grew to become the largest medieval city with a population of some 600,000. Although this Islamic influence was driven back and eventually largely obliterated in most of

Europe, it survived in Spain, coexisting with Christian and Jewish culture until the time of the Inquisition, established in 1233, and finally leading to the expulsion from Spain of both Muslims and Jews in 1492. In architecture and design, medieval Spanish work exhibits a parallel coexistence of two traditions: the Romanesque direction emanating from southern France and the Islamic or "Moorish" work coming from the east via northern Africa.

The Mosque

The special building type developed by the Islamic religion is, of course, the MOSQUE. A mosque is quite different from the temples, churches, and synagogues that serve other religions. It is a place for communal prayer, not the "house of God," not an auditorium where rituals are watched by a congregation. Byzantine churches were often converted to mosques as the Islamic faith came to dominate previously Christian territory in the Middle East.

Hagia Sophia, as a vast open space without a strong orientation to an altar, served quite well as a mosque, although monumental open space was not a usual characteristic of a mosque. Instead, a large space was most often developed by arranging rows of columns placed close together to support a roof structure. Columned halls were arranged around or adjacent to open courts where a fountain or pool provided for ritual cleansing. This is the kind of mosque that was built in Spain at Córdoba (beginning in 785 with additions from 848 to 987). Here a large prayer hall makes use of long rows of columns (a total of 860) supporting arches of a characteristic horseshoe shape (a semicircular arch with a downward extension at its sides); these support an upper tier of arches that in turn support the flat roof of wood (**fig. 3.27**). The arches are striped with alternate voussoirs of red brick and grey-white stone, making their forms appear very striking in seemingly endless receding repetition. Domes built from a lattice of intersecting arches cover the square MAKSURA (a special area for the prayers of a leader) and MIHRAB (a niche facing toward Mecca).

In Islamic design, arches are often built in a form that continues the curve of the arch below and beyond the semicircle, continuing to as much as 60 or 65 percent of a full circle. Many Spanish buildings that are now churches such as S. Maria la

Moorish Elements in Spanish Romanesque

Romanesque work in Spain closely parallels similar building in France. The monasteries of Santas Creus (1157) and Poblet (**fig. 3.29**; twelfth century) follow the typical Cistercian practices of southern France in planning and in detail. At Poblet the barrel vaults of the refectory and the arches that span the dormitory to support a wooden roof (both of the thirteenth century) are slightly pointed, raising a question as to whether this might reflect an awareness of Moorish practice or is simply a hint of the move toward the Gothic practice of the later Middle Ages. In the church of S. Isidoro at Leon, although concept and detail are generally typical of French Romanesque design, it is possible to note aisle arcade arches that create horseshoe forms and, where the barrel-vaulted transepts join the barrel-vaulted nave, arches that have cusped, scalloped edging—a strong hint of Moorish practice. In such details and in its use of strong abstractly patterned ornament, Spanish design reflects this special influence extending even into the much later work of the Gothic era.

3.28 Court of the Lions, Alhambra, Granada, Spain, 1354–91.

The palace courtyard is surrounded by arcades in which the arches are almost lost in the elaborate filigree of abstract carving. The Court of the Lions is named after the basin at the center, and this, and other fountains and pools create sound and movement. Plaster ornament and colorful tiles (visible at the lower right and left of the illustration) carry onward the sense of complex fantasy.

Blanca in Toledo (built in the twelfth century as a synagogue) have arcades of such MOORISH ARCHES. An aspect of Islamic belief that has had a strong impact on design is the strict interpretation of the second commandment of Moses which is taken to forbid any representation of natural plant, animal, or human form. With these sources of imagery forbidden, Islamic designers were led to develop abstract, geometric pattern and to make use of the calligraphy of Arabic writing as a basis for decorative design. Patterns developed in carved stone, in plaster, and through the use of decorative tile are often extremely elaborate and rich, with blue, green, gold, and white extensively used in a way that offsets any sense of austerity. Although its late date makes it contemporary with the later medieval Gothic architecture of Europe, the palace of the Alhambra at Granada (**fig. 3.28**; 1354–91) is a rich display of Moorish design at the end of its development in Spain. Arcades surround open courtyards, many with fountains and pools that reflect the richly decorated and colorful wall surfaces and arches of horseshoe, Moorish, and slightly pointed shapes.

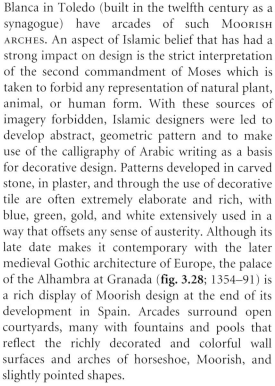

3.29 Poblet monastery, near Tarragona, Catalonia, Spain, twelfth century.

The dormitory of this Cistercian monastery (founded in 1157) has slightly pointed arches supporting a wooden roof. Screens of wood would have separated the areas occupied by the beds of each monk.

4 The Later Middle Ages

From *c.* 1250 onward, as feudalism became more established and all aspects of life improved, the crafts of building, woodwork, metalwork, and weaving produced a greater variety of objects. Knowledge of design, of interior spaces in particular, was greatly enhanced by the increasing use of pictorial illustration in manuscript books produced by artist monks and court illustrators (**fig. 4.1**). These books provide an important source of visual data for the historian.

Elements of Gothic Style

Great walled cities, large and elaborately defended castles, knights in armor on horseback, great cathedrals with their stained glass, buttresses, and gargoyles—all these make up our picture of Europe in the twelfth to fourteenth centuries, the era characterized as "Gothic" in recognition of the importance of the kind of architecture that has been given that stylistic name. The term "Gothic" was originally pejorative: it came into use in post-medieval times when the work of the Middle Ages

came to be regarded as crude and barbaric—like that of the Visigoths who were supposed to be lacking in the taste and elegance of succeeding generations.

Within the stone structure of the Gothic church, increasingly complex fittings, metal grilles and gates, carved stone screens, altars and tombs, wood stalls, thrones, and pulpits were developed in the later Middle Ages. The carved ornamental and representational sculpture applied to the stone structure was closely paralleled by the wood carving of choir stalls and the seats provided for the clergy. Candelabra, liturgical paraphernalia, and vestments of embroidered textiles which were used on altars and lecterns were movable elements that made the Gothic church richly elaborate and colorful. Paintings that illustrated religious subject matter were often placed at the back of altars—both the HIGH ALTAR in the chancel and other altars in side chapels. Altar paintings were often arranged in the form of a TRIPTYCH with a center panel painting and two painted hinged wing panels shaped to fit over the center panel when closed. The outside of these door-like panels might also be painted or carved, usually in quiet colors so that the triptych would, when opened at the time of a service, present a brilliant display of color. Color was often also present in painted pattern on walls and on the under surfaces of vaulting. Surviving examples of such interior treatment have often been restored and reworked in more recent times, or covered over or removed to leave the stone in its natural color.

The most important elements of color came from stained glass. The term is somewhat misleading since glass was not made clear and then stained, but made with integral color through the addition of various colorants melted into the glass as it was made. Glass was blown or cast in small pieces since no techniques for making large sheets were available. To make larger windows, small pieces of glass were joined with lead strips of H-shaped cross section. This way of making up large windows invited the use of patterns and images. Strong, clear colors—reds and blues predominantly, along with amber yellows and some greens—were assembled to make up pictorial images of saints and biblical figures illustrating religious legends and stories. These served the church as an important teaching device, a kind of "visual aid" at a time when the public making up churchly congregations lacked the ability to read and had no

4.1 (*below*) Limbourg brothers, a plate from *Les Très Riches Heures du Duc de Berry*, 1413-16. Musée Condé, Chantilly.

In this illustration of the month of January, the duke is seated at a banquet with his back to a great fireplace. The table is of boards, set on moveable supports. The colorful decoration on the chimney breast and ceiling suggest a space of great luxury.

4.2 (*opposite*) Abbey of S. Denis, Paris, France, *c.* 1135-44

This photograph, taken in the ambulatory at the left of the choir, looks across to the far side toward the pointed Gothic arches of the lower arcade, the triforium above, and the clerestory with its great windows of stained glass. Nine chapels radiate from the ambulatory to form the chevet end (apsidal liturgical east end) of the French Gothic cathedral plan. The emphasis on light is what chiefly distinguishes Gothic from Romanesque building.

4.3 (*right*) A fragment from a destroyed choir screen, Chartres Cathedral, France, *c.* 1220.

Realistic images of animals, birds, and even a giant snail, together with scenes of everyday events are displayed within the decorative rondels that act as framing elements. These carvings faced inward to the cathedral choir where they would be seen only by the monks and clergy.

4.4 (*top right*) Development of a pointed arch.

To lay out an arch with the desired width and height, width W and height H are drawn as shown. A and B are connected and a perpendicular from the mid-point of AB is drawn to reach the base line at C. With C as a center, AC can be used as radius R to draw a curve passing through A and B. This forms the profile of a Gothic pointed arch.

4.5 (*right*) Wells Cathedral, Somerset, England, *c.* 1175–1240.

In the 1330s "strainer arches" pointing downward were added at the crossing to aid bracing and the distribution of load below the crossing tower.

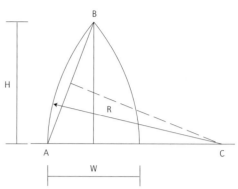

access to illustrated books or other pictorial material. Coming into a dark church interior with walls of brilliantly colored stained glass is still a moving experience. To the medieval church-goer it must have been deeply impressive and persuasive.

The Gothic era developed its own vocabulary of decorative detail, replacing the abstract vocabulary of the classical orders and the ornamental detail of dentils, Greek key, egg and dart, and similar forms with newer motifs that often drew on nature as a basis (**fig. 4.3**). Leaf forms such as the TREFOIL (a three-leafed cluster) and the QUATREFOIL (a similar cluster of four leaves) joined with CROCKETS (projecting leaf-shaped ornaments) to form a new style. Sculptural elements illustrating religious themes with images of saints and martyrs together with GROTESQUES and GARGOYLES that might amuse or frighten served both a decorative and a didactic role. Stained glass was subdivided with flowing bands of stone to form TRACERY. Such elements were introduced with increasing freedom unrelated to any systematic rules such as those attached to classical ornament.

New Construction Techniques

The arch and related vault remained, in the Gothic era, the most advanced technical devices for building lasting structures. Ancient Roman and medieval Romanesque work depended on arches and vaults for lasting construction and, in Romanesque work, the semicircular arch was occasionally modified to have a slightly pointed shape, but the pointed arch only came into its full development and wide use after the year 1150. It is often

stated and widely thought that the significance of the pointed arch related to its symbolism—its upward pointing that may lead the eyes and so the thoughts upward to the heavenly concerns of religion. However, pointed arches (**fig. 4.4**) came into use in many ways that have no religious implications. They appear in such mundane structures as castles, town gates, and fortifications, in town halls and other secular buildings, and in the details of furniture and decorative objects of every sort. There is even the astonishing example of the great Gothic "strainer" arches at the crossing of Wells Cathedral (**fig. 4.5**) in England that point *downward* toward the floor. Whatever the expressive impact of Gothic form may be to modern viewers, its development seems actually to have been the result of efforts to solve a technical problem in the structural design of churches, particularly the great cathedrals.

In Romanesque practice, the use of simple barrel vaults made it difficult or impossible to

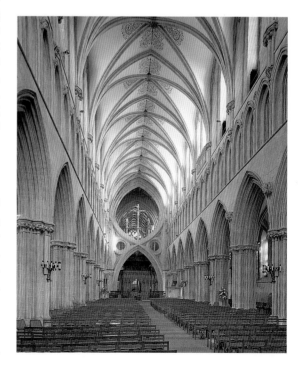

introduce windows large enough to light the interior space satisfactorily. Groin vaults made possible vaulted bays open on four sides, so that the front and back openings to adjacent bays created the lengthwise space of a church nave while the openings to the side could be used for the high windows of a clerestory. This left one problem: the vaulted aisles at either side below the clerestory level must either be topped with square vaults matching those of the nave, making the aisles too wide (and as difficult and costly to construct as the nave itself), or each bay must be split in two at the sides to match aisle vaults half the width of those of the nave. The latter approach was taken in a number of buildings such as S. Ambrogio in Milan or the cathedrals of Mainz and Worms in Germany. Another problem arises from the fact that a square groin vault, if built with semicircular arches at front, back, and sides, will either have diagonals that are not semicircular but elliptical, or will have diagonals that rise higher than the four surrounding arches. The first case makes the groins seem flattened while the second makes each vault a kind of dome-like unit that breaks the nave of a church into separate compartments that work against its unified spatial sense.

The problem became more acute when the technique of building vaults with ribs developed. Earlier vaults had been built on wood centering that filled the space that they were to cover. As vaults grew larger and were built above higher spaces, it became desirable to minimize the need for these temporary wood support structures. This was done by first building the arches that bounded the vault and the diagonals at the groin lines with centering, and then using these "rib" arches (**fig. 4.6**) as support for the limited wood scaffold needed to support the infilling between the ribs. The diagonal ribs became either difficult to lay out and construct as half ellipses, or they rose higher than the surrounding arches. If a vault that was rectangular rather than

square was desired to match the bays of aisles, the problem became worse, as the arches of the front and back, those of the sides, and those of the diagonals of the bay were all of different heights.

The solution to the problem was to build the diagonals as semicircular arches and to invent arches for front, back, and sides that would be of less span, but the same height. A strictly geometric solution to this problem would have used half elliptical arches for the four surrounding spans, but ellipses are geometrically complex forms, not parts of a circle, so that they cannot be drawn with a compass. The medieval architect and medieval stone mason were not prepared to lay out and cut the forms of elliptical arches. The Gothic solution was to turn to an arch that could be of any height in relation to any width which could also be laid out with a compass.

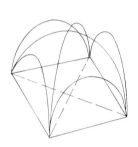 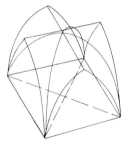 

The resulting arch will be pointed—a compromise that approaches the ellipse, but that is easier to lay out and to construct. Once this approach is adopted, a vault can be designed to cover any desired shape of bay—square, rectangular, or even trapezoidal (**figs. 4.7–4.9**). All of the arches, all four sides, and both diagonals can be of the same height, permitting a high ridge to run the length of a church nave in a straight, uninterrupted line that unifies the resulting space in a visually effective way. The diagonal groin lines can also be made into pointed arches. The pointed arch itself has its own aesthetic and symbolic appeal: pointed arches rapidly replaced semicircular arches, not only for vaulting, but wherever arches might be useful—for door and window openings, for example, and even in decorative details where no structural issues were involved.

The remaining issue involved the provision of buttressing to counter the outward thrust generated by vault construction. In the lengthwise direction of a church building, the thrust of each vault was countered by its neighboring vault, but the

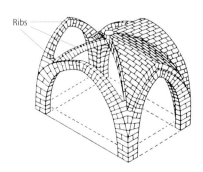

Ribs

4.6 Construction of a ribbed vault.

The diagonal ribs are semicircular. The arches at front and back are also semicircular and do not rise to the height of the center of the vault. The arches at each side are pointed and so permit a narrower span to fit the rectangular plan of the bay.

4.7, **4.8** and **4.9** Derivation of a Gothic vault.

The first diagram shows a vault with a square base and semi-circular arches. The diagonal arches rise higher than the arches on the four sides. In order to use the height determined by the diagonal arches for the arches on the four sides, pointed arches are laid out with required height and depth. This forms a Gothic vault, as shown in the second diagram. To construct a vault with a rectangular base, as shown in the third diagram, pointed arches for the four sides can be laid out with any required width and with heights equal to the height of the diagonal arches.

4.10 Cathedral of S. Etienne, Bourges, France, 1195–1275.

The Gothic groin vaulting has external, or flying, buttresses, which make it possible to have the large clerestory windows in the upper walls. The nave arcade is very high, bringing openness into a system of double aisles.

sideways, outward thrust required a structure that would rise above side aisles and not block the light reaching the clerestory windows. Solid masonry buttresses were possible, but their mass, resting down on the arches of aisle vaults, was not desirable. The use of open half-arch buttresses in one or more tiers solved the problem and generated the Flying buttress, such a striking element of the exterior of the medieval cathedral. Inside, the clerestory and the lower walls, no longer carrying any weight or thrust, could be opened up for windows to be filled with stained glass.

We have little information about the architects of the Middle Ages because they lived and worked in a era when the role of the individual creative person had not come to be recognized and recorded. Major medieval buildings were carefully planned and their construction and decoration was directed by experts who would now be called skilled professionals. This was still, however, a time when detailed drawings and specifications were not used, and when written communication was quite minimal. There were no manuals or handbooks documenting design and engineering techniques. The medieval architect worked on the basis of trial and error, aided by accumulated experience, rule-of-thumb practice, and intuition.

Medieval guilds provided training to the master masons who might become expert in the esoteric art of stereotomy, the technique of developing the geometry that governs stone cutting so that many individual stones could fit together to form the complex shapes of ribs and vaults. Some interesting studies have recently been undertaken, using modern techniques of structural analysis, in which cross-sectional models of several of the best-known cathedrals have been subjected to stresses that simulate those of gravity and wind forces of the sort that would be applied to the buildings in violent storms. Findings suggest that the engineering was in general surprisingly good, carrying loads down to the ground through vaults, columns, and buttresses that were logically sound and, within the materials and techniques available, quite economical.

Some cathedrals were, however, better engineered than others. Chartres (begun *c.* 1145), for example, was not as masterful in its structural design as Bourges (**fig. 4.10**; 1195–1275) where, with only vestigial transepts, double aisles are wrapped around the whole building with a double system of light buttresses that do their work with minimal material and great visual clarity.

Analysis of built structures demonstrates that design was not a casual or improvisational matter. It can be shown that one Gothic building after another makes use of theoretical geometric concepts in a way that parallels ancient Egyptian and Greek practice. Superimposed circles, squares, and octagons underlie the layout of many floor plans. Similarly, geometric figures can be developed to fit cross-sections and elevations, suggesting that aesthetic controls were established through sophisticated knowledge of theoretical systems of proportion. The west front of Notre Dame in Paris can be fitted to a grid of squares, six wide by nine high, with the main subdivisions of its design falling on the grid lines. The golden section proportion (**fig. 4.11**) shows up time after time, laid out with the aid of a simple geometric exercise that could easily be developed with cord and pegs as the only instruments required.

The simple 3-4-5 right triangle was used to establish a true right angle and as a basis for geometric modular planning. The south tower of Chartres has been shown to fit a 1:6 ratio of width to height, a ratio that corresponds to the vibration rates of the notes of the harmonious musical interval of a sixth.

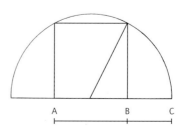

4.11 Construction of a golden section.

A golden ratio is derived by laying out a square, drawing a line from the center of the base to an upper angle, and swinging an arc with that line as radius. AB: AC is a golden ratio.

Gothic Cathedrals and Churches

Although it is possible to describe a "typical" Gothic cathedral, there is actually great variety. Albi in France (1202–1390), for example, is built of brick, has no aisles, a very wide nave, and buttressing contained inside the high outer walls of the building. Gothic churches of less than cathedral scale also vary widely. The church of the Jacobins at Toulouse (1260–1304) has a simple single space topped by two lines of vaults supported by a row of tall columns on the center line of the building, which generates a most surprising and dramatic interior. The famous small church, actually built as a royal chapel, of S. Chapelle (**fig. 4.12**; 1242–8) has a low, ground-level nave with a tall church above. The supporting structure has been reduced to thin stone ribs with the space between filled with stained glass, so that the interior seems entirely bounded by the brilliant light and color of the windows.

France

The Gothic cathedrals of France are both most fully representative of the type and most dramatically successful in design. The Gothic way of building went through a gradual process of change. The terms used to describe the development of French Gothic work are:

- Early and HIGH GOTHIC: These terms refer to the development of the building technique using pointed arches and vaults that took place from about 1150 to 1250. Cathedrals built over a period of several centuries, such as Chartres, often include both early elements and High

4.12 S. Chapelle, Paris, 1242–8.

The small royal chapel was built to house a revered relic. There is a lower chapel as well as the upper chapel, shown here. The walls were reduced to the thinnest possible piers so that the spaces between could be filled with stained glass. The result is an interior that seems made of light and color. The surfaces of the vaulting above are painted in blue and gold.

4.13 (*right*) Cathedral of Notre Dame, Amiens, France, *c.* 1220–88.

The tallest completed French cathedral, this is in many ways the most perfect example of its type. The grey stone of the structure is relieved by patterns of marble flooring and by the color of the stained glass. The great height of the nave and choir (140 feet) contributes to a sense of overwhelming intensity.

4.14 (*far right*) Church of S. Maclou, Rouen, France, *c.* 1436–1520.

The church is a late Gothic example of the style known as Flamboyant. The flame-like forms of the tracery, from which the style's name is derived, are visible in the windows at the far end of the choir. This church is not as large as the great cathedrals, but it displays the most elaborate of Flamboyant detail, especially in the west porch.

Gothic elements. Many of the most admired of French cathedrals—Amiens (**fig. 4.13**), Laon, Chartres, Bourges, and Beauvais—are characteristically High Gothic examples.

- RAYONNANT: This term refers to the elaboration of decoration in work from about 1230 to 1325 when radiating lines of tracery became an important element. The great rose windows of many French cathedrals are typically Rayonnant. S. Chapelle in Paris is the best-known Rayonnant building.
- FLAMBOYANT: Literally meaning "flame-like," this term describes the decorative detail of the late phase of French Gothic design. Complex patterns of tracery and elaborate, sometimes excessive, decorative detail are characteristic. S. Ouen and S. Maclou (**fig. 4.14**), both in Rouen, are Flamboyant examples.

The abbey of S. Denis (**fig. 4.2**), just north of Paris, had been founded in the fifth century. Its church was rebuilt several times in Carolingian and Romanesque times, but it was the rebuilding undertaken by Abbot Suger *c.* 1130 and continued in the thirteenth century by Abbot Eudes Clément that transformed the building into the earliest example of the prototypical Gothic cathedral. Like most cathedrals, it is of cruciform plan, with the entrance front facing west, the chancel at the east end, and the transepts to the north and south. The nave is made up of seven rectangular bays, with

aisles on either side and a choir (chancel) of three more bays ending in a semicircular apse. Around the choir there is a double-aisle passage or ambulatory. The entire building is topped with pointed vaults built to a consistent height for nave, transepts, and choir, generating a tall, open, and unified space. The slim structural supports make it possible for the walls to appear to be built almost entirely of stained glass windows.

Cathedrals that followed—Sens, Laon, Notre Dame in Paris, with double aisles for its whole length—are variations on this Gothic norm. Chartres (**figs. 4.15–4.19**), however, departs from the formula, with its two unmatched towers (built centuries apart), its Romanesque early portions, its later Gothic completion, and its extraordinary stained glass. The entrance from the west is made up of a triple grouping of doorways, each in an arched portal opening with richly sculptured panels (called TYMPANI). The triple arrangement makes reference to the Trinity of Christian belief. On entering, the vast interior seems to be a tunnel or cave, as one's eyes adjust slowly to the dim light. The nave stretches ahead with an arcade on each side opening into the aisles. Above the arcade the narrow band of the triforium is windowless. Above the triforium, the walls rise upward to form the clerestory, which is filled with stained glass. Each bay holds tracery, dividing the window into two tall, pointed panels with a round element above.

4.15 (*left*) West front, Cathedral of Notre Dame, Chartres, France, *c.* 1130–1290.

The lower portion of the west front of Chartres Cathedral is Romanesque in character, but above, the Gothic pointed arches assert themselves, and the two unmatched towers represent the advancing styles. The one on the right, the south tower, begun in 1145, is in the early Gothic style; the one on the left, the north tower, was begun in 1132 but displays the increasingly ornate vocabulary of later Gothic styles.

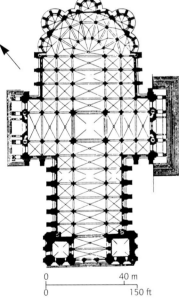

```
0                    40 m
0                         150 ft
```

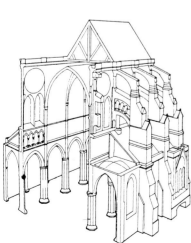

4.16 and **4.17** (*left and below*) Plan and diagrammatic perspective of the Cathedral of Notre Dame, Chartres.

The plan of the cathedral represents an ideal Gothic scheme, with its cruciform layout, nave and transepts with aisles, and a choir with double ambulatory aisles. Five projecting chapel apses form a chevet extending to the east. Massive piers on either side carry the loads of the structure, which are transferred to the ground by flying buttresses. Spaces between the buttresses allow for the windows of the clerestory.

4.18 (*above*) Nave, Cathedral of Notre Dame, Chartres.

The nave and choir are quite dim, largely because of the wonderful stained glass, which offers brilliant color while admitting only limited amounts of light. The external flying buttresses make possible the large windows, which begin below the springing of the vault arches.

4.19 North transept, Cathedral of Notre Dame, Chartres.

The giant round rose window in the north transept is more than 42 feet in diameter. Mary appears in the center of the rose and is surrounded by saints and prophets. Below, five lancet (pointed) windows show images of David, St. Anne, Aaron, and other saints.

4.20 (*right*) Salisbury Cathedral, Wiltshire, England, 1220-66.

The cathedral is a supreme example of consistent Early English Gothic architecture built from a single design in a comparatively short period. The almost black Purbeck marble, seen in the nave and choir, contrasts strongly with the lighter grey stone.

4.21 (*far right*) Exeter Cathedral, Devon, England, 1328-48.

The cathedral was built in the style known in England as Decorated Gothic. The nave is dominated by the fan vaulting, with its many radiating ribs. The massive screen separating the nave and choir, once present in most cathedrals, has survived here and forms a support for the large, later organ.

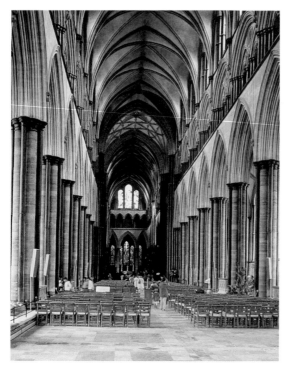

Ahead, the transepts open out to right and left while the choir extends toward the east. The choir is surrounded on three sides by a double ambulatory with, at the far end, five radiating chapels. The columns separating the inner and outer ambulatories and the windows that penetrate the walls and light the chapels form a complex and mystical space in the dim light, suggestive of infinite values.

The glass of the windows includes illustrative panels of apostles, saints, prophets, and martyrs. One window of the ambulatory aisle illustrates the legend of Charlemagne in twenty-two panels with abstract, decorative areas surrounding and separating the illustrations. The clerestory windows are too high to make the details easy to see, but the effects of their color and richness are overwhelming. Turning back to the western entrance front, the end wall above the entrance doors is filled with three large, Romanesque arch-topped windows with a huge, round Rose window above. The end walls of the transepts each have an entrance door with exterior porch and five narrow windows above, with a rose window high up.

Reims (begun 1211) is more consistent and so more formally "perfect" as an example of the Gothic cathedral type; Amiens (begun 1220) is more dramatic, with the amazingly tall proportions of its high nave. Beauvais, begun at about the same time, was to be even more spectacular in size and height, but suffered a disaster in 1573 when its central spire collapsed, giving notice that the limits of medieval technological skills in tall building had been reached. Its nave was never completed, so that only the choir and transepts survive.

England

The medieval cathedrals of England are closely related to those of France, suggesting close communication between the architects and builders on both sides of the English Channel. It is possible that itinerant architects worked on projects in both France and England. English work is never quite so adventurous and dramatic as its parallels in France, but it is varied in a way that makes each building a strongly individualistic expression. Salisbury (**fig. 4.20**; 1220–66), built in a short time with a consistent design, might be regarded as the prototypical English cathedral. Wells (1175–1338) may appear more interesting and original, with its strange and vaguely disturbing inverted bracing arches under the crossing tower. In English Gothic vaulting with extra ribs was sometimes used, dividing surfaces with radiating bands called Fan vaulting, in recognition of the supposed suggestion of the appearance of a palm fan. The fourteenth-century nave of Exeter Cathedral (**fig. 4.21**) is a spectacular

4.22 (*far left*) William Vertue, Henry VII Chapel, Westminster Abbey, London, 1503–19.

The most elaborate example of English Perpendicular Gothic was originally built for the private use of the king. The stone vaulting of the chantry chapel carries the concept of the multi-ribbed vault further with the development of pendants of stone, which are covered with such rich tracery that it seems to deny the stone structure.

4.23 (*left*) King's College Chapel, Cambridge, England, 1446–1515.

A simple rectangular space with walls of Perpendicular tracery holding richly colored stained glass. The spectacular fan vaulting dates from the last phase of building, 1508-15. Most of the interior is devoted to the choir, which was intended to hold all the students of the college. The screen divides this large choir from the small space reserved for the public. As at Exeter (see p. 62), the large organ mounted on the screen (1530s) is post-medieval.

display of the striking patterns of fan vaulting.

Most cathedrals were originally parts of abbeys or monasteries. The fan-vaulted cloisters at Gloucester and the octagonal chapter houses at Salisbury, Lincoln, York, and Wells are parts of the original groupings of monastic buildings. Westminster Abbey (**fig. 4.22**; 1045–1519) is often thought of as the most French of English cathedrals. The Gothic cloister and chapter house survive along with parts of the early Norman abbey, while the Henry VII Chapel dates from the late Gothic period when the richly decorated style called PERPENDICULAR was at its height. Enough is known of the building of English cathedrals to make it possible to identify some architects by name: William Joy at Wells, Hugh Herland and William Wynford at Winchester, and Henry Yevele at Westminster. Identification of such architects makes clear that, although craftsmen certainly had freedom to contribute to the totality of Gothic building, they worked under the direction of highly skilled professionals whose control of both concept and detailed realization was in some ways similar to modern practice.

Since many cathedrals were built over a long period, different parts of one building often belong to successive periods; different stylistic terms therefore often apply to different parts of a particular structure. The usual classification is:

- NORMAN: the English term for Romanesque. This is work of the early Middle Ages discussed in the previous chapter. Norman works falls between 1066 and about 1200.
- EARLY ENGLISH: This term refers to the Gothic work of the thirteenth century. Major parts of Lincoln and Wells cathedrals are Early English; Salisbury is a clear and complete example. Pointed arches and vaults are used with relatively simple decorative detail.
- DECORATED: Fourteenth-century work is usually of this period. Exeter Cathedral and the nave of Lincoln are examples. Carved decoration based on curving lines of foliage is a primary characteristic.
- Perpendicular: This is the term referring to the Gothic of the fifteenth century, the last phase of English Gothic work. Parallel vertical division of windows and the use of fan vaulting are aspects of this period. King's College Chapel at Cambridge (**fig. 4.23**) and the upper parts of the towers at Lincoln and at York are examples.

Elsewhere in Europe

The Gothic way of building spread from France in all directions so that Gothic design can be found in almost every part of Europe. In Germany, Cologne Cathedral (begun 1270) parallels French Gothic

4.24 Siena Cathedral, Italy, 1245–1380.

Italian medieval cathedrals tended to be conservative in construction, and semicircular arches were usually preferred to the pointed forms. To compensate for this simplicity, spectacular surface decoration was incorporated into the buildings. In Siena it took the form of black and white striped marble walls, both inside and out, a frieze of carved busts (portraits of the popes), and colorful vaulting.

architecture so closely that it can almost be classed as a French example. S. Stephen in Vienna is of a type called a HALL CHURCH, that is an interior space with nave and aisles of the same height so that there is no triforium or clerestory. There are Gothic churches in the Low Countries (now Belgium and Holland), such as the cathedral at Tournai or S. Bavo at Haarlem, the subject of a fine painting that shows its white-painted nave.

In Spain, Leon (begun 1252) suggests awareness of the design of Amiens, while Toledo (begun 1227) and Barcelona with its great cloister (begun 1298) seem closer to Notre Dame in Paris. In Spanish cathedrals, a vast and elaborately carved REREDOS behind the main altar is often a dominating element in the interior along with the richly decorative metal grills or REJAS that separate nave from choir. The vast cathedral of Seville (1402–1519), with dimensions established by the mosque that had previously stood on the site, has wide double aisles, almost as high as the flat-roofed nave and almost as wide, creating an interior similar to that of a hall church—there are flying buttresses above the aisle roofs that have only a slight slope.

Gothic design in Italy never completely escaped from the influences of ancient Rome. Italian work seldom fully exploited the possibilities of the Gothic pointed arch, stepping, it seems, from Romanesque almost directly into the post-Gothic Renaissance. Milan Cathedral (begun 1390) is the largest and most consistently Gothic work in Italy. It has a cruciform plan, high central nave, and double side aisles, all groin vaulted, and a rich overlay of decorative detail both inside and out. The very richness of the decoration has the effect of overwhelming the qualities of interior space, making Milan both impressive and, at the same time, disappointing. Siena (**fig. 4.24**; 1245–1380) stays close to Romanesque structural techniques, although the use of alternating light and dark stone in stripes gives the interior a special quality. The west front shows a plethora of Gothic decoration with some of the same florid excess that characterizes Milan.

Florence cathedral (S. Maria del Fiore, 1296–1462) has a Gothic nave leading to an octagonal crossing with three radiating half octagons that form the transepts and chancel and suggest an intended central plan building that the long nave converts to cruciform. The inability of the Gothic builders to solve the problem of completing the crossing octagon left the building incomplete until a Renaissance design completed the building with the great dome that will be discussed in the following chapter.

Secular Gothic Buildings

Medieval building in the Gothic era involved a wide variety of buildings other than cathedrals. Smaller churches were built in great numbers, sometimes using stone vaulting, but often with wooden roofs of the same sort that were used for a variety of secular buildings. Town halls, halls for the guilds of various crafts and trades, customs houses and other official structures were all built in

the Gothic style. In London, Westminster Hall (**fig. 4.25**; 1397–9), a surviving part of the Palace of Westminster, is roofed in wood with a series of great TRUSSES of the form called HAMMER BEAM. Here the Gothic arch appears supported on brackets, making it possible to span a greater width than would be possible with a simple, triangular truss structure.

In the latter part of the Middle Ages, with increasingly settled conditions, the developing complexity of society led to needs for a variety of special purpose buildings. The hospital developed as a part of a monastic institution devoted to the care of the sick and infirm. At Beaune in France the hospital (Hôtel de Dieu, *c.* 1443) is made up of a group of two-story buildings on three sides of a courtyard that housed various hospital functions and, on the fourth side, a large Gothic hall that was the main ward of the institution. The ward is a large open central space surrounded with curtained enclosures for the individual beds of patients (**fig. 4.26**). These do not back up against the walls; instead there is a passage for the use of the hospital staff behind the patients' enclosures. Visitors and ambulatory patients could walk about in the central space (where religious services also took place), while doctors and staff could move about behind the scenes in their own work space—an arrangement better in many ways than the often chaotic circulation mix in modern hospitals. The roof of the ward is of wood; the ceiling is curved in

4.25 (*left*) Hugh Herland, Westminster Hall, London, 1397–9.

A secular building, this great hall is the only surviving part of the old palace of Westminster. Its barn-like design is made spectacular by the great wooden roof of the type called hammer beam, for its projecting, bracket-like elements. It was probably designed and built by Hugh Herland, the king's carpenter. The windows between the roof trusses and at the end wall are rich with Perpendicular tracery.

4.26 Hôtel de Dieu, Beaune, Burgundy, France, from 1443.

The great hall of the monastery at Beaune served as a hospital ward. Booth-like curtained enclosures on each side contained beds. The wooden barrel-vaulted roof uses tie beams and vertical king posts to contain the outward and downward thrusting forces. The painting of the wood and the glass of the windows add color.

4.27 Market hall, Crémieux, Isère, France, c. 1300.

Although the wooden roofing has been reconstructed several times since it was originally built, it retains a form typical of the covered market halls of many European cities. Three parallel aisles, the central one higher than the ones at each side, provide space for farmers and tradesmen to set up shop on market days and shelter from the sun and rain.

4.28 Ca d'Oro, Venice, Italy, from c. 1420

In Italy Gothic design used pointed arch forms as decorative details even when they had no structural significance. In the central room of the piano nobile (principal floor) of this aristocratic town house, which looks out over the Grand Canal, the highly ornamental window tracery becomes the primary visual feature of the space.

the form of a barrel vault with wooden tie beams and a vertical member that forms part of the roof truss structure visible overhead. The building continued in its original use up until 1948.

Colleges and universities grew during this period, and the libraries of colleges became large enough to require their own rooms or buildings. The large library of Durham Cathedral and the smaller library of St. John's College at Oxford (1555) are examples of the timber-roofed halls equipped with shelves and tables to serve their special functions. The largest and most important spaces in the complex of buildings that made up a college were the chapel, actually often a large church such as the elaborately fan vaulted King's College Chapel at Cambridge (1446–1515), and the dining hall where all students assembled for an evening meal. The dining hall was an enlarged version of the great hall that was the main living space of a castle. The dining hall of St. John's College at Oxford (1555) has Gothic arched windows and doors, oak paneled wainscot, and a hammer-beam wood trussed roof.

Buildings with uses relating to trade activities were slow to appear. The shop of the craftsman or dealer in goods tended to remain a room on the lower floor of a house where the proprietor and his family (and often some of his employees) lived. Larger spaces eventually appeared for special purposes. At Valencia in Spain, the silk exchange (Lonja de la Seda, 1483–98) occupies a large Gothic hall topped by ribbed groin vaults. The ribs are carried down the columns as carved moldings twisting around the columns in a spiral. A wooden roofed hall, with open arches on all sides providing a sheltered market place, survives in many old European towns and cities. The handsome interior space of the market hall at Crémeaux in France is a good example (**fig. 4.27**).

Castles and Palaces

The building of castles continued throughout the Middle Ages. Some of the largest castles date from the very end of the period when the invention of gunpowder had begun to make the castle an obsolescent building type. The castles of the Gothic period had more elaborate and more comfortable living quarters than earlier examples, and many of these interiors are well preserved. Some large and impressive castles such as Caernarvon and Conway (both begun 1283) in Wales are in ruins internally, but many others have intact spaces such as the great hall at Stokesay in Shropshire (1285–1305) with its stone walls, windows topped by Gothic arches, and its trussed wooden roof. Bodiam Castle in Sussex (1386–9) has an orderly square plan, symmetrical about both axes, with towers placed at each corner and at the centers of each side in a way that suggests the more regular planning of later times.

In Italy, buildings such as the Palazzo Vecchio in Florence (1298–1314) have the qualities of an early medieval fortress or castle, although their function was the more modern one of a town hall. At the Ca d'Oro in Venice (**fig. 4.28**; c. 1420), the ornamental forms of tracery demonstrate the delicacy of Italian Gothic design.

With the more settled conditions of the later Middle Ages, the wealthy and powerful began to give up castle living in favor of large houses, sometimes with moat and drawbridge but without the elaborate defenses of walls and towers. In England many such manor houses (so called because they

housed the lord of a feudal land grant or manor) survive with interiors in good condition. The hall remains the main all-purpose room, as in the castle. At one end there is usually a kind of vestibule area, called the SCREENS because it was partitioned off by a wood screen. This also supported a balcony above—the minstrels' gallery where musicians or entertainers might perform—and connected with the kitchens and pantries. At the other end of the hall, a raised platform or dais isolated the table for family and important guests, while others were seated in the main space of the hall at temporarily placed tables and benches. A fireplace against one wall was the source of heat. Smaller rooms for special purposes—sitting rooms, bedrooms, chapels—were grouped about a court, often in a seemingly unplanned cluster that might be highly picturesque. Haddon Hall in Derbyshire (**fig. 4.29**) is a large and handsome example of the English manor house type dating from the fourteenth century (although with portions rebuilt after the end of the Middle Ages). Penshurst Place in Kent (1341–8) has a particularly fine and well-preserved great hall. Smaller manor houses such as Little Moreton Hall in Cheshire (sixteenth century) is built with a heavy wood frame visible externally in typical half-timber fashion. Its quaint jumble of rooms and chimneys, its moat and drawbridge are medieval in concept in spite of its late date.

Castles in France such as at Langeais (*c.* 1490) or La Brède (*c.* 1290) have interiors in good condition, although later changes have modified their medieval aspect. Pierrefonds (*c.* 1390), one of the most impressive of French castles, was so totally "restored" in the nineteenth century under the direction of Viollet-le-Duc that its medieval character has been almost completely lost. The Swiss castles of Aigle (thirteenth century) and Chillon (ninth to thirteenth centuries), however, are largely as they were in the Middle Ages, although original furniture and smaller details have disappeared. Many rooms at the lower levels of castle buildings and within towers are stone vaulted in Gothic fashion. Larger rooms are usually wooden roofed. Major rooms usually have a large fireplace, generally a hood projecting outward from the wall over a hearth rather than a recess made into the wall. Windows are generally small with leaded glass panes and internal wood shutters. Stone bench window seats, arranged below and at the sides of windows within the thickness of walls, provided seating close to the light and whatever heat the sun

might provide. Most furniture was movable and temporary although more elaborate beds, often with canopies and curtains to favor both warmth and privacy, appear in the chambers of the important occupants of castles. The most detailed information about aristocratic interiors of the Middle Ages comes from the paintings that illustrated manuscripts and books. Such books were often given by the wealthy and powerful as tokens of honor or love. Although knowledge of correct perspective drawing was not available to the medieval artist, spaces are often shown in quite realistic ways, including details in color of furniture, textiles, and small objects.

The paintings that have most to tell about the medieval interior fall into two classes—those that illustrate biblical or other religious subjects, in which figures are placed in settings familiar to the

4.29 Haddon Hall, Derbyshire, England, fifteenth century.

This banqueting hall, with its stone walls, wooden gable roof with tie-beams, and pointed-arch windows, was the gathering space for the lord of the manor and his dependants. The wooden paneling on the lower walls extends across one end of the room to form the "screens," a service area leading to the kitchens. It supports a gallery, traditionally the place of entertainers. The window niche seating, table, and chest are typical pieces of medieval furniture.

4.30 (*above*) Loyset Liedet, *The Birth of the Two Sons of St. Mary*, mid-fifteenth century. Bibliothèque Royale de Belgique.

The artist has set this scene in a late medieval interior with furniture typical of an affluent household of the period.

4.31 (*above right*) Master of Flémalle (probably Robert Campin), *The Annunciation*, c. 1427.

The event is shown as taking place in a room of the late Middle Ages. Mary sits on a bench that has a swinging back. There is a footrest along the side away from the fire. The floor is tiled, and the ceiling is of exposed wood construction, with beams resting on stone corbels. The windows contain frames filled with parchment. Shutters could be adjusted to control light and temperature.

artist in his or her own time; and illustrations of festivals, banquets, marriages, coronations, and similar events of the time. The painter Loyset Liedet (d. 1478), for example, shows the birth of the two sons of St. Mary as taking place in a medieval bedroom where there is a huge open fireplace, a canopied Gothic bed occupied by the mother, a Gothic arm chair alongside, and an elegant Gothic rocking crib for the newborn infants (**fig. 4.30**). The bedclothes, pillows, sheets, and blankets are all of colorful textiles that seem amazingly modern in character. The same artist painted a marriage banquet taking place in a hall with an elegantly tiled floor; musicians are playing trumpets on a balcony. The wedding party sits at the head table, while guests sit at a long side table, each covered with fine linens. An elaborate Gothic sideboard holds plates and tankards. The few plates are passed by servants to the banqueters, who appear to take food in hand as guests now take appetizers at a reception.

The artist Robert Campin (1375–1444) painted various religious subjects set in late medieval rooms. In the center panel of a triptych of the *Annunciation*, there is a large fireplace with a fire screen in front (**fig. 4.31**). Nearby there is a narrow wooden bench with a back rail arranged to swing from front to back so that the user, seated on plump cushions, has a choice of facing into the fire or facing away toward a table. The table itself has a silver candlestick with a single white candle and a blue and white pitcher holding flowers. Light pours in through windows equipped with shutters that

are hinged at the top and swung open by pulling cords that run on overhead pulleys. In a miniature of the fifteenth century, an artist is at work on a small painting in a kind of L-shaped work station oddly suggestive of the modern office. She is seated in a chair that displays the technique of barrel making—it has a round back made up of wood staves bound together with hoops. Such chairs developed in the late Middle Ages, an actual cut-down barrel later being adapted to support a seat and provide arms and back. The artist's work place is made up of boards of solid wood put together with TONGUE-AND-GROOVE joints, or with panels inserted into surrounding frames so as to make up larger surfaces from narrow boards while countering the warp and shrinkage characteristic of wood planks. Panels were often carved in Gothic arched motifs or with bands that suggest a folded textile—the so-called LINENFOLD paneling. Color is generally the natural grey of stone walls, the browns and tans of natural wood, and the clear, bright reds, greens, and blues of the dyed textiles that cover cushions and beds.

Medieval Houses

The scenes that appear in artists' paintings are most often based on the environment of the wealthy and powerful. The living places of the common people—the peasants or serfs—continued to reflect the simplicity, austerity, even poverty of the earlier Middle Ages. The typical house had only one, or at

4.32 House of Jacques Coeur, Bourges, France (c. 1443).

In this house of a wealthy merchant, almost a small palace, the hall or principal room of the main living floor is ornamented with an elaborately carved fireplace over-mantel. Each of the doors of wood paneling is set in an elaborately carved frame while a highly decorative cornice molding tops the wall. The ceiling is a simple structure of exposed wood beams. Royal coats of arms appear in the small windows between.

most two rooms, a dirt or plank floor, bare walls of stone or wood, and minimal furniture of benches, a table, and perhaps a chest or wall-attached cupboard. Beds were sometimes, particularly in colder regions, box-like constructions of wood, often so short that occupants must have slept partly sitting up. A hearth or fireplace serves both for cooking and heating. Candles became commonplace in the later Middle Ages, so that a variety of candlestick types ranging from the most simple to quite elaborate, portable, table-standing, or wall-attached developed.

The later Middle Ages also saw the development of a variety of trades and crafts so that shops—both workshops and retail shops—appeared in towns. Artists have provided many images of workshops for carpentry, weaving, and various crafts, as well as bakeries, butcher shops, and other stores. A shop was typically open-fronted toward the street, with a table or counter for wares and work and storage space to the rear. It was of strictly utilitarian character, having no decoration.

In the late Middle Ages, a few merchants

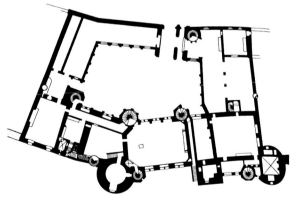

4.33 Plan of the House of Jacques Coeur.

The floor plan of the house shows the irregular grouping typical of medieval planning. Stairs are winding and utilitarian rather than ornamental.

became wealthy enough to own and occupy houses that could be fairly large, comfortable, and even elaborate. Such houses were generally in a town or city; living in open country was neither safe enough nor convenient in a time when transport was virtually non-existent. Only the nobility could own horses, and the poor state of roads made walking more practical in any case. Late medieval houses of affluent burghers survive in many European towns and cities. Medium-sized examples were similar to the houses at Cluny (see p. 50). More elaborate houses approached the scale of a miniature palace. The fourteenth-century house of the banker Jacques Coeur in the cathedral town of Bourges in France, for example, is a virtual chateau in the city (**figs. 4.32** and **4.33**). It is a cluster of multistory sections built around a courtyard with stair towers, arcaded galleries, gable roofs, and DORMERS in picturesque confusion. Interiors are full of elaborately carved doorways and fireplace mantels, and colorfully painted wooden ceilings. Tapestries would have added warmth, color, and richness to the main rooms.

Innovations in Domestic Comfort

Toward the end of the Middle Ages, both feudal aristocratic families who occupied castles and manor houses and affluent merchant families looked for ways to improve interior comfort. Lining rooms with wood paneling to cover cold surfaces of stone or plaster became common in regions where extensive forests made wood a readily available material. Wood was the usual material of floors and ceilings almost everywhere since it was the only alternative to stone vaulting as a means of spanning open spaces. Paneling walls created interiors that were entirely lined with wood, usually left in its natural brown color except for occasional decorative detail (coats of arms, for example) painted in bright colors. In the Tyrol, in southern Germany, there are many small castles, houses of prosperous burghers, and inns with wood-paneled rooms, often with built-in benches, cabinets, and washstands, so that the rooms are almost completely furnished without need for movable furniture other than a bed, a table, and perhaps a few stools. The development of stoves in Germany as a source of heat led to the introduction of elaborately ornamented tile stoves, almost small buildings in themselves, standing near a corner of almost every major room.

Since the width of wood boards is limited by the size of tree trunks, paneling of whole wall surfaces must inevitably make use of many boards placed side by side like the planks of a wooden floor. A floor must be smooth for practical reasons, but wall paneling can use strips of molding to cover the joints of boards, or can be made up of many separate wood pieces fitted together with moldings that form frames around the individual panels.

Elaboration of panel surfaces and moldings with carved detail became a favorite device for showing off the wealth and taste of the owners of Gothic houses. Ornamental detail might be simple and geometric, or it might draw on the vocabulary of Gothic stone architecture with its theme of pointed arch forms and carving of details based on leaves and flowers. Wood carving became a highly developed craft and art in some regions in Germany, Switzerland, and in England. Interiors in the Perpendicular style might include wainscoting or whole wall surfaces covered with panels carved in the linenfold design with its parallel, vertical lines. Important locations might use BAS-RELIEF (low-relief) carving, often taking themes from animals, flowers, and heraldic shields.

Utilitarian parts of medieval buildings, such as the cellars, kitchens, pantries, and stables, were generally designed in strictly functional ways but often have lost their original character through successive modernizations. The King's New Kitchen at Hampton Court Palace was built during the reign of Henry VIII (**fig. 4.34**; 1520). It is a huge room, 100 feet long and 40 feet high, with three enormous fireplaces each 18 feet wide and 7 feet high. There are bake ovens and various fittings to hold pots for roasting and boiling. The floor is stone and the walls are bare, but the windows, high up in the walls, are topped with pointed arches. In more modest houses, cooking was done in a fireplace which was also the main source of heat for the house, making the kitchen the most important—often the only—room.

The arches, vaulting, and ornamentation that differentiate Romanesque, Gothic, and subsequent architectural work were not present in simple town houses and farm cottages, so that there is little change over many centuries. In fact, houses like those of the Middle Ages continued to be built until modern times. A gradual increase in the size and number of windows can be noted as glass became more available and less costly, although windows were not always welcomed in cold climates where they might be a source of drafts, or, in the south, where too much sun was equally undesirable. In England, and to some extent in Holland, there seems to have been an understanding that, if facing south, windows would let in sunlight and heat that would more than offset winter cold. Wooden shutters served to cover windows at night and on dark days. The wood framing of half-timber buildings formed a grid that

4.34 Hampton Court Palace, London, from *c.* 1520.

The kitchen of Henry VIII's palace was a highly functional space with high windows for light and ventilation. The huge fireplaces served for cooking and baking all the food for the large population of the palace. The floor is stone, and the walls are whitewashed. The huge, roughly built wood table is the main work surface, and utensils such as those that would have been in daily use can be seen.

had to be filled in with some material—brick, stone, plaster, or rubble—to form a solid wall. Windows were a practical alternative where light was needed. Leading was required to make up windows from many small pieces of glass, the largest that medieval technology could produce. Multistory houses continued to be built in towns to conserve land use within wall-enclosed areas and, when wood was the structural material, upper floors were often cantilevered out over streets to increase the space within buildings. The habit of projecting upper stories was also carried over into building in villages and in open country. The diagonal bracing of the framing of half-timber buildings is often exposed inside some rooms where, along with other structural frame members, wooden ceiling beams, and leaded glass windows, it becomes a characteristic element of medieval interiors.

Although medieval ideas and medieval design remained extant in Europe for several hundred years after newer ideas and newer forms in design had surfaced, interest in the Middle Ages continues to be based on the realization that this was the last era in western history that was truly different from modern times in a fundamental way. The word "middle" in the designation of the period is significant in defining its position between the civilizations of classical antiquity and the modern world. In ancient Greece and Rome, literature, philosophy, and a probing curiosity about nature and human nature were current, even if in a form that now seems truly ancient. Gods and goddesses presided over a world of highly organized human institutions. In the Middle Ages, these classical traditions gave way to another world view in which faith and mysticism struggled, with gradually increasing success, against the forces of anarchy and chaos. After the latter part of the fourteenth century, a new world view began to surface in which human thought and human effort came to be seen as worthy means to improvement in the human condition.

5 The Renaissance in Italy

The modern western world can be thought of as having its beginnings in the Renaissance. The term describes a cluster of developments that gradually pushed medieval ways of thinking aside and made way for changes in human experience as great as those that came with the founding of the first historic civilizations around 5000 B.C.E. Exactly why these changes occurred when and where they did is unclear. What is quite certain is that in Italy, particularly in Florence, about 1400, medieval thinking began to give way to ideas that brought about changes in art, architecture, interior design, and every other aspect of human life. In Renaissance Europe there was a succession of styles that came to dominate the settings of life for the powerful and wealthy and the institutions of church and state that they controlled. For a major part of the population that was not wealthy and powerful, stylistic changes were less important—medieval ways survived with some small changes that were more cosmetic than basic.

The Rise of Humanism

By 1400, the city of Florence had established a stable form of government, great wealth through success in trade and the developing business of banking (based on the decline of the medieval prohibition against the "sin" of usury), and a kind of communal sense of optimism and power. The desire to progress and expand led to curiosity about the physical world and about the pre-medieval civilization that had left so many traces visible in Italy. These traces were both the ancient Roman ruins and the Greek and Roman manuscripts preserved in the libraries of monasteries. From Florence, Renaissance confidence, optimism, and curiosity spread out to Milan, to Rome, and to other Italian cities, and then, over centuries, to every part of Europe.

The term HUMANISM describes the Renaissance thinking that gave importance to the individual. It developed the idea that each human being had potentialities to learn, discover, and achieve. The medieval world view did not encourage individual curiosity and imagination—it taught that heavenly rewards outweighed anything possible on earth. Saints were identified with miracles and martyrdom while even feudal knights and kings rarely learned to read or write. Renaissance humanism did not reject religious values, but

rather augmented them with belief in the possibilities of human endeavors in a balanced relationship with the teachings of the church. It is interesting to notice how rarely individual names can be associated with medieval works of art and architecture. The cathedrals were designed and built by human beings, but there are few names known and scant records that associate a name with a work. The history of Renaissance art, by contrast, is a sequence of names, many of them known as distinct personalities; they were the subjects of biographies and were celebrities in their own times. Brunelleschi, Michelangelo, and Leonardo da Vinci, like Galileo, Copernicus, and Columbus, are Renaissance men whose names and achievements are widely, almost universally known. The ability to write, documentation of individual achievement in written texts, and the development of printing that made written texts widely available were all factors in making the individual significant.

Medieval thinking did not really believe in causal relationships. Supernatural powers willed events in the medieval view, and human questioning of reasons suggested a lack of faith. Miracles could occur, truth might be revealed in visions, but knowledge of the most basic actualities was often missing. The earth was flat because anyone could see that it was so; ships that sailed too far from land often never returned—they had fallen off the edge. The growth of humanism fostered the idea that the obvious could be questioned, that the mysterious could become less mysterious through probing and discovery. Even the human body could be studied in order to learn the secrets of its anatomy and functioning (**fig. 5.1**). The idea of the experiment that could demonstrate a cause and effect relationship and define it with precision is the basis on which modern science is built. It is a Renaissance concept, developed and made known in written materials newly available through printing.

Renaissance Interest in History

Along with scientific curiosity, aiding its development and being aided by it, came a new curiosity about history. The historical enthusiasms of the Renaissance are probably its most familiar aspect, the aspect that justifies the name Renaissance itself—literally "rebirth," a rebirth of the long forgotten wisdom and skills of ancient times. In ancient Greece and Rome there had been strong

5.1 (*below*) Francesco di Giorgio, drawing, sixteenth century.

The Renaissance humanist and architect Francesco di Giorgio (1439–1502) placed the human figure within a grid of squares, which he then developed as a plan for an ideal church, with nave, transepts, choir, and chapels.

5.2 (*opposite*) Michelangelo, vestibule and staircase, Laurentian Library, Florence, from 1524.

In the library's small, square vestibule half-columns pressed back into recesses, false windows in unique pedimented frames, and the great staircase itself assert the Mannerist movement toward a newly expressive vocabulary for classicism.

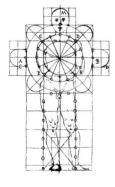

currents of humanism, important personalities who left written texts telling of their achievements and setting forth points of view in drama, poetry, philosophy, and mathematics. The Greeks had more scientific knowledge than the most learned of medieval alchemists. Plato, Archimedes, and Euclid were rediscovered in the Renaissance, while Vitruvius became an authority who could help to explain the Roman ruins and fragments built into later structures that were so visible in Italy. Learning through individual thought and experiment could be augmented by learning from history.

It may seem paradoxical that the movement that opened up the way to modern thinking should have turned back into history for stimulus, but Renaissance interest in history did not aim toward moving backward. It was rather another expression of the new curiosity that sought to learn what the ancients had known. The goal was to move forward on the basis of the best human achievements of the past, while pushing ahead into an advancing future. In the arts, it is easy to observe the ways in which ancient elements came to be admired and used, but it is a mistake to suppose that Renaissance design was merely an attempt to recreate the work of the Romans. Renaissance work is never narrowly imitative in the way that later revivalist and ECLECTIC work was. There is no Renaissance building that is a copy of an ancient precedent, no painting or sculpture that looks Roman or Greek. Details might be imitated, concepts rediscovered, but the Renaissance always generated new syntheses from the knowledge that came from study of the classicism of ancient times.

Elements of Renaissance Style

The homes of powerful and affluent citizens no longer needed to be fortified castles. Instead, the palace (PALAZZO) in towns and the villa in the country developed as residences offering considerable comfort and beauty. The typical palazzo in a town came to be three or four (or more) stories in height. The ground floor was devoted to entrance spaces, services, stables, and storage. The level above—the PIANO NOBILE—provided the large and richly decorated salons for formal life. Often, where space permitted, bedrooms were also on this level, arranged in suites for members of the owner family. A private suite usually included both bed

chamber and an outer private "studio," a room for use as a study, office, workroom, or for private conversation. A closet-like space adjacent was the equivalent of the modern bathroom; water was brought from a fountain or well. Many houses were built with a well below, connecting to a shaft rising through the building where water could be brought up in a bucket or other container. The level above the piano nobile was often similar in plan, providing similar living and bedroom spaces but with lower ceiling height. On an upper level, ceiling heights became lower still and the spaces were more open: here were living and sleeping accommodations for servants. Stairways, usually winding spiral or in narrow slot-like spaces in the Middle Ages, now became major visible elements with wide, straight flights turning to reverse direction at a broad landing. Secondary stairs, straight or winding, were often placed in obscure locations. The country villa could afford a more spread-out plan and so was often only two or three levels in height, but the same assignment of levels prevailed—services only at ground level, main rooms on the level above, and servants' accommodation in an upper floor or attic.

The style of the Renaissance interior is strongly influenced by the new devotion to classical precedents. Symmetry is a dominant concern and the details of moldings and trim draw on ancient Roman examples. In general, walls are smooth and simple, often neutral in color or painted in patterns suggestive of wallpaper. In elaborate interiors walls are often covered with mural fresco painting. Ceilings were often beamed or, in richly detailed interiors, coffered. Ceiling beams or coffers are frequently painted in rich colors. Floors of brick, tile, or marble may be patterned in checkerboard or more complex geometric patterns. Fireplaces, the only source of heat, were ornamented with mantels, some of great sculptural elaboration. Drapery and other accessories might be rich in color, as can be seen in contemporary paintings.

Furniture was more widely used in the Renaissance than in the Middle Ages, but it was still quite limited by modern standards. Cushions were used on chairs and benches and offered another opportunity for the introduction of strong color. Beds could be massive structures, up on a platform and with carved headboard, footboard, and corner posts supporting canopies and curtains. Carving, INLAYS, and INTARSIA were present according to the wealth and tastes of owners.

Renaissance church interiors using stone for walls and vaulted ceilings were of restrained color, but often richly elaborated with architectural detail derived from ancient Roman models. Stained glass for windows gave way to simple glass of limited color. Painting was widely used in altarpieces, triptychs, and easel paintings illustrating religious themes. Such art work was usually given by wealthy donors who sometimes appear as figures in the paintings they sponsored. Renaissance interiors, both residential and religious, tended to move from relative simplicity toward greater elaboration as wealth increased and knowledge of classical antiquity became more widespread.

In an attempt to find order in the complexity of Renaissance development, historians have identified three of its main phases. Many older histories view these phases as forming a symmetrical pattern, made up of a hesitant beginning, a triumphantly successful "high" period, followed by a period of decline and decadence. A more modern view recognizes the three phases, but considers them as differing in character of more or less equal merit: a progress from adventurous experiment through a period of developed and balanced achievement into a late phase of great freedom and elaboration.

The Early Renaissance

The Davanzati Palace in Florence (**fig. 5.3**) of the latter part of the fourteenth century is a beautifully preserved example of the kind of town house that existed at the transition point when medieval ways moved into a new era. The building stands on a narrow, irregular, and somewhat cramped site typical of the medieval town. On the ground floor there is an entrance loggia opening on the street that would have served as a store or shop. A central court gives access to stairs that lead up to the three floors of living spaces above—spacious and quite luxurious, but irregular and jumbled in plan in the manner of a medieval castle. Externally, the building is symmetrical and orderly and many of the rooms are handsomely detailed with patterned tiled floors, ornamentally treated wood beamed ceilings, and fireplaces with richly carved mantels. Evidence of a new awareness of classical antiquity can be found in small details, such as the moldings and the brackets that support the ceiling beams, but the leaded glass of the windows and the

tapestry-like patterned painting of walls still seem rooted in medieval practice. As now furnished (the building is a museum) the rooms are simple, quite bare, and, through their sparse but sturdy furniture, suggest an established aesthetic of dignity that holds luxury and austerity in a fine balance. In such a building it is possible to sense the Middle Ages giving way to something new.

Brunelleschi

The first or "early" phase of the Renaissance in Italy becomes clearly recognizable around 1400 and fits, roughly, into the fifteenth century. The first important personage whose name is well known was Filippo Brunelleschi (1377–1446), a Florentine trained as a goldsmith who eventually became a sculptor, geometrician, architect, and what would now be called an engineer, making him an example and prototype of the versatile "Renaissance man." He made a five-year visit to Rome and was able to study at first hand the surviving buildings and ruins of ancient architectural works. On returning to Florence, he was drawn into discussions about ways to complete the Gothic cathedral which had only a makeshift roof over its huge octagonal crossing. It is hard to

5.3 Palazzo Davanzati, Florence, 1390s.

The bedroom of the palazzo has been finely preserved. The floor is tiled, and the ceiling, which is of exposed wood construction, is painted with a decorative pattern. The furniture is minimal—a bed, a cradle, two chests, and two chairs—but the room is richly decorated by the fresco painting of wall surfaces, with repeating patterns on the lower surfaces, at the level of a frieze, and in the arcaded pattern above. Strong reds give an overall effect of warmth. A shuttered window and the corner fireplace complete the functional equipment of the room.

5.4 (below right)
Filippo Brunelleschi,
Cathedral, Florence,
1420–36.

*The great size and
height of the dome was
achieved without
external buttressing
and was an extraordi-
nary achievement.*

5.5 (below left)
Sectional axonometric
drawing of
Brunelleschi's dome.

*The ingenious system of
ribs made it possible to
construct the dome
without centering. The
chains that act as
tension rings are not
shown, but their posi-
tions can be located at
the base and at two
upper levels.*

5.6 (top right) Filippo
Brunelleschi, the nave,
S. Lorenzo, Florence,
1421–8.

*The church had a basil-
ican plan, with a tall
nave and vaulted
aisles. Corinthian
columns are topped by
an impost block, a tiny
bit of classical entabla-
ture on which the semi-
circular (Roman) arches
rest. The clerestory
above provides light
from windows, and the
wooden roof construc-
tion is hidden by a
coffered ceiling. There
are minimal transepts
(not visible here), which
create a nominally
cruciform plan.*

imagine how medieval builders could plan a building with no idea of how its most important element would be completed, but such an improvisational way of proceeding was not uncommon in medieval practice. Brunelleschi proposed a design for a vast dome to be built without buttresses and without the need for constructing wood centering (the latter would have required costly scaffolding that in itself would have been a huge engineering work). Although he was secretive about the techniques he planned to use, Brunelleschi was finally put in charge of the project and proceeded to build, beginning in 1420, the great dome that remains a dramatic landmark on the Florence skyline (**figs. 5.4** and **5.5**).

Brunelleschi's dome is not Roman in shape—its pointed form, well suited to the Gothic cathedral, suggests medieval vaulting—but the construction without external buttresses involved a number of ingenious technological devices. At each of the angles of the octagon there are stone ribs, plus additional ribs, two in each panel of the dome, all concealed between the outer roof surface and the inner surface visible inside. The hollow space between was used as working space during construction. Within this hidden zone, there are

great chains of stone, iron, and wood that wrap around the dome, tying the ribs with "tension rings" that resist the thrust that would tend to burst the structure outward. At the top of the dome there is an oculus that opens into a lantern. The lantern, virtually a small building in itself, was not completed until after Brunelleschi's death, but it follows his design and is the only part of the dome that has overtly classical details both outside and in.

Although the great dome (that has given the cathedral its informal name of Duomo) is Brunelleschi's most visible work, other projects demonstrate his approach to interiors more completely. In the Florentine churches of S. Lorenzo (**fig. 5.6**; begun *c.* 1420) and S. Spirito (begun 1435), Brunelleschi undertook the reworking of the typical Gothic cruciform plan with transepts, choir, and aisles into the new Renaissance vocabulary of classicism. Each church has a plan worked out on a strictly geometric grid of squares that establish a module for the complete design. In each there is a nave arcade of Roman arches, with vaults over the aisles supported on Corinthian columns. The ancient Romans did not support arches on individual columns, considering them, we assume, too weak either structurally or visually. In both Greek and Roman work, columns always support a continuous band of entablature, the basic character of a classic order. In Brunelleschi's designs, the columns are topped by a

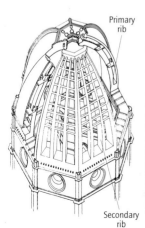

Primary
rib

Secondary
rib

fragment of entablature, a square block sometimes called an impost block or DOSSERET. This is an arrangement that was not unusual in Early Christian and Byzantine work, but its use in the Renaissance is typical of the early phase before Roman practice was fully understood.

Brunelleschi's earliest work at S. Lorenzo was the design of a small chapel-like SACRISTY (known as the Old Sacristy to distinguish it from the later New Sacristy by Michelangelo, now usually called the Medici Chapel). It is a square room topped by a dome on pendentives, with a smaller connecting chancel area (called a SCARSELLA), also a square space topped by a dome on pendentives (fig. 5.7). The interior of the room is lined with a classic Corinthian order using pilasters and an entablature. The problem of treating an interior corner with pilasters is dealt with by the curious Early Renaissance means of simply trimming and folding a pilaster to fit the corner. Eight rondels are arranged around the base of the dome, four on the wall surfaces and four in the pendentives. While unlike anything Roman, this space, with its orderly organization of square and circular elements, has a strongly classical feeling unlike anything in earlier Gothic design.

The small Pazzi Chapel in the courtyard of the church of S. Croce in Florence (fig. 5.8; 1429–61) has usually been attributed to Brunelleschi although there is uncertainty about the extent of his role in its design. It was not completed until after his death but its design is closely related to the Old Sacristy at S. Lorenzo. It is often thought of as the archetypal Early Renaissance work, with its symmetry, its use of classical Roman elements, along with a certain delicacy and tentative quality. A dome on pendentives is placed over a square space which is extended to either side with barrel-vaulted wings that convert the square plan into a rectangle. A square scarsella with its own dome balances a domed portion of the entrance loggia. This chapel was built as the chapter house of its monastery and so has a continuous bench around its internal perimeter as seating for the assembled monks of the chapter. The walls are treated with a pilastered order in grey-green stone, and there are rondels high up on the walls with medallion reliefs by Luca della Robbia (1400–82). The use of folded pilasters and slivers of pilasters at interior corners here repeats that characteristically Early Renaissance interior detail. The tentative quality of the design can also be traced in the curious scale of the space—it seems to be quite small while it is actually quite large. Such ambiguity in scale may derive from a somewhat uncertain exploration of the vocabulary of classical design.

5.8 Filippo Brunelleschi, the Pazzi Chapel, S. Croce, Florence, 1429-61.

The domed chapel is actually larger than it may appear (note the seemingly tiny door at the right of the chancel area). What color there is comes from the greenish-grey marble and the warmer tone of the plastered wall surfaces. The blue and white bas-relief rondels are by Luca della Robbia.

5.7 Filippo Brunelleschi, the old sacristy, S. Lorenzo, Florence, c. 1421-5.

The square, domed chapel has a small "scarsella" altar alcove. Originally, the color would have been limited to grey and white, but in the 1430s modifications were introduced by Donatello, the designer of the doors and their colorful surrounding, including the blue and white bas-relief panels. The doors are accurate reproductions of ancient Roman doors, such as those of the Pantheon. The central altar table is placed over the tomb of Giovanni di Bicci de' Medici and his wife, which is recessed in the floor.

5.9 (*above*)
Michelozzo di Bartolommeo, Palazzo Medici-Riccardi, Florence, from 1444.

The formal inner courtyard of the palazzo is an example of early Renaissance classicism in its use of semicircular arches, which rest directly on the slim Corinthian columns that surround the strictly symmetrical space. The tentative exploration of classical precedent can be noted in the relation of arches to columns, particularly at the corners.

Michelozzo

The Florentine Medici-Riccardi Palace (**fig. 5.9**; begun 1444) by Michelozzo di Bartolommeo (1396–1472) suggests medieval massing with its heavily RUSTICATED stonework and small windows, but its symmetrical plan which opens into a columned central courtyard and its use of Roman detail identify it as an Early Renaissance building. The central entrance passage leads to a square interior courtyard with a central exit on axis to a rear garden court. Twelve Corinthian columns support arches forming a surrounding loggia. The arches meet at the tops of the column capitals with a particularly awkward collision at each corner, indicating the designer's tentative understanding of the classical Roman way of relating columns to arcades. Room interiors are simple and largely unornamented except for elaborately coffered wood ceilings and classically detailed door frames and fireplace mantels. Rich and illustrative tapestries probably hung on the walls of major rooms. The chapel is lined with fresco painting by Benozzo Gozzoli (1420–97) showing the *Procession of the Magi* as an ornately costumed procession proceeding through a hilly landscape (**fig. 5.10**). The style and detail suggest tapestry translated into painted form. A later (1680) enlargement of the

5.10 Benozzo Gozzoli, *Procession of the Magi*, Medici Chapel, Palazzo Medici-Riccardi, Florence, 1459.

The simple interior form of early Renaissance rooms was often enriched by fresco painting, which frequently covered the walls. The subject here is the Procession of the Magi but the figures are portraits of members of the Medici family and their retinue. Gozzoli has included a self-portrait as a kind of signature.

building maintained symmetry externally, although the original symmetry of the plan now survives only in its left-hand portion.

Alberti

Leon Battista Alberti (1404–72) was a scholar, musician, artist, theorist, and writer. His book *De Re Aedificatoria* ('About Buildings') published in 1485 was the first major writing since Vitruvius to attempt a theoretical approach to architectural design. It was a powerful influence in moving the fifteenth century forward from the tentative Early Renaissance into the more strongly conceptual direction of the next phase. His text sets forth a

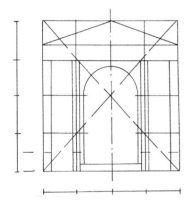

5.11 Elevation of the facade of S. Andrea.

The facade elevation of this church fits into a square. The square is then divided in four, both horizontally and vertically, creating sixteen squares. Elements are in proportion of 1:1, 2:1, 3:1, 6:1, and 5:6.

systematic way of using the classical orders and advances a view of aesthetics based on "harmony" and a system of proportions. In this view, paralleling the theory of musical harmony, relationships using simple number ratios such as 2:3, 3:4, and 3:5 (ratios of vibrations that generate pleasing chords in music) can be used as a basis for design in two- and three-dimensional space as well.

The church of S. Andrea at Mantua (**figs 5.11** and **5.12**; begun 1471) is Alberti's most influential work. The plan is cruciform, with a dome at the crossing and stone-coffered barrel vaults covering nave, transepts, and chancel. There are no aisles; in their place are massive transverse walls that carry the weight and thrust of the vaulting and separate a series of alternately large and small chapels. Giant pilasters take the place of free-standing columns. The rich surface decoration of the interior was added long after Alberti's death, but its simple and impressive character still strongly suggests Alberti's intention to model the space on one of the great ancient Roman baths. The walls of both the interior and the exterior demonstrate the use of simple proportional ratios. The facade is divided from side to side in a 1:4 ratio, the center 2 × 4 repeating the nave vault, the side 1 × 4 matching the side chapels. Vertically, there is a division in 1:3 ratio, with the giant pilasters representing five-sixths of the total height introducing the interplay of 1:6 against 1:3. The same relationships control the treatment of the interior surfaces.

The High Renaissance

Bramante

The transition from Early to High, or developed, Renaissance design can be traced in the work of Donato Bramante (1444–1514) whose career began in Milan with work at the church of S. Maria presso S. Satiro. A small ninth-century church (S. Satiro itself; **fig. 5.13**) on the site was remodeled externally in an Early Renaissance idiom, with classical moldings and pilasters applied to a form that rises in superimposed layers, cylindrical, Greek cross, square, and—in a topmost lantern—octagonal and round. The structure is thus curiously poised between a classical concept of organization and a sense of uncertain assembly of unrelated parts. The tiny interior is a centrally planned space, a square

5.12 Leon Battista Alberti, S. Andrea, Mantua, from 1471.

The interior of this great church represents an effort to adapt the design of ancient Roman baths and basilicas to the needs of a Christian church. The nave, choir, and transepts are roofed with coffered barrel vaults, and there is a dome at the crossing. Buttressing is provided by solid stone walls, which divide the side chapels. These chapels, in turn, are topped by smaller sections of barrel vault. Originally, the color would have been grey stone with off-white wall surfaces, but later modifications have covered surfaces with marble inlays and colorful painting.

5.13 Donato Bramante, S. Satiro, Milan, reconstruction begun 1476.

The effort to generate a cruciform plan was frustrated here because a street lay across the end of the church where a choir would normally have been positioned. Bramante's unusual solution was to create a trompe l'oeil effect, by adding a false choir, which is, in fact, virtually flat. The apparent space is actually a perspective image in bas-relief and paint.

converted to a Greek cross by four columns that support the lantern above. It serves as a chapel to the larger church which has a domed crossing at the intersection of barrel-vaulted transepts and nave. There is, surprisingly, no chancel because a street outside limited the plan to a T-shape. Bramante dealt with this issue by making use of his knowledge of the rules of optical perspective, a newly developed Renaissance artistic discovery. The end wall of the church is made into an illusionistic deep space by a painted bas-relief that, when viewed from the nave, appears as a barrel-vaulted chancel which seemingly completes a cruciform plan.

In 1499 Bramante moved to Rome. Here he began the second phase of his career, and became one of the first exponents of High Renaissance work in Italy. At the monastery of S. Pietro in Montorio in Rome, Bramante was given the task of reconstructing the existing cloister to make it the site of a small chapel. Only the chapel, now known as the Tempietto (**figs 5.14–5.16**; 1502), was built,

but surviving drawings show that Bramante planned a circular space surrounded by a ring of columns matching the order that wraps the round chapel with a portico of sixteen columns supporting an entablature. The enclosed center of the building is a drum that rises above the portico to be topped by a hemispherical dome. In elevation, the portico has a proportion of height to width of 3 to 5, the same proportion as the drum above the portico; total width to total height (including the dome) is 3 to 4. The enclosed drum has a ratio of width to height of 2 to 3; with the addition of the dome, 2 to 4; the width of the colonnade matches the height of the drum. Other choices of lines for measurement show up relationships that correspond to the golden section ratio of 1 to 1.618. The interior uses eight pilasters arranged in pairs separating window panels and larger niches, while the drum above has eight windows below the domed ceiling. There is also a round subterranean chapel reached by twin stairs leading to a door at the rear. Although it is not

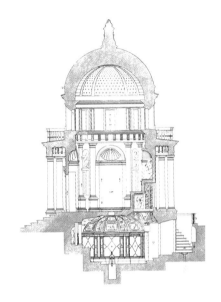

5.14 (*left*) Donato Bramante, Tempietto, S. Pietro in Montorio, Rome, 1502.

The Tempietto represented a highly successful effort to adapt the vocabulary of Roman classicism to a circular, domed structure. The building dominates the small monastic courtyard in which it stands.

5.15 (*right*) Engraving of the Tempietto from Paul Letarouilly's *Edifices de Rome Moderne (1825–60).*

This cross-section shows the domed circular space of the chapel and the subterranean space beneath, with its centrally located reliquary, the ostensible reason for the chapel's existence.

5.16 (*right*) Elevation of the Tempietto.

The elevation of the building is made up of two overlapping golden rectangles, one horizontal, one vertical. The entire elevation fits into an equilateral triangle.

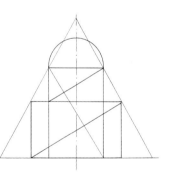

based on any one ancient Roman building, there is a quality of organization and coherence about the Tempietto that makes it seem truly classical in spirit. In spite of its small size, the richness and complexity of the design give the Tempietto a visual power that explains its influence on subsequent development.

Bramante was asked to prepare plans for the construction of a new St. Peter's Cathedral for Rome (**fig. 5.17**). His complex central plan called for a domed crossing, four identical radiating arms forming a Greek cross, and smaller domed chapels fitted into the resulting corners. Construction began in 1506 on the basis of this plan and, despite the modifications made by a sequence of successors, St. Peter's still incorporates the basic concepts of Bramante's plan. The change in plan concept to a Latin cross (cruciform) scheme seems to have been dictated by a feeling in the Vatican that a central plan carried a suggestion of Roman

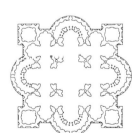

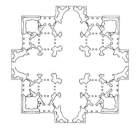

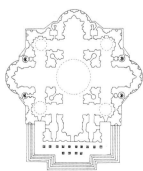

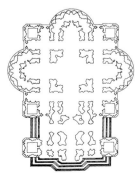

5.17 (*left*) Donato Bramante and others, plans for St. Peter's, Rome, 1506–64

The evolution of the plan for the great cathedral can be seen in the designs of Bramante, 1506 (top left); Bramante and Baldassare Peruzzi, before 1513 (top right); Giuliano da Sangallo, 1539 (below left); and Michelangelo, 1546–64 (below right). Further design modifications, made by Carlo Maderno in the seventeenth century were incorporated in the building as completed.

paganism and lacked both reference to the Christian symbol of the cross and a dominant orientation toward the east. As built, St. Peter's is largely based on Michelangelo's plan of 1546, although it was in turn extended to the west and elaborated by Carlo Maderno in the seventeenth century (see p. 94).

Palaces

The palaces (really town houses on a palatial scale) and country villas of the High Renaissance were built by wealthy and powerful families who were patrons of the greatest artists and architects of their time. The Farnese family made Antonio Sangallo the Younger (1484–1546) the designer in charge of their grand Roman palace (1513–89). He planned a large symmetrical block surrounding a central court in the manner of the earlier Florentine palaces, but moved toward a more perfect use of the classical Roman vocabulary than Early Renaissance architects had been able to manage. The entrance to the Farnese Palace (**fig. 5.18**) is through a broad, tunnel-like passage, vaulted over-head and with lines of six Doric columns on either side (actually antique columns of a red Egyptian

5.18 Antonio Sangallo and Michelangelo, courtyard, Palazzo Farnese, Rome, 1513–89.

The lower two levels of the courtyard, which are by Sangallo the Younger, follow the design of the ancient Roman Coliseum, while the upper level, which is by Michelangelo, exhibits a much freer interpretation of its Roman antecedents and hints at a movement toward Mannerism.

INSIGHTS

Vasari's Account of the Farnese Palace

The great palace built for the rich and powerful Farnese family had been started by the architect Sangallo, but was finished by Michelangelo. The Renaissance art historian Vasari records the story in his life of Michelangelo (spelt Michelagnolo), providing much insight into the rivalry and egotism of the artists involved:

And one day among others that he went to S. Pietro to see the wooden model [of St. Peter's] that San Gallo had made, he found there the whole San Gallo faction, who, crowding before Michelagnolo, said to him in the best terms at their command that they rejoiced that the charge of the building was to be San Gallo's and that the model was a field where there would never be want of any pasture, "You speak the truth" answered Michelagnolo, meaning to infer, as he declared to a friend, that it was good for sheep and oxen who knew nothing of art. [1]

Vasari records little about the inner comforts of the palace, probably because it was intended more as a public showpiece than as a private dwelling:

Pope Paul II had caused San Gallo, while he was alive, to carry forward the palace of the Farnese family, but the great upper cornice, to finish the roof on the outer side, had still to be constructed, and His Holiness desired that Michelagnolo should execute it from his own designs and directions. Michelagnolo, not being able to refuse the Pope, who so esteemed and favoured him, caused a model of wood to be made . . . It pleased his Holiness and all Rome. On this account, after San Gallo was dead, the Pope desired that Michelagnolo should have charge of the whole fabric as well . . . . Within the Palace he continued, above the first range of the court, the other two ranges, with the most varied, graceful and beautiful windows, ornaments and upper cornice that have ever been seen, so that through the labours and the genius of that man that court has now become the most handsome in Europe. [2]

1. Vasari, *Lives of the Artists*, 1550, trs. Gaston du Vere (New York, 1986), p. 276; 2. *Ibid*, p. 279

marble that had been excavated in the ruins of the ancient Roman forum). Beyond this dim passage, the bright central court is visible with an exit on axis leading to the garden at the rear. The court itself is a square, with colonnades in the classic orders at each of three levels. Unlike the earlier Florentine palaces, arches here do not rest on columns—they bear on solid piers with engaged columns on the faces of the piers running up to a

5.19 Annibale Carracci, ceiling frescos, Palazzo Farnese, Rome, 1597–1600.

A salon of the piano nobile of the palace, which was usually used as a dining room, had florid decorative elements on the walls, but the simple, vaulted ceiling was reserved for the frescos painted by Carracci. The panels illustrate a variety of mythological subjects while the apparently three-dimensional architectural detail and sculptural elements are, in reality, trompe l'oeil paintings on the smooth plaster surfaces.

continuous entablature. This is the system of the ancient Roman Colosseum, which gives the court a sense of solidity and, incidentally, solves the problem of corner treatment since arches bear on corner-angled piers and two columns stand on the adjacent surfaces without interference. At ground level the order is a correct Roman Doric; at the second-floor level the order is Ionic, with pedimented windows fitted within each arch. The third level was planned as Corinthian but, before it was built, Sangallo had been replaced by Michelangelo as architect in charge, leading to a more complex treatment that omits arches and substitutes overlapping Corinthian pilasters framing windows topped with curved pediments. The pilasters rest on a podium base with rectangular panels under each window. Some of these turn out to be small windows lighting a service mezzanine tucked between the second and third floor levels for part of the building perimeter.

A monumental stair leads to the main (second) floor where a passage runs around three sides of the court, giving access to ranges of rooms of various sizes. The largest room of the palace, the Salle des Gardes, is of double height, its two levels of windows continuing the external pattern of fenestration without change so that the exterior design gives no clue to what is within. There is an elaborate fireplace mantel, classically framed doorways, a coffered ceiling, and a decorative tiled floor. Otherwise, the room is simple and austere except for small relief rondels half way up the walls and tapestries hung high above. Other rooms vary from severe simplicity to elaboration with tapestries and fresco paintings. The room called the Carracci Gallery (**fig. 5.19**) at the center rear of the main floor level is treated in a way that became increasingly common in Renaissance practice. This involved the fresco painting of most or all of the surfaces of a room. In such an interior, the presence of furniture becomes no more than an incidental practical necessity. Here the barrel-vaulted ceiling is entirely covered by Annibale Carracci's (1560–1609) mythological scenes framed in

5.20 (*above*) Studiolo, Ducal Palace, Urbino, c.1470.

The studiolo of Federico da Montefeltro is ornamented with wooden paneling in which intarsia in colored woods created a series of illusory cabinets and niches, benches, and objects. The floor is tiled with a pattern in earth tones. Paintings high on the walls include portraits of famous men, including the duke himself.

5.21 (*right*) Baldassare Peruzzi, Palazzo Massimo alle Colonne, Rome, 1532–6.

The salon interior by Peruzzi is shown in an engraving in Letarouilly's Edifices de Rome Moderne. *Ionic pilasters support an entablature band, and above this, a frieze of decorative panels is inserted below the cornice. The ceiling is deeply coffered and richly decorated.*

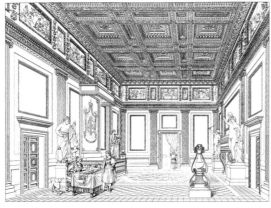

painted, simulated architectural details. The walls intermix niches and pilasters in three-dimensional plaster work, off-white with gilded details, with additional panels of fresco painting.

While framed (easel) paintings hung on walls were seldom used, the treatment of a complete interior with painting covering all surfaces had come into use as early as 1305 when Giotto (1266–1336) painted the interior of the Arena Chapel at Padua with religious paintings banked in rows. Gozzoli's frescos in the Medici-Riccardi Palace in Florence have already been mentioned. The Villa Medici at Poggio a Cajano, reconstructed in the 1480s by Giuliano Sangallo (1443–1516), has a central drawing room linking the front and rear

wings that make up its H plan with plain, smooth walls entirely covered with fresco painting by Andrea del Sarto (1486–1531) and others. Here simulated architecture, columns, pilasters, entablature, and moldings are all painted in illusionistic false perspective. In the Ducal Palace at Urbino there is a small room (the studiolo, *c.* 1470), lined with inlaid wood intarsia that simulates projecting shelves, cabinets with open doors, and a scattering of books, musical instruments, and other objects all in trompe-l'oeil on walls that are actually flat (**fig. 5.20**). The ability of Renaissance artists to create such effects stemmed from their new knowledge of perspective.

In 1532, Baldassare Peruzzi (1481–1536) began work on two smaller palazzi for two brothers, the Massami, in Rome. The houses, built on a constricted and irregular site, are ingeniously interlocked with entrances on both a front and a rear street. The larger of the two has a simple facade curved to match the curve of the main street it fronts on. The wall is simple, but the entrance is through a columned loggia that justifies the name Palazzo Massimo alle Colonne. The classically symmetrical facade masks a complex plan. There is a small but elegantly detailed courtyard and an elaborate salon on the piano nobile, as shown in beautiful detail in the engraved plates in *Edifices de Rome Moderne*, Paul Letarouilly's influential documentation of the Roman buildings of the High Renaissance published from 1825 to 1860 in three massive volumes (**fig. 5.21**).

The Late Renaissance and Mannerism

The term MANNERISM first came into use in art historical literature to describe painting that developed a freedom of personal expression within the Renaissance tradition. The term is equally useful in identifying the parallel developments in design. The design of the Renaissance had, by the middle of the sixteenth century, settled into a well-established system of classically based elements. The Roman orders and Roman ways of using them had been codified and made the subject of illustrated books; these showed "correct" ways of producing interiors that were serene and generally simple. As tends to occur when a style has arrived at a well-established norm, some artists and some designers came to feel unduly constrained by the set formulae. In painting, the style called mannerist introduced figures that seem in motion, gestures that appear theatrical, and compositions that are active and complex. In design, mannerism refers to the use of detail in ways that break away from the rules, that are sometimes eccentric, even humorous in their shifting and distortion of Renaissance serenity. Personal decisions began to take the place of the earlier rules.

Michelangelo

Michelangelo Buonarroti (1475–1564), one of the greatest as well as most versatile of Renaissance artists, imposed his personal modifications on classicism in a way that serves to define the concept of mannerism. At the solidly High Renaissance Farnese Palace he was responsible for inserting into its sedate facade the small but forceful balcony centered over the main entrance, and for adding the third level in the courtyard that introduces an adventurous variation on the Roman detail of the lower levels.

At S. Lorenzo in Florence, Brunelleschi's Old Sacristy discussed above (p. 77) was balanced by a symmetrically placed New Sacristy designed by Michelangelo beginning in 1519. The plan is the same simple square with a smaller square scarsella and a dome on pendentives above, as in Brunelleschi's project, but the treatment of the interior is as active, aggressive, and personal as Brunelleschi's was serene and classical. Pilasters and moldings in dark grey stone stand out against the white walls. Complex door and blind (false) window elements seem crowded in between the pilasters, and a whole attic story of arches, pilasters, and windows has been inserted below the level of the dome. Michelangelo's famous Medici tombs stand at either side of the space, giving it its more usual name of Medici Chapel (**fig. 5.22**). They are powerful and active sculptural works, adding intensity to the highly individualistic use of classical elements that gives the space its strongly mannerist character.

Also at S. Lorenzo, Michelangelo was given the task in 1524 of designing a new library at one side of the monastic cloister, a second story superimposed on a preexisting lower floor. The exterior, embedded amid the older structure, is scarcely visible. The library reading room within is a long narrow room with side walls given a strongly

rhythmic pattern by dark pilasters that separate the windows, upper and lower, arranged in the fifteen bays. Wooden reading desks are banked under the windows on either side of a wide aisle. The coffered ceiling is ornamented with a grid that matches the spacing of the windows, and the floor is patterned in a corresponding geometric rhythm. All of the detail, pilasters, window frames, floor and ceiling ornaments is delicate and subtle. In dramatic contrast, access to the reading room is from an entrance space that is a striking example of Michelangelo's mannerism. The vestibule (**fig. 5.2**) is a 34 foot square room, with its floor at ground level and its ceiling 48 feet above. The space is entered by small doors near the corners so that a visitor confronts the vast stairway that almost fills the space from one side rather than on axis. If the stairs are active and aggressive, the room that they fill is even more overwhelming in its powerful and unusual use of classical elements crammed into a space that seems hardly able to contain their energy. Paired columns divide each of the four walls into three panels. Their bases are raised up to the level of the stair top with great curving brackets below each column, while the columns themselves do not stand out from the wall, but are rather pushed back into recesses cut into the walls. The order used seems at first glance to be Doric or Tuscan, but a closer look at the capitals reveals

5.22 Michelangelo, Medici Chapel, S. Lorenzo, Florence, 1519–34.

The "new sacristy" was the setting for the famous Medici tombs, with their elaborate sculpture. The solemnity of the setting—the dark grey, almost black marble architectural detail and black and grey floor tiles—is in keeping with its mausoleum-like function. A dome on pendentives rises above the complex treatment of the walls. Michelangelo's highly personal use of classical elements justifies the use of the term mannerism to describe his work here.

5.23 (*right*) Giulio Romano, Palazzo del Tè, Mantua, 1525–35.

The loggia opens on to the extensive garden of this suburban palazzo or villa, and Giulio Romano's intention was clearly to recall ancient Roman villas, such as Nero's Golden House. The soft apricot-colored paint on the walls sets off the off-white floor marble, columns, pilaster, and other architectural detail. The paintings that are inserts in the ornamentation of the vaulted ceiling tell the biblical story of David and are the work of several artists associated with the workshop of Caravaggio.

5.24 (*below*) Sala dei Giganti, Palazzo del Tè, Mantua.

The walls and ceiling of the remarkable Sala dei Giganti (Room of the Giants) are covered with frescos based on the myth of the fall of the Titans. The images of giants hurling down the building around them amazed and horrified the Gonzaga family (whose palace this was) and their visitors. Giulio Romano was offering his patrons an ambiguous statement of virtuosity and anger. Only the floor stands apart from the painting, but, with its swirling circular pattern, it is itself dizzying.

them as an original variation on the classic model. Each panel of wall holds a blank, false window with a pedimented frame of unusual form. Actual windows are placed high up in an attic or clerestory level that repeats the pattern of columns with pilasters and real windows above the blank window frames below. All of the architectural detail is executed in a somber dark grey stone that seems to overwhelm the white plaster wall background. The total impact is highly dramatic—even tragic in tone.

Romano

If the mannerism of Michelangelo can be said to lean toward a tragic sense, the mannerist work of Giulio Romano (*c.* 1499–1546) can be seen as closer to theatrical comedy. The Palazzo del Tè at Mantua (**fig. 5.23**; begun 1525) is his most important work. It is really a suburban villa, a single-story building planned as a large hollow square surrounding a center court. The four facades facing into the court are each studies in Renaissance classic design, but each embodies odd irregularities, departures from symmetry, shifts in rhythm or deliberate "errors" that surprise, puzzle, or amuse the viewer. Pediments float above windows, sometimes with keystone blocks that are pushed up or seem to have slipped down out of line. Stones of the entablature that carry carved triglyphs are, here and there, deliberately placed in a slipped down position that suggests an almost mischievous disrespect for the rules of classic design. Many of the rooms of the palace are lined with fresco paintings, some with curious or strange subjects. A large room is lined with painted, simulated architectural detail with, high up on the walls, horses painted in full life size standing in incongruous positions (apparently a reference to the passion of the owner, Duke Federigo Gonzaga, for his famous stable). A smaller, windowless room known as the Sala dei Giganti (Room of the Giants) is lined, four walls and ceiling, with Romano's fresco paintings of giants rebelling against the gods and, in the process, tearing down the stones of some great building, possibly this palace itself (**fig. 5.24**). The desire to shift, modify, and distort accepted classical formulae along with a strongly dramatic tendency are the qualities that justify the designation mannerist.

Palladio

Andrea Palladio (1505–80), one of the most influential figures of Renaissance architecture, placed his personal stamp on Renaissance classicism but can hardly be viewed as a mannerist. Palladio was a northern Italian who worked in his home city of Vicenza as well as in Venice and the surrounding country of the Veneto. In 1549 he provided bracing for a late medieval town hall in Vicenza that was threatened with collapse. Palladio's way of dealing with this building, known as the Basilica, was to surround it on three sides with a two-story loggia that provided buttressing and converted the exterior appearance with classic columned arcades on two levels. Arches are placed between pilasters, Doric on the lower level, Ionic above, which support entablatures. Within each bay, the arch rests on small columns spaced away from the larger pilasters so as to leave a rectangular opening between. The arrangement of an arched opening with a rectangular opening on either side has become known as a "Palladian motif" (although this was not its first appearance), an arrangement that has caught the interest of subsequent designers and remained in use up until modern times. Palladio's influence was greatly enhanced by his *I Quattro Libri dell'Architettura* (The Four Books of Architecture) published in 1570. It is a thorough text on classical design including translations from Vitruvius and illustrative woodcut plates of ancient examples and of his own Renaissance work. This treatise became one of the most popular of Renaissance publications, known and used throughout Europe, particularly in England (where an English translation appeared in 1676) and eventually in America.

Palladio was the designer of a number of town houses in Vicenza and of villas in the surrounding countryside. The Villa Barbaro at Maser (**fig. 5.25**; begun *c.* 1550) has a temple-like central block between extended wings with farm-related functions serving the surrounding estate. The interior planning of the main house is typically Palladian, with a Greek cross plan using a central space with smaller rooms fitted into each corner. The interiors are architecturally simple, but the fresco paintings, largely by Paolo Veronese (1528–88), simulate architectural detail and include illusionistic painting of such elements as open doors, balconies, views into the out of doors, and even human figures—servants leaning from a balcony, a page looking out an open door, a parrot perched on a balcony rail.

The Villa Capra (or Rotonda), just outside Vicenza, is not really a residence but a kind of pleasure pavilion on a hill overlooking the town. A square structure with a domed central rotunda, it is one of the best known of Renaissance buildings. Each of its four sides has a pedimented, six-columned Ionic temple portico reached by a broad stair. Palladio's plan, symmetrical around the two main axes, is a study in modular layout. A grid of

5.25 Andrea Palladio, Villa Barbaro, Maser, Italy, *c.*1550.

In this room paintings by Veronese cover the walls and ceiling, making the actual three-dimensional elements of moldings and architectural details merge into the illusory imagery of landscapes, sculptural figures in niches, and doorway pediment. The stem of a vine in the panel on the left rises up and reappears in the panel above.

5.26 and **5.27** Plans of the Villa Foscari (or Malcontenta), Mira, Italy, c. 1558.

The plan uses a rectangle of 11:16 proportion. It is then subdivided in proportions of 4, 4, 3 from front to back and 4, 2, 4, 2, 4 from side to side. On this grid, rooms are laid out in proportions of 6:4, 4:4, 3:4, and 2:3. These ratios correspond to harmonic musical intervals of unison, octave, third, fourth, and fifth.

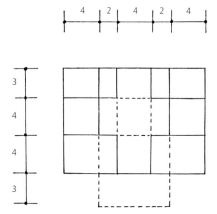

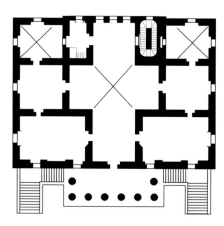

5.28 Andrea Palladio, S. Giorgio Maggiore, Venice, from 1566.

This Benedictine monastery has Roman classical detail in the columns and entablature within a barrel-vaulted cruciform space, with a dome at the crossing. The color scheme is grey and white, except for the warm tones of the marble floor. Beyond the altar there is a limited view into the space beyond, which was the monks' choir. An organ above the dividing screen provided music for both the choir and the main church.

squares can be overlaid on the plan, showing off the mathematically systematic proportions of the rooms which are all related to the proportions of the building as a whole. A balcony overlooks the rotunda and there is elaborate plaster ornamentation. The domed rotunda at the center of the plan invites a view outward through four passages leading to the four porches with their orientation to the north, south, east, and west, where views stretch out toward the infinite distance. The concept suggests the humanistic view of man at the center of an unlimited natural universe.

The Villa Foscari (often called the Malcontenta, begun *c.* 1558) at Mira, near Venice, has a pedimented portico only on the front, raised on a high base with stairs on either side. The plan can be fitted on a typically Palladian grid that gives each space "harmonic" proportions with simple ratios such as 2:3 or 3:5 (**figs. 5.26** and **5.27**). The British critic Colin Rowe has called attention to the way in which the plan of the modern villa at Garches (1927) by Le Corbusier uses the same grid as its basis. The combination of admiration for Palladio's works and the accessibility of information about them through his writing and related illustration made his work a source of inspiration and guidance in Renaissance England, where such buildings as Colin Campbell's Mereworth Castle (1723) or Lord Burlington's villa at Chiswick (1725) are clearly based on Palladian precedents. Even Thomas Jefferson's Monticello, near Charlottesville, Virginia (begun 1770), draws its concepts from Palladio.

Palladio's great churches in Venice, S. Giorgio Maggiore (**fig. 5.28**; 1565) and Il Redentore (1576–7), each apply classical vocabulary, with a barrel-vaulted nave with high windows and a windowed dome at the crossing. Arches at the sides

of the nave open into connected chapels at Il Redentore, and into aisles at S. Giorgio where there are full transepts repeating the vaulted form of the nave. At Il Redentore, the transepts are really apses on either side of the crossing. In both churches decorative detail is strictly limited to Roman order architectural elements executed in a darker stone that contrasts with the near white of the vaults and other plaster surfaces. The total effect in each church is open, bright, and restrained.

In the Teatro Olimpico at Vicenza (**fig. 5.29**;

1580) Palladio attempted to recreate an ancient Roman theater in a smaller, fully enclosed version. The tiers of seats banked in a semicircle rise to a colonnade at the rear, all beneath a painted sky. The stage has a richly ornamented fixed background (there is no provision for changeable scenery) that simulates the openings, windows, and statuary of a Roman stage. Three large openings each permit a view of a street scene executed in false perspective so that they seem to extend into the distance although they are actually quite short. Design as a major element in theatrical presentation surfaces here, introducing concepts from the theater into architectural and interior design.

Vignola

Along with Palladio's work and writing, the influence of Giacomo Vignola (1507–73) was important in spreading Renaissance design concepts. His best-known building, the Church of the Gesù in Rome (begun 1568), became a prototype for Jesuit churches in the seventeenth century. It can be regarded as an early Baroque church, and so is discussed below (see p. 94). Vignola's book *Regole delli Cinque Ordini* (Rules of the Five Orders, 1562), a systematic detailing of the classic orders, became a standard reference and a model of later manuals (that came to be called "Vignolas"). These were the basis for the acceptance of Roman classicism as a primary prototype for all design in much of the work of the succeeding centuries.

Interior Furnishings

Although the interiors of Renaissance churches and the more formal spaces of other large buildings survive much as they were when new, everyday living spaces have rarely remained unchanged. Furniture, textiles, and smaller artifacts that are easy to remove or replace generally survive only as museum exhibits or as antiques treasured by collectors. Fortunately, Renaissance painting turned toward increasingly realistic representation and, with the development of skill in linear perspective, artists were able to show interiors in ways that seem almost photographic. Religious subjects are usually shown set in locations of the artists' own times, so that the kinds of scenes that appear in medieval works in conventionalized form appear in Renaissance works in ways that are almost documentary. Carpaccio (1486–1525), for example, shows St. Ursula's dream as an event taking place in a handsomely furnished bedroom of the sort that might have been found in a Venetian or Florentine palace (**fig. 5.30**). The saint sleeps in a neatly made bed set on a raised platform

5.29 (*left*) Andrea Palladio, Teatro Olimpico, Vicenza, from 1580.

Semicircular tiers of seats rise up to a columned wall with statues above. The ceiling is painted with sky and clouds suggestive of the open nature of the Roman theater. The stage is backed by an elaborate architectural backdrop with three openings that offer views up streets.

5.30 (*below*) Vittore Carpaccio, *The Legend of St. Ursula*, 1490-98.

In this scene the saint sleeps in an elegant late fifteenth-century Venetian bedroom, on a bed elevated on a platform, with a high canopy supported by posts at the foot. Open windows have leaded glass above and wicker screens below, as well as shutters.

5.31 Carpaccio, St. Augustine in his study, c. 1502.

A spacious studio where the saint is seen seated at his desk on a platform raised a step above bare floor. The back wall is painted green and there is green wainscot. The door frames are of a reddish marble or are painted wood. A strange chair and reading stand at the left and the curious desk support seem to be fanciful inventions of the artist but the many objects on shelves, on and near the desk, and on the floor represent the cluttered possessions of a scholar. The central niche lined in red appears to create a small private chapel with suitable fittings. The ceiling is of wood; it is flat but painted in a geometric pattern.

base with painted ornamentation, with an elaborate headboard and tall posts supporting a high canopy. There is a small book cabinet and a stool pulled up to a table, and a book stand holds an open book—indications of the increasing knowledge of reading. A wall-hung candle holder suggests that lighting using candles must have been minimal. The door frame, window details, and moldings show Early Renaissance detail of considerable elegance. St. Augustine in his study, a favorite subject of Renaissance artists, is often surrounded with trappings of learning, shelves filled with books, reading stands, and furniture that is often medieval in character (**fig. 5.31**).

Furniture

For the wealthy and powerful, craftsmen developed artifacts of increasing variety and elegance to accommodate new tastes for luxury and artistic expression. Important people had books, papers, documents, maps, jewelry, changes of clothing, table coverings, and table wares, even such specialized objects as musical instruments, timepieces, scales, globes, and works of art. All of these things called for places for storage and display. Chairs appeared in increasing variety as alternatives to benches and stools. As they were gradually introduced into the basically simple living spaces of the Renaissance, all of these things began the movement toward the increasingly cluttered "fully furnished" interiors of the modern world. The new fashions, of course, were largely restricted to the homes of the wealthy and powerful (**figs. 5.32** and

5.33); the average interior remained much as it had been in earlier times.

Several different furniture types appeared in affluent Italian residences:

- CASSONE: This was a lift-lid chest, usually of solid walnut (the wood most used for Renaissance furniture), quite large and often elaborately carved with architecturally related details, with sculptural relief carvings of mythological or allegorical subjects, or with painted panels. The cassone was a traditional bridal or dowry chest and as such was treated as an important symbol of the wealth and power of the families being united. Small cassoni served as jewel or treasure chests.

- CASSAPANCA: A variation on the cassone resulting from the addition of a back and arms, this unit was usable for seating as well as for storage.

- CREDENZA: A somewhat taller cabinet, the credenza served as a sideboard or serving table. It also provided storage for silver, glassware, dishes, and linens.

- SEDIA: This was a somewhat massive chair with four square legs supporting arms. Seat and back were bands of leather attached to the frame with nails, the nailheads acting as a form of decorative trim.

- SGABELLO: This might be a stool or a small, simple chair—really a stool with a wooden slab back. It often was three-legged. The seat might be octagonal and elegant versions might have richly carved details. A sgabello from the Strozzi Palace survives as a fine example of the type.

- SAVONAROLA CHAIR: This folding arm chair made up from many curved strips of wood pivoted at the center of the seat was a widely used piece of furniture. It was named after the famous preacher who, it is thought, favored this design.

- DANTE CHAIR: A similar chair to the savonarola, this had a more solid frame, pivoted in the same way but with a cushioned seat and stretched cloth back.

Tables were solid planks placed on trestles, pedestals, or carved stone bases. Small paintings were often elaborately framed with many frames, their architectural detail suggesting a tiny temple facade. Mirrors, a development of Venetian glass production, remained small but were also often elaborately framed. Lighting came from candles placed in many varieties of table, wall mounted, or floor standing holders. Burning torches were also used for light out of doors and in large interior spaces, giving the name TORCHERE to the stands made to hold them; torchere also held candles. The candelabra is a stand that can hold many candles.

The Italian enthusiasm for music led to the production of fine musical instruments including keyboard instruments large enough to be articles of furniture. The small harpsichord called a spinetto was often semi-portable and small enough to be placed on a table. The larger harpsichords, although built with a thin and light wood shell, required an enclosing case with legs or a stand, making them somewhat similar in form to the modern grand piano. The cases of instruments were often decorated with carving, inlays, and paintings.

Coverings

Silks were the favorite textiles of the Renaissance; they display large-scale patterns woven in strong colors. Velvets and damasks were dominant in the Early Renaissance, with brocades and brocatelles coming into wider use in the sixteenth century. Loose cushions or pillows with fabric covering in bright colors were sometimes used on benches or chair seats. Floors were usually tiled in major spaces, or of stone on ground-floor levels. Tiling could be a simple pattern of squares or, according to the intended grandeur of the space, might be elaborately patterned. Marble and TERRAZZO (small marble chips embedded in cement and ground smooth) were used for floors of monumental spaces, also often in complex geometric patterns. Rugs were rarely used, although oriental rugs were valued and had occasional use as table coverings as well as on floors.

It is possible to follow the development of Renaissance design along either of two different paths. Geographically, the design of Italy tended to influence work in other regions, with a time lag of fifty to one hundred years. To the north and west, the Renaissance can be found as a developing concept in France, the Low Countries, Germany, England, and Spain. In Italy itself, in the sixteenth century, the design of the Renaissance ultimately shaded into the style called BAROQUE that had its beginnings in Mannerism. Whether it is viewed as a final phase of the Renaissance or as a totally new direction, the work of the Baroque era is an exciting development of design history. The

following chapter deals with the Baroque era in Italy and with its spread northward into the regions closest to Italy's northern border.

5.32 (*above*) Sala Bevilacqua, Fondazione Bagatti Valsecchi, Milan, *c.* 1500.

This richly decorated room has silk-covered walls and ornamental door frames and mantelpiece. The contemporary furniture includes a Savonarola chair at the left, a cassone, a cassapanca, and sgabello seat.

5.33 Gentile Mansueti, *The Miraculous Healing of the Daughter of Ser Benvegnudo of San Polo, c.* 1502–6.

The painting depicts a superb Venetian interior. The flat wooden ceiling with its painted pattern, the green walls, the overmantel, the artworks, furniture, and classical architectural details present a vision of idealized Renaissance space.

6 Baroque and Rococo in Italy and Northern Europe

The word Baroque designates a development, not a time period, and may be a source of some confusion because of its use in everyday speech to describe elaborate, or even over-elaborate, ornamentation. While ornamentation is certainly characteristic of much Baroque design, it is not the only, or even the most important, aspect of Baroque work. Further confusion can arise with the use of the term Rococo to describe a later, more delicate extension of Baroque style. Some historians seem to treat the terms as interchangeable, others see the Rococo as a kind of sub-species of Baroque, while in general use the terms have become virtually synonymous with the meaning "highly ornamental." The word "baroque" is thought to derive from a Portuguese word, *barocco*, that referred to pearls that were distorted or irregular in shape. The word "rococo" derives from French and Spanish words meaning "shell like."

As used here, Baroque refers to design as it developed in Italy following the mannerist transition from the High Renaissance of the sixteenth century. It flourished in Italy, Austria, parts of south Germany, in adjacent regions of Europe, and in Spain and Portugal in the seventeenth century. Related work in France, England, and northern Europe may be described as Baroque, although the rather different character of contemporary work in these regions makes the use of the term questionable. The term Rococo is used to describe work of the eighteenth century as it developed in France, south Germany, and Austria. Rococo development overlaps the severely restrained design referred to as Neoclassic. In general, Baroque design appears in religious building while Rococo work is more often secular, but there are certainly areas of crossover. It is, for example, possible to speak of a Baroque building with Rococo interior detail.

6.1 Vignola, Il Gesù, Rome, 1565–73.

The prototypical Baroque church, the home church of the Jesuit order, is shown here in a 1670 painting by Andrea Sacchi and Jan Miel with richly colored decoration superimposed on the normally elaborate ornamentation of the building. Effects of color and light make this interior space exciting and highly dramatic.

Elements of Baroque Style

Baroque architecture and interior design came to include a new emphasis on sculptural and painted forms. Shapes from nature, leaves, shells, and scrolls provided a vocabulary to enrich the classical form of earlier Renaissance design. The basic shapes of walls and ceilings were modified, even eclipsed, with three-dimensional sculptural decoration, figures, and floral elements. These in turn were painted in varied colors and merged into painted settings that offered illusionistic views of space peopled by figures full of movement and activity. The terms Quadratura for architectural space painted in illusionistic perspective; Quadro riportato, for images enclosed by illusionistic framing; and Di sotto in sù, for painting showing an illusionistic view upward into a seeming dome, sky, or heaven, have come into use to describe typically Baroque techniques of decoration.

Stage techniques developed in the Baroque. A proscenium arch was used to frame the opening to a stage so that it was a separate compartment in front of the audience seating area. Stage design, creating illusions of space through painting on flat scenic drops in order to introduce elements of visual excitement into drama, had a strong influence on Baroque and Rococo interior design. Stage design was in turn influenced by Baroque skills in the use of perspective and related spatial effects and in the use of light as an active element.

Baroque architecture and interiors served the aims of the Catholic Counter-Reformation. It provided exciting imagery that contrasted with the iconoclastic ("image-smashing") inclinations of the Protestant Reformation led by Martin Luther in northern Europe and offered new visual stimulus to a peasant population that had little access to rich and beautiful settings in everyday life. Entering a Baroque church where visual space, music, and ceremony combined was a powerful device for securing the loyalty of congregations. Along with decorative techniques, Baroque design turned to more complex geometry in spatial forms. Oval and elliptical shapes were preferred to square, rectangular, and circular. Curving and complex stairway arrangements and intricacy in planning offered a sense of movement and of mystery. The aims of design changed from simplicity and clarity toward complexity, readily augmented by illusionistic painting and sculpture.

The Baroque in Italy

The mannerist tendencies in the work of Giulio Romano and in Michelangelo's work at the Farnese Palace and the Laurentian Library suggest growing impatience with the classical code of High Renaissance design. The very perfection of that code, its presentation in the examples in Palladio's treatise, and the "rules" for the use of the orders set forth by Vignola invited rebellion at limitations on creativity. At St. Peter's in Rome (**fig. 6.2**),

6.2 (left)
Michelangelo,
St. Peter's, Rome
1546–64.

The majestic exterior of the cathedral seen from the southwest. The dome's structure is braced by internal chains, which makes buttressing unnecessary. The dome was completed in 1588-93 by Giacomo della Porta.

6.3 (below)
Gianlorenzo Bernini,
baldacchino, St. Peter's,
Rome, 1624–33.

The cathedral interior is given Baroque drama by the enormous baldacchino (canopy). The canopy is made of marble and bronze (said to have been taken from the pins holding stones of the Coliseum) with gilded details. At the east end of the choir is the ceremonial chair of St. Peter; above it a spectacular gilded sunburst.

Michelangelo took hold of the unfinished project begun by Bramante and gave it its final form with a gigantic order of pilasters supporting the huge barrel vaults that radiate from the crossing in a central plan. The provision of a clear entrance front for the west arm of the Greek cross modified the resulting biaxial symmetry. The vast dome is built with a triple shell reinforced with both hidden chains and external buttressing that takes the form of paired columns placed around the lower portion of the structure. The dome was completed, with some modifications, in 1590 after Michelangelo's death by Giacomo della Porta (1541–1604). The plan was altered by the addition of two additional bays to the west to create a clearly cruciform plan with a huge and dramatic facade by Carlo Maderno (1556–1629). This gave the building, at its completion in 1626, a strongly Baroque character. In its totality, St. Peter's embodies a full sequence of development from Early through High Renaissance, with hint of mannerist modifications, into a Baroque completion.

Rome

Vignola, although one of the rule makers whose efforts tended to rigidize Renaissance design, was a factor in the development of the Baroque. His design for the church of Il Gesù in Rome (**fig. 6.1**) became a prototype for the Baroque churches that the Jesuit order built or rebuilt during the Counter-Reformation era. Art, architecture, and design were intended to make the Roman church dramatic, exciting, and attractive. The interior of the Gesù as completed by Vignola was a study in the grandeur that Roman classicism could offer when combined with simplicity in giant scale. High windows penetrate the nave barrel vault, and a ring of windows in the drum of the dome create effects of daylight streaming in beams that penetrate the otherwise dim space in a way that approaches stage lighting. Later (c. 1670) painting and ornamentation of the Gesù (along with a 1577 facade by della Porta) added the color and richly complex detail that make it now seem entirely Baroque in impact.

Bernini

Gianlorenzo Bernini (1598–1680) began his career as a sculptor and continued to work on sculptural projects while turning his attention to architecture. Thus he brought a sculptor's way of thinking into the development of the Baroque. In 1629 he

became the architect in charge of work at St. Peter's, designing the huge BALDACCHINO of 1624–33 that stands in the central position under the dome (**fig. 6.3**). This introduced a Baroque focal point which dominates the space and moves its internal character into the Baroque vocabulary. It is both a work of sculpture and, in effect, a building made up of four huge bronze columns that support a roof or canopy at the height of a ten-story building. The columns are at least nominally Roman and Corinthian, but they have been twisted, as if by some giant, making them active and mobile rather than static supporting elements. Above the canopy top, S-curved half arches support a gilded cross on an orb. The whole structure is encrusted with sculptured vines, cherubs, and figures, making the surfaces alive with activity. Behind the altar at the apse end of the church there is another Bernini composition. The supposed chair of St. Peter, surmounted by a giant gold sunburst surrounding a yellow glass center, is visible from the entire length of the building.

Bernini's small Roman church of S. Andrea al Quirinale (**fig. 6.4**; 1658–61) is a single domed room of oval shape surrounded by small niches serving as chapels and chancel. The profile of the dome viewed in section exactly matches half of the oval of the plan. A Corinthian order lines the space, and sculptured figures seem to be perched around the windows at the base of the dome and the central oculus. The dynamic drive of the Baroque

also appears in the interest in passages and stairways, often tapered or curved to imply motion. The Scala Regia (1663–6) adjacent to St. Peter's, leading into the Vatican, was designed by Bernini with lines of columns on either side supporting a sloping barrel vault. The entire passage tapers in width and height as it moves upward; while windows light landings half way up and at the top of the stairs. The forced perspective of the tapered form and the contrast of light and dark spaces generates dramatic effect.

Borromini

Francesco Borromini (1599–1667) worked both for Maderno and for Bernini before undertaking independent projects in Rome. The small monastery and monastic church of S. Carlo alle Quattro Fontane (**figs. 6.5–6.8**; 1634–43) is often thought of as the archetypal Baroque achievement. The building stands at the intersection of two streets with fountains at each street corner (giving the church its name). One fountain is at the base of the tower that stands at the side of the undulating facade giving this church its powerful external presence. The small monastic courtyard is a simple rectangle with corners modified by convex, cut-off

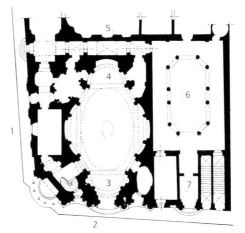

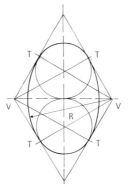

6.4 (*left*) Gianlorenzo Bernini, S. Andrea al Quirinale, Rome, 1658-61.

The church is based on an oval plan with radiating chapels and a dome above. Sculptured figures cling to the dome's surface. The classicism of the pilaster and entablature is given Baroque treatment by the complex plan and massed sculptures.

6.5 (*above*) Francesco Borromini, S. Carlo alle Quattro Fontane, Rome, 1634-43.

The exterior of this monastic church with its undulating facade and angled corner gives some hint of the complex interior within.

6.6 (*left*) and **6.7** (*below*) Plans of S. Carlo alle Quattro Fontane.
1 Via Quattro Fontane
2 Via del Quirinale
3 Church entrance
4 High Altar
5 Sacristy
6 Cloister
7 Monastery entrance

The plan is based on two equilateral triangles sharing a base line. A circle is placed in each triangle and arcs are swung from the meeting vertices of the triangles V with radius R to become tangent with the circles at T.

6.8 (*above*) Francesco Borromini, S. Carlo alle Quattro Fontane, Rome, 1634–43.

The interior of the monastic church embodies complex spatial relationships that have made it known as an outstanding example of Baroque design.

6.9 (*below*) Francesco Borromini, S. Ivo della Sapienza, Rome, 1642–62.

Looking up into the dome of this church demonstrates the complex geometry on which the plan was based. Six circles drawn on a six-pointed star create alternating convex and concave curves. It is possible to trace the forms of triangles, hexagons, overlapping circles and stars.

corners. The church is a tall space of complex form in plan, essentially oval with paired columns that press inward and an apse that bulges outward. A diagrammatic analysis shows the plan to be based on a pair of equilateral triangles with a common base line; a circle inscribed in each forms the basis for the oval that dominates the plan (fig. 6.7).

The oval is emphasized by the floor pattern and by the rim of the dome above, with its coffered pattern of octagons, hexagons, and cross shapes that diminish in size as they rise to the oval lantern at the top. Light comes from high windows at the lower edge of the dome and from windows in the lantern. The seemingly rubbery flexing of walls, the curved pediments, and the "rolled over" half domes over the altar and side apses, together with the complexities of the dome and the dramatic effect of the controlled daylighting, all add up to make this space extraordinary in its sense of activity and tension.

S. Ivo della Sapienza (**fig. 6.9**; 1642–62) is the chapel built by Borromini in the courtyard of della Porta's building for the University of Rome. Although it may appear to be a domed, centrally planned space, closer examination reveals the complexity typical of Baroque design. The plan is actually based on equilateral triangles but, instead of being abutted base to base as at S. Carlo, the triangles are overlapped to form a six-pointed star (**fig. 6.10**). Vertical support piers (each with two applied pilasters) are placed at the inner angles of the star to form a circle. Of the outward extending points of the star, the three that relate to one of the overlapping triangles define the positions of the altar apse and two apsidal niches on either side of the entrance, while the three that are the apexes of the other triangle locate the recesses of the entrance and those on either side of the chancel niche. This alternation of two differing treatments for the six points of the star sets up a complex rhythm which is continued up into the dome above.

The white, gold-starred dome is not simply

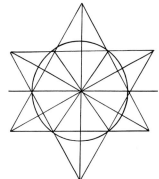

6.10 Plan of Sant' Ivo della Sapienza.

The plan is based on two overlapping equilateral triangles that create a hexagon and twelve smaller triangles. A circle contains the hexagon.

6.11 Sala del Senato, Doge's Palace, Venice, after 1574.

Venetian senators were provided with this spectacularly ornate setting for their meetings. Wooden paneling runs around the base of the walls where there is seating in stalls for the 200 or more senators. Above, the painted panels are surrounded by gilded frames so heavy that they almost overwhelm the paintings within, some of which are by Tintoretto and his pupils.

round, but is hollowed out to carry the forms of the six alternating concave and convex panels of the walls upward to the oculus with its windowed lantern. Externally, the lantern is topped by a sculptural element of spiral or helical form. Its symbolic significance is ambiguous and uncertain, but its visible wild gesture is highly characteristic of the Baroque.

Venice

Longhena

Venice is not a city where Baroque design established a major presence. The one exceptional Baroque building there is the church of S. Maria della Salute (begun 1631) by Baldassare Longhena (1598–1662). It is an octagonal building with an aisle or atrium surrounding a tall, round, domed central space. The eight sides of the octagon offer six radiating chapels, an entrance portal, and, on the eighth side, an arch opening into the chancel. The chancel, almost a separate adjacent building with its own smaller dome, is visible from the body of the church through the arch. The church is brightly lit by the sixteen large windows of the dome and has a geometrically complex patterned floor in bright yellow and black marbles. The chancel is relatively dim, while there is an opening into the CORO, or monks' choir, beyond. This establishes a sequence of varied light levels that is typical of Baroque spatial richness.

Venetian interiors, such as some of those in the medieval Doge's palace (**fig. 6.11**) that were reconstructed after a fire in 1574, display an amazingly rich surface frosting of paintings and ornate plaster work. In the Sala del Senato a giant wall clock shares space with paintings lined up above a band of wainscoting while the ceiling presses down on the viewer with its panels of painting framed in ornate gilt. Veronese was the artist who provided the paintings in 1585 for the similarly elaborate Sala del Gran Consiglio where Baroque architecture appears in quadratura illusionistic perspective as a setting for the figures acting out *The Triumph of Venice* above the Doge's chair.

Turin

Guarini

Baroque work was carried north by Guarino Guarini (1624–83), a Theatine monk who had worked in Portugal, Spain, and in Paris before settling in Turin, where his major work is located. Guarini was also a philosopher and mathematician; his *Architettura Civile* (1737) helped to spread his influence. His major secular work is the Palazzo Carignano in Turin (1679–92), a massive block built around a center court which is reflected externally by a central part of the facade that bulges forward in an undulating curve. The entrance leads into an oval, columned atrium that opens on the court. On either side small vestibules lead to twin

6.12 Guarino Guarini, S. Lorenzo, Turin, 1666–80.

The almost octagonal dome of S. Lorenzo displays Guarini's interest in geometric complexity. It is formed from the pattern of eight intersecting arches with eight windows at the base of the dome, and sixteen windows above as the construction rises to a tall cupolo. The dome is brightly lit, but the church below is dim and rich in heavily colored and gilded, complexly curved architectural elements.

6.13 Guarino Guarini, Capella della SS. Sindone, Turin, begun 1667–90.

The black and grey stones used to create the chapel of the Holy Shroud are topped by a dome with a ring of six windows at its base and with rings of many arches, each arch resting on the center of the arch below. Hidden windows illuminate both the dome and the small dome at its top in a way that emphasizes the mystery and enhances the dramatic impact.

stairways that curve as they rise, meeting at the top at the access point to the huge oval main salon. This room is topped by a ceiling dome which is open at its center to permit a view of a second ceiling high above, lighted by hidden windows.

Guarini's church of S. Lorenzo in Turin (**fig. 6.12**; 1666–80) is embedded in the buildings of the Royal Palace. Its square external block, with a projecting smaller block to house the chancel, is hollowed out in a complex pattern of bulging and receding forms that can be viewed in plan as Greek cross, octagon, circle, or a nameless shape created by overlapping curved forms that extend into the space from its edges. The chancel is an adjacent oval. All of this is treated with an overlay of rich Baroque architectural and sculptural decoration. The dome is not a simple half sphere but rather a lattice of eight intersecting arches that leave an octagonal opening at the center, opening into a windowed lantern above. There are eight small windows at the base of the dome, eight large oval and eight small pentagonal windows fitted between the arches, eight windows in the lantern, and a small eight-windowed dome at the top of this astonishing structure. The geometric complexity and bright light from the many windows of the S. Lorenzo dome are thought to make reference to the concept of infinity. The contrast with the dim lower space of the church itself is intensely theatrical.

In 1667 Guarini began work on a chapel for Turin Cathedral that was being prepared to house the religious relic known as the Holy Shroud, believed to be the cloth that held the body of Christ after the crucifixion. The resulting chapel of SS. Sindone (**fig. 6.13**) is a dark and somber space lined with black and dark grey marbles. It is approached by twin flights of dark, curved stairs that lead up from the cathedral. The entrances from the two stairs and from a doorway centered at the rear (leading to the adjacent palace) establish three points of an equilateral triangle. Three arches rise to support the circle that is the base of a six-windowed drum. Above it a conical dome is built up from six rings of flat arches, each arch resting on the centers of the arches below, each ring growing smaller in a way that creates a perspective effect of exaggerated height. Hidden windows light the space from behind the arches and, at the top, a small dome, also lighted by hidden windows, caps the top arch ring. A golden dove hangs from a sunburst at the center of the highest dome. The strange and complex forms and the theatrical effects of light and dark make the chapel seem dramatic, mysterious, and disturbing.

Juvarra

Filippo Juvarra (1678–1736) was the designer of the Superga (1717–31), a church and monastery complex outside of Turin on a hill overlooking the city. It is made up of a tall domed church attached to ranges of lower monastic buildings arranged symmetrically around a cloister court. Juvara seems, in this building, to draw back from the complexities of Guarini and to suggest a Baroque closer to the late phases of the High Renaissance. This church-monastery complex with its great dome and flanking towers is close to a pattern that appears in south Germany at about the same time. To what extent Juvarra influenced the work north of the Alps and to what extent he was influenced by that work remains uncertain.

At the huge Stupinigi Palace built for Vittorio Amedeo II of Savoy (**figs. 6.14** and **6.15**; 1729–33), outside Turin, Juvarra designed a complex of low buildings in a symmetrical pattern based on hexag-

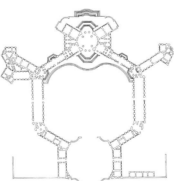

onal 30–60 degree relationships that spread out to tie into the surrounding park and landscape. A large, double-height central salon connects to radiating rooms and passages that create intricate spatial relationships. The surface decoration is a rich overlay of painted and gilded plaster work that suggests awareness of the contemporary French design in which basic forms tend toward simplification while surface ornament becomes increasingly rich. The term Rococo may be more appropriate here than Baroque.

6.14 (*above*) Fillipo Juvara, Stupinigi hunting lodge, Turin, 1729–33

The great hall of the hunting lodge incorporates galleries for musicians and singers as well as frescoes and stucco decorations. This is, in fact, really a royal palace, rather than a simple lodge, although the lavish decoration of the hall is in stark contrast to the low stable and service blocks that enclose the main courtyard.

6.15 (*left*) Ground plan of Stupinigi hunting lodge.

Juvara's ground plan is focused on the central hall, from which rooms radiate to form a rough hexagon around a central court.

6.16 Jakob Prandtauer and Antonio Carlone, Monastery of St. Florian, Linz, Austria, 1718–24.

The Marble Hall, which was the work of Prandtauer after Carlone's death, contains columns of faux marble with gilded capitals and ornate stucco work, and these form the base for an elaborate painted ceiling by the Italian artist Martino Altomonte. The painting, in faux perspective, glorifies Austria's then recent victory over the Turks.

6.17 Jakob Prandtauer, Abbey of Melk, Austria, 1702–38.

The Benedictine foundation of Melk included a collegiate church, which is a fine example of Austrian Baroque. The curving side walls, red-brown marble pilasters, and upper balconies frosted with stucco decoration contribute to the almost overpowering impression. The high windows illuminate the lavishly decorated transverse arches. The altar is backed by an ornate reredos. Only the floor, with its simple diagonal squares of marble, is a refuge from the ornamentation. After a fire in 1738 damaged the church, parts of it were rebuilt by Josef Munggenast.

Baroque in Northern Europe

In the regions of Europe north of Italy, Baroque design was taken up with zest, especially in the complex spatial concepts of monasteries and churches. The simpler spaces in secular buildings, with their overlay of elaborate surface decoration, draw on French Rococo influences.

Austria

The link between Italian and Austrian Baroque can be traced through the work of Carlo Antonio Carlone (1686–1708), a member of an Italian family of artists who relocated in Austria. Carlone was the designer of the Monastery of S. Florian (**fig. 6.16**; 1718–24) near Linz where the ceiling of the church is a series of slightly domed vaults (sometimes called sail vaults or given the German name of *platzlgewolbe*). Their surfaces of smooth plaster covered with paintings, they give illusions of high domed spaces with architectural detail

6.18 Jakob Prandtauer, library, Abbey of Melk, Austria, 1702–38.

The bookshelves line the walls, and above them ornamental brackets support the balconies, which contain additional shelving. The floor is simply tiled in marble, and only the ceiling is free for the exuberant painting of figures floating in a blue sky above a fringe of simulated architectural detail. The effect is close to rococo simplicity of form but with elaborate decorative overlay.

developed in false perspective. The monastic buildings were completed by an Austrian, Jakob Prandtauer (1660–1726), and include the ceremonial Marble Hall with decorative stucco work and *faux* marbling by F. J. Holzinger, an Austrian, and a painted ceiling by Altomonte and Sconzani, both Italians. The nearby abbey of Melk (**figs. 6.17** and **6.18**; 1702–38), a vast complex of connected buildings on a high bluff overlooking the Danube, is entirely the design of Prandtauer. The church interior with stucco architectural detail and illusionistic ceiling painting draws on Italian precedents. The secular spaces such as the library with its cantilevered balcony, both functional and ornamental, and the Marble Hall (or Kaisersaal) lean toward the Rococo ornamentation typical of Austrian, German, and French palace design.

In Vienna, Johann Bernhard Fischer von Erlach (1656–1723) was the designer of the Karlskirche (Church of St. Charles, 1716–37; **fig. 6.19**). The central space is topped by an oval dome; there are two large and four small radiating chapels, and a great arch that opens into a deep chancel backed

6.19 Johann Bernhard Fischer von Erlach, Karlskirche, Vienna, Austria, 1716–37.

The oval, domed interior of Karlskirche (the Church of St. Charles Borromaeus) is surrounded by chapels. The deep chancel is illumined by side windows that focus light on the sunburst design above the altar, and columns below permit a screened view into the monk's choir beyond. The high windows admit limited light into the generally dim interior, which is crammed with rich marble architectural detail and ornamentation.

6.20 (*right*) Kaspar Moosbrugger, Abbey Church of Einsiedeln, near Zürich, Switzerland, 1691–1735.

Moosbrugger showed a mastery of complex spatial relationships in the abbey church, where successive bays move toward the distant altar while an overwhelming overlay of stucco ornament and painted detail make the space dissolve into florid richness.

6.21 (*top right*) Peter Thumb, Monastery and Pilgrimage Church of Neu-Birnau, Germany, 1745–51.

This is a simple rectangular room with a projecting square chancel, but the simplicity of the underlying plan is lost in the lavish overlay of stucco and painted ornament.

6.22 (*right*) Domenikus Zimmermann, Die Wies, Füssen, Bavaria, Germany, 1744–54.

The interior of the Pilgrimage Church of Christ Scourged, known as Die Wies, is largely colored white and gold, and the intricate plaster ornamentation seems to dissolve forms into a kind of mist. The ceiling is bordered by a ring of architectural detail, partly real and in three dimensions, partly trompe l'oeil.

with a screen of columns that allows a glimpse of a monks' choir beyond. The wall surface detail uses a Corinthian pilaster order with generally restrained decorative detail so that attention is focused on the great sunburst (lighted by hidden windows) above the main altar.

Switzerland

The abbey of Einsiedeln (**fig. 6.20**; begun 1703) near Zürich, another huge church and monastery complex, was designed by Kaspar Moosbrugger (1656–1723). A small chapel stands within the large domed octagonal area at the entrance to the church; receding bays move toward the chancel and altar in a progression. The overlay of sculptured form and illusionistic ceiling painting generates the complexity of space and the theatricality typical of the Baroque. At S. Gallen, the ancient monastery was rebuilt in 1748–70 by the German architect Peter Thumb (1681–1766). The church has a long narrow-aisled nave with, at its midpoint, a round, domed interruption.

Germany

Thumb was the architect of the smaller German pilgrimage church at Birnau (often identified as Neu-Birnau) of 1745–51 (**fig. 6.21**). A cantilevered balcony that runs around the walls of the relatively simple rectangular church and projecting chancel adds to the spatial interest that is further amplified by sculpture and illusionistic ceiling painting. A clock is fitted into decorative banding that divides the ceiling painting into panels.

The pilgrimage church known as Die Wies (**fig. 6.22**; 1744–54) by Domenikus Zimmermann (1685–1766) and the monastic church complexes at Ottobeuren (begun 1737) and Zwiefalten (1739–65) by Johann Michael Fischer (1692–1766) each are unique variations on the Baroque themes of complex space, rich decorative sculpture, and illusionistic painting. In an agricultural region with few cities, and with a population having no experience of travel nor exposure to art in any other forms, entering one of these churches, flooded with light and filled with an overwhelming richness of color and ornament, must have been an exciting and inspiring experience.

In Franconia near the German city of Bamberg one of the best known of Baroque churches, the pilgrimage church of Vierzehnheiligen (Fourteen

Saints, 1742–72), stands alone on high ground (**fig. 6.23**). It is the work of Johann Balthasar Neumann (1687–1753), initially a military engineer who had been sent by his patron, the Prince-Bishop of Wurzburg, to Vienna and Paris before returning to Franconia to devote his efforts to architecture. The somewhat forbidding twin-towered exterior of the building hardly prepares the visitor for the Baroque complexity of the interior and its Rococo ornamentation. The plan is based on a Latin cross, but the arrangement of aisles and the related ovals of the low domes of the ceiling elaborate and obscure the plan form. A pilgrimage shrine-altar dedicated to fourteen martyred saints stands in the nave beneath an oval dome which overlaps, and is overlapped by, adjacent ovals and circles in a way that makes the whole interior full of implied motion. The windows are large and the glass is white so that light pours into the space; white, gold, and pink are the dominant colors. A frosting of Rococo plaster sculpture and painting contributes to the theatrical sense of light and movement.

Neumann was also the designer of the Residenz at Würzburg (**fig. 6.24**; begun 1735), a huge palace

6.23 Johann Balthasar Neumann, Pilgrimage Church of Vierzehnheiligen, near Bamberg, Germany, 1742-72.

The great pilgrimage church was built with a central shrine to house the venerated object, but the ground plan is based on interlocking ovals at floor, balcony, and ceiling levels of such complexity that the interior is almost incomprehensibly rich in spatial terms. This Baroque concept has been overlaid with Rococo ornament in white, gold, and pinks, and the painted ceiling merges into lavish plaster ornamentation. Only the floor of diagonal squares of marbles is simple.

6.24 Johann Balthasar Neumann. Residenz, Würzburg, Germany, 1735.

The Baroque fascination with movement, including vertical movement, made lavish stairways a favorite subject, and in his treatment of the staircase hall in the secular context of a palace, Neumann planned a setting for ceremonial movement. Most of the surfaces are white, embellished with rich decorative detail and sculptures in the Rococo manner. The colorful ceiling fresco (1751-3), with its view upward into a celestial realm, is by Tiepolo.

with a spectacular Rococo chapel, a ceremonial grand stair, and a Kaisersaal with fresco painted ceilings by the Venetian artist Giovanni Battista Tiepolo (1696–1770). Stucco decorative detail merges into painting with illustrations of endless space and foreground details that spill out of the painting over the plasterwork. Pink, blue, and gold form the color palette.

The Viennese architect Lukas von Hildebrandt (1663–1745) worked as a consultant to Neumann at the Wurzburg Residenz. His reputation had been established with his work on the Piaristen Church in Vienna (1715–21) and on the palace known as the Upper Belvedere (1700–23) also in Vienna. The palace stands at the upper end of a large formal garden and looks down toward another palace at the lower edge. A projecting central entrance element gives access to a grand stair hall. Here a lower flight of stairs at the center divides at a

landing into twin flights, leading to the salon that stands at the center of a long row of formal rooms. The stair hall is a simple square in shape, but it is lined with Rococo sculptural ornamentation. Huge ornamental lanterns supported by sculptured cupid figures stand at the upper and lower corners of the baluster railings, while one more lantern hangs from the center of the ceiling. Each of the formal rooms is treated with a different lining of Rococo architectural ornament and fresco painting.

The design of a palace often included individual rooms decorated in the newly current style. At Augsburg in Germany, for example, a *Festsaal* or ballroom was created in the Schaezler Palace (**fig. 6.25**; 1765–70). Its walls were covered with Rococo plaster work and wood carving, elaborately framed mirrors, wall bracket candle holders, candle chandeliers, and fresco painting on the ceiling and in

6.25 (*left*) Adam Liebert van Liebenhofen (architect, room designer unknown), Ballroom of the Schnaezler Palace, Augsburg, Germany, 1765–70.

In this Rococo interior the usual architectural elements of pilasters and entablature have been replaced by mirror panels between the windows and florid plasterwork, which covers every available surface. Candle brackets at the sides of the mirrors and the many hanging chande-liers provided for a spectacular level of night-time illumination.

6.26 (*below*) François Cuvilliés, Amalienburg, Nymphenburg Palace, Munich, Germany, 1734–9.

Silver and azure blue plaster ornamentation by Johann Baptist Zimmermann frame the windows and mirror panels. All of the Rococo ornamentation is in stucco, and there is little painting. The angles of the mirrors as they progress around the room create repeating reflection in kaleidoscopic complexity. The light of the candles of the great chandelier would have been endlessly repeated in the mirrors.

wall panels. All of this grandeur was intended to symbolize and emphasize the importance of the owner of the palace, a banker and silver merchant who had been elevated to the nobility in recognition of his financial help to the Empress Maria Theresa of Austria.

The influence of French Rococo interior design was a strong factor in shaping German palace interiors and also in small, less formal palace buildings, often almost pavilions placed in gardens. François Cuvilliés (1695–1768) spent four years in Paris working with the French designer Jacques-François Blondel (1705–74) and returned to Germany to produce the kind of restrained yet florid interior that had become fashionable in the salons of Paris. His best-known work is the Amalienburg (1734–9), a small garden palace, planned as a shooting box for pheasant hunting in the grounds of the Nymphenburg Palace in Munich (**fig. 6.26**). Its central room placed between adjacent rooms decorated in silver and lemon yellow is of simple circular shape; three windows open to the gardens. Mirrored panels on the walls have the effect of transforming the simple form of the room into seeming complexity—a kind of kaleidoscope effect that repeats and elaborates the silvery stucco decoration of the walls and ceiling and the glitter of the great central chandelier.

Cuvilliés was the designer of many other imperial interiors, including the gloriously elaborate Rococo interior of the court theater in the Residenz at Munich (1751–3). It is a miniature prototype for the Baroque-Rococo opera house interior, with horseshoe tiers of boxes and a huge central royal box. Such opera houses as La Scala in Milan (1776–8, by Giuseppe Piermarini) are similar spaces on a grander scale.

Furniture and Other Interior Features

Furniture of the Baroque era does not differ in basic character from that of the Renaissance, but since Baroque design served only the wealthy and powerful, elaboration—even ostentation—are typical of objects made for the rooms of palaces. The basic forms of cabinet furniture were modified to introduce curving or bulging shapes for door or drawer fronts. Legs were often turned on foot or on water-powered lathes to create round ball or bulbous, jug-like shapes. Carving of plant forms, figures, allegorical images, and coats of arms were favorite forms of ornamentation, along with architectural moldings, pilasters, and columns. The development of veneer made it possible to create wood surfaces in varied colors and patterns, often used together with inlays of other decorative and exotic materials. Ivory, tortoise-shell, and silver were sometimes used, and techniques for simulating materials by marbling, graining, painting, and gilding were valued not as economy measures, but as demonstrations of skilled technique.

Baroque furniture tends to be large and dominated by fat and bulging forms, while Rococo design, in contrast, strives for delicacy and elegance. Legs are slim and gently curved, inlay patterns are small in scale and often very elaborate. Applied ornamentation is often of pewter, silver, bronze, or gilded. Cabinet tops may be of colorful marble. There was increasing use of upholstered elements in seating furniture; wood frames of curving form support cushioning that may be edged with gimp, braid, cord, or with closely spaced nails with ornamental heads. Mirrors and pictures had carved and gilded frames which sometimes overwhelmed what they surrounded. Shell, scroll, or volute shapes were favorite S-curved decorative forms.

Since candles were still the usual source of artificial light, candlesticks, wall brackets, and chandeliers were functionally important and ideal vehicles for Rococo ornamentalism. The harpsichord, the basic keyboard instrument of Baroque music, was often decorated with paintings both outside and on the under surface of the lid. Its legs or stand followed the Baroque and Rococo fashions in table base design or, occasionally, became ornamental sculpture. The organ in the back gallery of the typical Baroque church was a massive construction, usually carved and ornamented in a way that rivaled the treatment of pulpit and altar. The clock, an important mechanical development of medieval technology, at first a large and costly device to be put to work in the tower of a church or town hall, gradually came to be made in smaller size with greater accuracy and at lesser cost, although it was still a status symbol to be put on display in the rooms of luxurious houses. Clock forms were elaborated with large decorated cases or with sculptured bases.

The color palette of the Renaissance with its basis in grey stone, marble, white (or off-white) plaster, and natural walnut wood survived in the Italian Baroque, although bright, chromatic color began to appear in textiles, rugs, and, of course, in paintings. Gradually, more daring use of color, such as marble in varied yellows, reds, and greens and gilding, contributed to the shift toward more theatrical visual effects in interiors. In Germany and Austria pastel tones of pink and light greens and blues were favored along with gilding and white stucco. The use of more color but in more delicate hues is a characteristic of Rococo design, where both wood and plaster are typically painted in soft colors with carved or stucco detail picked out with gold or some delicate pastel shade. The covering of walls with textiles in rich colors also came into use in residential interiors. Curtains were most often part of the appointments of the canopied bed where they were useful in controlling drafts and in maintaining the privacy that the plan layout of even the most luxurious houses generally ignored. Panels of textile were used occasionally for screens or at doors, but window curtains and decorative drapery at windows did not appear until well into the eighteenth century. Floors were usually of polished wood PARQUETRY (small blocks arranged in patterns), of marble or tile, also usually in patterns of several colors that relate to the shape of the room and the geometry of its other design elements. Carpets or rugs were rare luxuries.

Outside of major churches, abbeys, and the elaborate palaces and houses of the rich, Baroque and Rococo design had limited impact. Most people continued to live in houses that dated from medieval times or from the earlier years of the Renaissance, and new building continued to follow older traditions. Furniture in these houses was limited in variety and generally simple, although it is possible to trace some movement toward Baroque forms in "folk" or "provincial" furniture where curving forms appear along with surface decoration, sometimes carved and sometimes painted.

The richly complex aspects of Baroque and Rococo design were for many years labeled by historians as a decadent and declining phase of Renaissance work. Older books often provide no coverage of Baroque design or deal with it in only a few sentences of negative comment. A new appreciation for Baroque and Rococo design has emerged, however, with an understanding that the Baroque emphasis on spatial complexity relates to modern concepts of design. In his book *Space, Time and Architecture* (1943), for example, Sigfried Gideon began his study of modern trends with a discussion of the links between the Renaissance and the enriched spatial concerns of the Baroque. Far from being a decadent and declining aspect of the Renaissance, the Baroque era is now seen as the most significant link between the classicism of what went before and a new and adventurous spirit that can be traced to the best of recent design work.

Before discussing the role of Baroque and Rococo design in other parts of Europe, it is necessary to go back to an examination of the ways in which Renaissance thinking moved into France, Spain, the Low Countries, and England. This is the material of the following chapters.

7

Renaissance, Baroque, and Rococo in France and Spain

It is often said that the art and design concepts of the Renaissance spread outward from Italy into France, central Europe, and Spain. The use of the word "spread" suggests that this was a natural and inevitable process. New ideas do, it is true, tend to spread, but that process may be resisted or blocked as "foreign" and suspect, or welcomed and encouraged, depending on events and attitudes in a particular place at a particular time. French military involvements in Italy from 1494 to 1525 brought an awareness of Italian ideas to the French aristocracy. Primaticcio, Sangallo, Serlio, Leonardo da Vinci, and Bernini were all active in France and enabled Italian thinking to be translated into French practice. As in Italy, a tentative Early Renaissance shaded into a high style. The use of the term Baroque for later French work may seen questionable since French work toward the end of the Renaissance was more restrained and conservative in character than the developments in Italy and south Germany. The subtleties of Rococo work in France interlace with the Baroque style extending into the eighteenth century.

In Spain, a similar pattern can be traced, with ideas flowing both directly from Italy and indirectly from France. Spanish architects traveled and even, in some cases, worked in Italy; they brought back the High Renaissance style and incorporated it into the existing, somewhat restrained, approach. Spanish love for rich ornamentation aided the movement into richly ornamented interiors that are strongly Baroque in spirit. The Rococo character of Spanish design of the eighteenth century is clearly based on French examples, but developed with a unique regional character. The role of Spain in opening up the American continents helped to transfer Spanish Baroque and Rococo ideas into the New World.

France

In France at the end of the Middle Ages Renaissance ideas encountered both conservative resistance and some degree of encouragement. At the end of the thirteenth century feudal ways were deeply entrenched and their expression in Gothic architecture had reached a level of perfection unmatched elsewhere in Europe. At the same time, political centralization with government centered on a powerful king, the growth of cities, the development of trade, and the decline in the importance

of fortification of cities and castles (made obsolete by the development of firearms) led gradually to the abandonment of medieval ways.

As the power of the church was checked by an increasingly powerful monarchy, religious building tended to become less important as compared to secular building. France was already amply supplied with churches and monastic establishments, while the powerful aristocracy centered on the king felt a need for visible expression of power equivalent to the castle, but more practical and more comfortable. The palace, the country chateau, and the city residence increased in importance and, without the need for defense, their character could change.

Alongside these changes in society, French kings became involved in military efforts to expand their power and dominance. In 1494–5 Charles VIII (r. 1470–98) launched a campaign against the kingdom of Naples. In the course of this adventure, he and his followers had an opportunity to become acquainted with the art and architecture of Renaissance Italy. Twenty-two Italian craftsmen were brought back to France and put to work on various royal projects, including work at the chateau of Amboise where the king had established his principal residence. Louis XII (r. 1462–1515), who succeeded Charles, was also involved in Italian conquests, successfully taking both Milan and Naples. The wing added to the chateau of Blois that is called by his name (Louis XII wing) is conservative, that is, medieval in concept, but details of moldings and column capitals demonstrate that the craftsmen executing the work were aware of the latest Italian practices.

Early Renaissance

Francis I (r. 1515–47) had a four-day visit with the Pope at the Vatican in 1515 where he must have seen the High Renaissance work then current in Rome. At Francis's suggestion, Leonardo da Vinci moved to France in 1516 and lived near Amboise until his death in 1519. The Francis I wing at Blois (1515–19) with its famous exterior stair has three stories of classical pilasters, and moldings apparently based on the interior courtyard treatment of Florentine palaces. The prominent roof above, with its clutter of chimneys and dormers, remains both French and medieval in effect.

The most spectacular Early Renaissance chateau is the huge royal palace-hunting lodge at

7.1 Hôtel de Villette, Paris, 1712.

The reserved classicism of Louis Régence design is evident in the Ionic pilasters and the windows, mirror, and restrained ornamental panels. The color is a soft, warm grey with gilded detailing. The floor is dark natural wood parquet, while the ceiling is an oval framed painting. Light was provided by candles in wall brackets and from candlesticks placed on the furniture (now removed).

7.2 Domenico da Cortona (?) and Jacques and Denis Sourdeau, Château de Chambord, Loire, France, begun *c.* 1519.

The upper floor level, now missing (or possibly never built) makes it possible to view the double spiral stair that rises at the center of the main block of the chateau. It connects the principal floor levels and gives access to the roof. The supporting pillars are topped with Ionic capitals, and the ceiling is vaulted and coffered. The staircase is thought to have been based on a design by Leonard da Vinci.

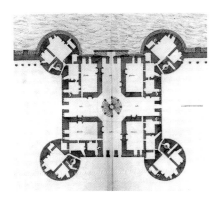

Chambord (**figs. 7.2** and **7.3**; begun 1519). It is a picturesque mix of moated medieval round towers and high roofs, with Renaissance concepts of symmetry and orderly planning and in the small details of arches, pilasters, and moldings. On the roof, an amazing collection of chimneys, towers, domes, and dormers are full of details that make reference to Italian Renaissance classicism, although the way in which they are applied haphazardly is typical of the Early Renaissance in France. The interiors of the main, central block at Chambord are organized by an open circulation space, a kind of lobby in the plan of a Greek cross. A double spiral staircase at the center dominates the space. Since Leonardo da Vinci was living at nearby Amboise, there has been speculation that he might have inspired the stair on the basis of sketches that appear in his notebooks. Living spaces are fitted into the four corners of the square,

while additional rooms, stairs, and passages are fitted into the corner towers and wings, making the building a complex labyrinth of spaces. The interiors have been stripped of their furnishings which, even when the building was new, would have been moved to and from Paris along with the royal court. The stone details of fireplaces, doorways, coffered ceilings, and the central stair are full of references to Italian practice.

It is thought that Domenico da Cortona (d. 1549) was the maker of the basic plan. He was a pupil of Giuliano da Sangallo, who was also in France in 1495 (Sangallo returned to Italy while Domenico remained in France). The French master mason Pierre Nepvau also had a role, but how much he was architect and how much simply a builder working under the direction of others is uncertain.

The smaller Loire valley chateau of Azay-le-Rideau (**fig. 7.4**; 1518–27) is the work of unidentified designers. It is an L-shaped building with a moat and lake surround, creating a visual composition of great charm. Its corner turrets and moat suggest castle architecture, but its rear elevation facing the moat is symmetrical, and the detail of pilasters and moldings clearly belong to the Early Renaissance. A grand stair is placed at the center of the main wing. A fanciful entrance bay marks its location on the front of the building, but the projecting L-wing places that entrance near a corner of the L, making the facade asymmetrical. Azay-le-Rideau is fortunate in having its interiors

7.3 Ground plan of the Château de Chambord.

The ground plan of the vast chateau reveals that the house is made up of a square central block with wings that stretch out to round towers on either side. Low wings complete a square. The central block holds rooms in each corner leaving a cross-shaped circulation space, which is focused on the central stairway. The symmetrical layout is evidence of the early Renaissance discovery of classical planning ideals.

7.4 Château de Azay-le-Rideau, Loire, France, 1518–27.

A typical room of the chateau, which could be used by the inhabitants for any purpose they wished. Here, a curtained bed has been set up but a table and chairs (including a folding Savonarola chair) are also available for the serving of a modest meal. The walls are covered with yellow silk. The huge fireplace and overmantel, carved in stone in the Italian Renaissance style, point to the emergence of French Renaissance design thinking.

7.5 Giovanni Battista Rosso and Francesco Primaticcio, Palace of Fontainebleau, near Paris, before 1533.

The Gallery of Francis I was a simple passage-like space made elaborate by the paneling on the walls with the ornately framed painting and stucco above, which was largely the work of the Italian artist and sculptor Giovanni Battista Rosso, known as Rosso Fiorentino. The beamed ceiling carries some decorative detail. The floor is simple wood parquet.

well preserved and restored with appropriate furniture and decorative details. In a building of such size and luxury, it is surprising to note that rooms are simply lined up in sequence on either side of the main stair, so that each room is the access passage to the next. There was no particular effort to differentiate room functions or to provide privacy. Each of the major rooms has a beamed wooden ceiling, stone walls covered by stretched cloth, and a large and richly carved fireplace mantel—probably the work of an Italian sculptor. Windows set in the thick stone walls open into a space in the wall thickness which can be curtained to give some privacy to the alcove. Since rooms had no fixed functions, furniture could be placed in any room to serve whatever function was chosen for it—a canopied bed in one room, a dining table and chairs, for example, in another. Color, other than the natural tones of the wood and stone, comes from wall coverings—green in one room, yellow in another, establishing a tonality for each room.

High Renaissance

The turn from the tentative experiments of the French Early Renaissance to the more assured High or developed phase of the era came about with the aid of several expatriate Italians who modified their Italian ways to create work that is specifically French. Under Francis I, Francesco Primaticcio (*c.* 1504–70) and Giovanni Battista Rosso (1494–1540), a Bolognese and a Florentine respectively, were put to work on the decoration of the Gallery of Francis I at Fontainebleau (**fig. 7.5**; before 1533). It is a long, narrow room with a beamed ceiling. The wood panels between the beams are geometrically carved, and there is a wood-paneled wainscot. Above the paneling, the

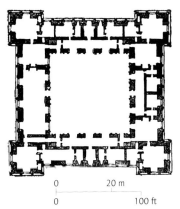

7.6 Sebastiano Serlio, Ancy-le-Franc, Burgundy, France, c.1546.

A symmetrical square plan with all spaces arranged around a central courtyard indicates the Italian influence on the design of this French chateau.

0   20 m
0   100 ft

walls are covered with a sequence of paintings of mythological and allegorical subjects framed with stucco sculptural figures and florid decorative details. STRAPWORK—the use of bands of relief that suggest straps of leather rolled out into patterns—appears here for the first time.

The Italian architect Sebastiano Serlio (1475–1555) was known for his published books on architecture before his arrival in France in 1540. He was the designer of the chateau of Ancy-le-Franc (**fig. 7.6**; begun 1546) in Burgundy. It is a hollow square, symmetrical on all four sides both outside and in the inner court. Classical pilasters and moldings are used with textbook precision, with an entablature at each floor level. At each corner a projecting tower block is three stories high, while the walls between rise only two stories. The entrance element at the center of each side is not strongly accented and the low relief of the architectural detail makes the walls almost flat planes, thus emphasizing the four-square simplicity of the basic plan concept. Arcades and niches elaborate the wall of the central court. A high tiled roof with many dormers and chimneys gives the building an especially French character, which remained the norm of French Renaissance work for more than a century. Internal planning takes a step forward with the introduction of passages that parallel the rows of rooms, permitting circulation to and from the four corner stairways and around parts of the square without passing through some of the rooms.

Pierre Lescot (*c.* 1515–78) took a further step in establishing the vocabulary of French Renaissance style with his work for Francis I and Henri II (r. 1547–59) at the Louvre in Paris. His design for one side of the square court (begun 1546) with two stories and an attic was a florid version of classicism that became highly influential.

François Mansart (1598–1667) was responsible for a series of projects that define the character of French Renaissance work as it developed a Baroque character during the reigns of Louis XIII (r. 1610–43) and Louis XIV (r. 1643–1715). The chateau of Balleroy in Normandy (*c.* 1626) is a symmetrical block with a taller central section flanked by lower wings. A high and prominent tiled roof with chimneys and dormers gives the building a typically French silhouette. The use of contrasting color masonry—lighter for window surrounds and quoins at the corners, darker for the intervening surfaces—creates a visual character that depends less on classical detail than on basic proportions of solid and void. The interiors also have a degree of reserve and dignity in spite of their rich ornamentation of plaster work and paintings that cover the wall surfaces. The Grand Salon that overlooks the gardens has a bare wooden floor of simple planks arranged in panels, contrasting with the elaborate *faux* marble painting of wall surfaces surrounding the paintings.

Mansart's name has come to be associated with the steep tile or slate roofs that so often top French Renaissance buildings. Attic space was exempt from real estate taxation and so was a desirable way of maximizing interior space at limited expense. In America in the Victorian era when such roofs became popular, they came to be known as MANSARD in recognition of their supposed originator. Such a roof tops Mansart's famous chateau of Maisons (or Maisons Laffitte, 1642–51) outside Paris (**figs. 7.7** and **7.8**). A U-shaped block, one room deep with high roofs, chimneys, and dormers, its white stone exterior is detailed with classical

7.7 François Mansart, Château de Maisons, near Paris, 1642-51.

The plan of this symmetrically perfect chateau, which is also known as Maisons Laffitte, forms a U-shape, with the rooms laid out in connecting sequence. Each room opens from its neighbors, and there are no independent corridors for circulation. There is a formal grand stair (to the right of the entrance hall), but all other stairs are tiny service elements tucked in unobtrusive corners.

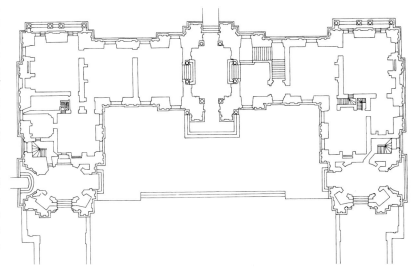

7.8 François Mansart, Grande Salle, Château de Maisons, 1642–51.

Elegantly correct classicism defines the formal entrance hall of this chateau. The Roman Doric columns and related detail show a degree of restraint relieved by the ornamental ceiling and sculptured bird above. The color is white throughout.

7.9 Salon, Paris *hôtel*, Île St Louis, Paris, eighteenth century.

An elegant interior with subdued rococo ornamentation and color. The harpsichord at the right has an ornamented leg base and painted imagery on its side and on the interior of the lid.

architectural trim, pilasters, moldings, and pediments. A grand stair, all in white, richly carved marble, leads up to a sequence of rooms, each opening into the next, each an elaborate but chilly display piece. While such aristocratic interiors may seem overbearing in their richness, the smaller houses (mostly eighteenth-century) built by powerful and wealthy families, the so-called *hotels* of Paris and a few other French cities, with their Rococo interiors, follow parallel stylistic trends on a more modest scale.

Royal favor was the source of power and wealth and those who had access to it wanted to live in circumstances that recalled royal living style in interior decoration and furniture. The Hôtel de Carnevalet in Paris (1655, now the City Museum), also by François Mansart, is a good example. Although its interiors have been subjected to various renovations and redecorations, they highlight the way in which the grandiosity of royal interiors was adapted to the life styles of the aristocracy.

The Hôtel de Sully (c. 1630–40) on the Rue S. Antoine in Paris was probably designed by Jacques II or Jean du Cerceau. Using a favorite plan, the entrance from the street is a gateway opening on a forecourt between twin buildings on either side that house stables, carriage house, kitchens, and service quarters, with the main house facade facing the court. Nearby, on the Ile S. Louis, the Hôtel Lambert (**fig. 7.9**; begun 1640) was an early but major work of Louis Le Vau (1612–70), a key figure in the development of French architecture and decoration. It has a grand stair in the space behind its main facade at the rear of a square court. From the top of the stair there extends a sequence of formal rooms—rectangular, octagonal, oval, and, in one case, a long and narrow gallery. Each room opens into the next except where small stairs and passages provide for some private circulation around bedrooms and for the use of servants. Some of the rooms have survived unchanged, their rich gilded plaster decoration surrounding paintings by various artists. The paintings provide the fanciful names given to the rooms: Cabinet de l'Amour or Cabinet des Muses. The painter Charles Lebrun (1619–90) worked with Le Vau here, and the two men collaborated in several later important projects

The spectacular chateau of Vaux-le-Vicomte, at the south edge of Paris (**figs. 7.10** and **7.11**; 1656), was designed by Le Vau for Louis XIV's Minister of Finance, Nicolas Fouquet. It is set in vast gardens planned with geometric order by André Le Nôtre (1613–1700), whose work established the French approach to landscape design. The chateau has a bulging oval central bay that houses a salon, the windows of which overlook the garden. Its mirrored doors opposite are arched and set between Corinthian pilasters. Above a classic entablature and below the ceiling dome, an upper

7.10 (*below left*) Louis Le Vau, Vaux-le-Vicomte, Melun; interiors by Charles Leburn, 1656.

This bedroom was intended for the king should he make a visit. The canopied bed stands in an alcove area fenced off from the room by a railing, thereby establishing privacy. The elaborate detail of the opening frame, the painted and sculpted ceiling, and ornate chandeliers expressed the symbolic status of the king.

7.11 (*below*) Ground plan of Vaux-le-Vicomte, Melun, 1656.

The ground plan of the chateau shows the oval salon that bulges from the garden front of the building and forms a focus for the various rooms of the interior. Elegant ceremonial bedrooms open in sequence, but there is no provision for private circulation. Stairs connecting levels are in unobtrusive secondary locations.

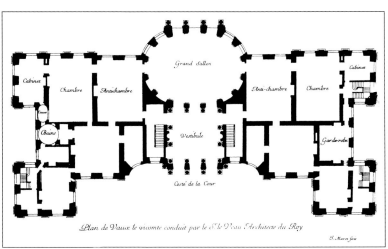

level of windows is surrounded by sculptured plaster figures and ornamental garlands. The sequence of rooms includes an overwhelmingly rich bedroom intended for the king, should he choose to visit, and special purpose rooms for dressing and bathing—even a billiard room for the game that had become popular as an aristocratic pastime. Vaux-le-Vicomte's interiors have survived with little change—even the kitchens are intact—to provide a particularly fine display of interior design in the time of Louis XIV. On Louis' first visit to the chateau, he was impressed with its beauty and its obvious cost. Investigations that followed led to the removal of its owner (to prison), and the transfer of the designers, Le Vau, Lebrun, and Le Nôtre to Versailles, where they were put to work transforming the royal palace. The oval exterior form and the vast extent of gardens with long vistas, waterways, and fountains at Vaux-le-Vicomte established the Baroque qualities of French landscape planning.

Baroque

Since work in the Louis xiv style comes from the latter part of the Renaissance in France, it is often designated as Baroque. In fact, French design never moved to the extremes of complexity and elaboration that characterize the Baroque work of Italy, south Germany, and Austria. Even at its most rich and heavily decorated, there is a certain reserve, an emphasis on logic and order, that makes it possible to argue that France simply skipped the mannerist and Baroque phases of the Renaissance and moved directly from the High Renaissance into the Rococo and Neoclassic phases that followed. Whatever terminology is used, it is certain that such vast projects as the palace and gardens at Versailles, and the related replanning of the whole town with radiating roadways focusing on the palace itself, demonstrate a Baroque love of grandeur used as a tool for the glorification of the king.

Versailles

At Versailles (**fig. 7.12**), the Sun King commissioned the creation of a setting that would justify his self-ordained status as the leader of victorious armies, the world's most powerful figure. Interiors were of staggering opulence. Marble walls and floors, stucco decoration, painted walls, paneling and ceilings, and furniture of gilded bronze or silver were designed by Le Vau and Lebrun. In

INSIGHTS

Louis XIV and Versailles

Louis XIV, the Sun King of France, created a palace at Versailles that was the wonder of all who saw it. The Duc de Saint Simon, a courtier, recorded amusingly and pithily in his memoirs what life was like there:

Louis XIV was made for a brilliant Court. In the midst of other men his figure, his courage, his grace, his beauty, his grand mien ... distinguished him till his death, as the King Bee. ... [1]

Towards women his politeness was without parallel. Never did he pass the humblest petticoat without raising his hat; even to chambermaids that he knew to be such .... He treated his valets well, above all those of the household. It was amongst them that he felt most at ease. ... [2]

His own apartments, and those of the Queen, are inconvenient to the last degree, dull, close, stinking .... I might never finish upon the monstrous defects of a palace so immense and so immensely dear. [3]

Mrs Thrale, a visitor to Versailles in the reign of Louis XVI, made the same observation:

The Queen has only two rooms ... a bedchamber and a drawing room—in the first she sleeps, dresses, prays, chats, sees her Sister or any other person who is admitted to privacy. She has no room for solitude, nor even a Closet to put her Close Stoole [chamber pot] in which always stands by her bedside. [4]

Another Versailles courtier, Mme Roland wrote along similar lines in the 1770s:

Mme Legrand, one of the Dauphin's ladies ... lent us her apartment. It was under the tiles [roof slates] opening out on to the same corridor as those of the Archbishop of Paris, and so close to his that the prelate had to be careful lest we should hear his talking, and the same applied to us. There were two rooms, meanly furnished ...with an approach rendered horrible by the darkness of the passage and the smell of the latrines. [5]

1. *Memoires of the Duc de St Simon*, trs. Bayle St John (London, 1902), p. 216; 2. *Ibid*, p. 229; 3. *Ibid*, p. 272; 4. Quoted in M.L. Kekewich, *Princes and People 1620–1714: Anthology of Primary Sources* (Manchester, 1994), p. 173; 5. Quoted in Evelyn Farr, *Before the Deluge: Parisian Society in the Reign of Louis XVI* (London, 1994), pp. 25–6

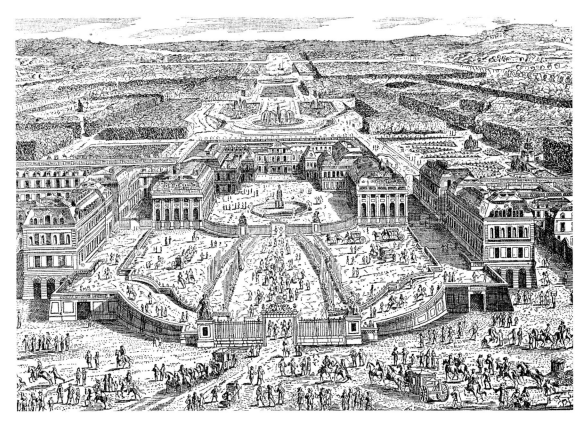

The famous palace, seen in this seventeenth-century engraving, was the result of many years of expansion and reconstruction. It turns its front face to the boulevards that radiated through the town and its other face to the vast gardens planned by André Le Nôtre.

1668, shortly after Le Vau's death, a second phase of elaboration was undertaken by Jules Hardouin-Mansart (1619–90), a nephew of François Mansart. He was responsible for the great gallery room that overlooks the gardens, the Galerie des Glaces (**fig. 7.14**) where mirrors on the inner wall face the windows that overlook the garden. The painted ceiling (by Lebrun) and the gilt and marble architectural trim generate a room of spectacular grandeur in spite of its somewhat unimaginative, even monotonous concept and detail. The adjacent anterooms, the Salon de la Guerre and the symmetrically matching Salon de la Paix, each have a huge oval decorative panel above a lavish fireplace and mantel. The rooms are rich with gilt, marble, paintings, mirrors, and chandeliers. They are, like the other seemingly endless formal rooms of the palace, showcases for the extremes of splendor that the style of Louis XIV produced. Among the more interesting spaces in the vast wings added to the palace by Hardouin-Mansart are the Royal Chapel (**fig. 7.13**; begun 1689) and the theater or small opera house known as the "Entertainments Room." The tall central space of the chapel is surrounded by an arcade at the lower level and a colonnade of Corinthian columns at the level of a balcony. There is a clerestory at the level of the painted, vaulted ceiling above, and windows at each level that flood the space with light. With the largely white and gold color, the space is remarkably bright. The gilded organ case at the gallery level above the altar is a reminder that the music of such composers as Rameau, Lully, and Couperin was given first performances here, as well as in the theater which was not completed until 1770 in the reign of Louis XV.

Louvre

At the Louvre in Paris (**fig. 7.15**), Louis XIV aimed to achieve a city palace comparable to Versailles through extensions and renovation of the existing somewhat diverse conglomeration of pavilions. Rooms such as Lebrun's Galerie d'Apollon (begun 1662), a long, barrel-vaulted room with sculptured and painted decoration (a forerunner to the Galerie des Glaces at Versailles), brought the interiors up to royal standards. Bernini was summoned from Italy to prepare designs for a renovation that would convert the exterior to a suitably Baroque structure. His three successive attempts were each found "too Italian"—too much like the palaces of Rome—and so failed to please the king. In 1665

7.13 Jules Hardouin-Mansart and Robert de Cotte, chapel, Versailles, 1689–1710.

The royal chapel, in the north wing of the palace, has an arcaded lower level and an upper, columned level for the king and his royal retinue. There are windows at both levels and in the clerestory above to provide ample daylight. Gilding is used with restraint for the railing balusters, for the altar and organ case above, and in the detail of the vaulted ceiling and painted half-dome. The floor is of colored marbles laid in geometric patterns. The ceiling fresco is the work of Antoine Coypel (1661–1722), and the marble altar is believed to have been by Van Clève.

7.14 Louis Le Vau and Jules Hardouin-Mansart, Galerie des Glaces, Château of Versailles, from 1679.

Charles Lebrun was the prime designer of the interior detail of the Galerie des Glaces (Hall of Mirrors). The simple basic design of this huge gallery was given its elaborate character by the many mirrors along one wall, which reflect the views of the garden through the windows opposite and, at night, the light of innumerable candles. Richly colored marbles and gilded plasterwork detail enrich the walls while the barrel-vaulted ceiling was painted by Lebrun in flame-colored and amber tones with elaborate allegorical scenes celebrating the early years of the reign of Louis XIV. The floor is of patterned wood parquet.

7.15 Louis Le Vau and Charles Lebrun, Galerie d'Apollon, Palace of the Louvre, Paris, after 1661–2.

The long gallery, of which one end is shown here, has a barrel-vaulted ceiling covered with sculptural and painted decoration celebrating legends of the sun-god Apollo—the reference to Louis as "sun-king" is obvious. Lebrun recruited a number of artists to work under his direction to produce the many images required. The room was left unfinished when Louis abandoned the development of the Louvre in favor of Versailles. The walls were decorated in a related style, following Lebrun's designs, by Eugène Delacroix with many paintings and much gilt.

7.16 Jacques Lemercier and François Mansart, Church of Val-de-Grâce, Paris, 1645–1667.

In this French Baroque church, the chapel of a great hospital, a spectacular baldacchino above the altar challenges the magnificence of that in St. Peter's, Rome. Bernini provided the design during his stay in Paris, and the six twisted Corinthian columns were the work (c. 1658) of the sculptor Gabriel Le Duc.

Bernini returned to Italy, leaving it to Claude Perrault (1613–88), a doctor and amateur architect, to provide the design which was finally built in 1667–70 as the east facade of the Louvre, often called the "New Louvre." It has a simple base with a long colonnade of paired Corinthian free-standing columns above. This forms a kind of loggia on either side of a pedimented entrance element with pilastered, slightly projecting end wings. The general effect is more strictly classical than the earlier work of Louis XIV's era and indicates a turn away from Baroque ostentation to the increasingly reserved Neoclassicism that was to follow.

Baroque Churches

Aside from royal building projects, the age of Louis XIV produced churches in which Roman architectural style was recreated in French terms. Among them are the church for the Sorbonne (1635–42) in Paris by Jacques Lemercier (1585–1684). This has a plan symmetrical about two axes to emphasize two major entrances, one from the street and the other from within the college. The similarly domed church of the hospital of Val-de-Grâce (**fig. 7.16**) in Paris (begun 1645) was by François Mansart and Jacques Lemercier. During his stay in Paris, Bernini

7.17 Jules Hardouin-Mansart and Libéral Bruant, Church of Les Invalides, Paris, 1677–1706.

The church that forms the central element of Les Invalides has a tall central space topped with a great dome, the work of Hardouin-Mansart. The interior is of grey stone, except for painted panels with gilded edging and the painting and gilt of the dome interior. The windows high up in the drum below the dome light the space with dramatic effects of light and shadow.

prepared the design for the baldachino at Val-de-Grâce. It is not unlike the huge baldacchino at St. Peter's in Rome, but has six twisted Corinthian columns (two more than Rome), each topped with a gilded figure of an angel. The most spectacular and best known of these Parisian domed churches is S. Louis des Invalides (**fig. 7.17**; 1677–1706)— the church, now the tomb of Napoleon, attached to the vast hospital and home for disabled veterans by Hardouin-Mansart. The central space, far higher than it is wide, is topped by a dome with an inner shell that is open at the top, permitting a view up to a painted upper shell that receives light from

windows that cannot be seen from the main floor below, and creating a dramatic effect of space and light that can be called truly Baroque. The somewhat overbearin grandeur of the space has made it an ideal setting for Napoleon's monumental tomb, which is now placed below the floor in a central well. The design of these churches leads French classicism toward the later S. Geneviève (see p. 129).

Furniture and Furnishings

Furniture made to suit the interiors of Louis XIV palaces and town houses shared the giant scale, heaviness of structure, and rich ornamentation that

7.18 (*above*) Jean Demoulin, commode, France, mid-eighteenth century.

Chinese lacquer indicates the interest in Chinese imports that became current in eighteenth-century France. The gilded metal Rococo decoration and florid shape set off the simplicity of the marble top. The owner was once the Duc de Choiseul at the Château de Chanteloup.

7.19 Musical clock, France, 1756.

The clock became a favorite ornamental element in aristocratic interiors of the eighteenth century. This example in gilded bronze is elaborately sculptured in Rococo taste with only its simple white enameled face to suggest its basic function. The clockmaker Michel Stollewerke provided the mechanism within, similar to a musicbox, that marked the hours by playing tunes.

characterized the architecture and interior design of the period. Oak and walnut were the usual woods, but inlays and applied decorative trim used exotic woods such as tulip and zebrawood, MARQUETRY, gilding, and silver. Chairs tended to be square and massive, with arms, seat, and backs upholstered. André-Charles Boulle (1642–1732) was a favorite cabinet maker to Louis XIV. He specialized in the design and making of ARMOIRES (large door-front cabinets that served the functions of closets) and COMMODES (table height storage units with drawers, invariably decorated with inlaid ornament in marquetry often using ivory, shell, brass, pewter, and silver; **fig. 7.18**); tops were often of richly colorful marble. Boulle also became known for the use of ORMOLU, a technique for gilding bronze ornament that was then attached to the corners and edges of furniture. Mercury was heated to plate the gilt onto the cast bronze trim— a process that generated poisonous fumes with disastrous results to the workers using it. The fact that it was costly in human lives as well as materials probably added to its role as an element of status display. Boulle's workshops were continued by his four sons and the term BOULLE has come to be identified with his style of work.

Along with this heavy and elaborate furniture, smaller objects followed parallel stylistic directions. Lighting came from chandeliers using metal, carved wood, and crystal in various combinations.

Complex candle stands were of various types— gueridons, candelabra, and TORCHIERS. Mirrors were made in various sizes, with carved and gilded frames similar to the richly ornamental frames used for paintings. Small mirrors were often placed in decorative frames with candle brackets on either side forming an illuminated looking glass called a GIRANDOLE. Clocks, valued more for ornament and the status they implied than for time-keeping (**fig. 7.19**), were favorite elaborate centerpieces on mantels, along with statuary (often busts on pedestals) and ornamental vases. The harpsichord was developed to a peak of technical excellence by makers such as Blanchet, Stehlin, and Pascal Taskin (1723–93). Their exteriors reflected the furniture styles of the time, and they often had fine paintings on the underside of the lid.

Colors tended to be strong and bright reds, greens, and violets, along with gilded trim in as great profusion as could be afforded. The importing of Chinese wallpapers began at this time and gradually became a favorite element for rooms, giving them an oriental, exotic flavor. Tapestries, especially those from the Gobelins workshops, were favorite wall hangings, while AUBUSSON and

SAVONNERIE CARPETS of woven wool sometimes covered floors that were otherwise bare parquetry, stone, or marble, usually in simple, geometric patterns. Since much of the movable furnishings of this era has been dispersed, replaced by later renovation or removed (even destroyed) at the time of the French Revolution, the best information on the character of complete interiors of the day comes from artists' illustrations. The engravings of Abraham Bosse, for example, depict various events taking place in the richly furnished rooms of upper-class homes.

Regency to Rococo

Between the death of Louis XIV in 1715 and the beginning of the reign of Louis XV when he came of age in 1723, there intervened a regency which gave the name RÉGENCE to the decorative styles that are transitional between the more clearly defined periods of Louis XIV and XV. In general, the work of the Régence is less heavy, clumsy, and overbearing than that of the earlier period. Curving forms became more commonplace; for example, the gently S-curved leg shape called CABRIOLE came into use. The artist-designer Juste-Aurèle Meissonier (1695–1750) published more than 100 engravings showing wall panel decorations, candlesticks, and furniture designs that make use of flowing curves, asymmetric ornament, and details based on the natural forms of shells and foliage. His work was a key influence on the design of the Régence and the periods that followed.

The style of LOUIS XV (r. 1723–74) is usually identified with the term Rococo, which describes the decorative style that characterized the later phases of French classicism. Régence design became more delicate, light, and florid, with flowing curves. It developed most strongly in the design of interiors and the associated elements of furniture and related decorative arts. Architecture of the Louis XV era moved from Baroque exuberance toward a more restrained classicism, finally deserving the stylistic designation Neoclassical, while rooms within can better be described as Rococo. French Rococo design was quickly imported and imitated in Austria and Germany and had considerable influence in England as well. François Cuvilliés was a key figure in carrying the style eastward. His work in Munich such as the Amalienburg Palace Pavilion is a masterpiece of French Rococo in spite of its German location.

Paris Hôtels

Military losses in wars with England led to financial constraints on royal building projects. With such vast projects as the palaces at Versailles and the Louvre and the domed churches such as those of Hardouin-Mansart complete, the time of Louis XV was more concerned with modest design of town houses, smaller royal projects, and the completion and renovation of interiors in the more delicate Rococo style. In Paris, many large houses built by wealthy and powerful families under royal patronage are interestingly varied in plan and generally richly decorated in Rococo style. Comfort became a major issue in the discreet private living accommodation of the élite (**fig. 7.20**).

Gabriel-Germaine Boffrand (1667–1754), a pupil of Mansart, planned the Hôtel d'Amelot in Paris as a forecourt of oval shape with services fitted around it at the front and side and with the curved facade of the house proper at the rear. Rooms of unusual shape such as a pentagonal anteroom and stair hall are neatly fitted into the ingenious plan that provides for convenience and privacy. In 1735 Boffrand designed an oval salon

7.20 Cross-sectional engraving of the interior of the Château de Petit-Bourg, France, eighteenth century.

The salon on the first floor of this luxurious house has rich Rococo detailing, including paintings, a fine mantel, and even a small fountain to the right of the chimney breast. On the second floor, the level of principal bedrooms, the paneled detail is simple except for carving above the door. On the third level, inside the mansard roof, bare rooms and shelves for storage indicate the territory of children and servants. The basement chambers are stone vaulted.

that was inserted into the earlier Hôtel de Soubise (**fig. 7.21**). Windows, doors, mirrors, and paintings are surrounded by gilded Rococo ornament applied to white paneled walls and a pale blue ceiling. The basic shape of the room is simple, but the filigree of sculptured and gilded cupids disporting on floral and shell ornament, along with a huge central crystal chandelier, all repeated in kaleidoscopic fashion by the mirrors, makes this an astonishing display of Rococo virtuosity.

The Petit Trianon

To the north side of the gardens of Versailles, the small palace called the Petit Trianon (**fig. 7.22**) was built in 1762–8 to the designs of Ange-Jacques Gabriel (1698–1782). It was intended as a modest house where members of the royal family could escape from the pomp and ostentation of Versailles. Externally, the four similar but subtly different facades relate to the surrounding gardens and reflect its plan. Three of the facades, each with four Corinthian columns (or pilasters), are composed with elegant simplicity controlled by a system of geometric proportions based on the golden section. Within, the spaces are superb examples of the Rococo style at its best. The stair hall is a simple square lined with cream-white stone. Florid detail is restricted to the metalwork of the iron stair rails, with gilded monogram inserts and a hanging candle lantern-chandelier. The living spaces are each paneled in wood painted in soft, pastel colors with restrained surface ornamentation in white and gold. Simple mantels with mirrors above are flanked by wall bracket candle holders. Two dining rooms, one larger and one smaller, each have circular elements centered in the parquet floors that were originally elevators arranged to lower the dining table into service areas

7.21 Gabriel-Germaine Boffrand and Charles-Joseph Natoire, Salon de la Princesse, Hôtel de Soubise, Paris, 1735.

The oval room, known as the Salon de la Princesse (Princess's Hall), contains elaborate Rococo details, mirrors, and paintings by Natoire (1700-77). An ornamental clock is placed on a marble mantel. White plaster cupids cling to the gilded ornamental detail at the edges of the ceiling, and a crystal ornamented chandelier hangs in the center of the room. The ceiling is blue but the walls are paneled in white.

7.22 Ange-Jacques Gabriel, bedchamber of Marie Antoinette, Petit Trianon, Versailles, 1762–8.

The low-ceilinged room fitted into a mezzanine level of the Petit Trianon, which became a favorite retreat for the queen. Simple paneling painted in a pastel tone sets off the casement windows, which gave a view over the gardens. The furniture, with its relatively simple neoclassical forms, is typical of the era of Louis XVI (r. 1774–92).

7.23 Lit à la turque, France, c. 1765–70.

Flowing curves and elaborate carving characterize French eighteenth-century furniture design, and the Rococo taste for the exotic generated furniture that was designed to suggest one or another faraway form of luxury. Couches that invited reclining became favorite objects for the rooms of the homes of the wealthy and aristocratic.

below, where servants could clear the table and set out a next course without intruding on the privacy of the royal party by entering the dining rooms. The bedroom that was occupied by Marie-Antoinette is a small room on a mezzanine floor. It is an elegant example of the Rococo, both simple and rich; its paneled walls are painted in pale grey with white and gold carved detail, while the marble fireplace surround with mirror above and curtained bed, chairs, and drapery are all in related golden yellow colors. Much of the interior detail in the Petit Trianon is the work of Richard Mique (1728–94) who became a royal favorite after the death of Louis XV. The Petit Trianon may be regarded as the peak expression of French Rococo design, while also beginning to turn toward Neoclassicism.

Regency and Rococo Furniture

The furniture of the Louis XV period follows the patterns developed during the Régence. Along with the introduction of curving forms, a new interest in comfort developed in such types as the FAUTEUIL, an arm chair with upholstered seat and back and open padded arms. The BERGÈRE was a somewhat larger arm chair with enclosed and upholstered arms and, usually, a loose seat cushion. The CANAPÉ was a small upholstered sofa, and the CHAISE LONGUE was an upholstered chair with an

extended seat for lounging: both furniture types developed in response to a new concern for informality and comfort (**fig. 7.23**). More varied storage furniture was also developed, along with various types of writing tables and desks. The DROP-LEAF and ROLLTOP (BUREAU À CYLINDRE) desk were developed in response to functional needs.

Rococo to Neoclassicism

Under LOUIS XVI (r. 1774–92), Rococo design survived in combination with a further move toward the more academic reserve of Neoclassicism. Gabriel's work at Versailles

7.24 François-Joseph Bélanger, Hôtel Baudard de Saint-James, Place Vendôme, Paris, c. 1775–80.

The grand salon of a palatial Paris house has been decorated with white paint and gilding, mirrors, and paintings in the ceiling. The rondels over the doors, an ornamental fireplace mantel, and candle chandeliers complete the image of fashionable luxury. The parquet floor includes a central sunburst motif. Furniture is absent but would, no doubt, have been in the Rococo neoclassical style to match the other detail of the room. An elaborate mantel clock is a small but suitable focal point.

(including the theater-opera house) and the well-known twin facades facing the Place de Louis XV in Paris (now the Place de la Concorde) are typical. Speculative real estate developments such as Jules Hardouin-Mansart's 1690 Place Vendôme, its buildings around a great central square, provided elegant living apartments for the affluent. Behind such elegantly classical fronts, various buildings are placed with no special regard for the formal facade. Inside, rooms were often richly decorated and redecorated according to changing fashion (**fig. 7.24**). Rococo rooms of simple shape with paneling in quiet, pastel colors and surface ornamentation of carved curvilinear ornament were typical. The furniture of the Louis XVI era takes on a more rectilinear and geometric quality than its predecessors. Mahogany became increasingly popular. Carved and gilded detail is typical, but the carving tends toward parallel bands of molding, FLUTING, or REEDING, while a new awareness of ancient design developed as knowledge of the work discovered in excavations at Pompeii and Herculaneum (beginning in 1748) spread. Even ancient Greek design began to be known, so that Greek ornamental details were introduced to further the connection with ancient classicism. Window draperies, previously rare, became increasingly common; colors included crimson red and golden yellow, often with trimmings of fringe and tassels. The Revolution of 1789 put an end to period styles based on royal patronage and encouragement, although a number of politically agile architects and designers managed to survive and resume their careers in the post-revolutionary climate.

The post-revolutionary style called DIRECTOIRE (named for the form of government that in 1794 followed the Reign of Terror) was developed under the influence of Georges Jacob (1730–1814) who had been a cabinet maker with commissions from the court of Louis XVI. His designs follow the general style of the Louis XVI period, but attempt a more austere classicism, with rather stiff forms and straight lines and details based on Greek and Egyptian precedents. Ornamental details are intended to make reference to the Revolution: the French tricolor, clasped hands, swords, and spears are common motifs. When Napoleon I came to power in 1799, such references increased in popularity, creating a sub-period sometimes identified as the CONSULATE STYLE. Egyptian motifs and military elements that could be identified with Napoleon's campaigns in Egypt often appeared. Window drapery and drapery covering wall surfaces came into increasing use, with striped silks and brocades arranged with valances and trimmings to suggest spears and lances. Tables with metal tripod bases and marble tops were made to imitate ancient Roman designs and suggested Roman military power.

The Empire Style

The Directoire and Consulate styles precede the EMPIRE style, which took its name from the self-proclaimed elevation of Napoleon I to emperor status in 1804. The partnership of Charles Percier (1764-1838) and Pierre-François-Léonard Fontaine (1762–1853), who had met as architectural students in Paris and Rome, led architecture and interior design under the emperor's patronage. They are often thought of as the first professional interior designers as that term has come to be used.

7.25 Salon de Jeux, Château of Compiègne, near Paris, 1786.

This room, associated with Marie Antoinette, is of simple, neoclassical Louis XVI style but has been furnished later in the Empire style. The black and gold of the cabinets, the simple stools and card tables, and the eagle-topped mirror suggest the end of the eighteenth century and the trends of the early nineteenth century.

7.26 Charles Percier and Pierre-François-Léonard Fontaine, design for a room in the Château de Malmaison, Paris, 1801 (room completed 1812)

In a publication of their works, the famous interior designers Percier and Fontaine show a room suggestive of an elaborate tented interior with various war-like trophies as decoration in the Empire style to honor the achievements of Napoleon. The Empress Josephine's tent bedroom at Malmaison was completed by the designers in 1812.

INSIGHTS

Charles Percier and Pierre-François-Léonard Fontaine: The Empire Style

The redecoration of the house of banker M. Recamier by French architects Charles Percier and Pierre-François-Léonard Fontaine gave birth to a new style in France entirely suited to the warlike nature of the times and the taste of Napoleon I. At the chateau of Malmaison, Napoleon gave the architects carte blanche. Fontaine described the military-style decoration designed for the Council Chamber at Malmaison:

It seems suitable to adopt . . . the form of a tent supported by pikes, *fasces* and standards, between which hang trophies of weapons, recalling those used by the most famous warlike people in the world. [1]

The precision of the decorative effects displayed the architects' concern for keeping strict control over all aspects of interior design and furnishings:

the structure and decoration are closely connected; and if they cease to appear to be so there is a defect in the whole . . . . [F]urniture is too much a part of interior design for the architect to remain indifferent to it. [2]

The Empire style did not find favor with everyone. Mme de Genlis, an acid commentator on all things modern, criticized the craze for chaises longues that had been initiated by Mme Recamier:

ladies should cover their feet when reclining. Decency demands it because, stretched out like that, the smallest movement may uncover the feet and even the legs. Besides a pretty *couvre pieds* [foot-cover] is a very decorative ornament—people do without them these days, but nothing looks so sloppy. [3]

1. Percier and Fontaine, *Recueil des décorations intérieurs,* 1812, quoted in Joanna Banham ed., *English Interior Design,* vol. 2 (Chicago, 1997), p. 942; 2. *Ibid*; 3. Mme de Genlis, *Memoires,* 1818

Previous interiors were generated by architects, artists, and craftsmen whose work came together through cooperation rather than under unified direction. Percier and Fontaine conceived of interior spaces developed under their full control in the manner of modern interior designers. Publication of albums of illustrations of their designs made their work widely known not only in France but in Germany and England and other European countries, and furthered the popularity and imitation of the Empire style. Fascination with Pompeian themes, the introduction of military and imperial references, and an intention to blend luxury with a sense of sternness and rigor are the typical qualities of their work. At the palace of Fontainebleau, suites of rooms were redesigned by Percier and Fontaine in the Napoleonic fashion. Pompeian red walls, gilded trim, mirrors, and black and gold furniture outfit the room called the Cabinet de l'Abdication. A room with a semicircular end and walls of green and gold silk held by vertical golden rods, it was designed as a workroom for the emperor himself. At the chateau of Malmaison near Paris (**fig. 7.26**), they undertook a redesign of interiors in order to create a setting for the occupancy of Napoleon's wife, Josephine, that would make her husband's role, status, and character apparent in every detail of every room. A bedroom at Malmaison was designed to suggest a luxurious tent interior of the sort that Napoleon might have occupied on a battlefield. The tent theme led to frequent use of loosely draped fabric along walls and around beds. The LIT EN BATEAU, a large bed surrounded by a virtual tent of fabric, was a favored furniture type. Detail based on the classical orders is rare in Empire design, although the library at Malmaison has Doric columns of polished light mahogany which appear to support the flat domes of the ceiling. Dignified furniture was often finished in black with gilded details such as carved eagles and FASCES, the bundled sticks that were the symbol of power of the Roman emperors. A gold N initial appears everywhere as a reminder of the emperor's identity. The rich red considered to be Pompeian was a favorite color, along with black and gold. Jacquard's invention in 1801 of the mechanical pattern-weaving loom made possible the quantity production of damasks and velvets with motifs such as wreaths, rosettes, or the bee, a symbol chosen by Napoleon as his own. Background colors were deep brown, green, and dark red; the small pattern elements were in bright colors. The inven-

tion of cylinder printing techniques led to an increase in the production and use of wallpapers, usually with patterns similar to those used for textiles. Scenic wallpapers also came into use, sometimes with groups of figures and architectural or landscape views that resembled fresco painting. Printed paper borders were also used in much the manner of architectural trim moldings.

In spite of political changes which are reflected in successive period names, there is a strong stylistic continuity in the Neoclassical theme that flows through work of the Louis XVI, Directoire, and Empire periods (**fig. 7.25**). The great domed

church of S. Geneviève in Paris (**fig. 7.27**; 1756–89), designed by Jacques-Germain Soufflot (1713–80) and built as a royal project, became, after the Revolution, the Panthéon, a secular hall honoring great men. The pedimented facade and high dome and the cold magnificence of the interior became a model for subsequent Neoclassical building.

Claude-Nicolas Ledoux (1736–1806) worked under royal patronage, avoided execution during the Revolution, and became an exponent of a highly personal type of Neoclassicism that guided his designs for thirty-seven toll houses for the gates of Paris (1785–9). Only four have survived (including the circular Barrière de la Villette) but his influence, extended by the 1804 publication of his designs, has remained and has attracted strong interest in recent years. His approach to interior design can be studied in the detailed engravings that show the magnificently Neoclassical interiors for the theater at Besançon (1775–84).

A striking example of post-revolutionary Empire architecture is the church of the Madeleine (**fig. 7.28**; 1804–49) in Paris, a focal point at the end of the Rue Royal, the grand avenue that begins at the Place de la Concorde and passes between the twin facades by Gabriel. The church, a work of

7.27 Jacques-Germain Soufflot, Church of S. Geneviève (Panthéon), Paris, 1756–89.

Originally built as a church, after the revolution this massive monument was converted to a pantheon, honoring the great of French history. Soufflot had ancient Roman and British classicism in mind as precedents for the domed interior. The plan is a Greek cross, with ambulatories all around. There is a high dome at the crossing and lower saucer domes over each arm of the plan. The marble patterned floor, paintings in the pendentives of the domed center, and statuary groups support the monumental current function.

7.28 Alexandre-Pierre Vignon, Madeleine, Paris, 1804–49.

Designed to fit the imperial ambitions of Napoleon and the nation that he led, the Church of St Mary Magdalene was originally going to be called the Temple de la Gloire; since 1813 it has been known as the Madeleine. The three domes of the interior admit light through oculae at the center of each. The intention was clearly to suggest an ancient Roman basilica or other monumental building, and huge Corinthian columns support arches, while smaller Ionic columns carry galleries and pedimented side chapels.

7.29 (*top*) Provençal kitchen; now displayed in the Musée Fragonard, Grasse, France.

This kitchen is typical of those that would have existed in the south of France between the sixteenth and nineteenth centuries. The tiled stove offers improved means of cooking, but the open fireplace on the right survives in its traditional role. There is no ornamentation other than the moldings along the lower edge of the smoke hood.

7.30 (*bottom*) Provençal bed-sitting room; now displayed in the Musée Fragonard, Grasse, France.

Rooms similar to this would have been found in country houses in the south of France in the eighteenth or nineteenth centuries. The carved fireplace surround and mantel introduce a degree of elegance, while a handsome bed fits into the arched and curtained alcove. A simple striped wallpaper covers the walls.

Alexandre-Pierre Vignon (1762–1828), was designed with the intention of reproducing a Roman peripteral Corinthian temple. Its interior is a Corinthian hall topped by three flat domes on pendentives with oculus windows. Although no such ancient Roman interior has survived, the space has the rather chilling effect of neo-Roman imperial grandeur—no doubt to Napoleon's taste.

Provincial Style

While styles of French Renaissance interior design developed in the service of the powerful and wealthy, citizens of modest means had to make do with rooms and with furniture that continued the functional craft traditions of the Middle Ages. When a bourgeois middle class of merchants, craftsmen, and professionals began to emerge in the seventeenth and eighteenth centuries there were an increasing number of householders who wanted and who could afford a rising level of comfort and luxury. It is not surprising that awareness of the elegance that was enjoyed in chateaux and palaces began to create a taste for something similar, even if on a more modest scale. As the makers of furniture, textiles, and all sorts of household goods became aware of this demand, they began to develop products designed to satisfy it. A "filter-down" effect in which the high styles of the aristocracy influence the larger public is a well-recognized pattern in the history of taste—a pattern that continues in the present. In France it was the impetus for the development of the style now called French PROVINCIAL. The term "provincial" implies a rural country style, but Provincial furniture became the norm of both country and town dwellings of those who felt able to take a small step toward the grandeur that the rich and powerful enjoyed (**figs. 7.29** and **7.30**).

Provincial furniture varies somewhat from one region of France to another, but it always takes elements from the high styles of Louis XIV or XV and simplifies them. Carved detail tends to be florid and curvilinear, but the material is usually solid (as distinguished from veneered) wood, most often oak, walnut, or one of the woods of fruit trees (apple, cherry, or pear, for example). A large storage cabinet with double doors, the armoire, was an important display piece that usually suggested Rococo design in its carved details. Metal hardware, such as hinges and escutcheons around keyholes, added decorative detail. Chairs were usually small and simple: ladder backs, rush seats, and tied-on cushions were commonplace. Chairs with some upholstery in seat and back followed the form of high style examples but with simplification of detail. As clock mechanisms became affordable, tall clocks with wood cases in carved, Rococo form became important display and status posessions.

Furniture made in the popular BIEDERMEIER style in early nineteenth-century Germany combined the Neoclassical direction of Empire design with forms borrowed from German peasant furniture. The style took its name from a German cartoon series that made a joke of the habits of the German bourgeois that tended to follow fashions set by French stylistic trends—particularly the Empire style. Made for a middle-class public, Biedermeier furniture was of considerable elegance, consisting of simple and practical forms which carried restrained ornamentation. Various woods were used, often of lighter colors (maple, birch, or elm) with black painted details. Marquetry ornamentation is used in some larger chests and cabinets. Seating furniture was generally upholstered, usually with cover fabric of velvet, often striped. Matching upholstery and drapery fabrics were popular. From its south German base, the Biedermeier style spread northward, and into Austria and Switzerland.

Spain

The Renaissance in Spain developed through the importing of ideas from Italy and, much later, through influences from France. In Spain, these stylistic directions came into contact with the preexisting Spanish traditions that mingled European Gothic architecture and the architecture and design of Islamic (Moorish) culture. The term MUDÉJAR is used to describe work of the late Middle Ages and early Renaissance (from about 1200 to 1700) in which Moorish and Christian traditions are intermixed. The geometric ornament that appears in wood, plaster work, and tile, and the use of bright colors (reds, greens, and particularly blues and white) are Mudéjar characteristics that influenced subsequent Spanish design.

Plateresco

The term PLATERESCO is used to identify work of the early Spanish Renaissance because, it is thought, of its relationship to the work of

plateros—silver (or gold) smiths who developed a vocabulary of florid ornamentation. From about 1475 until 1550, ornamental details from Italian work intermingled with Moorish details to form a distinctive mixture. Granada Cathedral (**fig. 7.31**; 1529), a Gothic structure, was detailed in Plateresque style by Diego de Siloe (c. 1495–1563) with classical moldings and column capitals and the huge iron screen or *reja* that guards the royal chapel there. It is a fine example of the metalwork characteristic of Spanish church interiors.

7.31 Diego de Siloe, choir with high altar, Granada Cathedral, 1529.

A double aisled nave leads to an east-end choir in the form of a rotunda. Classical forms are used with rich decorative detail typical of the Plateresco style.

Desornamentado

Around 1500, a new and more reserved style known as Desornamentado appeared in the never completed palace of Charles V at the Alhambra in Toledo. The plan is a square with a circular central court surrounded by two levels of colonnades of slim columns, Doric below and Ionic above. The somewhat academic classicism of this building belongs to the High Renaissance, a style most clearly developed in Spain in only one vast building, the Escorial (**figs. 7.32** and **7.34**). Commissioned by Philip II, it was begun in 1563 by Juan Bautista de Toleda (d. 1567), who had studied in Rome with Michelangelo, and completed in 1584 by Juan de Herrera (*c.* 1530–97). It is a huge rectangle that holds, arranged around fifteen inner courtyards, a monastery, a college, a multilevel church, and, projecting from the rear, a royal palace. The plan is said to be intended to suggest the gridiron on which St. Lawrence is supposed to have been martyred. The exterior is a symmetrical, sternly simple block of grey granite with towers at each corner. Within, the innumerable rooms are arranged around courts to serve varied functions. The library of the monastery is ornate, colorful, and Italianate in style, while the great domed church, simple and dark except for an elaborate reredos behind and above the altar, communicates an ominous quality that seems to relate to the infamous Spanish Inquisition of the same period. This one building dominates the Desornamentado and served as a model for the austere, simple, and stern interiors of lesser buildings of the time. Walls were

usually of stone or plaster, and were sometimes hung with cloth or leather. There was a minimum of furniture, which was of generally Italianate character with little ornamentation, and which served practical functions with little concern for comfort.

Churrigueresco

The following and final phase of the Spanish Renaissance, known by the stylistic term of Churrigueresco, extends from about 1650 to 1780 and parallels Baroque and Rococo styles elsewhere. The term is derived from the name of José Churriguera (1665–1725) who was a major exponent of the style. It can be understood as a reaction against the austerity of Desornamentado, an extreme reaction which led to surface ornamentation of the most exuberant and colorful sort. The most striking examples are in church interiors such as that of the Sacristy of La Cartuja at Granada (**fig. 7.33**; 1713–47), possibly designed by Luis de Arevalo and Fray Manuel Vázquez, where the walls are covered with a frosting of plaster sculptural decoration that overwhelms the basically classical forms of columns and entablature. In the Gothic cathedral at Toledo, Narciso Tomé designed an insert (completed in 1732) known as the Transparente, which was placed so as to make the sacrament displayed there visible through a small window (the source of the name) from the ambulatory where it passes behind the altar. The window itself is almost lost in the vast complication of Churrigueresco sculptural ornament that surrounds it, and is piled upward into the vaulting where a kind of dormer, itself surrounded with sculptured and painted ornament, admits light that beams down on the Transparente itself in a highly theatrical fashion. Such extremes of Spanish Baroque design found their way to Latin America along with the Spanish conquerors and became the basis for the religious architecture and design of those regions.

Furniture and Other Interior Features

Furniture of the Spanish Renaissance is generally simple, often almost crude, with its basis in the Italian Early Renaissance. Chairs, tables, and chests of walnut, oak, pine, and cedar were common. Massive arm chairs were sometimes made with

7.32 Juan Bautista de Toleda and Juan de Herrera, monastery and palace of San Lorenzo de El Escorial, near Madrid, Spain, 1563-84.

The engraving reveals the extent of the vast complex, known as the Escorial, which includes a palace, a monastery, a college, and a church. The austerity of the Spanish Renaissance/ Baroque can be seen here in its most extreme form, and the plan is said to have been based on the gridiron on which St. Lawrence was martyred. The grey granite used imposes its own somber quality on the solemn aspect of the building.

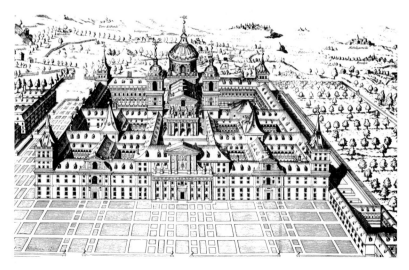

The overwhelming decorative plasterwork of the Spanish Baroque is an example of the churrigueresque style at its most extreme. The underlying forms of classical architecture are totally lost in the riot of surface ornamentation. Such an interior is hard to classify as related to Baroque, Rococo, or Mannerist directions. It seems to exist outside any such orderly classification.

7.34 Juan Bautista de Toleda and Juan de Herrera, the church of the Escorial, near Madrid, Spain, 1574–82.

The domed church at the center of the Escorial complex, with its high altar and richly painted reredos and vaulted ceiling, stands within a space of grey granite of a most solemn, even ominous quality. Philip II, the king whose project this was, had a palace area extending behind the church and arranged for hidden windows to be built into his bedroom so that he could have a view of the altar from a location high up on the right.

stretchers at front and back hinged so that the chair could be folded flat for moving about. The VARGUEÑO (**fig. 7.35**), a special development of Spanish furniture makers, is a drop-fronted case or writing cabinet that stands on a separable base. The front drops to provide a writing surface (supported by pull-outs in the base) and exposes an interior divided to provide many storage compartments and drawers. The closed exterior may be plain or decorated, but the interior is invariable richly ornamented with carved and often gilded detail, so that opening the door exposes an extremely rich internal display. Probably because of its practical use as a container for documents and valuables such as coins and jewels which had become common possessions of the wealthy (with no bank vaults for safekeeping), the vargueño was often imported into Italy and France where it can be seen in the rooms of chateaux and palaces.

Silk weaving as developed in Spain used brightly colored patterns and rich embroidery, often with threads of silver or gold. Textiles were often imported from Italy, but Spanish manufacture of damask, brocade, and velvet developed under Italian influence. Communication with the Low Countries made Flemish tapestries available. Chair seats and wall hangings were often of velvet. Leather was widely used as an alternative to textiles, and Spanish leather crafts centered at Cordoba specialized in finishing, coloring, tooling, and embossing leather. Cordovan leather became a highly regarded Spanish export. Metalwork of high quality provided elaborately ornamented candlesticks and wall brackets while candles remained the only source of artificial light. The brazier, a metal container on a metal stand served to hold burning

7.35 Spanish vargueño, seventeenth century.

This cabinet with a drop-front could be used as a writing desk. The body of the cabinet is filled with drawers and compartments for the storage of documents and valuables. Closing and locking the front makes the contents secure.

charcoal as a portable source of heat to augment open fireplace heating.

Under Charles V of Spain, Holland came under Spanish rule. In the Low Countries, Spanish influences interlaced with ideas that flowed from France and from northern Germany where the Protestant Reformation developed as an alternative to the Roman church. With England close across the English Channel and with trade between these areas active, it was inevitable that a transfer of ideas into England would take place. The next chapter will deal with the resulting developments in design.

8

Renaissance to Georgian in the Low Countries and England

The northward movement of Renaissance ideas continued into Holland and Flanders (now the Netherlands and Belgium) and to the British Isles. The movement of ideas, unlike the movement of goods or peoples, does not need to flow in a continuous stream, but can make leaps in both space and time. Ideas that originated in Italy moved into these regions by way of Spain, France, and Germany, but they were also conveyed directly by individual travelers and by printed materials. Increasing trade, both overland and by ship, meant that an increasing portion of the population were able to see new things in faraway places and to bring home ideas from abroad.

Low Countries

The Netherlands, parts of Belgium, and what was formerly called Flanders developed a Renaissance design vocabulary that is distinct from those of neighboring regions. The complex political history of the region, and certain distinctive traditions and social conditions were factors that help to explain the special character of Dutch and Flemish design. The political turmoil of the sixteenth century resulted from the conflict between the power of the Hapsburg Empire under Charles V (born at Ghent in 1500), who was also king of Spain, and the influence of the Protestant Reformation. The Catholic regime in Spain, particularly during the reign of Philip II, was brought into direct conflict with the religious teachings of Luther and Calvin. Opposition to Spanish rule led to the emergence of the Dutch nation, which eventually won independence from Spain by the Treaty of Munster in 1648.

In 1566, Protestant anger against repression, especially in the form of the Inquisition, was

expressed through the growth of Calvinism, with its doctrinal opposition to religious imagery thought to be too closely identified with Catholicism. The Iconoclastic Revolt in which churches were stripped of Gothic sculpture, painting, and other decoration (regarded as representative of Catholic traditions) left interiors plain, white painted, and flooded with light from the clear glass windows that replaced the destroyed stained glass (**fig. 8.1**). During and after this period of conflict, artists in the Low Countries produced work that documents the everyday life of the times in great detail. Bruegel's paintings of peasant life often show scenes in taverns or farm interiors. The works of Jan Steen, Jan Vermeer, and many other Dutch painters are full of wonderfully detailed images of the interiors of comfortable houses of the middle class and wealthy burghers who lived with an interesting mixture of simplicity and luxury in the town houses of Dutch cities.

Civic Buildings

Architects such as Cornelis Floris (1514–75) introduced the use of classical orders into buildings that were otherwise medieval in spirit, such as the spectacular Antwerp town hall (1561) or the Leiden town hall (1597) by Lieven de Key (c. 1560–1627), a native of Antwerp. The Leiden building mixes classical pilasters and pediments with a local style of ornamentation, making use of fretting, strapwork, and grotesque ornamentation in a style illustrated in the books of Vredeman de Vries such as his *Architectura* of 1577–81. Strapwork became popular as interior ornamentation developed in wood carving and in plaster. Strapwork plaster ceilings found their way to England through the work of Dutch and Flemish craftsmen and gradually came to exemplify Early Renaissance design there.

The Mauritshuis (c. 1633) at The Hague by Jacob van Campen (**fig. 8.3**; 1633–5), an architect who had traveled to Italy where he became acquainted with the designs of Palladio and Scamozzi, is a square block using a full-height order of Ionic pilasters and a central pediment. It is Palladian in character except for its high roof. The interiors were destroyed in a fire in 1704, but some idea of their design can be gained from the set of thirty-nine drawings done in 1652 by Pieter Post. Classical pilasters and molding appear in the major rooms. There is an unusual windowed cupola

8.1 (*below*) Frans Hagenberg, engraving showing Protestant Iconoclasts in Antwerp, August 20, 1566.

Protestants, in their rage against Catholicism, went on a rampage destroying religious paintings, sculpture, and stained glass. Churches and monasteries suffered irreparable damage.

8.2 (*opposite*) Great Hall, Hatfield House, Hertfordshire, England, from 1608.

The Marble Hall is a Jacobean English interior of exceptional richness. There was an underlying intention to recall the hall of medieval castles, but in this "great house" the theme has been transformed by richly carved woodwork and an ornate painted plaster ceiling. The woodwork, hanging tapestries, and elaborately carved furniture contrast with the simple tiled floor.

above the coved ceiling of the banqueting hall (**fig. 8.4**) on the upper story. This room also appears in an engraving showing King Charles II of England being entertained there as a guest in 1660. There was close communication between the Low Countries and England; the designs of many seventeenth-century houses in England resemble the Mauritshuis in their four-square simplicity and classicism.

Private Dwellings

The unique character of Dutch Renaissance interiors reflects several circumstances that were special to this time and place. The political troubles of the wars with Spain left the Netherlands without a powerful and dominating aristocratic class. Palaces and chateaux were not important building types, and Protestant churches aimed for simplicity rather than elaboration. The dominant social class was made up of merchants, officials, and professionals. They were prosperous, even wealthy, but they lived in houses that did not strive for extravagance and display. Awareness of Renaissance ideas came from artists and musicians who went to Italy to study and work, but there was no effort to imitate or equal the great buildings of Italy and France. Trade, carried on by the Dutch merchant fleet, brought both knowledge and actual objects

8.3 (*top*) Jacob van Campen, Mauritshuis, The Hague, Netherlands, 1633–5.

This house is a Dutch version of the classicism of the Italian Renaissance, and is based on a Palladian plan. Ionic pilasters on four sides of the square block, a pediment at the center of the front, and decorative swags complete the neatly organized composition.

8.4 (*center*) P. Philippe (after Toorenvliet), a banquet at the Mauritshuis in honor of Charles II of England, The Hague, c. 1660.

This engraved copy of Toorenvliet's painting shows a generally simple Dutch interior with a few touches of Renaissance decoration on the walls and in the central upper gallery. Most of the ornamental detail is temporary decoration for the festivity in progress.

8.5 (*right*) Cornelis de Man, *The Gold Weigher*, c. 1670–75.

A Dutch merchant is shown conducting his business in a room of his comfortable home. Wooden beams form the ceiling, and the floor is tiled in grey and brown stone squares. The wall at the rear and the mantel shelf are of carefully crafted wood, and painted tiles edge the fireplace. The table legs display the bulbous forms of the Dutch Baroque. The curtained arch gives access to the alcove bed.

from remote locations. Oriental carpets and other textiles, and oriental porcelains, were introduced into Dutch interiors; Chinese lacquer came into use as a furniture finish.

The typical medieval Dutch house survived into the Renaissance era. It was a narrow, multistory building where the ground floor was often a shop, the top floor a warehouse. The living floors between generally had large windows that took advantage of the increasing availability of glass, plain white walls, and a floor of marble squares or tiles. Wood came to be used for some paneling or trim (**fig. 8.5**). Pottery and tiles made at Delft were a distinctive part of the Dutch decorative vocabulary: plates and platters were treated as decorative display items, while tiles with painted images edged walls. Tiles were usually white, with painted figures, scenes, ships, and flowers most often in blue. Usually each tile carried a single image, often with a decorative border, but large scenes painted to cover many tiles were also produced, providing an effect similar to that of scenic wallpapers. Dutch tiles came to be widely known and were often exported to England and, eventually, to America.

Classical elements, moldings, and columns appear as ornament on the exteriors of buildings, but only to a very limited extent in interiors. Furniture was often large in scale and handsomely detailed. Beds were often enclosed in built-in, box-like DUTCH BED spaces or, when free-standing, were canopied and draped. Oriental rugs, imported

by Dutch merchant shipping, appear as table covers, but only rarely on floors. Music was an important part of Renaissance life in the Low Countries—the fine harpsichords and virginals made by the Ruckers family in Antwerp appear in many Vermeer paintings (**fig. 8.6**). They were usually made, like violins or lutes, of thin, soft wood and were then painted or decorated with patterned, printed papers. Chairs were similar to Italian and Spanish examples of the same period.

During the seventeenth century, massive storage cabinets with rich Baroque detailing came into use. Since closets were not provided as part of the fixed structure of houses, such pieces became important as wealth made possible the acquisition of much clothing and objects of every sort. Panels, carvings, rare woods, and classically derived details such as moldings and columns appeared in furniture. Bulbous feet and table legs were favorite Baroque details. A growing interest in scientific concerns, in exploration and discovery, is reflected by the presence of world and celestial globes, various musical and scientific instruments, maps and charts. Framed works of art are displayed alongside handsome pottery, glassware, and silver or pewter containers. In spite of the sense of affluence that stems from the rich variety of possessions present in Dutch interiors, objects are always placed without crowding, against plain and spacious backgrounds, in a way that communicates comfort along with simplicity.

The Low Countries lacked both quarries to provide stone suitable for building and forests as sources of plentiful wood supply. As a result, brick, with stone restricted to some details, became the major building material. Wood was used only where it was indispensable, as in roofs and upper floor structures.

England

The familiar pattern of Renaissance development through early, middle, and late phases can be traced in England, although stylistic terminology breaks up each phase into subdivisions named after successive royal reigns. English design was not as dominated by royal patronage as in the parallel periods in France, and styles often overlap. The usual period terminology is retained here, nevertheless, since it is widely used even if occasionally confusing.

8.6 Jan Vermeer, *A Young Woman Standing at a Virginal*, Delft, Netherlands, *c.* 1670. National Gallery, London.

The subject has been playing the small keyboard instrument, a box-like case with a simple exterior but rich painting within. The room in which it stands is of elegant simplicity, with a black and white tiled floor, a wall base of painted tiles, and a window of leaded glass. Only the fine paintings suggest the higher status that the house represents.

Tudor

The first evidence of awareness of Renaissance developments appears toward the end of the Middle Ages in the time of the Tudor monarchs, Henry VII, Henry VIII, Edward VI, and Queen Mary. The term TUDOR is often associated with the appearance of half-timber wood building which remained the usual VERNACULAR style until well into the seventeenth century, but it also defines the period when Italianate detail first began to appear in ornamentation, in trim around doors and fireplaces, in paneling, and in details of furniture. At Haddon Hall in Derbyshire, the typically medieval agglomeration of building that made up this large manor house was brought up to date by the introduction of a Tudor long gallery (**fig. 8.7**) which approaches symmetry in its plan, introduces large windows along its south side made up of many small panes of glass, has a plaster ceiling ornamented with strapwork (no doubt the work of craftsmen from the Low Countries), and wood paneling where pilasters and arches can be seen in arrangements suggesting Palladianism. The room dates from about 1530, although some of the ornamental detail may be later. The paneling of natural oak, the primary wood of the period, establishes the dominant color tone.

Elizabethan

The Elizabethan era (1558–1603) is generally recognized as a time of English greatness. The defeat of the Spanish Armada in 1588 established

British command of the seas and opened up possibilities for economic development that came from international trade and, eventually, colonialism. As power and wealth flowed into England, interest in the arts expanded: not only the poetry and drama of Shakespeare, and the music of William Byrd, but also the developing arts of Italy, France, and the Low Countries. The transition from Tudor to ELIZABETHAN design is gradual with increasing emphasis on symmetry and classical concepts of planning, along with more frequent introduction of Italianate classical detail. Some well-preserved rooms in the house in Conway called Plas Mawr (**fig. 8.8**; *c.* 1577) seem medieval in their irregular shapes, low ceilings, stone or planked floors, and leaded glass windows, but details of cornices and stone carved trim around fireplaces have a classical basis. Ceilings of strapwork plaster reflect the continuing contact with Holland and Flanders.

The recent reconstruction of the Globe Theater, where Shakespeare's plays were first performed, gives a good idea of what such a building was like. It was circular (or octagonal) with a central area (the "pit") open to the sky, while surrounding galleries provided seats for those who could pay for a better location. A stage in front was partially covered by a shed roof. The construction was medieval timber framing, and architectural ornamentation was minimal.

The first fully Elizabethan "great house" (as the mansions, comparable to the French chateaux, are called in Europe) is Longleat (begun 1568), a virtual palace designed, it is thought, by Robert Smythson (1536–1640) and built for Sir John Thynne to be ready for a visit by the queen in 1574. The house is a near-square rectangle, symmetrical

8.9 Robert Smythson, Long Gallery, Hardwick Hall, Derbyshire, England, 1591-7.

The gallery is on the uppermost floor of one of the most magnificent of English Elizabethan "great houses." Huge windows in bays on the right flood the space with light. The walls are covered with tapestries, and the fireplaces and chimney breasts above are of ornately carved stonework in an Italianate style. The paintings and most of the furniture is of a later date, but the plaster strapwork ceiling is original.

on all sides, with two inner courtyards. The exterior is divided into three stories by entablature bands and projecting window bays are trimmed with classical pilasters. Windows are many and large. The rooms are arranged in a complex plan, Tudor in its irregular spirit, but fitted into the order established by the exterior. Most of the interiors have been changed and redecorated over the years so that a better idea of interior spaces can be had at Hardwick Hall (1591–7), a considerably smaller great house, probably also designed by Smythson. Its symmetrical block is a rectangle with six projecting bays that rise one extra story above roof level. The exterior is without ornament except for moldings at each story level marking off the low ground level, the middle height second level occupied by rooms for everyday living, and the highest third level where the major ceremonial rooms are located. The towers extend above, ending in a picturesque topping of strapwork ornament. The entrance hall is a double height room with a gallery which recalls medieval practice, but is supported by four correctly detailed Doric columns. Wood paneling with tapestries above covers the walls; fireplace detail is classical, but the chimney breast above is covered with plaster strapwork. Wide stairs lead to the upper level where a long gallery runs the length of the building along one side (**fig. 8.9**). This room is entirely symmetrical with twin stone fireplaces and twin window bays. The exterior wall is largely window; other walls are covered with tapestry, and the ceiling has restrained strapwork detail. Other rooms at Hardwick are fine examples of the Elizabethan balance of almost modern simplicity along with luxury and grandeur.

Elizabethan Furniture

Elizabethan furniture differs from Tudor and earlier medieval practice in the introduction of more carved, ornamental detail, and in the development of some new types of furniture. One such was the court cupboard—actually an open shelf unit with three tiers intended for the display of silver ornamental and serving pieces. The supports and edges of the shelves were carved with a richness intended to equal the silver on view. In large houses, extremely large beds were made with a roof-like wooden canopy supported by headboard and foot posts that often stood free of the bed itself. In addition to simple square chairs with more or less carving, chairs were often made up of many lathe turnings, often three main turned uprights making a chair with a triangular seat. The ease with which a turner can make SPOOL AND KNOB forms led to designs of curious complexity. A massive folding chair known as a GLASTONBURY CHAIR also appeared, often with a carved back suggesting a two-arch arcade. Oak remained the usual wood, although ash, yew, chestnut, and other woods were sometimes used. Upholstery was limited to an

8.10 Inigo Jones, Banqueting House, Whitehall, London, 1619–22.

The high Renaissance, with its acceptance of Italian practice, came to England in the work of Inigo Jones. His plans for a vast palace were put aside and only the Banqueting House was built. Its galleried, symmetrical interior, with Ionic half-columns below and Corinthian pilasters above, demonstrates his expert handling of Italian-inspired Palladian detail. The elaborate ceiling, also Italianate in style, frames paintings by Rubens.

occasional cushion or a covering of cloth, sometimes embroidered with TURKEY-WORK. Colors were usually the natural tones of wood, stone, and plaster, with details sometimes painted in rich reds and dark greens.

Jacobean

The JACOBEAN period (1603–49) takes its name from James I, but also includes the reign of Charles I. Hatfield House (from 1608) is an irregular although symmetrical block, U-shape in plan. It is really two houses (intended as guest accommodation for the king and queen) linked by a connecting block containing a "hall" in the style of a castle (**fig. 8.2**), a long gallery, and many other rooms. Most of the exterior is quite plain red brick with large windows. A central facade, the work of Robert Lyming (*c.* 1560–1628), is of Italian marble in an Italianate style with an arcade, pilasters, and, for the entrance element, classical columns. A fantastic clock tower tops it off. Within, elaborate paneling,

carving, classically columned fireplaces, and plaster strapwork show off the Jacobean mix of Italian and Dutch influences.

Jones

Inigo Jones (1573–1652) was responsible for introducing the more consistent classicism of the High Renaissance into England. He had visited Italy, studied ancient buildings, and brought back some of Palladio's drawings to England. His first work was as a stage designer for the royal entertainments called masques. His appointment as royal surveyor (really official architect to the government) in 1615 led to his major works. The Queen's House at Greenwich (1616–35) is a simple, totally symmetrical square block (originally an H-shape, later filled in) with plain white walls, well-spaced windows of moderate size, and a loggia with six Ionic columns on the south side upper level. Jones' classicism included a continuing interest in forms related to the geometric perfection of the cube and its multiples. The brackets supporting the balcony, the elaborate ceiling with paintings in nine panels, the geometrically patterned marble tiling of the floor, and the details of door frames are all Italianate.

Jones was the designer of a vast new Whitehall Palace (*c.* 1638) that would, if built, have been the equal of the Louvre or Versailles although more rigorously classical than either. Only a small fragment was built, the Banqueting House (**fig. 8.10**; 1619–22), a single room of double story height with a strictly Palladian exterior. It has a double cube interior with a balcony on brackets, an Ionic order below, a Corinthian order above, and a ceiling with paintings by Rubens in panels surrounded by florid plaster ornamentation. The Queen's Chapel for St. James's Palace (1623–7) is another Jones double-cube room with a coffered, elliptical ceiling and a Palladian window above the altar. It is an early example of the classical form that so many English (and, later, American) churches were to take. Externally, it appears as a plain block except for its temple-like pedimented gable.

A larger London church by Jones, St. Paul's, Covent Garden (begun 1630), is also in pedimented temple form. It has a full columned portico facing into the garden that was the center of a planned group of row houses that has not survived. The church seems to have been based on Vitruvius' account of an Etruscan temple. Internally, it is a plain rectangular chamber—a striking contrast to the many surviving English Gothic churches.

Jones and John Webb (1611–72) were responsible for the design of a reconstructed wing of Wilton House (1648–50) in Wiltshire that contains two formal and elaborate state rooms called, for their geometric shapes, the single cube and double cube rooms (**fig. 8.11**). The walls are white with painted and gilded carved ornamentation, garlands, bunches of fruit, and simulated drapery framing areas where paintings are hung. A series of Van Dyke portraits hang amid doorways and the richly ornamented fireplace. Ceilings are coved with painted panels and COVE surfaces framed in plaster ornamentation. The richness of these rooms points toward the Carolean and later periods.

Jacobean Interior Furnishings

Jacobean furniture, although generally massive and straight-lined, became somewhat lighter and smaller in scale than its Elizabethan predecessors. Ornamental carving tended to be more elegant in

design. Lathe turnings with spool forms or spiral twist patterns were often used for legs and stretchers. Cushions came into use, loose or attached, often edged with ornamental nail heads used decoratively. Oak remained the most popular wood, but walnut was also used. An increase in textiles, silks, velvet, embroidered turkey-work, and tapestries contributed to a sense of comfort and luxury (**fig. 8.12**).

From Carolean to William and Mary

Oliver Cromwell's Puritan rebellion and the Commonwealth government that followed it from 1649 to 1660 interrupted the royal succession and the stylistic terminology based on it. With the return of Charles II in 1660, the RESTORATION PERIOD (1660–1702) begins. It is often subdivided into a CAROLEAN (or Caroline) period from 1660 to 1689 and a WILLIAM AND MARY period from 1689 to 1702.

Wren

The most famous of British architects, Sir Christopher Wren (1632–1723) was a mathematician, physicist, inventor, and astronomer, truly a versatile "Renaissance man." His only travel to the continent took him to Paris (where he met Bernini), but he was clearly aware of Italian Baroque work when he moved toward architecture as his major life work. This happened after the Great Fire of London in 1666, after which he was chosen to design replacements both for the many small city churches that had been destroyed and for the old Gothic cathedral of St. Paul's. In 1669 he was appointed surveyor-general, giving him responsibility for city planning in London and for many important architectural assignments. Wren's scientific and mathematical interests gave his work a theoretical or logical quality; this combined with his interest in French and Italian Baroque work to produce a specially English vocabulary. While

8.12 Jacobean furniture, Knole, Kent, England; shown in a 1907 engraving.

Crimson silk velvet cushions and gold fringes enrich this furniture, which dates from the time of James I (r. 1603-25). It is of basically simple form with small-scale carved detail.

8.11 John Webb, double-cube room, Wilton House, Wiltshire, England, 1648-50.

Webb had been an assistant to Inigo Jones, who was the original architect of the house, which was damaged by a fire in 1647. The term "double cube" refers to the geometry of the space. The basically simple form is filled with white and gold paneling, Van Dyck portraits, and a fabulously decorated, coved ceiling, with lush paintings by Edward Pierce (c. 1635-95). The central oval provides a view into a fantastic dome. The gilded and ornamented furniture by William Kent (c. 1685-1748) suggests an awareness of French Rococo themes.

8.13 Christopher Wren, St. Stephen, Walbrook, London, 1672–9.

In this small London church, Wren developed a scheme based on a geometric progression from rectangle to square, to Greek cross, to octagon to circle, with a dome divided into sixteen, eight and again sixteen coffers. The resultant space has been called one of the most beautiful interiors in existence.

8.14 (*below left*) Section of St. Paul's Cathedral, London, 1675–1710.

This vast cathedral was designed to rival St. Peter's, Rome. The great dome, ringed with windows at the lower drum, is made of three layers: the lower dome covering the interior space of the crossing, the structural cone above, and the wood-supported upper dome, which forms the visible exterior, a lasting London landmark.

8.15 (*far right*) Christopher Wren, St. Paul's Cathedral, London, 1675–1710.

The interior of the cathedral, with its great dome at the crossing and saucer domes covering the bays of the nave, transepts, and choir, is a spectacular display of Baroque grandeur. The vaulting is buttressed above the aisles by half-arches, which are invisible inside and hidden externally by screen walls.

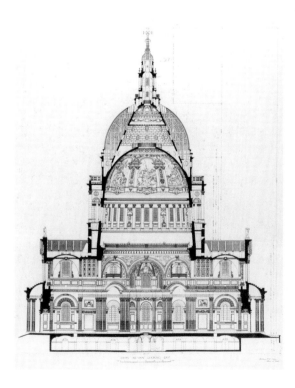

often described as Baroque, Wren's design was always restrained by a sense of order and discipline that makes it very different from the Baroque of Catholic northern Italy, south Germany, or Austria.

The many London city churches that Wren designed can be viewed as a set of textbook exercises in architectural geometry. Their varied plans are based on squares, rectangles, and other combinations of forms, including polygons and ovals. Each church steeple was given a unique form, each a study in vertical arrangement of classical elements. Many of the churches are very small, and some are so hemmed in on constricted sites as to make their exteriors insignificant. The church of St. Stephen Walbrook (1672–9), for example, is placed so that there is only a blank back wall visible on one street. A narrow entrance passage and tower are placed on another street. The interior is, however, one of Wren's great achievements (**fig. 8.13**). It is a simple, rectangular space made complex by the introduction of sixteen columns arranged so as to define a Greek cross, a square, and then, above, an octagon. The octagon is itself defined by eight arches that support a round dome coffered in sixteen, eight, and sixteen panels before reaching the small round opening into the lantern above. This remarkable exercise in geometry produces an

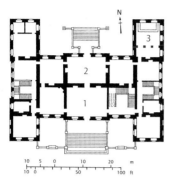

8.16 Plan of Belton House, Lincolnshire, England, 1685–8.
1 Hall
2 Dining room
3 Chapel

The plan is surprising in that access to each room is only possible by passing through an adjoining room.

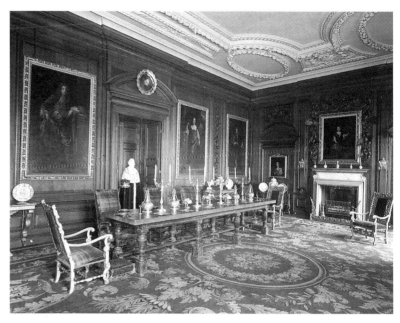

8.17 William Winde, Belton House, Lincolnshire, England, 1685–8.

The "saloon" or dining room is one of the principal rooms of this house said by some to have been designed by Wren but more probably designed by William Winde (d. 1722). The carved wood paneling may have been the work of the renowned wood carver, Grinling Gibbons, although there are records of payments to Edmund Carpenter. The ornate plaster ceiling is typical of the aristocratic interiors of the seventeenth century.

exceptionally beautiful interior lighted by oval and arched windows.

Other London churches by Wren such as St. James's Piccadilly and St. Bride's, Fleet Street, with barrel-vaulted (wood and plaster) nave ceilings and galleries supported on classical columns, established the typical English Renaissance church design on which many later English and American examples are based. Wren's churches are usually enriched by elaborately carved altar reredos, pulpits, and organ cases, the work of artist-craftsmen such as Grinling Gibbons (1648–1720). St. Paul's Cathedral (**figs. 8.14** and **8.15**; 1675–1710) is the most monumental and best known of Wren's works. It is an English Baroque rival to St. Peter's in Rome, with its saucer-dome vaulted nave, choir, and transepts forming a cruci-form plan with a giant dome at the crossing and a twin-towered facade reminiscent of the Italian Baroque. The vaulting is buttressed according to Gothic practice, but high screen walls hide the buttresses and present a strictly classical external appearance. The dome also hides ingenious arrangements. There is a lower inner dome set at a height planned to relate to the internal space below. Externally, a much higher dome, actually built of wood with a lead top surface, achieves the striking skyline silhouette of the building. In between, hidden from view, a cone of brick supports the wood dome and the stone lantern at its top. An oculus at the center of the inner dome allows a glimpse up into the cone (lit by hidden windows) and into the lantern. Hidden buttresses and an iron chain absorb the thrust of the stone inner dome and the cone above.

There is no house that can be proved to be by Wren, although tradition suggests that he may have been the architect of Belton House (**fig. 8.16**; 1685–8), a handsome mansion near Lincoln. It is a symmetrical H-shaped block of sedate grey stone with simple windows arranged in two story levels, pediments at the center of the front and rear facades, a tiled roof with dormers, many chimneys, and a small central cupola. Stables, kitchens, and other services are in outbuildings at one side. Front and rear doorways open directly into the two main formal rooms of the house, a marble-floored "hall" and the formal dining room or "saloon" behind it (**fig. 8.17**). Rich wooden paneling lines these rooms with carving said to be by Grinling Gibbons. The saloon has a decorative plaster ceiling. These rooms convey a sense of comfort and luxury that has been much admired and imitated in later work. It is interesting to notice that the plan of the house provides no corridors or vestibules, so that each room opens into its neighbors. With kitchens in a remote building, servants would have had to bring food into the dining room directly through a main outside door. Such seemingly impractical arrangements, in which formality outweighed convenience, remained commonplace until well into the eighteenth century.

Carolean and William and Mary Interior Furnishings

During the Carolean era, walnut came to be the most used wood, often with inlays of ebony and other woods. Curved forms appeared in chair backs and in the legs of chairs and cabinets. The cabriole leg with its gentle S-curve form began to appear. Round tables came into use. Very elaborate carving was not unusual, sometimes lacquered or gilded. An increasing emphasis on luxury, comfort, and practical convenience can be traced in the use

8.18 Engraving of furniture from several English great houses, 1660–1702, as shown in a book illustration of 1907.

Left: a silk-upholstered chair from Hampton Court Palace; center: a chair from Hardwick Hall (see p. 141); right: a silk-upholstered chair from Knole, a great house at Sevenoaks, Kent. The designs span periods from William III (r. 1689–1702) to Queen Anne (r. 1702–14).

ARM CHAIRS.

8.19 (*below left*) John Vanbrugh, the saloon, Blenheim Palace, Oxford, England, 1705–24.

In this room, the stone detail of doorways merges into the simulated architecture of wall painting that is filled with columns, pilasters, views of an imagined outdoors, and sculptural figures. The elegant furniture seems overwhelmed by the space and its decoration.

8.20 (*far right*) Nicholas Hawksmoor, Christ Church, Spitalfields, London, 1714–29.

The daring spatial composition includes columns supporting an arcade, which opens to side aisles. At the chancel end, columns support a high bar of entablature, introducing a sense of Baroque complexity into the otherwise simple, flat-ceilinged space.

of more upholstery and the appearance of such types as the WING-BACK CHAIR, various types of desks, and the development of drawer chests, previously almost unknown. Pottery imported from the Far East and oriental rugs from the Near East came into use in Restoration era houses as the increasing sea trade of British merchant ships brought such exotic materials into England.

From 1689 to 1702, during the reign of William and Mary, there was some retreat from the elaborate extremes of the Carolean period. Walnut was now the preferred wood for paneling and for furniture, veneer began to be used as a means of creating decorative surface treatments with wood grain matched in various patterns with edging of contrasting colored wood. Decorative lacquer

work, previously only available as an import, was developed in England as an alternative form of surface decoration for furniture (**fig. 8.18**). The HIGHBOY, a drawer cabinet raised on legs, became popular, along with such inventions as the GATE-LEG table. French weaving techniques were introduced into England, and printed chintz began to be used for window and bed curtains.

Queen Anne

The reign of QUEEN ANNE (1702–14) corresponds to Late Baroque design in English architecture. Furniture and interiors display a new sense of practicality, modesty, and comfort. Architecture, in contrast, continued to reflect Baroque grandeur. Wren's successors were Sir John Vanbrugh (1664–1726) and Nicholas Hawksmoor (1676–1734). Vanbrugh's Blenheim Palace (1705–24) was a vast and monumental gift to the Duke of Marlborough to honor his victory over France at the Battle of Blenheim. Its endless lines of state rooms, its huge three-story-high gallery (now the library), and its complex layout of kitchen and stable courts make it a rival to Versailles. The classical vocabulary is pushed into original variations that generate an active skyline and justify the Baroque designation—broken pediments, roof top

8.21 Room from Kirtlington Park, near Oxford, England, 1748.

This room, referred to in contemporary terms as an "eating room," is now installed in the Metropolitan Museum of Art, New York. It offers a view of a more restrained, yet rich and spacious interior, with Rococo plasterwork detailing by Thomas Roberts (1711–71), a local Oxford craftsman. The painting, furniture, oriental rug, and chandelier are suitable to the period, although they suggest a study or library of the era.

obelisks, and interiors such as that of the "saloon" (formal dining room; **fig. 8.19**) of overwhelming scale with illusionistic architectural wall and ceiling painting that is highly theatrical.

Hawksmoor's designs for London churches are ingenious, original, and forceful, with surprising interior spaces and exteriors of great power. Christ Church, Spitalfields, for example (1714–29), has a huge and astonishing tower, its arched elements stacked up with strange and disturbing overlaps below a tall spire. Inside, there is a high nave with a flat ceiling (**fig. 8.20**). The columns on either side carry arches that open to aisles, originally with galleries, now removed. At the chancel end, two columns support a bar-like entablature that spans across the nave, complicating the space and adding a surprising and theatrical sense. A contemporary critic described this interior as "Solemn & Awfull."

Queen Anne Furniture

Queen Anne furniture is generally somewhat smaller, lighter, and more comfortable than its predecessors. Curving shapes, the cabriole leg, cushioned seats, wing-back chairs, and practical secretary desk-book case pieces were in general use. The WINDSOR CHAIR with its back of slim turnings held by a bent hoop, a wood saddle carved seat, and legs that were usually turnings with turned

stretchers came into wide use. Elaborate carving and inlaid and painted decoration still appeared in more costly examples made for the houses of the wealthy.

Georgian

In the design of residential interiors and related furniture, the Queen Anne period merges with the beginnings of the GEORGIAN era, the dominant style of eighteenth-century England. The reigns of George I (1714–27) and George II (1727–60) cover the early Georgian period, usually defined as ending around 1750. A handsome room of this period from a lesser house, Kirtlington Park (1748), near Oxford, has been preserved in the Metropolitan Museum in New York (**fig. 8.21**). Its walls and ceiling are covered with decorative plaster work painted white. Mirrors, paintings, and a great gilded candle chandelier add color and glitter. A drawing of the room by its designer, John Sanderson, is also part of the museum collection. It shows the ceiling design surrounded by the four wall elevations rotated into their relative positions.

The building of great houses in which the influence of Italian Palladian practice often mingled with references to ancient Roman Pompeian ornamental detail continued on the estates of the wealthy. William Kent (1685–1748), whose furniture was used in the Double Cube room at Wilton, mentioned above, became a professional assistant to his patron, Lord Burlington (1694–1753), in the design of the great house of Chiswick (1725) at the edge of London. This is a square, domed building, clearly Palladian, its central rotunda and facade portico based on a free interpretation of the Villa Rotonda at Vicenza. The interiors use ornamental plaster work and painted details based on Pompeian precedents.

Robert and James Adam

Late Georgian architecture and interior design are characterized by the fine work of the Adam brothers. Robert Adam (1728–92) was the design leader of the partnership, while his brother, James Adam (1730–94), was more concerned with the practical aspects of carrying out their projects. The Adams were Scotsmen who established a reputation in London for their ability to organize large projects dealing with architecture, building construction, interior design, and decorative details efficiently but with a unique personal style that came to be greatly admired. Their work is partly Palladian in character, but also partly Rococo and, like French Rococo work, moves toward the restraint of Neoclassicism. Publication of examples of their work in the beautiful engravings of *The Works in Architecture of Robert and James Adam* (1773–1822) made their style well known in England and, eventually, in America as well.

Many Adam projects were renovations of pre-existing buildings. Some were never completed, some involved interiors only, but taken together their work can be understood as a suitably elegant final phase of Georgian design. The house called Luton Hoo in Bedfordshire (**fig. 8.22**; begun 1767) has been so much altered that the Adam design can best be studied in the plan and elevation that

8.22 James and Robert Adam, Luton Hoo, Bedfordshire, England, 1767.
1 Corridor
2 Bedroom of the 3rd Earl of Bute
3 Main staircase
4 Secondary stairs
5 Powder room
6 Water closet

Rooms are accessed from a corridor, although the Earl's bedroom is screened by adjacent rooms. Secondary stairs connect to the basement kitchens and servants quarters on an upper floor. The powder room is to provide for the powdering of the wigs worn by gentlemen at the time. All of this is within a classically symmetrical overall conception.

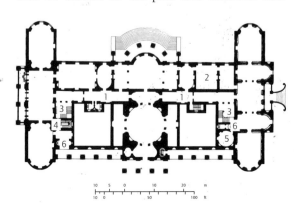

Robert Adam and Syon House

Robert Adam wrote in great detail in 1764 about his work remodeling Syon House for the Duke of Northumberland. He discussed the function of various rooms as well as their decoration:

the French style is best calculated for the convenience and elegance of life .... The hall both in our houses and those in France is a spacious apartment intended as a room of access where servants in livery attend. It is here a room of great dimensions, finished with stucco, as halls always are. [1]

With subtle discernment, he noted one of the principal differences between the French and the English:

To understand thoroughly the art of living, it is necessary, perhaps, to have passed some time amongst the French, and to have studied the customs of that social and conversible people. In one particular however, our manners prevent us from imitating them. Their eating rooms seldom or never constitute a piece in their great apartments, but lie out of suite, and in fitting them up, little attention is paid to the beauty of decoration. The reason of this is obvious; the French meet there only at meals, where they trust to the display of the table for show and magnificence, not to the decoration of the apartment, and as soon as the entertainment is over, they retire immediately to the rooms of company ... It is not so with us. Accustomed by habit or induced by the nature of our climate we indulge more largely in the enjoyment of the bottle .... The eating rooms are considered as apartments of conversations ... soon after dinner the ladies retire ... left alone [the men] resume their seats, evidently more at ease, and the conversation takes a different turn—less reserved and either graver or more licentious. [2]

Despite Adam's undoubted skill in creating beautiful houses in the Classical style, Lady Mary Wortley Montagu, a poet and essayist, trenchantly doubted their suitability:

Vistas are laid open over barren heaths, and apartments contrived for a coolness agreeable in Italy, but killing in the north of Britain. [3]

1. Quoted in Peter Thornton, *Authentic Decor*, (London, 1983), p. 145; 2. Robert and James Adam, *Works in Architecture of Robert and James Adam* (London, 1778), vol. I, pp. 10–11; 3. Lady Mary Wortley Montagu, *Diaries*, 1753, quoted in Peter Thornton, *Authentic Decor*, p. 88

appear in engravings. The plan shows off the Adams' concern for practical matters—rooms do not open directly one into another; instead a corridor runs the length of the building with rooms opening from it. The dining room has an adjacent pantry with stairs to the kitchens below. The Earl's bedroom can only be entered from adjacent rooms, but has a door leading into the huge library where, one assumes, the Earl could choose a book for late reading. Off the corridor, service stairs lead to other floors and small compartments contain water closets, early versions of the inside toilet. Externally, a central portico dominates the design with screen walls on either side hiding the light courts that gave light and air to minor rooms.

At Syon House (1762–9), outside London, a magnificent entrance hall (**fig. 8.23**), all grey and white with apsidal niches at each end, leads into an astonishing square anteroom where twelve green marble Ionic columns each support a golden statue. A colorful marble floor pattern is repeated in the beige and gold of the plaster ceiling. At Osterley Park (1762–9) nearby, there is another sequence of rooms including a small parlor in Etruscan style (**fig. 8.24**), that is, with wall decoration derived from Greek vase painting (then thought to be Etruscan) and a wonderfully colorful library with Pompeian detail. The library at

Kenwood House (1767–70), London, is probably the most famous of Adam rooms. It has a semicircular apse at each end, screened off from the center of the room by two Corinthian columns supporting an entablature bar. The plaster vaulted ceiling and walls are a soft grey-green, with details of Pompeian derivation picked out in white, pink, and gold.

Adam designs for London town houses, such as the house for Lord Derby on Grosvenor Square or the house at 20 Portman Square (1770s), fitted a complex layout of rooms into narrow sites with great ingenuity. The dining room from Lansdowne House, now demolished, is preserved in the Metropolitan Museum in New York, where Roman marble statues look out from simple niches beneath delicate Pompeian plaster detailing. Like many modern designers, the Adams dealt with a wide variety of projects, including a small London coffee house, a London theater in Drury Lane, a small country church, and a large and complex building for the University of Edinburgh that is a masterpiece of intelligent and orderly planning.

Georgian Town Houses

In contrast to such large and spectacular houses, more modest town houses were built in thoughtfully designed groupings, often around handsome, landscaped squares. The Covent Garden development by Inigo Jones established a model for such work in London, where land owned in large estates by titled gentry was laid out to form what would

8.24 James and Robert Adam, Osterley Park, Middlesex, 1762–9.

The ornamentation of the Etruscan room is colored with earthy yellow, umber, crimson, and black tones. The painting was done on paper by Angelica Kauffmann (1741-1807), and other artists completed doors, some wall areas, and the ceiling with some very shallow relief. The size of the room and the scale of the ornament create a sense of intimacy that contrasts with the grander interiors in the house.

8.23 (left) James and Robert Adam, Syon House, Middlesex, 1762-9.

The anteroom is a scene of colorful grandeur. Twelve green marble columns brought from Rome support gilded statues. Joseph Rose Jr. (1745-99), an English plaster worker, was responsible for the wall and ceiling decoration. The colors of the marble floor pattern mirror the design of the ceiling.

now be called speculative real estate subdivisions. Houses were planned in well-coordinated rows and built by developers to standard designs for sale (or lease) to individual buyers.

Less wealthy classes of English society had to make do with older houses, often dating back to medieval times, in neighborhoods that had deteriorated into slums. In the late seventeenth and eighteenth centuries, speculative building began to replace such neighborhoods and create new groupings of houses planned to serve a socially stratified, class society. Facing on the squares and major streets, large row houses were built, usually four or five stories high. The basements were occupied by kitchens, laundries, and service facilities. The ground floor was used for formal reception rooms and, sometimes, a dining room. The floor above held the largest formal entertaining rooms of the house. Above that, large bedrooms occupied the third floor; smaller rooms for children or guests occupied the floor above. At the top of the house, small rooms were provided for live-in servants. Back stairs made it possible for servants to move through the house without intruding on the formal spaces.

On lesser streets, rows of smaller houses were built for sale to middle-class owners, professionals, and tradesmen. On still lesser "back streets" and mews, small houses were built for the families of servants, artisans, and workmen, along with stables, coach houses, and servants' quarters, to service the large houses on major streets and squares. In the Georgian era, all of these houses, from largest to smallest, were of generally simple and functional design, fronted in red brick with painted wood window and door trim. The richness of trim and detail was varied to match the class of the occupants, but was invariably handsome, logical, and orderly. Such Georgian housing remains an example of good neighborhood design rarely equalled in modern times.

A rather primitive level of convenience remained the norm, however. Water came from a well, hand pump, or from the collection of rain water. It was carried to pitcher and basin in bed or dressing rooms. Hot water had to be heated in the kitchen and similarly carried. A bath tub, a luxury present only in some larger houses, was a small, portable affair set up in a dressing room and filled with water carried by servants—it was probably only rarely used. In a very few eighteenth-century houses, basins with running water and even "water

closets" (toilets), supplied with water from streams or springs, appeared. Heat came from fireplaces that burned wood or, as it became available, coal. Cooking was done in a fireplace, possibly improved with various iron accessories until the development of iron kitchen ranges at the end of the eighteenth century. Lighting depended on candles that required constant trimming and replacement. Oil lamps, although known in ancient times, did not come into wide use in England until the very end of the century.

Other Building Types

The Georgian era also produced examples of a variety of other functional building types. They included clubs where gentlemen could meet, converse, or doze in handsome and comfortable settings. Retail shops in towns and cities were generally small establishments, often the ground floor of their proprietors' homes. Shop fronts with large, often bowed windows of many glass panes and pleasantly designed signs gave access to interiors that were generally lined with shelves and cases displaying and containing the wares on sale. The Georgian theater developed into an enclosed auditorium with balconies on three sides facing a stage with a decorative proscenium.

Georgian Furniture and Interior Furnishings

Within Georgian houses, according to the wealth and status of the owner, the basically plain and dignified rooms were given ornamental plaster ceilings, decorated fireplace mantels, and furniture as comfortable and as ostentatious as the occupants might prefer. Paintings and mirrors, elegantly framed, might hang on the walls, while windows received increasingly elaborate drapery treatments. The taste for exotic imports, particularly those from the Far East, influenced furniture design so that actual imports, teak tables, and cabinets might mingle with CHINOISERIE carving of chair backs and table legs. Wallpaper from China displayed nature and scenic landscape themes (**fig. 8.25**). Imported porcelain (called, of course, "china") was fashionable for dishes but also for ornamental bowls and vases. Handsome Georgian silver bowls, candlesticks, boxes, and other accessories, often of very simple design, were also favorite objects for display, along with the useful and decorative silverware for table service. In addition to imported ceramics, a number of English factories made porcelains in florid ornamental designs, but simple

T. Sheraton del.

8.25 Thomas Sheraton, an engraved plate illustrating the south end of the Prince of Wales's Chinese drawing room, 1793.

Chinoiserie, a fondness for decorative detail derived from imports from China, was a phase in eighteenth century English interior design. In this plate from The Cabinet-Maker and Upholsterer's Drawing-Book *(1793-4) only a few details—the wall panels at right and left and the wainscot detail below them, and the ornamental candle-sticks and figure—do not seem to have any strong relationship to actual Chinese design, but they serve to inject novelty into an other-wise typically symmetrical eighteenth-century interior.*

designs also appeared. The plain Queen's ware made in the factory of Josiah Wedgwood (1730–95) is a model of classic simplicity and practicality, still produced and still appropriate for modern users.

English clock makers took great pride in the accuracy and quality of their products. Clocks were driven by gravity weights and regulated by pendulum motion so that means had to be found to deal with the hanging weights and swinging pendulum. Clocks were often made with a small wooden case that could be mounted on a high shelf or bracket, with the weights hanging below in the open. The tall ("grandfather") clock was an alternative arrangement in which the weights and pendulum could be enclosed. The cases of such clocks were large and followed the fashions of other furniture styles. A clock case often resembled a small temple building, complete with pediment and columns. Smaller clocks were made with spring drive mechanisms and cases ranging from restrained to ornate, intended as both functional and decorative elements to suit the style of particular rooms.

The major keyboard musical instrument of the Georgian era was the harpsichord. The main London makers were Jacob Kirkman and the firm of Schudi and Broadwood. Handel owned a fine double keyboard example of the latter makers'

work. English harpsichords followed the restrained design of other Georgian furniture. The mahogany case had veneer banding, and often satinwood veneer in the keyboard area. When pianos began to replace harpsichords, the same case design was retained. Beethoven owned a Broadwood piano. A smaller version of the harpsichord was called a spinet. It was made in a compact triangular case and was a popular instrument in smaller houses. Although pipe organs were most usual in churches, small versions called chamber or cabinet organs were often present in large houses A cabinet organ was housed in a large vertical case with doors that opened up to expose keyboard and pipes. Other designs displayed pipes in a decoratively carved surround. Even the smallest of such organs were inevitably massive and were often designed to be a major visual element in a room, with exterior decorative treatment to relate to the general style of their surroundings.

Georgian furniture can be classified as belonging to the three sub-periods, early, middle, and late. The early phase (1714–50) begins with a carry-over of Queen Anne practice. Walnut continued in use, but after 1735 the importation of mahogany, first from Spain and then from Central America, made that wood with its fine grain and reddish color increasingly popular. Cabriole legs, BALL AND CLAW FEET, carved lions' heads, and

8.26 Thomas
Chippendale, "Chinese
Chairs," 1754.

The plate from The
Gentleman and
Cabinet-Maker's
Director *(1754) shows
a typical design for an
eighteenth-century
chair with details
intended to suggest
Chinese influences.
Illustrations such as
this served as a kind of
catalog from which a
client might select their
preferred designs for
legs, backs, stretchers,
and arms.*

other fanciful decorative elements came into
general use. The influence of French Rococo can be
traced in the freer and more florid use of decoration. Some new furniture types appeared, such as
double chairs (small settees that appear to be two
chairs joined together) and reading chairs with a
book stand and candle holders. The high chest or
chest with many drawers was usually made in two
parts to permit easy moving.

The middle Georgian period (1750–70) is
particularly associated with the work of the famous
cabinet maker Thomas Chippendale (1718–79),
whose influence came not only from his own fine
design and craftsmanship, but also from the impact
of his book of engravings and instruction, *The
Gentleman and Cabinet Maker's Director*, published
in editions of 1754, 1755, and 1762 (**fig. 8.26**). A
kind of catalog or style book showing typical
Chippendale designs, it also served to make his
design known to many other cabinet makers in
England (and eventually in America) who based
their designs on Chippendale's work. The
Chippendale style might be called a restrained form
of Rococo combined with various exotic influences, particularly Chinese elements taken both
from Chinese furniture and from forms known
from Chinese landscapes as they appeared in wallpaper—pagoda forms, carved dragons, and lacquer
work. Chippendale furniture has an underlying
simplicity, is well made, sturdy, and practical, but it

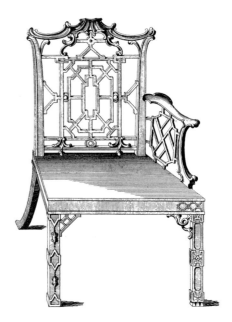

is also florid and decorative. Simple square legs,
cabriole legs, perforated back splats with carving in
Chinese or even Gothic style, ball and claw feet,
and carved arms are all used for chairs. Settees,
glass-fronted bookcases, and massive desks were
made in related designs. Massive bookcases or
breakfront units were often topped with pediments
suggestive of Baroque architecture. Broken pediments (with an open space at the center) and a
central urn or other finial are illustrated, along with
candelabra, stove grates, candle lanterns, cases for

8.27 George
Hepplewhite, a library
case, 1787.

*Fine books were
collected by wealthy
aristocrats, and they
had to be stored and
displayed in suitable
bookcases. This large
unit is made up of a
central, pedimented
element, which might
be ordered alone or,
should the client have
space, with the right
and left wings making
up an imposing unit.
The urns (and the
broken pediment) on
top were optional
elements, available to
suit the buyer's taste.*

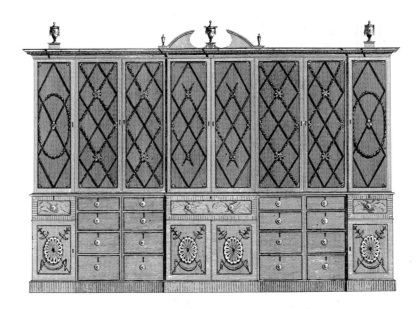

Plate 30.

A Library Table

8.28 Thomas Sheraton, a library table, 1793.

An illustration from Sheraton's The Cabinet-Maker and Upholsterer's Drawing-Book *(1793–4) shows an oval table with inlaid veneer surfaces. Slides can be pulled out from each end to open up easel stands to support the large and heavy books of illustrations that were favored by wealthy book collectors. The doors that open from the knee-hole to give access to spaces in the base pedestals are an amusing detail.*

clocks, and even a few designs for chamber organs. Chippendale was also a supplier of drapery window treatments, canopied beds, and framed mirrors in related rich, even fantastic, decorative styles. More modest furniture was made by many other craftsmen, who simplified and adapted the Chippendale vocabulary to suit a wider and less affluent public.

The late Georgian period (1770–1810) includes later work of Chippendale, but was dominated by the work of the two other famous Georgian cabinet makers, George Hepplewhite (d. 1786) and Thomas Sheraton (1751–1806). Each of these men developed a personal style, and each published a book of illustrations that served to promulgate that style. Hepplewhite's *The Cabinet Maker and Upholsterer's Guide* (1788–94) illustrates chairs with perforated backs in shield or oval shapes along with breakfront bookcases, and upholstered seating pieces. Legs are square, often tapered, and usually carved with parallel lines of reeding. Round tapered legs with a carved ring detail are also shown. Small tables and framed mirrors, pedestals topped with vases, elaborately draped beds, wash stands and "night tables" (incorporating a space for a covered chamber pot) also were made in Hepplewhite style (**fig. 8.27**).

Sheraton's *Cabinet Maker and Upholsterer's Drawing Book* (1790–4) illustrates a somewhat more rectilinear style, with small scale and delicate elements. Chairs have square backs and straight legs, cabinet pieces are veneered and often have curved parts, creating bulging fronts, curved ends, and whole pieces such as desks of oval form. Inlays of contrasting color, sometimes with painted and colored details, and much use of the light yellow satinwood establish a light and colorful character. Sheraton was an ingenious inventor of furniture gadgetry and illustrates many complex designs, such as dressing tables with pull-out compartments and swinging mirrors, tables with lift-up storage compartments, and a library table that opens into a ladder (**fig. 8.28**). He appears to be the inventor of twin beds. He also illustrates richly draped windows, alcoves, and whole rooms decorated according to his tastes. The writing table usually called a Carlton House desk is a Sheraton development.

The Georgian era of English design has become one of the most admired of all historic periods. It is a period in which consistency of character, order and logic in concepts, and elegance and restraint in detail became widely accepted by architects, builders, and craftsmen, so that a sense of unity extends from the largest works to the simplicity of modest terrace houses. In studying the beginnings of MODERNISM in the twentieth century, it is frequently suggested that a return to the consistency of style (but not the specifics of detail) of the eighteenth century is the logical starting point.

Eighteenth-century order and consistency gave way at the beginning of the nineteenth century to an era of technical innovation that upset Georgian traditions and presented challenges that designers struggled to resist or accept. Arkwright's invention of the spinning jenny in 1764 and Watt's successful steam engine of 1769 laid the foundations for developments that were to make the nineteenth century a time of sweeping change in every aspect of life in western civilization.

Colonial and Federal America

The discovery of the Americas by the explorers of the fifteenth and sixteenth centuries opened up a variety of possibilities to Europeans ready to uproot and relocate in the "New World." Motivations varied from the hope of financial gain to the desire to escape religious persecution; there was also the simple desire for new experiences and adventure.

Beginning in the seventeenth century, the American continents were settled by colonists from several European countries. The new settlers generally had little interest in or sympathy for the native populations they encountered, and either ignored or pushed aside (as in North America), or devastated in the search for plunder (as in Central and South America). A colony was invariably regarded as an effort to reproduce, insofar as possible, the European environment that had been left behind. This view of the New World as an empty space best filled with duplication of the old world may seem strange in view of the desire of many colonists to escape from poverty or repression in their old homes. Desire for new freedoms or new wealth rarely found expression in genuinely new design.

Typically, the aim was to build new houses and new towns to recall the European past. Thus the Spanish and Portuguese settlers in South and Central America built churches in the Plateresque, Baroque, and Churrigueresque styles that were current in Renaissance Spain and Portugal. French settlements in Louisiana followed the styles of contemporary Paris. Swedish, Dutch, and German settlers each developed a colonial style based on their memories of their countries of origin. The realities of climate, the availability of certain materials and the lack of others, and the simple necessity of managing survival in remote locations did, however, force colonists to make some modifications, often grudgingly, to the old and familiar ways of doing things.

Colonial Styles in Latin America

Buildings of Hispanic settlers involved a mixture of European Baroque design for the focal points (entrances and altars) of churches, with the vernacular traditions of native (Indian) building. In Mexico these were Mayan and Aztec, based on the use of sun-baked ADOBE brick with wood pole roof support for simple forms suggestive of the ancient PUEBLOS in the North American southwest. The

cathedral in Mexico City (1563–1667) follows Spanish Renaissance and Baroque traditions—its nave and aisles are of equal height, there are side chapels along both sides and twin towers flanking an ornate Baroque facade. Polychrome sculpture illustrating religious themes is rendered with powerful realism. Claudio de Arciniega, a Spaniard, was the principal architect. The Mexican Church of the Sanctuary of the Virgin Guadalupe at Morelia (**fig. 9.1**) is similarly ornate. The church of S. José at Teptzotlán (*c.* 1750) is an extreme example of the use of Baroque Churrigueresque ornamentation, more florid and more dense that anything in Spain itself. Some sixteenth-century churches in Peru also derive from Spanish practice.

In Brazil native craft skills were less developed, forcing the Portuguese colonials to depend even more heavily on importation—not only of design but of actual components. Stone carvings were brought by sea from sources in Portugal. S. Francisco de Assis at Ouro Preto, Minas Gerais (1772–94), and the nearby church of S. Francisco at São João del Rei are fine examples of the Brazilian Baroque style, their twin towers and white walls trimmed with a fantastic display of ornamental carving and sculpture, repeated internally with the addition of color and gilding. These churches are usually attributed to a sculptor-architect, Antonio Francisco Lisboa, known as O Aleijadinho (1738–1814), who was certainly a key figure in the development of eighteenth-century Brazilian church design. In contrast to the elaboration of religious architecture, secular building by Hispanic colonials in South, Central, and North America was generally plain and functional, following European vernacular traditions.

The Palace of the Governors at Santa Fe, New Mexico (1610–14 but much restored), is a simple, unornamented adobe structure with a long porch facing on the town square according to Spanish traditions. Catholic missionaries, as they built their convents or monasteries, adopted the native adobe traditions as at S. Estevan, Acoma, New Mexico (1629–42), where an unornamented, twin towered church stands adjacent to a square monastic courtyard with surrounding pueblo-like structures. By 1700, internal elaboration began, turned toward the Spanish Baroque as in the church of S. José at Laguna, New Mexico, of *c.* 1700 (**fig. 9.2**). The sophisticated design of the church of San Xavier del Bac near Tuscon, Arizona (1775–93), with cruciform plan, a domed crossing with Spanish Baroque

9.1 (*opposite*) Church of the Sanctuary of the Virgin Guadalupe, Morelia, Mexico, 1708–16.

The nave of this Mexican church has a vaulted, Gothic form and is covered with elaborate decoration.

154

9.2 Mission, San Jose, Laguna Pueblo, New Mexico, *c.* 1700.

This interior is a simple, rectangular room with a wooden beamed ceiling made rich through elaborate decorative ornamentation and painting around the altar and chancel area.

facade detail, and altar reredos can be credited to the Spanish architect, Ignacio Gaona.

The Spanish missions in California such as S. Carlos Borromeo at Carmel (1793) suggest the work of Plateresque Spain as modified by their development in Mexico. Residential interiors follow the vernacular Mediterranean traditions of white plastered walls, wood beamed ceiling, and tiled floors with a simple fireplace as the usual focal motif. A living space opening on a patio in the Palace of the Governor at San Antonio, Texas (1749), is a typical example that might be mistaken for a comparable space in Spain.

Colonial Styles in North America

English settlers brought with them the styles that were to become dominant along the eastern coast of North America, and it is the design of these English settlers that has come to be called COLONIAL. French colonial, Dutch colonial, or Spanish styles are generally thought of as

"regional" or in some way special, while the word "colonial," used without any modifiers, is almost universally understood as meaning the work derived from English design from about 1610 to 1800.

Early Colonial Houses

The earliest settlements established by arrivals from England were at Jamestown in 1607 and, with the *Mayflower* landing, at Plymouth in 1620. The first structures built were temporary "English wigwams," built of wattle (sticks), mud, and thatch. In spite of the name, they were not based on native American (Indian) practice, but were huts of a sort sometimes built by English peasant farmers. None has survived. Such huts were soon replaced by wooden houses built according to medieval English custom. These were half-timber houses, with sturdy framing of massive timbers. Wood was the most available of materials, since clearing forest land produced timber in quantity as a by-product. Sawing was, however, a laborious process so that the production of the neatly cut lumber of later times was not yet possible. Whole logs were cut, roughly squared up with such tools as the ax and ADZE, and then assembled into house frames with wood joints such as MORTISE AND TENON or PEGGED LAP JOINTS that could be produced with simple hand tools. In England, such frames are exposed on the exteriors of buildings (generating the familiar half-timber appearance), but on the American continent the plaster and brick infill used in England was not at hand. The climate also discouraged exposed framing because the variation from cold to hot and from damp to dry tended to break frame and infill apart, causing cracks and leaks. With wood so readily available, the natural solution was to cover the frame with a skin of wood that served as exterior wall. Planks could be nailed to the framing and then covered with an outer surface of overlapping SHINGLES or CLAPBOARDS made by splitting logs rather than by sawing. Internally, such houses exhibit their structure as a major element of their character.

The typical early colonial American house was simply an English medieval house with a wood exterior. It often had overhanging upper stories typical of medieval towns, and small windows with leaded glass. Gabled roofs were invariably shingled, while a chimney marked the location of the interior fireplaces. Brick, at first brought from England as

ballast in ships, but then made in local kilns, was the usual chimney material. Foundation sills generally rested on rough stones or even directly on the ground. Many early houses had only one main all-purpose room with an attic above, so that fireplace and chimney were placed at one end wall. An improved plan soon developed, with a center chimney separating two main rooms, each with a fireplace. A steep, winding stair in front of the chimney led to the upstairs spaces. This plan was further improved by the addition of a "lean-to" across the rear that made space for smaller rooms, one with its own fireplace. Such a house might also have a full second floor with rooms on either side of the chimney, sometimes with additional fireplaces. With the lean-to on the north, bringing the roof down close to the ground helped to protect against winter wind and storms and generated the typical SALT-BOX shape. The much admired and imitated CAPE COD COTTAGE was a house of this type, often built by ships' carpenters entirely without foundations so that it "floated" on the sand dunes of the cape. The carefully preserved and restored Hoxie House (**figs. 9.3** and **9.4**; *c.* 1637) at East Sandwich, Massachusetts, is of this type. It is one of the earliest of American colonial buildings. The more typical New England house on Cape Cod and inland has a center front door with two windows on each side. It may be one or two stories in height and usually has a simple gable roof, although roofs of more complex form with gables facing to front or back were not unusual. The Whipple House at Ipswich, Massachusetts (before 1669), is of this type; it also has an overhanging upper story which gives it a clearly medieval character.

Early Colonial Furniture and Interior Furnishings

Internally, early colonial houses were rigorously functional. The wood frame members were exposed, their diagonal braces often visible. The floors were wide wooden planks; the ceiling was simply the exposed wood framing and underside of the floor planks above. Wall surfaces might be of wood, or, between the frame members, plaster on SPLIT LATH, that is, LATH made by partly splitting thin boards so that plaster can be forced through the splits to form "keys" holding the plaster in place. A large brick fireplace dominated the main room, which was used as kitchen and all-purpose living space. Furniture, usually of pine but occasionally of cherry, oak, hickory, or some other native wood, might include a trestle table, benches, and a ladder-back chair or two made of wood turnings and with woven rush seats. Solid wood, often in very wide boards for tables and chests, was put together with hand-cut joints, BOX (FINGER) JOINTS, dovetails, or mortise and tenons. Storage was dealt with by hooks and pegs for hanging

9.3 (*above left*) Hoxie House, East Sandwich, Massachusetts, *c.* 1637.

An early American house on Cape Cod. The massive timbers of the braced frame are hidden by the shingled exterior. Only the chimney is of brick.

9.4 (*above*) Interior of Hoxie House.

The interior of the typical early American house was very dark because there were only a few, tiny windows. This view shows a half-attic loft, providing space for a simple rope bed. The spinning wheel in the corner of the space below and the two wool-winders in the loft reflect the home production of woolen textiles. Corn and other provisions are hung up for drying.

9.5 Bedroom, Stanley-Whitman House, Farmington, Connecticut, from 1664

The heavy timber corner post and timber ceiling are evidence of the braced frame structure. Plastered walls fill the spaces between wood members. The bed is a wooden frame with a laced rope support for the mattress. A trundle bed (on rollers) is stored beneath the bed, and it can be pulled out at night to provide extra sleeping space. The cradle accommodates the newest baby. There are woven coverlets on each bed. The windows are small and shuttered.

9.6 Old Ship Meeting House, Hingham, Massachusetts, 1681.

The dignified simplicity of early American religious buildings expresses the austere philosophy of the Puritan settlers.

objects, a few shelves, a box for salt, and possibly a small cupboard. Various kinds of candlesticks, holders, and lanterns would supply light to augment the fireplace. In bedrooms (**fig. 9.5**), the bed would have a wooden frame laced with rope to hold a straw, leaf, corn-husk, or feather mattress. Posts to hold a canopy were an occasional luxury. Cradles and trundle beds served children of various sizes. There might also be a blanket chest with a lift lid and possibly a spinning wheel since all textiles were homemade. A braided or "rag" rug would be a luxury on the floor, and homemade quilts on beds were a source of color. The functional austerity of such interiors accorded well with the religious attitudes of the Puritan inhabitants, whose beliefs found the display of wealth and status through ornamentation contrary to the need for simplicity, modesty, and a focus on virtuous living.

As time went on and the colonists became better established and more prosperous, various improvements were gradually introduced. Double hung window sash gradually took the place of CASEMENT windows (offering better control of ventilation with improved weather protection), and larger panes of better glass improved light and view. Specialized trades developed so that there were carpenters, weavers, chair makers, smiths, and tinkers (workers in tin and pewter) to make objects of improved design and function. Windsor chairs of the sort made in England came into use, some with arms; some (called tavern chairs) for use in inns have a special wide arm to hold food or drink. Drawer chests appeared, and chests that

combine some drawers below with a lift-lid blanket compartment above. Most early colonial furniture is unornamented, but gradually, in actual imports from England but more often in locally made versions of English designs, simplified Jacobean and Restoration style ornament appeared. Turned legs, round, ball-like "bun" feet, and surface carving served to show off the skill of woodworkers and the tastes of householders who could afford such luxuries. Highboy drawer chests and desks in William and Mary style were made in America by 1700 for use in the most spacious and comfortable homes of the time.

Churches and Meeting Houses

Aside from houses, barns, and sheds, the only common building types were churches and meeting houses. Few early examples survive; the Old Ship meeting house of 1681 at Hingham, Massachusetts, is a rare exception (**fig. 9.6**). It is a simple square wooden hall with windows at two story levels corresponding to the main floor and balcony on three sides. The exposed framing of the roof, said to be the work of ships' carpenters, resembled the interior of an inverted ship's hull (the source of its name). The framing supported a belfry centered on the HIPPED ROOF. Inside, the white walls and wood framing are entirely without ornament. A central pulpit is backed by a pair of arch-topped windows.

American Georgian

In the eighteenth century, colonial simplicity began to give way to more elegant and luxurious styles both brought from England by craftsmen and inspired by books that illustrated the architecture and furniture of the Queen Anne and Georgian eras. Ship owners, merchants, some tradesmen and craftsmen, and affluent land owners became sufficiently wealthy to be able to afford a style of life comparable to that of the "gentlemen" of England. In the southern colonies, particularly in Virginia and the Carolinas, vast plantations were established (often by younger sons of titled English families) that, with the help of slave labor, made their owners rich. Houses to please those owners began to approach the "great houses" of England, although none ever reached the extremes of their prototypes.

American Georgian Houses

The American Georgian house might be built of either brick or wood, but it generally followed Renaissance-based European models in its use of symmetrical planning and ornamental detail, including pediments, pilasters, and often a Palladian window. In a typical plan, a center hall was entered from the front door, and often ran through to a rear door. In the hall a handsome stair would lead to a matching second-floor hall. On either side of the entrance halls, one or two rooms would be placed as parlors, dining room and, upstairs, bedrooms. Chimneys to serve fireplaces were placed at the end walls and a hipped roof (sometimes with dormers) became more common than the gable roof. Kitchens and service quarters might be placed in wings or, particularly in the south, in outbuildings arranged in a formal plan.

9.7 Room from the Powel House, Philadelphia, 1765–6.

As wealth increased in colonial America, more luxurious houses with interiors rich in Georgian detail became more common. In this room, which is now installed in the Metropolitan Museum of Art, New York, there is fine wood paneling, an ornamental plaster ceiling, and, on one wall, imported Chinese wallpaper. The tall clock, Chippendale-style furniture, and oriental rug are indicative of the comfortable status of the owner.

Interiors in the Georgian house became more formal, with plastered walls or wood paneling, wood wainscot, and moldings and classically inspired details around fireplace mantels, doors, and windows and as cornice trim moldings.

In cities such as Philadelphia and Boston, brick row houses were built with Georgian detail in much the manner of English city houses. The Powel House in Philadelphia (1765–6) is a good example of the type. Rooms removed from the house have been reconstructed (one in the Philadelphia Museum of Art, one in the Metropolitan Museum in New York; **fig. 9.7**) and furnished with appropriate furniture and decorative details, giving a good idea of how such rooms appeared in the eighteenth century. A Chinese hand-painted wallpaper in the room in New York was added by the museum, but such wallpaper and the oriental rug on the floor are appropriate reminders that imports from Europe, the Middle East, and the Far East became available in America as its merchant shipping increased in importance.

In New England, the John Vassall House (later occupied by the poet Longfellow) of 1759 in Cambridge, Massachusetts, is a good example of the Georgian type, with its pediment and two-story-high pilaster order, all executed in wood. Outside of Philadelphia (now within the city's Fairmount Park) the house called Mount Pleasant (1761–2) is a beautifully preserved miniature version of the English great house. It has a simple symmetrical plan—a parlor on one side of the center hall (**fig. 9.8**), a dining room and stair on the other side, with bedrooms symmetrically arranged above. Services were placed in small twin outbuildings in front on either side. The material is brick plastered over with corner QUOINS. There is an elaborate pedimented entrance door with a Palladian window above. The interiors are well preserved with fine wood paneling, pediments over every doorway, and, in one upstairs room, twin-arch top-doored cupboards with broken pediments above on either side of a marble-edged fireplace. No architect or designer has been identified. The

9.8 Mount Pleasant Mansion, Fairmount Park, Philadelphia, 1761–2.

In the central hall of the upper floor of this handsome house the carved wooden detail is based on classical prototypes and includes a Palladian window, pediments over doorways, and Ionic pilasters and capitals. The woodwork is painted in a soft grey-blue to contrast with the white plaster.

9.9 David Minitree, Carter's Grove, near Williamsburg, Virginia, 1751.

The spacious Georgian mansion is reminiscent of its English precedents. The entrance hall opens through an archway into a broad stairway. Walls are paneled in natural wood and are rich in classical detail, with Ionic pilasters and a finely dentiled cornice. The candle chandelier, furniture, and rugs are typical of American eighteenth-century practice.

9.10 Mount Vernon, near Alexandria, Virginia, from *c.* 1740.

Mount Vernon was the Washington family plantation house. The Palladian window is in the ballroom (or State Banqueting Room as it was originally called), which was an addition to the older house developed at George Washington's request in the 1780s. He asked for the green wallpaper and buff paint for the woodwork. The detail is not as classically perfect as some other examples, but the overall effect is dignified and pleasantly decorative. A guest mentioned window curtains of "white chintz" with "festoons of green satin."

details seem to be derived from English pattern books, but they are used with extraordinary skill.

Farther south, great houses were sited on plantations. Stratford Hall (1725–30), the Lee mansion at Westmorland, Virginia, is designed with an H-plan in which two square blocks that rise up to chimney clusters are linked by a central waist. The plan seems to be based on Italian villas illustrated in Palladio's *Four Books*. The low-ceilinged lower floor houses a number of bedrooms, while the main floor above is a sequence of more formal rooms with rich classically based detail. Most of the furniture is English, imported to suit the taste of the wealthy owners. Other houses, such as Carter's Grove (**fig. 9.9**) in Virginia, are great brick mansions suggesting awareness of Wren and his followers in both plan concept and interior detail.

Mount Vernon, the plantation house of the Washington family, is unusual in having an eight-columned portico running the length of the rear, which faces the Potomac River. The house began as a smaller farmhouse in 1732, but was expanded over the years until it reached its present size in 1799. It is built of wood, with the entrance facade treated with nailed-on wood block painted to simulate stone. The window arrangement survives from the original house and is oddly non-symmet-

rical in spite of the pediment and cupola above. A ballroom added in George Washington's last expansion of the house is a double-height room with a large Palladian window dominating the end wall (**fig. 9.10**). The many rooms of the house follow Georgian formula treatments with wood paneling in some, ornamental plaster work in others. The smaller rooms have fireplaces placed diagonally on a cut-off corner, each with ornamental mantel and most with rich over-mantel detail.

In the deep south, in Louisiana and Mississippi, many-columned porches and porticos that provided shade and outdoor living spaces were typical exterior features of plantation house mansions. French doors and windows opened up interior spaces to connect with the surrounding verandas. Other regional differences derive from the points of origin of the settlers. Dutch settlers in New York built houses in wood or stone but preferred the GAMBREL (two-slope) roof that creates more usable attic space. The Dyckman House in New York (*c*. 1783), built in stone, has a gambrel roof that projects to form a porch across the full width of the house in front and at the rear. An idea of the interiors of Dutch colonial houses can be gained from the interiors of the Schenck

9.11 A kitchen from Millbach, Pennsylvania, *c.* 1752. (Preserved at the Philadelphia Museum of Art.)

The spacious kitchen of an American farm estate has a floor, ceiling, and trim of natural-colored wood. The walls are white plaster. The cabinets, tables, chair, and child's rocking-chair are all of traditional vernacular character, although the large storage pieces show evidence of a sophisticated knowledge of the ornamental detailing of European prototypes. The various containers and utensils are typical of the period.

House (1675–1730) now reconstructed within the Brooklyn Museum. Heavy wooden frame members with prominent corner braces, white plastered walls, a wood plank floor, and a large hooded fireplace dominate each of the two rooms. Two enclosed box beds, a massive Baroque KAS or wardrobe, and bands of blue and white Dutch tiles at the sides of the fireplace are characteristically Dutch elements of the second, more private room.

In Pennsylvania, German settlers (misleadingly called Pennsylvania Dutch) built simple wooden houses and great barns. The group of buildings built by a religious sect around 1742 known as the Cloister at Ephrata is of severely plain wooden construction, but the interiors, all natural wood and white plaster, have an impressive dignity that derives from their total simplicity. A more typical Pennsylvania German residential interior is a kitchen of 1752 from Millbach (**fig. 9.11**), now preserved in the Philadelphia Museum of Art. Wood beams overhead, a giant fireplace, white plastered walls, and simple wood furniture suggest a considerable level of unpretentious comfort. Wood furniture was often painted in bright colors with designs using birds, flowers, and decorative scrolls in the vocabulary of the peasant art of Europe.

American Georgian and Queen Anne Furniture

In the latter part of the Georgian era, American craftsmen and cabinet makers became increasingly skillful and expert in working in the styles fashionable in England. Queen Anne and Chippendale designs were both much used, sometimes even intermixed. The term Philadelphia Chippendale is often used to describe the work of cabinet makers in that city, such as John Folwell (active in the 1770s), who was sometimes called "the American Chippendale," and William Savery (1721–88), best known for fine highboys. Highboys and tall secretary desks often had plain tops, but pediments, particularly broken pediments with S-curved scroll shapes, were used on the most elaborate versions.

In Newport, Rhode Island, a unique version of the Queen Anne style developed in the workshop of Goddard and Townsend, makers of greatly admired tall secretary desks and low desks of the type called BLOCKFRONT. A fluted semicircular form suggestive of a scallop shell, a carved motif that seems to have

9.12 Ashley House, Deerfield, Massachusetts, c. 1730.

A "highboy," a tall drawer chest, can be seen in the far corner. The chairs, which are of the style called Queen Anne, have cabriole legs and simple backs. The walls are paneled, and the oriental rugs were imported. The candle holders with metal reflectors would have provided modest night-time lighting.

been only used in America, is much used in Newport furniture. New York and Boston were also centers of fine furniture production.

Chair design followed English patterns—Queen Anne designs (**fig. 9.12**) with simple splat backs, and versions of Chippendale and Hepplewhite with Rococo and Chinese-inspired detail. Windsor chairs were made in many types from simple to elaborate. The fully upholstered wing-back chair was also popular in America, where cold winters probably made its enclosing form particularly welcome.

Late Colonial Public Buildings

As the American colonies prospered, the need for more public buildings emerged. Churches were built in almost every town, and cities often had a number of churches. As the stringent beliefs of Puritanism gave way to more varied religious practices, churches tended to take on the character of English religious buildings. The Carolean and Georgian churches of Christopher Wren and James Gibbs became models for many American churches. Christ Church (begun 1727) in Philadelphia, variously credited to Robert Smith and to an amateur architect, John Kearsley, is a fine example of the Wren–Gibbs type. It is built in brick, with the upper part of the spire in wood; inside, white-painted wooden Roman Doric columns topped with square entablature blocks

9.13 Peter Harrison, King's Chapel, Boston, 1749–58.

The Georgian church interior suggests that Harrison was aware of English prototypes. Paired Corinthian columns support sections of entablature with a partly coved ceiling above. There is a Palladian window above the altar and a fine metal candle chandelier. Placing the seating in enclosed "box" pews was an attempt to minimize winter cold and drafts.

support galleries and a graceful arrangement of arches. A Palladian window forms a focal point above the altar. Peter Harrison (1723–1805) was the architect of King's Chapel in Boston (**fig. 9.13**; 1749–58) where paired Corinthian columns with entablature blocks carry the galleries and the coved forms of the plaster ceiling. St. Paul's Chapel in New York (1764–6) by the New York architect Thomas McBean is of similar design, but is of special interest because recent restoration efforts have discovered the original paint colors—not the conservative white, grey, or beige usually thought to be typical of the colonial church, but strong shades of blue and pink that set off the white-painted wood detail. Waterford crystal chandeliers imported from Ireland add to the sense of richness. Many American churches and meeting houses follow similar patterns in brick or in wood, with the level of elaboration adjusted to the religious beliefs and the wealth of their congregations.

Other colonial public buildings tend to follow the simple Carolean and Georgian tradition established by Wren at the Chelsea Hospital in London—red brick with white-painted woodwork, symmetry, and ornamental detail concentrated at doorways and, where there is one, in a spire. A building for the College of William and Mary in Williamsburg, Virginia (begun 1716), is known as the Wren Building because of a tradition that the design was actually provided in drawings by Wren. Certainly the design is a fine example of the Wren style, both outside and in the great hall within, modeled on the wood-paneled dining halls of English university buildings. The Williamsburg Capitol (1701–5) and Governor's Palace (1706–20) are also handsome examples of the Wren style, with beautifully detailed interiors, but it must be noted that these buildings were drastically reconstructed in 1928–34 on the basis of very limited documents and remains.

Federal Styles

With the signing of the Declaration of Independence in 1776, the term colonial ceases to be appropriate. Design produced from about 1780 until 1830 is usually described as belonging to the FEDERAL period. In stylistic terms, the tendency of the Federal period was to move toward an increasingly strict version of classicism based on sophisticated awareness of the published works of Renaissance authorities, such as Palladio and Serlio, and on knowledge of actual classical buildings. Books of detailed measured drawings made at archeological sites, such as the multivolume *Antiquities of Athens* by James Stuart and Nicholas Revett (1762), aided the movement toward Neoclassicism—and Greek rather than Roman precedents—that was also developing in Europe at this time.

Jefferson

Thomas Jefferson (1743–1826), although best known for his role as a statesman in the creation of the independent United States and as its third president, was a strongly influential figure in the development of American architecture and design. In the tradition of the Georgian English gentleman, Jefferson was a versatile intellectual with wide-ranging interests in political theory, science, agriculture, music, and the arts. From 1784 to 1789, Jefferson was in France serving as American ambassador. Direct contact with the classicism of French Renaissance architecture and with the Neoclassicism developing there at the time was augmented by a visit to Nîmes, where the best preserved of ancient temples, the Maison Carré (which Jefferson would already have known from Palladio's engravings), made a deep impression.

While still in France, Jefferson developed a design for a new Capitol for the State of Virginia to be built at Richmond (1785–8). The design is a fairly strict version of the temple form of the Maison Carrée, with a six-columned portico and pediment facade, but with windows introduced at two story levels to serve the practical needs of the spaces within. The columns have been changed from the Corinthian order of the Roman temple to an Ionic order. The four-sided capitals were promoted by the Italian Renaissance architect and author Vincenzo Scamozzi (1552–1616) because,

Jefferson explained, of the greater difficulty of carving Corinthian capitals—beyond, one assumes, the skills of American stone cutters of the time. Such direct appropriation of an ancient building's design for a totally unrelated modern purpose can be thought of as a first step toward the development of the stylistic revivals that were to follow early in the nineteenth century.

At Monticello and at the University of Virginia (1817–26), both near Charlottesville, Jefferson's use of Palladian and Roman concepts is more creative and imaginative. Monticello, his own house (1796–1809), with its columned porticos and domed octagon, is sometimes said to have been based on Palladio's Villa Rotonda. It is, however, very different and very original. The dome does not top an internal rotunda, but is rather the roof of a curious and hard to reach upstairs room. Although it appears to be a one-story building, Monticello actually had a full upper story of bedrooms (**fig. 9.14**) and an extensive lower floor of services that extend outward in long wings. A balcony overlooking the entrance hall

9.14 Thomas Jefferson, Monticello, near Charlottesville, Virginia, 1768-81 and 1796-1809.

Jefferson (1743-1826) was the architect for his house at Monticello. It was full of invention and ingenious and unusual arrangements. His bed can be seen in an alcove between the study and the bedroom, which is visible on the other side of the bed. The colors and details are simple. The book in the foreground and the microscope on a stand are reminders of Jefferson's wide-ranging intellectual and scientific interests.

9.15 Harrison Gray Otis House, Boston, Massachusetts, 1795.

The dining room shows influences of the Adam style known from England, possibly derived from the Adam brothers' published works. The delicate paper and molding at the top of wall surfaces, the window drapery, and the fireplace mantel design are characteristic. The furniture is based on Sheraton/Adam precedents. Note that the floor covering is wall-to-wall carpeting with a strong repeating pattern.

connects rooms on the upper floor, while stairs are hidden away in alcoves. The main living floor has a complex plan. Many rooms are fitted with closets, fireplaces, and alcove beds including, in Jefferson's own room, an alcove bed accessible from either his study on one side or the dressing room on the other. There are many ingenious and curious details such as the pair of double doors connected by an under-floor mechanism that makes both doors open when either one is swung. White woodwork, finely detailed fireplace mantels and door frames, and a full entablature cornice in the main hall are set off against generally plain wall surfaces—a bright Wedgwood blue in the hall, simple wallpapers in some other rooms.

At the University of Virginia, a central mall is surrounded by small college buildings (called "lodges") connected by columned covered walkways on either side and a domed rotunda at one end. In this case the rotunda is modeled on the Roman Pantheon, reduced in size by half, raised on a base and with six rather than eight portico columns. Internally it is a surprise to find that there is no large domed space; instead, its function as a library is served by smaller rooms, three of oval shape, fitted on three floors into the larger circle of the plan. The total concept is clearly based on Palladio's villa schemes, expertly adapted here to a different purpose.

Bulfinch

Charles Bulfinch (1763–1844) was the architect of the Massachusetts State House (State Capitol, 1795–7) in Boston. Bulfinch had visited England and become acquainted with the work of the Adam brothers, who were a major influence in the exterior design of the State House, as well as in the design of the large galleried and domed Representatives Hall. The golden dome that tops this building was the first example of the use of that architectural element as a virtually obligatory symbolic marker for the capitol buildings of various states, as well as for the national Capitol. The Adam style, with its Palladianism and awareness of French Neoclassicism, can be traced in many Federal period buildings, especially in their delicate ornamental detail.

The most dutiful effort at Adam style design, both externally and internally, appears at Boscobel (1805), Garrison, New York. It is a spacious house of frame construction built and presumably

designed by its owner, Morris Dyckman, a loyalist at the time of the American Revolution, who spent some years in voluntary exile in England where he became devoted to the Adam brothers' work. The house has a double-level, columned portico, a grand central stair with Palladian window, and much delicate plaster ornamental detail.

Oval rooms appeared in some houses, as in the house of William Hamilton in Philadelphia called The Woodlands (1788–9), or in the central rooms of Gore Place, a large Adams-like mansion at Waltham, Massachusetts (1797), by an unidentified architect. Sweeping curved stairs became an important feature of many houses and public buildings. Such stairs appear in Bulfinch's 1807 town house for Harrison Gray Otis in Boston, for example (**fig. 9.15**).

Thornton and Latrobe

The tangled history of the national Capitol in Washington begins with a 1792 competition in which none of the ten designs submitted was entirely satisfactory. In 1793 an amateur architect, a Dr. William Thornton (1759–1828), submitted a design that, with favorable comments from both Jefferson and Washington, was accepted by the Commissioners for Federal Buildings—to the annoyance of Etienne Hallet whose competition design had already been approved. Thornton's Capitol was burned in the War of 1812 so that extensive reconstruction was required, particularly internally. The English-trained Benjamin Latrobe (1764–1820) was largely responsible for the detail of the two large legislative chambers (**fig. 9.16**) and for the many smaller spaces that make up the intricate internal plan of the building. His invention of American variations on the Greek orders—column capitals using tobacco leaves and corn husks in place of acanthus leaves—was much admired by members of Congress. After 1819, the project was taken over by Charles Bulfinch who was responsible for the original rotunda with its low dome. The present dome and House and Senate wings are of much later date.

Thornton also designed the unusually shaped Octagon House (1799–1800) in Washington and the large house called Tudor Place (1816) in the Georgetown district of Washington. Both houses exhibit a reserved classicism based on Adam precedents, and both use a single projecting curved

element to accent the center, entrance axis. The triangular site of Octagon House gives rise to an interesting plan with a circular entrance hall (**fig. 9.17**) and round bedrooms above acting as a pivot between the two wings that angle to follow the adjacent streets. Recent restoration has repaired interior detail and recovered much of the furniture and related objects that were originally in the house. The round entrance hall has a grey and white marble floor, with walls of light yellow and grey woodwork. The same colors extend into the adjacent stair hall, where the floor and stair rail are natural, dark wood, the balusters and stair trim a dark grey-green. The walls of the drawing room are a warm grey with darker trim; dining room walls are green with a lighter green trim.

Although Thornton was a self-trained amateur architect and Benjamin Latrobe a London-trained professional, the work of the two men is closely parallel in defining the Federal style at its best. Latrobe had many more commissions for a variety of building types. His Bank of Pennsylvania in Philadelphia (1798–1800, now destroyed) is the

9.16 Benjamin Latrobe, Old Senate Chamber, The Capitol, Washington, D.C., 1803–11.

The semicircular room, topped by a half-dome ceiling, uses accurate classical detail for the Ionic columns, related moldings, and the coffered ceiling. Latrobe was anticipating the Greek revival when he wrote: "I am a bigoted Greek in my condemnation of Roman architecture." The simplicity and dignity of the architecture is rather overwhelmed by the canopy with its rich red and gold ornamentation, which is draped elaborately over the chair and desk of the presiding officer.

9.17 William Thornton, Octagon House, Washington, D.C., 1799–1800.

A circular entrance hall opens through double doors topped by a lunette window into a central hall where a stair leads to the floor above.

first American building to make use of a Greek order in its six-columned front and rear Ionic porticos. The banking room was a round chamber topped with a flat dome. The simple exterior suggested the Neoclassicism of Ledoux in France or John Soane in England.

Latrobe's design for the Philadelphia waterworks (*c.* 1801), a square block with a drum and dome ornamented with restrained Greek detail, included the design of the boilers and pumping machinery inside. It was a focal point in the city's

Centre Square until it was replaced in 1827. The domed Baltimore Cathedral (1814–18) is a monumental Neoclassical church with a broad and open interior space quite unlike the typical galleried Georgian churches of the eighteenth century. It combines John Soane's London Neoclassicism with a hint of the Baroque grandeur of Wren at St. Paul's.

Latrobe's house for Stephen Decatur on Lafayette Square in Washington (1817–19) is a well-preserved example of a Federal town house. It is an austerely simple square block of brick with a low ground floor for services and two floors of living spaces above. Externally, the only ornament is at the entrance where there are side windows and a delicate fan-light window above the wide door. Internally, the house has been changed many times over the years, but recent restoration has been based on available documentation. Latrobe's drawings for the entrance hall have survived, showing his careful treatment of the domed ceiling and niches, and subtle ornamental detail throughout. The original colors were a soft grey for the wall and an ocher yellow for the woodwork. Ceilings are entirely white.

St. John's Church (1815), across Lafayette Square from the Decatur House, was also a Latrobe project. Originally with a Greek cross plan, its lengthened nave, front portico, and spire are of later date. Like many of the educated professionals of the time, Latrobe had wide-ranging interests. He served as the first organist and choirmaster at St. John's, for example. His involvement in the engineering of various waterworks, utilitarian structures for the navy, canal building projects, even the introduction of a steamboat on the Ohio River are evidences of his technical versatility. Although Thornton and Latrobe can be regarded as equal leaders in the development of the Federal style, and although the U.S. Capitol resulted from their combined efforts, the two men became involved in bitter disputes. Thornton's verbal attacks became so excessive that Latrobe undertook a libel suit against him in 1808. In 1813 Latrobe won his suit and was awarded damages of one cent!

Furniture of the Federal Period

Furniture of the Federal period is sometimes classified as "early"—dominated by the late Georgian styles of Hepplewhite and Sheraton—or "late," showing the influence of French Empire fashions as interpreted by English cabinet makers and REGENCY design. Design of the early phase tended toward the delicate, straight-lined forms of Sheraton. Veneered surfaces often have decorative inlays and small carved details using shell, leaf, flower, and basket motifs. Legs are usually tall and slim, straight or turned. Mahogany remained the favored wood, with banding and inlays in contrasting woods such as maple or satinwood. TAMBOUR DOORS are often used for desk or sideboard storage compartments.

The late Federal period favored heavier, more massive forms with carved ornament, inlays, and brass trim elements. Claw and lion's paw feet, scroll-carved chair arms, lyre and CURULE (X-form) chair backs, and chair and couch forms suggestive of the images on Greek vases came into use in accordance with Empire and Regency tastes.

The best-known cabinet makers of the period were Samuel McIntire (1757–1811) and the even more famous Duncan Phyfe (1768–1854), whose name is often attached to the sub-style credited to him. McIntire was an architect based in Salem, Massachusetts, who began his career carving figureheads for ships. Houses that he designed for wealthy sea-captains and merchants were generally of simple form, ornamented by his carving outside and in. He often carved ornamental details for other cabinet makers, making it uncertain whether he ever designed complete pieces of furniture. His name is attached to Hepplewhite- and Sheraton-inspired furniture with details carved in his particular style. A carved basket of fruit or flowers was a favorite McIntire decorative motif.

Duncan Phyfe was born in Scotland, served an apprenticeship as a cabinet maker in Albany, New York, and then moved to New York City to establish his successful furniture business around 1792. Although his design incorporates the Hepplewhite and Sheraton influences that dominate Federal style furniture, his work took on a unique character that made his name widely known as a leading American designer-craftsman. His career lasted until he retired in 1847 and so spanned a time of stylistic changes—changes to which he adapted readily and which he sometimes led. His early work, close to Sheraton's models, included production of tables with a three-legged pedestal base, often with a folding top arranged so that the table could stand against a wall or be opened to make a free-standing dining table. Ornamentation varied from simple reeding to elaborate carving, ranging from spiral reeding to carved eagles, SWAGS, pedestals, and pineapple FINIALS. Applied brass ornament was common; legs of larger pieces were often equipped with casters. Mahogany was the wood most used, often in the form of figured and matched veneers, sometimes with inlays of contrasting colored woods.

Duncan Phyfe turned to imitation of the French Directoire and related English Regency styles and then, after 1815, to the French Empire style, as these became known successively in

America. Adoption of the PILLAR AND SCROLL style using carved versions of classical columns and S- and C-shaped scrolls was a late development (after about 1830) in his production. As the Federal period moved into the nineteenth century, the development of a sequence of historical revivals supplanted late Georgian influences, leading the adaptable and commercially ambitious Phyfe into production of designs suited to the interiors of revivalist architecture. These stylistic developments are dealt with in the following chapter.

Other cities grew to support local cabinet and chair makers who established high standards for both the design and the quality of their craftsmanship. In Boston, John and Thomas Seymour were experts in inlay work, while John Gogswell and Stephen Badlam made skillful use of sliding tambour doors in cabinet pieces. Thomas Affleck, Benjamin Randolph, John Aitken, and Joseph Barry became well known in Philadelphia. Barry also maintained a shop in Baltimore where John and Hugh Findlay worked with marquetry decoration.

A highly individual style of chair design was developed by Lambert Hitchcock (1795–1852) who established a factory at Barhamstead (now Riverton), Connecticut, to produce what he called "fancy chairs" based on Federal or Regency styles. They had turned wood front legs, a rush seat, and simple ladder back, but were characterized by their finish—black paint with brightly colored, painted (usually stenciled) decoration. These chairs became extremely popular in simple farmhouse interiors where they introduced a note of decorative fantasy into otherwise plain, vernacular interiors. Hitchcock chairs are still popular with some collectors and are often made in modern reproduction form.

Other Furnishings of the Federal Period

During the Federal period, a wide variety of objects were locally produced that had most often been imported during the colonial era. Among these were clocks of fine quality in various models, tall and shelf size, with weight or spring drive. Eli Terry and Seth Thomas became well known for the development of a shelf or mantel clock with detail based on Sheraton furniture. Simon Willard developed a wall clock with a round face at the top of a vertical element and box-like bottom that became

known as a banjo clock. The bottom element was usually glass-fronted to provide a view of the swinging pendulum within.

Makers of musical instruments who had begun building harpsichords and spinets changed over to the building of pianos—most often small instruments in a flat, rectangular case with the keyboard along the long side. Such instruments, called "square pianos" (**fig. 9.18**), were usually of handsome appearance but, unfortunately, of limited quality musically. Tall pianos built in the form of a secretary desk were also attempted, with limited success. They may be regarded as ancestors of the later upright piano. Organs built for churches were housed in simple cases with a frontal display of pipes as their main decoration. Tiny organs, often called harmoniums or melodeons, using reeds (like those of the accordion) instead of pipes for sound production, were built for use in small churches and homes.

Framed mirrors, sometimes with attached candle brackets, were popular ornamental and functional objects. The convex, round mirror that gives a condensed image became a popular decorative accessory, usually with elaborate, gilded frames, and often topped by the ever-popular carved American eagle.

American textile production included printed fabrics, at first hand-blocked but, after 1770, also cylinder-printed. Woven textiles were made in solid colors, narrow stripes, and in complex patterns woven with the recently developed JACQUARD loom. Favorite colors were strong blues and greens, golden yellows, and deeper shades of red. Woven horsehair became a popular upholstery cover material: its glossy surface and tough-wearing qualities made it practical, and availability was excellent as long as the horse remained the primary motive power for farm work and transport.

Wood paneling tended to be used for only one wall of formal rooms (the fireplace wall) or for the chimney breast alone. Other walls might display a wood wainscot and cornice, or might be painted, wallpapered, or covered with a woven textile above the wainscot. Direct trade with the Far East by American ships brought Chinese wallpapers, porcelain, and small decorative objects to America. These became popular accessories in affluent households. Chinese dinnerware was often made specially for the American trade, using pattern motifs such as stars and eagles that made reference

9.18 Gardner-Pingree House, Salem, Massachusetts, 1804–05.

A view from the dining room into a parlor showing wallpaper and decorative trim with Adam style influence. The furniture is of Hepplewhite character (note the shield back chairs) while woodwork (the work of Samuel McIntire) is of related design. There is a square piano at the front wall of the parlor with a round framed mirror above with an eagle crest, a favorite decorative ornament of the federal period. Elaborate drapery at each window contributes to a sense of opulence.

to the newly founded republic. Oriental rugs, Dutch tiles, French scenic wallpapers, and English silver and glass remained popular imports implying wealth and status as well as taste. Fine silver and glassware fully equal to the quality of any imports were also made in many eastern American cities.

Although 1820 is usually given as an end-date for the Federal period, the transition into subsequent developments was gradual. Emphasis on archeological correctness can already be detected in the Greek orders and detail used by Thornton and Latrobe. Duncan Phyfe, always ready to adapt to changes in taste, developed designs suggested by the furniture depicted in ancient Greek vase painting. In the 1820s and 1830s American architecture and interior design found a new devotion to Greek models, generating the first of several nineteenth-century revivals of the historic past that are dealt with in the following chapter.

10

The Regency, Revivals, and Industrial Revolution

The nineteenth century encompasses some of the most sweeping changes in human affairs since the beginning of history. Life experience as it developed through the Renaissance and into the eighteenth century had a continuity of qualities combined with gradual change. Scientific development and the coming of industrialization in the nineteenth century, however, has made modern life totally different from anything that preceded it. The enormous growth of world population along with the vastly improved nature of transportation and communication that characterize the twentieth century had their roots in the nineteenth century. The world of design had enormous difficulty in dealing with changes of such depth and magnitude. The nineteenth century is, therefore, a study in contradictions—in change and in the efforts to restrain change.

Regency

In 1811, George III of England was succeeded by his son who served in his place as Prince Regent. In 1820, on the death of his father, he became George IV, reigning until 1830. The design of this period, transitional between the end of the Georgian era and nineteenth-century developments that followed, is given the term Regency. The style has its origins in the Neoclassicism of the late eighteenth century and draws its form from Greek and Roman precedents with a mixture of elements drawn from more exotic sources—Egyptian, Chinese, and Moorish. The impact of the colonial holdings of England, France, and Belgium, and the newly extended knowledge of remote and varied civilizations made awareness of and fascination with the exotic an available theme. The most curious aspect of Regency design is its seemingly inconsistent vacillation between the restraint of classicism and the exuberance of fantasy.

Nash

The most spectacular building of the Regency period is the Royal Pavilion at Brighton (**figs. 10.1** and **10.2**; 1815–21), a residence and pleasure palace designed to please the whims of the Regent. It was designed by John Nash (1752–1835) in a mixture of oriental styles with great onion-shaped domes dominating the exterior and giving it a Moorish aspect. Internally the Royal Pavilion is a sequence of fancifully ornamented rooms. Fantastically elaborate chandeliers using the newly developed gas light introduce a new level of brilliance. Chinese wallpaper and bamboo furniture, elaborate drapery in reds and golds, gilded and carved furniture with brass inlays and trim, carpets in exotic pinks and greens, and strongly chromatic wall colors make the Brighton Pavilion representative of the playful, fantastic, and decorative aspect of Regency design.

A more restrained and classical aspect is represented by the work of the same architect when he designed groups of row houses—terraced houses as they are called in England—with simple forms, plain white walls, and details often based on Greek precedents. Houses arranged in a sweeping curve

10.1 (*top right*) John Nash, Royal Pavilion, Brighton, England, 1815-21.

In the music room of the Royal Pavilion the wall coverings and the gilded mirror surround above the fireplace make reference to Chinese decorative elements. The hanging lights add to the festive quality of the room, which should be visualized with piano, harp, and seating, all filled with gilded ornament and looking more French than Chinese is character.

10.2 (*bottom right*) Exterior of the Royal Pavilion.

10.3 (*opposite*) John Soane, Soane House, London, 1812-1813.

The small breakfast room in his own house, offered Soane the chance to experiment with architectural form. A flattened dome is supported by slim columns around the edges, but the walls of the room are in a square larger than the dome. The space between the dome and the walls allows hidden windows to add light. Mirrors appear over the mantel and in rondels at the dome's edges.

or crescent such as Park Crescent (1812) at the entrance to Regent's Park or the grand arches and Ionic columns of Cumberland Terrace (1827), both in London, with white-painted stucco detail covering simple brick, are typical of Nash in his most monumental phase. Ornamental iron railings, bow windows, and small hood roofs over porches or projecting bays set off against white stucco walls were typical of the Regency style groups built in London and many other English cities. These formal groupings were speculative real estate developments made up of individual houses owned or leased by occupants who treated the rooms within however they chose—most often in some version of the rich but reserved Georgian manner.

Soane

Sir John Soane (1753–1837) is a particularly interesting designer of the Regency era whose highly individualistic work is at once Neoclassical, sometimes austere in a way that seems to point toward modernism, and sometimes decorative and complex. His interiors for the London headquarters of the Bank of England (1788–1823), arranged around columned courtyards, now mostly altered or demolished and so only known through drawings and photographs, used arch forms, windowed drum clerestories, and domes to create spaces that arc intricate in form but simple in detail. The rooms within called the Old Dividend Office—where paired CARYATIDS stood in the high center drum—the Old Colonial (or Five Per Cent) Office, the Consols Office (**fig. 10.4**), and the great central rotunda were large public halls, dignified, spacious, and remarkably imaginative.

Soane's own house at 13 Lincoln's Inn Fields in London (1812–32) served as a kind of laboratory for architectural experiments and as a gallery to house his vast collection of art works and architectural fragments. The house is now a museum with remarkable interiors. A flat dome over the center of the breakfast room (**fig. 10.3**) is bordered by higher boundary spaces, with clerestory windows that admit daylight from hidden sources so that the dome seems to be a floating canopy. Round mirrors inserted into ornamental details here and in other rooms produce surprising effects of transparency, light, and illusion. The gallery space is a three-story-high chamber crammed with a fantastic collection of objects. Soane's highly personal way of putting together concepts drawn from ancient Greece and Rome, from the fantastic prison interiors of Piranesi's engravings, and from the Neoclassicism of Claude-Nicolas Ledoux and Etienne-Louis Boullée in France make him a key figure in the movement toward the ROMANTICISM of the later nineteenth century.

Regency Furniture

Furniture of the English Regency era was strongly influenced by French Directoire and Empire design, borrowing, as it did, from ancient Greek and Roman styles, and even from Egyptian, Indian, and medieval Gothic models. Mahogany and rosewood were favorite materials, usually in the form of veneers, and often with decorative inlays and ornamental details in brass. Black finishes and gilded details were also common. Table and chair legs often carried carving in fanciful, even bizarre, motifs such as a leg in the form of a lion or winged griffon with a head and body tapering to a single foot (called a MONOPODIA). Round and octagonal dining tables with pedestal bases became commonplace. Thomas Hope (1770–1831), a banker by profession, was also an enthusiastic furniture designer. His 1807 book *Household Furniture and Interior Decoration* illustrated his designs for what was then generally called "English Empire" furniture (**fig. 10.5**).

10.4 John Soane, Consols Office, Bank of England, London, 1798–9.

The various working spaces of the bank (now demolished) used monumental architectural elements to lend an air of grandeur to utilitarian functions. A dome on pendentives rises with a ring of statues below the skylight windows. Reserved classical detail edges the elements of the wall and ceiling surfaces.

10.5 Thomas Hope, illustration from *Household Furniture and Interior Decoration*, 1807.

Hope was a banker whose friendship with the French designer Charles Percier (see p. 127) led him to an interest in design. His book promoted what was sometimes called the "English Empire style," a Regency era development drawing on Percier's French work. In this grand room Hope suggests built-in couches with winged sphinx motifs, armchairs, and a table with other decoration of supposed Egyptian origin. The basic form of the room is simple, with framed pictures and ceiling surface ornament.

Revivals

The Romantic desire to experience life in the past—a past seen as wonderful, beautiful, perhaps sometimes frightening, but always rich in emotional content—developed in every aspect of art in the late eighteenth century. It came to a peak at the very time when the beginnings of the modern technological world were displacing so much of what had gone before. The Romantic novels of Sir Walter Scott, the poetry of Wordsworth, the music of Schubert, Beethoven, Schumann, and Brahms, the art of Géricault, Delacroix, Constable, and Turner all moved away from the logic and restraint of classicism toward more emotionally expressive directions. Romanticism in design led to an increasing interest in recreating or "reviving" the styles of the past. From the earliest Renaissance beginnings, there had been an interest in learning from the past and in borrowing elements to be used in a new context, but the idea of reproducing past design quite literally for modern uses is a nineteenth-century idea.

Greek Revival

The design of ancient Greece was the material for the first of a series of revivals. Visits by travelers to the Greek ruins at Paestum in Italy, as well as visits

to the Greek peninsula, the availability of books of beautifully engraved drawings, such as Stuart and Revett's *Antiquities of Athens*, and the exhibition of Greek vases and other artifacts in public museums and private collections encouraged enthusiasm for the idea that Greek art and design represented a peak in human aesthetic achievement. The step from Neoclassicism, with its roots in the Renaissance respect for ancient Rome, to the GREEK REVIVAL with its awareness of ancient Greek precedents fitted Romantic ideals of perfectionism very well.

Germany

The Greek Revival in Germany is usually associated with the work of Karl Friedrich Schinkel (1781–1841). Schinkel worked in a variety of styles ranging from Neoclassicism to Gothic, often providing designs for a particular building in several styles to permit a client a choice. His most successful works were adaptations of ancient classicism, using an order, entablature, and often a pediment, but his use of this material was quite free and imaginative. He never attempted a literal reproduction of any Greek building. Schinkel's best-known work is the museum in Berlin now known as Das Altes Museum (Old Museum, 1824–30). The facade is a simple portico of eighteen Ionic columns that stretch across the entire width of the building, supporting an entablature band. A simple

10.6 Karl Friedrich Schinkel, Upper Stair Gallery, Altes Museum, Berlin, 1824–30.

The engraving shows how the Greek revival in Germany was advanced by Schinkel's skilful adaptation of Greek architectural elements to this monumental building. In this engraving, based on Schinkel's own drawing, the many Ionic columns that surround the building externally can be seen through the four-columned entrance opening. The stair railings, floor, and ceiling designs are Schinkel's effort to extrapolate Greek practice into the forms of a nineteenth-century building.

10.7 Philip Hardwick and Philip Charles Hardwick, Great Hall, Euston Station, London, 1846–9.

A new building type, the railroad station, brought forth many monumental projects. This dignified hall (now demolished), which is lit by high windows, makes use of the Greek Ionic order at the far end, where stairs rise to give access to the doors and surrounding balcony.

attic block rises above at the center of the building. In this building, Schinkel faced a basic problem of the Greek Revival: the interiors of Greek temples, the only ancient Greek interior spaces of any importance, were relatively small and dark spaces not suited to any modern use. The Greek Revivalist had to invent a Greek approach to interior design and was thus driven to originality. This was at the time often criticized as unauthentic, but it now appears creative and interesting. In the Altes Museum behind the facade portico, an outdoor stair hall loggia gives access to a great central domed rotunda, the dome of which is fitted into the attic story and so is invisible externally. Stairs lead to an upper-level gallery (**fig. 10.6**) in the rotunda where exhibition galleries are placed in a rectangle with two inner light courts. The interiors are full of rich detail, paintings, sculpture, and Neoclassical architectural motifs arranged with great skill.

England

In England, the Neoclassicism of Regency design slipped easily into the more specifically neo-Greek of a revival. The British Museum, begun in 1823 by Sir Robert Smirke (1780–1867), has a pedimented, eight-columned portico using the Ionic order of the Erechtheum in Athens, which continues as a colonnade wrapped around the two side wings that project forward to form an entrance court—there are forty-four columns in all. The Greek Doric order was also put to use in England in ways that now seem surprising. The London terminal of the London and Birmingham Railway, Euston Station (1835–7), was approached through a pedimented Doric pavilion designed by Philip Hardwick (1792–1870). The station behind the entrance screen was an arrangement of outdoor sheds, destined to be replaced by a more monumental

station in 1846–9, also by Hardwick. It included a vast "great hall" (**fig. 10.7**) with stairs leading up to a screen of Ionic columns—a glorious space, but scarcely Greek in spirit. The difficulty of devising Greek interiors appropriate to Greek exterior architecture may have been a factor in bringing the Greek Revival to an early end in England.

United States

In the United States, Greek Revivalism was supported by an element of ideology. The newly independent nation was the first modern country to declare itself a democracy (actually a republic), just as ancient Greece had been. Towns were given Greek names—Syracuse, Utica, Schenectady, and Ithaca—in a flurry of enthusiasm for Greek art, literature, architecture, and governmental system. The aim was to recreate the glory of the Periclean age on the North American continent. In architecture and design, the Federal style, already inclined toward the use of Greek detail, moved into a Revival phase in which the aim was to create whole buildings that would appear to be Greek.

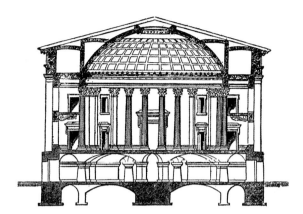

The Second Bank of the United States in Philadelphia (1818–24) by William Strickland (1788–1854) is the first American building to be designed in the form of a Greek temple; it has an eight-columned pedimented portico on the model of the Parthenon at front and rear. Windows were introduced along all four walls to make the interior spaces functional. In the interest of fire safety as well as monumentality, the building is entirely of stone, and all interior spaces are vaulted in a manner unknown to ancient Greece. The main banking room that occupies the center of the building is a handsome chamber with six columns along each side supporting an entablature below the simple barrel-vaulted ceiling.

The new federal government encouraged Greek Revivalism by commissioning a number of official buildings in the increasingly popular style. In New York, the firm of Town and Davis (Ithiel Town, 1784–1844, and Alexander Jackson Davis, 1803–92) produced another Parthenon-like temple to be the U.S. Customs House (1833–42; now called the Federal Hall). It is also an all-stone building with Doric porticos front and back and windows along the sides alternating with pilasters. The interiors were largely the work of John Frazee (d. 1852), who was the designer of the main public room, a rotunda with a circle of Corinthian columns and pilasters supporting a coffered dome fitted under the main gable roof (**fig. 10.8**). This totally non-Greek interior space is another reflection of the continuing problem of dealing with interiors of what appear externally to be Greek temples.

Greek Revival buildings that made freer adaptations of Greek precedents were often functionally successful as well as dignified and impressive. Robert Mills (1781–1855), best known for his 1836 design for the Washington Monument, was the architect for a number of government buildings

including the Old Patent Office (now the National Portrait Gallery) with its Doric portico, and the Treasury Building (1836–42) with its seemingly endless Ionic colonnade. The Patent Office has many simple and dignified stairways and vaulted spaces, with only restrained efforts at Greek detail.

William Strickland worked in a freer and more creative version of the Greek idiom after his temple bank in Philadelphia. In Philadelphia, his Exchange building (1832–4) uses the Corinthian order for a semicircular portico that is topped by a tower imitative of the ancient Choragic Monument of Lysicrates in Athens. A similar tower motif tops the building usually considered to be Strickland's masterpiece, the Tennessee State Capitol at Nashville (1845–59). It is a simple, rectangular block with eight-columned pedimented Ionic porticos at each end and six-columned porticos without pediments at the center of each side. The monument-topped tower makes this one of the few American state capitol buildings without a dome. Internally, lobbies and stairs and the legislative chambers all use Greek details in ways that are restrained and handsome.

The Greek Revival quickly became a favored style for residential building, with results that spread from the northeast states into the south, and into the mid-west as far as the Mississippi River. The Lee Mansion at Arlington, Virginia (1802–26), largely the design of its original owner, G. W. P. Custis, in simple Federal style, was transformed by the addition of a massive Doric portico and pediment by George Hadfield (c. 1764–1826). The wood paneling, fireplace, and window and door trim are typical of Federal style, although there are arched openings and a triple-arch separation between parlor and dining room that give these rooms a special character. The Greek portico gives the building the form that became known as a TEMPLE HOUSE. Hundreds of such houses were built, often with designs developed by local carpenter-builders who found their Greek details in books. One such was the *Modern Builder's Guide*, by Minard Lafever (1798–1854), a successful professional practitioner in the Greek vocabulary. Small houses were generally built entirely of wood, and the skill with which the stone detail of Greek temples was reproduced in that material is remarkable. Temple houses often exhibit strange compromises in the effort to fit reasonable dwelling plans—complete with windows and chimneys where needed—into Greek

10.8 Town and Davis with John Frazee, U.S. Customs House (now Federal Hall), New York, 1833–42.

A large public hall was required within a Greek revival, temple-like exterior, something not developed in ancient Greece. Frazee approached the problem by inserting a round domed hall with an oculus skylight. Although surrounded by Greek Corinthian columns, the effect is more Roman than Greek.

10.9 Row house, New York, 1832.

The typical city house in Greek revival style is now called the Merchant's House Museum. The dining room and front parlor are separated by an opening with sliding doors. Greek Ionic columns flank the opening, and plaster detail uses Greek-inspired elements. The furniture seen here is by Duncan Phyfe, and the patterned carpet is typical of the period. The elaborate window drapery would be usual in the home of wealthy people. The hanging gaslight fixtures are of a somewhat later date than the house.

temple forms. Row houses in the large cities could not be made into temple houses, but they were often fitted with small doorway porticos such as those surviving on the handsome row along Washington Square North in New York. Within such houses, major rooms were made Greek with woodwork and plaster details, egg and dart or Greek key moldings, and even pilasters or columns using one of the orders—Ionic was a special favorite. There is a fine rendering of such a room, thought to be designed by Town and Davis for a New York City town house, showing two pairs of Ionic columns separating front and back parlors in a city house. Greek-inspired furniture, klismos chairs, and a sofa with upholstery embroidered in Greek motifs are set beneath Greek cornice moldings and a plaster ceiling rosette. Even the wall-to-wall carpeting of the floor uses a vaguely Greek pattern. The modest row house built in New York for Joseph Brewster in 1832 (now called the

Merchant's House Museum), is remarkable for having quite well preserved interiors (**fig. 10.9**).

From about 1820 until the 1850s, Greek Revival design was applied to almost every kind of building. Greek churches were built in great numbers. Some, such as St. Paul's in Richmond, Virginia (1845), add a quite un-Greek tower to a temple plan with, in this case, Corinthian columns in a semicircle behind the altar. Others, like the 13th Street Presbyterian Church in New York (1847), are simple brick meeting houses made Greek by the addition of a Doric portico, well executed here in wood. There are Greek college buildings (Amherst, Washington, and Lee), Greek insane asylums (Raleigh, North Carolina), Greek courthouses, and Greek hotels.

In the south, Greek porticos turned out to be genuinely functional for the great mansions built on plantations where their shade helped keep interiors comfortably cool. The Hermitage near Nashville (*c.* 1835); Oak Alley (also called Bon Sejour, 1839); Madewood, an Ionic temple house of 1848—both near New Orleans in Louisiana—and D'Evereux (1840) near Natchez, Mississippi, are all examples of the many surviving great plantation houses of simple symmetrical plan with porticos rich in Greek detail.

Gothic Revival

United States

Impatience with the less practical aspects of Greek Revivalism, criticism of departures from archeological accuracy, and probably simple boredom with the monotony of such wide use of a limited design vocabulary eventually began to undermine the Greek Revival. Also, the taste for Romanticism turned toward more varied and more flexible sources. After all, although ancient Greece could be seen in a Romantic light by a Lord Byron viewing ruins by moonlight, Greek art and architecture were at base classical and disciplined. Readers of Romantic novels longed for settings evocative of Sir Walter Scott's *Ivanhoe*. The English Pre-Raphaelite painters with their rediscovery of medieval art as a precedent for their work offered another connection to the Gothic era.

Medieval Gothic design, known in America only through verbal description and the engravings in European books, was inherently exotic and appealed to a public satiated with ancient Greece.

10.10 Richard Upjohn, Trinity Church, New York, 1846.

The Gothic revival produced this carefully detailed version of an English parish church of medieval date. Upjohn had wanted to design a church with a simple timber roof, but his client's building committee wanted vaulting, here executed in plaster in imitation of stone. With its colorful stained glass, the interior gives an impressive illusion of the Gothic of the Middle Ages, despite its nineteenth-century origin.

Richard Upjohn (1802–78) was born and trained as a cabinet maker in England. His Trinity Church (**fig. 10.10**; 1846) at the end of Wall Street in New York is a convincing version of an English Gothic parish church; it stands only a short distance from the Greek temple Federal Hall by Town and Davis completed only four years earlier. The vaulted nave, stained glass, and rich Gothic detail gave Americans a first view of medieval design of the sort that was already being revived in England.

Almost immediately, other specialists in Gothic design emerged. James Renwick, Jr. (1818–95), won a competition with a Gothic design for Grace Church on Broadway in New York (1843–6), a rival to Trinity Church in its sensitive and accurate recreation of English Gothic church building. Renwick's most important GOTHIC REVIVAL work was St. Patrick's Cathedral in New York (completed 1878). This was modeled on French Gothic examples, complete with cruciform plan,

aisles, ambulatory, clerestory, and stained glass. The vaulting which appears to be stone is actually papier-mâché, with the result that the external flying buttresses that would restrain the thrust of stone vaulting are absent. While Gothic forms may seem to have a certain appropriateness in the design of churches, the style quickly spread to every phase of architecture and interior design, including many sorts of public buildings and residential design. Renwick's design for the original Main Building of the Smithsonian Institution in Washington (1844–6) is also medieval in style, although in this case it is Romanesque or Norman in inspiration, with picturesque towers externally and Gothic detail internally.

Town and Davis, alert to the shift in popular taste, abandoned their Greek enthusiasm and, particularly in the contribution of A. J. Davis, became Gothic Revivalists. The mansion overlooking the Hudson River near Tarrytown, New

10.11 Town and Davis, Lyndhurst, near Tarrytown, New York, 1838–65.

The interiors of this mansion, which is in Gothic revival style, have some Gothic detail to match the building's ornate exterior. Pointed arches, paneling, tracery, and crockets executed in wood relate to the leaded glass of the windows. Statues stand in niches to the right and left of the window bay. The furniture attempts to offer related style with carved wood detail.

York, called Lyndhurst (1838–65) is a remarkable essay by Davis in the application of Gothic elements, including a grand tower, to the design of a country house. The plan of the house as originally built was symmetrical, but when it was enlarged in 1864 (by Davis) for a new owner, the changes converted the plan to one of picturesque ASYMMETRY. Most of the rooms are filled with Gothic detail—ceilings with plaster ribs suggestive of Gothic vaulting, pointed windows with tracery and stained glass inserts, and much carved ornamental detail (**fig. 10.11**). The billiard room–art gallery has a wooden roof structure suggesting a baronial hall. Davis designed furniture in what was supposed to be a Gothic mode for the house: chairs with carved backs (called WHEELBACK), suggesting Gothic rose window tracery, an octagonal dining table with Gothic carving, and beds with massive Gothic pointed-arch head- and foot-board details.

Davis was friendly with the landscape gardener Andrew Jackson Downing (1815–52). Downing's

books *Cottage Residences* (1842) and *The Architecture of Country Houses* (1850), with their many engravings showing plans and perspectives of houses in a range of sizes, became popular and influential. Designs were shown in a variety of styles, including a simplified version of Gothic intended for wood construction. The kind of building called CARPENTER GOTHIC, produced by local builders cutting pointed-arch forms in wood with the aid of the widely used SCROLL SAW, became a staple of American house building for many years. Exterior walls given vertical emphasis with board and batten siding and pointed-arch windows, often with leaded glass, were favorite elements for houses and small village churches.

England

The Gothic Revival in America was at least in part stimulated by a comparable revival in England. Even in the late eighteenth century there were English forays into the Romantic implications of medievalism, with the building of country houses such as Strawberry Hill, near London, a modest cottage remodeled in 1750 by Horace Walpole (1717–97) with interiors that are lacy, delicate, and playful interpretations of the Gothic mode. It is a surprise to learn that Robert Adam was among the professionals that Walpole employed, working here in his notion of a Gothic vocabulary. Beginning in 1796, a wealthy English eccentric, William Beckford, commissioned the building of a huge mansion on Salisbury Plain in Wiltshire, designed by James Wyatt (1746–1813) and given the name Fonthill Abbey (**fig. 10.12**). It was an astonishing agglomeration of battlements, pinnacles, and towers with vast Gothic halls and a 276 foot high tower above an octagonal vaulted chamber—all conceived as a kind of stage set on which the dramas of medieval life could be replayed. Fonthill Abbey is known only from paintings and engravings; built largely in wood and stucco, the tower collapsed in a wind storm, turning the entire structure into a suitably romantic ruin.

The emotional and aesthetic leanings toward Gothic medievalism were soon backed up by a body of criticism and philosophy. As the Regency gave way to the Victorian era, a movement toward a sternly moralistic religiosity developed. Queen Victoria, herself a model of piety and rectitude, became a symbolic leader for this turn toward a desire for a Christian mode of design, in contrast to the classicism of Greece and Rome which were, after all, pagan civilizations. The era in which Christianity dominated Europe was, of course, the Middle Ages, and its Gothic design had an obvious connection with the church. The romantic spirit and moralistic theories thus joined to urge Gothicism as the only virtuous and acceptable style. Several writers became polemicists for this philosophical line of criticism. John Ruskin (1819–1900), in his *Seven Lamps of Architecture* (1849), sets forth a highly moralistic theory of architecture in which "good" design is not merely an aesthetic matter, but a matter of moral virtue as well. According to Ruskin, a return to the "Christian" style was the only proper and acceptable direction for art and design to take.

Ruskin was not himself a designer, but his themes were advanced with parallel force by a highly professional architect, Augustus Welby N. Pugin (1812–52), the author of *Contrasts* (1836), *True Principles of Pointed or Christian Architecture* (1841), and a number of other works in which illustrations are used to make direct comparisons between classical and Gothic approaches to similar design problems—always much to the disadvantage of the classical which was made in many of the plates to seem foolish or absurd. The intensity of Pugin's attack on classicism and the moralistic tone of his arguments set off what is often called "the battle of the styles" in which Greek and Gothic Revivalists aired opposing views with considerable heat. Many architects and designers were happy to work in either style as their clients might request.

Pugin not only propagandized in favor of the Gothic mode, he also urged a *true* or *pure* Gothic that would rise above the decorative trivialities of the first Gothic Revivalists. When the time came to build the Houses of Parliament (the New Palace of Westminster) in London, the architect chosen was Sir Charles Barry (1795–1860), whose previous work had been in a sedate Neoclassical style. His logical and orderly plans for this large and complex building were well received, but pressure was brought (probably generated by Victoria herself) for an English Gothic treatment, outside and in. Barry turned to Pugin for direction, and the two men together produced the famous building that became a symbol of British strength and power at its Victorian peak.

Externally, the Houses of Parliament display the symmetry and formal organization of a classical building, except for the variations introduced by towers and the presence of the genuinely medieval Westminster Hall. The surface detail, however, is Gothic, representing Pugin's knowledge and skill— marred only by a certain mechanical repetitiousness, more modern than medieval. Iron joists, products of the Industrial Revolution, were used, hidden behind the seeming Gothic detail. Pugin was the leading designer of the interiors, which include some of the finest work of the Gothic Revival. The Peers' Lobby, the Victoria Lobby, St. Stephen's Hall, the Central Octagon, and St. Stephen's Porch added at the end of the genuinely medieval Westminster Hall all demonstrate Pugin's Gothic Revivalism at its best. The chamber for the House of Lords (**fig. 10.13**) is probably the most spectacular of these rooms—the chamber for the House of Commons went through several alterations that left it not to the satisfaction of either Barry or Pugin (or, for that matter, of the Members who met there).

Pugin designed many churches in the Gothic idiom, but their very correctness in imitation of

10.12 James Wyatt, south end of St. Michael's Gallery, Fonthill Abbey, Wiltshire, England, from 1795.

This extraordinary house, shown in a 1823 engraving, was built for an eccentric English client, William Beckford, who was early in demanding the style that was to dominate the Gothic revival. Despite its name, it was not an abbey, but the stained glass, tracery, and fan vaulting, simulated in plaster, was typical of the many grand spaces with subtle coloring. Red carpet, curtains, and chair cushions set off the more delicate pink and grey of painted surfaces. In 1825 the building was destroyed when a wind storm blew over its 276 foot high wooden tower.

10.13 Charles Barry and Augustus Welby N. Pugin, New Palace of Westminster (Houses of Parliament), House of Lords, London, 1836–52.

Barry's orderly plan for the extensive cluster of buildings was clothed in a Gothic ornamental treatment, which was urged by Pugin who had primary responsibility for the interiors. This great chamber, with its traceried stained glass, Gothic arches, and paneled ceiling, could easily be mistaken for a medieval interior, although it was built during the early Victorian era.

their medieval prototypes makes them seem some-what dull. The small country church of St. Mary's at West Tofts, Norfolk (1845–50), is one of the most successful. Although many examples have beautifully detailed furnishings and ornament, the vitality that came from slow building with contri-butions of carving and ornament from generations of craftsmen, is missing in these works that were produced from drawings made by (or at the direc-tion of) one architect working in a modern profes-sional way.

Pugin had few opportunities to apply his theo-ries to residential projects. He was active and successful as a designer of furniture, textiles, wall-paper, decorative tile, stained glass, and metalwork, and published illustrated books of designs in these fields that exerted strong influence in the develop-ment of design in the Victorian era for many years after his death.

The work of William Butterfield (1814–1900) is not as archeologically correct as the Gothic of Pugin, but it has qualities of originality and strength that make it interesting even when it may border on ugliness. All Saints, Margaret Street, in London (1849–59) is a brick building squeezed on to a cramped site along with its vicarage and a church school together with a massive tower. The red brick walls are striped and patterned with bands of darker brick. Inside, simple Gothic forms are covered with glazed brick, tiles, and marbles in various colors forming strong geometric patterns (**fig. 10.14**). Butterfield's intention in his use of Gothic style was not romantic or even aesthetic; it grew rather from the conviction that it was the only structurally valid system of building. His ornament was an original approach to expressive detail for sound structure—a foretaste of the emphasis on "honesty" and struc-tural expression that would develop in the modernism of the twentieth century.

The Industrial Revolution

The term Industrial Revolution is used to describe the complex of developments that transformed Britain, then other western European nations and the United States, into modern industrial nations. It is helpful, in trying to grasp the extent of change in the last two centuries, to consider what tech-nology was available in the eighteenth century. The French encyclopedist Denis Diderot (1713–84) produced in his many-volume work documenta-

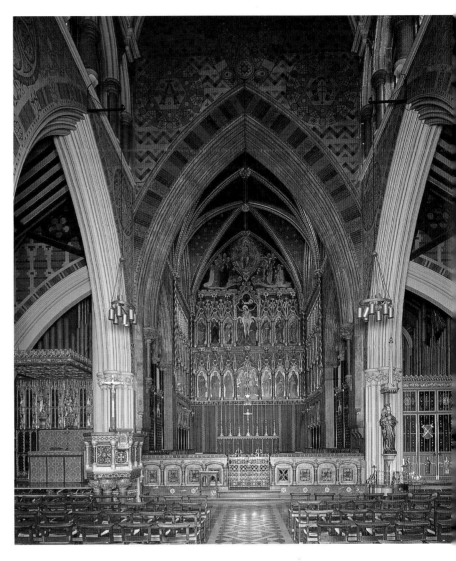

tion of the processes of industry in the eighteenth century. The articles, illustrated with wonderfully detailed engraving, show the techniques of glass blowing, shipbuilding, cabinet making, and dozens of other trades. Virtually all work is *hand* work—not, of course, without tools and equipment, but the tools are simple and the equipment is hand made. There is no assembly line, no machinery.

The most advanced machinery shown by Diderot is the wooden gearing of a mill grinding hops for the making of beer. The power is supplied by four horses walking in a circle in the basement of the mill. A windmill is shown, entirely built of wood even to the wheels and gears. The only sources of power are human, horse, water, and wind, all of the last three only used in limited ways. Through all of human history from the stone age until the late eighteenth century, these had been

10.14 William Butterfield, All Saints, Margaret Street, London, 1849-59.

Although Butterfield's work can be viewed as belonging to the Gothic revival, it has an energy and originality that goes beyond historic imitation. The great arches and buttress half-arches have an almost harsh forceful-ness, which is accented by the generous use of floor and wall tiles, which are in the strongly contrasting colors typical of much Victorian work.

the *only* ways in which things could be made. A quick survey of the possessions of any modern family will reveal few, if any, hand-made objects. The plumbing fixtures, the lamps, the stove, and refrigerator; the telephone, radio, television, and computer; the furniture, the bedding, the clothing—not to speak of the car, the lawn mower, even the children's toys: all are factory made, and most would be useless without the ready supply of pumped water, electric current, gasoline, and spare parts which are in turn products of industrial processes.

Early Industrialization and Inventions

The first wave of industrialization was based on a few key inventions. The steam engine, the first great "prime mover" to be turned to use as a source of power for pumping water and running the machinery of textile mills, was developed by a series of inventors culminating with James Watt (1736–1819) of Glasgow. His stationary engines of 1769 to 1788 offered the first practical alternative to hand, horse, wind, and water as a source of power. Steam engines and the boiler that fed them required metals for their working parts. Iron had been known and steel made in small quantities for special purposes (armor, weapons, and knife blades) since ancient times, but the quantities needed for engines required mines and blast furnaces, foundries and steel mills. Transport of coal from mines, of iron from foundries, and of steel from mills to the shops where engines could be made called for something better than ox carts pulled along muddy roads. Making a road of metal rails, a "rail road" with cars—no longer pulled by horses or oxen but by the special mobile version of the steam engine, the locomotive—made it easier to build more steam engines, to make more rails for more railroads, and to bring raw materials to factories and take their products to markets. The building of iron ships powered by steam engines introduced similar improvements in sea travel and the inter-continental transport of goods. The power loom of Joseph Cartwright (1785) and the steam engine together made possible a textile mill capable of producing cheap cloth in quantity.

The products of engine-powered factories required less hand labor and so could be inexpensive. Profits earned by mills and factories could be used to build more factories, making their owners wealthy and, eventually, making the countries that turned to industrialization rich and powerful. England became a dominant world power. France, Germany, the United States, and, eventually, other countries rose in wealth and status as the process of industrialization progressed. While all of this was happening, the world of design paid little attention except to offer a few complaints about the noise and dirt associated with the new inventions. The revivalists, Greek or Gothic, took little notice of the great changes taking place in their world. John Nash used iron columns in the Brighton Pavilion, Euston Station had a Greek entrance gate, Latrobe designed a steam-powered water pumping station with Greek detail. Steam engines often incorporated structural parts of cast iron in the form of classical columns. Locomotives sometimes had domes shaped like Roman temples or curiously squat versions of Greek columns. Wealthy clients were less often titled aristocrats and more frequently self-made industrialists or the managers and professionals who served industry. The segments of populations who would have been "peasants" working in agriculture and living in farm houses became the "mill-hands" who worked in factories and lived in cities, most often in grim slums made up of squalid tenements.

Industry and Interiors

The impact of the early phases of the Industrial Revolution on interior design was more technical than aesthetic. First steps toward modern plumbing, lighting, and heating appeared, making some important elements of earlier interiors obsolescent. Cast iron became an inexpensive and practical material for the making of stoves. Stoves heated with wood, and then coal, had major advantages in terms of efficiency and convenience over the open fireplace (**fig. 10.15**). Ready availability of coal resulted from improved mining and rail transport. For cooking, the special form of stove called a kitchen range, also of cast iron, made kitchen fireplaces obsolete. Kitchen ranges were developed, with water reservoirs kept warm by the stove fire to provide hot water as needed. In cities, central piped water systems began to appear, the pressure provided by steam pumps that could lift water to a high reservoir or water tower so that gravity would make water available to bathrooms on the upper floors of buildings. Running water, flush toilets, and the drain trap that blocks the escape of sewer gases were all introduced into general use in the 1800s. Bath tubs and showers were luxuries at first but eventually became standard in city houses and at least sometimes in rural houses as well. Systems of central heating gradually replaced stoves. Coal-fired furnaces were placed in cellars to heat warm air which was circulated to living spaces through pipes and grilles called "registers." The larger spaces of churches, theaters, schools, hospitals, and public buildings could also be heated by warm air systems. Furnaces were also arranged to heat water so that piped hot water could be available in bathrooms.

Artificial lighting, confined to candles until the end of the eighteenth century, was improved through a series of inventions. Oil lamps that burned a fuel called colza oil (made from a vegetable seed) were developed with wick holders and feed mechanism. That could be factory made in quantity and provided better light than candles with less inconvenience. Whale oil replaced colza oil as a fuel and was eventually replaced by "mineral oil," that is, petroleum and its derivative, kerosene. Various improved burners such as those using a mantle, a curtain of ash that produced a bright incandescent glow, gave better light than a direct flame. The development of oil lamps with their functional advantages and varied appearance displaced candlesticks, sconces, and chandeliers in many applications. The invention of illuminating gas, originally coal gas, made possible the gradual introduction of piped gas for lighting supplied by centralized city systems. The same gas was also usable for cooking ranges and for various heating devices such as the gas grate which could be placed in fireplaces to make an open fire unnecessary.

The visible evidences of these technological developments remained minor in the early nineteenth century. The bathroom emerged as a new kind of space, but it was usually given a minor place in house and other building plans and treated in a utilitarian way, perhaps with some marble trim or colorful tiles in luxury examples. Kitchens, viewed as the workplaces of servants, were often early exercises in functional design by default since they were not given any particular aesthetic attention. In living spaces, the role of the fireplace and mantel diminished, giving way to a small coal grate, a "parlor stove," and finally to a hot air register inserted where the fireplace opening would have been.

10.15 Restored flat, tenement building, Glasgow, c. 1892.

The Industrial Revolution brought workers into parts of cities where living space was scarce and expensive. Factory workers and their families often were crowded into tiny quarters, such as this room, where cooking stove, alcove bed, and clothes drying lines share the same small space. The restoration has probably made this room less squalid than it would have been in its original state. The neat wall clock and small objects introduce an improbable touch of elegance. The radio is, of course, modern.

Iron and Glass

The Industrial Revolution brought new ways of building that resulted from the interaction of new needs and new technology. The availability of iron as a material of great strength and low cost, produced for engines and railroad rails, introduced a new alternative to wood and masonry as building materials. At the same time the need for great bridges to carry railroads and great train sheds for stations presented new engineering problems. Engineering emerged as a technological profession which had little connection with the gentlemanly aesthetic concerns that had been the bases of earlier architectural practice. Although early engineering structures at first had little impact on the designers of Greek and Gothic Revival buildings, they demonstrated new techniques that were destined to bring about basic changes in design comparable to those developing in every other aspect of life.

The first iron bridge was built in England to span the River Severn at Coalbrookdale, Shropshire, in 1779, its arches cast in sections in the foundry of Abraham Darby III. Thomas Telford (1757–1834) was the designer of a major aqueduct, Pont-Cysylltau in Wales, built in 1805 to carry a canal across the River Dee. Great stone piers support nineteen arches made up of cast-iron segments bolted together. Telford designed a great suspension bridge to carry a carriage road from the mainland of Wales to the island of Anglesey across the Menai Strait. This opened in 1826: it had a span of 579 feet, and the roadway was held high enough above water level to permit large sailing ships to pass underneath. The suspension elements are not cables, but chains made of great iron bars bolted together so that the chain could hang in the graceful catenary curve typical of all such bridges. The bridge is still in regular use carrying modern traffic. A giant ship built of iron, the *Great Eastern* of 1851 designed by Isambard Kingdom Brunel (1806–59), was powered by two sets of steam engines, one driving paddle wheels and the other turning a screw propeller. Its luxurious passenger accommodations were decorated in the prevailing ornate taste.

While the building of engines, railroads, ships, and bridges may seem to have little connection with interior design, it was the techniques for the use of industrial materials developed in these projects that made new ways of constructing buildings possible. Railroad terminals needed sheds to protect trains, passengers, and baggage on a scale that would reach across many tracks. Wood and masonry were not ideal materials for the purpose and engineers designing railways found it logical to apply their knowledge and build in iron. Glass, now factory made in quantity in large sheets, was an ideal light and transparent material for filling in iron frames to make train sheds. The two side by side that covered King's Cross Station in London (**fig. 10.16**; 1850–2) were designed by Lewis Cubitt (1799–1883); here the masonry facade reveals the iron sheds within in two great arches separated by a simple clock tower. There is no Gothic, Greek, or other historically inspired detail. London's Paddington Station (1852–4) has glass and iron train sheds by Brunel.

England: Paxton

The greatest nineteenth-century glass and iron building was built in London in 1851. It had been decided to hold a "Great Exhibition," what would now be called a World's Fair, in London to celebrate the greatness of Victorian England. The nations of the world were invited to send exhibits of their finest products in art and industry to be shown in Hyde Park in a huge exhibition hall. Queen Victoria's consort, Prince Albert, was put in charge of organizing the project, and turned his

attention to finding proposals for a suitable building. Various architects presented schemes too elaborate, too expensive, or otherwise impractical. It was reported that a chief gardener (really an estate manager) for the great estate of Chatsworth, Joseph

INSIGHTS

The Public's Perception of Crystal Palace

The radical nature of Joseph Paxton's design for Crystal Palace in London drew sharp condemnation from many quarters, adding to criticism of the very notion of a "Great Exhibition." The writer and art critic John Ruskin dismissed it as a "cucumber frame between two chimneys," adding,

In the year 1851, when all that glittering roof was built in order to exhibit all the petty arts of our own fashionable luxury—carved bedsteads of Vienna, glued toys of Switzerland and gay jewellery from France—in that very year, I say, the greatest pictures of Venetian masters were rotting at Venice in the rain for want of a roof to cover them. [1]

Politicians followed suit:

Are the elms [of Hyde Park] to be sacrificed for one of the greatest frauds, greatest humbugs, greatest absurdities every known .... [T]hey are going to expend £26,000 on this building when the Irish poor are starving. [2]

However, when Paxton's design was completed, and the exhibition opened, Queen Victoria made the following entry in her journal:

The glimpse of that transept through the iron gates, the waving palms, flowers, statues, myriads of people filling the galleries and seats around, with the flourish of trumpets as we entered, gave us a sensation which I can never forget, and I felt much moved .... The sight as we came to the middle, with the beautiful crystal fountain just in front was magical—so vast, so glorious, so touching—a day to live forever. [3]

Even *The Times*, an early critic, conceded:

There was yesterday witnessed a sight the like of which has never before and which in the nature of things can never be repeated. They who were so fortunate as to see it hardly knew what most to admire or in what form to clothe the sense of wonder...the edifice, the treasures of art collected therein .... Above them rose a glittering arch far more lofty than the vaults of our noblest cathedrals. [4]

1. John Ruskin, *The Opening of the Crystal Palace*, 1854, p. 1; 2. *Hansard Parliamentary Report*, June 18, 1850; 3. Patrick Beaver, *The Crystal Palace* (London, 1970) 4. *The Times*, editorial, May 2, 1851

10.16 Lewis Cubitt, train shed, King's Cross Station, London, 1850–2.

The two parallel train sheds (one of which is shown here) that Cubitt designed are typical of the engineering achievements developed to meet the demands of the Industrial Revolution. The semicircular arches supporting glass skylights were originally constructed in laminated wood and later replaced with iron. Victorian ornamentalism here gives way to a functional emphasis that points toward the modern era.

10.17 Joseph Paxton, Crystal Palace, London, 1851.

The famous building, seen in a contemporary lithograph, housed the Great Exhibition, a showcase of Victorian prosperity and taste. It occupied one of the first buildings of truly modern concept. Its iron frame and the glass walls and roof, with their functional simplicity, contrast strangely with the display of florid, overdecorated goods and sentimental statuary. The great trees in this interior predated the building and remained after its removal.

10.19 (*right*) Pierre-François-Henri Labrouste, Bibliothèque Nationale, Paris, 1859–67.

A square reading room is topped by nine domes, each with an iron frame supporting panels of tile. Light comes from the oculae in the domes. The extreme thinness of the columns, permitted by the strength of the iron, makes for an open and beautiful space.

10.18 Pierre-François-Henri Labrouste, Bibliothèque St. Genevieve, Paris, 1844–50.

The reading room, the main space of the library, has one of the first all-iron structural systems to be put to architectural use. The outer walls are stone, but the support structure is iron, with the slim row of columns down the center of the space supporting the iron arches of the roof. The detail of the arches is ornamental but also suited to the wrought-iron structure.

Paxton (1803–65), had constructed a conservatory for tropical plants—a greenhouse—all of iron and glass. A meeting was arranged where Paxton proposed to Prince Albert a vast greenhouse of similar construction for the exhibition. Despite uncertainties and protests, Paxton's proposal was finally accepted and constructed with the aid of the engineering firm of Fox and Henderson.

The building, soon known as the Crystal Palace (**fig. 10.17**), was made up of iron frames, columns, and girders produced in quantity at a foundry, bolted together on site, and glazed with sheets of factory-made glass. It was unlike anything ever built before: a vast internal space (it was 1851 feet long and had an area of more than 800,000 square feet) with structural elements so slim as to be almost negligible, glass walls and roof. A giant elm tree on the site was left undisturbed within the building. The beautifully simple and airy interior was greatly admired by the crowds that attended the exhibition so that, when the time came to remove the building, it was decided to dismantle it and reassemble it at Sydenham, then on the edge of London. It stood there until 1936 when it was destroyed by a fire.

We can see from the many engravings and color prints that were made of the building how strikingly modern the vast interior space was—indeed, Crystal Palace appears in every architectural history as the first fully realized achievement of what much later came to be called modernism. The

exhibits that filled the Crystal Palace during the Great Exhibition were also thoroughly documented in well-illustrated publications. They form a strange contrast with the building, as they are generally of the decorated or over-decorated sort that became the norm of "high Victorian" design (see Chapter 11).

Iron and glass were increasingly used as building materials in the second half of the nineteenth century, most often for buildings that were thought of as strictly utilitarian—train sheds, market halls, mills and other factory buildings, and exhibition halls—all structures where the economy and ease of iron construction were more important than monumentality.

France: Labrouste, Baltard, and Eiffel

The French architect Pierre-François-Henri Labrouste (1801–75) was trained at the Ecole des Beaux-Arts in Paris and won the Grand Prix de Rome that gave him a five-year period of study in Italy. His first major work was the library of St. Geneviève in Paris (**fig. 10.18**; 1844–50). Its design is forward looking in a way quite independent of the teachings of the Ecole des Beaux-Arts. The building has a simple exterior of stone, its rows of arched windows framed with Neoclassical detail so restrained as to be hardly noticeable. Carved into the stone panels below the upper windows are the names of 810 authors, arranged in alphabetical order. A central entrance door leads to a large hall where square Neoclassical columns support iron segmental arches that in turn support a plain, flat ceiling. On either side of this vestibule are stacks and a room for special collections. The entrance hall passes through the building like a tunnel to

reach a grand double stair at the rear; this in turn gives access to the great reading room that occupies the entire upper floor. The walls are lined with bookshelves with windows high above. A row of thin iron columns on the center line of the room supports the two simple barrel vaults, made up of iron arches, that support the curved plaster ceiling. The ironwork is perforated in a decorative pattern with no historical precedents. The provision of gas light made it possible for this to be the first French library to remain open after dark.

The much larger Bibliothèque Nationale in Paris (1859–67), also designed by Labrouste, is a more complex building. In the main reading room (**fig. 10.19**), sixteen thin iron columns support interconnecting iron arches to form nine square bays. Each is topped by a dome made up from curved plates of earthenware ceramic. An oculus window at the center of each dome floods the space with light. The outer walls are of masonry, independent of the iron structure, and are lined with three tiers of bookshelves with balconies for access. Adjacent to the reading room, the *magasin central* or stacks occupy an equally large space filled by four tiers of stack shelving, all of iron with open

grid stairs and floors, permitting daylight from roof skylights to light all of the levels. A glass wall permits a view from the reading room into the stacks. A high, open central space runs through the stack room, with bridges for easy access from one side to the other. Ornamentation is minimal, giving the stack room an entirely functional, and therefore surprisingly modern, aspect.

Other iron structures for various uses gradually became more common in the nineteenth century. The great wholesale food markets of Paris, Les Halles Centrales, begun in 1853 by Victor Baltard (1805–74), were a virtual neighborhood of iron pavilions with covered streets until their demolition in 1964. Exhibition buildings, such as the Galerie des Machines built for the Paris International Exhibition of 1889, used giant trusses with pivot points at their bases and at a center point where the trusses meet to form a "three-hinged arch" with a span of more than 480 feet. The purpose of the pivots is to allow movement as thermal expansion and contraction occur in the metal of the trusses. The French desire to demonstrate equality or superiority in engineering as compared to English achievements is demonstrated by these stuctures and, close by, for the same exhibition, by the famous tower by Gustave Eiffel (1832–1923). It was for many years the tallest structure ever built. The elevators that serve the tower were evidence that tall buildings could be made useful to the general public. The restaurants on the platforms of the tower combined the engineering vocabulary of iron with the fashionable taste for decorative clutter. Eiffel's earlier work had included several great iron railroad bridges and the iron-structured interior of a large Paris department store, Bon Marché (**fig. 10.20**; 1876), where the iron structure and glass roofs above open courts allow daylight to flood the interior.

The Regency and the several revival styles that followed it can be thought of as ending the sequence of stylistic developments dating back to antiquity. The changes brought about by the Industrial Revolution upset this long continuity in design history. Social and economic changes relating to the mechanization of so many aspects of production created new circumstances that designers struggled to deal with. The VICTORIAN era in the second half of the nineteenth century, the subject of the following chapter, is marked by the successes and failures of the efforts to come to terms with new realities.

10.20 Louis-Charles Boileau and Gustave Eiffel, Bon Marché, Paris, 1876.

Grand stairways lead to the upper levels of this Paris department store, seen in an engraving. The slim and elegant iron structure permits spectacular views of the open central space and supports the roof of glass skylights. The crowds of fancily dressed shoppers found the store a source of entertainment as well as a place to purchase goods.

11

The Victorian Era

Until the nineteenth century, European society had been made up of a small, powerful, and wealthy "upper class" of titled aristocrats whose wealth was based on feudal land holdings inherited from generation to generation, and a very large class of "peasants," mostly agricultural workers on the land owned by the titled class. The middle class of tradesmen, skilled craftsmen, and professionals was so small as to be a minor factor in the social and economic order. In the nineteenth century, the aristocratic upper class began to lose its domination for both political and economic reasons. The class of agricultural peasants decreased in size as work in mills, factories, and mines supplanted farm work. The growing middle class was made up of a rising stratum of society that learned to turn the Industrial Revolution into a source of new wealth. The rich and powerful who lived in great houses, chateaux, and palaces had always been surrounded by richly decorated objects, ornate rugs, and draperies, all hand made of costly materials by skilled craftsmen. The new middle class could afford such things now that they were inexpensively produced in quantity; the decorative and the ornamental became the dominant theme of all design.

The Roots of Victorian Style

The long reign of Britain's Queen Victoria (1837–1901) overlapped the period of revivals and the "battle of the styles," and coincided with a major part of the Industrial Revolution and the ARTS AND CRAFTS or AESTHETIC MOVEMENT in England. As a style, however, "Victorian" has come to mean an aspect of nineteenth-century design in England and America (and parallel developments in other European countries) characterized by proliferation of decorative, sometimes over-decorative, ornamentation. Many twentieth-century design historians and critics have dismissed Victorian design as representing a nadir of quality, a riot of tasteless excess verging on absurdity.

However, Victorian design often has an energy, a vitality, and a freedom that the more "tasteful" design of the preceding and following years sometimes lacks. One aspect of Victorianism has been much neglected—the development of a simple vernacular vocabulary in areas dealing with technical, practical, and functional design where decorative elements were restrained or absent. Such

functionalism is a precursor of twentieth-century developments. Victorian design thus seems to be strangely split into two worlds, with florid decoration dominating the formal and "respectable" worlds of home life, religion, and government, while the functional tradition developed in industry, transport, and in the growing fields of science and technology.

A striking demonstration of this seemingly inconsistent design view can be studied in the documentation of the Great Exhibition of 1851 at the Crystal Palace. This famous proto-modern building (see pp. 187–8) was a dramatic demonstration of the possibilities of the new industrial materials, iron and glass. Within, however, the materials exhibited were a riot of decorative frosting, each exhibitor seemingly trying to outdo all competitors in an excess of tastelessness that now seems ludicrous. A complete illustrated catalog of the exhibition and a fine set of colored lithographs make it possible to study these curious contrasts in considerable detail (**fig. 11.1**).

In the background and overhead, the wonderful simplicity of the great structure can be

11.1 (*below*) Catalog page, Great Exhibition, London, 1851.

Despite the logic and simplicity of the Crystal Palace, where the exhibition took place, the objects on display varied from the "Light Park Phaeton" (top) to the riot of meaningless architectural ornament intended to beautify a chimneypiece (bottom).

11.2 (*opposite*) Frank Furness, Pennsylvania Academy of Fine Arts, Philadelphia, 1871-6.

The Victorian-type institution incorporated an art school on the ground floor and a museum on the second floor, which was reached by the grand stairway shown here. Furness's highly personal and original version of Victorian style made frequent use of stubby columns and pointed arches to generate interiors that depart from any historic precedents. The strong colors and patterned wall surfaces are unusual and lively in an era that the critic Lewis Mumford called the "brown decades."

THE INDUSTRY OF ALL NATIONS.

glimpsed. The hoop-skirted ladies and stovepipe-hatted gentlemen in the illustrations are viewing, and one assumes admiring, chairs and tables, mirrors, and pianos, stoves and mantels, china and glassware, all encrusted with an amazing variety of ornamentation. In general, the ornament is not based on any historic precedents. Greek columns and Gothic arches are rarely to be seen; instead forms borrowed from human and animal figures, leaves and flowers, and complex florid arabesques having no discoverable sources cover almost every object. Here and there a locomotive, a pistol, an astronomical telescope, or the gears of machines offer some contrast, but these functional objects are almost lost amid the plethora of "artistic" decorative works. There were tables supported by cast-iron swans, chairs of papier-mâché decorated, the catalog states, with "two winged thoughts," carved sideboards and cradles, a metal bed "with details of the French Renaissance," industrially produced AXMINSTER carpets, flowery chintzes. The pianos of Collard and Collard, one grand and one upright, are barely visible beneath their overlay of ornamental carving.

The reasons behind this typically Victorian frenzy of decorative excess seem to be based in the congruence of two related developments. The Industrial Revolution and its impact on manufacturing had, by 1851, made it easy, and therefore cheap, to produce ornamentation that would previously have required slow and costly skilled handwork. Power looms could weave elaborately ornamented textiles and carpets as easily as plain and simple equivalents. Cast iron was an ideal material for making ornamental carving—once molds were made, repeating an elaborate design was cheap, easy, and cost effective. In fact, ornamentation could conceal minor defects in castings that would be objectionable in plain surfaces. The scroll saw and more complex carving machines could produce details in wood reminiscent of hand carving of the past. Industrial production also generated wealth. The owners of factories and mills became rich, while their industries created a need for a new class of managers, salespeople, and accountants, and the supporting systems of banking, securities markets, insurance, and all the related professions that make up modern business. People who worked in these fields also became increasingly affluent, and so able to afford to buy the products of industry that would make for a comfortable life.

That the *quality* of ornamentation declined so dramatically calls for further explanation. In the pre-industrial world, design was produced by a small number of creative people—artists, architects (often self-taught), and craftsmen-designers who worked within traditions that had developed slowly over long periods. The cabinet maker learned his trade as an apprentice, and learned the ornamental detail of his period in relation to the best art and architecture of the time. The weaver was the designer of the cloth he wove and had a knowledge of and respect for the materials and patterns that he produced. The silver smith, the glass blower, the clock maker, the wood carver, and the plaster craftsmen all worked in related traditions for a clientele that respected excellence in aesthetic as well as materialistic terms.

When weaving became an industrial operation, the mill hand had no role in the design of the textiles that the factory produced. When textile printing became a mechanical process, the design to be printed was no concern of the workers producing the cloth. Factory-made furniture was not constructed by cabinet makers, but instead produced from machine-made parts that were assembled by workers who had no role in design. Design became increasingly separated from the crafts, and control of design passed into the hands of the factory owners and managers who had no tradition of involvement in such matters. They knew only that the buying public wanted a maximum of ornamentation and that industrial production could deliver what was wanted easily, cheaply, and profitably. As garish ornamentation became the norm of Victorian style, the ever-present desire to be "in style" made such design virtually a universal norm.

The Victorian fondness for free combinations of decorative elements in all styles finally defeats efforts at classification. The term "eclectic," meaning borrowing from many sources, is descriptive, but that term has become so attached to a more formal practice of the twentieth century that its use for Victorian examples creates confusion. The interior design of Victorian buildings is, if anything, even more difficult to classify. The mixture of styles and the use of invented ornament having no clear stylistic bases were typical of the design of furniture and other objects of the time, while the owners and occupants of buildings felt free to mix, alter, and redecorate according to whim.

Britain

The Gothic Revival, itself a highly professional exercise in historicism, lasted until well into the 1880s as one of a number of stylistic directions that competed for the patronage of newly wealthy merchants, manufacturers, bankers, and other "self-made" men who were all anxious to have great houses comparable to those of the titled aristocracy. The great houses of Tudor, Elizabethan, Jacobean, and Carolean times were at hand as models, and castles could sometimes be bought in ruined states, so that real antiquity could combine with sham extensions.

Mansions

Architects and interior decorators who worked on houses for the English nouveaux riches were generally quite knowledgeable about historic styles they tried to reproduce, although the results always seem to reveal their synthetic qualities. Victorian mansions in England were large, even gigantic, buildings with great halls, chapels, dozens of bedrooms, and service wings to house the small army of servants that were needed to staff them. Half-timbered, gabled blocks, keeps with battle-

mented defenses, and clock towers visible for miles around were favorite external features. In Cheshire, John Tollenmache commissioned his architect, Anthony Salvin (1799–1881), to build Peckforton Castle (1844–50), a surprisingly convincing imitation of an actual medieval castle, complete with round tower keep, stone-vaulted great hall and chapel, but with a billiard room, a school room for the children, and a bathroom adjacent to the master's chamber. Tyntesfield in Somerset, a work of John Norton (1823–1904), was built in 1863 in a more typically Victorian muddle of styles, generally with some relation to Gothic, but with bay windows, turrets, and towers unlike anything built in medieval times. The interiors, full of carved pseudo-Gothic woodwork and harshly colored polychrome tile, are crowded with furniture in every style, while walls are covered with ornamental detail, displays of pictures, vases and pottery of Chinese and Japanese origin, all in picturesque confusion (**fig. 11.3**). Dozens of such mansions dot the English countryside, inviting confusion with historic buildings of earlier times.

Middle-class Houses and Public Buildings

Town houses of the sort that wealthy owners might want to live in were usually parts of rows, or even whole neighborhoods, that adhered to restrained design based on Georgian traditions of classicism, Internally, however, restraint often gave way to acquisition and display in ornamental chaos. It is hard to imagine how the occupants managed to walk about or sit down.

Interiors of more modest houses were also cluttered and decorated with patterned materials on every surface, but some restraint seems to have been applied either through taste or through financial constraints, so that the effect is often one of cozy charm. The front parlor of the house in the Chelsea neighborhood of London that was owned by the writer Thomas Carlyle has been carefully preserved as a museum and gives an idea of what this kind of middle-class residential interior was like in the mid-nineteenth century (**fig. 11.4**). Suburban neighborhoods grew up around English cities during the Victorian era. Here houses were built in rows for those of modest means, and "villas" in pairs or free-standing for those who could afford more. The design character externally

11.3 John Norton, Indian Hall, Elveden Hall, Suffolk, England, c. 1870.

The hall, sometimes known as the Marble Hall, of the Victorian mansion was remodeled into what was thought to be Indian style for the benefit of a new owner, an Indian maharajah, who wanted to create a marriage gift for his new wife, the half-Abyssinian, half-German Bamba Müller. It is only the overhead plasterwork detail that justifies the stylistic designation. The furniture seems to be stolidly English.

11.4 Robert Taft, *A Chelsea Interior*, Carlyle's House, London, 1857.

This painting of the parlor of the house occupied by Thomas Carlyle shows Victorian comfort at its best. This simple but handsomely detailed interior is of a typical London row house with the moderate ornamentation that a literary couple might find comfortable and pleasing.

is usually some version of Regency or Gothic Revival, sometimes with touches of decorative detail in the Victorian mode. Inside, the occupants arranged whatever level of Victorian detail that appealed to them. Most public spaces, clubs, restaurants, theaters, hotels, and railroad stations were carpeted, padded, and stuffed in order to achieve a special comfort typical of the "gas-light" era that provided the settings in which Arthur Conan Doyle's famous fictional detective, Sherlock Holmes, conducted his practice.

Shaw and the Queen Anne Revival

Richard Norman Shaw (1831–1912), in a long and productive career, produced a large body of work quintessentially English Victorian in character. His early work belongs to the Gothic Revival, using, for country houses, a mix of half-timber and masonry often called "Old English;" but by about 1870, he developed a more creative and individualistic style which came to be called Queen Anne. This design has little to do with the Queen Anne style of the early eighteenth century. Shaw's Queen Anne country houses and London town houses are based on intricate internal plans that generate asymmetrical, irregular exteriors. Red brick and white-painted wood trim are the primary materials, while windows are large with many small panes of glass. Bay windows are common. There is a hint of Gothic Revivalism along with some reference to Dutch Renaissance work, but Shaw's work is unique and original. Interiors in his houses, rich in decorative detail, are full of asymmetrical spaces with nooks, bays, and other irregularities that favor comfort and charm (**fig. 11.5**). Shaw's clients, and Shaw himself in his own house, filled Queen Anne interiors with framed pictures, ornamental objects, and the ornate furniture so beloved by Victorians .

Shaw was also the designer of a number of office buildings (New Zealand Chambers of 1871–3 in London is the best known), banks, and churches. New Scotland Yard, London, is a Shaw design of 1887–90. Shaw's churches are invariably in a Gothic Revival mode, so carefully correct as to be virtually indistinguishable from medieval buildings. He was much concerned with technical matters, such as the arrangement of efficient chimney flues and bathroom drains; he used iron structural elements where they seemed advantageous and was the designer of the first English house to be entirely lighted by the recently developed Swan electric lamp. Shaw's country houses were usually rambling in plan, their rooms

arranged for both convenience and picturesque external effect; some were staggeringly vast in scale. Shaw remained aloof from the Arts and Crafts movement (the subject of the following chapter) in a way that emphasizes the gulf between Queen Anne and the Aesthetic movement. At the end of his career, Shaw turned toward classicism, anticipating the twentieth-century reaction against the norms of Victorian design.

United States: Victorian Variations

Victorian design in America produced work of similar elaboration, although English work of the period tends to be somewhat more ordered and disciplined, more "professional" and therefore perhaps less creative, than the free improvisation of much American Victorian design.

Although Americans aimed for a classless society after the Revolutionary War, the same processes operated as in Victorian Britain. Simple farmers became middle-class city dwellers, managers, professionals, and businessmen. Awareness of the mansions of the wealthy, the prosperous merchants, and the plantation owners created an appetite for the fancy and the elaborate. Ornamentalism was supported by an increasing flow of imports from Europe. The American clipper ship, the McCormack reaper, the Colt revolver, and the Waltham watch represented a strain of Yankee ingenuity, honesty, and simplicity, but architecture and interior design turned away from such functional concerns in order to embrace the other, more pretentious and ostentatious, aspect of Victorian taste.

There are several sub-species of Victorianism often referred to by historians. They include:

11.6 Richard Upjohn with later additions by McKim, Mead and White, Kingscote, Newport, Rhode Island 1839, additions, 1881.

The entry hall with its simple parquet floor, stained glass, and red walls carries the love of Gothic pointed arch forms forward into the Victorian era.

- Carpenter Gothic: the term applied to the vernacular adaptation of the Gothic Revival style in America (**fig. 11.6**). The material used is usually wood, often with board and batten siding. Pointed-arch forms are used along with applied woodwork in spiky decorative patterns. Leaded glass windows are common, sometimes with colorful stained glass. Small railroad stations and village churches were often built in this style.
- ITALIANATE: This term describes designs using low-sloping hipped roofs, porches, and loggias with columns, bracketed roofs, and cornices, and often a tower. Windows and doors are often topped with semicircular arches.
- MANSARDIC: These designs take their name from the mansard roof (see p. 113). A mansard roof has a steep, visible front surface, usually of slate, visible from the street. Cast-iron decorative trim is often present, along with as much carved detail as the owner could afford. Mansardic design was often used for public buildings, courthouses, and

railroad stations as well as for houses. The term GENERAL GRANT style is often given to mansard-roofed Victorian buildings.
- Queen Anne (or Queen Anne Revival): This is a term applied to late Victorian design that uses a somewhat sophisticated application of ornamental detail as it developed in England in parallel with the Arts and Crafts movement. Typical features are the asymmetrical arrangement of elements, bay windows, mixtures of brick, terracotta, shingles, and decorative inserts of bas-relief ornamentation and stained glass in some windows.

The Centennial Exhibition in Philadelphia in 1876 was a showcase for Victorian design in America, much as the Great Exhibition had been in England. A number of halls showed off machinery, horticulture, and art, while various industries and individual states erected smaller buildings in a chaotic variety of styles. An actual pagoda was brought from Japan and stimulated interest in

Japanese design, adding one more element to the Victorian stylistic mix. One of the most impressive exhibits was a giant steam engine built by the Corliss Iron Works to power a city pumping station. It was shown in operation and drew crowds to admire its impressive functional beauty. At the same time, exhibitions of products for household use leaned toward excesses of decorative detail. A Mason and Hamlin organ suitable for the Victorian parlor is encrusted with ornamental inlays, carvings, and crockets, but was described by Walter Smith, a contemporary critic, as "free from all the abortions in the shape of ornament with which many pretentious instruments are disfigured."

The style of the organ and of much furniture of the time is often called EASTLAKE in recognition of the aesthetic values advanced by an English designer and writer, Charles Locke Eastlake (1836–1906). His book, *Hints on Household Taste* (1868), was widely read in America and exerted considerable influence (**fig. 11.7**). Eastlake urged simplicity and restraint, but the illustrations that accompany the text seem only additional examples of the Victorian taste for excess elaboration.

Mansions

Those made rich through factory production of newly invented products usually chose to build mansions in which ornamentation in any and all styles crowded every available space, inside and out. Colonel Samuel Colt, the inventor of the revolver, had a house (named Armsmere) built close to his factory in Hartford, Connecticut, in an amalgam of styles– vaguely Italian with Moorish domes in prominent locations. Frederick E. Church, a landscape painter, built his dreams into his house called Olana, overlooking the Hudson River (**fig. 11.8**). He was his own designer, working in what he believed to be the "Persian" style, with some assistance from the professional architect and landscape designer Calvert Vaux (1824–95).

Vaux was English by birth, but made his reputation in America (in parnership with Frederick Law Olmstead) designing great public parks, including New York's Central and Riverside parks and South Park in Chicago. In 1857 he published *Villas and Cottages*, a manual based on his architectural work with A. J. Downing. The book begins

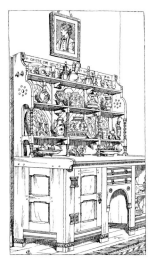

11.7 Charles Locke Eastlake, dining room sideboard, 1874.

Eastlake was an active arbiter of Victorian taste, using his work as a journalist to make suggestions to his readers and promote his own designs. An Arts and Crafts orientation is evident in his work, but it shows an urge toward extra elaboration. The craftsman-built sideboard shown in this plate from Hints on Household Taste in Furniture, Upholstery, and Other Details *(1868) is modified by the extensive display of ceramics rich in "art" ornamentation.*

11.8 Calvert Vaux and Frederick E. Church, Olana, near Hudson, New York, 1874–89.

This hallway displays a love of Victorian fantasy, incorporating elements intended to be "Persian" and therefore romantic and artistic. Curtains edge the raised landing from which stairs move up to Moorish arches with a stained glass window lighting the area.

with highly practical suggestions for logical, functional planning of homes, and designs for improved water closets. It then proceeds to illustrate the ornamental details, both exterior and interior, and then presents thirty-nine designs for houses ranging from modest cottages to gigantic mansions. Given such titles as "Picturesque Villa with Wing and Attics" and "Irregular Stone Villa with Tower" (with twenty-nine rooms not counting the attic and tower; cost $30,000), it is not surprising that the designs express ornate Victorian taste.

Vernacular House Styles

The American farmhouse of the Victorian era moved away from its colonial and Georgian predecessors to give up symmetry and classical detail in favor of "picturesque" irregular plans, more vertical proportions, and detail that varied from the severe plainness of the houses of the settlers of the mid-west to the ornate GINGERBREAD favored by more affluent families in the east and south. Around the factories of mill towns, districts of small houses were built to accommodate workers and mid-level managers, somewhat in the manner of modern suburbia. Houses varied from minimal rows or groups of two (twin houses), built to house workers, to more generous single family houses standing on their own lots even when placed close together. Such houses were usually built by specu-

lators or developers for sale or rental, and the value of fashionable decorative detail to attract occupants was well recognized. Books and magazines offered "ideal" plans and designs incorporating ornamental details that could be factory made, bought from a lumber yard, and added to a basic house. Internally, paneling, fancy mantels, stair rails, and moldings served to introduce a level of clutter that the occupants could then amplify with wallpapers, drapery, and furniture to taste.

The Gothic Revival slipped into the mode of carpenter Gothic, which in turn led to the production of gingerbread ornament in scroll-sawn wood or in cast iron. Thus a simple wooden house could turn into a Victorian house fully decorated with trim. Inside such houses, flowery wallpaper covered the walls; patterned carpeting covered the floors. Woodwork was full of carvings and turnings, usually finished in dark tones. The parlor stove might be a fantasy of decorative elements in cast iron, the parlor organ (or harmonium) a comparable fantasy in wood. Furniture was crowded into every room, filling up space with carving and upholstery. Oil lamps, now the usual source of artificial light, invited elaborate shapes and colorful decorative shades. Any otherwise unused spaces could be filled with such newly developed furniture types as the WHAT-NOT, a shelf unit intended to hold a display of generally useless ornamental objects. Blank wall spaces could be hung with "artistic" prints in decorative frames while the small sculptural groups in plaster produced in vast quantity by John Rogers (1829–1904) illustrated sentimental themes of love and sadness.

A curious Victorian fad favored the building of octagonal houses. The idea was generated by Orson Squire Fowler (1809–87), an eccentric theorist known for the invention of the pseudo-science of phrenology (the discovery of human character by exploring the shape of the skull). A particularly ornate octagonal example is the Armour-Stiner house (1860) at Irvington, New York. It is surrounded by a porch with florid cast-iron columns and railings, and has a huge mansardic dome topped by a cupola and spire. The richly ornamented interiors include such oddities as a triangular library and music room, created by the need to fit the octagonal floor plan.

In large cities, town housing was provided by solid blocks of row houses (**fig. 11.9**). The uniformity of such rows—the BROWNSTONES of New

11.9 Blakely Hall House, New York, 1896.

The contemporary photograph of the stairhall of this typical New York City row house on West 45th Street shows how the owners assembled a characteristically late Victorian interior with dark woodwork, dull wallpapers, and a profusion of draperies, carpet and fabric-covered furniture to generate the sense of richness through ornamentation that was the norm of late Victorian taste. The elaborate newel post at the base of the stair baluster sets the tone for the space.

York, the brick rows of Philadelphia and Baltimore, for example—produced overall monotony, but had the virtue of establishing visual order which, when streets were planted with trees, created attractive neighborhoods that can still be admired where they have survived intact. The Italianate mode was a favorite for brownstone rows, while mansardic roofs and veranda porches raised the status of free-standing houses that often were intermingled with the rows. Internally all of these house types showed evidence of technical progress through the introduction of central (usually hot air) heating, gas lighting, bathrooms, and kitchens. These were improved with the introduction of running water, first coal and, then, a few years later, gas ranges, and ice boxes for refrigeration. Built-in closets and cupboards were worked into house plans, along with extra dressing spaces adjacent to bedrooms, often with wash basins with running water. Larger houses had such luxuries as marble top surfaces and built-in mirrors. Long flights of ornamental stairs led to upper floors (often three or four) and narrow "back stairs" were usually provided for the use of servants.

Victorian taste favored vertical emphasis in proportions so that ceilings were often unreasonably high while doors and windows were made both tall and narrow. Ornate overmantels above the now largely useless fireplace (often with a gas grate or hot air outlet) reached up to the high ceilings where plaster moldings ran around the tops of walls. Minimal daylight entered the narrow windows by day; oil and gas lamps provided light at night. Colors of brown, black, olive green, and mauve made such interiors seem cluttered and gloomy—more quaint than beautiful by modern standards.

Shingle Style

Queen Anne style, developed in Britain by Shaw, was taken up with considerable enthusiasm in America alongside Gothic, Italianate, and Mansardic alternatives. A book by the architectural historian Vincent J. Scully, *The Shingle Style* (1971), has led to that term being used to describe American country and suburban houses that echoed the Queen Anne of Shaw and his followers. Wood was the dominant material of such building, the basis of Carpenter Gothic, and the simplified version of that style that Scully calls "the stick style"—a reference to board and batten exteriors which featured external frame members. Shingle style buildings often use some masonry—particularly for ground-floor walls—sometimes of rough rubble stonework, but otherwise exterior walls and roofs are generally covered with cedar wood shingles left to weather to a natural grey. Exterior ornament is usually sparse or absent, but building forms are often complex, with gables, projecting wings, porches, dormers and rounded bays, turrets, and occasional towers.

Most Shingle style buildings are houses, but

11.10 Henry Hobson Richardson, Watts Sherman House, Newport, Rhode Island, 1876.

The drawing of this interior was probably by Stanford White who was often the interior designer for Richardson projects. The paneled walls and elaborate woodwork with its typically Victorian Gothic references typify the early work of Richardson and White.

11.11 Camp Cedars, Forked Lake, Adirondacks, New York, 1886.

The "camps" built as summer vacation houses in the mountains were often quite luxurious, but they made a point of rusticity through the choice of furniture and the style of interior decoration. The rough stone fireplace is trimmed with rough-hewn logs, and the bed is built of similar wood members. The lanterns, fans, and curios are typical of Victorian taste.

hotels, casinos, and clubhouses were built in this idiom as well. Kragsyde, a coastal private mansion at Manchester-by-the-Sea (Peabody and Stearns, *c.* 1882), is a good example of the type, with its rambling layout, picturesque porches, turret, and great arch where a drive passes through a wing of the building. Inside, paneling, small-paned windows, fireplaces, and nooks with built-in settees generate a typically Queen Anne mix of complexity and cozy charm.

H. H. Richardson (1838–86) worked in the Shingle style when designing the W. Watts Sherman House at Newport, Rhode Island (**fig. 11.10**; 1874). The firm of McKim, Mead, and White was responsible for many examples of the style, such as the seaside mansion at Elberon, New Jersey (1880–81), for Victor Newcomb, and casinos at Newport and Narragansett Pier, Rhode Island (1879–84). These are architects better known for more formal works mentioned in later chapters, but these less formal buildings are among their most lively and original works. The "artistic" clutter of the great living hall at Elberon shows off the mix of informality, complexity, pretension, and comfort that was characteristic of Queen Anne at its full flowering in America.

Adirondack Style

A minor sub-style of Victorian design has been recently given the name ADIRONBACK in recognition of its development in that mountainous region of New York. As railroad networks developed and train travel became reasonably fast and comfortable, those who could afford summer vacations sought out locations in unspoiled natural regions where the mountainous landscape and cool summer climate provided an escape from city life. In the Adirondack mountains, cabins and camps were built as summer houses and as lodges for hunters and fishermen. Although camps and lodges tended to grow in size and comfort in the latter part of the nineteenth century, the rustic character of simple cabins was usually retained and even developed as yet another Victorian form of decoration. Adirondack furniture is often made up of tree branches (frequently still with bark remaining) cleverly assembled to make benches, tables, and chairs, with smaller twigs used for ornamental detail. Great stone fireplaces dominate rooms lined with wood boards left in their natural color. Camps with quaint names such as Pine Knot and Camp Cedars (**fig. 11.11**) were made up of

cottages and lodges filled with rustic furniture, rugs and cloth wall hangings, hunting trophies, and oil lamps.

Shaker Design

A drastically different alternative to the florid excesses of Victorian design developed in the modest and, in their day, obscure, communities of the religious sect known as Shakers. The first Shakers came to America from England in 1774 seeking freedom from religious persecution. Shaker communities were villages built at the center of agricultural lands where members shared property and work in a simple form of communism. By 1800 a number of these villages had been established. Large communal dwelling houses provided separate living quarters for men and women. In pursuit of the goal of total independence from "the world" or outsiders, Shaker communities built their own buildings and produced, insofar as possible, all of their needs through subsistence agriculture and workshops. Religious beliefs that forbade "worldly" ostentation and favored efficient use of human efforts led to the production of a wide variety of objects of total simplicity and remarkable functional excellence. Shaker design reached a peak of achievement around 1830 and continued to hold to its idealistic standards throughout the Victorian era.

The interiors of Shaker buildings were totally free of ornament. Walls were plain and white-painted. Floors were wood boards that were

INSIGHTS

The Shaker Philosophy

The English religious mystic Ann Lee, known as Mother Ann, left England in 1774 to set up her own form of Quaker community in the freer religious atmosphere of the New World. She founded the Shakers and summed up her philosophy in the following phrase:

put your hands to work and your hearts to God . . . . [W]ork as though you would live a thousand years, and live as though you were to die tomorrow. [1]

The austerity of the Shaker lifestyle was expressed in a series of Millenial Laws governing everything from behavior,

Ye shall have no talking, laughing, sneering, winking, blinking, hanging and lounging on the railings, hugging, fumbling and fawning over each other when going to the table [2]

to decorative finishes,

Beadings, mouldings and cornices which are merely for fancy may not be made by believers. [3]

Elder William Denning, a mid-nineteenth-century Shaker builder noted for his work on the Church Family Dwelling at Hancock, Massachusetts, commented on the Shaker habit of preserving neatness by suspending chairs and clothes from wooden pegs:

we hang everything but people and that we leave for the world to do. [4]

The Shakers' opinion of the furnishings of the outside world is captured by a report made by one member from Massachusetts on a visit to Harvard in 1850:

I think they have gathered into their habitations too much furniture which belongs to Babylon! Mother [Ann] used to say "You may give such things to the moles and the bats." [5]

1. Holy Orders of 1841, quoted in David Larkin and June Sprigg, *Shaker: Life, Work and Art* (London, 1987), p. 43; 2. Millennial Laws of 1845, quoted in *ibid*, p. 33; 3. *Ibid*, p. 92; 4. *Ibid*, p. 168; 5. *Ibid*, p. 168

11.12 (*top*) Hancock Shaker Village, Hancock, New York *c.* 1820.

The typical bedroom of an elder or eldress in the Shaker communal residence hall contains a simple rope bed and wooden wash-stand. The wood-burning stove in the foreground incorporates a Shaker invention, the upper smoke box, which extracts extra heat from chimney gases. The wood trim is painted in a tone the Shakers called "Heavenly blue."

11.13 (*bottom*) American Shaker Meeting House, Sabbathday Lake, Maine, 1794.

Shaker simplicity is evident in the meeting house, where religious gatherings took place. The bare interior, with its simple benches, uses painted woodwork as the only concession to visual variety. The color is "heavenly blue."

painted, often in strong colors. Furniture included benches, tables, chairs, storage cabinets, and work tables of utmost simplicity, but of great subtlety in proportion and detail. Floors were kept bare for easy cleaning, storage was provided in banks of built-in drawers; pegs mounted in bands along walls made it easy to hang up hats, cloaks, and even chairs when not in use. Boxes for storage of small objects, baskets, cast-iron stoves of remarkable efficiency, clocks, and woven materials were all produced with design of fine aesthetic quality, although Shaker societies advanced no aesthetic theories and established no central control of design practice. The ascetic pursuit of simplicity and efficiency alone seems to have been the driving principles that produced design that seems to presage twentieth-century modernism. Shaker communities offered some products for sale—most notably their LADDER-BACK chairs, rockers, and straight chairs of simple wooden parts with woven tape seats—objects that achieved surprising popularity in spite of their total independence from the norms of Victorian taste. Although Shaker communities are now reduced to a handful of members, a

number of Shaker villages, including those at Hancock (**fig. 11.12**), Massachusetts, Sabathday Lake (**fig. 11.13**), Maine, and Pleasant Valley, Kentucky, are preserved in a form suitable for modern study and admiration.

Early Skyscrapers

As cities grew larger, central districts developed that were devoted to business activities. Before telephone communication was available, proximity was an important consideration in making business communication fast and easy. The resulting need for offices crowded into a central "business district" led to high rents and high land values. Real estate owners realized that their earnings were limited by the quantity of rental space that could be squeezed onto a lot of given area. Taller buildings became profitable with the development of passenger elevators, but the height of buildings was still limited as long as masonry walls and columns were the main structural elements.

Cast iron, an extraordinarily useful and versatile material, was put to work for a great variety of uses,

11.14 Schuyler, Hartley & Graham shop, New York, 1864.

Guns and military goods were in great demand during America's Civil War. The shop interior makes use of counters, cases, and cabinets in a vernacular of the period, while upper walls and ceiling are decorated according to Victorian taste.

11.15 Office of a publishing firm, New York, *c.* 1890.

The development of larger business firms generated a need for extensive office spaces, where clerks and book-keepers could handle the tasks that were, before the advent of typewriters and computers, conducted by hand. Cast iron columns support wood beams, ceiling, and floors. Gas light augmented daylight on dark days. An industry developed to supply suitable office desks and chairs for the paper processing that was the work of an office.

including the building of early skyscrapers. American cities often have "cast-iron districts" where rows of buildings were built with iron structural columns and with exterior walls made up, like the Crystal Palace, of prefabricated units of iron holding glass windows. The ease with which iron could be cast in any desired form made it possible for these iron facades to be made up of classical columns, Gothic arches, or any other ornamental themes that owners and builders might think appropriate. Floors were of wood, with the result that such buildings were vulnerable to disastrous fires, made more dangerous by lack of adequate exit stairs to serve upper floors. Many cast-iron buildings were utilitarian loft buildings, warehouses, and factories, often housing sweat-shop industry of the grimmest sort. Others were retail stores, "dry-goods" shops, the ancestors of department stores (**fig. 11.14**).

Cast iron enabled building to go higher, because its high-strength characteristics made it possible to reduce the size of support columns within buildings. Masonry, however, remained the preferred material for outer walls because it offered a degree of fire safety by enclosing each building in a non-inflammable barrier. Fire safety within a building was improved when wooden floors were replaced with systems using arches of brick or terracotta tile supported on iron beams and columns wrapped with tile heat insulation. Fireproof structural framing and elevators together made it possible to build to heights of eight, ten, or twelve stories. Still higher "skyscrapers" finally became possible at the very end of the nineteenth century when the Bessemer process made steel available for columns and beams. The tall buildings of the late Victorian era presented difficult problems to their designers. Architectural history offered few models for high building. George B. Post's Western Union Building (1873–5) or Richard Morris Hunt's Tribune Building of the same date, both in New York, are each curious conglomerations of masonry detail, arches, dormers, mansard roofs, and clock towers—cobbled up pieces of the past.

Offices inside such tall buildings, and many smaller buildings, tended to strictly utilitarian treatment (**fig. 11.15**). The typical office building had rows of small offices arranged along corridors so that every office could be close to windows for light and ventilation. Private offices were screened from the adjacent outer offices and waiting rooms

by glazed wood partitions that allowed inner spaces to borrow some daylight. Operable transoms over doors made possible ventilation from outer windows into interior rooms and corridors. Larger "general offices," where many clerks or stenographers worked in a common open space, appeared as larger businesses, railroads, newspapers, and manufacturing corporations grew to a level that required such hives of workers. Business equipment, file cabinets, typewriters, adding machines, and time-clocks were gradually introduced into the late Victorian office, along with roll-top desks and swivel chairs. Gas light, followed by electric light, reduced dependency on window proximity, while the telegraph followed by the telephone became vital communication devices. Floors, ceilings, partitions, and furniture were usually of wood—most often oak—in some shade of brown. Even the offices of powerful chiefs and board of directors' meeting rooms only differed from the norm in having a rug on the floor, leather-cushioned chairs, and a few pictures on the walls.

Taller multistory hotels and apartment houses were encouraged by the same economic values that spurred tall office buildings. The problems of suitable exterior design were also similar. The Waldorf Hotel (1893) and the Dakota Apartments (1884), both New York works of Henry J. Hardenbergh (1847–1918), are amazingly complex warrens of rooms ingeniously arranged around light courts so as to give daylight to every major space. Externally they are in what the designer called "German Renaissance" style, conceived as a Victorian massing of arches, bays, balconies, turrets, dormers, chimneys, and tile roofs. Hotel interiors were elaborated with all the grandeur of High Victorian style. Apartment houses were planned, their main rooms rich with paneling, fireplaces with mantels, sliding pocket doors, stained glass, parquet floors, and rich, luxurious materials. Servants' quarters were provided within apartments or sometimes, as at the Dakota, in attic rooms. Individual tenants could, of course, decorate as they chose with carpets, wallpapers, drapery, and furniture of the same sort that would have been used in a private house of comparable luxury.

Public Buildings

Public buildings were built in styles as ornamental as those of private dwellings, but on a more formal and grander scale. The official architecture of

France during the reign of Napoleon III (1852–70), known as Second Empire style, was much admired by Americans. An ornate reworking of Mansart's work in France, it was used for such projects as Philadelphia's enormous City Hall (**fig. 11.16**; 1872–1901) by John McArthur, Jr. (1823–90), a giant hollow square with an overpowering Mansardic tower. The interiors, many now carefully restored, have a boldness and vitality that seems to be indifferent to all issues of taste and restraint. U.S. government buildings designed by Alfred B. Mullett (1834–90) while he served as Supervising Architect for the U.S. Treasury, such as the massive State, War and Navy Building in Washington, D.C. (1871–87), now the Executive Office Building, follow a similar pattern. Mansard roofs and architectural detail applied with a heavy hand are external characteristics, while internal elaboration makes up for anything lacking in stylistic quality.

Furness

The work of the Philadelphia architect Frank Furness (1839–1912) was quite unrelated to any particular school or movement. It is easy to characterize it as ugly, with its heavy and aggressive forms, but it is also full of strength and originality, drawing on such varied bases as the Gothic Revival, the Victorian Stick and Shingle styles, and the Arts and Crafts movement. Furness had an extensive practice which included the design of churches, railroad stations, banks, and many private houses. His building for the Pennsylvania Academy of the Fine Arts (1871–6) houses an art school on the ground floor with museum galleries on the upper floor. A great entrance stair hall, now carefully restored to its original color and detail, uses florid iron railings and lighting standards, heavily textured wall surfaces, and Furness's unique stubby columns and pointed arches loosely based on Gothic sources (**fig. 11.2**). The library for the University of Pennsylvania (1888–91), now renamed the Furness Building and housing the architectural school of the university, is even more original. The vast reading room and "rotunda" are lined with brick and stone. There are complex arch details and a great fireplace with a clock above of original and curious form with much florid carved detail. Access to upper levels is provided by an extraordinarily complex iron stairway with ornamental iron railings. Houses and other smaller buildings by Furness are full of interesting and

11.16 (*opposite*) John McArthur Jr. and Thomas U. Walter, City Hall, Philadelphia, 1872–1901.

This space, known as "Conversation Hall," is a monumental interior in the huge building that was the governmental center for the large city that Philadelphia had become. Admiration for the architecture of the French Second Empire style had led to some rather florid and excessive efforts at grandeur in the public buildings of a democratic society. This space, carefully restored to its original appearance, glories in colored marbles, a spectacular gaslight chandelier, and a ceiling rich in color and gilding.

Belter built a large business specializing in the production of furniture in the style called "rococo revival." His invention of techniques for carving and pressing elaborate ornament by mechanical means made it possible to produce at modest cost the complex ornamentation that the style demanded. The resultant, widely popular forms are typical of the Victorian view of luxury as symbolized by decorative ornament.

unusual decorative details in wood, stone, and tile. As American tastes changed in the early twentieth century, Furness's work, already somewhat controversial when it was designed, came to be disliked—even hated. He had employed Louis Sullivan, however, and influenced his development, and his work has been studied and valued by such later architects as Louis I. Kahn and Robert Venturi.

Furniture and Other Interior Furnishings

Factory production in the Victorian age made richly decorated objects relatively inexpensive and so available to a very large public. New materials and techniques were developed that made whole new categories of objects possible. In Austria, the Thonet brothers developed the technique of using steam in pressure chambers that made it possible to bend thin strips of solid wood into curved forms. Thonet chairs and other furniture types made up of a number of pieces of BENTWOOD were strong, light, and inexpensive, and so came into wide use as seating in cafés and restaurants and in informal residential interiors.

Plywood, developed in continental Europe, was made up of many layers of thin wood veneer. It became an alternative to solid wood, less costly and less subject to warping and splitting. Plywood panels, chair seats, and curved parts that could form seats and backs for benches and church pews were used in combination with solid wood components to form new furniture types. Industrial materials such as iron and brass tubing, at first made as plumbing pipes, were turned to use to make bed frames, creating the popular iron and brass head- and foot-boards. All of these new materials could produce simple and practical objects, but they were also adaptable to decorative designs that appeared in forms as ornate as any traditional furniture types.

Most Victorian designs were ornate. The products of the New York shops of John Henry Belter (1804–63), particularly his chairs (**fig. 11.17**), sofas, and tables, used curving forms, bulging upholstery, and frames carrying elaborate floral carving. Much of it was made by mechanized processes using plywood, built-up surface carving, and mechanically duplicated ornamental details. The resulting designs, much imitated by other makers, are highly

characteristic of American Victorian interiors. The style is often called Rococo Revival, and Belter's name is also applied to the work of other shops that produced work in the same style.

As Victorian fashion sought out exotic themes, furniture makers responded with designs intended to relate to one or another popular style. Oriental references were popular in England and America for a time, leading to furniture detailed in imitation of bamboo construction. Real bamboo objects were imported or sometimes made locally from imported material. Folding screens with painted surfaces or stretched fabric on wooden frames were a popular means of introducing some privacy in part of a room, or simply to add an extra element of decoration. Wicker furniture made from woven rattan or similar flexible material was also popular in Victorian interiors, particularly in informal spaces—porches or children's rooms or simply mixed in with other furniture in the typically Victorian desire to display and enjoy whatever came to hand in any and every style.

Upholstery, desired both for comfort and for the appearance of opulence, is a dominant element in Victorian seating furniture. Cushions, usually attached to wood frames, tend to be thick and bulging, with quilting and tufting to emphasize their forms. Metal springs hidden under cushions were widely used to create soft and bouncy surfaces. Cover materials with elaborate and colorful woven patterns were the norm, with woven horsehair (usually black) and leather as alternatives. Leather was particularly favored in rooms intended to suggest a "masculine" atmosphere—smoking rooms, "dens," and the rooms of men's clubs.

Furniture of the Victorian era tended to massive size along with excesses of ornamentation. Huge mirrored hat-racks were favorite elements for halls and vestibules. Pianos, many made in rectangular "square" form, as well as in the familiar grand and upright patterns, were important items for status-oriented display, and were designed with particularly rich, complex, and generally heavy ornamentation.

Victorian textile design, separated from the process of hand weaving by the use of powered looms set up in large and efficient mills, emphasized heavy, elaborate, and colorful pattern, both woven and printed. Floral designs were particularly favored. Trimming materials such as braiding, fringe, and tassels were added to make drapery rich and complex. Lace curtains were a popular, more modest window treatment. Interior doorways were often equipped with curtain rods so that, in addition to doors, portières could be hung to discourage drafts and add a touch of decorative richness.

Carpets, now generally made on power looms, were designed with themes similar to those used for textiles. Leaves, flowers, arabesques, and scroll forms were developed in repeat patterns so that carpet could be had by the yard to be sewed together and tacked down wall-to-wall. Linoleum, a newly invented floor covering material, was similarly produced in floral patterns and in designs imitating woven rugs. Wood floors or hardwood in parquet patterns, and floors of colored tile in varied patterns were also common.

Wallpaper became a particularly popular form of wall treatment, used whenever plain plaster might be visible above wainscot or other wood trim. Factory-printed papers provided a simple way to cover surfaces with pattern which might be geometric, floral, or even scenic; oriental themes were also popular. Some papers were embossed to create a bas-relief effect. Printed paper borders were available using designs based on architectural molding and trim details such as egg and dart or Greek key motifs. By cutting, arranging, and pasting, the paperhanger could create pattern compositions customized to a particular room or wall.

Victorian color tastes gradually shifted from bright and daring toward heaviness and gloom. Owen Jones's book *The Grammar of Ornament* (1856) illustrated ornamental motifs in brightly colored plates that encouraged the use of strong, chromatic colors. As time passed, darker and more muted colors, browns, olive greens, and mauves, came to be regarded as more "tasteful." The end of the Victorian era has been described by Lewis Mumford as "the brown decades"; these somber colors were carried over into the Edwardian era at the beginning of the twentieth century.

Distribution of the elements of Victorian interiors was furthered by several new commercial techniques. Department stores in cities offered a wide choice of goods of every sort, so that the Victorian shopper could compare, select, and order delivery of everything needed for household decoration at one stop. Away from American cities, particularly on the farms of the middle and far west, mail order catalogs from Sears Roebuck, Montgomery Ward, and many smaller firms illustrated an even more extensive range of products that could be ordered for shipment to even the most remote locations. In addition to furniture, textiles, carpets, and wallpapers, the mail order firms offered heating stoves, plumbing fixtures, kitchen equipment, and all sorts of useful and decorative objects. Stoves and kitchen ranges made of cast iron are ornate in form but full of practical features to aid heating and cooking. Coal supplanted wood as a fuel, to be followed by gas in cities. The patented 1871 Wilson adjustable chair uses cushions supported on an iron frame that permits adjustment into a wide variety of configurations. Bathroom fixtures include flush toilets, bath tubs, and wash basins in a variety of styles from the sternly utilitarian to elaborately ornate.

Oil lamps in great variety, from simple to ornate, were the most used lighting devices, but city gas led to fixtures in forms similar to candle brackets. Chandeliers were popular, often similarly ornamented with brass work and hanging crystal prisms. With the development of electric light, older lamps and gas fixtures were regularly converted to use the new Edison bulbs wherever electric service became available. The first electric fan was made in 1889 and, by 1893, a fully electric

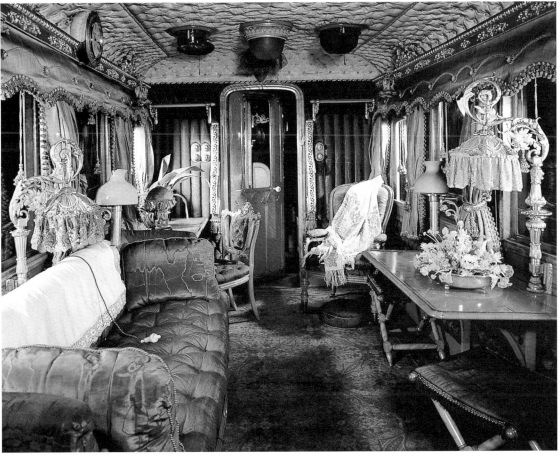

11.18 (*opposite*) Horace Trumbauer, The Elms, Newport, Rhode Island, 1901.

Trumbauer's work marks a transition from the creative ornamentalism of the Victorian era into the more disciplined historicism of the eclectic work that followed after the turn of the century. This grand house attempted to recreate a French Renaissance chateau. It captured the elaboration of its models, but without their aesthetic discipline. Carved wood detail, columns, marble at the fireplace and above, crystal chandeliers, Aubusson carpet and richly carved furniture all serve to support the ambitions of the wealthy owner.

11.19 (*left*) Queen Victoria's Royal Saloon (railroad car), 1869.

The major Victorian technological advance represented by the building of railroads came face to face with the Victorian taste in interior design in this special private car, which was built for the queen by the London & North Western Railway. Surfaces are padded and quilted, fringed drapery is everywhere, furniture is carved and quilted, lamps are shaded and fringed. The door at the end of the car is of wood carved in Gothic, pointed detail.

kitchen was ready for display at the Columbian Exhibition in Chicago. Singer's first sewing machine of 1851 developed into a household necessity. In its developed form, the mechanism was embedded in a table supported on a cast-iron base that carried the foot treadle and flywheel. The iron parts, perforated to save material and weight, were invariably made into ornamental forms, while the machine itself carried gilt-stenciled designs. A plywood top cover was usually provided.

The astonishing mixture of the functional and the practical with ornamentalism and sham is the characteristic of Victorian design that makes this period so complex, so contradictory, and so interesting (**fig. 11.18**). The Victorian design dilemma can be summed up at British transport museums where it is possible to view steam locomotives of great elegance and simplicity. The great Stirling

Single, named for its designer, Patrick Stirling (1820–95), and for its single pair of giant eight-foot driving wheels in gleaming green paint with no decoration except simple stripes emphasizing the form of its mechanical parts, contrasts with a passenger coach outfitted as a private carriage for Queen Victoria (**fig. 11.19**). The coach interior is padded and quilted, trimmed with woodwork in Gothic style, and furnished with opulent upholstery. Fringed curtains hang at the windows, and no trace of its role as transportation, intended to speed along steel rails behind a steam locomotive, can be discovered.

The contradictions and problems of Victorian design did not go unnoticed, and eventually movements dedicated to reform emerged. The most effective and interesting of these movements is the subject of the following chapter.

12

The Aesthetic Movements

During the Victorian era, various reactions developed in opposition to the historicism, decorative display, and excess of the prevailing design fashions. Opposition coalesced in several more or less organized movements that are now usually thought of together as constituting the Arts and Crafts movement or, as it is sometimes called, the Aesthetic movement. These movements had their beginning in England and developed there in the second half of the nineteenth century. Eventually, these developments generated the CRAFTSMAN MOVEMENT in the United States. Influence can also be traced into Germany and Austria in later styles and movements which in turn have direct links to the modernism of the twentieth century.

In this chapter, developments are considered in relation to the theorists, philosophers, and designers whose names and works define the movement of design history. The individual becomes increasingly important in this respect as the nineteenth century advances. The emergence of the celebrity designer was promoted by the expanding availability of publications that served to make the work of individuals known to a broad public.

Britain: Arts and Crafts

Ruskin and the Roots of Arts and Crafts

12.1 Charles Rennie Mackintosh, Hill House, Helensburgh, Dunbartonshire, Scotland, 1902–3.

Mackintosh's work stands at a border between the Arts and Crafts emphasis on simplicity and honest craftsmanship and the Art Nouveau urge toward more adventurous new forms. In this interior the use of geometric forms in the furniture and hanging lights is combined with directions that point toward later modernism. The carpet uses small pattern elements of tiny squares in contrast to its simple overall color.

The first such person to be considered here is not a designer but a writer, theorist, and critic. John Ruskin, whose moralistic approach to art and design critiscism has been mentioned already as a significant influence in the development of Gothic Revivalism (see p. 178), was also the source of many of the ideas that dominated Arts and Crafts design. There are substantial areas of overlap and cross-influence between Gothic Revival and Arts and Crafts ideas, but whereas the Revivalists simply advocated return to medieval Gothic practice, the Arts and Crafts movement sought original design of its own time based on the ideology of Ruskin and his followers. Ruskin's admiration for Gothic work arose from his conviction that it was "honest" in its use of materials and in its emphasis on craftsmanship of the highest available quality.

In *The Seven Lamps of Architecture* (1849) Ruskin asserts, "Until *common sense* finds its way into architecture, *there can be but little hope for it.*" The "seven lamps" of which he wrote were designated as "sacrifice," "truth," "power," "beauty," "life," "memory," and "obedience," suggesting the strongly idealistic tone of Ruskin's ideas. It was Ruskin's bitter denunciation of the design of industrially produced objects that impacted most strongly on the Arts and Crafts movement. The assumption that machine-made things would inevitably be tasteless and garish led to advocacy of a return to hand craft as the only possible route to reform.

This combination of a desire for honesty in terms of expression of function, material, and techniques of production, combined with a conviction that only hand craft can achieve such honesty, is the central doctrine of the movement. Excessive and ugly ornamentation is to be banished, but "meaningful" decoration devised by the craftsman is to be welcomed. Since craftsmen with the inventiveness and taste that this might require hardly existed, Arts and Crafts designers either turned into craftsmen themselves, or produced designs on paper of the sort they thought craftsmen *should* invent.

Morris

The best known and most influential of Arts and Crafts figures was William Morris (1834-96). Morris was educated at Oxford and there met the Pre-Raphaelite painter Edward Burne-Jones (1833–98), who was involved in attempting to reform the art of painting based on a return to what he considered to be pre-Renaissance ideals. Ruskin's writings had a powerful influence on both men who favored the idea of a close relationship between art and craft. Morris worked for a short time in the office of George Edmund Street (1824–81), a Gothic Revivalist architect in London. Morris did not himself practice architecture, but, at the time of his marriage, turned to his friend Philip Webb (1831–1915), another former employee of Street who had established an architectural office, for the design of a house to be built at Bexleyheath, then on the edge of London.

The Red House (**fig. 12.2**; 1859–60) that Webb designed is a demonstration of the ideas that Morris had formed. Its red brick walls and red tiled roof carry no ornamentation, while its plan, external form, and placement of windows and doors are strictly the result of internal function.

The pointed arch of an opening is a real brick arch; the chimneys serve actual fireplaces; large windows and small windows relate to the spaces within; the well house on the lawn serves a real water well. The irregular plan is based on functional realities, not on a desire for Gothic quaintness. Both the formalities of classicism and the picturesqueness of the Gothic have been rejected in exchange for functional simplicity.

As a result, the Red House thus can be viewed as a step toward the modern view of design, although its rustic informality seems completely unrelated to the technological pioneering of the Crystal Palace of 1851. Ruskin hated the Crystal Palace, describing it as a "cucumber frame," and cited its internal exhibits there as evidence of the disastrous level that Victorian design had reached. Morris was equally belligerent in his denunciation of the industrial products that were featured in the exhibition. By 1861 he had founded the firm of Morris, Marshall, Faulkner, and Co. to design and produce tapestries, wallpapers, furniture, and stained glass (**fig. 12.3**). Morris himself only designed a few three-dimensional objects—some furniture for the Red House and a simple rush-seated wood chair of 1862. His name, however, is connected with all examples of arm chairs with adjustable tilt backs—MORRIS CHAIRS, so named because Morris was the first to develop a prototype example.

Morris's far-reaching interests constantly changed, moving through poetry to political involvement in the cause of socialism, with its teaching that factory production tended to alienate workers from any creative contribution to the products they produce. He focused on two-dimensional design for textiles, wallpapers, books, and typography. His textile designs were always based on nature motifs, showing great respect for the natural subjects, the plants, flowers, and birds that were their themes. Superficially similar to factory-made Victorian prints, Morris's designs have qualities of simplicity and dignity that make them remarkably lively when so much of Victorian design appeared as pretentious, heavy, and overly decorative. In 1875, Morris became sole owner of the firm, called then Morris & Co., which produced many of his designs as well as work by a number of followers. The output included designs for printed chintzes and hand-tufted carpets and, eventually, carpet designs for Wilton and Axminster factories. The firm was also active in interior design, taking

12.2 (*opposite*) Philip Webb, Red House, Bexley Heath, London, 1859–60.

Webb designed the Red House for his friend William Morris, and this room contains many typical details, including the white-painted walls and a large bookcase-and-bench unit (called a settle) of Morris's design. It is painted white, and the hand-forged iron hinges are painted black. The ladder on the left gave access to the door opening to an attic. The furniture and rugs are of later date; the radiator is modern.

12.3 (*left*) Edward Ould, Wightwick Manor, Wolverhampton, Staffordshire, England, 1887–93.

The chair, which was designed by Violet Hunt and produced by Morris & Co., stands in front of a wall of Morris's Honeysuckle patterned linen. The painting by Frederick Sandys (1829–1904) is in a Rossetti frame. The fireplace detail and mantel complete an Arts and Crafts interior.

on whole rooms for treatment in consistent Arts and Crafts related themes. The Green Dining Room (1866), now preserved in the Victoria and Albert Museum in London, is an example of Morris's interior work; Philip Webb was the primary designer, and the artists Burne-Jones and Charles Fairfax-Murray contributed painted panels. The wall paneling and paper, the ceiling treatment, the art work, and the furniture all maintain a relationship orchestrated by Morris. The room is richly colorful, with green as a unifying theme.

Webb

Philip Webb maintained a close association with Morris throughout his career, designing furniture for use in Morris's interiors as well as for his own architectural projects. He was the designer of the massive wardrobe with a front painted by Burne-Jones presented to Morris for the Red House. Webb also designed a number of country houses that form an interesting contrast with the Queen Anne work of Norman Shaw. Although some of Webb's houses were very large, he aimed for a

*The drawing room of
this fine house contains
a carpet and many
pieces of furniture to
William Morris's
designs. The simple,
white-painted paneling
is characteristic of Arts
and Crafts design at its
best.*

certain modesty drawn from English vernacular examples—goals developed through his Arts and Crafts involvement. His interiors seem, in contrast to Victorian love of crowding and clutter, remarkably simple and original and so are perhaps the best examples of Morris's aims in interior design. Clouds (1881–91), a Wiltshire house designed by Webb, is a large and rambling mansion, but its interiors, including the White Drawing Room with white walls and a Morris carpet and the library with its white-painted woodwork and plaster and simple fireplace, seem free of clutter and surprisingly modern in spirit.

Another Webb design is Standen in Surrey (**fig. 12.4**; 1891–4), also large, but with the character of a cluster of simple brick farm buildings. Inside, most of the rooms have walls paneled up close to the ceiling; some are papered with Morris patterned papers instead. Paneling is generally white-painted, although in the dining room it is blue-green. The detailing is straightforward, and the color, coming from Morris carpets, textiles, and paper, has a pleasant simplicity.

Other British Designers

In the latter half of the nineteenth century a number of other English designers took up the themes of Morris's Arts and Crafts movement, or the related Aesthetic movement that drew inspiration from such sources as Japanese prints and ceramics. Christopher Dresser (1834–1904) began his design career with a study of botanical forms which he urged as a basis for "applied art," that is, decorative design. Dresser became interested in Japanese art and design in the 1860s and eventually established himself as a commercial designer; he is sometimes spoken of as the first industrial designer. He produced designs for pottery, porcelains, glassware, textiles, wallpapers, silver, and ironwork. Although he had no reservations about designing for industrial production, he was a vocal advocate of simplicity and "honesty," making connections between his botanical knowledge and the model for design excellence that nature has to offer. Many of his designs, particularly those for silver and glassware, are amazingly modern in concept (**fig. 12.5**).

Edward W. Godwin (1833–86) concentrated his work on furniture design based on Japanese precedents. His firm, the Art Furniture Company (founded 1860s), was devoted to the production of "Anglo-Japanese" furniture that attracted a following among a somewhat limited aesthetically inclined élite (**fig. 12.6**). His designs were light and delicate with decoration that was, by Victorian standards, restrained and simple. A catalog of Godwin designs was published in 1877, illustrated with drawings grouped under headings such as "Anglo-Japanese Drawing Room Furniture" or "Students' Furniture." Other plates show complete rooms in Godwin's own version of the Arts and Crafts approach. His later works were generally one-of-a-kind objects, hand craft made for his own use or for clients, who included such leaders of the Aesthetic Movement as Oscar Wilde and James McNeill Whistler (1834–1903).

Godwin was the designer of the White House in Tite Street, London, for (and probably in cooperation with) Whistler in 1887–8. Although Whistler's reputation is primarily based on his work as a painter, he was often involved in decorative projects that ranged from painted picture frames and screens made up of painted panels to the decoration of a room in a London house called the Peacock Room (**fig. 12.7**), which has been reassembled in the Freer Gallery of Art in Washington, D.C. The room was originally designed in 1876 by Thomas Jeckyll (1827–81), a designer who shared the enthusiasm for Japanese themes with Godwin and Whistler. The Peacock Room was a dining room with Godwin furniture, walls covered with

12.5 Christopher Dresser, pattern in the "Japanese Manner," 1886.

Dresser moved from this typically Victorian decorative pattern, which was included in his book Modern Ornamentation, *to increasingly creative forms that make him a precursor of modern industrial design.*

12.6 Japanese Court, International Exhibition, London, 1862.

The Victorian discovery of Japanese design promoted a new interest in orientalism. Visitors to the exhibition came away with an awareness of an exotic theme that fitted into the Aesthetic Movement's urge to bring the forms of oriental design into the decorative practice of nineteenth-century England.

INSIGHTS

Rossetti and the Aesthetic House

Lady Mount Temple, a respectable Victorian society hostess, encountered at first hand the starkly expressed artistic sensibilities of the pre-Raphaelite poet and painter Dante Gabriel Rossetti. She recorded the meeting in her *Memorials*:

You remember our dear little house in Curzon Street; when we furnished it, nothing would please us but watered paper on the walls, garlands of roses tied with blue bows! Glazed chintzes with bunches of roses, so natural they looked, I thought, as if they had just been gathered (between you and me, I still think it was very pretty) and most lovely ornaments we had in perfect harmony, gilt pelicans or swans or candlesticks, Minton's imitation of Sevres, and gilt bows everywhere.

One day Mr Rossetti was dining alone with us, and instead of admiring my room and decorations, as I expected, he evidently could hardly sit at ease with them. I began to ask if it were possible to suggest improvements! "Well," he said, frankly, "I should begin by burning everythng you have got." [1]

Rossetti's own house, with its artistic approach to decor, was described by Henry Treffry Dunn after a visit in 1863:

I was ushered into one of the prettiest, and one of the most curiously furnished and old fashioned sitting rooms that had every been my lot to see. Mirrors of all shapes, sizes and designs, lined the walls, so that whichever way I gazed I saw myself looking at myself. What space remained was a most original compound of Chinese black lacquered panels, bearing designs of birds, animals, flowers and fruit in gold relief, which had a very good effect, and on the other side of the grate a series of old Dutch tiles, mostly displaying Biblical subjects treated in a serio-comic fashion that existed at the period, were inlaid [2]

1. Lady Mount Temple, *Memorials* (London, 1890);   2. Henry Treffry Dunn, *Recollections* (London,1882)

12.7 Thomas Jeckyll and James McNeill Whistler, Peacock Room, 49 Princes Gate, London, 1876-7.

Within this dining room Whistler introduced Japanese themes into an Arts and Crafts environment. The room, with its shelves to display Japanese porcelain, had been designed by Thomas Jeckyll. Whistler's decoration used blue and gold wall painting inspired by peacock feathers. The furniture was by Edward William Godwin, a former assistant of William Burges.

leather and lined with an intricate system of shelves on thin wooden support members intended for the display of a collection of Japanese blue and white porcelains. Whistler converted this setting into what he called "A Harmony in Blue and Gold" by painting the entire room—even the doors, walls, and window shutters—with decorative forms based on the feathers of the peacock, a favorite theme of the Aesthetic movement. It was the drift of this movement toward the exotic, toward extremes, and toward pretentiousness that became the basis for the satire by W. S. Gilbert in the Gilbert and Sullivan operetta *Patience*. It is amusing to note that Gilbert himself lived in a Norman Shaw London house, Grims Dyke, with interiors that exemplify the pretensions that *Patience* satirizes.

Charles Eastlake (see also p. 197) was another influential figure in the movement through his publications, but his own very limited work and the work of his many imitators was closer to the heavy High Victorian tradition than to the spirit of the Arts and Crafts movement. The term "art furniture" was Eastlake's name for the aesthetically "correct" design that he advocated. Bruce Talbert (1838–81) was a designer of furniture and metal-work in a style he called Gothic, but which appears in the drawings he published to be close to Arts and Crafts intentions. Robert W. Edis (1839–1927) was an architect working in the Queen Anne vocabulary, but in his book *Decoration and Furniture of Town Houses* (1881) he illustrates interiors where Morris wallpaper and Godwin furniture are to be used (**fig. 12.8**).

Ernest Gimson (1864–1919) met Morris in 1886, became skilled as a plaster worker and as a wood turner, and produced both furniture and ironwork. The simple forms recall a medieval vernacular, but also suggest the simplicity that was to become a primary value in twentieth-century modernism. He produced chairs for an organization called the Art Workers' Guild that was for a time a gathering point for Arts and Crafts oriented personalities. Charles R. Ashbee (1863–1942) was also associated with the guild, acting as its leading designer of furniture, silver, and jewelry. In 1901 he was instrumental in moving the guild, by then numbering some 150 craftsmen, to the Cotswold village of Chipping Campden where it continued production until 1907. Mackay Hugh Baillie Scott (1865–1945) designed furniture for the guild, as well as interiors that were published in Germany and the United States around the turn of the century (**fig. 12.9**). His work forms a link with European developments in the twentieth century, including the Deutsche Werkstätten.

A number of details helped to make the interiors of Arts and Crafts designers seem open and airy, even when ceiling heights were lower than

12.8 Robert W. Edis, interior, London, 1881.

The plate from Edis's Decoration and Furniture of Town Houses (1881) shows an interior with furniture by Edward William Godwin, a frieze by Henry Stacy Marks, and wallpaper by William Morris. Edis was an active propagandist for the ideas of the Aesthetic Movement and the Arts and Crafts Movement. His book urged readers to follow the design lead shown by these movements and to adapt them for use in their own homes.

12.9 M.H. Baillie Scott, design for a music cabinet, Marvel Hill, Witley, England, c. 1914.

Mackay Hugh Baillie Scott continued to design in the spirit of the Arts and Crafts Movement well into the twentieth century. This cabinet is covered with painted ornamental detail in the manner that Morris had introduced fifty years before.

those favored in typical Victorian work. Walls were often paneled up to a height of six or seven feet, while a frieze or band of lighter tones, paint, or paper introduced a horizontal element that suggested openness. Bulbous lamps and lighting fixtures were often replaced by box-like forms with frosted or colored glass to screen the newly introduced electric bulbs.

Links to Modernism

Voysey

An important figure in the transition from Victorian to twentieth-century design was Charles Francis Annesley Voysey (1857–1941). Voysey was an architect but began his career with designs for wallpapers, textiles, and carpets. He became a member of the Art Workers' Guild and eventually developed furniture designs in a simple, craft-based style well related to his architectural work. Voysey designed a large country house, Broadleys (1898), overlooking Lake Windermere. It has three curving bow windows facing toward the lake. The

interiors, originally with furniture of his design, have a directness based on craft orientation. His own house, The Orchard (1900), at Chorley Wood, Hertfordshire, is a simple gable-roofed mass suggesting English country vernacular design. Interior spaces are of great simplicity and elegance (**fig. 12.10**). Although they appear close in spirit to modernism, Voysey actually disliked modernism as such. The living room at The Orchard has walls covered with violet fabric up to eye level, with white paint above. The woodwork is natural oak or painted white. Bedroom walls are covered with wallpapers of his own design. His designs for such objects as clocks, silver flatware, and ironwork are highly original and strikingly successful. Voysey's work carries hints of the ART NOUVEAU movement on the continent (see Chapter 13).

Mackmurdo

The work of Arthur Heygate Mackmurdo (1851–1942) suggests an even closer link to Art Nouveau—indeed, he is often viewed as one of the originators of that style. Early in Mackmurdo's career he acted as an assistant to Ruskin during a trip to

12.10 C.F.A. Voysey, The Orchard, Chorley Wood, Hertfordshire, England, 1900.

In the living space of his own house, called the "hall" Voysey works with simple elements that point to the ideas of Modernism that were to surface in the following century.

Italy. In 1877 he was in contact with Morris, and in 1880 with Whistler. His book *Wren's City Churches* (1883) carried an oddly inappropriate title page—a Mackmurdo woodcut showing sinuously curved leaves, flowers, and lettering in the graphic style that came to be typical of Art Nouveau design (**fig. 12.11**). His furniture design made use of related flowing curved forms. He was also the founder of the Century Guild, yet another organization devoted to furthering Arts and Crafts ideals through publications and production of various decorative objects.

Mackintosh

In Glasgow, Scotland, work related to Art Nouveau was produced for a short time by a few designers led by Charles Rennie Mackintosh (1868–1928). Mackintosh's work grew out of Arts and Crafts bases, but moved toward the freedom of Art Nouveau and became greatly admired by continental designers, including those based in Vienna (fig. 12.1). The most important building by Mackintosh is the Glasgow School of Art (1896–1909), which is devoted to studio spaces with large windows that dominate the exterior. Internally, lobby, stairway, office, and library spaces use simple timber and masonry constructional elements set off by unusual furniture and details of lighting and metalwork that move toward Art Nouveau inventiveness. The building was not well liked by the Glasgow public. Mackintosh also designed a few private homes, such as Hill House at Dunbartonshire, Scotland (1902–3; **fig. 12.1**), a church, and several tea-room restaurants in Glasgow operated by a Miss Cranston. The latter had remarkably creative interiors, with decorative wall murals, fireplaces, windows and doors with stained-glass inserts, and special furniture. For private clients and for his own Glasgow flat, Mackintosh developed furniture designs that most often used simple, geometric forms, but then introduced exaggerated proportions, extreme high chair backs, and white or black paint finishes with decorative details in violet, silver, or gold. Painted ornamental elements were often added by Mackintosh's wife, Margaret Macdonald (1865–1933), who, along with her sister Frances (1874–1921), was an active participant in the Arts and Crafts movement and related design activities that were centered in Glasgow in the 1890s.

It is a curious fact that the Arts and Crafts Movement, despite its aim to bring about a broad reform in Victorian design and taste, only succeeded in influencing a small group of supporters and enthusiasts able to afford its costly productions. However, in its rejection of meaningless mass-produced ornamentation, in its emphasis on honesty in the design expression of realities of function, material, and technique, Arts and Crafts pointed toward the future, almost in spite of itself. Its link to Art Nouveau, with its total rejection of historicism, makes it the starting point for all studies of modernism.

United States: The Craftsman Movement

The close link between England and the Americas made it inevitable that there should be an Arts and Crafts movement in the United States. While the ornate Victorianism discussed in the last chapter remained dominant in America after the Civil War, a divergent movement, limited in size and acceptance, surfaced and offered alternatives to the dominant taste of the time.

Stickley and the Roycrofters

The leading figure in what came to be called the Craftsman movement in America was Gustav Stickley (1858–1942), a member of a family that

12.11 Arthur Heygate Mackmurdo, title page, *Wren's City Churches*, 1883.

Mackmurdo, a devoted supporter of Arts and Crafts ideals, was the author of a book urging the preservation of Christopher Wren's London churches. His highly original title page seems unrelated to the content and suggests the Art Nouveau direction that, at the time, had not yet fully surfaced.

operated several furniture factories. Stickley began his career running a furniture store selling a variety of historic reproductions. He became interested in the writings of Ruskin and Morris and, in 1898, made a trip to England to see the Arts and Crafts work being produced there. He also made a stop in Paris to visit Bing's Art Nouveau shop. On his return to America he began to design and produce simple furniture, generally of massive form and made in solid oak, assembled with craftsmanly wood joints, iron hardware, leather cushions and other details. Ornamentation was minimal or non-existent except as it resulted from constructional detailing. The style was often given the term MISSION because of its supposed similarity to simple furniture made for the earlier California missions, or was designated GOLDEN OAK for the typical yellow-brown tone given the oak wood by a process called "fuming." Some of the most interesting examples of Stickley furniture were produced during the brief period when Harvey Ellis (1842–1904) was associated with the firm. His designs incorporated ornamentation suggestive of Voysey and later English and Scotch designers.

In 1901 Stickley began publishing a magazine, *The Craftsman*, which promoted Arts and Crafts ideals in architecture and design and illustrated "Craftsman houses" (**fig. 12.12**). The magazine also carried articles promoting various causes such as women's rights, improved child care, and social justice, along with art photography, poetry, fiction,

and any other materials that came to Stickley's attention that would appeal to an audience both tasteful and idealistic. Voysey contributed an article on the design of houses, illustrated with photographs of several of his designs including The Orchard. Advertisements in *The Craftsman* offered products by other craft-oriented firms. Stickley eventually established his headquarters in New York, where offices and showrooms for Craftsman enterprises were grouped.

The commercial success of Stickley's efforts encouraged various imitators until a number of factories were producing Craftsman furniture and other products. As the excesses of Victorian design began to lose popularity at the turn of the century, the Craftsman movement grew in importance. Gustav Stickley's factory at Eastwood, New York, found itself in competition with the Onondaga, New York, shops of his younger brothers Leopold and John George Stickley. Elbert Hubbard (1856–1915) established his own craft-oriented venture at East Aurora, New York, with the name of Roycroft. Hubbard produced books and pamphlets dealing with art and literature designed in a style clearly based on Morris's precedents. The Roycrofters also produced Mission style furniture in direct competition with Stickley, and moved even further than Stickley toward the establishment of an aesthetic cult. Although it faded in importance after World War I, when "period" decoration in various historically imitative styles became increasingly popular, some traces of Craftsman influence survived into the 1930s. Themes related to the Craftsman movement included the development of a "bungalow style" based on a kind of vernacular one-story house that became popular in California. A typical bungalow had porches, overhanging eaves, walls of shingle or stucco, and minimal ornamental detail.

Bradley

Will Bradley (1868–1962) was a commercial illustrator who developed an enthusiasm for the Craftsman style, for bungalows, and for English work of related character. He was commissioned by the popular and influential *Ladies' Home Journal* magazine to develop designs for houses, rooms, and furnishings (**fig. 12.13**). They were published in the form of his skillful and attractive renderings, showing colorful versions of the Mission style, often with amusing decorative

12.12 U.S. dining room, 1904.

The Craftsman, *from which this illustration is taken, was a magazine that promoted the ideals of the Arts and Crafts Movement, which was known in America as the Craftsman Movement. The magazine suggested designs for rooms and objects that were clearly inspired by the thinking of Morris, Webb, and Voysey. Traditional ladder-back chairs stand around a table and sideboard from the shops of Gustav Stickley. The room itself, with its wood wainscot and plain window detail, is in strong contrast to the florid ornamentation of most Victorian design of the time.*

12.13 Will Bradley, interior, 1902.

Colorful renderings of house interiors of Bradley's design became familiar to an extensive American public through their publication in the popular magazine Ladies' Home Journal. *His support for designs in the Arts and Crafts or Craftsman style and his hints about the designs of Charles Rennie Mackintosh and the Vienna Secession designers helped to lead to the acceptance of the furniture that came to be called "Mission Style."*

12.14 Henry Hobson Richardson, Trinity Church, Boston, 1877.

Richardson's work was, in its day, often called "Romanesque Revival," but it was far more creative than that designation suggests. This church contains forms unlike any known in the Romanesque era, and they resulted in an impressive space, rich in color, with stained glass by Tiffany and painting by John La Farge.

details. The making of "artistic" wares—lamps with stained-glass panels, decorative objects of metal, most often hammered copper, and pottery such as that of the Rookwood Pottery in Ohio—rounded out the presence of Arts and Crafts design in the United States. The influence of Art Nouveau ideas developed in America at the same time, so that the resulting overlap reflects a fusion of these two, quite separate alternative challenges to the patterns of Victorianism.

Richardson

Henry Hobson Richardson (1838–86) was the first American architect of international importance. Richardson's early works were in versions of various Victorian styles—Gothic, second Empire, Stick, Shingle, or, with increasing frequency, Romanesque. His first masterpiece, Trinity Church in Boston (1877), uses semicircular arches and other Romanesque motifs, but they are combined around a great central crossing tower in a way that is entirely original. Externally, the rough-cut stonework is beautifully detailed but the interior space suffers from the brightness of stained-glass windows, some of indifferent quality. The interior (**fig. 12.14**) is dominated by the ceiling form, wood and plaster vaulting of trefoil shape with iron tie-beams encased in wood. Richardson's stated intention was for "a color church" where all surfaces would be covered with painted stenciling or with

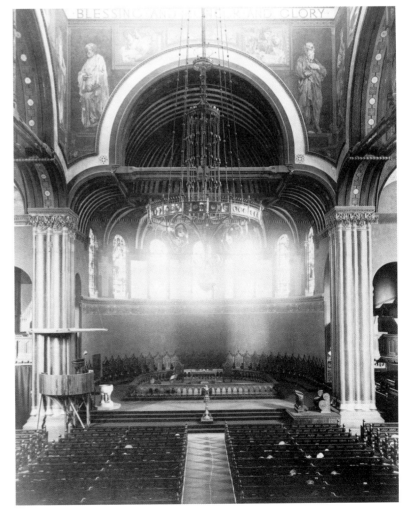

the figurative paintings of John La Farge (1835–1910) in dull reds and red-browns with some blue-greens and gold. La Farge also designed the windows of the west front. Although Richardson's work seemed for a time to be another revival—in this case of Romanesque—his work gradually moved from historicism toward simplification while retaining fine stonework and semicircular arches as dominant themes. A series of library buildings, each based on functional plans, became progressively more innovative in design. The Crane Library at Quincy, Massachusetts (1880–2), is the best known. Its main space is a double-height stack room with an open reading space at its center. The beamed ceiling, wood shelving, and access balconies and floor are all of wood. An elaborate fireplace and mantel forms a focus at one end of the room. Tables, chairs, and (gas) lighting fixtures are all of Richardson's design. The chairs used here, and similar chairs designed by Richardson for other projects, are spindle-backed arm chairs of simple but elegant form, far superior to the typical furniture designs of the time.

The Richardson work that became most influential, the Marshall Field Wholesale Store in Chicago (1885–7), has, unfortunately, been destroyed. It was a block-long seven-story stone mass with windows in orderly arch-topped groups. The interiors were simple open lofts and warehouse spaces of strictly utilitarian character. The fame of the building rests on the simplicity of its exterior form, which can be considered a precursor to the even more advanced work of Louis Sullivan, one of the building's most vocal admirers.

Greene & Greene and Maybeck

In California, the brothers Charles Sumner Greene (1868–1957) and Henry Mather Greene (1870–1954) established an architectural practice with a highly personal style that drew on the Craftsman tradition, on the Stick style, and on the bungalow vernacular. Greene and Greene houses are of wood with low sloping roofs having long overhangs. It is the quality of the interiors of these houses, such as the Pasadena, California, Blacker House of 1907 and the Gamble House (**fig. 12.15**) of 1908 (now preserved as a museum), that distinguishes Greene and Greene work from other California work of the same era. Wood is used with careful and intricate joinery detailing that draws on oriental precedents in combination with parallel

Arts and Crafts respect for quality handwork. Ornamentation is present but generally very restrained, while panels of stained glass, lantern-like lamps, and hanging light fixtures (now for electric lights), and simple furniture of great elegance and full of craftsmanly details fill the spacious entrance halls and other generous interior spaces. Color is dominated by red-brown tones of wood, mahogany, some teak, some rosewood, ebony, and maple, with polished oiled natural finishes. Reds, blues, and greens appear in stained glass and in rugs.

Bernard R. Maybeck (1862–1957) was the designer of houses in a related California-based vocabulary sometimes called the Western Stick style. His Christian Science Church in Berkeley (1910) uses highly original, craft-oriented wood detail to generate a handsome and original church interior. His most spectacular work, the Palace of the Fine Arts for the Panama Pacific Exposition of 1912 in San Francisco, with its great central rotunda, turns away from vernacular and craft traditions toward historicism, albeit incorporating a highly personal and creative view of its classical precedents. The more modest works of the Greene brothers and of Maybeck established a California bungalow tradition, encouraged in the east by the Craftsman movement, that became a staple of modest suburban development. At best it offered simple and sensible alternatives to Victorian pretensions. At worst, it became a cliché adopted by real estate speculative developers to lend a kind of spurious charm to subdivisons crammed with poorly designed and badly built houses offered to a public eager to satisfy the dream of "a home of one's own."

Developments in Continental Europe

The Arts and Crafts movement and its parallel Craftsman movement in America did not transfer to the European continent and the Scandinavian countries in any clearly recognizable form. As the nineteenth century came to an end, an extraordinarily complex variety of developments surfaced in the design fields. On the European continent, the emergence of Art Nouveau in Belgium and France presented a new approach to design suited to the modern world (see Chapter 13).

12.15 (*opposite*) Greene and Greene, Gamble House, Pasadena, California, 1908.

The work of the Greene Brothers is based on an understanding of craft ideals with woodwork detailing in a way that appears based on Japanese traditional design. Finely detailed furniture, original lantern-like light fixtures, and stained-glass inserts in windows generate interiors that are both original and full of a sense of tradition.

Germany: Muthesius

In Germany, although no direct parallel to English Victorian design surfaced, the English Arts and Crafts movement became a model for attempted design reform furthered by the efforts of Hermann Muthesius (1861–1927). An architect for the Prussian government, Muthesius was sent to the German Embassy in London in 1896 to study English design practice. He was the author of a number of magazine articles and books dealing with English Arts and Crafts and related design activities. After returning to Germany he published the three-volume *Das Englische Haus* (1904–5) illustrating work by Shaw, Baillie Scott, Voysey, and other leading figures in English architecture and interior design. As a government official, he urged improvement in German design and was a key figure in the formation of the Deutsche Werkbund in 1907, an organization that promoted design excellence. The Werkbund was a powerful influence on the development of modernism in Germany, and made a link between nineteenth-century English design reform and twentieth-century developments on the European continent.

The Netherlands: Berlage

In the Netherlands, the effort to find an alternative to Victorian excess is represented by the work of Hendrik Petrus Berlage (1856–1934), an architect best known for the massive Amsterdam Stock Exchange (**fig. 12.16**; 1898–1903). The building is constructed of Dutch brick with a facade that is symmetrical except for the great clock tower on one side. The arched entrance openings and simple brick walls suggest the later work of Richardson—there is no attempt at historic imitation and the ornamental detail is restrained. The interior is largely devoted to a vast open exchange room, with balconies on two upper levels looking out into the central space through brick arches. Overhead, exposed iron trusses with iron tie rods span the open space and support glass skylights that flood the interior with daylight. Most of Berlage's later work was in city planning for Amsterdam, but this building established his reputation as an important figure in the reform efforts that ultimately led to modernism.

If design history had progressed according to a strictly logical pattern, the Arts and Crafts movement and the parallel Art Nouveau design of continental origin would have come together and moved into the modernism of the twentieth century in a smooth progression. These efforts at reform, however, were pushed aside by a new wave of enthusiasm for historical imitation usually called eclecticism (see Chapter 14). It required a new wave of reform to push eclecticism aside and open up the way to the twentieth-century directions now called modernism.

12.16 (*opposite*) Hendrik Petrus Berlage, Bourse, Amsterdam, 1898-1903.

The carefully detailed brickwork in the walls and upper galleries of the Bourse (stock exchange) forms a dignified shell for the exposed steel trusses that roof the space with extensive areas of glass skylights. The work of Berlage, with its strong base in Dutch traditions of fine masonry (particularly in brick and tile), embodied elements of functionalism as it was to develop in the twentieth century.

13 Art Nouveau and the Vienna Secession

The late nineteenth century was a period of relative peace and prosperity in continental Europe. Economic prosperity generated larger upper and upper-middle classes that could support new and experimental directions in design. Belgium and France became the leading regions for the development of Art Nouveau (with some extension into Germany, Spain, and the Scandinavian countries). In Austria, Vienna became the center for the design direction that became known as the Vienna SECESSION. Awareness of design in remote locations, such as the orient (particularly in Japan), increased as travel became easier and communication brought objects and art works into European culture.

Roots and Characteristics of Art Nouveau

Many of these developments were quite unrelated to one another and had, at least at their beginnings, no central core of direction or leadership. It is only in retrospect that it has become possible to see commonalities and relationships that justify speaking of Art Nouveau as "a movement." Even the term Art Nouveau had no currency at the time the movement was developing—it was the name of a Paris shop whose wares displayed the qualities that were characteristic of the movement.

In Germany and the Scandinavian countries the German term JUGENDSTIL (the "young style" or "style of youth") was generally used. In England, where Art Nouveau was at first simply an aspect of the Aesthetic movement (see Chapter 12), the term LIBERTY STYLE came into use—also taken from the name of the London shop that offered objects related to Art Nouveau directions. Art Nouveau work in Spain, Scotland, and America had only remote relationship to what had surfaced in Brussels and Paris. In Vienna, the development called Vienna Secession can be viewed as a separate but parallel manifestation of Art Nouveau. The characteristics that make Art Nouveau design recognizable as a unique development are:

- A rejection of Victorian styles and of historic imitation in revivals or through eclectic combinations of precedents.
- A willingness to take advantage of modern materials (iron and glass), modern techniques (industrial production), and such innovations as electric lighting.
- A close relationship with the fine arts, incorporating painting, bas-relief, and sculpture into architecture and interior design.
- The use of decorative ornamentation based on nature forms—flowers, vines, shells, bird feathers, insect wings—and abstract forms derived from these sources.
- Curvilinear forms as dominant themes in both basic structural elements and in ornamentation. The relationship to the generally curving and flowing forms of nature gave rise to the S curves or "whiplash" curves usually regarded as the most visible Art Nouveau motif.

Art Nouveau directions can be traced in graphic illustration, typography, posters and advertisements, painting and sculpture, and fashion design, and the design of jewelry and decorative objects such as ceramics, glassware and silver, picture frames, and lamps, arriving at a synthesis in complete interiors and in architecture. Because Art Nouveau surfaced in many fields and in many places, it is difficult to trace an orderly developmental progression. It is usual to say that Art Nouveau first appeared in France and Belgium, but it is probably more accurate to identify England as the point of origin. A number of individuals identified with the Arts and Crafts movement designed

13.1 (below) C. F. A. Voysey, decorative design, England, 1907.

Voysey stands at a crossroads between the Arts and Crafts Movement prevalent in England (see p. 210) and the Art Nouveau style that was developing on the continent of Europe. This design, which comes from late in his career, makes use of the nature-based and curvilinear forms that are characteristic of Art Nouveau.

13.2 (opposite) Eugène Vallin, Masson House, Nancy, France, 1903–14; now in the Musée de l'Ecole de Nancy.

Vallin was responsible for the design of every detail in this dining room. The built-in woodwork of the cabinet, the fireplace surround and over-mantel, the ceiling detail, the hanging light fixture, the rug, and the furniture are all of Vallin's highly original design and full of the flowing curves typical of the Art Nouveau movement.

13.3 Victor Horta, Tassel House, Brussels, 1892.

Stairways offered the Art Nouveau designer opportunities to develop flowing curves in steps, railings, and, as in the Tassel House (now the Mexican Embassy), painted or stenciled color patterns on walls and ceiling. The slim column is an indication of the acceptance of metal as a legitimate material for interior detail, while the hanging lighting fixture exploits the possibilities of the then new electric light.

objects that embodied characteristics of Art Nouveau. The term proto-Art Nouveau has been used by S. Tschudi Madsen to describe the work of Arthur Mackmurdo, such as his chair of 1882 with its perforated back carved in swirling flower-like forms, some of his metalwork, textile print designs, and the graphic design of the book cover of 1883 (see p. 219). C. F. A. Voysey's textile prints also make use of plant forms in free curves (**fig. 13.1**), and Christopher Dresser's design philosophy was largely based on his knowledge of botany. Aubrey Beardsley (1872–98) is well known for his style of illustration using fantastically curving linear forms. In France similar themes appear in the posters of Alphonse Mucha (1860–1939), and then in the posters and other works of such major arists as Henri Toulouse-Lautrec (1864–1901) and Pierre Bonnard (1867–1947).

Belgium

Horta

The Belgian architect and designer Victor Horta (1861–1947) produced an extensive body of work that shows off all of the qualities that are typical of Art Nouveau design. The Tassel House in Brussels (1892) has a symmetrical row-house facade that uses fairly conventional architectural motifs. Within, however, there is a complex open stair using flowing iron railings, support columns, and electric light fixtures with curving lines that are then carried into the stenciled wall and ceiling painted decorations and the mosaic tile patterns of floors (**fig. 13.3**). Spaces are more open and flowing than Victorian practice would have permitted. The Van Eetvelde House in Brussels (1895) contains a remarkable salon where iron columns support a glass dome in a relationship technically suggestive of the Crystal Palace, but here with the introduction of the florid curves of Art Nouveau.

In his own house and adjacent office-studio in Brussels (**fig. 13.4**; 1898), with its asymmetrical facade with twisted iron balcony supports and large glass windows, Horta was able to design every detail—furniture, light fixtures, stained-glass panels, door and window frames, even hardware— so that every element is an expression of Art Nouveau, curvilinear, nature-related decorative

---

INSIGHTS

Victor Horta and Art Nouveau

The architectural magazine *L'Emulation* described the Art Nouveau movement in Belgium during the 1870s and 1880s in the following terms:

We are called upon to create something which is our own, something to which we can give a new name. We are called upon to invent a style . . . . We must free ourselves from foreign influences . . . . Nothing is beautiful in architecture unless true. [1]

The editor, Edouard Allen, went so far as to advise his readers to "shun painted plaster and stucco." [2]

Such views found expression in the unique and influential buildings of Belgian architect Victor Horta. In describing the design concept for his celebrated Tassel House in Brussels, Horta declared,

I discard the flower and the leaf, but I keep the stalk. [3]

New technology was central to his work and he presented his designs and ideas to clients through "photographs projected on to the end wall of the drawing room and dining room space where the audience sat." [4]

The radical nature of Art Nouveau did not impress many outside a small avant garde. The writer R. D. Benn criticized the style in 1904:

With regard to this "new art," it has been said, and with some measure of reason, that, on the one hand, most of it which is really new, is not art, and, on the other, that which is art, is not new; and I do not think that the situation could be summed up more correctly or concisely. [5]

1. Edouard Allen, *L'Emulation*, quoted in Kenneth Frampton, *Modern Architecture*, (London, 1992), p. 67; 2. *Ibid*, p. 68; 3. Victor Horta, *Memoirs*, quoted in J. M.Richards, *Who's Who in Architecture* (London, 1977), p. 151; 4.*Ibid*, p. 151; 5. R. D. Benn, *Style in Furniture* (London, 1904), p. 37

---

detail. The house is now preserved as a museum. In the Hôtel Solvay (not a hotel but a luxurious private house), also in Brussels, there are interiors with an even richer display of Art Nouveau decorative vocabulary. Horta's Maison du Peuple (1896–9), now demolished, was a larger building with an iron and glass facade curved to follow the form of the adjacent street. Its top-floor meeting hall with exposed iron structural elements and great electric light standards suggests directions that the twentieth century was to explore. Having achieved remarkable success with his early work, Horta retreated into a rather dull, conventional

13.4 Victor Horta, Horta House, Brussels, 1898-1911.

In his own house (now the Horta Museum) Victor Horta included tiled walls and ceilings, built-in cabinets, woodwork with stained-glass inserts, electric lighting fixtures, and furniture with flowing Art Nouveau curves all to his own design. The white tiles and the use of color are typical of Art Nouveau style.

13.5 Henri Van de Velde, magazine advertisement for Van de Velde's Atelier, *Dekorative Kunst*, Vol. I, Belgium, 1898.

In this advertisement, Van de Velde offers various materials for use in interior design, including papers and paints, textiles, tiles, and light fixtures, all of which were available from his shop at Uccle, near Brussels. The design of the advertisement, with its flowing curves, is evidence of Van de Velde's commitment to Art Nouveau.

vocabulary and had a long and successful career that never moved to exploit or extend his early achievements.

Van de Velde

The second significant Belgian Art Nouveau practitioner was Henri Van de Velde (1863–1957) whose own house of 1894 also exemplified the Art Nouveau desire to create everything in a new and unified mode. He designed the house and all its furniture and contents, down to table silver and kitchen cookware. He moved from Brussels to Paris where he was the designer of the shop established by Samuel Bing (1838–1919) that carried the name L'Art Nouveau and gave that name to the style and period. Van de Velde was strongly influ-

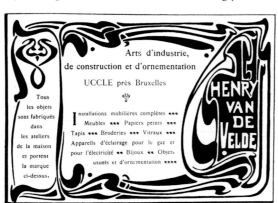

enced by English work of the time, and established a bridge between English and continental Art Nouveau beginnings. He eventually relocated in Berlin, and most of his Art Nouveau furniture design, on which his reputation largely rests, was developed during these years. It is full of the flowing, curved forms typical of Art Nouveau, complex and decorative but without any references to historic precedents. The Art School Building at Weimar that he designed in 1904–11 became the building that housed the post-World War I BAUHAUS at its inception. Van de Velde was a key figure in promoting the ideals of a new and progressive direction in design (**fig. 13.5**).

France

The School of Nancy

In France, Art Nouveau developed in two main centers, in Paris and in the smaller city of Nancy. In Nancy, Eugène Vallin (1856–1922) was the designer of interiors for a house (now a museum) of 1903–6 which included a dining room that might be regarded as an archetypical Art Nouveau achievement (**fig. 13.2**). Every detail of woodwork, ceiling moldings, wall treatment, carpet, light fixtures, and furniture were his designs, creating a fantastic environment of closely related, original, curvilinear, and complex forms. There arose a School of Nancy, which included other designers such as the master of decorative craftsmanship in glass Emile Gallé (1846–1904) and the furniture designer Louis Majorelle (1859–1926), each a master of a vocabulary of ornate and complex decorative form. Majorelle was a specialist in the design of furniture using carving, inlay, and ormolu or other metal decorative elements; the curving themes were generally based on floral patterns. He developed a successful business with showrooms in Paris and other French cities.

The work at Nancy is amazing in its variety, originality, and beauty, although there is a tendency toward an excess of decorative richness.

Guimard

In Paris, the most significant figure was Hector Guimard (1867–1942). Guimard was an architect, but his work included the interior design of many

and its stenciled ceiling is an integrated essay in the curving, whiplash forms and pastel colors of the Art Nouveau vocabulary. Stairs rise in a tower, while the water hydrant in the court has been made into a fantastic sculpture in bronze. The interiors of apartments vary, of course, according to their histories and the tastes of occupants, but old photographs show Guimard in the studio of his own apartment surrounded by his furniture, woodwork, and plaster details, many of the elements that were offered for sale in a brochure titled *Le Style Guimard*.

Guimard's own Paris town house of 1909–12 is a four-story corner building on an awkward triangular site. The two street fronts of stone with ornamental iron balcony railings are full of unusual asymmetrical, flowing, curving, carved forms. The interiors as they appear in contemporary photographs consist of rooms of unusual shape, with every bit of furniture and decorative detail an example of Guimard's highly individualistic style.

Apart from a number of Paris apartment houses, an office building, and many private houses in and around Paris, Guimard designed the entrance kiosks and many detail elements for the Paris Métro (subway) system around 1900. The entrances differed in size and shape; some had glass roof shelters, most incorporated signs, light

13.6 (*left*) Hector Guimard, Castel Béranger, Paris, 1894–9.

In the vestibule of this apartment, Guimard uses uniquely designed terracotta wall tiles, metal wall details that continue up to a painted ceiling, and an entrance gate of metal. All these elements use the flowing curves of Art Nouveau. The cream background and blue-green painted detail explore the pastel palette favored by Art Nouveau designers.

13.7 (*below*) Hector Guimard, entrance to Porte Dauphine Station, Paris, c. 1900.

In the entrances to stations for the Paris Métro Guimard used standard elements of metal that could be assembled to form entrance kiosks of varied size and form. All made use of curved details with nature-related forms.

of his buildings, the design of furniture and smaller objects, and of decorative elements such as tiles, window and door trim, and fireplace mantels that could be reproduced in some quantity for sale as products. He was, in a way, a pioneer industrial designer of a wide variety of objects. He worked on such forward looking projects as the design of visible components for the Paris Métro, the subway system that was under construction at the end of the nineteenth century. Many of Guimard's earliest works and some of the small houses and villas he designed throughout his career have a bizarre and fantastic quality, but his major works can be thought of as Art Nouveau at its best.

Castel Béranger (1894–9) is a six-story Paris apartment house built around a central courtyard which is entered through a vestibule passage (**fig. 13.6**). The entrance arch hints at the Romanesque, but a closer look at the stubby columns at either side with their swirling carved ornament makes it clear that the design is original, not derivative. The iron entrance gate and the vestibule with its molded terracotta tiles, its metal tile retaining bars,

fixtures, and panels for advertising posters and identification signs (**fig. 13.7**). Guimard dealt with this project by designing a number of standardized elements—metal railing panels, signs, light standards, and wall panels—that could be prefabricated in quantity and assembled in various configurations to suit the need of the individual Métro stations. Some of the larger entrances were unique designs, but most shared typical elements assembled in varied ways. Many of the Métro entrances have been destroyed, but the surviving examples have come to seem essential elements of the Paris street scene, beautiful and full of local color. They are among the most successful of all Art Nouveau designs.

Guimard was still practicing as late as 1929, although his later work moves away from the more florid manifestations of Art Nouveau toward a more restrained but still richly decorative style. Guimard's work, like most Art Nouveau design, demanded costly handwork. The flowing forms of a chair, for example, were not the result of the use of a flowing material—they demanded a high order of woodworking skill. Such work was only affordable by affluent clients who were also avant-garde in their tastes—a very limited public that could never support quantity production.

Other French Designers

A number of other French designers worked in the Art Nouveau vocabulary, specializing in interior design, furniture, and smaller decorative objects in ceramics, metals, glass, and jewelry. The shop established in 1895 in Paris by Samuel Bing with the name L'Art Nouveau helped to make such work accessible and widely known. Among the designers promoted by Bing, Edouard Colonna (1862–1948), and Eugène Gaillard (1862–1933) were both known for their design of furniture and jewelry. René Lalique (1860–1945) was a designer of textiles, jewelry, framed mirrors, and lamps, but is best known for his work in glass. A relationship to Paris fashion developed that helped to make the style popular with a fashion-oriented audience. However, once a style is established, fashion tends to seek new and different directions. As a result, Art Nouveau faded in the early twentieth century and had virtually disappeared by World War I (1914).

Spain

Gaudí

The use of the term Art Nouveau, at first confined to work in Belgium and France, has gradually been extended to include work in related style, using non-traditional, decorative design generally based on nature forms, wherever it appeared. The term is also used, therefore, for work in Spain, England, Scotland, and America that shares some or all of these characteristics. In Barcelona, Spain, although there is a variety of work in this style, the dominant figure of Antoni Gaudí (1852–1926) stands out as the inventor of a highly personal vocabulary of flowing curves and unusual decorative details. His 1904–6 reconstruction of an older building, Casa Batlló (**figs. 13.8** and **13.9**), included a new facade of complex, bone-like forms with a fantastic roof line and, for some apartments, remarkable interiors. Paneled doors are studded with small mirrors of irregular shape; ceilings are of plaster in swirling curved forms.

The nearby, much larger Casa Milá, informally known locally as La Pedrera ("the rock quarry;" begun 1905), is a large, six-story apartment house built around open courtyards. Its rippling cement exterior with iron-railed balconies is wrapped around a most unusual plan in which each apartment is a suite of rooms of irregular shape fitted together like stones of a mosaic. At rooftop level, terraces are covered with broken, colorful bits of tile combined as a mosaic. Fantastic sculptural forms are developed for chimneys and vents. Gaudí developed fantastic curving, sometimes bone-like, sometimes wiry forms for furniture designed to be custom made by skilled craftsmen for specific projects. The Guell Park (1905–14) and unfinished Sagrada Familia church (1903–26) exhibit Gaudí's fantastic and highly personal stylistic vocabulary on a major scale.

Germany: Jugendstil

The name Jugendstil derives from a periodical called *Die Jugend* (Youth), founded in Munich in 1869, but the style is essentially identical to the Art Nouveau directions practiced elsewhere in Europe.

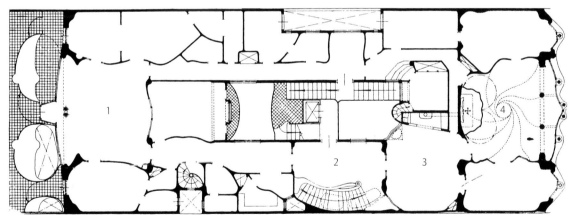

13.8 (*left*) Antoni Gaudí, Casa Batlló, Barcelona, 1904-6.

The dining room of the Casa Batlló contains table and chairs, door and window frames, paneling, hanging light fixture, and flowing plaster ceiling forms in Gaudí's highly personal form of Art Nouveau.

13.9 (*center*) Antoni Gaudí, plan of second floor, Casa Batlló.
1 Dining room
2 Grand staircase
3 Waiting room with fireplace
4 Salon

This building, which stood on a narrow city site, was an already existing structure that was reconstructed to Gaudí's design. There is a central court with stairs and elevator, and many rooms had unusual shapes produced by curving walls. The street front of the building is on the right-hand side of the plan, and the dining room illustrated above is on the left (number 1). Note the swirling ceiling forms indicated with dotted lines in the "salon" (number 4) at the right.

Endell

A relatively minor work of the Jugendstil designer August Endell (1871–1912) in Munich seems to sum up Art Nouveau design directions in a single project. Atelier Elvira (**fig. 13.10**; 1896, now destroyed) was a small, two-story building housing the studio of a photographer. The facade was penetrated by a doorway and a few small windows placed asymmetrically. The openings are of curious shape, rectangular with curving upper corners. There is no hint of any historical reference. Overwhelmingly powerful decoration—a great

13.10 August Endell, Elvira Studio, Munich, 1896 (destroyed 1944).

This small building for a photographer's atelier embodies the essence of Art Nouveau (Jugendstil) in the avoidance of historicism and the use of curving forms and artistic elements that relate to nature forms.

233

13.11 Lars Sonck, St John's Cathedral, Tampere, Finland, 1902-7.

Art Nouveau concepts were strongly welcomed in Finland, where they were known by the German term Jugendstil. Sonck was influenced by brick-built churches in Germany, but the flowing curves of the architectural elements, the painted ornamental details, the murals and stained glass, and the hanging lights all suggest Art Nouveau with a strongly individualistic Finnish accent.

bas-relief of curving form, abstract, yet suggestive of waves or sea creatures—dominated the blank upper wall surface. Window mullions were curved irregularly, as if made from stems of vines. The entrance hall and stairway made use of related fantastic decorative motifs. Endell was the designer of several less spectacular buildings and some Art Nouveau furniture, but his reputation rests on the Elvira shop alone.

Riemerschmidt and Behrens

Jugendstil themes were also developed by Richard Riemerschmidt (1868–1957), the designer of a music room for a Dresden exhibition in 1899 which included his furniture, lighting, and wall decoration. Its relative simplicity makes it seem predictive of later design directions. A simple Riemerschmidt chair incorporating a diagonal side support has come to be regarded as a "classic" design, the basis for several modern variants. In 1900, Riemerschmidt worked with Bernhard Pankok (1872–1943) on the design of a dining room shown at the Paris exhibition of that year, while Pankok alone produced a "smoking room" for the same exhibition, lined with wood in carved and shaped forms that related to windows, ceilings, and light fixtures, all expressive of Jugendstil fantasy form. The early work of Peter Behrens (1868–1940) is also in the Jugendstil mode, such as the interiors of his own house at Darmstadt (1901), for example. He later moved toward a more reserved, modernist style in his work for the German electrical industry (AEG), which included a variety of products such as electric fans, kettles, and lighting devices.

Scandinavia

Jugendstil spread northward into the Scandinavian countries where, particularly in Finland, it found a unique regional expression. Toward the end of the nineteenth century, Finland had experienced a design development usually called Romantic Nationalism, in which ancient Nordic themes dating back to the Viking era combined with vernacular craft traditions to produce work not unlike the American Adirondack style (see p. 200). The originality and decorative inclinations of Art Nouveau blended into this work to produce such buildings as the cathedral (really a church of

modest size) at Tampere (**fig. 13.11**; 1902–7) by Lars Sonck (1870–1956). Its stony exterior is suggestive of H. H. Richardson, but with details that balance Nordic and Art Nouveau influences. The interior, a wide open space surrounded on three sides by broad balconies, uses stained glass, wall painting, and ornamental plaster work in a Jugendstil decorative vocabulary. In the Helsinki Railroad Station (1906–14), Eliel Saarinen (1873–1950) displays a style transitional between Jugendstil and an early form of modernism.

Austria: The Vienna Secession

Vienna Secession is the term that was used by a group of artists and designers who withdrew from the exhibitions of the Vienna Academy in 1897 in protest against the refusal of the academy to accept their modernist works. The leader of the group was the painter Gustav Klimt (1862–1918).

Olbrich

Joseph Olbrich (1867–1908) designed the Secession Gallery (1897) in Vienna as an exhibition space and headquarters for the movement. The building is symmetrical, rectilinear in form, and hints at classicism with its cornice moldings and other details, but there is also decorative detail based on nature-related motifs, carved leaves, and mask-like Medusa faces. On the roof above the

entrance there is a great hollow dome of metal with a surface of gilded leaves (**fig. 13.12**). The interior of the building has been altered, but old photographs show it as it was at its opening: the great central gallery room has an arched ceiling and skylight and painted wall decoration in flowing Art Nouveau patterns (**fig. 13.13**).

Other work by Olbrich included a number of houses in the Mathildenhohe art colony, founded in 1899 at Darmstadt in Germany under the patronage of the grand duke of Hesse. An exhibition hall there and the Hochzeitturm (Wedding Tower, 1905–8) make use of geometric decorative elements along with proto-modernist rectangular forms. Olbrich's residential work combines traces of an Austrian peasant vernacular building style with the more original forms of Secession experimentation. Interiors are filled with carefully detailed woodwork that often incorporates fantastic forms. A creature with huge outstretched wings forms a window frame in the 1898 Villa Friedmann near Vienna, for example. Walls carry painted decoration; beds are sometimes enclosed in a virtual tabernacle of canopies and hangings.

Wagner

Otto Wagner (1841–1918), who had an established architectural career working in a conventional revivalist style, moved toward a new direction with the publication of his book *Moderne Architektur* (1895), which called for the abandonment of

13.12 (*above left*) Josef Olbrich, Secession Building, Vienna, 1897.

Olbrich's Secession building had a symmetrical scheme with a strongly rectilinear basis and moldings suggestive of classicism, but with decorative detail using floral motifs that relate to Art Nouveau. The gilded sculptural dome has a laurel-leaf theme and the balance between straight and curving forms typifies Secession work.

13.13 (*above*) Interior of Secession Gallery.

In the central gallery of the Secession Building the severely geometric forms of door and other openings and the pattern of squares on the wall indicate the rectilinear emphases of Secession design, while the wall painting uses the flowing forms similar to those of Art Nouveau work in Belgium and France.

13.14 (*below*) Otto Wagner, Post Office Savings Bank, Vienna, 1904–6.

The main banking room uses an exposed metal structure and a glass barrel-vaulted roof. The rivets of the steel columns act as decorative elements, while other ornamental detail is confined to a few black and white bands in the tiling of the floor, which is largely glass to admit light to the basement below.

panels of marble and glass. The gilded decorative detail reflects the Art Nouveau related ornamentalism of the Secession style. Interior detail in white, green, and gold ornamented the lobby.

Wagner's large church of S. Leopold Am Steinhof (1905–7), Vienna, has a tall dome of iron construction supporting a copper exterior. Inside the church, a broad crossing formed by the cruciform plan is topped by a low internal dome lined with a light, suspended ceiling of square, white panels held by thin metal strips painted gold. The liturgical fittings, the altar with baldachino, the pulpit and confessionals, the hanging light fixtures, the pictorial mosaics above the altar, and the stained-glass windows are all examples of the geometrically based decorative vocabulary of the Secession movement.

The best known of Wagner's projects is the large headquarters for the Austrian Post Office Savings Bank (**fig. 13.14**; 1904–6). The exterior of the building is sheathed in panels of stone held by bolts with heads exposed as decorative detail. Interior lobbies, stairs, and corridors are enriched with Secessionist detail in metal and stained glass. The central main banking room has a high central area with lower side spaces on either side (a "nave and aisles" in strictly modern terms) all roofed in metal and glass; support columns are steel with exposed rivet heads. The metal is all white; the floor of structural glass gives light to the space below. Electric light fixtures and tubular ventilator outlets are functional elements that also serve a decorative role. Simple wooden counters, check writing desks, and stools are all in Wagner's increasingly simple design. Although a work of the Vienna Secession, this room can be viewed as the first truly modern interior. It brings modern concepts first visible in the Crystal Palace into use in an interior that is totally practical and aesthetically successful through form and structure, without dependence on any applied decorative ornament.

Hoffmann

Josef Hoffmann (1870–1956) had a long career in architecture and design that extended from the early days of the Secession movement into twentieth-century modernism. His most important works date from early in his Secessionist period. In 1903 he was one of the founders of the Vienna WERKSTÄTTE, the loose guild of craft shops that produced objects of his design and work by other

historical revivalism in favor of design based on "purpose." His major civic projects of the 1890s included parts of a Danube canal system incorporating locks, bridges, and dams, as well as viaducts, buildings, and architectural elements for the Stadtbahn, an urban rail transport network. Entrance kiosks such as the twin structures at the Karlsplatz station in Vienna (1898) used a metal cage structure, externally visible, to hold wall

Secessionist designers. His design moved toward strict rectangularity (he usually made his drawings on graph paper); themes of small squares in patterns for textiles and papers, for perforations in metalware, and as ornament in architectural contexts were common. The Puckersdorf Sanatorium near Vienna (1903–6) is an austere, symmetrical block with white walls and minimal external ornament. Interiors are also simple, but patterns of squares in black and white tiled floors, and specially designed furniture including a simple chair for the dining hall look toward the austerity of later modernism. He also designed various exhibitions, residential projects, retail shops, bars, and restaurants, as well as furniture, china, table silver, and glassware.

The most famous Hoffmann work is not in Vienna but in Brussels. The large and luxurious house commissioned by the Belgian Adolphe Stoclet, usually called Palais Stoclet (1905–11), is an extraordinary building, an asymmetrical mass with a large tower topped with sculpture. The walls are covered with thin sheets of marble edged with narrow bands of gilded metal ornament. The many rooms include a double-height hall with overlooking balconies, a small theater or music room; all are of rather formal character and use rich materials (marbles in various colors) and restrained, geometric ornament. The dining room (**fig. 13.15**) has large mosaic murals by Gustav Klimt. There is an exceptionally large bathroom with tub, wall panels, and flooring all in marble. Hoffmann even designed the silver toilet articles spread on a dressing table shelf.

13.15 Josef Hoffmann, Palais Stoclet, Brussels, 1905-11.

In this formal dining room Hoffmann designed the marble walls, built-in cabinets, floor tiles, carpet, and furniture. The black and white floor tiles and the dark furniture are brightened by the warm color of the marble walls and by the mosaic murals of the side walls. These were designed by Gustav Klimt and were executed in marble, glass, and semi-precious stones by Leopold Forstner.

13.16 Adolf Loos, apartment, Vienna, c. 1903.

Loos's 1908 attack on ornament is presaged in the geometric simplicity of his own home. The exposed beams and brickwork suggest the vocabulary of twentieth-century modernism. Built-in shelving, seating, and cabinets support a functional approach to design. The decorative rugs and an orna-mental clock on the shelf may seem surprising, but Loos did allow such older orna-mental objects within his austere interiors.

Loos

Adolf Loos (1870–1933) was an architect and designer associated with Secession for a time, but he became disenchanted with what he regarded as the superficial decorative concerns of that move-ment. His reputation rests in large degree on his writings, which include early statements of theory that became central to the development of modernism. His essay "Ornament und Verbrechen" (Ornament and Crime) of 1908 attacks the use of ornament, which he viewed as a needless expression of degeneracy that modern civilization could best eliminate. While Loos's attempt to make a clear association between orna-ment and criminality now seems odd, his view of ornament as inappropriate to modern mechanized

production is central to much of the design of the twentieth century (**fig. 13.16**). His own work included simple bentwood furniture for the Thonet firm, and glassware (still in production) for Lobmeyr. His architectural work was, oddly, by no means free of ornament. A Vienna retail shop of 1909–11 for the firm of Goldman & Salatsch used Greek Doric columns as exterior ornament for its lower floors, but nevertheless attracted anger and ridicule because the upper, residential apartment floors have plain, white walls with rows of plain, square windows. The tiny Vienna Kärntner Bar of 1907, with its ceiling of rectangular panels, floor tiled in squares, and rich woods and leathers for the furnishings, is hardly an austere space. By contrast, Loos's Steiner House of 1910 carries austerity to the brink of brutality with its blocky white-walled masses punctured by scattered window openings. Interiors are less doctrinaire, with a clutter of contemporary Viennese comforts.

Secession design proved to be the most influen-tial aspect of Art Nouveau. While the florid curves of Belgian and French Art Nouveau came to be regarded as eccentric and willfully decorative, the more geometric forms of the Vienna work were more easily related to modernism. The writings of Loos underlined the modernist emphasis on puristic simplicity, while the craft-oriented concerns for honesty of materials and workman-ship expressed through the Werkbund and Werkstätte movements carried Arts and Crafts concepts into the modern world. Peter Behrens, although a member of the Munich (rather than the Vienna) Secession, formed a personal link from Jugendstil to modernism through his employment of the three most famous European modern pioneers—Gropius, Mies van der Rohe, and Le Corbusier.

United States

The role of Art Nouveau in America is almost completely confined to the work of two individ-uals—Tiffany and Sullivan—both of whom were highly influential.

Tiffany

Louis Comfort Tiffany (1848–1933) was the son of the founder of the well-known New York jewelry firm. As a young man he studied painting in

13.17 Louis Comfort Tiffany, window, Rochroane, Irvington-on-Hudson, New York, 1905. The Corning Museum of Art, Corning, New York.

Tiffany's fame rests on his skills in the use of stained glass in a variety of ways. Windows such as this one in a reception room at Rochroane were executed in a pictorial style that related to painting of the period. This landscape becomes luminous as it is lighted by outdoor daylight. Tiffany developed his techniques for use in lamps with glass shades and in bowls and vases that took on the qualities of Art Nouveau design.

America and Paris before settling in New York to devote his attention to art. Toward the end of the 1870s he became increasingly interested in the decorative arts, and in 1897 he established the interior decorating firm Louis C. Tiffany & Associated Artists. This offered both design and workshop production of many of the elements that went into such spaces as the Veterans' Room of the Seventh Regiment Armory in New York (1879) and residential interiors for wealthy New York families.

These rooms tended to follow the Victorian taste for crowded rich elaboration, modified by an awareness of the standards of the Arts and Crafts movement. In 1885 Tiffany reorganized his business, the new name Tiffany Glass Company indicating his increased concentration on the art of stained glass (**fig. 13.17**). He was commissioned to produce windows for many American churches (including H. H. Richardson's Trinity Church in Boston; see p. 221), often using conventionalized

13.18 Louis Comfort Tiffany, Tiffany Residence, New York, 1883–4.

In his work as a decorator Tiffany made use of a variety of ornamental elements based on Victorian taste, Arts and Crafts influences, and his own artistic urges. The florid wall covering, elaborate standing lamp, ornamental fireplace surround, and shelves for books and ceramics come together with hints of the urgings of Eastlake and Edis. The illustration is reproduced from a plate in a publication entitled Artistic Houses.

pictorial treatment of religious subjects in a Victorian version of medieval practice. Gradually, his stained glass came into demand in settings other than churches.

In residences (**fig. 13.18**), clubs, and similar locations his landscape, floral, and semi-abstract themes showed increasing similarity to French Art Nouveau work in glass. A window titled *Four Seasons*, with landscape panels for each season, was exhibited in Paris in 1892; it established an international reputation for Tiffany and drew the attention of Samuel Bing, who added Tiffany designs to the roster of works shown in his Paris Art Nouveau shop.

Skill in working with glass led Tiffany into the production of ornamental vases, bowls, paper weights, and other objects that used colorful patterns with floral motifs or purely abstract color and texture patterns. Terms for the various kinds of glass included Favrile, Cypriote, Cameo, and Lava, referring to the various processes and the resulting designs. Iridescent color effects were often used in the greatly admired Jack-in-the-pulpit and Morning glory designs. Tiffany's glass resembled

and often surpassed the work of such great French glass workers as Gallé and Lalique. His famous Tiffany lamps use metal bases with glass shades in a great variety of forms. The shades are often of leaded, pieced stained glass, and often single-piece globes of colorful, patterned Favrile glass. Some lamps are clusters of many small glass shades held by complex metal bases suggesting the stems of flowers or vines. Nature forms, peacock feathers, or insect wings often appear as alternatives to plant forms. Tiffany also designed mosaics, rugs, and some furniture. The tremendous popularity of Tiffany designs faded as tastes changed after World War I, but more recent interest in the Art Nouveau era has established Tiffany as a major figure in the movement.

Sullivan

Louis H. Sullivan (1856–1924) has an important though complex place in design history. Sullivan is often thought of as a pioneer of modernism, the advocate of the idea that "form follows function." He was the first American modernist architect, as well as the early employer and mentor of Frank Lloyd Wright. Yet Sullivan was not opposed to the use of ornament. Most of his work includes rich ornamentation in a highly personal style that has its basis in nature forms—thus he can also be understood as an exponent of Art Nouveau in architecture and interior design in America. Sullivan studied briefly at the Massachusetts Institute of Technology and then worked for a time in the Philadelphia office of Frank Furness. In 1874 he went to Paris to take up architectural study at the Ecole des Beaux-Arts, but he was dissatisfied and moved to Chicago in 1875.

He entered into a partnership with an older, German-trained architect, Dankmar Adler (1844–1900). The firm's Chicago Auditorium Building (1886–90) is a great opera house, hidden in a central space, surrounded by a multistory hotel and office building. The iron structural framing permits the ten-story height, but the outside walls are of masonry treated with detail reminiscent of H.

H. Richardson's Marshall Field Warehouse, although visually less successful. Sullivan's principal contribution was in the interior spaces that were the great glory of the project (**fig. 13.19**). Lobbies, stairways, public spaces in the hotel, and those serving the auditorium display Sullivan as an extraordinary designer both in terms of spatial organization and of ornament. The auditorium is topped with great arches that span a space studded with electric light bulbs and surrounded by florid, gilded relief ornament in Sullivan's personal vocabulary of Art Nouveau related detail. The sightlines and acoustics of the auditorium were excellent and there were ingenious arrangements for movable ceiling panels that could be lowered to reduce the 4200 seat capacity when an event did not require so large a hall. The main dining room of the hotel, placed at roof level, was a magnificent arched space with windows overlooking Lake Michigan, skylights, and painted wall and ceiling surfaces edged with Sullivan's elaborate decorative detail.

13.19 Louis Sullivan, Auditorium Building, Chicago, 1886–90.

With Dankmar Adler as his partner, Louis Henry Sullivan was co-designer of the great building that combined offices, a hotel, and an opera house (which gave the building its name) in one large complex. Sullivan was the designer of many interior spaces, the auditorium itself being the most spectacular. The arches of the ceiling with their painted detail, the proscenium design, and the organ grilles combined to produce a large space with jewel-like light, color, and form. It was unlike any older theater or concert hall and a striking success in both functional and decorative terms.

13.20 and **13.21**
Louis Sullivan,
Guaranty Building,
Buffalo, New York,
1894.

*The identification with
Art Nouveau of the
decorative detail
designed by Sullivan for
many of his buildings is
supported by these
examples of stair rail-
ings and door knobs
used inside the 12-story
Guaranty building.
Although his approach
to architecture empha-
sized function in a way
that pointed to
modernism, Sullivan
produced a highly
personal form of deco-
rative detail based on
the forms of nature.*

Adler's role in the subsequent work of the partnership was strictly technical, while Sullivan
controlled design. His interest in the tall building
as a design problem deserving of non-historical
solution led to a sequence of famous buildings with
exteriors that were increasingly austere and close to
the modernism of the twentieth century. Interiors
and details continued to use nature-based, florid
ornament. The Schiller Building in Chicago
(1891–2) was an office tower with a theater with a
richly ornamented interior—almost a smaller
version of the Auditorium. The Wainwright
Building in St. Louis (1890–1), the Guaranty
Building in Buffalo, New York (1894–5), and the
Bayard Building in New York City (1897–8) are
each studies in Sullivan's approach to skyscraper
architecture. All have a simple vertical emphasis
externally, rich but appropriate decorative detail,
and public space interiors filled with fine ornament
(**figs. 13.20** and **13.21**).

Other Sullivan projects included private
houses, such as the Charnley House of 1892 in
Chicago (in which Frank Lloyd Wright had a major
design role) with its particularly fine interior detail,
now carefully restored; the Transportation
Building for the Chicago Fair (World Columbian
Exposition) of 1893; and the Schlesinger & Mayer
(now Carson Pirie Scott) Department Store in
Chicago (1899–1904). This store building was in
many ways the most forward-looking of all
Sullivan buildings. The upper ten floors of the
twelve-story mass are treated externally as a simple
grid of vertical bands covering the structural steel
columns within, and horizontal bands at each floor
level. The resulting spaces are filled with large
windows, generating a "curtain wall" of glass
divided by narrow bands of white terracotta. The
band of ornament surrounding each window is so
thin as to be almost unnoticeable, leaving the exterior startlingly modern in character. On the two
lower levels around the entrance and the shop
windows, there is a rich overlay of decorative ornament in metal. An overhanging roof cornice that
topped the building has been removed, to the
detriment of Sullivan's overall design.

Sullivan's career declined after 1900 as
American tastes changed. His Transportation
Building at the Chicago Fair in 1893, with its
fantastic arched, ornamented, and gilded entrance
portals, was unique in its originality. It stood in
contrast with the other buildings of the fair that
were designed in the historically imitative classical
style that was coming into increasing favor among
east coast architects, many of whom had been
trained at the Ecole des Beaux-Arts in Paris. Both
public and many critics were drawn to the white-
columned classical pavilions around great
reflecting pools, and tended to find the Sullivan
Building a discordant note. As time went on,
Sullivan had fewer clients and less work.

Sullivan's St. Paul's Methodist Church in Cedar
Rapids, Iowa (1910–12), combines a rectangular
school block with a semicircular church auditorium that gives the building its external form. A
great bell tower rises from the center of the
building. The church interior has seats arranged in
curving rows, as in an amphitheater, with more
seats in an overlooking balcony. Unfortunately,
Sullivan fell out with his clients who, in order to
save money, omitted much of his decorative detail
and substituted cheap "art glass" for the original
stained-glass windows he had designed. The

building is still a striking and unusual work.

The later commissions of Sullivan's career were mostly small bank buildings in mid-western cities, but they include some of his finest works in their simple and original concepts and in their rich external and internal detail. The National Farmers' Bank of Owatonna, Minnesota (1907–8), the People's Savings Bank of Cedar Rapids, Iowa (1911), the Merchants' National Bank of Grinnell, Iowa (1914), the People's Savings and Loan Association Bank of Sidney, Ohio (1917–18), and the Farmers' and Merchants' Union Bank of Columbia, Wisconsin (1919), all belong to this final phase of Sullivan's career. Each one is a brick box ornamented with sculptural and decorative detail in terracotta. Each has great round or arched

windows. Each uses stained glass, beautifully detailed counters, and furniture and lighting fixtures that relate to Art Nouveau and Secessionist forms so as to make a small building in a small town into an exceptional work of art. Sullivan expressed his ideas about design in various writings, most notably in *Kindergarten Chats*, a series of articles presenting his theoretical ideas, written in 1901 and 1902 and later published in book form; *The Autobiography of an Idea*; and in his drawings for *A System of Architectural Ornament* (both of 1922–3).

The most important immediate successor to Sullivan was Frank Lloyd Wright. When Wright was working for Sullivan, he was referred to by his employer as "the pencil in my hand," and Wright throughout his lifetime gave great credit to Sullivan, his only significant teacher, whom he referred to as "Lieber Meister" (beloved master). Wright played a significant part in Sullivan's work during the years between 1887 and 1893 when he established an independent practice, but Sullivan's influence can be noticed in many of Wright's early works. Wright, unlike most pioneer modernists, continued to use decorative ornament throughout his long career, although he moved away from the curving Art Nouveau forms used by Sullivan toward a more geometric vocabulary that was entirely his own. Wright's role as one of the key figures in the development of modernism is discussed in Chapter 15.

American Art Nouveau directions had, in the end, no more lasting presence than they had in Europe. Critics and historians in the early twentieth century took to referring to Art Nouveau as a "style that failed," or to dismissing it as frivolous, tasteless, and overly decorative. Rediscovery of Art Nouveau only began after World War II when exhibitions, publications, and fresh study brought it back into its rightful place as an important step in the development of modernism.

14 Eclecticism

Toward the end of the nineteenth century and until the middle of the twentieth century, the design professions developed both skill and enthusiasm for the imitation of work of the past. Historicism, which means relying on history for inspiration (and for detail), has been common since the Renaissance and is a natural part of progressive development in design. Revivalism refers to efforts to return to a particular historic style, as in the Greek and Gothic revivals of the early nineteenth century. The term TRADITIONALISM also came into use to describe an alternative direction opposed to modernism. The public often came to believe that a choice between "traditional" and "modern" had to be made. Traditionalism expressed the new belief that design was primarily a matter of imitating the work of some, even of *any*, historic "period." Thus "period styles" came to be viewed as a stockpile of possibilities to inspire every new project.

The term "eclecticism" seems to be the best word to describe the view that all design should be a matter of choosing some historic precedent and imitating it as convincingly as possible. The dictionary definition of the word is "selecting what appears to be the best in various doctrines, methods, or styles." The term has had currency in philosophy where an "eclectic philosophy" is based on multiple sources. In design, it has come to mean the practice of selecting from historical precedents whatever seems suitable or attractive for a particular project. Total originality was eschewed. However much the revivalists and the Victorians may have drawn on historic precedent, they all aimed to make something new, something of their own time from the origins on which they drew. The essence of eclecticism, by contrast, is a slavish aim to reproduce the past—some past, any past— as long as the reproduction can be made convincing.

Eclecticism thrived in America, in particular, perhaps because there was so little past on which to build. The idea of importing something from the past that would bring with it culture, style, and status became an obsession that offered to the newly rich and powerful in America some identification with the European aristocracy. It offered to American institutions visible monuments that could compete with the universities, cathedrals, and monumental governmental buildings of the old world.

The Ecole des Beaux-Arts, Paris

The Paris Ecole, really the first truly professional school of architecture, had developed a teaching method that was spectacularly effective in presenting an orderly and logical theory of architectural planning. It also taught history through the making of magnificent drawings and renderings of the great monuments of classical antiquity. The new designs that students produced in the ateliers of their Beaux-Arts mentors were studies in the application of classical historicism to skillful planning. The great teachers at the Beaux-Arts were also designers of hallmark buildings that demonstrated the validity of the Beaux-Arts doctrines.

Nineteenth-century design in continental Europe moved only gradually from the Empire style of France and Biedermeier of Germany through Neoclassicism toward the more ornate taste so strongly developed in England and America. In France, the style called SECOND EMPIRE developed a form of ornate classicism that later had so much influence on contemporary American work. French professionalism in architecture and design was furthered by the increasing importance of the national school of art and design in Paris. Previous apprentice learning and self-teaching were replaced at the Ecole by a rigorous and organized program that included classroom lectures on history, construction, and other specialized topics, and by design teaching using a method now generally adopted by almost all design and architectural schools. Under this method, students were given a written "program" of requirements for a building desired by some imagined client. Each student then prepared designs under the direction of a "critic" who operated an atelier or studio. On a given date, all of the designs by the many students in a class were presented in the form of elaborate drawings to be criticized and judged by a "jury" of established professionals. High marks in many such judgements could earn a diploma that certified a high level of achievement and skill. The Beaux-Arts method was so successful it attracted students from all over the world, and the kind of design encouraged at the Ecole came to be called BEAUX-ARTS style.

A number of leading French architects were teachers at the Beaux-Arts at the same time that they produced work typical of Beaux-Arts style.

14.1 (*opposite*) Jean-Louis-Charles Garnier, Opera House, Paris, 1861–75.

The festive character associated with attendance at an opera is expressed through the florid elaboration of lobbies and stairs. Sculptured figures hold up giant candelabra, and marble columns in varied colors and gilded detail make the grand staircase an experience to match the excitement of the opera that will take place in the main auditorium. This engraving shows off the architectural detail with great clarity but cannot convey the actual effects of color and light.

14.2 (*right*) and **14.3** (*center*) Section and plan of the Opera House, Paris.

1 Entrance for those arriving by carriage
2 Entrance for those arriving on foot
3 Stage
4 Emperor's entrance

The most admired of Beaux Arts architectural works combines a Victorian-style love of ornament with a monumental presence. The functional arrangement of the building, a basic strength of Beaux Arts thinking, provided ample circulation spaces for the movement of large audiences. The working spaces backstage were also logically planned.

The Paris Opera House (1861–74) by Jean-Louis Charles Garnier (1825–98) is a fine example of Beaux-Arts design at its best (**figs. 14.1–14.3**). It has a logical and highly functional plan, realized in richly decorative exterior and interior detail that rises to the level of over-elaboration without ever overstepping the line into vulgarity. The building remains a model for what a festive hall should be. Garnier was also the designer of the equally successful Casino and Concert Hall at Monte Carlo (1878–82).

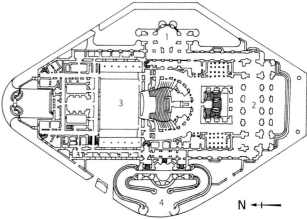

The final phases of French Beaux-Arts design reached a pinnacle of decorative excess in some of the exhibition buildings for the Paris world fairs, such as the Petit Palais of 1897–1900 built to the designs of Charles-Louis Girault (1851–1932), or the great Paris railroad station of 1898–1900, the Gare du Quai d'Orsay, by Victor Laloux (**fig. 14.4**; 1850–1937), now recycled into a highly successful museum of art. The vast iron-framed vault of the main train shed, where electric trains came and went at a lower level visible from the passenger circulation spaces above, is one of the finest interior spaces of the nineteenth century. Its typically florid Beaux-Arts sculptural decoration is skillfully integrated into a highly functional scheme. Giant clocks facing out toward the Seine and facing into the public area provide decorative accents and are, in a railroad station, highly functional as well.

14.4 (*right*) Victor Laloux, Gare du Quai d'Orsay, Paris, 1898–1900.

Laloux overlaid the great railroad station in the Beaux Arts style with classical detail. Tracks carried trains through the station at a lower level, and the platforms were reached by stairs from street level in the vast, skylit main hall. The huge clock dramatizes the railroad company's commitment to schedule. The building has survived to be put to modern use as the Orsay Museum.

Louis Sullivan studied at the Beaux-Arts, but left it when his drive toward personal expression and individuality was not accepted. Other Americans were more accepting, and brought home Beaux-Arts classicism as the cornerstone of their eclecticism.

United States

In the United States, as elsewhere, styles formed a stock of treatments from which the designer could choose whatever seemed appropriate for each project. Cities, towns, and countryside were turned into exhibits of varied, unrelated works—classical for banks and courthouses, Gothic for some churches, Georgian colonial for others. Houses might be colonial, Norman, French Renaissance, Tudor half-timbered, Gothic, Spanish Mission, ranch-house, or even odd combinations of styles. The only firm rule came to be that originality was forbidden, only imitation of the past tolerable. For many years this approach was defended as "traditional" and, it was claimed, as satisfactory to the general public that tended to like whatever was familiar.

Key Architects and Designers

Hunt

Richard Morris Hunt (1827–95) was at the vanguard of the Beaux-Arts invasion of America. He had studied at the Ecole from 1846 until 1855 and brought back to New York the skills and prestige that his Parisian training had given him. His typically eclectic viewpoint made it possible for him to work in whatever style suited a particular project or the taste of a particular client. For William K. Vanderbilt's New York town house (1879–91) he adapted the design of early French Renaissance Loire Valley chateaux to a corner city lot. Hunt's Marble House, the Newport, Rhode Island, mansion of 1885–92 for the same William K. Vanderbilt, has interiors that match the grandiosity of the palaces of French royalty.

Hunt's design for The Breakers (**fig. 14.5**; 1892–5), another great Newport, Rhode Island,

14.5 Richard Morris Hunt, dining room, The Breakers, Newport, Rhode Island, *c.* 1895.

Hunt brought back from France to America his devotion to the classicism of his Beaux Arts training. In this building he reproduced his own version of Italian Renaissance design, and the interiors matched the lavish scale and detail of external architecture.

mansion, this time for Cornelius Vanderbilt II, is in a classical Renaissance style with rooms symmetrically arranged around a two-story central court designed to be used as a ballroom. The walls are ornamented with Corinthian pilasters and the entrance portico uses four free-standing Corinthian columns. For the bedrooms on the second floor, Ogden Codman (1863–1951) developed interiors of relative simplicity of the sort suggested in his book *The Decoration of Houses* (1879), written in collaboration with Edith Wharton.

The huge country chateau named Biltmore (**fig. 14.6**; 1890–5) near Asheville, North Carolina, was designed by Hunt for George W. Vanderbilt. The style is again the French Renaissance of the time of Francis I, with elements recalled from Chambord and Blois. Within each of these houses, interiors were designed to follow the overall stylistic character of the house, making each room a virtual museum piece of antique decorative style.

Hunt's unhappy struggle to apply historicism to the problem of the tall building in the New York Tribune Building has been mentioned in Chapter 11 as an example of late Victorian uncertainty in the face of new opportunities provided by advancing technology. Hunt was able to design with greater confidence monumental buildings for which antiquity offered more reasonable precedents. The great front entrance hall of New York's Metropolitan Museum of Art (1895–1902) was designed as a Renaissance version of Roman classicism, with a facade and monumental vaulted interior of impressive dignity.

At the World's Columbian Exposition of 1893 in Chicago, Hunt was a key figure on the board of architects responsible for the general concept of monumental columned white palace-like structures around a great lagoon. The Administration Building that he designed had a dominant central position and, in spite of its rather poorly conceived domed mass, served to symbolize the ascendency of the kind of eclecticism that Hunt favored. The rich classical detail of the gleaming white buildings (all temporary structures, using plaster to simulate stone) captured the popular imagination and made Louis Sullivan's far more original Transportation Building with its strong colors and Art Nouveau detail seem odd and out of place. The fair is often viewed as a turning point, where the promising directions developed by H. H. Richardson and by Sullivan were overwhelmed and defeated by the

superficial appeal of the monumentality of Beaux-Arts eclecticism.

Hunt's place in design history depends less on his own work than on his role in setting the course of American design toward eclecticism. He can be thought of as having brought the Beaux-Arts approach to America, but with his own urge toward emphasis on imitative historicism. At the Paris Ecole, such historicism was not a primary focus. Students studied and made drawings of historic buildings (most often ancient Greek and Roman monuments) in order to understand their qualities. In design projects, the emphasis was on skillful planning and composition, not on imitation. The works of Garnier and Labrouste were not narrowly imitative and can hardly be considered examples of eclecticism. Hunt was most successful when he was most narrowly imitative (as at Biltmore) and least successful when confronting problems (as in the Tribune Building) where historicism offered no ready models.

McKim, Mead, & White

Charles Follen McKim (1847–1909), another member of the architectural board for the Chicago 1893 Fair, was also a product of the Paris Ecole des Beaux-Arts. He had worked for a time for H. H. Richardson, where he met Stanford White (1853–1906). McKim established his own practice in 1872, then joined in a partnership with William Mead (1846–1928) in 1877 and with White in 1879 to form the successful and influential firm of McKim, Mead, & White. Early work of the firm, such as the house Kingscote (1880) at Newport, Rhode Island, or the William Low House (1887) at Bristol, Rhode Island, was in the picturesque idiom of the Victorian Shingle style, but the originality of such work gave way to eclectic historicism as larger commissions offered opportunities for classically based monumentality. McKim was a specialist in carefully "correct" adaptations of Italian Renaissance and Roman classicism, White was a brilliant and imaginative designer inclined to a freer use of historic precedents, while Mead provided organizational back-up for the design partners and dealt with matters of construction. In the group of six New York town houses for Henry Villard (1882–5), the firm established its mastery of eclectic practice with a sober Italian Renaissance palazzo exterior housing richly decorative interiors. The Villard group has been preserved, serving in part as an entrance to the adjacent modern hotel.

14.6 (*opposite*) Richard Morris Hunt, Biltmore, Asheville, North Carolina, 1890–5.

In this building, sometimes described as French Gothic, Hunt attempted to reproduce a French chateau on a grand scale. Some of the interiors, like the banqueting hall, go beyond anything actually built in Renaissance France in order to satisfy the desires of the client for a fantasy version of ancient grandeur. The monumental scale of the room makes the table and chairs appear lost amid the tapestries, carved bas-relief sculpture, banners, and trophies of the hunt.

14.7 McKim, Mead, & White, Public Library, Boston Massachusetts, 1895.

In the majestic delivery hall, library users could wait for the delivery of books brought from the stacks, which were not open to the public. The detail is drawn from the Italian Renaissance, with painted wood beams overhead, a massive fireplace and mantel, Corinthian columned doorways in marble, and a band of mural painting above. Any citizen of Boston could enjoy the glories of a Beaux Arts inspired interior while waiting for a book.

14.8 McKim, Mead, & White, Pennsylvania Railroad Station, New York, 1904–10.

The growth of railroads in the early twentieth century inspired the building of monumental terminals that provided both functional services to travelers and a symbolic assertion of the railroad's importance. This grand concourse, modeled on the ancient Roman Baths of Caracalla, was reached by monumental stairs that descended from street level. It housed ticket office windows, where the traveler could stop before continuing onward into the train shed beyond. The building was destroyed in 1963–6.

The Boston Public Library (**fig. 14.7**; 1895) established the primacy of McKim, Mead, & White in the design of American public buildings. It recalls the Labrouste Bibilothèque S. Geneviève in Paris with its line of upper-story arched windows above a simple base, but internally a grand stair gives access to the upper level where a richly decorated reading room stretches across the Copley Square front. The work of several distinguished American artists—John Singer Sargent, Augustus Saint-Gaudens, and Daniel Chester French—enriches the interior spaces, which are arranged in a hollow square around a central court.

McKim, Mead, & White's block square station for the Pennsylvania Railroad (**fig. 14.8**; 1904–10) in New York was a vast complex loosely based on the baths of Caracalla in ancient Rome. The vaulted, majestic main concourse with its tremendous Corinthian columns and coffered vaulting was one of the most majestic interior spaces of the twentieth century. The adjacent train shed made use of glass and iron in a roof structure equally impressive even if hemmed in by a surround of neo-Roman classicism. The building was destroyed in 1964.

Stanford White is usually credited with the more delicate and decorative character of other works of the firm, such as the first Madison Square Garden (1887–91, now demolished) and the Century Club (1889–1891), both in New York.

14.9 Carrère and Hastings, Public Library, New York, 1902–11.

The monumental library building was designed in the style the architects had absorbed when they studied at the Ecole des Beaux Arts in Paris. The handsome interior of the main reading room with its surrounding open shelves of books on two levels is flooded with light from the windows above. It remains in current use with its original function.

After White's death, the firm continued to prosper. Its many commissions for monumental buildings and groups of buildings included the college campus for Columbia University, with its central domed Low Memorial Library (begun 1897) in New York. The firm continued in practice for many years after the original partners were no longer involved, producing innumerable major buildings, usually monumental.

Public Buildings

Around the turn of the century, state capitols, city halls, public libraries, courthouses, churches, and private homes on a palatial scale were built by eclectic architects—projects that remain among the important structures of every major American city. Where planning followed the sound concepts of Beaux-Arts teaching, and where eclectic historicism was controlled by a sense of what might be appropriate, the resulting buildings of what is sometimes called the American Renaissance remain serviceable and impressive. The New York Public Library (**fig. 14.9**; 1902–11) by John M. Carrère (1858–1911) and Thomas Hastings (1860–1919), both Beaux-Arts trained and both ex-employees of McKim, Mead, & White, has a complex plan which arranges many handsomely detailed spaces around two interior courtyards with admirably efficient circulation. The building continues to serve modern needs and recent restoration has made the interiors as impressive as they were when new.

Another surviving example of highly successful Beaux-Arts eclecticism is New York's Grand Central Station (1907–13) by Whitney Warren (1864–1948) and Charles D. Wetmore (1866–1941). The ingenious planning includes viaducts for traffic, arrangements for train movements on two levels, and remarkably efficient movement of passengers, baggage, and, at least as originally provided, vehicles. The main concourse, a vast space roofed with a simple vault (painted with a star-studded sky), and the adjacent public spaces are among the greatest interiors in America. The classic columns of the facade and the florid sculptural detail at its top represent the Beaux-Arts style at its best. Other great American railroad stations were built in various cities, such as the Union Station in Washington, D.C. (1908), by Daniel H. Burnham (1846–1912).

Early Skyscrapers

Tall buildings, increasingly important in major cities as business needs and elements of civic and commercial pride pressured for height, posed problems for their designers that were only rarely well solved. The Monadnock Building in Chicago (1889–91) by Burnham and his partner, John Welborn Root (1850–91), was remarkable for its early simplicity. It is a totally unornamented sixteen-story slab with bearing walls of red brick, enormously thick at the lower levels to carry the huge weight of the walls above. A slightly projecting base story and a simple rolled cornice give the mass an articulated bottom and top of great dignity. Internally, the iron structure and elevator cages provide the only decorative elements. The Reliance Building in Chicago (1890–5) by the same firm (but completed after Root's death) finally abandons masonry exterior walls in favor of "curtain walls" of iron, terracotta, and glass that do not support floors but are themselves supported by the metal structural frame. This is the system that became universally adopted for tall buildings, even when a masonry exterior was desired.

The distinguished tall buildings of Louis Sullivan (see Chapter 13) suggested an appropriate direction for skyscraper design that did not attempt to disguise the structure within but simply sheathed it in an aesthetically satisfactory fashion without the pretense of massive masonry. Eclectic designers, determined to cling to the traditions of pre-industrial constructional techniques, insisted instead on developing designs that had little relation to the realities of modern high-rise construction. Internally, tall buildings were sometimes given distinguished spaces for entrance halls and elevator lobbies. The Chicago office building called The Rookery (1886) by Burnham and Root has a central court roofed over with glass and iron at the ground-floor level, creating a space that was given a distinguished ornamental interior by Frank Lloyd Wright in 1905. Sullivan provided beautifully detailed Art Nouveau decoration in his buildings. The upper floors of office towers were hives of small offices, partitioned with walls of wood and glass or solid partitions like those on the guest room floors of hotels. Tenants could, of course, decorate as they chose, but most were content with a strictly utilitarian "business-like" space. A few buildings had a central court with skylights at roof level and open balconies to take the place of corri-

14.10 George Herbert Wyman, Bradbury Building, Los Angeles, 1893.

The emergence of the modern large office building posed new problems for architects of the eclectic era. Wyman introduced the skylights of a central atrium to provide light for the galleries that took the place of dark corridors and gave access to offices on many floors. The elevators moving in open cages and the stairs connecting the various gallery levels present an image more functional than eclectic.

dors giving access to offices. This approach created an impressive internal atrium where stairs and elevator cages could be seen as interesting visual elements. The Bradbury Building (**fig. 14.10**; 1893), Los Angeles, by George Herbert Wyman is an outstanding example of this approach.

Ernest Flagg (1857–1947) was unusually successful in applying the florid decoration of the Second Empire style to the forty-seven-story Singer Building in New York (1907–8, now demolished). It was the headquarters of the prosperous Singer Sewing Machine Company and served to glorify that firm as the owner of the world's tallest building—a status soon lost to competitors. Its highly original exterior mass, a mansard-topped tower rising from a larger massive block below, and the florid public space interiors with stairs and balconies and vaulted ceilings made it strikingly superior to the high buildings that rose around it in lower Manhattan. Flagg had designed an earlier, smaller Singer Building (1904) on Broadway in

New York that survives, showing off a finely detailed glass, terracotta, and metal exterior that fronts a twelve-story loft building of L-shape plan, fronting on two streets. A fine interior by Flagg survives in the ground-level store of 1913, originally the retail outlet for the Scribner publishing firm's headquarters that occupied the entire building. The store has a remarkable glass and metal facade, permitting a view of the vaulted and balconied interior space within.

The long struggle to find an appropriate eclectic style for skyscraper design produced many strange, even absurd, efforts. The 1915 design by Welles Bosworth (1869–1966) for the New York headquarters of the American Telephone and Telegraph Company (now known simply as 195 Broadway) is made up of nine Roman Ionic colonnades stacked one on top of another, each representing three floors of the building. At ground-floor level, the public lobby spaces are a virtual hypostyle hall with their rows of huge Greek Doric columns—certainly

impressive but oddly unrelated to the purposes and ownership of the building.

For many years the world's tallest building was the Woolworth tower (1913) in New York, the work of Cass Gilbert (1859–1934), a prominent eclectic designer who had developed Beaux-Arts skills as an employee of McKim, Mead, & White. Gilbert reasoned that the only historic precedent available for a tall tower structure was to be found in the towers of Gothic cathedrals. The Woolworth building is a simple block from which a tall central tower rises, all clothed in white glazed terracotta sheathing detailed with the vertical lines, tracery, and pinnacles of French Gothic church architecture. The steel framing, elevators, and sixty stories of offices were thus converted into a "cathedral of commerce" that both ornamented the city skyline and advertised the success of the famous chain of five and ten cent stores. The public interiors include spacious elevator lobbies (**fig. 14.11**) with arcades, stairs, and balconies detailed in a curious but quite effective mix of Gothic and Byzantine styles. There is much marble and mosaic decoration. Interior gargoyles include small caricature portraits of both Woolworth (clutching money bags labeled "5c" and "10c") and Gilbert holding a model of the building. Executive office interiors displayed an amazing variety of carving, tapestries, and ornamental furniture in a truly eclectic mixture. Gilbert was the designer of a number of later eclectic works—state capitols (West Virginia and Arkansas), libraries, and the sternly Roman temple for the U.S. Supreme Court in Washington (1933).

The Rise of the Interior Decorator

Eclectic architecture created a need for interior design specialists who had the knowledge and skill to produce rooms in styles appropriate to the building that housed them. The profession of interior decoration developed to fill this need. The typical decorator was trained to know period styles, to be skillful in assembling the many elements that go into an interior, and, often, to be an expert in acquisition of antiques, art works, and whatever else might be required to complete a project. Many decorators were also dealers or agents who acquired and resold to their clients furniture, rugs, and decorative accessories. The ability to charm, cajole, and adjust to the whims of wealthy clients was also essential.

De Wolfe

Elsie de Wolfe (1865–1950) is usually thought of as the first successful professional decorator. She was an actress and a society figure before she began to remodel her own home, transforming typically Victorian rooms with stylish simplicity by using white paint, cheerful colors, and flowery printed chintzes. Her distinguished guests often admired what she had done and began to ask her for help with their decorating problems. Stanford White, for example, asked for her help with some residential interiors, as well as with the interiors of the New York Colony Club (**fig. 14.12**; 1905–7). De Wolfe also gave public lectures; she published *The House in Good Taste* in 1913. While historicism was not a primary concern of the de Wolfe view of design, the nature of her clients and of the houses that eclectic architects designed for them pushed her work toward historic imitation. Henry Clay Frick, the millionaire steel magnate, employed de Wolfe in 1913 to deal with the second-floor family quarters of his Fifth Avenue mansion (designed by Carrère and Hastings, now the museum housing the Frick Collection), for which she assembled French antique furniture and placed it in suitable settings.

Wood

Ruby Ross Wood (1880–1950), originally a newspaper reporter, after working for Elsie de Wolfe as a writer (she probably wrote most of *The House in*

14.11 (*opposite*) Cass Gilbert, Woolworth Building, New York, 1913.

Called a "Cathedral of Commerce," the outside of the Woolworth Building was clothed in Gothic style detail. In the public lobby, however, Gilbert turned to Byzantine detail, for which he used marbles and mosaics. Gargoyles provided a setting for entrances to the elevators that served the many stories of what was, for some years, the tallest building in the world.

14.12 (*below*) Elsie de Wolfe, Colony Club, New York, 1905–7.

In this private dining room, as illustrated in her book The House in Good Taste *(1913), de Wolfe demonstrated her personal style through the use of delicate colors, wallpapers, and simple forms to suggest a truly eclectic sense of inspiration derived from many historic sources but without showing a concern for the accurate reproduction of any particular past era.*

Good Taste), became her assistant, and eventually established her own business as a decorator. Her own book, *The Honest House* (1914), urges simplicity and "common sense." The eclectic historicism of her own work is characterized by the use of English period furniture, often with florid wallpapers and strong colors. William (Billy) Baldwin (1903–84) started his career as an assistant to Ruby Ross Wood and pushed the work of her firm in a theatrical and fantastic direction that became typical of his own output as an independent decorator after World War II.

McMillen

McMillen Inc. was established in 1924 by Eleanor McMillen (1890–1991). Her leaning was toward French period furniture arranged within rooms that mixed period details in a truly eclectic fashion. The firm provided many wealthy and powerful families with residential interiors that showed off their wealth and taste for display. Eventually she turned to work for business and corporate clients as well.

Other American Decorators

Rose Cumming (1887–1968) was less concerned with accuracy of period reproduction than with the use of period elements in settings with strong and aggressive color, elaborate draperies, much use of gilt, and smoked-glass mirrors. Other American eclectic decorators who established successful practices included Nancy McClelland (inclined to a more conservative and "correct" use of historic precedents), Elsie Cobb Wilson, Francis Elkins, Syrie Maugham, and Dorothy Draper (whose work was largely in commercial rather than residential practice). The work of these and of many others became well known through such magazines as *House and Garden, House Beautiful,* and other publications that were showcases for the homes of wealthy and famous people. Another tier of magazines that combined coverage of decorating with other household matters—*The Ladies' Home Journal, Good Housekeeping, Delineator,* and others—carried word of eclectic period decoration to the middle class. The idea that every interior had to be in a style that could be named—"Spanish," "Tudor," or, most popular of all, "Colonial"— came to have almost universal acceptance. This idea, and many of the people who promoted it, continued to dominate the interior design of the twentieth century at least until after World War II.

Eclecticism in Professional Practice

In the design of larger, more public, institutional and commercial interiors, eclecticism was the norm. Designers with specialized knowledge and skill in a particular style became well known and admired for their ability to achieve a convincing reproduction of the work of a particular historic era. Ralph Adams Cram (1863–1942), for example, was both a propagandist for the virtue of Gothic design and a skilled practitioner in that style. In his book *Church Building* (1901) Cram makes a case for the virtues of medieval English Gothic work, illustrates examples of medieval excellence, and makes comparisons with illustration of "vicious," "affected," and "unintelligent" design. His design for All Saints' Church, Dorchester, Massachusetts (1891), was a careful and accurate recreation of a typical English parish church. Cram and his firm, Cram, Goodhue, and Ferguson, came to be enormously successful in producing Gothic churches and Tudor Gothic groupings for college campus construction that made the Gothic style the eclectic norm for such projects. The term "collegiate Gothic" came into use to describe such works as the dormitory groupings at the University of Pennsylvania in Philadelphia (1895–1901) by Cope

14.13 Ralph Adams Cram, St. Thomas's Church, New York, 1906–13.

Although Cram worked in various eclectic styles, he became best known as an expert in producing Gothic design that convincingly recreated the architecture of the Middle Ages. In this large city church forms that merge French and English traditions create a rather cold ambience that is, in reality, enriched by strong blues and reds in the stained glass that fills the clerestory and end wall windows.

and Stewardson, or the quadrangles at Yale with the spectacular Harkness Tower (1931) by James Gamble Rogers (1867–1947).

Cram's own firm designed a number of buildings for Princeton University, including some impressive interiors. Those of the refectory for the Graduate College (1913) and the University Chapel (1925–8) are convincing reworkings of their Tudor Gothic equivalents at Oxford and Cambridge. The large New York City church of St. Thomas (1906–13) is an outstanding work. Its strikingly impressive interior (**fig. 14.13**), with stone vaulting, stained glass, and a huge sculptured reredos that combines details from many Gothic precedents, made aspects of medieval work available to an American public that, at least at that time, had little chance to experience the original sources.

Saarinen and Cranbrook Academy

In 1922, a competition was held in Chicago to design a skyscraper tower for the *Tribune* newspaper company. Howells and Hood's winning design was a piece of Gothic eclecticism suggestive of a medieval cathedral. Many professionals and critics, however, noted that several entrants— among them the forefathers of modernism Adolf Loos, Walter Gropius, and Adolf Meyer—had submitted designs far more imaginative and advanced than the winner's. The most admired design was that of the second-place winner, a submission by the Finnish architect Eliel Saarinen. He proposed a relatively simple massive tower of stepped form with strongly emphasized vertical masonry lines between bands of windows. Although details carried a suggestion of tradition,

14.14 Eliel Saarinen, Saarinen House, Cranbrook, Michigan, 1928-30.

Saarinen brought from his native Finland a sense of Scandinavian simplicity along with a respect for fine craftsmanship. The quite formal symmetry of the living room is enlivened by tapestries, a rug by Loja Saarinen, furniture by Eliel, and lamps by Eero Saarinen.

14.15 Eliel Saarinen, Kingswood School, Cranbrook, Michigan, 1931.

The dining hall is a dignified space with light grey walls and a dark oak floor. Color came from coral-painted details of the chairs and the seat cushions of the same color, and window curtains in vermilion, silver, and grey. The tapestry on the end wall, The Festival of the May Queen, was designed by Eliel and Loja Saarinen.

there was no overt imitation of any historic work.

Saarinen was invited to America to head the Cranbrook Academy of Art at the Cranbrook Foundation, an educational and cultural complex near Detroit. As the head of that school and as the architect and designer of various buildings at the center, Saarinen exerted considerable influence in the development of American architecture and interior design. From 1925 onward, he headed a group of designers at Cranbrook who moved away from eclecticism toward a modern vocabulary that retained strong roots in traditionalism. At Cranbrook, Saarinen was asked to design a number of buildings that gradually created a campus complex of great beauty.

The Cranbrook School for Boys (1927), the Saarinen House (**fig. 14.14**; 1928–30), Kingswood School for Girls (1931), the Cranbrook Institute of Science (1933), and the Cranbrook Academy of Art (1942) form a progression from the Nordic eclecticism of the 1920s to a near approach to modernism. The interiors of all of these buildings are full of interest. The great dining hall of the School for Boys is a long chamber with a high, barrel-vaulted plaster ceiling, arched windows on both sides with leaded glass, hanging Orrefors glass bowl light fixtures, and simple wooden tables and chairs. At Kingswood, the dining hall (**fig. 14.15**) and auditorium are impressive spaces with finely detailed leaded glass windows, oak woodwork and furniture, and textiles in grey, vermilion, and silver. In the Saarinen House, simple spaces are furnished and ornamented with custom-designed tapestries, lighting fixtures, and other decorative details. At Cranbrook, other ornamental details such as ironwork for gates, special lamps, ANDIRONS, and works of art were by the students and faculty of the school. Graduates of the Cranbrook Academy had an important role in the development of design in the 1940s and 1950s; it continues to be a major center of American design education.

Stripped Classicism

After World War I, eclectic design began to move away from the literal reproduction of historic examples toward a simplified, less ornamented version of Roman and Renaissance precedents, often called STRIPPED CLASSICISM. In America, a French Beaux-Arts graduate, Paul Phillipe Cret (1876–1945), was influential in promoting the Beaux-Arts approach to design teaching at the architectural school of the University of Pennsylvania, where he became the principal teacher in 1903. His own work moved from the imitative classicism of the Pan American Union Building in Washington, D.C. (1903) to a gradually more simplified version of classicism, as in the Folger Shakespearean Library (**fig. 14.16**; 1930–2) and the Federal Reserve Office Building of (1935–7), both in Washington. Although the library contains a curious attempt to reproduce an Elizabethan theater, Cret's interiors generally follow a pattern of classically inspired forms and proportions; ornament is reduced to a simple,

geometric vocabulary that seems almost diagrammatic. Fine marbles and handsome woods are typical materials, while the introduction of "indirect lighting" in which sources are concealed so as to create an overall, near-shadowless illumination gives such interiors a dignified, solemn, sometimes rather chilling quality. Stripped classicism often echoed the form of the more fashion-oriented ART DECO design (see Chapter 16), but its dignity and reserve made it more acceptable for governmental and other monumental buildings. When the United States government backed a vast program of public building as a form of work relief in the depression years of the 1930s, Cret's stripped classicism came to be regarded as ideally suited to the many post offices, courthouses, and other buildings that were built under WPA (Works Progress Administration) and other Federal programs. Indeed, this style came to be informally labeled WPA STYLE.

Eclecticism for the Masses

Eclectic design, as developed by professional architects and interior decorators, was at first only accessible to the general population in public buildings, museums, libraries, office buildings, banks, hotels, theaters, and stores. Magazines, however, illustrated and recommended the eclectic designs commissioned by the wealthy and powerful, and so contributed to a trickle-down effect in which people of moderate means became acquainted with period styles and developed an appetite for something of the sort for themselves. A 1917 issue of *House and Garden* magazine, for example, devotes pages to interiors of the magnificent New York mansion designed for Adolph Lewisohn by C. P. H. Gilbert (1863–1952) and decorated by the firm of Hoffstatter and Baumgarten, specialists in eclectic residences for the very wealthy. The typical reader was not prepared to commission similar work, but the advertisers in such magazines offered furniture and other products in various "styles" that could provide an economy version of eclectic grandeur.

Houses and Apartments

The houses and apartments where average people lived were generally given some details of trimming that could justify the real estate agents' claims that they were of some named style. Suburban houses and city apartment houses were not built to order

14.16 Paul Phillipe Cret, Folger Shakespearean Library, Washington, D.C., 1930-2.

Although Cret was best known for his "stripped classical" design, which characterized the exterior of this building, inside he turned to an eclectic urge to present an Elizabethan English interior that would relate to Shakespeare. In the reading room, a hammer-beam wood truss ceiling, candle chandeliers, and carved woodwork assert a period orientation.

14.17 Puritan interiors, 1926.

The desire for period interiors in America filtered down to a general public where "colonial" design came to be a favorite theme. In this advertisement, from a Sears Roebuck catalog (1926), the illustration of the house and an assortment of interiors was intended to support the colonial ideal, albeit with a kitchen and bathroom more familiar to a 1920s family than to the eighteenth century.

reproductions of the styles of Chippendale and Sheraton to crude mass-produced maple furniture unlike anything known to the American colonies. For those far from major cities, mail order catalogs offered as many styles as could be found in big city department stores. Even complete houses could be ordered by mail; a Sears Roebuck catalog illustrated dozens of designs with a plan and picture of each (**fig. 14.17**). All the materials and trimmings would be delivered to any location, ready to be assembled by a local carpenter who was thus relieved of any responsibility for providing design in a recognizable style. Sears Roebuck houses can be found all over America and can be readily recognized as matching their catalog illustrations.

In the 1930s a special impetus was given to the colonial fad by the restoration of the old Virginia capital at Williamsburg. With the support of Rockefeller financing, the rather meager traces of the colonial town were recreated by the Boston architectural firm of Perry, Shaw, and Hepburn, specialists in eclectic Georgian design. The recreated town is far more "correct" and perfect than anything that eighteenth-century America could have produced. As a famous tourist attraction, Williamsburg, Williamsburg style, and Williamsburg reproductions became widely known and fueled the popular desire to live in pseudo-colonial settings. The Boston architect Royal Barry Wills (1895–1962) built his practice on exquisitely charming reproductions of Cape Cod cottages. Kitchens with modern electric stoves and refrigerators were regularly made "colonial" with knotty pine cabinets and "country style" window curtains. Crude versions of such colonial reproduction houses were built in rows and clusters by the hundred in suburban real estate subdivisions. In England, a parallel vogue developed for country cottages suggesting the days of Henry VIII but built in grim suburban rows. In France, miniaturized chateaux, in Italy Mediterranean stucco cottages are all evidence of eclectic ideals. Eclecticism still lives on in catalogs of furniture and decorative accessories offered to an eager public, in odd bits of half-timber trim, "quaint" details in development houses, and in an occasional brand new Georgian bank branch or ranch-style restaurant.

Furniture and Accessories

Furniture stores and department stores featured "traditional" products and often provided model room settings where customers could see furniture

for their occupants; they were produced by developers or speculative builders as saleable commodities, just as furniture, carpets, and wallpapers were produced. A population moving upward from the poverty of farm life or factory work welcomed the decorative elements of style and convenience that the magazines suggested were necessary as evidence of wealth and culture.

Stylistic preferences varied somewhat regionally. Spanish styles were favorites in California and the southwest, New Orleans ironwork in the south, but "colonial" spread in popularity from its home base in New England to become the style most widely desired. The term could mean anything from a Cape Cod cottage to a Georgian mansion. Furnishing ranged from fine quality accurate

and accessories arranged by "store decorators" who were also prepared to offer advice and decorating help to hesitant customers. Furniture manufacturers took to making "suites" (often called "suits") of furniture that claimed to represent one or another period, especially colonial. Even such a modern invention as the radio, as it became a universally desired object in every home, changed from the laboratory functionalism of the early wireless set into a piece of furniture, a wooden box made in some traditional style—Georgian, Louis XV, or Spanish (**fig. 14.18**). The round form of the radio speaker stimulated designs that used wooden tracery like that of a medieval rose window and pointed arch-shaped cases, so that Gothic radios in wooden cabinets became widely popular.

Movie Theaters

The development of moving pictures as a medium of mass entertainment provided another vehicle for eclectic designs. The magnificent Hollywood sets were, more often than not, great mansions richly decorated in period styles, either for historic dramas or as modern environments for the rich and famous. The moving picture theater itself became a part of the eclectic visual experience. Theaters and opera houses had always been elaborately decorative, but now a mass audience could

come into a gigantic Loew's, Fox, or Roxy and find lobbies loaded with rich decorative furniture and a vast auditorium designed to suggest a Moorish harem, a Spanish palace, or some assortment of decorative treatments. The ceiling might simulate a sky with stars and moving clouds, while the giant theater organ rose out of the orchestra pit, filling the hall with its sentimental vibrato. Thomas W. Lamb (1871–1942) became a specialist in the design of theaters with interiors suggesting exotic and fantastic settings—Persian, Hindu, Chinese, or some amalgam of styles. Loew's 175th Street Theater in New York and the Loew's Pitkin in Brooklyn, the Stanley and Fox in Philadelphia (Adam style), and the San Francisco Fox (Baroque) (all of the late 1920s and early 1930s) were among the more than 300 theaters credited to him. John Eberson was a specialist in the "atmospheric theater," where the ceiling was a false sky with moving clouds, stars, and moon floating above architectural and sculptural detail of fantastic complexity. The Paradise in Chicago (1928) was one of dozens of theaters of this type. Grauman's Egyptian (1922) and Chinese (1927) theaters in Hollywood, by Meyer and Holler, were extravaganzas in their respective styles that became nationally famous. Hotels and restaurants followed this drift toward story-book historical settings that the householder might then attempt to imitate at home.

Europe

In Europe, although the practice of eclecticism was not unknown, it did not develop the near-universal grip of the American experience. Perhaps the presence of real historic buildings and interiors gave imitation less appeal. Historicism, present since the Renaissance, tended to seek new interpretations rather than slavish reproduction. Some eclectic European buildings on a grand scale, such as the Palace of Justice in Brussels, Belgium (1866–83), by Joseph Poelart, or the Monument to Victor Emmanuel II in Rome (1885–1911) by Giuseppe Sacconi, achieved an unmatched level of overbearing grandiosity. Hotels, banks, churches, and private homes were built in great numbers in one or another historic style, but these tended to be the works of indifferent practitioners. Leadership in design meant creativity rather than historicism.

Stripped classicism came to be the official style of governmental design in Europe in the 1930s (**fig.**

14.18 Harold Van Doren and J.G. Rideout, Air-King Radio, Brooklyn, 1930–3.

Eclectic home interiors in assorted traditional styles demanded furniture and equipment to match. Console radios were housed in wood cabinets in a variety of period styles. This example is intended to suggest a Renaissance design, perhaps Spanish.

14.19 Grigorii Zakharov and Zinaida Chernysheva, central hall, Kurskaya Metro Station, Moscow, 1949.

The totalitarian regimes of Europe took on eclectic design as it suited their various orientations, whether fascist, communist, or, in this example, Stalinist. A form of stripped, classic Doric architecture serves the unlikely role of subway station entrance.

14.20 Ragnar Östberg, City Hall, Stockholm, 1908–23.

The Nordic accent of Swedish design in the early years of the twentieth century had strong popular appeal. It seemed to offer a design vocabulary that was of modern times but was firmly rooted in tradition. This formal and monumental hall, known as the Golden Chamber, was one of several rooms of the Stockholm town hall that had strong appeal to a widely varied audience around the world.

14.19). The combination of a sense of formality, of tradition along with a touch of modernism and—in the depression years—a certain sense of economy and efficiency contributed to its appeal. A fine example is the Finnish Parliament House at Helsinki (1927–32) by J. S. Siren. Its facade of fourteen classical columns at the top of a broad, monumental flight of steps screens an orderly symmetrical plan arranged around the circular legislative chamber at its center. The same style had the misfortune to become the architectural expression of fascism in Mussolini's Italy and Hitler's Germany. Great halls lined with marble were favorite settings for dictators who wished to pretend to greatness and to intimidate with the impersonal vastness of the spaces they built and occupied. Albert Speer (1905–81) was the favorite architect of the Nazi regime and produced a number of buildings in this chillingly ostentatious style, such as the new Chancellery in Berlin (1938). Although the U.S.S.R. under Stalin was ostensibly the adversary of fascism, the official style of design in Russia became similarly heavy and intimidating. Even after World War II, buildings such as the Lomonosov University in Moscow (1948–52) continued to be designed in a way suggestive of the American eclecticism of the pre-World War I era.

Scandinavia

The eclecticism of Scandinavian design, built on folk traditions reaching back to the Norsemen, never became narrowly imitative and so was able to make a smooth transition into the simpler forms that came to characterize modern design. "Scandinavian modern" in its earliest forms really belonged to the eclectic era and so avoided the qualities that made early modernism unpopular with a major part of the general public. Almost universal admiration met the eclectic Stockholm Town Hall (1908–23) by the Swedish architect Ragnar Östberg (1866–1945). It is a romantically composed block of brick, with green copper roofs and a great tower beautifully sited by a lake. The Blue Hall, really a covered courtyard or atrium where exposed pink brickwork contradicts the name (blue mosaic was intended but never installed), the Golden Chamber (**fig. 14.20**), a great assembly hall with walls of gold and colorful mosaic, and the Prince's Gallery with murals painted by Prince Eugen offer both grandeur and charm to match the exterior.

In Finland, development of what became known as National Romanticism introduced a unique aspect into eclecticism. Eliel Saarinen (see pp. 234, 257–8) began his career in 1902 with the design and construction of his own house and studio group near Helsinki that he named Hvittrask. It was a cluster of structures in the red tile roofed Nordic Romantic style that had connections with Jugendstil work, but also had original qualities, particularly in the spacious interiors where rugs and tapestries, metalwork, and furniture were all fine examples of design based in craft tradition. Saarinen's wife, Loja, a sculptor, weaver, and designer of textiles and carpets, was an active participant in the design of Hvittrask and continued to participate in many of her husband's projects throughout his career.

Saarinen's European reputation was established with a design for the Helsinki Railroad Station (1906–14), a distinguished masonry building with a tall tower and handsome interiors that carry a hint of Nordic traditionalism. With his move to the United States in 1925, Saarinen became highly influential in the development of design in America.

Britain

In England, eclecticism surfaced in some of the later work of Norman Shaw as Arts and Crafts influence faded and Beaux-Arts classicism asserted

14.21 Richard Norman Shaw, Cragside, Rothbury, Northumberland, 1870–84.

The drawing by W. R. Lethaby of Shaw's design for a chimney breast at Cragside indicates how Shaw used local buildings and vernacular details to create a personal style of nineteenth-century English design, which projected a sense of the traditional without attempting a direct imitation of past examples. This florid, decorative composition satisfied a wealthy client's desire for baronial splendor while still having a basis in its own time.

itself. Shaw's enormous mansion, Bryanston in Dorset (1889–94), is a symmetrical U-shaped mass with hints of both Wren and French eighteenth-century chateau architecture. Interiors are filled with heavy classical detail. Cragside at Rothbury (1870–84; **fig. 14.21**) is heavy with ornament. The Northumberland mansion Chesters (1890–4) used even more formal and monumental forms of classical symmetry, with a massive Ionic portico at the entrance and interiors notable for size rather than interest. Shaw's Piccadilly Hotel (1905–8) in London is a massive block mixing Dutch Baroque flourishes with a screen of Ionic columns.

Lutyens

England's most creative eclectic was Sir Edwin Lutyens (1869–1944). He started out as a follower of Norman Shaw and Philip Webb, but soon found a direction of his own in the design of some of the last great country houses around the turn of the century. Deanery Gardens at Sonning, Berkshire (1889), is an original and handsome grouping of familiar elements—brick and tile, an arched entrance, great chimneys, a great projecting bay with small-paned windows—all set in a beautifully landscaped garden site developed with his frequent collaborator Gertrude Jekyll (1843–1932). At Tigbourne Court in Surrey (1899) he produced a complex grouping in a native stone with gables and chimneys clustered to suggest medievalism, although there is no overt reproduction of Gothic

14.22 Edward Lutyens, Castle Drogo, Drewsteignton, Devon, England, 1910.

Lutyens achieved a delicate balance between traditionalism and a forward-looking approach at Castle Drogo. This passage in a large country house— it is not a castle at all— leads from the drawing room to the hall and uses simple detailing in stone to create space that can be understood as traditional or as pointing to a new, twentieth-century simplicity.

detail. The only departure from austere simplicity is in a low entrance porch with classical detail. He turned to his own free and somewhat eccentric adaptation of classicism for Heathcote (1905–7), a country house in Yorkshire. Castle Drogo in Devon (**fig. 14.22**; 1910) is a fortress-like battlemented manor house, less original and more narrowly imitative. In these houses, Lutyens developed a remarkable talent for offering to his clients the comforts they desired, a sense of belonging to an aristocratic tradition, and a genuine element of creative originality.

Lutyens's status rose rapidly as he came to be regarded as the leading figure of his time among British architects. His commissions gradually became larger and more monumental in character, culminating in the planning of the Indian capital city at New Delhi (1913–30). There buildings are arranged according to traditional concepts of formal symmetry, but individual buildings of Lutyens's design (such as the Viceroy's House) combine elements of Indian traditional design with British classicism in a truly eclectic mix.

Ocean Liners

Eclectic interior design reached remarkable extremes in the interiors of the great ocean liners (**fig. 14.23**). Aboard the British Cunard liner *Mauretania* (1907), first-class passengers could enjoy halls, lounges, and smoking rooms in Italian Renaissance and Francis I French styles designed by the British architect H. A. Peto (1854–1933), who had established a reputation for town houses, country mansions, and hotels with lavish eclectic interiors. Paneling, columns, pilasters, gilt, and

crystal were everywhere. The smoking room of the Cunarder *Franconia* (1923) was a Tudor half-timbered hall with a huge brick fireplace. The great German pre-World War I liners excelled in excess eclectic decor—the swimming pool of the *Vaterland* (1914) (later renamed *Leviathan*) was "Pompeian," with Roman Doric columns two stories high along the decks surrounding the tiled pool. The Italian liner *Conte di Savoia* (1931) had a main lounge that reproduced the gallery of the seventeenth-century Colonna Palace in Rome, complete with statuary and fresco painting.

The Spread of Eclecticism

Ships with eclectic interior decor carried colonists to undeveloped parts of the world where they immediately demanded the recreation of their home countries through eclectic building. The westernized architecture of India, Australia, and other colonial regions is full of Roman classicism, Gothic and Renaissance motifs that comforted colonists and either impressed or exasperated native populations. Even China and, to a lesser extent, Japan produced eclectic work inspired by the British presence in Hong Kong and Shanghai, and by Chinese and Japanese architects who had been trained at American architectural schools where Beaux-Arts eclecticism was the universally accepted direction. The Bank of Japan (1895) by Kingo Tatsuno and the Akasaka Palace (1909) by Tokuma Katayama closely parallel eclectic work in Europe and America.

A long struggle to root out the devotion to historicism that had come to dominate design schools took place in the 1930s and 1940s. As design training turned away from eclecticism, the design professions gradually were taken over by a new generation rooted in the modern, technological world and devoted to the rejection of all historic imitation. Eclecticism became a surviving direction only in a few backwater design schools, and in the practice of the manufacturers and builders who remained convinced that the public still desired design that clothed every object, every setting, and every building in forms borrowed from centuries long past.

14.23 SS *France*, 1910.

Some of the most spectacular eclectic interiors were, oddly enough, not in buildings but on ocean-going ships. This grandiose space, the grand stair and dining room, with its rich, supposedly Baroque decoration was intended to convince first class passengers that they were dining in a grand hotel or palace rather than on the Atlantic Ocean. When intercontinental travel could only be accomplished by sea, passengers, none too happy with the time and possible discomforts of sea travel, could be lulled into a feeling of contentment with the aid of such design.

15

The Emergence of Modernism

By the first decades of the twentieth century, it had become apparent that industrialization and the technology that it relied on had brought about changes in human affairs as great as any that had occurred since the discovery of fire and the invention of language. Telephone, electric light, travel by ship, rail, automobile, and by air, and structural engineering using steel and REINFORCED CONCRETE brought about the extensive changes in human experience that are often characterized as those of the "first machine age." Through all of earlier history, handwork had been the primary means by which things were made (aided by limited use of wind, water, and horse power). In the modern world, very little is hand made and factory production has become the norm. Accelerating population growth and the increase in urban poverty were new and pressing problems. The rise of communism and fascism and the distress engendered by World War I presented problems that technology did little to solve. In art, architecture, and design it became increasingly evident that the traditions that had served past ages were no longer relevant to this modern world.

The nineteenth-century efforts to find new design directions—the Arts and Crafts Movement, Art Nouveau, and Vienna Secession—all remained tied to the past. Arts and Crafts asked for a return to the handcraft of pre-industrial times. Art Nouveau and Vienna Secession sought new decorative vocabularies but did not recognize the extent of the changes that were overwhelming every aspect of modern life. Eclecticism was devoted to the application of bygone design to modern reality. The heavy elaboration of nineteenth-century ornamentalism (in Victorian and parallel examples) and the superficial historicism of eclectic work became a focus for attack. The leaders of modernism were, in a sense, revolutionaries, although not directly connected with revolutionary ideas in politics. In design, just as in music, literature, and art, new ideas were disturbing and frightening to major elements of society.

The most important development in early twentieth-century design was the emergence of a design vocabulary appropriate to the modern world of advanced technology and the new patterns of life that it brought about. Modernism is the name given to the new forms that appeared in all of the arts—in painting, sculpture, architecture, music, and literature. Four men are regarded as pioneers of modernism in design. They defined new directions with such clarity and force that they can be thought of as the originators of the "modern movement." All four were architects, but all four were also active in interior design and in the design of objects and other elements that characterize twentieth-century modernism. They were the Europeans Walter Gropius (1881–1969), Ludwig Mies van der Rohe (1886–1969), and Le Corbusier (1887–1965), and the American Frank Lloyd Wright (1867–1959).

Frank Lloyd Wright

Wright produced an enormous body of work—more than four hundred constructed buildings and many other projects—in a long career that can be divided into two phases. Each phase is of sufficient importance to support his major place in design history. The first or "early Wright" phase, extending from the beginning of his career up to about 1920, clearly established his role as the first major modern architect. The second "later Wright" phase, which surfaced after 1930, will be discussed in Chapter 18.

Wright had a brief training in engineering at the University of Wisconsin in 1886. It was his period of employment in the offices of Adler and Sullivan in Chicago (1887–93) and the close relationship that he established with Sullivan that established the direction he was to take in his own work. Sullivan's dedication both to the concept embodied in the phrase "form follows function," and to a style of ornament that was non-historic, original, and "organic" was central to Wright's own early work. In spite of his great admiration for Sullivan and his important role in Sullivan's office (he was the primary designer of Sullivan's Charnley House of 1892 in Chicago), Wright was uncomfortable in the role of an assistant to someone else and so moved to establish his own practice in 1893 in the Chicago suburb of Oak Park, Illinois. Oak Park and the neighboring suburb of River Forest were situated in open country where well-to-do businessmen who traveled daily into Chicago had houses built in pleasant surroundings. Wright built a house for his own family in Oak Park (1889), with an adjacent studio, and began to receive commissions for other houses there and in nearby communities.

15.1 Frank Lloyd Wright, Larkin Building, Buffalo, New York, 1904.

The office building was for a mail-order company, and Wright arranged space for office workers on several levels surrounding a central, skylit court. Filing cabinets are neatly fitted into alcoves, and specially designed furniture included chairs attached to their related desks and each with a swinging arm support. Daylight was augmented by electric light clusters of Wright's design. The building was demolished in 1950.

The Early Commissions

The earliest Wright houses are somewhat tentative, with hints of Victorianism, Arts and Crafts, and Queen Anne aesthetic touches and, usually only when demanded by a client, eclectic elements (half-timber work in a few examples) as well. The Winslow House of 1893 in River Forest is, however, a decisive step toward original expression (**fig. 15.2**). The front facing the street is symmetrical and has a classic dignity not unlike some early projects of the Vienna Secession. Unlike the typical Victorian house with its vertical emphasis, horizontal lines are emphasized. There is a low hipped roof with a broad overhang. Decorative bands of ornament are arranged around the entrance door, and the upper-floor windows are placed in a continuous frieze of terracotta ornamentation. The plan is a more complex interlocking of varied spaces, with rooms clustered around a central chimney. The entrance hall has an arcaded alcove with seats on either side of a fireplace. The dining

room, on the other side of the central chimney, extends outward from the rear of the building in a semicircular conservatory. Ornamental detail including stained-glass inserts in some windows suggests Sullivan's vocabulary, but is shifted toward a more geometric approach that Wright gradually developed as his career moved onward.

The Hickox House (1900) at Kankakee, Illinois, retains symmetry only for the open living, dining, and music room grouping across its front. Its gable roof has long overhangs and horizontal bands of windows, and low walls extending outward at ground level give it the long horizontals characteristic of what Wright called the Prairie house form, implying a relationship to the broad, flat landscape of the American mid-west. The side of the house facing the street is entirely asymmetrical. Its white plaster wall surfaces divided by strips of wood give it a vaguely Japanese flavor. This is not the result of any imitative drive, but may reflect Wright's awareness of oriental aesthetic ideas as expressed in Japanese prints—favorite works with

15.2 Frank Lloyd Wright, Winslow House, River Forest, Illinois, 1893.

In his early work Wright often used details that carry a hint of traditional architecture, and the influence of his association with Louis Henry Sullivan is evident. Here, off the entrance hall of this house, this small loggia provides a fireplace flanked by built-in seating. The rails on either side end with a pedestal topped by sculpture.

the Aesthetic movement in England and a continuing interest for Wright. Interiors were carefully developed in all of Wright's prairie houses. Drawings that Wright made for publication in the *Ladies' Home Journal* in 1901 show the open suites of living spaces, the extensive built-in woodwork, and specially designed furniture that were typical of Wright's residential projects.

Wright's growing reputation brought him a number of non-residential commissions, including the large four-story office building for the Larkin Company at Buffalo, New York (1904, now demolished). Open general office spaces are arranged around a central skylit courtyard, a majestic interior space with Wright's unique decorative detail introduced only at the top level just below the skylights (**fig. 15.1**). Highly innovative metal furniture and light fixtures were designed for this building so that every interior element would be part of a unified design concept. Unity Church at Oak Park, Illinois (1906), is Wright's first work in reinforced concrete. It is made up of two linked blocks, the church proper and the related parish house with entrances in the linking element. Roof slabs project out above bands of windows placed near the top of the church auditorium walls. The interior with projecting balconies, a ceiling incorporating a grid of square skylights, linear decorative bands of wood along the white walls, hanging light fixtures, and stained-glass windows of geometric form generate an abstractly complex space suggestive of directions that were to surface in European art and design a few years later.

In 1907, the large suburban residential grouping designed for Avery Coonley was built at Riverside, Illinois, another Chicago suburb (**fig. 15.3**). The house is surrounded by elaborate gardens, a pool, and various service buildings. The plan is developed on a modular grid of squares, a means of establishing unified control of proportional relationships that Wright frequently used

throughout his career. Squares are the theme for decorative tile and plaster patterns on exterior wall areas, and for interior details such as pattern motifs in specially woven rugs and stained-glass window inserts. The forms of the sloping roofs are visible as ceiling internally, with wood strips suggesting the patterns of structural members and with decorative ceiling panels covering concealed lighting. As in most of Wright's interiors, there is a sense of warmth and color, although his use of color is generally very restricted according to his conviction that the natural colors of materials should not be altered. The warm tones of natural wood, brick, or stone and the beiges of woven materials generate the basic color; leaded glass and an occasional small detail in bright red provide decorative accents.

The large house for Frederick Robie in south Chicago (1906) is one of the most successful of all

15.3 Frank Lloyd Wright, Coonley House, Riverside, Illinois, 1907.

Wright had, by the time of this house, established his personal early modern style. The drawing, reproduced in the magazine and book illustrations circulated in Holland and Germany, displayed Wright's approach to design. The ceiling pattern reflects the roof structure but is also strongly decorative. Geometric design is present in the stained glass and in the specially designed rug. The furniture is of Wright's design.

The Philosophy of Frank Lloyd Wright

Frank Lloyd Wright's first years as an architect were spent drawing together his responses to his surroundings. The romanticism inherent in his approach to architecture was expressed in 1928 as he reflected on his career in the 1890s:

When in early years I looked south from the massive stone tower of the Auditorium Building, a pencil in the hands of a master, the red glare of the Bessemer steel converters to the south of Chicago would thrill me as pages of the Arabian Nights used to with a sense of terror and romance. [1]

His aims as an architect were, as he expressed himself, to exalt the health, lift the spirit, and create a complete environment in response to the immediate surroundings. The prairie houses he designed were a specific response to the landscape he saw around him, and he wrote of his theories in an essay in 1908, describing the inspiration for such houses as Highland Park and Riverside in Illinois:

We of the Middle West are living on the prairie. The prairie has a beauty of its own and we should recognise and accentuate this natural beauty, its quiet level. Hence, gently sloping roofs, low proportion, quiet skylines, suppressed heavy set chimneys and sheltering overhangs, low terraces and out-reaching walls sequestering private gardens. [2]

1. Frank Lloyd Wright, "The Nature of Materials," *Architectural Record* (Chicago, 1928); 2. Frank Lloyd Wright, 1908, quoted in Kenneth Frampton, *Modern Architecture* (London, 1992), p. 137

Wright's houses. Low walled gardens and terraces and extended sloping hip roofs surround living spaces that flow together. The main living and dining rooms (**fig. 15.4**) are a continuous space, their windows forming an uninterrupted band along the main street front of the house. A central fireplace and chimney backed by an open stairway separate the two spaces without walls or doors. Stained glass in the windows, wood bands across ceiling surfaces, and built-in woodwork fittings and lighting fixtures give the interiors a unified character. Originally, furniture, rugs, and textiles were all designed by Wright. The high-backed dining chairs were intended to give a sense of enclosure to those sitting together around the table. The table itself was unusually low, and supported by corner posts that rise above the table top to become lighting fixtures.

Wright's American career gradually slowed and then came to a halt between 1910 and 1930. A series of unhappy and tragic events in his personal life combined with the drift in public taste away from work of such striking originality combined to leave him with little work. An invitation by a group of Japanese business men to design a major hotel in Tokyo was accepted and led to a number of years spent in Japan designing and directing construction of the Imperial Hotel (1916–22, now demolished). The large building with its vast and elaborately decorated public spaces survived a great

earthquake in 1923. This event brought Wright to public notice in a favorable light, so that he was able to build a second career after his return to America.

De Stijl

It was Wright's frequently expressed conviction that he was the only originator of modernism in architecture, and that European modernists were merely (inferior) imitators of his achievements. Reality hardly supports such claims, but it is true that Wright's work was exhibited, published, and admired in Europe long before it had comparable recognition in America. The Dutch artists, sculptors, architects, and designers who in 1917 began publication of the magazine *De Stijl* (The Style), which appeared until 1927, may well have known of Wright's work. Certainly, it is possible to notice some similarities in form between such Wright designs as the Gale House of 1909 in Oak Park and the Dutch Huis ter Heide at Utrecht (1916) by Robert van't Hoff (1887–1979), an architect of the De Stijl movement.

Mondrian and van Doesburg

De Stijl was primarily concerned with concepts of pure abstraction in painting and sculpture which had surfaced in cubist art of the time and which were taken to their logical limits by such artists as Piet Mondrian (1871–1944), Jean Arp (1887–1966), and Theo van Doesburg (1883–1931). Mondrian is famous for his abstract paintings using bands of black arranged in rectilinear grids on a white background, with some areas filled in with pure primary colors. Although he confined his work to painting, Mondrian's work was destined to become a strong influence in design and architecture. As historicism fell into disrepute, abstract form became a primary interest. Mondrian and van Doesburg developed a theory, called Neoplasticism, set forth in a number of manifestos that asserted the superiority of abstract values of form and color (the primaries and black) over all naturalistic and subjective values in art. Van Doesburg developed a number of architectural projects in which abstract forms and primary colors are translated into three-dimensional compositions that could become buildings. Although he developed many projects on paper

15.5 (*left*) Theo van Doesburg, Café l'Aubette, Strasbourg, France, 1926–8.

In this entertainment center, with bars, ballrooms, and a cinema, van Doesburg used De Stijl abstract geometric forms to generate a strikingly modern interior. In the Cinema Dance Hall (seen here) the films were projected on to the central screen, while patrons occupied booths or danced on the central dance floor. Van Doesburg worked with Jean Arp and his wife, Sophie Taeuber-Arp, on the abstract designs, which were disliked by the public when the complex first opened.

15.6 (*below*) Gerrit Rietveld, Schröder House, Utrecht, The Netherlands, 1924.

Rietveld worked with the designer Truus Schröder-Schräder (1889–1985) on the house in Utrecht. The upper level of the house was fitted with sliding panels, making it possible to screen off individual rooms or open up the space as it appears here. The typical De Stijl color scheme, with white, black, red, and blue, enlivens the rectilinear geometry of the space. Rietveld's red and blue armchair is in the foreground.

that had considerable influence, van Doesburg's only works that were executed were his own small house at Meudon (1930) and a complex of restaurant interiors known as l'Aubette at Strasbourg in 1926–8 (**fig. 15.5**). Geometric, abstract diagonally placed three-dimensional forms, tubular stair and balcony railings, and wall paintings using the "modern" materials of concrete, steel, aluminum, and glass (avoiding wood), with black, white, and primaries as the only colors, are all important features.

Rietveld

The best known De Stijl work was produced by Gerrit Rietveld (1888–1964), whose Schröder House at Utrecht (**fig. 15.6**; 1924) is the most complete realization of the movement's ideas. It is a rectilinear block made up of complex, interpenetrating planes of wall, roof, and projecting decks, with voids filled by glass in metal sash. The (upper) main living floor is divided by a system of sliding panels that permit rearrangement to achieve varying degrees of openness. Built-in and movable furniture of Rietveld's design is geometric and abstract in concept. Only primary colors and black are introduced within the generally white and grey tones of most surfaces.

Rietveld's most familiar works are two geometrically formed chairs, the small and simple "Z

chair," made from four flat wooden rectangles arranged in a Z configuration, and the more complex "red and blue" arm chair of 1918 where a cage of thin wooden strips painted black with yellow ends supports the flat seat and back planes painted red and blue. Although they appear somewhat forbidding, they offer a reasonable degree of comfort while acting as abstract sculpture in visual terms. Both are currently in production. Other Rietveld furniture and lighting designs follow a parallel pattern of conception in strictly abstract, sculptural terms.

Because of its few members, short life, and limited accomplishments, De Stijl influence in the development of modernism has been less obvious than that of the pioneers in Germany and France.

Pioneers of the International Style

In Germany, Peter Behrens, mentioned above as a significant figure in the Deutscher Werkbund, the design organization promoting excellence in German production (see p. 225), had established an active practice in architecture and design and developed a reputation as a leader in advanced design thinking. In 1910, three of the employees working for Behrens were the Germans Walter Gropius and Ludwig Mies van der Rohe and the Swiss-born Frenchman Charles Jeanneret who later became famous under the pseudonym Le Corbusier. It can be assumed that Behrens and these three apprentices all were aware of the early work of Wright.

Gropius and the Bauhaus

Walter Gropius established his own architectural practice in 1911 and began to produce work in an unornamented, functional style directly descended from Behrens's industrial building practice. Gropius's historical importance is not so much related to his own work as to his role in design education. After World War I he was offered the directorship of the schools of fine art and of applied art at Weimar. He merged the two schools under the name Staatliches Bauhaus (**fig. 15.7**). The German verb *zu bauen* (literally, to build) has a broader meaning in this context, implying creation of the kind that, in English, is simply

called design. The Bauhaus developed a new educational program that attempted to establish a relation between the emerging modernism of the fine arts and a broad range of design and craft fields, including architecture, town planning, advertising and exhibition design, stage design, photography and film, and the design of objects in wood, metal, ceramics, and textiles—in short, what has come to be known as industrial design.

The Bauhaus program began with an introductory year of studies devoted to abstract design in two and three dimensions, and studies of materials, textures, and color that would form a sound basis for later specialization. Gropius recruited an extraordinary faculty that included a number of distinguished modern artists, such as Paul Klee, Wassily Kandinsky, and Lyonel Feininger, and many other distinguished teachers, such as Josef Albers, László Moholy-Nagy, and Marcel Breuer. In 1925 economic and political problems led to the closing of the Bauhaus at Weimar and its relocation to the industrial city of Dessau, in a new building designed by Gropius (**figs. 15.8** and **15.9**). Completed in 1926, the Bauhaus building was an impressive grouping that embodied Bauhaus ideals in both plan and aesthetic expression. The most striking part of the complex was a four-story block devoted to workshops where students could actually produce, at least in prototype, the objects that they designed. Printed materials, woven textiles, furniture, ceramics, lamps, metal objects, stage scenery, and costumes were all turned out in the shops and, whenever possible, manufacturers were persuaded to take on production of Bauhaus designs. A bridge across a public street contained a library and offices and formed a link to a classroom block. A low link element contained an auditorium and dining hall; this led to a small dormitory unit where advanced students had studio bedrooms, making it possible for them to live full time within the school. The striking appearance of the Bauhaus building resulted from the three-story-high glass curtain walls of the shop block, the austerely ornament-free white walls of the other wings with their large ribbons of glass windows, and, for the dormitory, tiny projecting balconies with tubular railings. The form of the building was derived from its plan; the roofs were flat in accordance with modern industrial practice. The resulting appearance was sternly functional—as shockingly disturbing to traditionalists as it was exciting to the new generation of modernists.

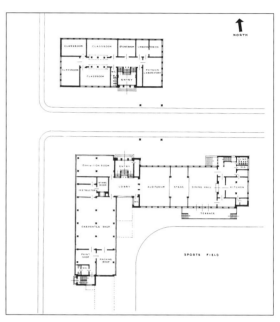

15.8 (*top*) Walter Gropius, Bauhaus, Dessau, 1926.

In the ground floor plan the shop areas appear at the lower left, and the lecture hall and dining room extend to the right. A bridge at upper floor levels connects to the classroom block, shown above. A street passes under the bridge element, and there are entrances to the building on both sides.

15.9 (*above*) Exterior of the Bauhaus, Dessau.

The large, four-story block, with its curtain walls of steel and glass, housed the many work-shops that served the Bauhaus instructional programs. To the left, an entrance and stair area is visible before the bridge element that extends out of the photograph to the left.

The Bauhaus building and all similar modern works were described as being in the INTERNATIONAL STYLE by the historian and critic Henry-Russell Hitchcock when he (with Philip Johnson) organized an exhibition of such work in 1932 at the Museum of Modern Art in New York. The term reflects the fact that modernism was not marked by the strong national differences typical of earlier design history. As related work began to appear in France, Italy, England, and the Scandinavian countries, it became clear that such modernism was truly international. Interiors at the Bauhaus were as simple and functional as the

15.7 (*above left*) Walter Gropius, Bauhaus, Weimar 1923.

While the Bauhaus was still at Weimar, Gropius designed his own office using abstract geometric forms. The rug, tapestry, furniture, and hanging lighting fixture are the work of the Bauhaus faculty or students. The desk and chair are Gropius's own designs.

exterior. Gropius designed a remarkable interior for the director's office, a study in rectilinear geometric form. Furniture and light fixtures designed by various Bauhaus students and instructors were used wherever possible, while the use of white, grey, and primary color accents suggested the design of the De Stijl movement.

The Bauhaus came under financial pressures and, with the hostility toward all avant-garde ideas that marked the rising Nazi movement, political pressures as well. Gropius resigned in 1928, to be succeeded by Hannes Meyer and, in 1930, by Mies van der Rohe. When the school was finally forced to close in 1933, many students and faculty members left Germany as refugees. As they found design work and positions as teachers, they achieved a remarkable dispersal of Bauhaus ideas that became central to the wide acceptance of International Style modernism. Gropius practiced for a time in England but in 1937 he moved to America to become the head of the Graduate School of Design at Harvard.

Mies van der Rohe

After his apprenticeship with Behrens, Mies van der Rohe spent the year 1912 in Holland working on designs for a large house for H. E. L. J. Kroller in a style that relates to the Neoclassicism of Schinkel, although with less emphasis on symmetry and less use of historic detail. A full-size model of the house, made like stage scenery of wood and canvas, was built on the intended site, but the the house was never actually constructed. In 1913, Mies (as he is most often known) established his own practice in Berlin. After World War I, he worked on a number of projects for tall buildings with exterior curtain walls entirely of glass, and for an office building of concrete construction where continuous horizontal bands of windows were to alternate with concrete bands at each floor level. Although unbuilt, through published plans and drawings these designs strongly influenced the modernism of the 1950s and 1960s in both Europe and America.

Work of the 1920s and 1930s

By 1927, Mies's reputation in Germany was sufficient to bring him the role of director for an exhibition of modern housing design at Stuttgart called the Weissenhofsiedlung. A number of leaders in the growing modern movement (including

Behrens, Gropius, and Le Corbusier) were invited to design model houses that were built to form a demonstration neighborhood in the new style. Mies was the designer of the largest building, a three-story and roof-deck apartment house with the smooth white walls and large bands of windows typical of the International Style. Other exhibits in the late 1920s and early 1930s offered Mies opportunities to demonstrate his approach to interior design. Lilly Reich (1885–1947) was a collaborator in many of these projects, and probably had a role in the development of furniture designs such as the MR chairs which used a frame of steel tubing bent into a cantilever form to support seat and back of stretched leather. The austere simplicity of these interiors, where colors and textures of rich materials provided the only ornamentation, were clear demonstrations of Mies's belief in the validity of his phrase "less is more."

Mies won an international reputation with his design for the German Exhibit Pavilion at the Barcelona Exhibition of 1929. The Barcelona Pavilion (as it is now generally known), placed on a wide platform of marble with two reflecting pools, was a simple structure made up of eight steel columns that supported a flat slab roof. There were no enclosing walls, but screen-like walls of glass and marble were arranged in an irregular but recti-linear abstract pattern, with some walls extending into outdoor space (**fig. 15.10**). Visitors could move through the open spaces to admire the rich materials, the abstract composition of the planes, and a few works of modern sculpture. The color—gleaming chrome on the steel columns, marble walls in rich greens and orangy red, scarlet red drapery, and both clear and opal glass—made the pavilion an abstract work of art in itself. Simple chairs, ottomans with chrome-bar frames and leather cushions, and related glass-topped tables were provided for use at a ceremonial visit by Spain's king and queen. These furniture designs have become modern classics, which are still in

production. The Barcelona Pavilion seems to have been the first building to fully exploit the ability of modern structural technology of steel and concrete to make walls optional elements—they have no role in holding up the roofs, so that interior space can be freely planned without division into rooms and with as much openness as may be desirable for a particular function.

Similar ideas were introduced in residential design in Mies van der Rohe's Tugendhat House at Brno in the Czech Republic (**figs. 15.11** and **15.12**; 1928–30). The house is on a hillside, its entrance and garage at the upper (street) level. Bedrooms occupy something like a penthouse on this top floor. The main living area on the floor below is an open space subdivided only by an onyx marble screen separating living space from an adjacent library-study area and a curving screen of Macassar ebony that defines an open dining area. The exterior walls on the downhill side of this space and across its end are entirely of floor-to-ceiling glass. The curtains can be drawn back and the walls lowered by mechanical means into the basement,

15.10 Ludwig Mies van der Rohe, German Pavilion, International Exhibition, Barcelona, 1929.

The open space of the area, which had no identified rooms but screen walls of glass and marble to define spaces, has been a key influence on modern ideas of interior planning. The walls at the right are floor-to-ceiling glass, and structural support is provided by slim steel columns. The area was finished with luxurious materials, including marble, travertine, onyx, green glass, and polished steel. The chairs and ottomans, now called Barcelona, are visible in their original positions.

15.11 Ludwig Mies van der Rohe, Tugendhat House, Brno, Czech Republic, 1928–30.

The idea of open planning is apparent in the living area of this house. The floor-to-ceiling glass walls could be lowered into the basement level to make the house a totally open pavilion. The furniture is of Mies's design, while color comes from richly veined marbles and fine, polished woods used for the screen-wall elements. The structure is of steel columns.

15.12 Plan of the Tugendhat House.

The openness of this plan in which living spaces omit walls of separation has exerted great influence on subsequent design thinking.

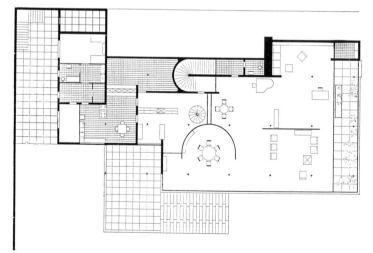

leaving the space totally open to the out of doors. Slim steel columns are the unobtrusive structural elements, barely noticeable with their mirror-polished steel surfaces. The Barcelona Pavilion and Tugendhat interiors have had tremendous impact on modern interior design, emphasizing abstract arrangements of spatial elements, with the colors and textures of the materials taking the place of ornamentation.

Emigration to the United States

After serving as a teacher and then as director of the Bauhaus, Mies could find little work in Nazi Germany. He developed designs for several houses that were never built—designs known from his remarkable drawings that show interiors comparable in simplicity and openness to those of the Barcelona Pavilion. The drawings are works of art as minimalist as the spaces they describe. In 1937 Mies relocated in America to become the head of the architectural program at Illinois Institute of Technology in Chicago.

His role as a teacher was another factor in transferring the ideas of International Style modernism into the mainstream of American design practice. His own work in America included a campus plan and many buildings for Illinois Institute. Among them is Crown Hall, housing the architectural and design departments. It is a simple rectangle of open interior space with all-glass walls on all four sides. There are no internal columns since the roof is supported by steel girders that project above roof level. Internal subdivisions are movable screen and storage units, while stairs lead

The Emergence of Modernism

15.13 Mies van der Rohe, Farnsworth House, Plano, Illinois, 1946–51.

Late in his career, while he was working in the United States, Mies was able to apply the concept of open living space in the country weekend house he built for Dr. Edith Farnsworth, in which all four walls are of glass. The wall elements to the left are for an island with fireplace (visible here), bathrooms and utilities within, and kitchen elements on the opposite side. A storage unit forms a screen (seen ahead). All furniture here is of Mies van der Rohe's design.

down to a basement, partially above ground, where all enclosed rooms are located. Externally, structural elements are painted black so that they become unobtrusive elements in the wall surfaces of glass. The term MINIMALIST is often applied to such design, in which extreme care in the simple detailing of the structure and a subtle sense of proportion give the building a serene, classical feeling comparable to that of ancient Greek architecture.

Later Commissions

In the latter part of his American career, Mies van der Rohe's commissions included skyscraper apartment buildings in Detroit, Newark, New Jersey, and Chicago, and office buildings there and in Toronto and (in collaboration with Philip Johnson) in New York. The Seagram Building in New York (1954–8) is one of the most admired of modernist American tall buildings (see p. 323 below). His most famous late residential design is the Farnsworth House (**fig. 15.13**; 1946–51) at Plano, Illinois. The house stands in an open but secluded country location near the Fox River. The

floor is raised a few feet above the ground, allowing open space beneath. It is supported by the same eight steel columns that support the roof, which is of identical size and shape. About two-thirds of the space between floor and roof is enclosed by glass on all four sides—the remaining space is an outdoor deck reached by five broad steps that lead up from a wide platform reached in turn by wide steps. The columns and steel edges of floor, roof, and platform are all painted white. The open glass box that forms the interior is subdivided only by an enclosed "island" that houses bathrooms and utilities and forms a back wall for the equipment of an open kitchen area. A few pieces of furniture (all of Mies's design) are placed in the open living space.

One of Mies's last major works was the National Gallery in Berlin (1962–8). A broad raised terrace base enclosed galleries, offices, and a restaurant. On its upper surface, set back at its center, is a simple, glass enclosed exhibition space. Its steel roof is supported by eight columns at its outer edge. Set back under the roof, floor-to-ceiling glass walls enclose the unencumbered open space that can be arranged as necessary for temporary exhibitions.

15.14 Le Corbusier, Villa Schwob, Chaux-de-Fonds, Switzerland, 1916–17.

Le Corbusier demonstrated his interest in the geometric aesthetic generated by the golden ratio proportion in this early work. In the diagram, diagonals are drawn across golden rectangle elements. The parallel angles of these lines and their right angle intersections demonstrate their relationships. Although not apparent in the finished building, the resultant visual unity of the design can be sensed.

Le Corbusier

As a young man, the fourth pioneering leader of modernism, Le Corbusier, designed several houses in or near his home in the town of Chaux-de-Fonds, Switzerland, near the French border. The style is romantic with a hint of Art Nouveau or Secessionist influence. Le Corbusier spent five months in the office of Peter Behrens in 1910 and then stopped briefly in Vienna to work for Josef Hoffmann. The influences of these experiences can be traced in the largest of the early houses at Chaux-de-Fonds, the Villa Schwob (**fig. 15.14**; 1916–17). It has the symmetry and orderly sense of Neoclassicism, while the material (reinforced concrete), the openness of planning, the large windows, and flat roofs suggest the direction of modernism. The aesthetic design of Villa Schwob derives from a system of geometric controls that Le Corbusier called "regulating lines"—intersecting

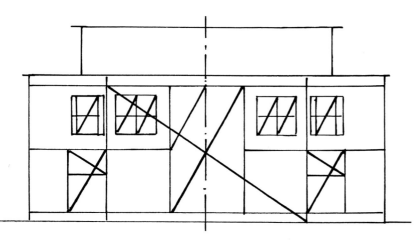

diagonals with right-angle relationships that govern the placement of elements according to a systematic method recalling the practice of Renaissance masters. Throughout his career, Le Corbusier used such geometry in systems that he developed more and more fully. The impact and aesthetic power that can be felt in even his minor works may derive in some part from this methodical way of bringing order to what might otherwise be entirely arbitrary forms.

Paris: Developing the Machine Aesthetic

For a time, Le Corbusier gravitated toward the fine arts, concentrating on painting under the influence of Picasso, Braque, Duchamp, and others. After moving to Paris in 1917, he joined the artist

Amédée Ozenfant in developing a form of cubist abstract painting that they named Purism. In 1920 they joined in the publication of a magazine, *L'Esprit Nouveau*, which dealt with every aspect of modern art. In 1922–3, Le Corbusier was the architect of a Paris studio-house for Ozenfant. It is a small four-story building at the end of an attached house row, austere and geometric in form, with large windows for the top-level studio which is topped by a saw-tooth skylight of the sort often used to light industrial buildings. The rigorously International Style white walls and steel-framed windows, an outdoor projecting spiral stair to the second-floor level, and, above all, the skylights gave the house an exterior that was shockingly unlike any conventional architecture. The geometric system of regulating lines controlled the form and placement of elements, while proportions approach the golden section ratio of 1:1.618. The top-level studio, with giant corner windows on two sides meeting the skylight area of the ceiling in a three-way corner defined by the thinnest possible structural elements, is a dramatically impressive space deriving its effect entirely from the arrangement of its abstract geometric elements. The building has undergone some unfortunate minor alterations, but still has a visual intensity out of all proportion to its small size.

Although Le Corbusier continued to be active as a painter throughout his life, his interest in architecture and design increased during the 1920s. His ideas became widely known through the publication of some theoretical texts and some drawings of unbuilt projects. His 1923 book *Vers une Architecture* (given the title *Towards a New Architecture* in English translation) is a collection of essays that set forth the basic ideas of modernism in design with great force and clarity. Historic architecture, particularly that of ancient Greece, is praised for its abstract, formal qualities, while eclectic imitation is condemned with such phrases as "The styles of Louis XIV, XV, XVI or Gothic, are to architecture what a feather is on a woman's head; it is sometimes pretty, though not always, and never anything more." Pictures of factories, grain elevators, ocean liners, automobiles, and airplanes appear along with details of the Parthenon. The beauty of modern machinery is cited as the true artistic expression of the modern world. "A house is a machine for living" is the memorable quotation that has drawn both anger and praise, but it is often misinterpreted as an

expression of hostility to aesthetic values. In fact, Le Corbusier had a deep understanding of the aesthetics of historic design, and his own aesthetic is comparable to that of any past age.

Early Houses, Villas, and Apartments

With the help of his cousin and frequent collaborator Pierre Jeanneret (1896–1967), Le Corbusier designed a pavilion (1925) sponsored by *L'Esprit Nouveau* magazine for an exhibition in Paris. It was conceived as a model apartment that could form a module in a large apartment building that would, in turn, be an element in a newly planned city. There is a double-height living space with a balcony above (**fig. 15.15**). The furniture includes simple, mass-produced bentwood chairs from Thonet, modular storage units of Le Corbusier's

own design, and simple, anonymous upholstered chairs. Purist paintings hang on the plain white walls, the rugs are vernacular craft Berber weavings, laboratory glassware is used for flower vases, and stones and shells are the only decorative accessories. The resulting interiors demonstrate the ideals of 1920s modernism with dramatic clarity. The pavilion was reconstructed in 1977 in a park plaza at Bologna, Italy.

In 1927 Michael Stein (brother of Gertrude) and Gabrielle de Monzie commissioned the design of Les Terraces, a large house at Garches at the edge of Paris (**figs. 15.16–15.18**). The resulting building is a cubistic International Style block with white walls, ribbon windows, and flat roof. It is symmetrical as seen from the street front except for minor deviations to provide a garage door and a canopy

15.15 Le Corbusier, Pavillon de l'Esprit Nouveau, Exhibition of Decorative Arts, Paris, 1925.

Within the exhibition space, Le Corbusier presented an interior of a model apartment, designed according to his theories. Modular storage units, simple arm chairs, and Thonet bentwood chairs suggest furniture far from the norms of the decorative furniture of the period. The art works on the wall typify the purist style advocated by Le Corbusier.

15.16 (*right*) and
15.17 (*far right*) Le
Corbusier, Villa Stein de
Monzie (Les Terraces),
Garches, near Paris,
1927.

*The plan of the house,
similar to that of
Palladio's Villa Foscara
at Mira (see p. 88) is
based on a rectangle of
11:16 proportions. Its
planning grid is
however divided in 4, 3,
4 proportions from
front to back, and, like
Palladio's, in 4, 2, 4, 2,
4 from side to side. Fig.
15.17 shows the archi-
tect's own isometric
drawing of the house.*

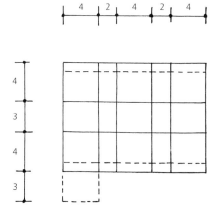

above the entrance door, but, from the rear and in
plan, symmetry is abandoned in favor of a complex
scheme based on internal function. An analysis by
the British historian and critic Colin Rowe has
shown that the plan is based on the geometry of
Palladio's Renaissance Villa Foscari at Mira. While
no overt resemblance can be observed, a sense of
classical order is clearly present in the completed
building. Le Corbusier's diagrams show that his
forms are here again based on golden section geometry. Interiors of Les Terraces have been drastically
altered, but old photographs show (in black and
white) the complex spatial organization as it

15.18 Interior of Villa
Stein de Monzie (Les
Terraces).

*An interior of this early
Le Corbusier house,
seen in Le Corbusier's
own drawing, reveals
the open plan relation-
ships, the simplicity,
and the austerity that
characterized the space.*

15.19 Le Corbusier, Villa Savoye, Poissy, France, 1929–31.

Living spaces open out to a terrace enclosed within the walled geometry of this house. Originally, since no appropriate furniture was available, the interiors made use of nondescript designs then in production. The house has now been restored and furniture of Le Corbusier's own designs has been put in place. The rolled-back glass walls demonstrate the open relationship between interior and outside that Le Corbusier favored.

appeared before furnishing. The opinion sometimes expressed that Le Corbusier interiors are colorless and "cold" may well be based on photographs that suggest that these spaces are all black, white, and chrome. In actuality, Le Corbusier made extensive and quite daring use of strong color in a way that derives from his work as a painter. Even exteriors were not always, as often supposed, plain white boxes. Walls of many of the small workers' houses built for the industrialist Henri Fruges at Pessac outside of Bordeaux (1926) were painted yellow, blue, pale green, or a dark maroon. Similar colors were used in interiors; often one wall of a space was strongly colored in contrast with the other walls, which were white. The group is thus richly colorful in ways that suggest cubist paintings.

One of the best known of Le Corbusier's works, and one of the most influential, is the house at Poissy, near Paris, known as Villa Savoye (**fig. 15.19**; 1929–31). The main block of the house is a near square raised up to second-floor level on slim, tubular steel columns. Its walls are white with continuous bands of ribbon windows. The space at ground level is occupied by a curving driveway leading to a garage, an entrance hall area, and several service rooms. Walls are set back beneath the mass of the floor above and are either of glass or painted a dark green that minimizes their visual impact. A ramp leads up to the main living floor, doubling back on itself to reach into the center of the space. A large living–dining area stretches across one side of the building. The floor-to-ceiling wall of glass faces into an internal patio, open to the sky; an unglazed portion of the exterior ribbon window band gives a view of the surrounding landscape.

The ramp continues out of doors to give access to roof-deck living spaces protected by straight and curved screen walls painted in pastel colors. Services with their own curving stair, bedrooms, and baths are arranged within the box-like block of the house, generating complex, surprising, and dramatic relationships. The house has now been carefully restored, although it is without furniture. Old photographs do not convey how colorful the interior spaces are. Those photographs do, however, show the level of comfort and charm that was generated in the main living area, when a modest table and chairs, a few nondescript uphol-stered chairs and several small oriental rugs furnished the space. A continuous indirect lighting strip hanging from the ceiling was the primary source of artificial light. Walls are bright blue and orange; the floor is of square yellow tiles laid diago-nally. The master bathroom, opening without wall or door into the adjacent bedroom, is a remarkable interior—tile-surfaced, with a blue-grey tile-lined sunken tub and a built-in contoured chaise.

In 1928 and 1929, in collaboration with Charlotte Perriand (1903–99), Le Corbusier devel-oped a number of furniture designs including an arm chair, an adjustable chaise, and a group of

upholstery designs in which loose cushions are held in a cage structure of chrome-plated steel. This furniture was used in a house at Avray, and shown to the public in a demonstration apartment at the Paris Salon d'Automne of 1929. Modular box storage units that could make up room dividers or storage walls appeared here, along with glass-topped tables and model kitchen and bath arrange-ments, all reflecting the concept of a house as "a machine for living." The furniture continues in production and frequent use.

In 1931, Le Corbusier designed a nine-story apartment house in Geneva named Immeuble Clarté. Most of the apartments are on two levels, with double-height living rooms overlooked by balconies. The glass walls flood the spaces with light. There are two identical entrance lobbies, dark spaces that lead to the elevators, and stairs serving one half of the building. The stairs are largely of glass and are topped by skylights that pull natural light down through the public spaces.

The Maison Suisse (1932), a dormitory-resi-dence for Swiss students living in Paris, is a four-story block consisting of three floors of dormitory rooms with a roof-deck floor above, raised up on concrete supports—"pilotis," as they came to be called—leaving the ground under the building open. Stairs and elevator are in a vertical element that rises from a one-story wing that contains entrance and communal facilities. A curving end wall of the long wing is of rough stone work that contrasts dramatically with the smooth walls of the taller mass. Inside, this wall was originally covered with photomurals made up of magnified images of microscopic natural forms. The wall is now covered by a painted mural executed by Le Corbusier at the time of a post-World War II reha-bilitation of the building. A Paris apartment house at Porte Molitor designed by Le Corbusier and built in 1933 contains a top-floor and roof-level apartment and studio with large glass areas, curving ceiling surfaces, and contrasting surfaces of smooth plaster and rough brick. This was Le Corbusier's home for the rest of his life except for regular visits to a tiny cabin on the coast of southern France.

Le Corbusier designed many major projects that were never built. His designs were often rejected for trivial reasons, as when his competition entry for the Palace of the League of Nations at Geneva was disqualified for being drawn in the wrong type of ink. Many ink-line drawings ranging

---

I N S I G H T S

The Philosophy of Le Corbusier

Le Corbusier explained his theories and ideas at length in his book *Vers une Architecture* (Towards a New Architecture) published in 1923:

The machinery of society is profoundly out of gear, oscillates between an amelioration of historical importance and a catastrophe. The primordial instinct of every human being is to assure himself of a shelter. The various classes of workers in society today no longer have dwellings adapted to their needs; neither the artisan or the intellectual. It is a question of building which is at the root of the social unrest of today; architecture or revolution [1]

The difference between construction and architecture is vividly expressed in the following words:

You employ stone and wood and concrete, and with these materials you build houses and palaces; that is construction. Ingenuity is at work. But suddenly you touch my heart, you do me good. I am happy and I say: "This is beautiful". That is Architecture. Art enters in. [2]

For Le Corbusier, the house was a "machine for living":

If we eliminate from our hearts and minds all dead concepts in regard to houses and look at the ques-tion from a critical and objective point of view, we shall arrive at the "House Machine", the main production house, healthy (and morally so too) and beautiful in the same way that the working tools and instruments which accompany our existence are beautiful. [3]

1. Le Corbusier, *Vers une Architecture*, 1923, quoted in K. Frampton, *Modern Architecture* (London, 1992), p. 178;   2. *Ibid*, p. 149;
3. *Ibid*, p. 153

from casual sketches to meticulous constructed perspectives show Le Corbusier's ideas for houses, offices, apartments, whole neighborhoods, and cities. The frequency with which resistant and resentful clients and authorities managed to block Le Corbusier's projects made him, as years went by, combative and irascible to a degree that may have further limited his success in achieving built projects.

Town Planning

Le Corbusier's ideas about town planning were first developed in his Plan Voisin for Paris (1925), in which most of central Paris was to be demolished to make room for a futuristic city of giant skyscrapers set within a system of elevated roadways. It included the concept of large buildings that would each become a small neighborhood, with apartments of various sizes, a shopping street high up in the building, and various communal facilities such as a restaurant, a school, recreational spaces, and even a small hotel. Such a building he called a UNITE D'HABITATION.

In 1946 the government of the city of Marseille commissioned a group of such Unité buildings to form a new housing district. Only one Unité was built there (1945)—a huge slab-like block with

seventeen floors of apartments raised up off the ground on PILOTIS, creating open space at ground level (**figs. 15.20** and **15.21**). The typical apartment is a long and narrow DUPLEX (an apartment on two floors), with one floor passing all the way through the building to open decks on both sides. The other level is only half as deep, with an open balcony and stair connecting the two levels. The interlocking of two apartments leaves a central space for a corridor that occurs only on every third floor. From the corridor, apartments on one side are entered at the upper level, with a stair leading down to the larger level, while those on the other side are entered on the lower level, with stairs leading up to the larger level—an arrangement clearer in a sectional diagram than in words.

There is a shopping street half way up the height of the building, and communal functions on the roof, where there is a small two-story nursery school—really a building on top of a building—and great funnel-like ventilator stacks of strongly sculptural form. The small but adequate apartments are ingeniously planned, exceptionally light and airy with their open decks facing in two directions, and surprisingly rich in spatial qualities. The grid of sunshades (brise-soleil) that makes up the exterior surfaces of the building is brightened by brilliant colors painted on the side walls of the outdoor decks that they shade. The building has aroused much controversy. Some critics blame it as the source of the evils of later high-rise public housing, while others note its many advantages over even luxury apartment buildings as they are conventionally built. Le Corbusier designed other Unités at Briey-en-Forêt, Firminy-Vert, and Nantes-Rezé in France, and in Berlin. At Firminy there is also an interesting House of Youth and Culture, with a tension cable roof structure that helps to generate unusual and striking interior spaces.

15.20 (*left*) Le Corbusier, Unité d'habitation, Marseilles, 1945.

The vast apartment house was designed to be a complete neighborhood within itself. Such buildings, spaced apart in a park-like setting, were intended to take the place of the crowded and chaotic conditions found in most modern cities.

15.21 (*below*) Le Corbusier's elevation of the Unité d'habitation.
1 Kindergarten/nursery
2 Ramp
3 Tower for escalators
4 Ventilator stacks
5 Wind shield
6 Gymnasium
7 Upper terrace
8 Corridor
9 Shopping street
10 Sunshaded areas
11 Fire escape
12 Air conditioning plant and machineries
13 Pilotis

The scheme of the Unité called for apartments of double height opening on both sides of the building on one floor and on one side of the building only on the other so that central corridors could serve apartments that, alternately, had a second level above and below the corridor level. Corridors thus occurred only at every third level, minimizing the number of elevator stops.

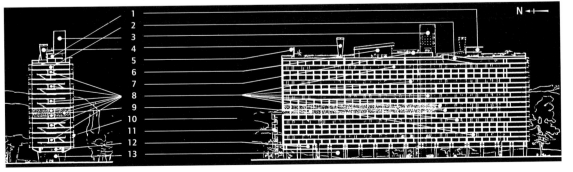

15.22 Le Corbusier, Church of Notre-Dame-du-Haut, Ronchamp, 1951.

The emotional character of the dark interior of the pilgrimage church is intensified by the effects of light coming from small windows, which are filled with colorful stained glass. The curving roof is held above the walls by metal pins, permitting a continuous band of light at the wall to roof intersection point. Le Corbusier was the designer of all the interior fittings.

Post-War Years

After World War II, the character of Le Corbusier's work tended to shift away from the cubistic rectangularity of earlier projects toward freer, more sculptural forms. The church of Notre-Dame-du-Haut at Ronchamp (1951) in France, near the Swiss border, is a dramatic example of this later design vocabulary. Curving concrete walls enclose an irregularly shaped interior. The roof is a curved construction of reinforced concrete, hollow in section like the wing of an airplane. Three chapels, two low and one higher, rise above the roof level to curving tops. The interior space is very dark: the light comes into the three chapels from hidden windows at their tops (**fig. 15.22**). The roof is raised above two walls on pins, leaving a glass-filled slot that makes the roof seem to float in the air. One wall is very thick, with rectangular funnel-shaped openings, large on the inside but tapering to small windows on the outside where stained glass in various colors fills the openings. Although the walls are white, the light from the glass makes the openings light up in brilliant colors. Behind the altar, the wall is pierced by tiny glazed openings that light up or are cut off as a viewer moves about within the space. The colorful windows, an enameled ceremonial entrance door (which swings on a pivot), the seating, and the chancel fittings were all

designed by the architect to create a mysterious and moving space that is suggestive of Gothic church interiors.

The Dominican convent of La Tourette (1960) near Lyon groups monastic buildings on three sides of a central open court. The church forms a large block on the fourth side. The building is of concrete, with surfaces left rough as they are when the formwork into which concrete is poured is removed. The uncompromising austerity of finish suited the ideals of the monastic order, but also derived from Le Corbusier's inclination toward strong forms executed in rough, even brutal materials. The term "new brutalism" was coined by British critics (perhaps derived from BETON BRUT, the French term for rough concrete) to describe such work. A visit to the Romanesque monastery of Le Thoronet in southern France (see p. 49) was a stimulus to seeking a modern equivalent to such medieval simplicity. The interior of the church is a simple box-like space with a central altar. The roof is separated from the walls by a narrow ribbon window that admits a diffused daylight from above, and slot-like windows shielded by exterior planes admit light reflected from above in brilliant colors generated by simply painted reflective surfaces. Adjoining the church, a projecting sculpturally contoured unit houses many small chapels arranged on two levels. Funnel-like skylights are painted on the inside in bright colors, creating effects that suggest stained glass through totally simple means.

Late Commissions

Toward the end of his career, Le Corbusier was involved in the planning of a new capital city for the Indian state of Punjab, Chandigarh in Pakistan. The basic plan of the city and many of the buildings are by Le Corbusier. The bold, sculptural forms of the larger buildings—the High Court (1956) where open-air circulation leads to offices and courtrooms with tapestries designed by Le Corbusier, the Secretariat (1958), and the Assembly (1961) with the main legislative chamber, a round funnel form placed off-center in a broad "forum" circulation space—with their rough concrete surfaces and bold colors, make them among Le Corbusier's most powerful late works.

There is only one building by Le Corbusier in America. It is Carpenter Center (1963), a small structure devoted to art studios for graduate students on the campus of Harvard University in Cambridge, Massachusetts. A central ramp plunges through the building, giving access to studio spaces in adjacent wings with curved forms. The rough "brutalist" surfaces of concrete with occasional accents painted in bright colors are particularly well suited to studio functions.

A very late work, completed after Le Corbusier's death, is the exhibit pavilion in a Zürich park known as Centre Le Corbusier or La Maison de l'Homme (1963–7). It is a geometric arrangement of cubical modules with wall panels of glass and bright, primary colors and a long projecting ramp for access to its upper level. A great roof umbrella of steel, supported on thin columns, shelters and contains the entire building. Internally, open galleries provide for exhibitions, while one area is arranged as a kind of ideal house complete with kitchen and bedroom. In this building, as in all of Le Corbusier's work, systematic use of a geometric system of proportions was a governing factor in every detail of design. This systematic approach, first described in some of his earliest writing, was gradually developed throughout Le Corbusier's career, leading to the publication of a two-volume work, *Modulor I* and *Modulor II*. Here text and diagrams propose a dimensional rule in which scales of feet and inches or metric scales are replaced by a progression of MODULAR dimensions intended to govern every element of design, from the smallest details of furniture up to whole buildings or communities. Human dimensions are fundamental, and the concept is related to the golden section proportion. The several Unité buildings and all of Le Corbusier's work thereafter made use of the modular system.

Although subject to frequent—sometimes bitter—criticism and attack, the work of Le Corbusier has had enormous impact on modern design practice. Its success in bringing about a relationship between aesthetic values and the realities of the modern technological "machine age" world became clear in the 1920s. Just as criticism became focused on its cubistic and supposedly "harsh" and "cold" materials and forms, movement into freer, sculptural forms and more richly textural materials undermined such attacks. A rather artificial contrast between the "organic" and nature-related work of Wright and the "mechanistic" qualities of Le Corbusier's design ultimately faded as Le Corbusier came to seem in many ways as organic and romantic in orientation as Wright. In late work, Wright often turned to forms related to the International Style, however bitter his criticism of it might have been. Recent "late modern" works often draw on Le Corbusier as a source of inspiration. His furniture remains in production and wide use. Visits to actual buildings confirm their merits and make it clear that photographs, however impressive, never fully convey the complexity and richness of Le Corbusier's work.

Aalto

In addition to the four pioneers already discussed, there were a number of other European figures who made major contributions to the development of modernism. For some, their secondary status may derive from the lesser quantity of their production, for others from a late start that makes their work seem derivative, or even from the remote or unfamiliar location of their works. The most important of these "second-tier" pioneer modernists is the Finnish architect and designer Alvar Aalto (1898–1976). Aalto's career began amid the romanticism and Nordic nationalism of Sonck and Eliel Saarinen, with its links to Neoclassicism and Jugendstil movements of the late nineteenth century. The Workers' Club and

15.23 Alvar Aalto, Turun Sanomat Building, Turku, Finland, 1927–9.

The tapering concrete columns generate rhythmic forms that make this essentially industrial interior—the press room of the newspaper Turun Sanomat— *a space of great beauty.*

INSIGHTS

The Vision of Alvar Aalto

Alvar Aalto described his thinking behind the design of the Finnish exhibit at the World Fairs in Paris (1937) and New York (1939) as follows:

One of the most difficult architectural problems is the shaping of the building's surroundings to the human scale. In modern architecture where the rationality of the structural frame and the building masses threaten to dominate, there is often an architectural vacuum left over, which is filled with formal gardens. It would be good if the organic movement of people could be incorporated in the shaping of the site in order to create an intimate relationship between Man and Architecture. In the case of the Paris Pavilion, this problem could fortunately be solved in this way. [1]

Humanity and a sense of the organic were always at the heart of his work:

I would like to add that architecture and its details are connected in a way with biology. They are perhaps like large salmon or trout. They are not born mature, they are not even born in the sea where they will normally live . . . as the fish egg's development to a mature organism takes time, so it also requires time for all that develops and crystallises in our world of thoughts. [2]

The architect and writer Stanley Abercrombie, one of Aalto's contemporaries, observed this emphasis on the "human" qualities of architecture:

He once advised the architecture students at MIT to design their windows as if the girls they loved were sitting in them. [3]

1. Alvar Aalto, *Collected Works,* quoted in K. Frampton, *Modern Architecture* (London, 1992), p. 197;   2. Alvar Aalto, *The Trout and the Mountain Stream,* quoted in *ibid,* p. 201;   3. Stanley Abercrombie, *Contemporary Architects* (Chicago and London, 1987), p. 4

Theater at Jyvaskyla (1924), an early Aalto work, even makes use of Doric columns and entablature to form a loggia-like band at ground level. By 1929, however, his building for the *Turun Sanomat,* a Turku newspaper, is clearly a work of International Style modernism with its white walls and asymmetrically arranged ribbon windows. In the press room, columns of reinforced concrete slope inward (**fig. 15.23**). The sequence of their curved edges and flared tops that flow into the ceiling slab above forms a distinguished space for a strictly utilitarian function. Interior details such as lighting fixtures, railings, even doorknobs, were carefully studied so that a unity of design extended from the general concept to the tiniest elements.

Aalto's international reputation was established by a large hospital building, the Paimio Sanatorium, built in 1930–3 for the treatment of tuberculosis patients. Connected wings placed at angles house the various parts of the building—a long six-story block for patients' rooms, all facing south to trap the sunlight, a shorter wing of open-air terraces, a central entrance block, and units for communal dining and utilitarian services. Internally, the spaces are open, simple, and logical, but details are extraordinarily sensitive. The reception office, stairs, elevators, and such small elements as lighting fixtures and clocks were all specially designed with great care and subtlety. Aalto continued to be involved with furniture and other interior elements that became factory products, many of which are still in production.

The Library at Viipuri (1935, but virtually destroyed in the Russian war with Finland) was a simple building made up of two rectangular blocks, the larger block containing the main reading room spaces, with a small auditorium and other minor

functions in the attached longer but lower block (**fig. 15.24**). The reading rooms were top-lighted by round skylights that could be artificially lighted at night. The auditorium ceiling was an undulating surface of strips of natural wood. Aalto's furniture had the simplicity of the International Style, but the material—molded plywood of Finnish birch— suggested warmth and introduced color that contributed to the "humane" character typical of all of Aalto's work. The firm Artek took up production of Aalto-designed furniture, and eventually other Finnish manufacturers of lighting, glassware, and other products brought Aalto's designs to international recognition.

The Villa Mairea at Noormarkka (**fig. 15.25**; 1938–41), built for the Gullichsen family, a wealthy industrialist and his wife (who directed the Artek firm), is a singularly successful blending of the order and logic of International Style thinking with a sensitive, almost romantic use of natural materials and freer forms. Gallery, studio, and entertainment spaces are arranged with easy and flowing forms that offer flexibility of use along with great visual variety. Americans were able to see an Aalto design at first hand at the New York World's Fair of 1939. The box-like interior space of the Finnish exhibit was made remarkably interesting by the introduction of flowing, free-form walls (**fig. 15.26**). A wall of wood strips leaned out over the main exhibit space that screened additional exhibit space on an upper level. A balcony restaurant with provision for film projection from a startling suspended free-form projection booth completed the exhibit. In spite of its small size and somewhat obscure location at the fair, Aalto's design attracted highly favorable critical comment and eventually led to a teaching appointment at the Massachusetts Institute of Technology. His design for Baker House (1947), a dormitory at MIT is the most important Aalto work in America. It is a long six-story block of undulating shape stretched out along the bank of the Charles River. An adjacent single-story block houses a common room, a large open space lighted by circular skylights which become the sources of artificial lighting at night. All bedrooms face the river, while two stairs climb up the inland side of the building in strong, angular forms.

After returning to Finland, Aalto received a steady flow of commissions. The Pensions Institute in Helsinki (1952–6) is a complex facility of government offices, but the modest scale of its massing and the warm brick of its exterior walls

15.24 (*top*) Alvar Aalto, City Library, Viipuri, Finland, 1927 and 1933–5.

In the lecture room of this small city library, the undulating ceiling is covered with strips of naturally colored wood, and these, together with its large windows opening on to an exterior landscape, give the room a sense of calm and comfort. Aalto was also the designer of the various chairs used here, notably the three-legged stacking stool.

15.25 (*bottom*) Alvar Aalto, Villa Mairea, Noormarkku, Finland, 1938–41.

The large windows of the living room of this spacious country house flood the space with light, while seating benches stand near flower boxes. Moveable chairs offer seating comfort, while a lamp and hanging lantern-light provide night-time illumination. The sense of calm and warmth are typical of Aalto's residential work.

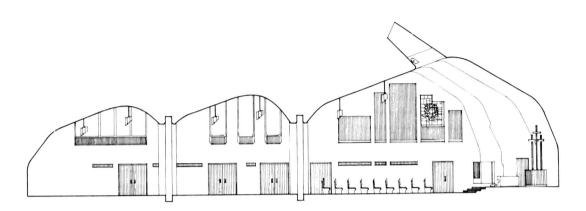

relate to interiors that are pleasant and practical. A skylighted hall with small booths for interviewing visitors, a library recalling the building at Viipuri, and the detailing and lighting throughout the building are a model for such public facilities.

The buildings of the Technical Institute at Otaniemi (near Helsinki, 1964) combine several low classroom wings with a large lecture hall element that generates a striking external form. Inside, the tiered seating of the hall is arranged in curves that parallel the forms of a stepped ceiling that conceals windows that light the space by day and also contain the artificial lighting that becomes the primary light source during the long Finnish winter.

The Vuoksenniska Church at Imatra (**fig. 15.27**; 1956–9) provides a large interior space that can be subdivided by curving sliding walls to accommodate varied uses by different sized groups. Daylight floods into the space, which is largely white with floors and furniture of natural wood. Aalto also designed the chancel fittings (even to vestments), the small inserts of colorful stained glass in the large windows, and the striking display of pipes for the large organ in a side balcony. Most of Aalto's works remain in good repair and in active use, offering impressive evidence of the practical and aesthetic success of his work. Furniture and glassware of Aalto design is in continuing production.

The work of the pioneer modernists has been vastly influential, and so, perhaps inevitably, it has become the subject of considerable criticism. New thinking always meets resistance from critics devoted to past values. Modern art, modern music, and modern architecture have all been subject to such resistance. The wide acceptance by historians of this modernist work has stimulated a revisionist literature seeking out its real and imagined weaknesses. One hears of leaking roofs, streaked white stucco walls, rusting window frames, excessive glass areas leading to winter heat loss and summer heat gain, unhappy clients, and similar complaints. Negative criticism most often comes from commentators who have not visited—let alone lived in—the projects in question. It often turns out that poor maintenance, inappropriate usage, and problems of client–designer friction are behind such reports. Reports of great satisfaction can also be found, from clients such as Frederick Robie or Herbert Jacobs (Wright), Fritz Tugendhat (Mies van der Rohe), or the tenants of the houses at Pessac (Le Corbusier).

The merits of International Style modernism can best be appreciated by visiting the buildings in question. The Robie House, Unity Temple Church, the Lakeshore Apartments in Chicago, Crown Hall at Illinois Institute of Technology, Villa Savoye, the Unité at Marseille, the Paimio Sanatorium, the church at Imatra are all accessible and each gives testimony to the lasting merit of modernist work. Although design has moved onward, the modernist pioneers retain their stature as the inventors of a design vocabulary for the twentieth century.

15.26 (*opposite*) Alvar Aalto, Finnish Pavilion, New York World's Fair, 1939.

Although a small space within a larger building, Aalto's Finnish Pavilion was a major critical success at the Fair. The slanting wall of undulating wood strips and the balcony (barely visible at right) formed an exciting space, within which products of Finnish industry could be seen in a stimulating setting.

15.27 (*above*) Alvar Aalto, Vuoksenniska Church, Imatra, Finland, 1956-9.

The sectional drawing shows the way in which the space has been divided into three sections separated by moveable walls. The main church at the right, with altar, stained glass, and organ, serves for normal services. On special occasions, the walls can be rolled back to add one or two additional spaces to hold larger congregations. Note the skylight at the right, which floods the chancel area with daylight from an unseen source.

16

Art Deco and Industrial Design

After World War I Europeans struggled to find a design direction that would be a true expression of the twentieth century, a truly modern design. In France the word MODERNE came to be understood as a designation for a new style, a style which in English took on the name MODERNISTIC. The term served to distinguish the word modern, which simply meant recent or current, from the idea of a new, that is, Modernistic style.

Art Deco

The 1925 World's Fair in Paris carried the title *L'Exposition Internationale des Arts Décoratifs et Industriels Modernes*. It was a showcase for the exhibition of interior design, objects, and rooms in the new, post-war style. A number of French designers had already produced designs for furniture, lamps, textiles, and various accessories that showed stylistic similarities. Sharply angled and cubistic forms, the use of aluminum, black lacquer, and glass, and zig-zag shapes that were thought to relate to electricity and radio served as symbols of the modern world. The term "jazz modern" was sometimes used to suggest an affinity with the nervous rhythms of the jazz music of the 1920s that became popular in France and elsewhere in Europe.

The term Art Deco has come into use to identify design of this character. Unlike modernist

design (see Chapter 15), Art Deco design was not strongly concerned with issues of functionalism and technology. It was primarily a fashion-oriented style which was expected to take its place in the sequence of styles from past history—styles among which designer and client could choose as their preferences might suggest. A room in the Salon des Artistes Décorateurs in Paris (1928) by Michel Roux-Spitz (1888–1937) sums up the essence of Art Deco design (**fig. 16.1**). The carpet pattern suggests awareness of cubist art. The folding screen carries a pattern derived from African tribal art. The stepped forms of furniture suggest the architecture of skyscrapers, while the large mirror and prominent lighting units call attention to modern materials and electric lighting. The total effect is in no way suggestive of anything from the past but neither is it related to the functional interior of the International Style; it is, rather, fashion-oriented and strongly decorative. With France as its point of origin, the style gradually moved to other European countries and to the American continent until the beginning of World War II.

France

Furniture Designers

The design of furniture became a readily available field in which the ideas of the French *moderne* style could develop. Art Deco furniture made extensive use of such rich materials as Macassar ebony, zebrawood with inlays of ivory, tortoise-shell, and leather. Polished metal, glass, and mirrors appear in many designs. Glass was a favorite medium for decorative vases, bowls, and lamps by such designers as René Lalique (1860–1945) and by the designers of the firm of Daum. Their earlier work in Art Nouveau idioms was now converted to Art Deco forms.

The furniture of Jacques-Emile Ruhlmann (1879–1933) made use of rich materials and fine craftsmanship similar to those of traditional design. Louis Süe (1875–1968) formed a partnership with André Mare (1885–1932) to produce similar designs on a commercial basis, but with emphasis on rich materials in simplified forms (**fig. 16.3**). Jean Dunand (1877–1942) was a figure in the Art Nouveau movement before World War I, but in the 1920s turned to the more geometric form of Art Deco. He established a factory where he produced screens, cabinets, chairs, and tables,

16.1 (*below*) Michel Roux-Spitz, Salon des Artistes Décorateurs, Paris, 1928.

Art Deco had its origins in displays in Paris in the 1920s, notably the Exposition des Arts Décoratifs et Industriels in 1925. In this room, the stepped forms of the dressing table, the African themes of the folding screen, the carpet pattern, the light fixtures, and the use of mirrors are typical of Art Deco.

16.2 (*opposite*) Ellis & Clarke with Owen Williams, Daily Express Building, Fleet Street, London, 1931.

The entrance lobby of this building, designed by R. Atkinson, was an early example of the Art Deco style as it surfaced in England. Black glass and chrome with Deco style murals and a spectacular ceiling light fixture make up a 1930s period piece.

usually with areas of decorative lacquer work. He also worked as a decorator, creating rooms for wealthy clients that could serve as settings for his furniture.

Maurice Dufrène (1876–1955) made a similar transition from Art Nouveau to Art Deco style. He was well known and widely influential as a result of his writings and teaching as well as his actual work as a designer of furniture, textiles, glass, metalwork, and complete interiors (**fig. 16.4**). Jean-Michel Frank (1895–1951) developed a Deco style that shares many of the same characteristics, but also draws on new directions in modern art such as surrealism. His couch in the shape of a mouth is based on a painting by Salvador Dalí. He opened a Paris shop in 1932 where his furniture designs were made available to English and American designers such as Syrie Maugham and Frances Elkins. He also designed residential interiors for many wealthy clients, including the Nelson Rockefellers for whom he produced a typically Deco New York apartment in 1937.

Eileen Gray (1878–1976) was born in Ireland but had a long career in France, her work spanning several periods and styles. She became an expert in lacquer work before World War I but after the war began to design screens and other furniture and, when opportunity permitted, complete interiors,

16.3 (*above*) Louis Süe and André Mare, Grand Salon, Exposition Universelle, Paris, 1925.

Süe and Mare's company, La Compagnie des Arts Français, aimed at the luxury market. At the Paris Exposition, their room design indicated how traditional period design had been replaced by newly devised forms that still retained a link with the past. The over-stuffed upholstery, the fabrics and carpet with florid patterns, the grouping of clock and vases on the bookcase at the left, and the mirror over the mantel at the right suggest an effort to modify traditional forms without rejecting them.

16.4 (*below*) Maurice Dufrène, Hall, La Maîtrise Pavilion, Exposition Universelle, Paris, 1925.

To the architectural space designed by architects J. Hiriart, G. Tribout, and G. Beau, Dufrène added a decorative overlay of painting on walls and ceiling, slim metal railings, hanging lights, and decorative objects. The Art Deco effort to find a new style is apparent in every detail.

often using her own lacquer panels. Her furniture was highly original, ingenious, and cubist in character. The Bibendum arm chair of 1925, the Transat chair of 1924 (patented in 1930), and a variety of cabinets, couches, tables, lamps, and rugs with colorful geometric patterns appear in interiors designed for her own use and for various clients. By 1929 her work turned increasingly toward architecture with a simple, cubistic character that related to the work of Le Corbusier.

Textile Design

Textile and carpet manufacturers produced patterns to suit the demand for Art Deco designs. Some manufacturers used leading designers; others simply asked their in-house designers to develop patterns in this new style. Cubistic themes, zig-zags, stripes, and plaids in Deco colors by anonymous designers became widely available. A particularly well known figure in textile design was the artist Sonia Delaunay (1885–1979) who began to design textiles for a manufacturer in Lyon in 1922.

Ocean Liners

Art Deco of the 1920s, with its strong ties to fashion and with emphasis on decorative forms that were inevitably costly to produce, was limited to wealthy clients and customers. Acquaintance with the style reached a wider public, however, as Art Deco interior design came into use in restaurants, hotels, and in the interiors of the great ocean liners of the 1920s and 1930s. The French liner *Normandie* (1935) was a showcase for the work of French architects, decorators, artists, and craftsmen whose way of expressing modernity was to adopt Art Deco themes. Overall responsibility for the interiors of the *Normandie* (**fig. 16.5**) was placed in the hands of Richard Bouwens (1863–1939) and Roger Expert (1882–1941). Although they designed some of the spaces, they were assisted by a number of French artists and decorators, including Raymond Subes, Jean Dupas (1882–1964), and Jacques Dunand (1887–1942). Those working on the project were a virtual roll-call of the French masters of the Deco idiom.

16.5 Roger Expert and Richard Bouwens, Grand Salon, SS *Normandie*, 1935.

In the double-height, first class main lounge of the great French oceanliner Normandie, *tall murals of etched and painted glass, designed by Jean Dupas (a portion now installed in the Metropolitan Museum in New York), took the history of navigation as their theme. The tower-like, glass lighting fixtures were designed by Labouret. Great urns, visible on the right, emerge from round seating clusters and contain lights directed upward to the ceiling. This room, like most others on the ship, was a showcase of Art Deco concepts.*

16.6 (*right*) Paul T. Frankl, skyscraper furniture, 1930.

The excitement of skyscraper building in New York and the stepped, set-back forms typical of these tall buildings led Frankl to designs for furniture using similar stepped forms. Skyscraper profiles became a favorite part of the Art Deco design vocabulary.

16.7 (*below*) Reinhard & Hofmeister, Corbett, Harrison & MacMurray, Raymond Hood, Godley & Fouilhoux, International Building, Rockefeller Center, New York, 1935.

The monumental lobby contains gas escalators leading to upper and lower concourse levels. Green marble and a gold-leaf ceiling establish a level of luxurious grandeur for this formal entrance to one of the several skyscrapers that make up the Rockefeller Center complex.

16.8 (*top right*) Donald Deskey, Radio City Music Hall, New York, 1932.

The huge theater, designed as a major feature of the Rockefeller Center development, was intended as a setting for film and stage productions. Deskey's furniture used Bakelite and aluminum, among other materials, and was in a style that combined the luxury of French Modernism with the functionality of the Bauhaus.

The style spread internationally so that the German, Italian, and British liners each showed off the Deco idiom in a particular national version and carried Art Deco, both figuratively and quite literally, from Europe to America.

United States

Designers from Europe

Some American designers working in the style were themselves immigrants from Europe. Paul Frankl (1878–1958), for example, was trained in Vienna, but had an extensive career in the United States. It was he who observed the stepped forms of American tall buildings (forms created by the requirements of zoning laws rather than for any aesthetic reasons) and applied them in furniture such as his "skyscraper" furniture of the 1930s (**fig. 16.6**). Shelves were cantilevered in a way that demonstrated the characteristics of plywood, the newer material that replaced solid wood typical of older furniture.

Joseph Urban (1872–1933), who also had trained in Vienna, came to America as a stage designer. He also turned to interior and furniture design, working in an Art Deco vocabulary. His interiors for the New School for Social Research of 1930 in New York are a fine example of his work. His more spectacular Ziegfeld Theater (1928), with its elliptical auditorium and richly painted walls, as well as his exotic roof-top restaurant at the St. Regis Hotel in New York (1929) have, unfortunately, been demolished.

Frederick Kiesler (1892–1965), originally a stage designer in his native Vienna, associated briefly with the De Stijl movement in Holland before coming to America in 1926. His first American project was a small theater in New York, the Film Guild Cinema on 8th Street, which was one of the first modern interiors known to the general public. His work was largely in sculpture, but he became known as something of a theorist and futurist, most closely associated with his never-built proposal for a curvilinear Endless House exhibited in drawings and models.

Radio, a new means of communication and entertainment, was widely understood as one of the key innovations of the post-World War I era. It seemed natural, then, that fresh Art Deco forms should be applied to the cabinets of table- and console-model radio receivers. The material was wood, but the slick and curving forms of the enclosures were no longer historically based. They carried Art Deco into almost every home. The studios of radio stations such as those of NBC in New York's Rockefeller Center (often called Radio City in the 1930s), where the public was often invited to watch radio programs being broadcast, were also typically Art Deco spaces, both in form and in their daring use of colors. Blue was thought to suggest electricity, and black and chrome hinted at new technology.

Many of the lobbies and other public spaces at Rockefeller Center are of Art Deco character. The lobby of the International Building (630 Fifth Avenue), with its rich materials and subtly concealed lighting, is a prime example (**fig. 16.7**). The vast Radio City Music Hall, a spectacular display of Art Deco design, is largely the work of the American designer Donald Deskey (1894–1989). Lobbies and lounges are as interesting in their color and detail as is the huge auditorium itself (**fig. 16.8**). Deskey also designed the interiors of a number of apartments and houses for wealthy clients. The dining room of a New York apartment has walls covered with thin sheets of cork commonly used to insulate refrigerated storage rooms. The furniture is of maple veneer bleached to near white, with black lacquer details. Walls, doors, and furniture are all free of moldings and paneling typical of traditional design. The Mandel House at Mount Kisco, New York, designed by Edward Durell Stone, contained typically Deco interiors by Deskey set into an International Style shell. Deskey designed textiles in Art Deco modes for several American manufacturers and, as he moved toward an industrial design practice, his work included clocks and lamps in Deco forms.

Deco Architecture

The architectural forms of New York's Chrysler Building (**fig. 16.9**; 1930), designed by William van Alen (1883–1954), with its stepped setbacks and stainless steel spike top, were ornamented with details intended to suggest the headlights and radiator caps of the automobiles that were Chrysler's products. The building created a perfect setting for van Alen's Deco interiors of lobbies, stairs, and elevators. Many other office and apartment buildings have similar characteristics, and many retain interiors of the period that are still in very good condition.

16.9 William van Alen, Chrysler Building, New York, 1930.

The Art Deco style borrowed forms from skyscraper architecture, and at the same time architects incorporated decorative elements from Art Deco into their buildings. The Chrysler Building, with its stepped, set-back forms and its decorative details leading up to the great stainless steel spike, is the most dramatic example of this style of skyscraper architecture. When it was built, it was Manhattan's tallest building, crowned by the steel spire, which weighed 27 tons.

The relationship between Art Deco design and modern architecture was an uneasy one, despite many overlaps. As the architectural profession became increasingly loyal to the ideals of the International Style in the 1930s and 1940s, Deco design came to be called "modernistic"—superficial and decorative, a mere whimsical expression of popular fashion—while the word "modern" was reserved for work that was more clearly based on theoretical underpinnings. Still, many parallels can be discovered.

A series of World's Fairs, occurring in a time of deep depression in the 1930s, provided a forum for 1920s and 1930s design. The Chicago fair of 1933–4 called A Century of Progress was a cluster of Art Deco buildings, many with brightly colored exteriors, that displayed interiors and objects of Deco character. While public acceptance was often hesitant, some manufacturers launched furniture and other products of clearly Deco character. The "waterfall modern" design of factory-made inexpensive furniture of anonymous origin with its curving veneers, perhaps suggestive of Niagara Falls, brought Art Deco into at least some homes of people of limited means.

Britain

The Art Deco style was taken up in England to a limited extent, usually surfacing in the interior design of theaters, hotels, and restaurants. In London's Strand Palace Hotel, for example, public interiors were filled with angles and zig-zag forms in glittering glass and metal. The London building for the *Daily Express* newspaper (1931) by Owen Williams (1890–1969) with the firm of Ellis and Clark is a gleaming example of Art Deco design, with its rounded corners and bands of polished black glass edged with chrome. Public interiors such as the main entrance hall show off comparable Deco detail (**fig. 16.2**).

The Art Deco interiors of British ocean liners such as those of the Cunard Line (*Queen Mary* and *Mauretania* of the 1930s) and those of the Orient Line by Brian O'Rorke (1901–74) have already been mentioned (p. 293). Art Deco exposure for a wider public came from the design produced for the London Underground system under the direction of Frank Pick (1878–1941). Many stations (with architecture by Charles Holden) had interiors with strong Deco character, as did the interiors of train carriages and buses. The work of the

ceramicist Clarice Cliff (1899–1972) included many hand-painted pottery objects with colorful semi-abstract patterns of Deco character.

A plastic table radio designed in 1933 in typically Deco form by the English architect and designer Wells Coates (1895–1958) for Ekco is considered the first truly modern design to appear in England. Other English designs for table radios were developed by Serge Chermayeff (1900–92) in 1933, Misha Black (1910–77) in 1937 (also for Ekco), and by Gordon Russell (1892–1980) and his brother Richard, with cabinets of plywood, for Murphy Ltd. from 1930 to 1938. Gordon Russell, along with several partners, was also a designer of Deco furniture. He became something of a spokesman for British design and was responsible for an exhibition room at the Paris Exposition of 1937, with furniture by W. H. Russell and textiles by Marian Peplar.

Scandinavia

While the Scandinavian countries are not generally thought of as having any significant involvement with Art Deco design ideas, work there in the 1920s and early 1930s parallels developments in other countries to a considerable degree. Scandinavian designers also sought new directions appropriate to the twentieth century, but for some time did not participate in the development of International Style modernism. Instead, a somewhat cautious advance took place that had strong roots in traditions of craftsmanship and wise use of materials. The resulting work avoided the mechanistic qualities of De Stijl and Bauhaus to appear "warm" and comfortable in order to a broad consumer public. The International Style still seemed "cold" and forbidding.

In Sweden, the Stockholm Town Hall by Ragnar Östberg (see p. 262), with its beautifully decorated Blue Hall, became famous as an example of a charming kind of modernism which hinted at tradition. National Romanticism is the term often applied to such work that did not attempt imitation of past achievements but seemed rather to seek a way to recall the past in more contemporary terms. Whatever the aims, such work had an immediate appeal to a large audience. The term "Swedish modern" came to suggest furniture and interiors that were not reproductions of historic design, but that had a warmth and appeal that was easy to accept.

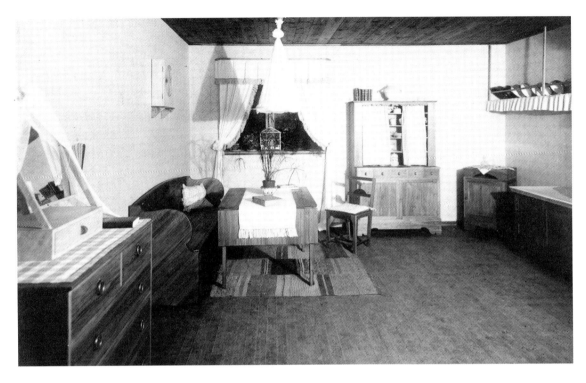

16.10 Gunnar Asplund, room setting, Slöjdföreningen Exhibition, Stockholm, 1917.

In Asplund's kitchen and living room for the exhibition of Slöjdföreningen (Society of Arts and Crafts), the simple Scandinavian wood detailing of furniture and the craft-woven rug indicate an acceptance of modernism while the window drapery and the shaded hanging light pay homage to earlier traditions.

The 1917 room settings designed by Gunnar Asplund (1885–1941) for an exhibition in Stockholm helped to define and publicize the Swedish approach to interior design (**fig. 16.10**). His Senna chair of 1925, with its smoothly curved seat, high back, and stubby arms, suggests a simplified version of some classic prototype. Asplund was the architect of the Stockholm City Library of 1928, an example of a restrained and classically based modernism, while his role in the design of the 1930 Stockholm Exposition asserted Sweden's modern Scandinavian direction. An extension table of 1938 by Bruno Mathsson (born 1907) is typical of the simplicity and logic of 1930s Swedish design.

Danish design of the 1920s and 1930s maintained a conservative respect for traditions of craftsmanship and became known for furniture that was simple, practical, and well made. Neither International Style nor Art Deco influences ever overcame Danish traditions, which were more rooted in a logical vernacular than in any particular style. The resulting "Danish modern" style has a history that extends from the early years of the twentieth century until recent times. Kaare Klint (1888–1954) was a leading influence in the development of furniture based on human proportions and human needs. His updated version of the traditional safari chair and deck lounge chair have become classics. Another Danish classic was the hanging light unit PH, developed in 1925 by Poul Henningsen (1895–1967). Mogens Koch (1898–1969) became known for a variety of folding furniture designs based on a traditional vernacular, as well as some simple and comfortable upholstered chairs. Finn Juhl (1912–89) designed furniture that was produced in Denmark and then, in the 1950s, designs for production by the American firm of Baker Furniture. His most important interior project was the Trusteeship Council Chamber of the United Nations headquarters building in New York (1952–3). It has a wall of undulating woodstrips and a ceiling open to the ducts and equipment overhead.

(For the work of Eliel Saarinen, particularly his interior and furniture design at Cranbrook, Michigan, which has strong links to Art Deco concepts, see Chapter 14.)

Industrial Design

In the late 1920s and early 1930s, a number of designers, some of whom had been proponents of Art Deco and others more oriented toward the International Style, developed an interest in design for industrial production. The term "industrial design" came into use to describe a new profession that would focus on products for industry. In

16.11 (*below left*) Raymond Loewy, mock-up office, New York, 1934.

Loewy created this office interior as a display for a design exhibition. The designer is surrounded by examples of his work in furniture, lighting, clock, drawings, and automobile model. The circular forms testify to the industrial designers' adoption of streamlining as a decorative theme.

16.12 (*below right*) Raymond Loewy, stateroom interior for the ships Panama, Ancon, and Cristobal of the Panama Line, 1934.

Ingeniously compact furniture arrangements, use of strictly fireproof materials, and an overall sense of the combination of streamlined and Deco concepts were part of the effort to introduce modern design to American passenger ship interiors.

promoting their services, the new generation of industrial designers spoke to their clients not so much of aesthetic goals, but rather of the strictly commercial goals of increased sales. In the years of depression, when manufacturers were faced with sagging sales, the idea that new design could make products attractive to consumers brought clients to the industrial designers. The new forms became typical of the 1930s. The sources of these forms were, logically enough, in new technology—in particular, the technology of aerodynamics.

During World War I, Germany developed and made use of large dirigibles, usually called Zeppelins after Count von Zeppelin, their leading designer and producer. After the war dirigibles were adapted as transport vehicles. Such craft as the British R-34 and R-100 and the German Graf Zeppelin became well known to the public. Called airships, dirigibles were indeed as large as ocean liners and could transport passengers in comparative luxury.

It was discovered that efficient flight could be best achieved if the form of the airship featured a rounded, bullet nose and a tapered tail with a slightly bulging curve between. Such form was called "streamlined" because it encouraged the smooth flow of an airstream over the dirigible hull. Smaller airplanes that were rivals of the dirigibles also turned out to benefit from streamlined form.

Public excitement over the exploits of Dr. Hugo Eckner piloting the Graf Zeppelin on long trans-oceanic flights and Amelia Earhart's and Wiley Post's record-setting flights in the beautifully streamlined Lockheed Vega airplane came to fix the streamlined form in the public mind as a visual symbol of future-oriented achievement. The minds of industrial designers were turned in the same direction, so that streamlined forms became a theme for 1930s industrial design.

Loewy and Other Designers

Raymond Loewy (1893–1986) began his career with a modernized form for a Gestetner mimeograph machine (a small office printing device) producing a dramatic upturn in sales. His streamlined design for automobiles for Hupmobile and Studebaker had similar success. Other American designers, including Henry Dreyfuss (1904–72), Walter Dorwin Teague (1883–1960), and Norman Bel Geddes (1893–1958) followed suit. Success with industrial products led these designers to expand their practice into interior design and even some efforts in architecture (**fig. 16.11**). Donald Deskey (see p. 295) now practiced as an industrial designer, working in every field of design. His furniture and lighting fixtures of the 1920s and early 1930s helped to make his reputation.

16.13 Russel Wright, "American Modern" tableware, 1939.

Wright's designs introduced the American public to simple modernism that could be put to use in any home. The enormous success of this dinner service helped to convince American industry of the value of modern design in products offered to the general public.

(1889–1936) was a German-born industrial designer who came to San Francisco to work on the Panama-Pacific International Exposition there. He remained in California and worked on furniture designs for Baker and Widdicomb of Grand Rapids, on retail store interiors, and on clocks and other objects. His Airline chair of 1934 is his best-known work.

Russel Wright (1904–76) was a successful American industrial designer. His most significant work, a line of tableware known as "American Modern," achieved enormous popularity from 1939 onward (**fig. 16.13**). It was the first simple and functional china to be introduced in America. Its success brought attention to his other designs for furniture, metal accessories, cutlery, and table linens. With his wife, Mary, he was an effective promoter of modern design in room-setting exhibits and in his book, *A Guide to Easier Living* (1951). Wright's sculpturally formed wood-framed arm chair of 1934 was used in the members' lounge of the newly built Museum of Modern Art in New York, but no manufacturer could be found to undertake its production.

The visual character of the work of the early industrial designers was usually a blend of Art Deco ornamentation with the slick forms of stream-lining. The goal was to convince a large public that a newly designed vacuum cleaner, railroad train, or ship was in some important way better and there-fore would become commercially successful. The philosophic and functionalist goals of the early European modernists were not concerns of the industrial designers although they often borrowed forms from the International Style, softening, diluting, and decorating those forms to make them more palatable to a consumer public.

In addition to the increasingly popular forms of trains, buses, automobiles, and ships, streamlining became well known to Americans in the form of a curious vernacular type, the diner, a short-order restaurant in the form of a railroad dining car (**fig. 16.14**). The first diners were actually railroad or street cars blocked up on fixed foundations. As streamlined trains became well known, the building of diners to imitate the cars of luxury trains became popular. Often at roadside locations where they could serve the increasing flow of auto-mobile traffic, the diner was a popular symbol of depression era life. Diner interiors with curving metal trim, mirrors, and bright color accents were produced by anonymous designers working for the firms that built these units.

Loewy (and his increasingly large firm) developed interior design for ships, retail stores, and offices. He not only redesigned railroad locomo-tives, but also provided interior designs for the passenger cars of the Pennsylvania Railroad and for the three sister ships of the Panama Line, *Panama* (**fig. 16.12**), *Ancon*, and *Cristobal*. Dreyfuss produced similar work for the rival New York Central Railroad, and interiors for four ships of the American Export Line. Later, his office was respon-sible for design of the larger ships *Independence* and *Constitution* for the same steamship line.

Teague worked on passenger car interiors for the New Haven Railroad. Bel Geddes moved from a distinguished career in stage design to focus on futuristic proposals for vast airplanes and stream-lined ocean liners. These never came to realization, but his modest Elbow Room Restaurant in New York (1938), with its curved walls and mirrored areas, showed that he was a talented interior designer.

Gilbert Rohde (1894–1944) is best known for his work in furniture design. In the 1930s he introduced the American firm of Herman Miller to the ideas of modernism, although the character of his design was more closely allied with Art Deco than with the functionalist directions that later became the norm of modernism in furniture. Kem Weber

16.14 Supreme Diner, Boston, Massachusetts, 1946.

The diner, a short-order restaurant intended to simulate the dining car of a railroad train, became a popular feature of roadside America. As real railroad cars took on the qualities of streamlined and Deco design, the diner followed, adopting rounded forms, chrome trim, and harsh lighting that created the atmosphere for a quick meal.

Design Training

The pioneer industrial designers were not actually trained in design. Loewy's training was as an electrical engineer in France; Dreyfuss's background was in stage design; Teague was an illustrator who had studied at the New York Art Students' League; Deskey studied and taught painting in Paris but appears to have been self-taught as a designer. Formal training in this field only began when industrial design was developing as a profession. Carnegie Institute (now Carnegie Mellon University) in Pittsburgh offered a program in industrial design as early as 1935 under the leadership of Donald Dohner (1907–44), who later introduced the subject at Pratt Institute, Brooklyn, in 1937. Such programs remain within an art school setting and so continue somewhat removed from the training offered to architects. The reality that buildings have interiors led to a relationship, however uneasy, between architecture and interior design, bringing about a style somewhere between modernism and Art Deco. The austerity of International Style modernism was widely felt to be too forbidding, while the less doctrinaire quality of Art Deco design appealed to at least some architects. It was the style of many public buildings in the United Sates, particularly those built under the sponsorship of depression era work relief projects such as the Works Progress Administration (WPA). The Tennessee Valley Authority (TVA) built great dams and power houses. Roland Wank (1898–1970), who was in charge of its architectural and interior design, produced remarkably fine examples of industrial interiors within the power-generating facilities at the dams. Here Deco and industrial design idioms made an unusually fortunate meeting.

Just as some architects began to incorporate Art Deco ideas, many interior decorators took up the style as an addition to the portfolio of historic styles on which they had previously depended. The terms "moderne" or "modernistic" were used to describe English and American work, such as the rooms by the English decorator Syrie Maugham (1879–1925), which had an all-white color scheme along with mirrors and glass. In America, Dorothy Draper (1889–1969) designed public spaces such as the lobbies of the Carlyle Hotel and the 770 Park Avenue apartment house. In each, a black marble floor with white banding, white walls, and glossy black doors in symmetrical arrangements are used, with a few strong color accents of red and blue in limited areas.

Residential Design

Architects of residential buildings were generally restrained by their clients from introducing Art Deco and modernist concepts, although flat roofs, rounded corners, and such newly developed materials as glass block were occasionally used. Many proposals for prefabricated house construction that would bring the economic benefits of factory mass production into housing were developed and publicized, but none achieved popular acceptance.

Kitchens and Bathrooms

Industrial design, with its connection to Art Deco and its love of streamlining, came into the homes of the twentieth-century middle classes through kitchens and bathrooms rather than more formal living spaces (**figs. 16.15** and **16.16**). Kitchens, even after the introduction of electric appliances, had remained rooms housing a collection of unrelated

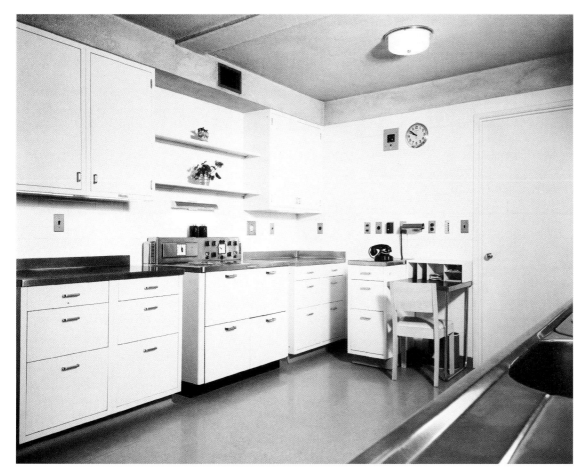

16.15 Kraetsch and Kraetsch, Butler House, Des Moines, Iowa, 1936.

The modern kitchen, as it had developed by the 1930s, made use of a continuous counter with overhead cabinets modeled on the practice of scientific laboratory design. Ease of cleaning and efficiency of work patterns are implied, while the visual impact relates to the streamlining typical of industrial designers' work of the time. Kitchen appliances—such as the range visible in this illustration—were designed to fit into this concept of the modern kitchen.

16.16 Paul Nash, bathroom for Edward James and Tilly Losch, London, 1932.

The idea of the bathroom as a place for decorative pleasure rather than a minimal utilitarian room developed in the 1920s and 1930s. In this example, mirrors, metals, and lighting elements make the room a showplace of Deco concepts. Note the mirror element in the ceiling lighting fixture.

items—the cooking stove, the ice box (now electrified), and the sink and drainboard unit, each in forms that dated back to the early nineteenth century. Industrial designers persuaded manufacturers to transform the old wooden ice box into a slick, white, mildly streamlined form. Loewy designed the 1935 Coldspot, soon to be followed by similar designs for General Electric, Norge, and other manufacturers. White and smooth surfaces then became the norm for ranges, beginning with Bel Geddes's simple, white-painted, smooth metal-formed unit for the Standard Gas Equipment Corporation (1933). An almost identical design by Teague appeared in 1934. These simple cubical forms with their standard height flat counter tops suggested to many designers and manufacturers the idea of continuous counters that could be topped with metal or linoleum to produce a laboratory-like band of equipment. Only the smooth refrigerator needed to poke up above the line. With gleaming white cabinets and smooth tops, banks of overhead cabinets and floors of colorful linoleum, such kitchens became favorite elements in houses of the 1930s.

Bathrooms also became eligible for modern treatment, with a built-in tub and shower, and often with wash basins made into cabinet units. The makers of plumbing fixtures became enthusiastic clients of industrial and interior designers, who produced model bathrooms in bright colors and advertised them in magazines. Houses that were otherwise still designed in sentimentally duplicated historic modes would nevertheless sport modern kitchens and baths. In the basements of houses, industrial designers provided smoothly styled exteriors for furnaces, now generally fueled by oil or gas rather than the earlier coal.

Lighting

The conversion of oil and gas lighting to electricity gave lighting design a new lease of life. Art Deco lamps and light fixtures appearing in the 1930s claimed to have "sight-saving" virtues. Indirect lighting—that is, lighting in which the light sources are concealed in coves or other housings so that the light produced was reflected from ceilings while the sources remained hidden—came into wide use. In the 1930s, tubular light sources became available,

16.17 Norman Bel Geddes, Futurama Exhibit, New York World's Fair, 1939.

Visitors to the General Motors exhibit were transported in moving booths above a scene of the "World of the Future" built in highly realistic model form. The illustration shows a city of the future as conceived by the industrial designer, Norman Bel Geddes (1893-1958), a strong advocate of stream-lined design. This exhibit is often thought of as a primary stim-ulus to the design and construction of modern superhighway networks.

first in incandescent versions and then, with the development of fluorescent light, tubular light sources became the norm in public, commercial, and institutional interiors. Neon lighting, first only used in signs, became an occasional source of decorative light effects. Practical, functional lamps began to appear in the work of designers such as Kurt Versen (born 1901), whose own firm manufactured a range of such lamps and lighting fixtures. They were used in interiors designed by architects and interior designers, but remained little known to the general public for residential use.

Textiles, Carpets, and Furniture

Textiles and carpets in geometric and abstract patterns suggestive of cubist art became available from sources catering to the professional design fields, but rarely found their way into average homes. Dorothy Liebes (1899–1972), for example, had a successful career as a designer of modern fabrics popular with the designers of public and commercial interiors. Manufacturers catering to mass markets still found it expedient to produce flowery prints, designs with illustrative motifs, and rugs based on oriental and other traditional designs.

Just as the era of Art Deco was introduced by the Paris Exposition of 1925, the World's Fair that opened in New York in 1939 can be thought of as summarizing and bringing to a close the era of Art Deco and streamlining. It included work by many of the important designers of the 1920s and 1930s and offered examples of each of the directions that the preceding decades had developed. German and Italian exhibits displayed the stripped classicism that had come to symbolize the aggressive trends of fascism. In contrast, the French pavilion was a modernist work of Roger Expert, who had been one of the designers responsible for the interiors of the liner *Normandie*. The designs of Dreyfuss (a city of the future in model form in the fair's theme center), Bel Geddes's Futurama, a whole world of the future viewed from moving overhead booths in the General Motors exhibit (**fig. 16.17**), Loewy (for Chrysler), and Teague (for Ford and Eastman Kodak), among others, showed off the commercial merits of the industrial designers' devotion to both Deco and streamlining themes. Modernism of a more serious kind could be found in the works of Lescaze (the Aviation building), Aalto (the Finnish exhibit, an interior that introduced Aalto to America), and the handsome Swedish pavilion by Sven Markelius (1889–1972). The modernism of the 1920s and 1930s is the subject of the next chapter.

17 The Spread of Early Modernism in Europe

Although design in the first half of the twentieth century continued to be dominated by eclectic historicism, awareness of the ideas of modernism began gradually to spread. In 1932, at the Museum of Modern Art in New York, the architectural historian Henry-Russell Hitchcock and Philip Johnson, the museum's director of the department of architecture and design, organized an architectural exhibition entitled The International Style.

Of the seventy-five projects presented, only seven were in the United States. Sixteen were works of the modern pioneers discussed in Chapter 15. There were buildings from across western Europe, the U.S.S.R., and Japan. They shared several stylistic qualities, including flat roofs, smooth (and usually white) walls, large areas of glass, and asymmetrical planning, along with a total absence of any historical or ornamental detail. The designs were examples of "functionalism," that is, they placed the requirements of function ahead of any preconceived aesthetic goals. It is interesting to notice that the images exhibited were, in eleven cases, illustrations of interiors. It was one of the key principles of modernism that architectural design should begin with interior arrangements that would lead to logical external expression. The illustrated interiors share the same functional simplicity, the same absence of historic and ornamental detail that characterize the external form of the buildings in question.

In omitting the work both of Frank Lloyd Wright and of Scandinavian designers whose design might be seen as having a romantic leaning, the organizers of the exhibition defined International Style modernism as having the abstract, cubistic, and mechanistic qualities that represented the twentieth century, the "machine age." The style became increasingly visible in magazine articles and book publications. Among the stimuli encouraging the simplicity and mechanistic reference of the new work were the impressive engineering structures that made use of steel and reinforced concrete to create forms that would have previously been impossible. The great airship hangars of 1916 at the Orly airfield outside of Paris (now destroyed) by Eugène Freyssinet (1879–1962) and the many concrete bridges in Switzerland by Robert Maillart (1872–1940) suggested the ways in which new structural techniques could promote new forms of great power. Concrete, since it is in semi-liquid form before being poured, has the ability to take shapes, such as smooth curves, that are difficult to achieve in other building materials such as wood and steel (**fig. 17.1**). Steel reinforcing rods, placed in formwork before concrete is poured, accept tensile stresses and generate the great strength of this material. In practice, the habits of using materials in straight columns and beams carried forward into the use of concrete in most buildings. The difficult engineering calculations and the complex formwork required for freer forms have tended to restrict the use of concrete. Maillart's bridges and his designs for warehouses and water storage facilities, where columns flow into overhead slabs in smooth curves, suggest interior forms that had rarely been seen outside of such utilitarian structures.

The early spread of modernism was blocked in parts of Europe by political factors. In the U.S.S.R. a repressive government was fearful of the implications of a freely developing vocabulary in the arts. In Germany and Austria, the rise of fascism brought all progressive thinking to a stop. Early Futurist and Rationalist work in Italy was pushed aside by burgeoning fascism that favored the "stripped classicism" of Hitler's Germany. In the countries of Europe that remained free, modernism also encountered much opposition. Governments and the established professions were firmly wedded to eclecticism and to the conviction that excellence could only be found in imitation of historic examples. Nevertheless, the ideas of modernism gradually established a hold.

Among the ideals of the modernist pioneers and their followers was the belief that design should serve the needs of all people. All users of designed buildings and objects were to be treated as equals. Although the clients who commissioned much modern work were generally wealthy and powerful, many projects, housing schemes, public buildings, and products such as furniture were

17.1 (*below*) Robert Maillart, Salginatobel Bridge, near Schiers, Switzerland, 1929–30.

A reinforced concrete bridge in an obscure alpine valley in Switzerland drew attention to the aesthetic possibilities that modern technological techniques offer. An engineer, Maillart was not concerned with visual effect when he designed this 300-foot long structure in terms of functional performance and economy.

17.2 (*opposite*) Mendelsohn and Chermayeff, de la Warr Pavilion, Bexhill-on-Sea, Sussex, England, 1935–6.

One of the first major buildings in England to demonstrate the ideas of modernism, this public pavilion in a seaside resort is a fine example of modern architecture at its best. The building houses an auditorium, exhibition space, restaurants, and indoor and outdoor lounge spaces. The architects drew inspiration from the Schocken Store in Stuttgart for the curving, cantilevered stair, which is seen against an ocean view through curving areas of glass.

planned to serve the needs of a broad spectrum of the general population. This respect for individual people, for their needs and desires, was at odds with the fascist view of individuals as helpless servants of an all-powerful state.

It is not surprising, therefore, that modernism developed most rapidly and fully in the parts of Europe where democracy and social idealism thrived during the difficult years between World Wars I and II. Holland, the Scandinavian countries, and England became the countries where modernism found most acceptance during the late 1920s and 1930s until World War II interrupted progress.

The Netherlands

Several architects carried forward the traditions of H. P. Berlage and other late nineteenth- and early twentieth-century architects and designers whose work avoided the narrow historicism of the eclectics. Willem M. Dudok (1884–1974), for example, who worked in the small city of Hilversum, near Amsterdam, designed the town hall there (1924–30), a distinguished and monumental structure in brick, its interiors pointing in both Deco and modernist directions (**fig. 17.3**). J. J. P. Oud, one of the architects included in the Museum of Modern Art exhibition, is best known for public housing projects that demonstrate the connections between modernism and enlightened social and political policies (see Chapter 15).

17.3 Willem Dudok, Town Hall, Hilversum, The Netherlands, 1924–30.

In the council chamber of this government building, Dudok has achieved a sense of formality and official dignity while working in the vocabulary of modernism. Warm colors and rich materials make the space seem comfortable while maintaining its authoritarian role.

Germany and Austria

Before its repression by the Nazis, modernism was developed not only by the major Bauhaus figures Gropius and Mies van der Rohe, but also by a number of other architects and designers whose work in interiors, furniture, and textiles had wide influence. Lilly Reich (1885–1947) worked closely with Mies van der Rohe and had a role in the interior design of a number of exhibitions, in the famous Barcelona Pavilion, and in the design of furniture credited to Mies. Marcel Breuer (1902–81) was active at the Bauhaus working on interiors, but is particularly known for his furniture designs. His early work in wood suggests De Stijl connections but, it is said, after a visit to a bicycle factory, he began experimenting with steel tubing as a structural material. The side chairs given the name Cesca (1928) and the arm chair called Wassily (1925) have become well known classics of the modern movement.

The exhibition housing group called the Weissenhof Siedlung, built in Stuttgart, Germany, in 1927, included examples of the design work of most of the leading figures of modernism, including Mies van der Rohe, Le Corbusier, J. J. P. Oud, Ludwig Hilberseimer, Josef Frank, Mart Stam, and Hans Scharoun. All of the houses were furnished according to the designs of the architects, and all were open to the public for the duration of the exhibition. Public awareness of the ideas of modernism was encouraged, with considerable impact on German design directions.

A comparable housing design exhibition called the Werkbundsiedlung was introduced in Vienna in 1930. There the designers included Josef Frank, Adolph Loos, Josef Hoffmann, André Lurçat, Richard Neutra, and Gerrit Rietveld, among others. The impact on the Austrian public was comparable to that of the Stuttgart exhibition in Germany. These exhibitions marked a peak achievement of the Werkbund (see p. 225). The influence of the Werkbund increased with modernist ideas, but it was dissolved in 1934.

Erich Mendelsohn (1887–1953) is known for a major early work, the Einstein Tower astronomical observatory (1921) at Potsdam. It is a unique example of EXPRESSIONISM in architecture, a direction that Mendelsohn abandoned as his work moved more toward the International Style. His work in Germany included several major department store projects before he left for England in 1933. He finally settled in the United States, where his work followed International Style directions.

Italy

The movement called Futurism developed in Italy before World War I. In various manifestos, Futurists advocated modernity, technology, speed, and the power of the machine. Although Futurists such as Antonio Sant'Elia (1888–1916) made architectural proposals, none was built. It remained for the Italian Rationalists of Gruppo 7 and others to take up the modernist cause between the end of World War I and the rise of the fascists in Italy. "Electrical house," a model house designed by I. Figini and G. Pollini for a 1930 exhibition at Monza, was the only Italian work included in the International Style exhibition in New York. At Como, a town administrative building was built in 1933–5 by G. Terragni, a handsome modernist building with an open-grid facade organizing its four-story interior which surrounds a central court (**figs. 17.4** and **17.5**). Its exterior elevation is of

17.4 Giuseppe Terragni, Casa del Popolo, Como, Italy, 1938.

Originally known as Casa del Fascio, this public building was intended to accommodate political meetings, but in spite of Fascist preferences for monumentality in design, Terragni managed to produce a fine work of modernism. The open, grid-like sides lead to a glass-topped atrium. It has survived under its new name as an expression of a democratic spirit.

17.5 Exterior of Casa del Popolo.

A work of the Rationalist movement, this building has a strict geometric program controlling the proportions which are the basis for its aesthetic qualities.

exactly half-square dimensions and the proportions of the grid are geometrically derived. A main meeting room with abstract wall treatments suggestive of De Stijl art has tubular metal chairs around a glass-topped table. This opens onto a large central court which is accessed from the street through a bank of glass doors that could be simultaneously opened by electrical controls. Under fascism, it was renamed the Casa del Fascio; more recently it has become the Casa del Popolo.

In 1938, the Milan firm known as BBPR (for its members, Banfi, Belgioioso, Perressutti, and Rogers) was responsible for the Institut Héliothérapeutique at Lugano. It was a kind of health camp for children where sun exposure was expected to offer therapeutic benefits. The building is largely devoted to a large double-height dining hall seating 800. South-facing glass areas and a red-tiled north wall are of typically International Style character.

Although Italian fascism was, in its early years, not overtly hostile to modernism, as the influence of Hitler in Germany became dominant, modern work faded. It did not resurface until after the war.

Switzerland

The orderly and homogeneous nature of Swiss society, and the strong development of engineering and technical skills in Switzerland, made that country hospitable to the rational and logical concepts of modernism. The engineering of Robert Maillart, the art of Paul Klee, and the egalitarian nature of Swiss society were all important for its development. St. Anthony's Church (1925) at Basel by Karl Moser (1880–1936) is a bare concrete structure, with a long coffered vault carried on columns placed close to the side walls. The tall windows are glazed in small panels of stained glass. It is probably the first Protestant church of successful modern design.

Also in Switzerland, two small apartment houses of 1935–6 at Doldertal near Zürich were designed by A. and E. Roth, together with Marcel Breuer who was in Switzerland for a time between his departure from the Bauhaus and his move to England. The buildings were commissioned by Sigfried Giedion, the well-known architectural historian and advocate of modernism. One of the flats belonged to Alfred Roth and included his architectural office. Large areas of glass, simple

smooth walls of white and light color tones, and a variety of examples of modern furniture, most by Breuer or Aalto, characterize the interiors. Breuer designed retail stores in Zürich and Basel in 1933 for the firm of Wohnbedarf, which had connections with the Werkbund. The best of modern furniture and other household items were on display there and available to the Swiss public. The firm played a significant role in bringing modernism into prominence in Swiss design.

Max Bill (1908–44) had been a student at the Bauhaus and, after his return to Switzerland, became something of a spokesman for modernism through his association with the Swiss Werkbund. He was also involved in publishing, including the multivolume series presenting the work of Le Corbusier. He was the designer of the Swiss exhibition area at the Milan Triennale in 1936 in which exhibit panels and cases were placed freely in an open space which formed a white surround for units in strong, bright colors.

Le Corbusier, although thought of as a French architect, was, in fact, Swiss. The small, lakeside house at Vevey that he designed for his parents in 1924 is a clearly realized International Style project. Although conceived as a "dwelling machine," the interior space is full of subtleties such as the darkness of the end spaces that form a contrast for the main interior space, a long band lighted by continuous glass, facing south and offering a view of Lake Geneva. Furniture comprised simple, traditional country tables, chairs, and beds. The relationship between the older furniture and the austere modernism of the space is strikingly happy. (The work of Le Corbusier is dealt with in more detail in Chapter 15.)

France

Although Le Corbusier produced most of his work in France, and has come to be France's most famous modernist, he always remained somewhat outside of the mainstream of French design—he was too radical to achieve wide acceptance. Another pioneer, Auguste Perret (1874–1954), was one of the first designers to understand the possibilities of reinforced concrete as a structural material that offered new aesthetic directions. His early work, such as the apartment building at 25 bis Rue Franklin in Paris, has close ties to the spirit of Art Nouveau, but his church of Notre Dame at Le

Raincy (1922–4) presents a dramatic interior of clearly modernist character (**fig. 17.6**). The concrete structure made it possible to use supporting columns of extreme thinness rather than solid walls or massive columns. As a result, the outside walls are entirely of stained glass—of modernist design but of strong and rich color. The resulting space suggests a modern version of the medieval Sainte Chapelle.

A somewhat less famous figure of French modernism is Robert Mallet-Stevens (1886–1945), whose early work seems close to the *moderne* direction of Art Deco (**fig. 17.7**). His 1924–33 house at Hyères for the Vicomte de Noailles had a number of interiors of forward-looking design. The Pink Salon used simple, geometric forms as a setting for rubber upholstered furniture and steel tube designs by both Mallet-Stevens and Breuer. The large Villa Cavrois (1931–2) at Croix has handsome interiors that stand at the border between Deco and International Style concepts. The kitchen and bathrooms are particularly forward-looking. His role in the design of settings for films of the 1920s made his work visible to a larger public, as did his Bally shop in Paris of 1928 and his designs for the Hygiene and Electricity Pavilions at the 1937 fair in Paris. Mallet-Stevens designed furniture for a number of projects—his simple 1928 side chair of metal is still in production and frequent use.

Pierre Chareau (1883–1950) is best known for his 1928–32 Maison de Verre (House of Glass) in Paris that made use of steel framing and large areas of glass block and plate glass (**fig. 17.8**). His furniture designs included both chairs of rich woods and heavy upholstery and simple folding seating with metal framing and wicker seats and backs, suggesting a move from Art Deco to the International Style.

17.6 Auguste Perret, Church of Notre Dame, Le Raincy, France, 1922–4.

In this building the slim columns and flat vaulted ceiling of concrete clearly express the qualities of the material, while an ambience suggestive of Gothic churches is generated by the walls that appear almost entirely of stained glass. The glass is mounted in screens of concrete, which enclose the interior on all sides.

17.7 (*left*) Robert Mallet-Stevens, House at 12 rue Mallet-Stevens, Paris, 1927.

For his own house, Robert Mallet-Stevens designed a living room that marked a transition from Art Deco design to Modernism.

17.8 (*below*) Pierre Chareau and Bernard Bijvoet, Dalsace House (Maison de Verre), Paris, 1928–32.

The early and dramatic use of metal and glass generated this dramatic and handsome interior shown. Chareau was the primary designer, but he worked with a Dutch architect, Bernard Bijvoet (1889–1979), on this project. The exposed steel frame and glass blocks predate Le Corbusier's use of the materials. Although Chareau's work was not extensive, this famous house remains an important work of modernism.

Scandinavia

The Scandinavian countries, with their generally democratic political orientation and openness to ideas of social equality, were strongly drawn to the ideas of modernism in design.

The work of Alvar Aalto in Finland has already been discussed (see pp. 285–9). His furniture using molded plywood as a primary material was manufactured by the firm of Artek in Finland and exported to the United States and other countries where it became some of the best known of all modern furniture designs. Aalto taught architecture at the Technical University outside of Helsinki, and supported many other Finnish architects, such as Erik Bryggman whose chapel at Turku (1939) presents a serene, mostly white space of great dignity.

Swedish modern design, at first in the cautious vocabulary discussed in Chapter 16, became more clearly identified with the International Style in the Stockholm Exhibition buildings of 1930 by Sven Markelius and his Halsingborg Concert Hall of 1925, where a handsome interior was developed in large part on the basis of acoustical considerations. Modernism became the accepted stylistic direction for Swedish public and commercial buildings of the 1930s and early 1940s, such as the Kingholmen Girls' School of 1941, Stockholm, by Paul Hedquist. Modest modern furniture, textiles, and accessories were widely available and had general public acceptance.

England

Modernism in England met with considerable resistance, both from a degree of conservatism in public taste and from more specific objections on the part of architectural professionals and governmental restrictions. Building laws were often interpreted to cover aesthetic choices that demanded adherence to existing traditions of design. Nevertheless, the arrival in England of architects and designers exiled from Germany and Austria in the 1930s brought an influx of modernist ideas. These resonated with the thinking of British designers, whose ideas were moving along the directions that had their origins in the Arts and Crafts movement and in the English versions of Art Nouveau.

Walter Gropius came to England in 1934 for a brief stay before moving on to the United Sates in 1937. While in England he formed a partnership with Maxwell Fry (1899–1987) with whom he designed a fine educational group for Impingten College in Cambridgeshire in 1936. It is a prototype for many later one- and two-story school buildings in the modern design vocabulary. The two men also designed a modern house in Old Church Street, London (1936), for Benn Levy. It is a fine example of International Style modernism in plan, exterior character, and interior design. Close by, on the same street, is a house by Erich Mendelsohn and Serge Chermayeff (1935). The two houses in an accessible city location made modernism visible to Londoners, as did Sun House (**fig. 17.9**; 1936) by Fry. Its large glass areas facing the street brought light flooding into simple interiors with typically modernist furniture and details. Chermayeff had been born in Russia but was educated in England; Mendelsohn had come to England in 1933 after being forced to leave Germany.

Mendelsohn and Chermayeff were responsible for one of the most successful of larger public buildings in England, the de la Warr Pavilion at Bexhill-on-Sea (1935–6). This is a seaside pavilion with restaurants, an auditorium, and extensive terraces and other public spaces for recreation and

17.9 Maxwell Fry, Sun House, Hampstead, London, 1936.

One of the first modern residential interiors in England, the Sun House makes use of the large glass areas typical of International Style architecture.

17.10 Marcel Breuer, plywood long chair, London, 1936.

After the closing of the Bauhaus in Germany, Breuer spent several years in Britain, where he was involved in designing a group of furniture intended for production by the firm Isokon. The material is molded plywood, using techniques made familiar by Alvar Aalto's designs for Artek.

17.11 Adams, Holden & Pearson, Underground Station, Gant's Hill, London, 1934.

Under the design directorship of Frank Pick (1878–1941), the London Underground system became a leader in introducing modernism to the British public through the design of train carriages, graphic elements, and stations. This interior—jokingly called "Moscow Hall"— is an example of the functional simplicity and fine aesthetic quality of much of the work produced in the 1930s.

lounging. The interiors with a fine winding stair and large open spaces exhibit International Style modernism at its best (**fig. 17.2**). The building has been well maintained and is in current use.

Breuer had come to England in 1935 and was the designer of an exhibition building in the form of a house at the Royal Show in Bristol (1936). It made

use of rough, exposed stone walls that offered an alternative to the smooth white more often thought of as characteristic of International Style modernism. The interior of the pavilion offered visitors a glimpse of what modern interiors could be. In this project, Breuer collaborated with an English architect, F. R. S. Yorke (1906–62). Yorke had been one of the first native British architects to undertake modern work, including several houses in strongly cubistic form. Gropius, Fry, and Breuer were among a number of modernist designers who worked on furniture using plywood and some metal parts intended for factory production under the name Isokon. The best known of Isokon products is a Breuer chaise with a frame of molded plywood (**fig. 17.10**). Breuer also designed some furniture using molded and flat panels of plywood for Heal's department store in London. Heal's included a room interior designed by Breuer in a 1936 exhibition showing the work of seven architects.

Many street-level entrance buildings for stations of the London Underground from 1934 onward were of modern design, usually with brick wall surfaces that seemed less aggressive in character than the white of most early modernism (**fig. 17.11**). The firm of Adams, Holden, and Pearson

17.12 Tecton (Berthold Lubetkin *et al.*), Highpoint, Highgate, London, 1936–8.

Berthold Lubetkin was the leader of a group of seven architects who practiced under the firm name of Tecton. In the apartment blocks known as Highpoint I and Highpoint II, they demonstrated the qualities of modern architecture that could serve residential as well as public roles. The entrance lobby illustrated here leads from the front entrance up a few steps to corridors seen at the right, which, in turn, lead to elevators. The airy and simple space continues to serve the building and its residents and to appear modern in spite of its early twentieth-century date.

were the architects for the London transit system, which brought modernism into the everyday life of Londoners.

Wells Coates, mentioned earlier (p. 296) for his role in industrial design, was also an architect who helped to bring the International Style to England. His Lawn Road Flats in Hampstead, London (1934), and the Embassy Court Flats at Brighton (1935) were among the first large buildings in England of International Style character. Similarly, his tiny Sunspan Bungalow at Welwyn (1935) offered the same qualities in a small, family house. Coates was also a designer of interiors and furniture. For the Lawn Road flats he detailed a typical, tiny apartment with built-in fittings that made conventional furniture largely unnecessary. Coates designed some ingenious furniture for his own home, including a desk on rollers that could be inserted into a bank of cabinets so as to merge into the total grouping.

Berthold Lubetkin (1901–90) was born and trained in Russia, studied in Paris, and came to England in 1930 where he founded the firm Tecton. Tecton designed the multistory apartment house at Highgate, London, called Highpoint, in 1936–8, one of the first striking successes of the modern movement in England. Its plan provides for eight large and luxurious flats on each of its seven floors, each disposed so as to provide cross-ventilation and open views without overlooking the windows of neighboring flats. The entrance foyers, fine examples of simple modern interior design, are still in good condition and in regular use (**fig. 17.12**). Tecton also produced a number of buildings at the London Zoo in Regent's Park, including the famous Penguin Pool (1933), a classic demonstration of the possibilities for reinforced concrete to create abstract forms in space.

The development of modernism in England and in continental Europe was brought to a temporary halt by World War II in 1939. In the United States, in spite of the early pioneer work of Louis Sullivan and Frank Lloyd Wright, development of modernism was relatively slow. However, many European designers moved to America to escape the upheavals in Europe and to explore the possibilities of the New World. The following chapter traces the progress of modernism in the United States.

Modernism in America

In the United States, the most successful architects and designers maintained the dominant role of eclectic historicism based on the concepts of the Paris Ecole des Beaux-Arts. The work of Sullivan and Wright at the turn of the century was generally ignored or regarded as a curious footnote to American design history, while the work of European modernists was rarely published and therefore little known.

Architects and Designers

Gill

The work of the Californian architect Irving Gill (1870–1936), although it attracted little contemporary attention, includes a number of buildings that seem to presage later modern developments, while his design shows some influence from the Spanish California missions. His interiors had simple, unornamented white walls and, sometimes, arched openings. Smooth wooden walls without moldings and grilles of wood generated spaces with modern sensibilities. Gill's best-known works are the Dodge house in Los Angeles (**fig. 18.1**; 1915–16) and the Scripps house at La Jolla (1917).

18.1 (*below*) Irving Gill, Dodge House, Los Angeles, 1915-16.

Before wide acceptance in the United States, modern ideas of simplicity were the basis for the interiors of houses designed by this American architect.

18.2 (*opposite*) Philip Johnson, Glass House, New Canaan, Connecticut, 1949.

While he was working in close association with Mies van der Rohe, Johnson planned his own glass house in a way that relates to Mies's Farnsworth house (see p. 277). The house is a simple rectangle, with all four walls of floor-to-ceiling glass. The red tiles of the floor and the outward view into surrounding greenery establish color. The furniture, all of Mies van der Rohe's design, uses brown leather on chrome frameworks.

Wright: 1920s and 1930s

In 1932, when Henry-Russell Hitchcock and Philip Johnson organized the exhibition The International Style for the Museum of Modern Art in New York, they included only seven American projects. Of those seven, one is a single room interior by Mies van der Rohe, three are small projects, in retrospect hardly memorable, leaving only three examples of genuine significance. These constituted a fairly complete survey of modern work in America at the time, with the exception of the work of Frank Lloyd Wright—excluded from the exhibition, one must assume, because his early work had already passed into history or because it did not fit the concept of modernism that the term International Style implies. Between his return to America from Japan in 1922 and the mid-1930s, Wright produced comparatively few buildings. Hollyhock House, Los Angeles, was designed and constructed for Aline Barnsdall during Wright's Japanese years, and was completed in 1921. It is a large, almost monumental structure in poured concrete with bands of cast geometric ornament. Externally, it suggests Mayan architecture, while internally, its large rooms have surprisingly limited openings onto the elaborate surrounding terraces and gardens (**fig. 18.3**). Several of Wright's subsequent house designs used concrete block in a similarly creative way in place of poured concrete. Each block was cast with a decorative patterned face, giving the wall surfaces an overall repeat pattern that Wright called TEXTILE BLOCK because of its recall of the repeat patterns of printed fabrics.

La Miniatura, the Millard house in Pasadena (1923), is probably the most successful of Wright's houses of this period. It is a hillside building with kitchen and dining space on a lower, garden level with a large, double-height living room above overlooked by a balcony. There is a bedroom and bath on each level. The patterned block appears in the interior walls, and blocks with perforations in some exterior walls, generating internal patterns of light and dark. Several other textile block California houses hint at Mayan architecture, although it may be a fortuitous by-product of the use of patterned block rather than a deliberate reference.

As Wright's work gradually became known, young people interested in studying architecture often approached him for advice. He always advised them against studying at the established architectural schools and, instead, began to invite

18.3 Frank Lloyd Wright, Aline Barnsdall House (Hollyhock House), Los Angeles, 1916–21.

Decorative patterns on the ceiling reflect the structural support members. A skylight with ornamental detail lights the area in front of the massive fireplace and chimney, which form a spatial anchor for this large room. Indirect light comes from the coves at the lower edge of the ceiling. Some of the furniture can be recognized as being of Wright's design.

18.4 Frank Lloyd Wright, Taliesen, Spring Green, Wisconsin, from 1925.

The complex of buildings that forms Wright's estate includes many dramatic interior spaces. This living room with sloping ceiling planes and massive stonework for walls and fireplace is shown here with many small objects from Wright's collections. Much Wright furniture and a rug and hanging were designed late in his career. The name, Taliesin (meaning "Shining Brow"), was that of a mythical Welsh poet.

those interested to work as apprentices with him at his home at Taliesin, near Appleton, Wisconsin (**fig. 18.4**). This arrangement became known as the Taliesin Fellowship. It was, in effect, Wright's office and continued to grow and prosper during his lifetime. It still exists under the direction of former apprentices.

The full impact of Wright's approach to modernism did not become widely known until, in 1938, the *Architectural Forum*, an American periodical, devoted an entire issue to previously unpublished Wright buildings. The large complex of living and work structures at Taliesin first appears here. Many photographs show the richness of interior spaces, where rough stone walls contrast with smooth plaster, elements in natural wood, and varied window areas—often in continuous bands or in high clerestories. Wright's own furniture designs are everywhere, but decorative detail is minimal. Plants, material textures, and objects collected in Japan generate a sense of warmth and richness that is a characteristic of Wright's interiors.

In the same issue, the first published pictures of Fallingwater, the most famous of Wright's houses, first appeared. This house, built in 1936 for the Kaufmann family on a wooded site at Bear Run, Pennsylvania, near Pittsburgh, its balconies of concrete projecting out over a stream and waterfall, is one of the most romantic examples of modern architectural form anywhere (**figs. 18.5** and **18.6**).

18.5 Frank Lloyd Wright, Fallingwater, Bear Run, Pennsylvania, 1936.

One of Wright's best known commissions, Fallingwater was undertaken at the request of Edgar Kaufmann Jr. for his father. It was built over a waterfall and has cantilevered concrete balconies and roof planes that project from the vertical elements of rough stonework. The relation of the house to its natural setting is remarkably effective.

18.6 Interior of Fallingwater.

The great open living space of Fallingwater uses large areas of glass to look out into the countryside beyond and includes floors and fireplace of local stone. The ceiling patterns relate to hidden electric light elements. The built-in seating benches and moveable stools are of Wright's own design.

18.7 Frank Lloyd Wright, Johnson Wax Building, Racine, Wisconsin, 1936–9.

The "great room" of the administration building, which was constructed at the S. C. Johnson Wax Factory, is dominated by concrete structural columns, which spread out to form disk elements of the roof. Between the concrete circles, glass tubing skylights provide daylight.

18.8 (*below*) Private office, Johnson Wax Building.

The distinctive furniture designed by Wright for the S. C. Johnson Wax Building used circular and semicircular elements to relate to the structural design of the building. Desk drawers swing out on pivots and desk tops end in semi-circles. Many desks also have an upper shelf along the rear edge to provide extra storage space.

The unornamented cantilevers and the bands of windows with thin metal frames suggest an awareness of the International Style modernism of Europe, although Wright would never acknowledge such influences. The much photographed and published interiors (which can now also be visited), in which natural stone, built-in furniture in natural wood, and a miscellany of other furniture and possessions combine in relation to views of the surrounding outdoors, have great charm. The spaces are at once open to views of the surrounding woods and closed in circulation and private uses.

The same magazine also carried drawings and construction photographs of the S. C. Johnson Company office building, then still being built in Racine, Wisconsin. On its completion in 1939 it became one of the best known of Wright's non-residential projects. Most of the building is devoted to a single large "great room" general office space. The structure is a cluster of "mushroom" concrete columns which are not, in fact, mushroom-shaped, but are formed with slim tapered shafts that spread out into large disks at their tops (**fig. 18.7**). The spaces between the disk tops are filled with glass tubing made into skylights that flood the space with daylight. Perimeter walls of red-brown brick are windowless, but glass forms a band between wall tops and the edges of the column tops. There is a balcony mezzanine surrounding the main space, and some private offices and related spaces in a penthouse on the roof. Wright designed unique furniture for this building, making use of circular motifs, for chair seats and backs, for the ends of desk tops and shelves, and even for desk drawers which do not pull out but swing on pivots (**fig. 18.8**). These are among the most successful of Wright's furniture designs.

The Winkler-Goetsch house of 1939 at Okemos, Michigan, is an example of Wright's work in modest residential projects. Its clerestory-lit, simple interior spaces with surfaces of natural wood and brick, and the concrete floor that holds the pipes that circulate warm water for radiant heating, are typical of what Wright called USONIAN house design. The term was coined by Wright to incorporate the letters U.S., to suggest his conviction that his style was unique to the United States of America.

A modest desert camp near Phoenix, Arizona, gradually grew into the complex called Taliesin West where Wright and the apprentices worked together during the winter months. Its interiors with rough stone and wood used in a romantic interplay are among the most interesting of Wright's works. For the rest of his life he was able to produce an increasing flow of work of striking originality. In spite of his success and fame, however, Wright remained something of an outsider to the architectural and design professions. As long as eclecticism remained dominant, the architectural establishment ignored his work or viewed it with horror. As modernism became more accepted, it was the European International Style that was more widely admired than Wright's more organic work, with its emphasis on natural materials and a highly personal idiom. Wright's freely expressed contempt for virtually all work but his own did nothing to draw other practitioners' sympathy or understanding.

Some of Wright's apprentices went on to produce distinguished work of their own. Harwell Hamilton Harris (1903–1990) established his own office in Los Angeles in 1934. His own tiny house at Fellowship Park, Los Angeles (1935), brought him wide recognition. It was a single, simple space with windows on three sides, a floor of rush squares, plus a few bits of simple furniture. The glass areas that made up the walls can be removed to transform the house into an open pavilion. Kitchen and bath occupy an enclosed area at one end of the main living space. As in much of Wright's work, there are strong connections with traditional Japanese house design.

Schindler and Neutra

Several other American pioneer modernists had at least a tenuous relationship with Wright early in their careers. Rudolph Schindler (1887–1953) had a stormy relationship with Wright that began with collaboration but ended in bitter conflict. Schindler conducted his own practice in California (**fig. 18.9**) designing a beach house (1926) for the Lovell family in Newport Beach, California, in a geometric modern vocabulary suggestive of De Stijl. Richard Neutra (1892–1970) was born in Vienna and studied there with such early modernists as Loos and Otto Wagner. He came to the United States in 1921 where he met Louis Sullivan and worked for a short time with Frank Lloyd Wright. In 1926 he moved to Los Angeles to establish his own practice. The Lovells (who had been Schindler's clients earlier) commissioned a large house in 1927 in Los Angeles (included in the Hitchcock-Johnson exhibition). It is the first clear example of the International Style in the United States (**fig. 18.10**). The client was a doctor much associated with advocacy of health practices involving sun and exercise. The house became known as the Health House, with pool, gym, outdoor sleeping porches, and huge glass areas admitting sunlight throughout the interior. With white, unornamented walls outside and in, with grey carpeting in all living areas, and simple, largely built-in furniture, the house represented a dramatic introduction of the new, modernist style in America.

Neutra's own house of 1932 and a series of houses for private clients in the Los Angeles area established the character of a large body of his work. A particularly spectacular project was a house in the California desert for the film director Joseph von Sternberg (1935, demolished 1971). Walls surrounding a pool and driveway extended the basic box form of the house outward in long horizontals. The walls were of steel and painted

18.9 (*right*) Rudolph Schindler, Schindler House, North Kings Road, Los Angeles, 1921–2.

Sliding walls open out this house to its surround, and clerestory windows admit light above a continuous shelf. The fireplace and chimney are of unornamented simplicity. The chairs are of Schindler's design.

18.10 (*below*) Richard Josef Neutra, Lovell House, Los Angeles, 1927–9.

The large glass areas and undecorated white wall surfaces are evidence of Neutra's commitment to the International Style. This steel-framed house was largely made of components chosen from catalogs.

aluminum. The interior spaces, with unornamented stretches of white and large glass areas, were exceptionally fine examples of how modern interior space was organized. Neutra designed a large number of houses, apartment buildings, and schools in which he remained a consistent advocate of a severe, geometric modernism.

Lescaze

The importation of European ideas of modernism was furthered with the arrival of William Lescaze (1896–1969) in America in 1920. He had been a pupil of the Swiss architect Karl Moser in his native Geneva, and he opened a practice in New York in 1923. In partnership with George Howe (1886–1955) he was the leading designer of the building for the Philadelphia Saving Fund Society (**fig. 18.11**; 1929–32). Howe had been a successful designer of houses and small bank buildings but was persuaded of the logic of modernism by Lescaze. The resulting building is the first truly modern tall building anywhere and the first large, readily visible work of the International Style in America. Its great size, sternly geometric mass, and black stone-surfaced base with a huge corner area of glass shocked the conservative Philadelphia public, previously unaware of the nature of modern architecture. The building was, however,

highly successful. With no suitable modern furniture available in the United States, Lescaze was forced to design special furniture for the project in the general idiom of Bauhaus design, using metal tube frames supporting the seats and backs of chairs, and tops and drawers of tables. After the partnership with Howe was dissolved, Lescaze worked on residential projects, radio studios (for CBS) and a variety of other projects, always clearly International Style in design.

Goodwin and Stone

New York's Museum of Modern Art opened in 1931 and immediately became a strong influence in promoting interest in the modernism that was by then well established in Europe. The museum's own building on 53rd Street in New York, a fine example of modernism, was designed by Philip L. Godwin (1885–1958) and Edward Durrell Stone (1902–78) in 1939. Its interior spaces, lobbies, stair, auditorium, and members' rooftop lounge (**fig. 18.12**), all designed by the architects, made modernism visible to a New York public in an institution with an avowed educational purpose. For a number of years it was the best, indeed almost the only, example of International Style architecture and interior design of a high level of excellence in New York City.

In 1940 Edward Durrell Stone designed a house for Conger Goodyear at Old Westbury, Long Island, New York, a flat-roofed essay in International Style modernism. Floor to ceiling glass and plain white walls form a gallery space for a major collection of modern art works.

Gropius and Breuer

The direct influence of International Style modernism increased hugely when several of the European leaders of the movement arrived in the United States. Walter Gropius and Marcel Breuer were invited to Harvard University in Cambridge, Massachusetts, in 1937. Gropius became the head of the Graduate School of Design. Architectural training abandoned its tradition-oriented content in favor of a fully modern program. In 1938, Mies van der Rohe became Director of Architecture at Armour Institute (now Illinois Institute of Technology). As faculty and graduating students from the programs at these institutions began to teach and practice in America, a vast change in professional attitudes took place. Modernism, and particularly the modernism of the International Style, began to replace the tradition-oriented and modernistic directions of the 1920s and 1930s.

Walter Gropius was the architect of his own house at Lincoln, Massachusetts (**fig. 18.13**; 1937).

18.11 (*above left*) William Lescaze and George Howe, Philadelphia Saving Fund Society (PSFS) Building, Philadelphia, 1929–32.

The large, main banking room is flooded with light from large glass areas. Concealed indirect light comes from lowered ceiling area panels. The columns are faced with polished black marble, and the floor is dark grey.

18.12 (*above right*) Philip Goodwin and Edward Stone, Museum of Modern Art, New York, 1939.

The members lounge occupied a penthouse of the newly constructed building of the Museum of Modern Art. Floor-to-ceiling glass opened to an outdoor terrace. Modern chairs, including examples by Breuer, Mathsson, and Russel Wright were used.

A fine example of International Style design, it has a typical flat roof, large glass areas, and such details as an entrance shelter supported by tubular columns, an external spiral stair, and generous use of glass block. The white walls are, surprisingly, not of concrete or stucco but of the tongue-and-groove wood boards typical of vernacular New England building. The interiors are of elegant simplicity and display many pieces of furniture by various members of the modern movement (**fig. 18.14**). The house is now landmarked and open to visitors.

By 1949 Gropius had organized a firm which he named the Architects' Collaborative. It was responsible for the extensive group of residential buildings grouped around courtyards known as the Harvard Graduate Center, the first modern building on the Harvard campus at Cambridge, Massachusetts. The simple forms, exterior and interior, gradually became the vocabulary of most institutional building in the United States. Interiors included distinguished art work by Joan Miró, Josef Albers, and Herbert Bayer.

Mies van der Rohe

Mies van der Rohe planned a new campus for the Illinois Institute of Technology where his first American project was the Metallurgical Research Building (1943). Its austere patterns of exposed steel structure with filled-in areas of brick and glass established the vocabulary of his hugely influential late work. As the campus developed, it included a number of Mies's buildings that demonstrated the possibilities of minimalist simplicity.

The concept of the glass skyscrapers that Mies had developed before leaving Germany finally found realization in the twin-tower apartment buildings in Chicago overlooking Lake Michigan. The Lake Shore Drive apartments (1948–51) were simple rectangular blocks, with all four faces of black-painted steel and glass. A central core of stairs and elevators served the eight apartments on each floor. The apartment interiors were, of course, each decorated as the occupant might choose but the outside walls of floor-to-ceiling glass still dominated the interior space, and the ground-level

18.13 Walter Gropius, Gropius House, Lincoln, Massachusetts, 1937.

In 1937 Gropius took up a teaching post in the Graduate School of Design at Harvard, and his own house is a fine example of International Style design, the first to be built in New England, although it is constructed in wood in traditional American fashion. An outdoor spiral stair connects the second-floor terrace with the ground floor.

18.14 Interior of Gropius House.

The study in the architect's own house has windows above the built-in deskwork surface. A door gives access to the outside of the house, while a wall of glass block isolates this small room from the main living and dining areas.

entrance areas show Miesian interior design at its simple best. (Mies's work in America is discussed more fully in Chapter 15.)

Johnson

Philip Johnson (born 1906) left his post as chairman of the department of architecture at the Museum of Modern Art in order to study architecture as a student at Harvard under Gropius. His 1942 house in Cambridge, Massachusetts (said to have been designed and built as his graduate thesis), demonstrates his developing devotion to the ideas of Mies. It is a simple walled rectangle of which about two-thirds are a garden open to the sky, and the remaining third an enclosure open to the garden, with a floor-to-ceiling glass wall. The furniture, of Mies's European design, gives the house a striking International Style character.

In 1949, aware of Mies's Farnsworth house, Johnson designed his own house at New Canaan, Connecticut, as an all glass-walled box with only a small cylindrical brick enclosure to house a bathroom and to provide a location for a fireplace (**fig. 18.2**). The kitchen was a counter with lift tops giving access to equipment. The furniture was all of Mies's design, while major works of art introduced a variety of less rigorous forms into the space. This

"glass house" has become a famous example of the possibilities of an open plan carried to its logical, extreme conclusion.

Johnson and Mies van der Rohe were collaborators on the New York skyscraper Seagram Building of 1954–8, a simple rectangular tower rising from a broad plaza. The exterior walls are of bronze-tinted glass held in by vertical bands of bronze. The interiors of lobby and circulation space are lined with travertine in totally simple forms. The ground-floor restaurant (called the Four Seasons) was designed by Johnson in collaboration with the decorator William Pahlmann. It is a majestic space using Mies's Brno chairs and glass walls curtained with brass- and copper-colored aluminum chains hanging in curved swags. A Richard Lippold sculpture is hung over the bar. The entrance area contains a curtain painted by Picasso.

Skidmore, Owings, and Merrill

Large architectural firms with a number of partners and a large staff (often more than a hundred) began to emerge to take on major design projects generated by large corporate, institutional, and governmental requirements. The firm of Skidmore, Owings, and Merrill (now known as SOM), founded in 1936, was responsible for both the

18.15 Skidmore, Owings & Merrill, Terrace Plaza Hotel, Cincinnati, Ohio, 1945.

SOM became known especially for its work on buildings in landscaped settings. This hotel's small dining room is on one of the upper floors, and there is a large glass area offering an attractive view. The built-in banquette seating and chairs are covered in light brown leather. The mural by the Spanish painter Joan Miró (1893-1983) on the curving inner wall enlivens the space.

architecture and the interior design of the Terrace Plaza Hotel in Cincinatti, Ohio (**fig. 18.15**; 1945). Interiors included art works by Joan Miró, Saul Steinberg, and Alexander Calder. Benjamin Baldwin, Davis Allen, Marianne Strengell, and Ward Bennett (born 1917) participated in various aspects of its interior design. The firm came to favor the minimalist direction of Mies van der Rohe, particularly in projects developed by Gordon Bunschaft (1909–1990), the partner in charge of design, such as the New York skyscraper Lever House (1952), the first truly modern tall building to be built in New York City.

Eero Saarinen

Eliel Saarinen's son Eero (1910–61) entered into partnership with his father at Cranbrook, Michigan, to design the Kleinhans Music Hall in Buffalo, New York (1938). The first twentieth-century American concert hall to achieve acoustic excellence, it has simple, dignified interiors in which unornamented wood surfaces generate a sense of warmth. Their First Christian Church (also known as the Tabernacle Church) at Columbus, Indiana (1942), presents a comparably simple and impressive interior with white walls and brickwork generating a serene sense of space (**fig. 18.16**). The Saarinens, in partnership with the firm of Perkins and Will, were the lead designers for the Crow Island School (1939), an impressive demonstration of the possibilities of modernism for the typical American public school. In partnership with J. Robert F. Swanson, the Saarinens won a competition in 1939 for a Smithsonian Gallery of Art to be built in Washinton, D.C., a superbly organized, asymmetrical composition that would have been the first important work of modernism in that city. Unfortunately, it was never built. The intended site on the mall was ultimately given over to the National Gallery in an eclectic, backward-looking style, the work of John Russell Pope (1874–1937), completed in 1941 after his death.

Interior Decoration: the Reaction to Modernism

American schools of design taught historic imitation in programs modeled on the Beaux-Arts system, often requiring students to execute problems in a particular historic style. Interior decoration was taught in many schools as a branch of home economics, with the idea that students would use their knowledge in the decoration of their own homes. Among professional decorators, Syrie Maugham worked on residential projects in the United States as well as in England. American designers working in an eclectic vocabulary included Ruby Ross Wood, Rose Cumming, Nancy McClelland, and the firm of McMillen, Inc. Smyth Urquhart & Marckwald were responsible for ship interiors, including those of the *America*. Frances Elkins worked in California, while Dorothy Draper, best known of American decorators, worked on both residential, hotel, restaurant, and office interiors in her overscaled ornamental style (**fig. 18.17**). Mrs. Henry ("Sister") Parish II (1910–94) was known for her easy-going English country-house style.

18.16 Eliel and Eero Saarinen, First Christian (Tabernacle) Church, Columbus, Indiana, 1942.

This may be regarded as the first U.S. church of modern architectural design. The extreme simplicity of the finely proportioned space, with its tall windows, its dignified cross on the end wall, and its use of white and natural wood tones as the only color, generate a space promoting calm meditation.

18.17 Dorothy Draper, Pompeiian Court Restaurant, Metropolitan Museum of Art, New York, 1948.

The interior decorator was retained to make over an older space, originally used for museum exhibits, so that it could be used as a restaurant. The lively color scheme chosen for the floor and walls was augmented by the very large and ornamental hanging lights. The Doric columns are part of the pre-existing architecture.

store in New York became well known, and Billy Baldwin (1903–84), whose fashionable interiors were favorites of many wealthy clients.

Furniture and Other Interior Furnishings

Modern interior design in America in the 1930s and 1940s was hampered by the lack of available modern furniture. Office furniture of steel construction from such firms as Globe-Wernecke and General Fireproofing (now G.F.) was, even if somewhat pedestrian in design, available for office and institutional use, but furniture for residential and commercial interiors hardly existed. The designs of Gilbert Rohde manufactured by Herman Miller were one exception, but they displayed a strongly Art Deco character not quite in line with the simplicity sought by International Style designers. The Finnish firm of Artek found outlets for the imported designs of Alvar Aalto and Thonet, and manufactured some products suitable for modern interiors. However, designers were often compelled to design furniture to be custom made for their interiors, or to settle for whatever nondescript designs they could find in production.

Knoll

A step forward occurred when, in 1937, Hans Knoll (1914–55) came to New York from his native Germany to begin production of modern furniture. Knoll was not himself a designer, but he had learned in Germany an appreciation of the kind of furniture that modern interiors called for. He made an alliance with Jens Risom (born 1915), a Danish designer who had arrived in New York in 1938. Risom designed for Knoll a number of simple chairs and tables that could be made in readily available wood with chair seats and backs of stretched webbing. As wartime restrictions tightened in the late 1940s, most furniture manufacturers were diverted into military production. Knoll's furniture could, however, be manufactured in small shops using available basic materials; the webbing was said to be available as reject material from the making of parachutes. The simple designs also turned out to be highly suitable to wartime needs for the interiors of military facilities, officers' lounges, servicemen's clubs, and similar installa-

Several other decorators, however, moved away from historic imitation. They attempted to develop styles that were more related to the modern world, while avoiding the functionalist aspects of International Style modernism. T. H. Robsjohn-Gibbings (1909–73), who had been born and trained in England but who worked in America, designed furniture in a stripped classical vocabulary that suited his rather simple but elegant interiors. He became particularly interested in the furniture of ancient Greece and developed a modern Klismos chair that was for a time offered as a factory-made product from the Widdicomb Furniture Company in Grand Rapids, Michigan.

Edward Wormley (1907–95) became known for his tastefully simple furniture produced by the Dunbar Furniture Company in Berne, Indiana. His showrooms for Dunbar placed the furniture in suitably reserved settings. Other versatile decorators working in a variety of styles included William Pahlmann (1906–87), whose floridly elaborate model rooms for the Lord and Taylor department

18.18 and **18.19**
Florence Knoll, furniture, 1940s and 1950s.

Knoll Associates was founded in New York in 1946 by the German-born Hans Knoll and his wife, formerly Florence Schust. As design director, Florence Knoll was a key force in maintaining the company's determination to produce furniture of the highest design quality. The company made available the classic designs by the early modern pioneers, including Breuer and Mies van der Rohe, but, when a need surfaced, Florence Knoll undertook new designs in the modern idiom.

tions. As a result, Knoll secured a foothold in the production of modern furniture (**figs. 18.18** and **18.19**). The 650 chair of 1941–2 remains in production and is as suitable to modern interiors as it was when first introduced. As the only supplier of modern furniture suitable for use in the interiors that architects and designers were producing in the 1940s, the Knoll firm established a long and fruitful relationship with the design professions.

In 1943, Florence Schust (born 1917) joined the Knoll firm to deal with interior design projects that were often referred to Knoll by architects. She had spent some of her youth with the Saarinens at Cranbrook, and she was able to use her Cranbrook contacts to bring into the Knoll orbit the classic designs of Marcel Breuer and Mies van der Rohe. She also persuaded other leaders of the developing American modern movement to assign designs to Knoll. Eero Saarinen was the designer of a series of objects, including the lounge chair of 1948 (now often called the "womb" chair) and the pedestal-based chairs and tables of 1955–6. Harry Bertoia (1915–78), a sculptor who was another Cranbrook contact, was the designer of the wire chairs that joined the Knoll line of classic designs in 1952. Florence Schust (now Hans Knoll's wife) herself undertook the development of a number of straightforward modern designs for upholstered seating and office furniture.

The Planning Unit at Knoll, originally a modest service that offered help in the selection and placement of furniture, gradually grew into a complete interior design service. Under Florence Knoll's direction, it became a favored source of interior design for architects of modern works who were unable or unwilling to undertake the interior design for their own projects. A textile division was added in 1949, with Eszter Harastzy (1910s–95) as director. The Knoll Planning Unit produced some of the best interiors of the period, including distinguished interior design for the office building of the Connecticut General Life Insurance Company at Bloomfield, Connecticut (1954–7), an architectural project of Skidmore, Owings, and Merrill. Florence Knoll's awareness of the aesthetic of Mies van der Rohe is evident, along with a sense for strong color.

Herman Miller Furniture Company

The Herman Miller Furniture Company had curtailed production during World War II to devote its facilities to war-related products. After the war, without their designer Gilbert Rohde, who had died in 1944, the firm turned to George Nelson (1908–86), an architect who had written and edited several magazines dealing with design. Nelson was asked to develop a complete line of modern furniture to be introduced in 1946. Working with several associates, Nelson produced a full range of modular cabinet units with related seating and beds. He also advised the inclusion in the product line of a few designs by the sculptor Isamu Noguchi, the Hollywood decorator Paul Laszlo and, most significantly, seating and storage units by Charles Eames.

Eames (1907–78), who was also an architect, had been at Cranbrook from 1937 and had established a friendship with Eero Saarinen. Together, Eames and Saarinen took two first prizes in a 1940 Museum of Modern Art competition entitled Organic Design in Home Furnishing (**fig. 18.20**). The chairs, intended to be of molded plywood, turned out to be too difficult to produce, but Eames persisted in working on molded plywood seating during the war years until they were introduced by Herman Miller. They were the first of a long series of Eames furniture designs.

The design program of the Herman Miller Company was further enhanced when Alexander Girard (1907–93) became head of a textile division in 1952. Girard was trained in Europe but came to New York in 1932 and relocated to Detroit in 1937 where he was active as an architect and interior designer. His own house at Grosse Pointe, Michigan, was a showcase of lively and colorful interiors filled with objects from his vast collection of folk art. His Herman Miller textiles used abstract form in a range of cheerful colors. He was also responsible for the interior design of a large house designed by Eero Saarinen for Irwin Miller in Columbus, Indiana (1952). Girard moved to Santa Fe, New Mexico, in 1953. Here he acquired and reconstructed a traditional adobe house, making it a virtual museum of folk art collected in Arizona, Mexico, South America, and India. Girard's color

CONVERSATION

18.20 Charles Eames and Eero Saarinen, competition drawings, 1940. The Museum of Modern Art, New York.

A prize-winning design submitted in the Museum of Modern Art's Organic Design in Home Furnishings competition. Although production problems prevented the design from being manufactured, the concept led to later chair designs developed by each of the designers separately.

sense was in part a product of his study of and love for the bright and daring color typical of the objects he collected.

By 1950, modernism was firmly in place as the established norm of all major American designers. The wider public, however, looked in a different direction, translating modernist ideas into the language of commercial production. Suburban houses of questionable merit, interiors filled with gross versions of "modernistic" furniture, kitchens with appliances in pastel colors, and, above all, gigantic automobiles sporting meaningless tailfins became the design icons of the post-World War II world. Interior design, in the work of thoughtful professionals, moved forward in contrast to this unfortunate dominant direction.

The Ascendency of Modernism

19

If World War II had limited design activity in America, it had brought design to a virtual stop in Europe. After the war, design began to come alive again in Europe. As countries recovered from the war and its economic impact, there was a gradual return to prosperity. In the United States, economic health rapidly encouraged new building to make up for the suspensions of the war years. Expanding businesses required new offices and other facilities. The expansion of programs in colleges, hospitals, and other institutions created an extensive need for interior design work. Design firms grew and prospered in Europe and in America.

Modernism with a basis in the International Style became the norm of professional design work. There was a new willingness to move beyond the vocabulary of flat roofs, white walls, and maximal glass. The glass-walled skyscraper became a symbol of success for businesses and municipalities, so that central city districts were clogged with such tall buildings. This tendency was most marked in the United States, but even such traditionally conservative cities as London and Paris became studded with new tall buildings.

Buildings and interiors produced without benefit of professional design tended to remain attached to "traditional" stylistic directions, however poorly understood and reproduced. Housing developments, usually the work of speculative builders, occupied increasing areas of land in suburban districts fed by extensive highway networks. "Suburban sprawl"—the clutter of unplanned commercial development surrounding cities and their related suburbs—became endemic, with buildings of indifferent design. It is not surprising that the interiors were also rarely of outstanding design quality. Residential interiors were normally assembled by the householders that were to occupy them. Design resulted from the nature of the home furnishing products offered at retail, which were rarely of great technical or aesthetic quality. It is in the work of professional designers as they served business, institutions, and government agencies that the better design of these years is to be found.

Many technical developments led to changes in the nature of interior spaces. Synthetic materials, such as plastics, became available as replacements for older, natural materials. Textiles and carpets using synthetic fibers (often in combination with some natural fibers) came into general use. Vinyl became the most used material for floor tiles (replacing asphalt-asbestos). Melamine plastic came into wide use as an impervious material for furniture and counter-top surfaces. Glass fiber reinforced plastic became a highly useful material for chairs made in body-fitting curvilinear forms. Plastics were the binders for various forms of paneling made of wood chips, which could be used for wall surfacing and furniture construction. Plaster as a material for walls and ceilings gave way to factory-produced boards known as "sheet-rock" or "dry-wall." Ceilings, particularly in offices and institutional buildings, were hung from above by a system of metal strips that held panels of acoustic sound-absorbing material. Lighting and air circulation grilles could be integrated into ceiling design.

The traditional dependence on windows as a source of light and fresh air began to be displaced by mechanical air conditioning systems that delivered air, at the desired temperature and humidity, into buildings that could have fixed windows or no windows at all. Inexpensive fluorescent lighting became the norm for commercial and institutional spaces in spite of its often undesirable aesthetic qualities. Residential design was influenced by these developments in ways that were often unobtrusive. Plastics could be made to simulate traditional materials in carpets, textiles, and furniture. Air conditioning could be concealed with only small inlet and return grilles visible. Fluorescent lighting came into acceptance in business interiors, kitchens, and bathrooms but remained less used in living spaces.

Design became more truly international than ever before. There was an increasing flow of information through magazines and books, while the coming of regular intercontinental air transportation made movement easier both for designers and an interested public. European modern design became increasingly familiar to and popular with the more affluent population in the United States, while developments in materials and technology spread from their points of origin (often in the United States) worldwide.

Italy

Italy became a leading center for exciting post-war design and exported furniture and other products to other countries hungry for new and imaginative design. Anyone arriving in Rome by train would be

19.1 Joe Colombo, furniture, Milan, Italy, 1970.

In a futuristic apartment using circular forms as a theme, Colombo arranged rotating elements including a dining table-shelf and, on the right, a Cabriolet Bed with a folding canopy.

Gio Ponte: Pirelli Tower

In his early life as an architect Gio Ponte faced the dilemma of trying to steer between the modernist Rationalist movement and the more accepted fascist orthodoxy which advocated a more classical style. Eduardo Persico, the Turinese art critic and designer, wrote about this struggle in 1934:

Today artists must tackle the thorniest problem of Italian life; the capacity to believe in specific ideologies and the will to pursue the struggle against the claims of an anti modernist majority. [1]

After the war Ponte was free to follow his true instincts and express beauty and excitement in his work. The architect Richard England, who studied under Ponte after the war, comments on the individuality of the Pirelli Tower and the way its design attempts to transcend purely materialistic requirements:

Ponte's belief, plea and commitment was essentially for the individual, the particular and the unique . . . . The Pirelli Tower in Milan must be considered as the jewel of modern skyscrapers; a diamond well cut and beautifully facetted. In the best Italian tradition (and what a tradition that is!) Ponte's work evokes in its spectators a magical sense of ecstasy and fantasy. This is an expression of love and joy that transcends purely intellectual technological values into the realm of the spiritual. [2]

1. Quoted in K. Frampton, *Modern Architecture* (London, 1992), p. 205; 2. Quoted in *Contemporary Architects* (London and Chicago, 1987), p. 708

19.2 Pier Luigi Nervi, Palace of Labor, Turin, Italy, 1960–1

Concrete columns with spreading, leaf-like arms form the structure for the large Exhibition Hall of the Palace of Labor. The photograph is of a scale model viewed from above. The structural system establishes a visual character that unifies the changing exhibits that the hall was designed to contain.

struck by the new railroad station, the Stazione Termini (1951) by Eugenio Montuori (born 1907) and associated architects. The great galleria leading from street entrance to train shed is a dramatically impressive space.

Pier Luigi Nervi (1891–1979), an engineer whose reputation was formed by his stadium in Florence (1930–2), had the opportunity there to create interior spaces through the imaginative geometry of reinforced concrete construction. In his exhibition building in Turin (1948–50) great pylons of concrete branch out to form a support for a vast roof shell, in which the ribs are formed in corrugations permitting bands of glass between them, generating a space and structure of great vitality. His exhibition hall called the Palace of Labor (or Italia 61 Pavilion) at Turin (**fig. 19.2**; 1960–1) is formed as a cluster of sixteen square units, each with a tapering center column of concrete supporting a roof panel created by branching rib-spokes of steel carrying the roof decking. Bands of glass separate each square while the perimeter enclosure is entirely of glass.

Nervi was the engineering collaborator with Marcel Breuer in the design of the Unesco headquarters building (1953–7) in Paris. He was also the engineering collaborator in the design of the Pirelli building in Milan (1955–9). Gio Ponte (1891–1979) was the architect responsible for the basic plan of this impressive skyscraper, one of the first modern tall buildings to be built in Europe. Ponte's interiors of the ground-floor public spaces are examples of post-war Italian interior design at its best. The gleaming floors of rubber in yellow and green marbleized veining have islands of colorful rugs containing Ponte-designed furniture; the ceiling is made up of bands of acoustic materials separated by grooves providing air inlets. Ponte was also responsible for a widely admired side chair based on traditional craft precedents. This 1951 Superleggera—a modern classic—was simple, elegant, and light in both physical weight and visual character.

Italian design became visible in New York with the Olivetti showroom on Fifth Avenue (1954, destroyed). Its typewriter outside on a marble pedestal, its elegant use of marble in the interior, and its enormous wall bas-relief mural by the sculptor Constantino Nivola made it one of the city's most beautiful interiors.

Many other Italian designers became famous for their furniture. Franco Albini (1905–77),

Marco Zanuso (born 1916), Tobia Scarpa (born 1935), Carlo Molino (1905–73), Vico Magistrettti (born 1920), and the Castiglionis (Achille, born 1918, and two brothers) all became known for their furniture, lamps, and other products. Joe Colombo (1930–71) was one of the most adventurous of the Italian designers, producing a variety of chairs and many interesting furniture units that combined various functions into single packages. Many other Italian design products, such as the colorful glassware produced by Venini, made Italian modernism well known and influential.

Scandinavia

Denmark, known before the war for its warm, attractive modernism, became a leader in post-war interior design. Finn Juhl (1912–89) made use of traditional Danish woodworking craftsmanship to produce elegantly sculptural furniture. Juhl designed many interiors where his furniture and built-in shelving and other units generated a quiet and subtle sense of space. His designs were made available in the United States for a time, produced by the Baker Furniture Company in Grand Rapids, Michigan. His most important interior project in America was the Trusteeship Council Chamber in the United Nations building in New York (1953). Simple wood paneling on the side walls frames a great window looking out over the East River that can be closed off by drapery. Overhead, the ceiling is a series of metal grids that hold box-like lighting units, each in a bright color, giving the space a lively and active character.

Arne Jacobsen (1902–71) was a leading Danish architect who produced some fine private houses, schools, and town halls. Many of these buildings, such as the town halls at Sollerod, Glostrup, and Rodovre, had simple and handsome interiors, often with Jacobsen-designed furniture. He was also responsible for such major projects as the high-rise SAS Royal Hotel in Copenhagen (**fig. 19.3**; 1958). His Egg chair designed for that hotel became widely known, as did several simple chairs using molded plywood for seat and back with metal legs produced by Fritz Hansen. He was also the designer of textiles, lamps, silver flatware, ceramics, and glassware that represented Danish design at its best.

Jorn Utzon (born 1918) is best known for his winning competition design for the opera house in

Sydney, Australia (1956). Its repeated sail-like shell forms create a landmark externally and remarkable interiors within. His design for Bagsvaerd Church in Copenhagen (1979) also deserves attention. It includes a number of spaces designed with a rectilinear plan on a square module, which rise into a remarkable complex in the ceiling of the church itself. As a furniture designer, Utzon developed the Utsep Mobler seating system which used a number of modules that can be combined into a variety of curved and straight groupings.

The modern furniture of Denmark became popular worldwide. Its somewhat conservative design combined with traditional craftsmanship in finely finished teak and other hardwoods and favorable economic conditions to make it particularly popular in the United States. Designers included such pre-war established individuals as Hans Wegner, Borge Mogensen, and Paoul Kjaerholm. Younger designers were Peter Hvidt, Grete Jalk, and Verner Panton, along with Finn Juhl and Arne Jacobsen, who are mentioned above. Modern Danish cabinetry and shelving systems also became popular, while the availability of related ceramics, silver, and other household products made "Danish modern" an internationally popular style.

The design of post-war Sweden was strongly concentrated on advanced ideas of town and city planning, but many individual works also came into notice. Gunnar Asplund's last work, the Forest Crematorium at Sockenvagen near Stockholm (1934–40), is a serene grouping with a woodland cemetery and a main chapel with a bronze and glass gate forming its front wall. The gate can be lowered into the ground, making the outdoor court and the chapel interior into a single space. Sven Markelius continued his distinguished career with such works as the Stockholm Folkets Hus (**fig. 19.4**; 1934), a grouping of meeting rooms and other facilities to serve Swedish trade unions. The largest meeting hall has been called Markelius's finest work. He was one of several architects responsible for the UN headquarters in New York, where he produced the interior design for one council chamber, a space similar in form to that designed by Finn Juhl but with a ceiling formed as a large, smooth panel studded with recessed lights. The impact is more formal and sedate than Juhl's chamber.

The fine quality of Swedish design is evident in many private homes and housing groups.

19.3 Arne Jacobsen, SAS Royal Hotel, Copenhagen, Denmark, 1958.

A room interior designed in the quiet form of modernism typical of Jacobsen's Danish work. All the furniture is by Jacobsen, including the curving arm chair often called the Egg chair.

19.4 Sven Markelius, Folkets Hus, Stockholm, Sweden, 1934

The large auditorium has seating in curving rows that are widely spaced to permit easy access. The simple, functional forms are enlivened by the ceiling design, in which lighting takes the form of bright discs that seem to float against a darker background.

Household products of superior design quality are sold in retail stores. Swedish furniture, textiles, and decorative objects, such as the glass of the Orrefors firm, became well known and popular. The AGA cooker (kitchen range) and the unique Ericofon telephone continue to offer Swedish design available for any suitable interior.

Finland has maintained a high standard of design, its roots going back to traditions of simplicity and craftsmanship. Alvar Aalto continued to exert a strong influence in Finnish design through his later work and his role as a teacher. Aalto's Technical University at Otaniemi (1955–66) with its distinguished lecture hall is close to the student union building called Dipoli (**fig. 19.5**; 1964–6), by Raili Paatelainen and Reima Pietilä, a sprawling building of irregular shape with interiors enriched by natural rock formations that have been preserved as interior walls. The Helsinki City Theater (1967) by Timo Penttilä has an extraordinarily successful theater auditorium.

Viljo Revell (1910–64) was first known for a factory building at Hango (1954–6) that included simple, brightly lit office spaces. He became better known internationally with his winning design for a new city hall for Toronto, Canada (1958). Its two curving tall buildings look across lower buildings that hold council chambers and other facilities.

Finland has had a particularly distinguished history in the design of furniture and other household products. The hollow ball chair by Eero Aarnio (born 1932) of 1963–5, and his 1967 arm chair, cup-shaped on a pedestal base, are among the designs that made Finnish furniture internationally

19.5 (top right)
Paatelainen and Pietilä, Dipoli, Otaniemi (near Helsinki), Finland, 1964-6

In the interior space of the students' union natural outcroppings of rock have been retained to form wall surfaces. The irregular forms of the building's interiors generate a sense of comfortable informality. Raili Paatelainen and her husband Reima Pietilä carried out many other projects together.

19.6 (bottom right)
Paatelainen and Pietilä, Kaleva Church, Tampere, Finland, 1964-6.

The tall interior space is created by fin-like concrete walls, which have been widely spaced to make room for bands of windows. The roof is made up of concrete panels, positioned to match the spacing of the walls. The color scheme is subdued greys, except for the warm wood tones of the seating and case for the pipe organ on the right.

known. The Finnish shipyards of Wartsila at Turku produced an outpouring of passenger ferry ships, large floating hotels with many handsome interior spaces. The ferry *Finnjet* (1973), for example, provides handsome staterooms and distinguished public spaces on its five passenger decks.

The Kaleva Church at Tampere (**fig. 19.6**; 1964–6) by Raili Paatelainen and Reima Pietilä, with walls of tall, curved slabs of reinforced concrete separated by bands of glass, is a space of impressive dignity. In contrast, the small chapel at Otaniemi by Kaija and Haikki Siren is a simple, box-like form facing a front wall of glass looking out on a beautiful landscape.

France

Le Corbusier's later works dominate post-war design in France. The chapel at Ronchamp and the Unité d'Habitation at Marseille have already been discussed (see p. 283). His idea for city planning that focused on large, tall, residential buildings that would each constitute a complete neighborhood finally came to reality with the building of the Unité. Le Corbusier was commissioned to build several other Unité buildings at Nantes and Firminy in France and in Germany and Belgium.

One of Le Corbusier's last works is the interesting Centre Le Corbusier of 1967 at Zürich, Switzerland. A group of mostly cubical, modular elements enclosed in glass with a few solid panels, this virtually complete building stands below a steel "umbrella" of triangulated panels supported by just four steel structural columns. Part of the building is a demonstration ideal house, part an exhibition center with a projecting enclosed ramp connecting two levels.

Germany

One of the other great pioneers, Mies van der Rohe, demonstrated his idea of "universal space" in Germany in the great, open glass-walled enclosure of the National Gallery in Berlin (see p. 277). The Philharmonic Hall of 1959–63 in Berlin by Hans Scharoun (1893–1972), with its tent-like curving roof forms, includes handsome foyer spaces leading to the vast concert hall within. In the hall, angled planes define platform-like elements for the seating; a large organ with exposed pipes occupies an asymmetrical position on the right. The orchestra is placed in a central area, surrounded by the audience.

At Ulm an effort was made to reconstitute the Bauhaus in a new institution, the Hochschule für Gestaltung, founded in 1952. The building (1955) was designed by its first director, Max Bill, and is appropriately International Style in character. It became a center for the development of the

19.7 Kurd Alsleben and Quickborner Team, open office plan, Germany, 1968.

The plan for a large German corporation's administrative offices adopted the approach called Burolandschaft *(meaning "office landscape"). Private offices and closed spaces are replaced by freely positioned groups of furniture, which are sited according to patterns of communication. The swirling lines indicate circulation paths.*

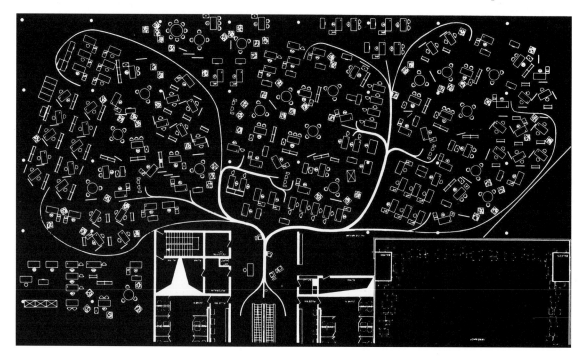

austerely minimalist style favored by Dieter Rams (born 1932) and Hans Gugelot (1920–65). The elegant products of the Braun electrical industry and furniture such as the M125 modular furniture group of 1953 were typical examples of the influence of the school of Ulm. The school was closed in 1968 but its influence continues.

Several major office buildings for German corporations sprang up during the post-war years. Most are of typically restrained International Style modernist character. Many of their interiors made use of a concept developed by management consultants, the brothers Eberhard and Wolfgang Schnelle working in the organization known as the Quickborner Team. Their approach to office planning called for the elimination of all partitioning into separate office rooms and the substitution of open space called *Burolandschaft* ("office landscape") in which furniture and movable screens could be freely placed to permit easy communication (**fig. 19.7**). Early examples of such open planning were at first considered radical but acceptance, in somewhat modified form, has become the norm of modern office planning. The Buch und Ton offices at Guttersloh (1961), those of Krupp at Essen (1962), and the 1963 offices of Orenstein-Koppel at Dortmund-Dorsfeld are typical early examples of office landscape.

The works of Frei Otto (born 1925) generate exceptional tent-like interior spaces as a result of dependence on suspended cable structures. His German Pavilion at the Expo 67 World's Fair in Montreal (**fig. 19.8**) made the possibilities of such structure visible to a large audience of visitors. The Munich Olympic Stadium (1972) is a larger and more dramatic example of such a structure.

The Netherlands

The architect Aldo Van Eyck (born 1918) has criticized the aim of modernist designers who seek an "ideal" solution to problems, usually on the basis of their own Euro-centric and middle-class values. He has urged a freer view in which constructed space leaves openings for user and occupant participation in the organization of interiors. Herman Hertzberger (born 1932) employed similar ideas for the office building of Centraal Beheer (**fig. 19.9**; 1973), an insurance company at Apeldoorn. The building is made up of modular units stacked in rectilinear but irregular patterns. The interior space is, as a result, a complex of small spaces where the individual workers are encouraged to arrange furniture, equipment, and personal accessories in any desired way. The resulting clutter is surprisingly humane, quite unlike the uniform order that is the effect of so many office projects.

19.8 (*left*) Frei Otto, German Pavilion, Expo 67, Montreal 1967.

The use of tension cables hanging from masts and supporting a net of cables, which, in turn, supports a plastic skin, encourages the development of freely curving shapes. The translucency of the roof material made it possible for the interior to be filled with light by day while at night interior lighting made the exterior glow in the dark.

19.9 Herman Hertzberger, Centraal Beheer, Apeldoorn, The Netherlands, 1973.

The office building that Hertzberger designed for the insurance company Centraal Beheer, moves away from the concept of the open plan office in favor of a more cellular organization. Modular platforms or balconies at various levels are placed in a complex, constantly varied pattern. More than 1000 office workers are placed in locations that offer each worker a unique setting, and workers are encouraged to arrange furniture and personal belongings in any way they wish to create lively settings with no sense of regimentation.

19.10 R.H. Matthew and J. L. Martin, Royal Festival Hall, London, 1951.

The large concert hall was part of a complex built on the South Bank of the Thames. The ceiling forms and curved fronts of boxes on side walls were planned to favor acoustical considerations. The ceiling incorporates concealed lighting, and the natural wood of the three panels at the front focus attention on the platform area. The exposed pipes of the large organ provide a decorative element above the stage.

Britain

Post-war work in Britain was dominated by the planning of new towns and by housing projects of a generally high level of design. The Royal Festival Hall, built as part of the Festival of Britain exhibition of 1951, remains as the only permanent survivor of that fair. The architects were R. H. Matthew and J. L. Martin of the London County Council. The 3000-seat main hall is one of the first distinguished concert hall interiors to be built in the post-war era (**fig. 19.10**).

The Smithsons (Alison and Peter) are thought of as leading proponents of the new brutalist direction (see p. 284). Their best known work is the Economist building (1964)—actually three towers—in St. James's Street, London. The interior spaces of the original entrance lobbies and other public areas display the austerity of brutalism.

The last great ocean liner, the *Queen Elizabeth II* (1968), had interiors coordinated by Dennis Lennon and Partners that were examples of British design at its best. Theo Crosby of the firm Pentagram was the designer of a particularly handsome room on the upper deck, a bar and lounge called The Lookout. The room was an observation lounge stretching the width of the ship; its forward bulkhead (wall) slanted inward and was studded with large windows overlooking the bow of the ship. There is a piano in bright vermilion, the only touch of strong color. Pentagram has been responsible for a number of other interior and exhibition design projects of outstanding quality, including office interiors for Reuters, British Petroleum, and Pentagram's own London offices.

David Hicks (1929–98) established his practice in 1955 and became a leading British designer. His distinctive designs for textiles and carpets are based on rectangular blocks. Patterned floors, with strong colors, often in rooms with large paintings and traditional furniture, marked his personal style. Furniture by Robin Day, Ernest Race, and a number of other designers was assembled by Terence Conran to provide designs for the highly successful Habitat retail shops.

United States

Gropius, Breuer, Mies van der Rohe, and Aalto continued to exert their influence in post-war America. Eero Saarinen designed the TWA terminal at Kennedy airport (**fig. 19.11**; 1956–62), its free forms in reinforced concrete generating large, open, sculptural interior spaces with curving elevated walkways looking out over the complex, curving surfaces. Access to the aircraft was through tubular passages, also curving but contrasting in their sense of closure with the openness of the main terminal building.

Saarinen's design for the terminal building for the Dulles airport serving Washington, D.C., located at Chantilly, Virginia (1962), used a different approach. Its cable suspended roof structure generates an impressive and vast interior concourse. Special vehicles called "mobile lounges" transported passengers to and from the terminal to airplanes waiting on the field. This scheme made a more compact terminal possible than would have been required to give direct access to planes. At the Massachusetts Institute of Technology (MIT; **fig. 19.12**), Saarinen designed a small, round chapel lighted by the changing reflections from a surrounding water-filled moat, and the related Kresge Auditorium within a great shell structure (1955). His austere black tower skyscraper for CBS in New York (1965) housed elegantly colorful interiors designed by Florence Knoll.

After Saarinen's death, the successor firm of Roche Dinkeloo designed the office complex for John Deere at Moline, Illinois (**fig. 19.13**; 1955), and the distinguished New York headquarters building for the Ford Foundation (1967). The John Deere space has the character of a two-story garden conservatory, which makes the office furniture a minor element in an area dominated by growing plants. In the Ford Foundation building, office

19.11 Eero Saarinen, TWA Terminal, Kennedy Airport, New York, 1956-62.

Saarinen explored the possibilities inherent in reinforced concrete as a structural material to create the freely curving forms that characterize the building both inside and out. Curving stairs give access to upper levels, while simple metal railings act as decorative detail. Large glass areas admit light in ways that accentuate the sculptural forms of the structure. Even the information desk, visible at the right, is made up of freely flowing curved forms.

floors form an L-shape on two sides of a high garden atrium. Windows look into this skylit interior space, where trees and smaller plantings make the garden equal in importance to the surrounding offices. Warren Plattner developed its interiors of great dignity and simplicity, often with furniture of his own design.

Richard Neutra continued to produce many distinguished projects after the war, including schools, medical facilities, and private houses, all in the International Style vocabulary of rectilinear simplicity. His house of 1946–7 at Palm Springs in the California desert for the Kaufmann family (who had been Wright's clients for Fallingwater) is a particularly fine example (**fig. 19.14**). Vast areas of floor-to-ceiling glass connect the simple interiors with the surrounding outdoor spaces.

Modernist residential design was particularly welcomed in Calfornia. William Wilson Wurster (1895–1973) was one of several architects who developed what is often called a Bay Region vernacular, centered around San Francisco and its bay. The style draws on the tradition of farms and ranch structures to produce a form of modernism that is unpretentious and direct. The Pope ranch house of 1958, for example, has a gable roof and is surrounded by wide verandas. The Coleman city house in San Francisco (1962) has crisp white-painted steel framing with broad glass areas giving views of the bay. Interiors use simple, white-painted walls, and natural wood for floors, doors, and trim.

19.12 (*opposite*) Eero Saarinen, Kresge Memorial Chapel at MIT, Cambridge, Massachusetts, 1952-6.

This building is a cylinder of brick, illumined only by reflected light from a surrounding moat admitted through arches at the base of the walls. The altar reredos is a screen of golden bronze elements, a sculptural work of the Italian-born sculptor Harry Bertoia (1915-78).

19.13 (*top left*) Kevin Roche and John Dinkeloo, offices for John Deere & Co., Moline, Illinois, 1955.

Work spaces are arranged on two floors of two rectangular blocks, which have a spacious garden atrium between them. Every work station is within sight of either the atrium or the park setting in which the building stands. Structural members are of COR-10 steel.

19.14 (*left*) Richard Neutra, Kaufmann House, Palm Springs, California, 1946-7.

The simplicity of the International Style continued to characterize Neutra's later work, and the influence of Mies van der Rohe can be seen in the Kaufmann House. The large, roll-away glass areas and simple treatment of floors and ceiling give the interior space a unity with the carefully planned garden areas outside.

19.15 Pietro Belluschi, Central Lutheran Church, Portland, Oregon, 1951.

Belluschi was born in Italy and moved to the United States in the 1920s, when he joined the Portland architectural practice of Albert Ernest Doyle (1877-1922), a practice he took over on Doyle's death. An altar and reredos form the visual focus within this dignified interior. The pattern of the reredos is random except as the cross image develops at its center. The white railings that define the chancel area are of utmost simplicity.

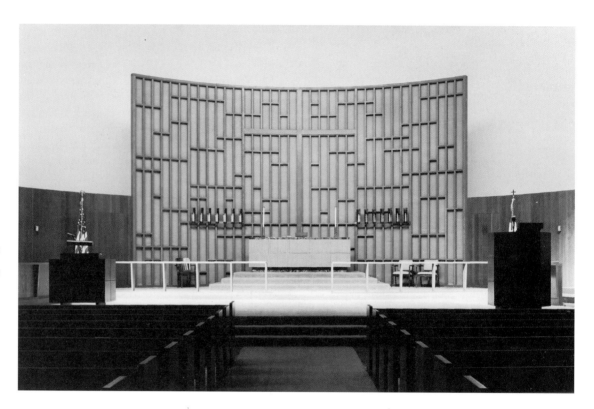

Farther north, in Portland, Oregon, Pietro Belluschi (1899–1994) became known for his Equitable Building of 1948, one of the first tall buildings in America of strict modernist character. Built three years later, his Central Lutheran Church, also in Portland, is a construction of redwood, inside and out, suggesting an affinity with the vernacular barn structures of the Pacific Northwest (**fig. 19.15**). Belluschi became dean of the architectural school at MIT in 1951 and managed to continue his practice on the west coast while accepting commissions in the east as well. He was the designer of many churches, such as that of the Portsmouth Priory at Portsmouth, Rhode Island (1961), an octagonal building with walls of redwood and fieldstone, the warmth and texture of wood dominating the interior. (For Belluschi's role in the design of the Pan Am Building and the Juilliard School in New York, see pp. 342, 343.)

Frank Lloyd Wright had a continuing, active career in the post-war era which led to one of his most famous (and final) works, the Guggenheim Museum in New York (1942–60). Its interior, a round funnel-like space holding a winding spiral ramp, is one of the most remarkable designs in any modern building (**fig. 19.16**). Controversy has centered on its suitability as a museum space, with critics suggesting that the strength of its

architectural form overwhelms any art work displayed there.

Another museum of comparable importance to the Guggenheim is the Whitney Museum of American Art in New York (1963–6) by Marcel Breuer. The massive, heavy structure houses spaces of austerity and dignity. The entrance across a bridge over an open garden leads to a lobby area. It and the basement café prepare the visitor for the gallery spaces—open areas with a ceiling structure of concrete in a triangulated grid (**fig. 19.17**). One large projecting window, asymmetrically placed, allows the visitor a glimpse of the out-of-doors and the outside world a glimpse into the galleries. Breuer had a number of major commissions in the United States, including a dormitory building, Ferry House, at Vassar College, Poughkeepsie, New York (1950), and St. John's Abbey Church and library at Collegeville, Minnesota (1953–68). The church interior is a large, auditorium-like space with walls and ceiling of folded concrete slab. A balcony is an indepedent concrete structure standing within the church auditorium.

Breuer's office in New York designed many churches, college buildings, office complexes, and private houses. The giant headquarters building for the U.S. Department of Housing and Urban Development in Washington, D.C. (1963–8),

19.16 Frank Lloyd Wright, Guggenheim Museum, New York, 1942–60.

The museum's main rotunda space is formed by the great spiral ramp. Art works are displayed against the outside wall, which follows the curve of the ramp. Visitors can look down to the ground below or up to the skylight dome above. Color is a cream off-white with plants providing green accents.

19.17 (*below*) Marcel Breuer, Whitney Museum of American Art, New York, 1963–6.

The floor of stone rectangles and the functional overhead grid, which contains adjustable lighting fittings, combine with the white walls to provide a setting in which works of art may be seen without competition. In the center of the far wall can be seen one of several trapezoidal windows that project out from the building's exterior walls.

houses nine floors of routine office space within an exterior grid of concrete above an entrance floor bordered by sheltered outdoor passageways.

Urban Office Buildings

Walter Gropius organized The Architects' Collaborative (TAC) in 1945. Together with Pietro Belluschi he was a consultant in shaping the design of the New York office tower of 1963 originally known as the Pan Am Building. The firm of Emery Roth and Sons carried out the execution of the project. Gropius's influence can be seen in the plan of the tower with its tapered ends, and in the public spaces at ground level (now unfortunately badly modified) enlivened by distinguished art works by Josef Albers, Gyorgy Kepes, and Richard Lippold. The Architects' Collaborative has designed many school and college buildings, as well as governmental and institutional buildings, such as the Johns Manville office building in Colorado, near Denver (1976–7), with its open stretches of office space treated in office landscape fashion.

Other exceptions to the indifferent quality of many office towers include the Citicorp building in New York (1977), a tall office building of outstanding quality by Hugh Stubbins (1912–94). Its handsome inner atrium is a shopping center, its

19.19 I. M. Pei and Partners, National Airlines Terminal, John F. Kennedy International Airport, Queens, New York, 1972.

This open space roofed with a space-frame structure has exterior walls of glass.

many stores and restaurants surrounding a high open space with escalators connecting several levels. An unusually interesting office interior can be found on a high floor of that building: the offices of BEA by Tod Williams and Associates. Partitions of sand-blasted glass and red-brown columns housing lighting give the space a quiet and attractive quality.

Skidmore, Owings, and Merrill were the architects and interior designers for the American Republic Insurance Company building in Des Moines, Iowa (1965), with its distinguished interiors. The firm produced many projects outside the field of office design. The Mauna Kea Beach Hotel at Kamuela, Hawaii (1965), for example, has interiors that refer to local traditions through their materials and craft-related forms. Guest rooms use furniture of local wicker and sliding screens of narrow strip louvers. Rooms face on galleries that surround an open court with tall palm trees.

Edward Larrabee Barnes (born 1915) was the architect and designer for several IBM projects including the World Trade offices at Mount Pleasant, New York (**fig. 19.18**; 1974), its three floors of open office space surrounded by windows opening onto the countryside. Where the program called for the enclosure of private spaces, clear glass has been used for floor-to-ceiling partitions that allow visual openness.

Philip Johnson was the designer of the A.T.&T. headquarters office building of 1984 in New York (now the Sony Building). It is an architecturally controversial project discussed in the following chapter. The office interiors by the firm ISD are in many ways backward-looking, with their rich areas of marble, elaborate wood paneling, and similar references to the corporate styles of the past. The lobby of 885 Third Avenue (also a Philip Johnson project) of 1986, jokingly called the Lipstick

Building in recognition of its stepped, elliptical shape, has ground-floor lobby space more allied to the Art Deco directions of the 1930s.

The work of I. M. Pei (born 1917) extends from his own serenely simple country house at Katonah, New York (1952), to a range of major projects for which his office also provided interior design. Apartment buildings in New York, Philadelphia, and Washington, D.C., are typical examples, as is the Denver Hilton Hotel (1960) where Alexander Girard cooperated in the interior design. The National Airlines Terminal of 1972 (now TWA terminal B) at Kennedy airport in New York is a vast open space topped by a space-frame truss roof supported by columns that stand outside the glass walls of the building (**fig. 19.19**). It suggests a strong attachment to Mies van der Rohe's concept of universal space. (For later work by Pei and his partners see Chapter 20.)

The group of buildings forming New York's Lincoln Center for the Performing Arts is a monumental cluster with disappointing interior spaces. The best of the three major buildings from an interior design point of view is the New York State Theater (1964) by Philip Johnson. The entrance-level lobby and the grand foyer above it are distinguished spaces where travertine floors and walls and, in the foyer, balconies on several levels provide a setting for two major sculptural works by Elie Nadelman. The auditorium expresses some of the sense of the great opera houses of the past, with much gold leaf and red plush. It is far more successful than the banal interior of the Metropolitan Opera House adjacent. The nearby Juilliard School of Music of 1968 by Pietro Belluschi and Eduardo Catalano (**fig. 19.20**) is the best of the Lincoln Center buildings: its moderately sized Alice Tully Hall auditorium is an outstanding interior both visually and acoustically.

19.18 Edward Larabee Barnes, IBM World Trade Offices, Mount Pleasant, New York, 1974.

The three-story building has walls of continuous glass. A circulation space follows the glass walls, while work stations are grouped within so that all workers have equal access to the light and views of the pleasant exterior space. Each floor is carpeted in an identifying color, here red, pleasantly contrasting with the many green plants.

Office Planning

The design of office facilities has become so important an aspect of interior design practice that a specialized profession has grown up, usually called SPACE PLANNING. Space planners also deal with institutional, hotel, and retail projects. Their approach begins with the development of the plan, and moves into furniture placement and the more decorative aspects of interior design. The goal of such planning is to provide for efficient office functioning along with comfort for workers and flexibility for growth and organizational change.

ISD (Interior Space Design) has been one of the best known and most successful of space planning organizations. Their office interiors in the Boston City Hall, the A.T.&T. Building in New York, and the Xerox headquarters building in Stamford, Connecticut, are good examples of ISD practice. The interiors of the Boston building for the American Academy of Arts and Sciences (1961) by the architectural firm of Kallmann, McKinnell, and Wood finds ISD working with more varied spaces where a sense of calm and dignity is developed through the use of wood surfaces with other carefully chosen materials and objects.

Other space planners include the firms SLS Environetics, the Space Design Group, and Designs for Business (the latter responsible for fourteen floors of offices for Time-Life Inc. in the New York Time-Life building of Rockefeller Center). Sidney Rogers Associates were the planners for the twenty-six floors of the Montgomery Ward headquarters building in Chicago. Carpeting in differing bright colors serves to differentiate the floors of the project, which are otherwise almost totally similar.

19.20 Belluschi and Catalano, Juilliard Theater, Lincoln Center, New York, 1968.

This theater-concert hall is housed within the extensive building that contains the Juilliard School of Music. Its moderate size and extensive use of natural wood give it a comfortable quality, which makes it a highly successful setting for recitals and chamber music concerts.

All use landscape planning (discussed below). Rogers Associates were also office designers for the headquarters building in Tacoma, Washington, for the Weyerhaeuser Company. Knoll office furniture was used in open-plan configurations with broad areas of glass opening onto the surrounding landscape. The building architects were Skidmore, Owings, and Merrill.

The office of George Nelson (1908–86) produced an exceptional interior for the Aid Association to Lutherans building (1976) by John Carl Warnecke (born 1919) in Appleton, Wisconsin. The special open-office furniture system was produced under the firm name Storwal International. An unusual feature was the use of small conference areas made up of movable panels arranged in a circle, with a central umbrella forming a kind of internal roof. On a smaller scale, the New York restaurant La Potagerie (1971, now demolished) shows the Nelson office (with Judith Stockman in charge of design) producing spaces that were colorful and cheerful as well as highly functional.

Office Furniture

With the vast expansion of office building, and increased use of Bürolandschaft (office landscape) planning, American furniture manufacturers soon began to develop systems in which work surfaces and storage were integrated with screens or panels that provided a degree of privacy and also dealt with the plethora of electric and telephone wiring that modern office equipment requires (**fig. 19.21**). Robert Propst developed a system which he called Action Office for the Herman Miller Furniture Company in 1964. Before long an increasing number of similar systems began to appear, each system named for its designer. The Stephens, Zapf, Hannah, and Morrison systems were introduced by Knoll. There were also the Haller system from Switzerland, the Marcatre and Olivetti systems from Italy, the Lucas system from England, the Race system from Canada, the Voko systems from Germany, and the products of Hayworth and Steelcase in the United States.

The discovery that full-time office work seated in a chair at a work station could generate physiological problems led to the development of so-called ergonomic chairs that offered designs intended to be beneficial to the physical comfort and health of the user. Designs by Bill Stumpf (the Ergon chairs), Niels Diffrient, and then a host of other designers all aimed at providing superior office seating. They have become essential elements in modern office design.

19.21 Bill Stumpf, Ethospace Interior, Herman Miller, Inc., 1985.

The office furniture and screen partition system from a major American manufacturer is shown in a typical grouping with work surface, ergonomically designed chairs, and a lamp contained in a space defined by wall panels. The interchangeable panels may be fabric covered in a variety of colors, or made of clear or obscure glass to provide privacy, light, and open vision or closure as desired.

19.22 Sarah Tomerlin Lee, Helmsley Palace Hotel, New York, 1980.

The fine houses designed in the eclectic era by McKim, Mead, & White were preserved when the new Helmsley Palace was built and made into public rooms for the hotel. The designer has made adjustments in relating the elaborate traditional interiors to modern use and modern taste, but the rich color and detailing of the original spaces are echoed in the choice of furniture and color scheme.

Interior Designers

Interior design is often undertaken without strong involvement in architecture, especially by those active in the design of residential interiors. The work of some designers is regarded as so exciting and glamorous that it can enhance the status of their clients. Among such "star" designers working in America, Mario Buatta (born 1935), Mark Hampton (1940–98), and Angelo Donghia (1935–85) are best known for lush interiors using antique furniture and colorful fabrics to generate spaces recalling the work of the eclectic decorators of the 1920s and 1930s. The work of John Saladino (born 1939) places historic references in more clearly contemporary settings. Ward Bennett (born 1917), mentioned earlier for his work at the Chase Manhattan tower, designed simple interiors suggestive of the International Style together with his own furniture. Joseph Paul D'Urso (born 1943) was trained both as an interior designer and as an architect and worked for a time with Ward Bennett before establishing his own practice. His work, sometimes called "minimalist," used simple surfaces along with elements of industrial products (shelving, table bases, light fixtures) to generate what may also be called an industrial style.

Sarah Tomerlin Lee (born 1910s) developed a practice that specialized in hotel interiors, many called "romantic" in their use of period furniture and textiles, in hotels such as the Parker Meridien of 1981 (made over from an older hotel) in New York, or in interiors of traditional design dating from an earlier era. The Helmsley Palace in New York is made up, in part, from the great Villard houses of 1884 by McKim, Mead, and White. The 1980 conversion to hotel use gave Sarah Tomerlin Lee a setting of eclectic opulence in which her richly ornamental interior style seems entirely at home (**fig. 19.22**).

Benjamin Baldwin (1913–93) was a product of the Cranbrook Academy, who became known for some of the most distinguished interior projects of the 1960s and 1970s. His style, close to minimalism but with a strong sense of color and form, made it possible for him to work with a number of modern architects, including Edward Barnes, Louis Kahn, and I. M. Pei. For Kahn, he was responsible for interiors of the library and dining hall at Phillips Exeter Academy, Exeter, New Hampshire (1967–72), and for furniture and related details at the Yale Center for British Art at New Haven, Connecticut

(1969–74). The exceptionally fine interiors of the Americana Hotel in Fort Worth, Texas (1980), are also his work. His own house at East Hampton, New York, is a fine example of his approach to design.

Furniture and Other Interior Furnishings

Modern furniture that came into use post-World War II includes many of the "classic" designs of the 1920s and 1930s, such as those of Aalto, Breuer, Le Corbusier, and Mies van der Rohe. Charles Eames, the office of George Nelson, Warren Platner, and many other Americans joined the classics and imports of more recent designs from Italy and the Scandinavian countries to provide interior designers with a rich variety of available furniture of excellent design quality. Charles Eames provided a steady flow of distinguished designs, often by-products of interior projects that he and his wife, Ray, worked on together. Such designs were generally only familiar to architects and designers; most households of middle-class families made do with shoddy products in designs that pretended to be "colonial" or "French provincial." Exceptions to this pattern are the designs of Paul McCobb (1917–69)—simple wooden cabinets and chairs that seem to have a basis in American colonial or Shaker precedents without being in any way imitative. McCobb's inexpensive furniture, available in department stores, and the designs of Jens Risom (born 1916), as well as the more costly designs of Edward Wormley, found their way into at least some American homes.

Textiles

The wide acceptance of the modernist aesthetic propelled the major manufacturers of textiles toward production of a vast range of simple, solid color patterns, plus stripes, checks, and other geometric designs suitable for use in upholstery and drapery. There was also continuing production of the floral and other decorative prints and weaves used in traditional interior decor. Among American designers, Dorothy Liebes (1899–1972) became known for rich, over-scaled textures in thick yarns. Boris Kroll (born 1913) established a firm offering varied textiles of high quality in both design and structure.

19.23 Larsen Design Studio, foyer of the Rainbow Room, Rockefeller Center, New York, 1996

Strong patterns in a jacquard fabric on the curving wall and a pattern of rings in the Wilton carpet demonstrate the way in which woven materials can elaborate a basically simple space.

Most production textiles and carpets were anonymous patterns produced by staff designers employed by manufacturers, but some furniture manufacturers turned to offering proprietary lines of textiles. The designs were then coordinated with a special stylistic approach using distinguished designers identified with individual styles. The work of Alexander Girard for Herman Miller, based on the color and pattern of Mexican and South American folk art, has already been mentioned. Knoll employed a sequence of able designers including Eszter Haraszty for such patterns as the linear Tracy, and Anni Albers (1899–1994) of Bauhaus origins for abstract geometric patterns. Angelo Testa (born 1921) contributed some of the first abstract prints offered by Knoll.

At Cranbrook, Loja Saarinen (1879–1968) organized a weaving studio and was the designer of many craft-based weavings. Later Cranbrook textile designers included Ed Rossbach (born 1914) and Marianne Strengell (born 1909). The work of Jack Lenor Larsen (born 1927) in developing a great variety of creative weaves, often using newly developed fibers (metallics and synthetics) and abstract prints, has established textile design as a distinctive art form (**fig. 19.23**). He has been the most influential of Cranbrook influences in the world of textiles.

The color and bold patterning of Finnish textile art became widely known under the trade name Marimekko with design by Armi Ratia (1912–79) and Marja Isola (born 1927). Imports such as the Thai silks of Jim Thompson (1906–77), Danish designs by Verner Panton (born 1926), and Swedish and German textiles by lesser known designers came into wide availability and use.

Modernism has been a significant style for many decades. Its emergence in the 1920s, its rise in the 1930s and 1940s, and its dominance in the 1960s, 1970s, and 1980s mean that it has lasted through two to three generations of designers and public, always finding new forms and new expressions. It was inevitable that the ascendency of modernism would continue to evoke criticism. Some work that often adopted the superficial qualities of modernist design without understanding its underlying intentions helped to encourage a backlash against it. Modern design was accused of ignoring the needs and desires of occupants and users in pursuit of abstract ideals that had more significance among professional colleagues than among a wider public.

Modernism is a stylistic designation that takes in a broad spectrum of design; early and recent, thoughtful and dull, original and imitative. By selecting the least successful of modernist works for attack while ignoring inspired successes, hostile critics have built up a body of negative criticism to the effect that modernism is a "failure," citing the many vast housing projects of indifferent design and the monotonously dull glass tower office buildings as evidence. This criticism has at least had sufficient resonance to encourage exploration of the directions that design is to take after modernism. Possible answers to such questions are the subject of the following chapter.

20

Late Twentieth-Century Design

The urge to identify a new style or direction that may develop to replace the International Style as a theme of modernism is active among critics and historians alike. Recent work seems to have moved in several competing directions, each suggesting a possible future dominance, or some further development in another direction not yet surfaced, or as a result of amalgamation of several directions. There has also been a growth of internationalism. Neutra, Lescaze, Eliel Saarinen, Gropius, Breuer, and Mies van der Rohe brought the International Style and variations of that style to England and to America. One of Frank Lloyd Wright's most important early projects was built in Japan. After World War II, air travel, and particularly the coming of jet air travel, made movement anywhere on the globe a matter of hours. Increasing ease and speed of communication have made awareness of design throughout the world readily available through magazines and books. As a result of these developments, design work has become a truly international profession.

Prophets of Future Design

Two examples of this internationalism can serve to make this point. Louis I. Kahn (1901–74) is an internationally known and admired figure, little known until the 1940s and 1950s when reputations began to develop quickly and dramatically through printed communication. Cesar Pelli (born 1926) is still in active practice with work on both sides of the globe. Both are architects whose work has a special concern for interior space; both are hard to classify as proponents of any particular stylistic direction.

Kahn

Kahn was born in Estonia, graduated from the architectural school of the University of Pennsylvania in 1924, and then worked as a draftsman and designer in a number of architectural offices. In 1941 he joined George Howe in

20.1 (*below*) Louis I. Kahn, First Unitarian Church and School, Rochester, New York, 1959–69.

The austerity of the interior is relieved by the daylight that enters at each of the four corners of the room from windows above the ceiling, which are not readily visible from normal seating or standing positions. Color comes from the woven tapestry panels on the side walls, the work of Jack Lenor Larsen.

20.2 (*opposite*) Cesar Pelli, Winter Garden, World Financial Center, Battery Park City, New York, 1980–8.

With its obvious echoes of London's Crystal Palace of 1851, this structure offers a huge space that can be used for concerts, exhibitions, and other special events. When not so used, it forms an atrium circulation space, from which there is access to surrounding shops. Color comes from floor patterns, painted columns, and the green of trees.

20.3 Louis I. Kahn, Center for British Art, Yale University, New Haven, Connecticut, 1969-74.

A door opens into the round stair enclosure of brick which houses steps connecting the floors of this museum. Daylight enters the stair well from above contrasting with the subdued lighting focused on art works. The colors are warm tones of wood and masonry materials.

architectural practice. After beginning teaching at Yale in 1947 he became better known within the design professions as an outstanding theorist-philosopher than for his executed work. His first important building was an art gallery for Yale University (1951–3). The gallery floors are open spaces made special by ceilings formed by triangular coffers of concrete structural slabs. There are four levels connected by an elevator and stairs housed in a cylindrical enclosure.

The Yale Art Gallery was followed by the even more striking Richards Medical Research Laboratories (1957–61) at the University of Pennsylvania in Philadelphia. Here Kahn developed a concept of separation between what he called "serving spaces" and "served spaces." The serving spaces are tower-like enclosures that stand outside of the larger laboratory spaces that they serve, with stairs, ducts, plumbing, and similar utilities. The serving towers are windowless and of brick, while the laboratories are arranged on five floors of pavilion-like units with glass walls and concrete-framed structure. The external forms of the building were unlike any modern work previously built and, although the resultant interiors are of generally utilitarian character, this building made Kahn a major figure in American architecture.

Kahn was deeply concerned with expression of materials and with the ways in which light reveals form and creates the nature of interior spaces. The Unitarian church at Rochester, New York (1959–69), is a cluster of multipurpose rooms surrounding a central church sanctuary where light enters from windows high up on roof projections (**fig. 20.1**). The windows cannot be seen from most positions within the church—the light seems to enter from mysteriously invisible sources. With its simple, grey masonry walls the space is austere, but it is enlivened by brightly colored fabric tapestry hangings by Jack Lenor Larsen. The effects of light in relation to the limited color create an atmosphere that is powerfully moving.

As his reputation grew, Kahn's practice became international. The Indian Institute of Management at Ahmedabad, India (1962–74), and the new Capitol of Bangladesh at Dhaka (1962–83) are some of Kahn's most impressive works. In each, masonry forms are penetrated by openings planned to create interiors where a constant play of light modulates the interior space. The National Assembly building at Dhaka is a cluster of cylindrical and rectangular masonry units with round and triangular openings into interior spaces. They surround a central assembly chamber with a vault-like roof and high clerestory windows.

In the United States, a library for the Phillips Exeter Academy at Exeter, New Hampshire (1965–72), has stacks arranged on balcony floors that surround a central atrium looked into through huge circular openings. Light comes from skylights above the atrium. The Yale Center for British Art at New Haven, Connecticut (**fig. 20.3**; 1969–74), provides gallery space on levels surrounding two skylit courts. The Kimball Art Museum at Fort

Worth, Texas (1966–72), is a single-story building, a kind of pavilion made up of parallel concrete vaulted elements where light is led in from hidden sources at the top of each vault. Artificial light comes from the same locations as daylight. As a teacher, Kahn tended to speak in mystical phrases about form, light, and materials that had a fascination for his students and, ultimately, for the design professions that came to regard him as a prophet and leader.

Pelli

Cesar Pelli, born in Argentina, is a far more worldly figure—a maker of gigantic projects where interiors seem to be a by-product of massive building structures. In 1972 he designed the U.S. Embassy in Tokyo, a rectilinear mass clad in mirror glass and aluminum. In 1984 he was the architect for work at the Museum of Modern Art in New York, adding an adjacent apartment tower and extending the original museum building with a glass-enclosed atrium-like space that houses escalators connecting the exhibit floors. At the World Financial Center at Battery Park City in New York, Pelli designed a group of similar tower buildings. The interior of the Winter Garden (**fig. 20.2**; 1980–8) suggests the famous Crystal Palace of 1851 (see p. 190).

The 1995 NTT building in Tokyo by Cesar Pelli is made up of a thirty-story tower, basically triangular but with a curved hypotenuse, giving typical office floors light and view out over the adjacent plaza and small service building. Workplaces are fully computerized as are the building management (power and security) systems. The public entrance lobby at plaza level is marble floored and has a ceiling of perforated aluminum plate. A curving open stair to the mezzanine level above provides a visual accent.

The twin towers of Pelli's Petronas Center in Kuala Lumpur, Malaysia (1998), are the tallest buildings in the world. They house, at base level, a variety of lobby and shopping atrium spaces; upper levels form balconies surrounding open areas, one topped with a flat dome. The works of Kahn, with their introspective sense of restraint, and of Pelli with their exuberant excesses form an interesting contrast, but both defy classification as representative of any recognizable emerging style or school.

The long domination of the established norms of modernism has invited a mannerist era of explo-

ration and experiment. These experiments can be viewed as falling into a number of competing categories, each of which has developed a popular title. They are: hi-tech, post-modernism (incorporating a revival of tradition), late modernism, and deconstructivism.

Hi-tech

The modern movement viewed new technology (steel, concrete, and glass) as one of its prime bases. In recent years technology has made vast forward steps, particularly the technology associated with aircraft, with space exploration and the associated advances in communication and, most recently, computers. The popular term given to design based on advanced technology is Hi-tech. The designers of hi-tech projects point to the reality that more than 50 percent of the cost of any modern project is generated by the systems that provide electrical, telephone, plumbing, and air quality services. When basic structure and mechanical transport (elevators, escalators, and moving sidewalks) are added, technology can be seen as the dominating portion of any building or interior. The decision to make these systems visually apparent and to maximize their impact leads to the special quality of hi-tech design.

Fuller

Even before this way of thinking took on a name, it was the basis of the work of Richard Buckminster Fuller (1895–1983), the American engineer-designer-inventor-philosopher whose activities became known as far back as the 1920s. Fuller was the inventor-designer of many projects that were usually called "futuristic" and therefore not implemented beyond the few prototypes that he could manage to build. He coined the word Dymaxion (made up of "dynamic" and "maximum") to identify such projects as his Dymaxion house of 1927, its elevated living floor cable suspended from a central mast. The Dymaxion three-wheeled automobile of 1933 followed, as did a factory-made, prefabricated bathroom in which the fixtures and plumbing were an integral part of a unit that could be shipped to a site completely assembled. Although each of Fuller's projects attracted interest, none came to the mass-production realization that he had visualized. However, his devel-

20.4 (*right*) Richard Buckminster Fuller, United States Exhibit Pavilion, Expo 67, Montreal, 1967.

A partial sphere constructed with the geometry of Fuller's geodesic domes housed exhibits on platforms reached by escalators. The geodesic domes were hemispherical, space-frame constructions, formed from lightweight rods, joined to create hexagons. The design of the exhibition was by a company called the Cambridge Five. Automatic shutters controlled the daylight, which poured in through the plastic panels that formed the outer skin for the metal structure.

20.5 (*right*) Charles Eames, Eames House and studio, Santa Monica, California, 1949.

Better known as the designer of the Eames chair (1940–1), Eames's own house was an early example of the direction known as "hi-tech" in its use of metal and glass. Exposed open-web joists support the roof, while the exterior walls are made up of glass and solid panels in standard industrial window and structural elements. In this view of the studio, a stair leads to an upper level where the primary colors of an Eames storage unit can be seen.

opment of a geometric concept that made possible the building of hemispherical dome structures from triangulated units resulted in the geodesic dome, an idea that turned out to be workable in many different materials and at many different scales. The most spectacular use of the Geodesic dome was the U.S. exhibit pavilion at Expo 67, the World's Fair at Montreal in 1967. The huge structural dome (more than a hemisphere) was enclosed by plastic panels admitting light controlled by mechanically operated shades. The interior housed exhibits on platforms accessed by escalators, while the enclosing structure formed an independent membrane high above (**fig. 20.4**). The resulting interior was generally judged to be both dramatic and beautiful.

Rogers and Piano and the Centre Pompidou

Richard Rogers and Renzo Piano won the competition to design the Centre Pompidou early in their careers and their original design concept was informed by the architects' firm belief in freedom of space and movement:

It is our belief that buildings should be able to change not only in plan but in section and elevation. A freedom which allows people to do their own things . . . . This framework must allow people to perform freely inside and out, to change and adapt in answer to technical or client needs, this free and changing performance becoming an expression of the architecture of the building—a giant Meccano set rather than a traditional static transparent or solid doll's house. [1]

Such a design allowed the managers of the Pompidou to adapt the interior space according to the changing requirements of the programme of events, yet while the building was hugely popular with the exhibition-going public, some contemporary commentators, such as Alan Colquhoun, an architectural critic, criticized the design for not being discriminating enough:

[the design] assumes that the purpose of architecture is merely to accommodate any form of activity which may be required, and has no positive attitude to those activities. [2]

In 1999, the building underwent much needed restoration, the results of which were strongly condemned by Richard Rogers. The following letter printed in the *Architects' Journal* articulated the disappointment that Rogers and others felt at the way in which the flexibility of the original design (as well as the original paint colors) had been compromised:

The original masterly handling of the circulation which was part of the joy of the building has now been weakened, and the clarity of expression muddled. Rogers and Piano are right in deeming it a tragedy. How would Leonardo da Vinci have felt if Jacopo Blogski had repainted the face of the Mona Lisa? [3]

1 Rogers and Piano, "A Statement," quoted in Deyjan Sudjic, *Foster, Rogers and Stirling*, (London, 1986), p. 24;   2. Alan Colquhoun, *Architecural Design*, quoted in *ibid*, p. 29;   3. Letters page, *Architects' Journal*, January 20, 2000, p. 23

Charles Eames's own house built from standard industrially produced parts (see p. 346) has also often been cited as a demonstration of the way in which technologically based design could produce interior spaces of great beauty, even for residential uses (**fig. 20.5**).

Rogers and Piano

Probably the best known and most accessible of hi-tech projects is the Centre Pompidou in Paris (1971–7), a multipurpose cultural center. Its design is by the team of the Italian Renzo Piano (born 1937) and the Englishman Richard Rogers (born 1933). The large, multistory building exposes and displays its structure, mechanical systems, and vertical transport (escalators) on its exterior in a way that suggests, on the west side, the scaffolding of a building under construction, and, on the east side, the pipes and tubes of an oil refinery or chemical plant. The spaces within are equally honest in their display of overhead ductwork, lighting, and piping, the elements that are carefully concealed in most more conventional construction (**fig. 20.6**). The building has been intensely popular with the public, a mecca for tourists and Paris residents alike.

The partners went their separate ways after the Pompidou project. Piano designed the Menil Collection Museum in Houston, Texas (1981–6), its exterior structure supporting overhead louvers which continue inside to form gallery ceilings. His Galerie Beyeler Museum (1998) in Basel, Switzerland, is a work of great dignity.

Rogers's most spectacular independent project is the Lloyd's Bank office building in the financial

20.6 Renzo Piano and Richard Rogers, Centre Georges Pompidou, Paris, 1971–7.

Part of the interior space is used as a gallery, housing work from the French national art collection. The wall and ceiling panels are moveable, while the quality of the space is established by overhead patterns developed by the way in which the structural and mechanical system elements are left entirely exposed. The emphasis on the technological elements supports the Center's popular designation of "hi-tech."

20.7 (*above left*)
Richard Rogers,
Headquarters of Lloyd's
of London, 1978-86.

*The floors occupied by
office workers surround
an open atrium, where
structural columns and
a network of escalators
assert the dominance of
modern technology.*

20.8 (*above right*)
Norman Foster,
Sainsbury Centre for
the Visual Arts,
University of East
Anglia, Norwich,
England, 1976-8.

*The university building
that houses the arts
courses is a large, open
structure, into which
any element can be
inserted, moved, and
changed as circum-
stances demand. A
major part of the
building is an open
exhibition hall, seen
here. The ceiling is an
open grid, providing
lighting and other tech-
nical requirements.*

district of London (1978–86). Like the Centre Pompidou, the building carries much of its structure and mechanical systems (including elevators) on its exterior. Inside, office floors surround and overlook an enclosed central court topped by a half-cylinder glass skylight. Banks of escalators rise within the lower levels of this central space (**fig. 20.7**). The building gives a sense of being entirely of glass, structure, and services. Rogers has offices in Berlin and Tokyo and works on many international projects.

Foster

Norman Foster (born 1935) was in partnership with Richard Rogers from 1963 to 1965. Foster later became widely known with the completion of his Sainsbury Centre at the University of East Anglia at Norwich, England (1976–8). The building is an unobstructed interior space created by a tubular truss structure, a series of frames that rise on each side and cross overhead (**fig. 20.8**). At each end of its rectangular interior, a wall of glass opens to the out of doors. The side walls and roof are made up of square corrugated aluminum panels held in place by Neoprene rubber gaskets. Some glass panels and some door panels occur as

interruptions in the otherwise uniform exterior skin—all of the panels are easily interchangeable. The main, ground-level interior space is an exhibition gallery, while a second level provides for a raised common room and study area above the quarters of the school of fine art. The open space at the end of the building away from the gallery is a restaurant. The eight-foot truss structure houses services on either side of the building and overhead,. where louvers partially screen the lighting and other services. Although highly technological in concept and realization, the interior spaces give a sense of serenity and simplicity.

The office building of Willis Faber and Dumas at Ipswich, England (1970–5), was also designed by Foster's firm. Glass walls follow the form of an irregular site. An open central area inside is surrounded by two floors of offices and various services on the ground floor. Escalators within the central space connect the three floors (**fig. 20.9**) and a roof penthouse which houses a restaurant. Open planning links all of the interior to the glass perimeter and the central atrium, where the overhead structure of open trusses underlines the hi-tech character of the space. In the United States, Foster developed a fine addition to the Art Deco Joslyn Art Museum building in Omaha, Nebraska

20.9 Norman Foster, Willis–Faber–Dumas Offices, Ipswich, England, 1970–5.

A three-story office building for the insurance company has an open central atrium, in which the escalators connect the floors and introduce movement into the areas where 1300 workers are accommodated. The visible structural framing of the skylight at roof level and the aluminum strips forming ceiling panels emphasize the technological focus of the building's design. Yellow wall panels and green flooring establish a bright and colorful atmosphere.

20.11 (*opposite*)
James Stirling,
Staatsgalerie, Stuttgart,
Germany, 1977–84.

*A central courtyard—
really a room open to
the sky—forms the core
of the art gallery, which
was a modern addition
to an older museum
building. Statuary, an
arcade of stone faced
in marbles, and stubby
Tuscan columns at the
entrance point on the
left hint at a movement
toward post-modernism.
A winding ramp leads
to an upper level.*

20.10 (*below*) James
Stirling, History Faculty,
Cambridge University,
Cambridge, England,
1964–7.

*This building, largely
devoted to library func-
tions, has several floor
levels overlooking an
open atrium, which is
enclosed in glass.
Projecting enclosures
with windows allow
passers-by to look down
into the gallery space.*

(1994). In it, serene white space with a ceiling curved to trap daylight from hidden skylight sources establishes ideal gallery space for the display of modern art. Other hi-tech projects by Foster include the Law Faculty building at Cambridge, England (1995), which uses a hi-tech truss structure of half-cylindrical form as a glazed shell above multiple level platforms holding stacks and reading areas; a spectacularly tall skyscraper tower office building in Hong Kong for the Shanghai National Bank (1986); and the Sackler Galleries, a new interior inserted into a court space in the buildings of the Royal Academy in London (1991), which makes use of subtle detail to relate the classicism of the older buildings and of the art displayed there to the technically advanced new spaces.

Stirling

James Stirling (1924–92), a British architect, can be thought of as belonging to the hi-tech direction. The Engineering Building at Leicester University in England (1959, with James Gowan as a partner) attracted wide attention with its glass office tower, wedge-shaped adjacent blocks containing lecture halls, and ship's funnel-like ventilator. There is a

large, low adjacent area devoted to shop facilities. The interiors share the mechanistic qualities of the exterior, their exposed structure suggesting the engineering-related role of the building. The History Faculty building (1964–7) at Cambridge University, which is mostly devoted to a library, contains a large gallery atrium topped with glass skylight roofing. Here again the mechanics of structure set the character of the large and impressive interior space (**fig. 20.10**). As Stirling's career moved ahead, the technological emphasis of his work gradually moved toward a more complex range of values. At the Olivetti training facility at Haslemere in England (1969) interior spaces were more varied, so that a "multispace"

could be converted to accommodate meetings of varying size and character. Glazed galleries with ramp circulation paths connect elements of the building.

Stirling's last major work, the addition to the Staatsmuseum at Stuttgart, Germany (1979–84), moves away from technology and toward a more adventurous direction. Gallery spaces are set around a circular courtyard (**fig. 20.11**) where marble walls, statuary (from the museum's collection), and a portal using stubby versions of Tuscan columns make references to past architectural styles. The building is totally original, but still suggests complex relationships to art and architecture of the past. It is tempting to suggest that Stirling had moved toward the approach now called post-modern, although the building certainly retained some of the rigors of hi-tech design. The exhibition gallery spaces are restrained in form and color, while the entrance lobby, shop, circulation spaces, and restaurant use brilliant, saturated color as do many details of the exterior.

Post-modernism

The term POST-MODERN would seem to identify any work that post-dates the style now called modern but, in current use, it identifies a particular recent direction that is actually a part of the continuing development of modernism.

Venturi and Scott Brown

Robert Venturi (born 1925) developed the theoretical basis of post-modernism in his *Complexity and Contradiction in Architecture* (1966). It suggests that the devotion to simplicity and logic which was the cornerstone of the modern movement was a limitation, leading ultimately to dullness and

boredom. The book cites many examples from architectural history (Blenheim Palace, Hôtel de Maignon, Jefferson's Monticello, and Butterfield's All Saints, Margaret Street, for example) in which greatness derives instead from complexities and contradictory forms. He suggests that acceptance of such qualities can bring design into closer touch with human qualities, which are full of complexity and contradiction. It is interesting to note that Venturi uses many examples drawn from the work of the pioneer modernists, Le Corbusier and Aalto in particular, in which these masters felt free to be complex and contradictory in violation of the announced goals of modernism.

The house Venturi designed in 1964 for his mother, Vanna Venturi, at Chestnut Hill, a suburb of Philadelphia, is the first important demonstration of the ideas that characterize post-modernism (**figs. 20.12** and **20.13**). Its basic symmetry is modified by unexpected asymmetries. Interior spaces have unexpectedly angle. Its basic symmetry is modified by unexpected asymmetries. Interior spaces have unexpectedly angled forms that upset

20.12 (below) Robert Venturi, Vanna Venturi House, Philadelphia, 1964.

In this interior, the visual consequences of its unusual planning can be seen in the stair and fireplace-chimney element that constricts it. Conventional furniture contrasts with these unusual forms..

20.13 (bottom) Ground floor plan of Vanna Venturi House.

In the plan, Venturi demonstrates some of the complexities and contradictions that are central to his design thinking. Rooms have corners cut off at diagonals, a central entrance requires a sharp turn to reach the doorway, and a stairway that begins at an angle widens and is suddenly narrowed.

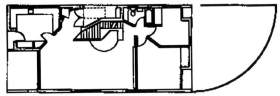

20.14 Venturi, Scott Brown Associates, Venturi House, Philadelphia, 1980s.

The Venturis occupy an older house as their home, and they have introduced into it their design idiom in which traditional and modern elements are easily mixed. The painted frieze above the picture molding, the glass and wood built-in cabinets, the hanging light fixture, and the dining room furniture all suggest this highly personal blend.

20.15 Venturi, Scott Brown Associates, Sainsbury Wing, National Gallery, London, 1986–91.

The gallery spaces in this addition to the original museum are of simple design, with the smooth walls setting off the paintings that are on display. The galleries are connected by arched openings, which create appealing vistas, drawing the visitor onward. Above, windowed clerestories admit daylight, while arched forms in ceiling coves make a transition between the arched openings and the clerestories high above.

their routine rectangularity. The furniture is traditional and nondescript rather than the modern classics that might be expected. Guild House, a residence for the elderly in Philadelphia (1960–3), and the Brandt house of 1970 in Greenwich, Connecticut, embody similar complexities.

In later unbuilt projects and actual buildings, Venturi has embraced decorative ornament and references to historic precedents. A 1997 proposal for a house in Greenwich, Connecticut, is a version of George Washington's mansion at Mount Vernon, oddly condensed and distorted. Venturi's furniture designs of 1984 for Knoll introduced both decorative pattern and references to historic precedents. A number of chairs were developed, all structurally alike—simply two elements of molded plywood, one the seat and front legs, the other the back and rear legs. A variety of versions were generated by cutting out the plywood planes in decorative forms reminiscent of Chippendale, Queen Anne, Sheraton, and Art Deco. The surfaces of some are silk-screened with playful, decorative designs suggestive of conventional wallpapers, while others have patterns in bright color. A sofa of exaggeratedly over-stuffed proportions is covered

in a flowery tapestry textile. In their own home, Venturi and Denise Scott Brown (his partner and wife) have used traditional furniture and decorative patterns in wallpapers to generate an atmosphere that is both eclectic (in the literal sense) and comfortable (**fig. 20.14**).

As his career advanced, Venturi began to receive commissions for major architectural projects in which his interiors generally showed the whimsical and contradictory qualities of post-modernism. A faculty dining room at Penn State University, State College, Pennsylvania (1974), has screen walls with decorative perforations, a truncated arched opening on a balcony, and an ornamental lighting fixture overlooking the sedate dining room with chairs of traditional design.

Venturi and Scott Brown added the outstanding Sainsbury Wing (1986–91) to the 1835 National Gallery on Trafalgar Square in London. Externally, the classical detail of the older building is repeated in the form of variations on its theme. Openings lead to a monumental stair with arch-shaped metal frames overhead. The stair gives access to lower levels housing an auditorium, restaurant, shop, and other facilities. At the top of the stair a bridge link element connects with the older building. The stair and the bridge give alternative access to the main galleries, sixteen rooms connected by arched openings, some edged by stubby versions of Tuscan columns. The galleries (**fig. 20.15**) are sufficiently simple in character to form ideal settings for the painting on display, but the subtle details of moldings and columns offer a reminder of the unique nature of the building's design. The more recent museum in Seattle, Washington, follows many of the same conceptual patterns on a more modest scale.

Graves

Michael Graves (born 1934) began his professional career working in a modernist direction together with four other New York architects. They became known as The New York Five, or the Whites for their devotion to that color in all their works. Graves pulled away from this group, however, and moved in a more post-modern direction, embracing decorative details, strong color, and forms that might seem arbitrary and even eccentric. His 1978 design for the Kalko house (unbuilt) shows a house that is basically symmetrical but its two sides do not match. A stair, too narrow to

20.16 Michael Graves, furniture showroom, Houston, Texas, 1980.

Graves's use of such unexpected elements as the paired columns supporting blocky capitals that support indirect lighting units and his use of a palette of strong secondary colors supports the view that such an interior is post-modernist. The showroom for the Sunar Furniture Company offers visitors visual entertainment together with a display of furniture designed by, among others, Massimo Vignelli and Graves himself.

20.17 Michael Graves, Public Services Building, Portland, Oregon, 1980–3.

The exterior design of the Portland building provoked a shocked reaction among many critics, but the interiors are, in comparison, quite conservative. Only the colors, the capital-like lighting units above the mezzanine level, and the upper wall and ceiling lighting units suggest the qualities of post-modernism.

climb and with steps too high for any but giants, moves up one side of the facade, while a pergola ornaments the other side.

Graves interiors appear in several showrooms designed for the Sunar Furniture Company in 1979 (**fig. 20.16**). A complex of chambers with unusual forms and pastel and strong colors provided settings for furniture, including some examples of Graves's own design. His growing reputation as the foremost proponent of post-modernism was dramatically advanced when he won a competition in 1980 for a city office building for Portland, Oregon. The building is a massive cubical block, but its varied surface treatment with projecting wedge-shaped elements, changes in surface material and window shapes, and its bands of ribbon-like decoration shocked the established architectural profession. One critic asserted that it had "set American architecture back by fifty years." The interiors of the building are largely unremarkable, although the main entrance lobby is an essay in the eccentric vocabulary of post-modernism (**fig. 20.17**). Graves's San Juan Capistrano Library (1980) is a low building with a central courtyard using clerestories and exterior pavilions to modulate light entering quietly detailed reading areas. A winery, Clos Pegase at Calistoga, in the Napa Valley, California (1984), explores post-modernism by hinting at the design of the eighteenth-century French Neoclassicist Ledoux.

Two hotels for the Walt Disney World at Buena Vista, Florida—the Swan and the Dolphin (1990)—are huge masses each sporting sculptural ornaments on roof tops. They have offered Graves the opportunity to design interiors with flamboyantly eccentric forms and colors. The Disney connection with entertainment has provoked a design that is playful, even foolish, in a way that flaunts a disregard for what is usually thought of as "taste." Graves has also designed offices for Disney and a Paris Disney project in much the same vein. These buildings and their interiors are a source of amazement and delight to the public. Such design is always at the border of "kitsch," that is, design that is deliberately foolish and tasteless in an effort to reflect the human appetite for mischief.

The determination of post-modernism to escape from logic and order may be a reflection of a modern world in which logic seems to have disappeared into the excesses of the affluent 1980s and 1990s. Eccentricity and tastelessness have become tools of design, and the garish and the banal are seen as legitimate means of communication with a population whose ideas come from the entertainments offered by television, film, and the cults of celebrities. Graves has also designed a large number of major projects in Japan. At tiny scale, his designs for a tea kettle, scarves, and kitchen tools bring his work to a large public of fashion-oriented shoppers.

Johnson

Philip Johnson, once a modernist in the manner of Mies van der Rohe, seemed to have joined the post-modernists when his New York skyscraper headquarters office building for A.T.& T. (1978–83) was topped by a whimsical motif thought to be based on the pediments that topped Chippendale bookcases. The entrance is through a vast arch-form portal which leads into a marble lobby with details that suggest a medieval monastery (**fig. 20.19**). In

20.18 Sottsass Associati, Museum of Contemporary Furniture, Ravenna, Italy, 1994.

Simple geometric shapes combine with strong colors to create visual surprises that are used to generate interior space in the spirit of the Memphis design movement. The openings in rectangular and arched forms produce changing patterns of sunlight, which contribute to the surprisingly calm overall impression.

the center is the gilded statue that once topped the old A.T.&T. building in downtown New York. The majestic claims of a giant corporation appear to be interpreted ironically in whimsical and decorative terms.

Post-modernism in Europe

In Europe the claims of modernism encountered a major challenge in the work of the Milan-based group that took the name Memphis in 1981. Ettore Sottsass (born 1917), the leader of the group, along with his associates Andrea Branzi, Aldo Cibis, Marco Zanuso, and others, broke away from mainline modernism by designing furniture, textiles, and decorative objects of deliberate eccentricity and playfulness. Bright color, decorative surface pattern, and shapes that have little reference to function are characteristics of Memphis design. Michael Graves provided a dressing table design for Memphis in 1981. Its stepped forms, strong color, and pinnacle top relate clearly to such designs as Sottsass's Casablanca sideboard and Cariton bookcase (1981) with their bright colors and angular shapes.

Sottsass's firm, Sottsass Associati, created a new gallery for the Museum of Contemporary Furniture in Ravenna (1994). The resulting spaces, enclosed gallery, portico, and open courtyard use simple rectangular and arch-shaped openings that generate spatial complexity accented by bright color (**fig. 20.18**). The fantasy of Memphis can be traced here in the perspective illusions of wall painting, while a tranquil serenity dominates the spaces intended for "open studio" gatherings of artists.

Hans Hollein (born 1934) was the designer of a remarkable post-modernist interior in 1978, the Austrian Travel Bureau office in Vienna (**fig.**

20.19 Philip Johnson, A.T.& T. (now Sony Plaza) Building, New York, 1978-83.

The ground-floor entrance lobby of this building, a modern skyscraper, introduces such surprises as arched and vaulted spaces, with columns reminiscent of a Romanesque cloister in front of paneled elevator doors, a geometrically patterned marble floor, and, on a central pedestal (to the right of the photograph), a gilded statue of a winged male figure. The shadow of the statue flickers on the wall in this view. Johnson's design is not altogether surprising when it is remembered that he had long since abandoned Mies van der Rohe's precepts.

20.20 Hans Hollein, Austrian Travel Bureau Office, Vienna, 1978.

Decorative elements are meant to suggest possible destinations for travel. The green floor and skylight form a setting for metal palm trees representing tropical destinations; a fragment of a column evokes Greece or Rome.

20.20). Its toy-like elements are intended to symbolize travel to various regions—a column fragment to suggest Greece and Rome, a garden kiosk pavilion, and, most obvious, metal palm trees to suggest exotic tropical and desert destinations. A floor in pale green patterns and a glass skylight ceiling create a restrained setting for the elements of fantasy.

The Revival of Tradition

Along with the fantasy and freedom of post-modernism, another, related development is the appearance of a return to classicism—not the accurate reproduction of past design that characterized the eclecticism of the 1920s and 1930s, but an effort to produce new work on the basis of classic principles. Palladian design ideals, the classic orders, columns, and pediments reappear in such work not as playful inserts, but in literal quotations from history used as a basis for new design.

Greenberg

The most extreme form of this new Neoclassicism appears in the work of Allan Greenberg (born 1938). His design for a large house for a horse farm in Connecticut (1979) takes the scheme of Washington's Mount Vernon, enlarges it, and corrects the "errors" present in the original design (**fig. 20.21**). The columns of the original veranda have become paired columns and all minor irregularities have been eliminated. His courthouse for Manchester, Connecticut (1978–80), could easily be mistaken for an eclectic design of the 1930s.

Stern

Robert A. M. Stern (born 1939) is usually thought of as a post-modernist although most of his work stands in a position somewhere between the adventurousness of the post-modernists and the constraints of classic revivalism. In interiors Stern focuses on small details that look back to strict clas-

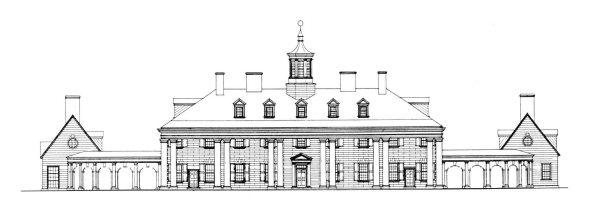

20.21 Allan Greenberg, farm house, Connecticut, 1979.

The drawing shows a design for a house based on George Washington's eighteenth-century mansion in Virginia. A proposal by Robert Venturi in 1997 had a similar theme: the condensation of the famous house into a post-modernist fantasy. In Greenberg's design, however, the house is not condensed but, if anything, expanded, with the veranda columns made into six paired twins in place of Washington's eight single columns.

sicism and forward toward post-modern variants. Much of his work has been residential, including city apartments and country houses. In both, logical planning creates rooms that have a strongly traditional flavor, although details are often given enlarged and exaggerated form. Country "villas" suggest the eclectic work of Stanford White or Edwin Lutyens recast in contemporary terms. Pediments, domes, classically inspired columns, urns, and other details place his interiors for office buildings, hotels, and other large projects between revivalism and post-modernism.

Stern's Disney Yacht and Beach Club Resorts at Buena Vista, Florida (1987–91), close to Graves's hotels, form a virtual village of large buildings suggestive of resort hotels of the nineteenth century. Interiors are richly ornamental without slipping into excess. Disney projects tend toward flamboyance. The Feature Animation Building at Burbank, California (1991–4), and the Casting Center at Lake Buena Vista, Florida (1987–9), are both filled with colorful decorative detail. In France, at Villiers-sur-Marne, a visitors' center for Euro Disney (1990) exhibits the playfulness of an amusement park. In contrast, the interiors of the Columbus Indiana Regional Hospital (**fig. 20.22**; 1988–96) resemble early Frank Lloyd Wright in their extensive use of brick and natural wood in warm colors. Stern's international practice includes projects in the Netherlands and in Japan.

20.22 Robert Stern, Columbus Indiana Regional Hospital, 1988-96.

Materials in warm color tones generate an atmosphere of calm in this public space of a large hospital complex.

20.23 I. M. Pei, East Wing, National Gallery of Art, Washington, D.C., 1968–78.

An atrium space leads to exhibition galleries on several levels. The plan of the building, based on triangular forms, makes for complex, interesting spatial relationships. Balconies overlook the atrium, where a skylight roof floods the space with light. The color scheme is neutral but is enlivened by the bright red of the mobile by Alexander Calder (1898–1976).

20.24 I. M. Pei, Pyramid, Louvre Museum, Paris, 1983–9.

The public space acts as a new entrance to the many traditional spaces that make up the famous museum. Although it inspired much doubt and controversy, the glass and metal structure has come to be recognized as a great success. Glimpses of the surrounding Renaissance architecture are set off by the pyramidal geometry and the flow of the great winding stair that leads to the lower level entrance concourse.

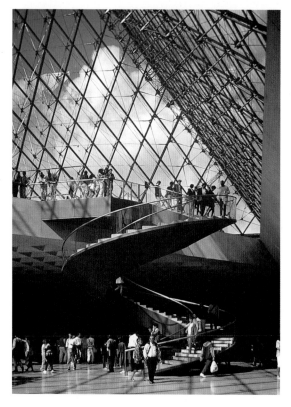

Late Modernism

An alternative theme in recent design rejects the characteristics of post-modernism in favor of continuing loyalty to the concepts of earlier modernism. LATE MODERNISM describes work that does not imitate that of the modern pioneers, but that moves ahead in ways that they might have been expected to develop if they were still active.

Pei

The work of I. M. Pei (see p. 342) can, as his career moved onward, be thought of as late modernism. The County Library at Columbus, Indiana (1963–9), is a simple rectangular block of brick with asymmetrically placed areas of glass at the entrance. Inside, a balcony level overlooks the main reading area where natural colors of materials and simple forms generate a sense of calm and order. An addition to the Des Moines Art Center (1966–8), Iowa, has strong geometric forms that create a simple setting for sculpture and painting in the gallery spaces.

In the Municipal Center (City Hall) Dallas, Texas (1977), the vast public space flooded with natural light is overlooked by balconies that give access to the various city offices. The concrete surfaces of a warm beige color are surprisingly pleasant despite their vast areas; it is one of the most successful of American governmental public buildings. Another Pei project, well known and well liked by its public, is the East Building added to John Russell Pope's older eclectic classical main building of the National Gallery in Washington, D.C. (**fig. 20.23**; 1968–78). The building is based on triangular forms that dominate the main atrium space; the skylight roof is formed by a triangular structural grid. Balconies on several levels overlook the main open space and give access to galleries and other secondary spaces on seven levels. A giant mobile by Alexander Calder introduces brilliant red color into the otherwise neutral tonality of the space established by its marble wall surfaces.

Glass and steel also form the structure of the huge exhibition areas of the Javits Convention Center in New York (1979–86). The building recalls the Crystal Palace of 1851 with its glassy overhead grid braced with triangulation along its edges. Triangulation is a central theme for the pyramid structure in the court of the Louvre in Paris (1983–9). The steel and glass pyramid forms a new entrance to the Louvre, giving access to stairs and an elevator leading to a vast lower concourse that acts as an entrance foyer and location for shops, exhibits, and a café (**fig. 20.24**). Although the introduction of the modern structure into the court of the historic Louvre raised much controversy, the completed project has come to be recognized as a major success. Pei's firm became I. M. Pei and Partners, and then Pei, Cobb, Freed, and Partners as the important roles of Henry Cobb and James Freed became recognized. The Myerson Symphony Hall by Pei, Cobb, Freed, and Partners

20.25 Charles Gwathmey, De Menil House, East Hampton, New York, 1983.

A double height living room has an overlooking balcony and seating area facing a fireplace. The mounted trophy is a favorite possession of the owner.

in Dallas, Texas (1982–9), is an extraordinary success both in the visual qualities of its main hall with its rich, warm wood and brass tones and in its acoustical excellence. The firm has been responsible for a huge number of major projects, with international representation in Singapore, Hong Kong, Japan, and China.

Gwathmey and Meier

Charles Gwathmey (born 1938) and Richard Meier (born 1934) were both associated with the New York Five, but both have moved to practices producing work that adheres to the modernist themes of simplicity, geometric form, and total absence of decorative detail. Gwathmey designed a small house for his parents at Amagansett on Long Island, New York (1966). Its abstract, geometric forms suggest the work of Le Corbusier. Now in partnership with Robert Siegel, the firm has produced work that ranges from the residential (the Cogan house of 1972 at East Hampton, for example, or the De Menil house of 1983, also at East Hampton; **fig. 20.25**, p. 365) to increasingly major works. The addition to Whig Hall at Princeton University at Princeton, New Jersey (1970–2), is, in effect, a late modern building inserted within the shell of the preexisting 1893 classical structure which had suffered fire damage.

The Shezan restaurant interior in New York (1976) uses glass block walls and a gleaming metal ceiling along with Breuer Cesca chairs to generate a room related to the modernism of the 1930s. Gwathmey's addition to Wright's Guggenheim Museum in New York is, like many of his office interior projects, late modernist in style. The Sony takeover of the former A.T.&T. building in New York gave the Gwathmey and Siegel firm an opportunity to generate such spectacular interiors as the "sky lounge" reception area, its simple furniture in a setting of travertine marble dominated by a brilliantly colorful wall fresco.

In 1996, Gwathmey Siegel inserted into an older former department store building a new Science, Industry, and Business Library for the New York Public Library. The entrance at street level gives access to a lower-level lobby by elevator and an open stair. Original columns, now encased in green surfacing, emphasize the height of the space. Electronic signage provides directions, many stations are fully computer-equipped, while all 500 reading desks provide connective sockets for portable computers. Five levels of stacks above the lobby level occupy floors of the old store.

The work of Richard Meier has gradually moved from the complex late modernist geometry of early residential projects, such as the Smith house (1965) at Darien, Connecticut, the Saltzman house (1967–9) at East Hampton, New York, and the Douglas house (1971–3) at Harbor Springs, Michigan, to increasingly complex large projects, such as the Atheneum at New Harmony, Indiana (1975–9), and the Hartford Seminary at Hartford, Connecticut (1978–81). In the Bronx Development Center in New York (1973–7), a four-story cluster around a central court, the usual white walls have been abandoned in favor of aluminum surfaces with rounded corners. The Getty Center in Los Angeles (1984–98), claimed to be the largest building complex of the twentieth century, is almost a village of separate units with a variety of classically conservative interior spaces.

20.26 Richard Meier, Stadhaus, Ulm, Germany, 1993.

A complex arrangement of interior spaces with smooth white surfaces forms a contrast with the medieval cathedral nearby.

Meier's practice has become international with projects in Germany, the Netherlands, Spain, and France. The Stadhaus (town hall) at Ulm, Germany (1993), is a complex building woven into spaces in the old city. It stands in a plaza, its curving, white forms creating a striking contrast with the medieval cathedral tower opposite. Open space is threaded into the center of the building, giving access to offices and public spaces, including gallery spaces, on a top floor (**fig. 20.26**). The interior is flooded with light from triangular gabled skylights that offer glimpses of the cathedral tower, maintaining contact between the ancient and the modern building.

Individual Stylists

Starck

Some late twentieth-century work of great interest does not fit any of the stylistic designations that critics like to use. Philippe Starck (born 1949) first became known as a furniture designer, but his work has moved onward to interiors and architectural projects that are often flamboyant and exotic.

Starck's furniture designs often use plastic and metal parts in unexpected combinations, and similarly unexpected mixes of cubistic straight-line and flowing curved forms. The cast aluminum three-legged stool of 1990, with its tiny seat on tapered flowing legs, can be viewed as more sculpture than functional object. The whimsical nature of Starck's chair designs is emphasized by the names he gives them (Lord Yo, Dr. No, Miss Trip, and Prince Aha). As an industrial designer, Starck has produced toothbrushes, an orange juice squeezer, and other objects, all more sculptural than practical. In interior design, Starck has been similarly unpredictable. The Café Costes in Paris (1987; no longer in existence) was dominated by a staircase that widened as it ascended, facing a gigantic wall clock at its top (**fig. 20.27**). Fantasy elements appear in his designs for restaurants, nightclubs, and hotel interiors.

The Royalton Hotel in New York (1988) has a large two-level lobby with a blue carpet with a calligraphic pattern in white along one edge defining the main circulation path, while a zone at one side is filled with groupings of Starck's erratic furniture. At New York's Paramount Hotel (1995) a double-height lobby houses a dramatic stair that also starts narrow and widens as it rises. Starck's selection of

20.27 Philippe Starck, Café Costes, Paris, 1987 (no longer in existence).

Shades of apricot and olive and the giant clock at the head of the tapering stair demonstrate the post-modernist acceptance of unconventional, often fantastic elements.

367

20.28 (*right*) Philippe Starck, Paramount Hotel, New York, 1995.

In this hotel guest room the floor is carpeted in black with squares of grey. All walls, ceiling, and furniture are white, allowing the large framed reproduction picture to dominate the room.

20.29 (*far right*) Philippe Starck, Asahi Building, Tokyo, 1994.

A tapering stairway with adjacent sculptural forms and lighting aimed upward from floor level generate a mood of futuristic fantasy in this public space within the Asahi office building.

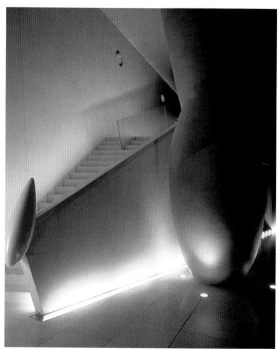

post-modern furniture is arranged in groups on a carpet of large squares placed diagonally on a marble floor. Bedrooms are dominated by a massive framed reproduction of a detail from a Vermeer painting forming a headboard for the bed, while typically curious Starck furniture rests on a carpet of two-toned checkerboard squares (**fig. 20.28**). The bathroom washbasins are round stainless steel bowls fitted to the top of a stainless cone that tapers to a point at floor level.

Starck demonstrated his approach to a tall building with the Asahi building in Tokyo (**fig. 20.29**). An exterior of reflective glass covers a tapering block form; on top, a gigantic gilded sculptural form is described by Starck as a "flame." In the ground-level café, an angled mezzanine, a slanting wall, and twisting sculptural columns form a setting for Starck furniture in bright red. The adjacent bathrooms use glass and marble in unexpected ways; the men's urinals are golden vertical half-cylinders, the women's room is an essay in fine marbles and glass.

Putman

Like Starck, Andrée Putman (born 1925) maintains an international practice. From 1978 to 1997 she headed Ecart International and she now runs her own firm. Ecart began producing early modern furniture classics including those of Eileen Gray

and Mallet-Stevens. She has now also designed a number of offices, showrooms, and shops around the world. The showrooms and offices of Ecart are outstanding examples of her approach, which relates the simplicity of early modernism to restrained decorative detail and quiet colors. In 1988 she designed new office interiors for the Villa Turque (**fig. 20.30**) in Chaux-de-Fonds, an early work of Le Corbusier.

Putman's museum interiors in older buildings in Bordeaux and Rouen adjust simple details to existing spaces, such as the magnificent stone vaulting of the Bordeaux building (**fig. 20.31**). Club, hotel, and restaurant interiors in Kawaguchiko-Cho and in Kobe, Japan, in Monaco and Seville and many shops and private apartments in England, France, and the United States follow the same patterns of quiet serenity, often combining elements of an existing space with furniture of the early modern era and, occasionally, antiques. The Wasserturm Hotel in Cologne (1990) is fitted into a gigantic water tower built in the nineteenth century and preserved as a historic monument. The round form of the tower and its massive brick construction generate spaces that Putman has put to good use with thoughtfully related interior detail. In New York, interiors for the Morgans Hotel (1984) and the elegantly simple jewelry shop for Ebel (1989) are fine examples of her work.

Deconstructivism

The term DECONSTRUCTIVISM has come into use to identify a strain of design practice that emerged in work of the 1980s and 1990s. The term was given legitimacy with a Museum of Modern Art New York exhibition in 1988 organized by Philip Johnson and Mark Wigley. Drawings and models of unbuilt works in which broken up, loosely assembled parts, and elements seemingly torn apart and reassembled in chaos were typical. The term itself refers both to the works of the Russian constructivists Tatlin, Malevich, and Rodchenko, who often focused on assembly of broken fragments, and to deconstructionism, a significant theme in French philosophy and literary criticism which aims to break up the elements of any text into its components in an effort to reveal meaning not apparent on the surface of its narratives. Application of such theory to design stretches the concept of a text to include any built reality.

The projects that Johnson and Wigley selected for the MOMA exhibition included the Park at La Villette in Paris (**fig. 20.32**; 1982–5), in which Bernard Tschumi (born 1944) placed small pavil-

20.30 (*left*) Andrée Putman, interiors at Villa Turque, Chaux-de-Fonds, Switzerland, 1988.

The 1916–17 villa by Le Corbusier (see p. 278) became an office facility for an advertising firm in 1988, and it was decided that the interiors required total renovation while the character of the historically important early modern work was preserved. A sitting room area is viewed here from the upper floor level. The high window facing a garden is original, but now has Roman blinds of net and silk. The two dark chairs are Transat chairs, from 1927, by Eileen Gray, who had exhibited with Le Corbusier at the Paris Exhibition in 1937.

20.31 Andrée Putman, Musée d'Art Contemporain, Bordeaux, France, 1984.

The old Lainé warehouse for spices, originally built in 1824, was converted to accommodate offices and a museum of modern art to house the city's collection of the Centre d'Arts Plastiques Contemporains (CAPC). The brick and masonry arches of the old building and the wooden roof that they support have been carefully preserved. The restaurant space is dominated by the circular weaving used as a wall hanging. Metal frames hold woven seat and back surfaces of the Topacio chairs by Ecart.

20.32 Bernard
Tschumi, Exhibition
Building, Parc de la
Villette, Paris, 1982–5.

*This is one of a number
of structures distributed
through the large Park.
A ramp leads to an
upper level accessible
to the public. Red and
blue elements enliven
the mostly white
interior.*

20.33 Peter
Eisenman, Miller House
(House III), Lakeville,
Connecticut, 1970.

*Intersecting cubes
generate a complex
geometry, which is
emphasized by the all-
white paint. Only the
natural wood of the
flooring and the distant
glimpse of outdoor
greenery contrast with
the white architectural
elements.*

ions, all formed from basic cubes deconstructed
into complex geometric realities, painted bright red
and placed according to a geometric grid in an
open park. These pavilions have various functions—a café, a children's play space, a viewing
platform—so that most can be entered, making it
possible to see their cut-away forms from within.
Several larger building units contain complex
elements in intricate relationships that can seem
accidental. Tschumi has become the dean of the
architectural school at Columbia University in
New York. For Columbia, he has designed a
student center, Lerner Hall, where long glass ramps
cross through a glass-walled atrium facing into the
college main campus.

Eisenman

Peter Eisenman (born 1932), first known as one of
the New York Five, has developed work in terms of
complex deconstructivist geometry. A series of
houses of his design (given Roman numeral identification) use grid plans, with several grids overlapping. White remains the color inside and out. The
Miller House (House III) at Lakeville, Connecticut

(1970), is developed from the forms of two cubes that intersect and overlap in collision, one at a 45 degree angle to the other. The resulting interior space is an abstract study in rectilinear sculptural forms, all in white (**fig. 20.33**). Some simple furniture accommodates the realities of the occupants' lives. In the Museum of Modern Art exhibit, Eisenman was represented by drawings and models showing a building called The Biocenter for the University of Frankfurt, Germany. A long spine circulation path penetrates and connects a series of laboratory blocks, each a small building in itself. The sense of elements torn apart and then loosely recombined is typical of the deconstructivist direction.

In the Wexner Center for the Visual Arts for Ohio State University at Columbus, Ohio (1985–9), Eisenman again used a long spinal passage to tie together in a loose relationship a series of units including, at the main entrance point, some curved tower-like units. An all-interior Eisenman project was an exhibition of his work called Cities of Artificial Excavation, organized by the Canadian Centre for Architecture and installed in their existing museum building in Montreal, Canada (**fig. 20.34**; 1994). The exhibit inserts into the conventional older building new galleries designed on the basis of overlapping Greek cross forms. The four arms use strong colors to identify the separate themes of the projects that they house. Green stands for Long Beach, California, rose for Berlin, blue for Paris, and gold for Venice. The complex forms and strong colors make the installation the most important element of the display.

Gehry

Despite his disclaimer of a deconstructivist identity, Frank Gehry (born 1929) has become the best-known practitioner working in this idiom. He first attracted attention with an unconventional renovation of his own modest suburban house in Los Angeles (1978–88). Elements appear to have been torn away and then attached to the house exterior in arrangements that imply chance collisions. In this house and in other residential projects in the Los Angeles area, Gehry has brought the seemingly random and chaotic interplay of common materials and colors inside (**fig. 20.35**). As major projects have come to Gehry, he has moved toward a vocabulary of complex, curving forms that seem in collision externally and that produce interior space of unusual variety. The Vitra Museum at Weil-am-Rhein, Germany (1990), is such an assembly of white boxes of varied shape coming together at unexpected angles. Internally, the complex provides spaces suitable to the display of modern chairs and other objects from the Vitra collection. The American Center in Paris (1991–4) juxtaposes similarly complex forms with masses of more conventional character to express the varied functions for which the building was planned.

The Frederick R. Weisman Art Museum in Minneapolis, Minnesota (1994), combines a simple, almost conventional gallery plan with complex curving skylight forms and an entrance area of amazing complexity, emphasized externally by its cladding in gleaming stainless steel. The gallery spaces are simple, white-walled rooms at eye level, but become startling overhead where great truss forms (all in white) and curving skylights challenge the simplicity of the plan.

Gehry's Guggenheim Museum in Bilbao, Spain (1998), applies the concepts of the Weisman Museum to the total mass of the building, a complex of forms all wrapped in gleaming titanium metal. The internal spaces reflect the external forms in their intricate and varied forms (**fig.**

20.34 Peter Eisenman, exhibit installation, Canadian Centre for Architecture, Montreal, 1994.

In this exhibition, which was devoted to his own work and was entitled "Cities of Artificial Excavation," Eisenman retreated from his customary practice of using white to introduce strong color. Each color identifies the location of the projects on display. The green, for example, relates to design for projects intended for Long Beach, California.

20.35 Frank Gehry, Gehry House, Los Angeles, 1978–88.

In the kitchen of his remodeled suburban house, Gehry demonstrated his enthusiasm for elements that appear to have been torn apart, tossed about, and reassembled in surprising relationships. Although the working level of the kitchen is quite functional, the skylight elements above justify the term deconstructivism.

20.36 Frank Gehry, Guggenheim Museum, Bilbao, Spain, 1998.

The complex, titanium-wrapped exterior forms of the museum house similarly complex spatial relationships. Walls slope, overlap, and curve, leaving only the flat floor plane as a reference to familiar patterns of architectural geometry.

20.36). The development of complex and curving spatial volumes has always been limited in the past by the practical problems of making drawings and engineering calculations, as well as by the cutting and assembly of actual building materials in ways that depart from the basic geometry of orthogonal shapes. Gehry has exploited the potential of computer-aided design to make freer forms possible.

Gehry is also interested in furniture design. In 1972, he introduced a group of furniture products made from corrugated cardboard, laminated to form wide slabs several inches thick. Their surprising strength permits curving forms that retain springiness. The Wiggle chair is the best-known design of the group; it was reintroduced by Vitra in 1992. In 1990–2, Gehry was commissioned to develop a group of chairs and tables for Knoll. The resultant designs use strips of laminated wood that are assembled into a variety of configurations, ranging from a small side chair to a massive arm chair and ottoman.

Other Trends

East–West Crossovers

The emergence of several Japanese architects and designers as prominent figures in current practice in Europe and America reflects the growing internationalism of design practice. Earlier, western design had exerted its influence in Japan through such projects as Frank Lloyd Wright's Imperial Hotel in Tokyo or Le Corbusier's Tokyo National Museum of Western Art (1955–9). Increased availability of publications, and travel and study in Europe and the United States made many younger Japanese professionals more aware of modern design in the west. The simplicity and logic of traditional Japanese architecture generated an affinity between Japanese traditions and western modernism.

The Chikatsu-Asuka Historical Museum in Osaka, Japan (1994), by Tadao Ando (born 1941) is at once a minimalist work of modernism and a seemingly timeless cluster of spaces relating to the ancient tombs that are the focus of the museum's

exhibits. Interior spaces are dark and somber, their exposed concrete walls permitting play of light and shade, constantly changing with the movement of the sun (**fig. 20.37**). The same architect's Suntory Museum (1994) also at Osaka, Japan, is a seafront structure with a great IMAX theater rising in a tapered cylinder drum from stepped plazas leading down to the waterfront. Rectangular elements house a restaurant and a gallery and contribute to the strongly geometric forms of the building.

In the Kirishima International Concert Hall at Aiura, Japan (1994), by Fumihiko Maki (born 1928) an entry hall and foyer wrap around the main auditorium with an outer glass wall giving views of the surrounding mountain terrain (**fig. 20.39**). The main hall is leaf-shaped in plan, with balcony seating stepped down in terrace platforms on either side of the central space. Walls are of natural wood, while the ceiling is made up of triangular white panels in an irregular arrangement that is visually interesting and acoustically effective.

Just as western influences have moved into the Japanese design world, a reverse flow of Japanese design into Europe and America has become commonplace. Arata Isozaki (born 1931) has a

20.37 Tadao Ando, Chikatsu-Asuka Historical Museum, Osaka, Japan, 1994.

In the main exhibition space, a model of an ancient burial mound occupies the focal circle at the lower level. A ramp rises to an upper level, which gives visitors access to surrounding cases and objects on display. The subdued ambience reflects the traditional Japanese respect accorded to the ancient materials exhibited.

20.38 Tadao Ando, Kidosaki House, Setagaya, Toyko, 1982–6.

Simplicity of form and restrained use of furniture suggest a meeting point for the ideas of Japanese tradition and International Modernism.

20.39 Fumihiko Maki, Kirishima International Concert Hall, Aiura, Japan, 1994.

Maki developed the idea of the angled ceiling planes and the leaf-shaped plan of the auditorium to improve the acoustic of the space. Balcony seating is extended in a series of stepped levels as it bears the stage. Natural wood surfaces introduce warm color.

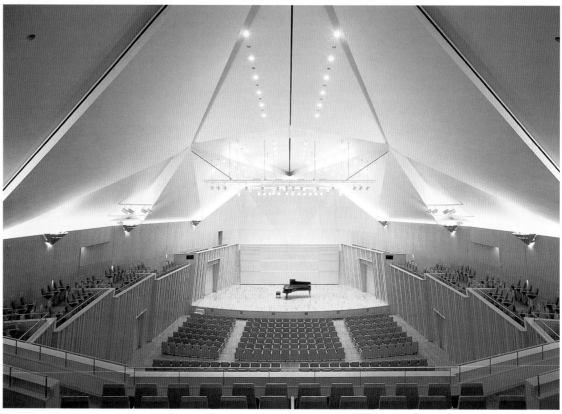

striking presence in the United States. In his four-story administrative center building for Team Disney at Lake Buena Vista (1990) a variety of masses are grouped in seeming collision. The selection of Yoshio Taniguchi (born 1937) as the designer of a major reconstruction of New York's Museum of Modern Art is another indication of the extent of internationalism in the design fields.

Preservation

In the last decades of the twentieth century, interest has increased in preserving older structures, inspired by the waste and loss associated with the destruction of so many buildings in response to economic pres-sures. Railroad stations, now often made obsolete by changing modes of transportation, are obvious candidates. The loss of New York's old Penn Station, an impressive work of eclectic Roman classicism by McKim, Mead, and White (1911, destroyed 1963), has inspired the restoration and reuse of the old Union Station in Washington, D.C. (*c.* 1975), for example, and the careful on-going restoration of New York's Grand Central Station. In Paris, the restoration and conversion of the Gare d'Orsay into the Musée d'Orsay (1986) by Gai Aulenti (born 1927) is an extremely successful demonstration of the way in which the details of historic architecture can serve as background for modern elements standing within an existing structure.

20.40 Erick Van Egeraat Associated Architects, ING Bank, Budapest, Hungary, 1995.

A sliding door of frameless glass opens into the boardroom of the bank. The laminated wooden ribs that form the shell of this space, which was sited above an existing nineteenth-century landmark, give the room its futuristic character. A glass-enclosed elevator shaft is at the left. Chairs designed by Charles Eames surround the gleaming top of the boardroom table.

A nineteenth-century building in Budapest, Hungary, became the basis for a drastic reconstruction by EEA—Erick Van Egeraat (born 1956) Associated Architects—in 1995 for the ING Bank. The new construction is inserted into the center courtyard of the old building and rises above the roof to become a virtual new building on top of the old. Offices occupy the floors surrounding the center space, while the roof-top structure becomes an amorphously shaped "whale" of wooden ribs and glass that serves as the boardroom for the bank (**fig. 20.40**). The unique interior shape is reflected in an irregularly shaped rug in blue with abstract forms in tan.

Green Buildings

Along with the desire to preserve and reuse older structures has come a realization that the increasing dependence on technology to solve problems has brought with it increased consumption of raw materials and increased demand for energy use. The typical mid- to late twentieth-century building depends on artificial lighting, heating, and air conditioning, along with mechanized vertical transportation. As resources have become strained by increasing demand, it becomes logical to look toward design that is oriented to conservation rather than consumption. Older buildings offer many suggestions: more dependence on daylight and natural ventilation, on solar heat and solar energy supply. The concept of green buildings refers to structures that make minimal demands on their environment and take maximum advantage of natural ways to provide desired functions. While buildings are designed by architects and engineers, their nature is largely determined by the interiors that they house. As interior design turns to intelligent use of materials, to minimal dependence on energy-hungry mechanical systems, buildings can be made less destructive of environment and natural resources and, incidentally, often more economically sound.

In New York the National Audubon Society elected to demonstrate its commitment to environmental concerns in the design of its national headquarters building (**figs. 20.41** and **20.42**). Croxton Collaborative, the designers, bought a neglected 1891 eight-story loft building for a fraction of the cost of new space. A full renovation preserved windows that can be opened and used window and skylight illumination to reduce power require-

20.41 Croxton Collaborative Architecture Designers, National Audubon Society Headquarters, New York, 1992.

An older building, dating from 1891, which might well have been designated for destruction, was rescued through a renovation that focused on environmental concerns to minimize energy consumption, to provide efficient waste recycling and disposal, and to use materials from renewable sources. The office space shown retains the old, arched windows as sources of light and ventilation. Paint colors were selected for maximum reflectivity to conserve light, and the lighting system was designed for maximum efficiency. The space profits aesthetically from its natural ambience.

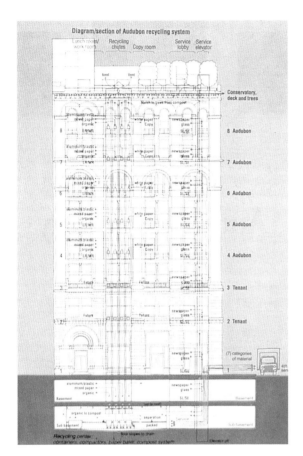

Diagram/section of Audubon recycling system

Technology now enables designers to visit, modify, and develop images of proposed spaces on screen without the slow and unreliable processes of making models and renderings. Amazingly accurate simulations of reality can be produced, which offer the experience of spatial environments without their having to be built, and tempt suggestions for eliminating much constructed structure altogether. Such proposals may suggest the dreams of science fiction, but realization of design in this form is very close to becoming commonplace.

What form will interior design take in the future? Some critics have suggested that postmodernism, once considered the direction of the future, is already slipping into the past. The excesses and extremes of the 1980s and 1990s will almost certainly be curtailed by a rising sense that the rationality of the earlier modern movement still has an ability to assert itself through its underlying intellectual strength. The idea that big is always better is subject to question in many contexts. The ability of new materials and new structural techniques will inevitably be exploited within whatever philosophical intentions designers may adopt. Concern for human needs, for better relationships between built and manufactured elements of the environment and the people they intend to serve, is a growing issue. The idea of universal design—design that is adapted to the needs of all people—is increasingly important. The idea of social responsibility in design—concern for users of spaces who cannot project their desires through economic or political power—is under active discussion. Design will continue to establish the settings for human civilization and exert influence on the character of life in the future, just as it always has in the past.

20.42 Croxton Collaborative Architecture Designers, National Audubon Society Headquarters, New York, 1992.

In this diagram the waste-recycling systems are illustrated. Metals and glass, paper, and organic wastes are separately delivered to a basement area to be prepared for shipment to suitable recycling processors or disposal. Organic materials are processed into mulch, which is used around the trees in a rooftop garden and conservatory. The project demonstrates economic gains as well as environmental responsibility.

ments. Windows incorporate a heat shield film that reduces heat buildup from the summer sun and helps to retain winter heat. Materials were chosen to minimize consumption of scarce raw materials and to eliminate materials that give off fumes. The completed project is aesthetically satisfying, economically advantageous, and a fine demonstration of the possibilities of design that reflects concern for environmental values.

Glossary

Guide to Pronunciation

Pronunciation guides for selected terms appear in parentheses. Strongly stressed syllables are shown in large-size capital letters; lightly stressed syllables are shown in small-size capital letters. Most of the symbols, which use ordinary letters or combinations of letters, should be self-explanatory. The following may need clarification:

a	c<u>a</u>t
ah	f<u>a</u>ther, cl<u>o</u>ck
ay	d<u>a</u>te, pl<u>ay</u>
dh	<u>th</u>at, mo<u>th</u>er
e	n<u>e</u>t, b<u>e</u>rry
i	<u>i</u>t, b<u>i</u>g
igh	<u>i</u>ce, l<u>igh</u>t
kh	Ba<u>ch</u>
n	French bo<u>n</u> (shows that the vowel is nasalized)
ng	thi<u>n</u>k, si<u>n</u>g
oe	French d<u>eu</u>x, German sch<u>ö</u>n
oh	<u>o</u>pen, c<u>o</u>ld
ou	s<u>ou</u>nd, c<u>ow</u>
u	p<u>u</u>t, b<u>oo</u>k
ue	French r<u>ue</u>, German <u>ü</u>ber
uh	c<u>u</u>p, <u>a</u>bout, b<u>i</u>rd, pap<u>er</u>
zh	mea<u>s</u>ure, bei<u>g</u>e

abacus The topmost block of a Greek Doric column capital.

acanthus An ornamental leaf element surrounding the capital of a Corinthian column.

Adirondack style (AD-uh-RAHN-dak) Interior and furniture style developed in the American Adirondack mountains using rough tree branches.

adobe (uh-DOH-bee) Brick made of dried earth and straw. Also structures built of this material.

adze A heavy chisel-like long-handled tool.

Aesthetic movement 19th-century British art and design movement

agora (AG-uh-ruh) The open market square of an ancient Greek city.

aisle A passage at the side of the nave of a church.

alignment Prehistoric arrangements of large stones in straight lines.

ambulatory (AM-byuh-luh-TAWR-ee) A passage around the sides and rear of the chancel of a church.

andiron (AN-digh-uhrn) One of a pair of metal stands used to support logs in an open fireplace.

apse (aps) The semicircular end of a basilica or church chancel.

aqueduct A bridge structure supporting a water channel.

arabesque (AR-uh-BESK) A light and flowing surface decoration.

arcade A series of adjacent arches.

arch A structure of wedge-shaped blocks bridging over an opening.

architrave (AHR-ki-TRAYV) The lowest horizontal band of an entablature.

archivolt (AHR-ki-VOHLT) A molding on the face of an arch following its curve.

armoire (ahrm-WAHR) A movable wardrobe cabinet with door front.

arris (AR-is) The sharp edge formed where two surfaces meet.

Art Deco (AHR(T)-day-KOH, -DEK-oh) A decorative style of the 1920s and 1930s using elements intended to suggest modern technological developments.

Art Nouveau (AHR(T)-noo-VOH) A late 19th-century stylistic development using flowing curves and nature-inspired elements to replace historic decorative elements.

Arts and Crafts An aesthetic movement of the latter half of the 19th century in England, led by the teaching of William Morris.

ashlar (ASH-luhr) Building stone cut in regular rectangular blocks; walling made up of such blocks.

astragal (AS-truh-guhl) A small concave molding, often ornamented with carved beads.

asymmetry Avoidance of symmetrical balance.

atrium (AY-tree-uhm) In ancient Roman architecture, the central open courtyard of a house. By extension, any central open space.

attic The upper story of a building; interior space beneath a roof.

aubusson (OH-bue-SAWn, OH-buh-SAHN) A handmade French rug or carpet with a flat weave.

axminster (AKS-min-stuhr) A traditional carpet construction using a cut pile of wool in a wide variety of pattern and color.

baldacchino (BAHL-duh-KEE-noh, BAL-) A canopy supported by columns, usually above an altar or tomb.

ball and claw foot A decorative element at the bottom of a furniture leg in which a carved claw grasps a spherical ball element.

ball foot A decorative element of spherical form at the bottom of a furniture leg.

baluster (BAL-uh-stuhr) A post or column supporting a handrail.

Baroque The architectural and design style of the latter phase of the Renaissance which developed in 16th-century Italy. Spaces of complex form with elaborate decorative detail are typical.

barrel vault A masonry vault of semicircular form. Also called a tunnel vault.

barrow An ancient tomb in the form of an artificial hill.

basilica (buh-SIL-i-kuh) Originally, an ancient Roman courthouse of a type that became a Christian church, having a high central nave with lower aisles on either side.

bas-relief (BAH-ri-LEEF) Sculptural carving of a flat surface in low relief.

batter Inward slope of a vertical wall surface.

Bauhaus (BOU-hous) A German school of art and design of 1919 to 1932. Under the direction of Walter Gropius the school was strongly influential in the development of modernism in all aspects of design.

bay A unit of a structural system using repeated identical elements.

bay window A projecting window element.

bead and reel A carved ornamental treatment using alternating elements of semi-spherical and semi-cylindrical form.

beam A horizontal element providing structural support.

Beaux-Arts (boh-ZAHR) An architectural style developed at the French school of art and design in Paris, the Ecole des Beaux-Arts.

bentwood A technique of forming strips of wood into curves by applying steam heat and placing the softened wood on molds. Furniture made by this technique is designated as bentwood.

bergère (ber-ZHER) A low upholstered armchair developed and used in France.

beton brut (bay-tawn-BRUET) The French term for exposed reinforced concrete.

bilateral symmetry Design using elements in two symmetrically placed locations.

blockfront Furniture unit with a three-part front, projecting on either side and recessed in the center; a popular type with 18th-century American (especially New England) cabinet makers.

bombé (bahm-BAY, baw^n-) French term for furniture using outward-swelling curves.

boulle (bool) Metal and tortoise-shell inlay work as developed in France by Charles Boulle.

box (finger) joint Wood joint with interlocking projecting teeth.

breakfront desk A furniture unit made up of an upper bookcase with a projecting desk below.

broken pediment A pediment with a central opening.

brownstone Soft brown sandstone. Also, buildings of this material.

brutalism (or new brutalism) Modern architectural style using massive elements, usually of exposed concrete.

bureau à cylindre (bue-ROH-ah-see-LA^n-druh) Writing desk with cylindrical roll-top closure.

burl Decorative veneer made from wood with irregular growth patterns.

buttress A element of masonry structure providing bracing or support. (See also *flying buttress*.)

cabriole (KAB-ree-OHL) A curving, tapered furniture leg.

caldarium (kal-DER-ee-uhm) Chamber of ancient Roman bath for hot steam bath.

canapé (KAN-uh-PAY) French term for a couch or sofa.

cantilever (KAN-tuh-LEE-vuhr) A horizontal projecting beam or other structure supported only at its inward end.

Cape Cod cottage A much-imitated colonial American house type of one story with a gable roof.

capital The top element of a classical column.

Carolean (KAR-uh-LEE-uhn) The English style of the time of Charles II.

Carolingian (KAR-uh-LIN-j(ee)

uhn) The Romanesque style of France and Germany from 750 to 1000 C.E.

carpenter Gothic American Victorian carpenter-built structure using Gothic decorative elements cut from wood.

caryatid (KAR-ee-AT-id, KAR-ee-uh-TID) A column used as a structural support carved in human form.

casement window Window with side-hinged sash.

cassapanca (KAS-uh-PANG-kuh) Italian Renaissance ornate chest with paneled back and arms so that it can also be used as a bench.

cassone (kuh-SOH-nay, -nee) Italian Renaissance elaborately carved chest.

cella (SEL-uh) The enclosed chamber of an ancient Greek temple.

centering Temporary wood structure used in building an arch or vault.

chaise (shayz) Side chair.

chaise longue (SHAYZ-LAWNG) A chair with an extended seat area usable as a lounge.

chancel (CHAN-suhl) The sanctuary area of a church or cathedral, also called choir.

chevet (shuh-VAY) A grouping of chapels around the choir and ambulatory of a Gothic cathedral.

Chinoiserie (sheen-WAH-zuh-ree) Use of decorative elements derived from Chinese traditional design in 18th-century France and England.

choir The chancel area of a cathedral or church, originally occupied by the choir of monks.

churrigueresco (CHOOR-ee-guh-RES-koh) Spanish Baroque design of 1650 to 1780.

cimborio (sim-BAWR-ee-oh) Spanish term for a lantern or elevated structure above a main roof to permit window openings.

clapboard (KLAB-uhrd) Exterior building siding using overlapping horizontal, flat boards.

clerestory (KLEER-stawr-ee) Windows or openings in the upper part of a wall.

cloister Enclosed open courtyard of a monastery. Also, by extension, a monastery or convent.

coffer A hollowed out panel in a ceiling, vault, or dome.

colonial Design from a period of colonial history, especially American work before 1776.

colonnade A series of columns.

commode A piece of furniture containing drawers or shelves.

Composite order Architectural order using a combination of Ionic and Corinthian elements.

compression A force tending to squeeze or compress materials to which it applies stress.

Consulate style French decorative style of the Napoleonic era.

corbel A projecting element supporting a structural element such as a beam or the base of an arch.

Corinthian (kuh-RIN-thee-uhn) The most elaborate of the Greek and Roman orders of architecture using a grouping of carved (acanthus) leaves around the capital of each column.

cornice The topmost element of an entablature or any projecting element at the top of a wall.

coro The choir of an Italian and Spanish Gothic or Renaissance church.

cove A concave projecting molding or element, a trough or recess.

Craftsman Movement American design and furniture style based on Arts and Crafts movement in England.

credenza (kri-DEN-zuh) A horizontal cabinet with shelves or drawers.

crocket Ornament using projecting form based on foliage.

cruciform Having the shape of a Latin cross.

crypt An underground space

below the floor of a church or cathedral, often used as a chapel or burial place.

curule (KYOOR-ool) Ancient Roman seat intended for person of high rank.

dado (DAY-doh) Lower portion of an interior wall with a special finish; also, in woodworking, a groove.

Danish Modern 20th-century decorative and furniture style developed in Denmark.

Dante chair (DAHN-tay, -tee) Italian Renaissance folding chair using stretched leather for seat and back.

deconstructivism In late 20th-century architecture, design making use of broken and separated elements.

decorated The second period of English Gothic architecture (14th century).

dentils (DEN-tlz) Tooth-like projecting decorative details used in Ionic and Corinthian classical architecture.

desornamentado (des-AWR-nah-MEN-tah-doh) Late Spanish Renaissance decorative style using minimal decorative detail.

De Stijl (duh-STIGHL) A Dutch movement (1917–31) of early modernism in art and design.

Directoire (dee-rek-TWAHR) French design of the post-revolutionary period (1795–1804) emphasizing ancient Roman decorative elements.

di sotto in su (dee-SAW T-taw-in-SOO) Ceiling painting in perspective with upward-looking illusion.

dolmen A prehistoric grouping of stones made up of two or three upright stones topped with a horizontal. Probably part of an ancient tomb.

dome A circular vault derived from rotation of an arch; may be hemispherical, flattened (saucer dome), or elliptical in plan.

Doric The simplest of the Greek and Roman classical orders of architecture.

dormer A projection on a

sloping roof providing location for a window; also, a window placed in such a projection.

dosseret (DAHS-uh-RET) A block placed above a column capital, often supporting arches above.

dovetail A woodworking joint using interlocking elements of tapered form.

dowel A round pin fitted into matching holes to join two elements; also a type of joint used in carpentry and cabinet making.

drop-leaf desk A box-form desk with a down-swinging panel to form a writing surface. (Also called a fall-front desk.)

duplex An apartment or flat of two stories.

Dutch bed A bed fitted into an enclosing alcove.

Early English The earliest of the periods of English Gothic architecture (13th century).

Eastlake style A florid Victorian decorative style introduced by Thomas Eastlake.

echinus (i-KIGH-nuhs) The round element of a Doric column capital at the top of the column and below the abacus.

eclecticism The borrowing of design from various earlier periods, common in architectural and interior design of the first half of the 20th century.

egg and dart A decorative detail used to ornament molding in classical architecture with alternating egg-shaped and dart-like elements.

Elizabethan English design period corresponding to the reign of Queen Elizabeth I (1558–1603).

Empire A period of French Neoclassical design corresponding to the reign of Napoleon (1804–14).

entablature (in-TAB-luh-chuhr, -choor) The horizontal band supported by the columns of classical architectural orders. It is made up of the three elements, architrave, frieze, and cornice.

entasis (EN-tuh-sis) The swelling or outward curvature of the shaft of a classical column.

Etruscan style Decorative style based on early ancient Roman precedents.

exedra (pl. exedrae) (EK-suh-druh) Room or other area of semicircular shape intended for conversation.

Expressionism Art and design style striving for emotional expression.

fan vault A vault with many ribs radiating in a pattern suggesting a palm fan.

fasces (FAS-eez) An ancient Roman symbol of imperial power, in the form of a bunch of sticks tied together. The form was revived in decorative design of the Empire period in France to symbolize the power and ambitions of Napoleon.

fauteuil (foh-TUH-ee) A French Renaissance upholstered armchair with open arms.

Federal A period of American architecture and design (1780–1830) following the colonial era.

feudal system The governmental system of medieval Europe based on the holding of land and the authority of a hierarchy of rule.

finial (FIN-ee-uhl) A top or crown ornament.

Flamboyant The last period of French Gothic architecture (14th to 16th centuries) characterized by elaborate flame-like decorative tracery.

fluting Carved parallel grooves as used on the shafts of classical columns.

flying buttress A buttress of half-arch form, spanning over an open space to a point where pressure is applied to resist the thrust of an internal vault.

folded pilaster A pilaster fitted into a corner by giving it bent or folded form.

frieze (freez) The second or middle band of a classical entablature and, by extension, any horizontal decorative band.

frigidarium (FRIJ-i-DER-ee-uhm) Chamber of ancient Roman bath containing a cold water pool.

frosting Decorative surface elaboration suggesting cake icing.

Futurism Italian art and design style of the 1920s featuring movement, mechanization, and speed.

gable The triangular end wall of a structure with slanted roofs.

gambrel roof (GAM-bruhl) Gable roof having two angles of slope, steeper below and flatter above.

gargoyle (GAHR-goil) A projecting water spout carved in fantastic form.

gate-leg table A table with hinged leaves supported by swinging leg(s) when lifted.

General Grant style American Victorian architectural and decorative style of the time of Ulysses Grant's presidency (1869–77).

Georgian The style of the English and American periods corresponding to the reigns of the English kings George I to George IV (1714–1830).

ger see *yurt.*

gingerbread Informal term for elaborate Victorian surface ornament.

girandole (JIR-uhn-DOHL) A decorative candle holder, often a mirror with a candle holder on either side.

Glastonbury chair An English Tudor folding chair with X-leg base.

golden mean A ratio or proportion in which the smaller number is to the larger as the larger is to the sum of the two, or A:B=B:A+B.

Golden Oak style American furniture style of the late 19th century using brown colored oak.

Gothic The architectural style of the later Middle Ages characterized by the use of pointed arches.

Gothic Revival A 19th-century style in which the forms of medieval Gothic architecture are used.

Greek cross A cross having four arms of equal length.

Greek key A decorative pattern used in ancient Greek design in which a key-like motif is used.

Greek Revival A 19th-century style in which the forms of ancient Greek architecture are used.

groin vault A vault formed by the intersection of two vaults producing the intersecting edge lines called "groins."

grotesque Fanciful and distorted form; carving of such form.

half timber A system of wood construction in which posts and beams with bracing are exposed on the outside of a structure with in-filling of brick or plaster.

hall church Church having one large interior nave space without aisles.

hammer beam A type of truss in which a horizontal tie at the base is omitted.

high altar The most important central altar in a church or chapel where there are several altars.

highboy A tall chest with many drawers.

high Gothic Medieval Gothic architecture of the most fully developed periods.

high tech 20th-century modern architecture and design featuring elements typical of advanced technological design, such as that of aircraft and spacecraft.

hipped roof Roof with slanted surfaces at ends as well as at front and back.

historicism The practice of using historic forms in design.

humanism Thought or

philosophy based on human actions and values.

hypocaust (HIGH-puh-KAWST) A hollow space beneath the floors of some ancient Roman buildings providing heat from flue gases passing through the space from a remote furnace.

hypostyle hall (HIGH-puh-STIGHL) A space containing many columns supporting a roof structure above.

impluvium (im-PLOO-vee-uhm) In ancient Roman architecture, a pool or cistern in the center of a courtyard open to the sky.

impost block (IM-pohst) A masonry block at the base of an arch.

inlay Decorative surface ornament made by inserting forms of contrasting color or material in spaces cut out from a background material with a flush surface finish.

intarsia (in-TAHR-see-uh) Elaborate decorative inlay work often forming abstract or pictorial design, as used in the Italian Renaissance.

International style A 20th-century architectural style based on function, usually without ornament, and characterized by flat roofs and large glass areas.

Ionic (igh-AHN-ik) The second of the three orders of ancient Greek and Roman architecture. Column capitals are characterized by the use of a pair of *volutes* of spiral form.

Italianate (i-TAL-yuh-NAYT) Design imitative of Italian precedents.

Jacobean (JAK-uh-BEE-uhn) English design dating from the reigns of James I and Charles I (1603–49).

jacquard (JAK-ahrd, juh-KAHRD) A type of loom developed in France, capable of weaving elaborate patterns. Also, a fabric made by the jacquard process.

Jugendstil (YOO-guhnt-SHTEEL) The term for late 19th-century German, Austrian, and Scandinavian design of Art Nouveau character.

kas (kahs) Large Dutch wardrobe cabinet with hinged door front.

keep The most securely defended, usually central, part of a medieval castle.

kitsch Low quality, often playful, design of poor taste.

klismos (KLIZ-mahs) An ancient Greek form of chair with forward curving front legs and curved rear leg and back supports supporting a concave curved back.

laconicum (luh-KAHN-i-kuhm) Chamber of an ancient Roman bath using hot, dry heat to promote sweating.

lacquer An Asian varnish used as a wood finish, with many coats forming a high gloss surface. The term is used for modern finishes of similar character made from synthetics.

ladderback chair Chair with a back using several horizontal slats.

lantern A windowed structure rising above the top of a dome or roof.

late modern A term used to describe late 20th-century architecture and design that continues the qualities of early modern (often International Style) design.

lath Thin wood strips that form a base for plaster surfaces. Modern lath may also be of metal mesh or plaster board with holes to help bonding of plaster.

Latin cross A cross having three equal arms and one longer one.

Liberty style A British term for Art Nouveau style.

linenfold Carved wooden surface ornament suggesting folded linen.

lintel A horizontal member bridging an opening such as door or window. A lintel also provides support for the wall or other structure above.

lit en bateau (LEE-ahⁿ-bah-TOH) A French form of elaborate bed in a form suggesting a boat, developed in the Empire period.

loggia (LOH-jee-uh) A covered porch or verandah with columns supporting the roof.

Louis XIV style (LOO-ee-kuh-TAWRZ) The French style of architecture and design typical of the period of the reign of Louis XIV (1643–1715). The term Baroque is used to describe the character of the style.

Louis XV style (LOO-ee-KAⁿZ) The French style of architecture and design of the period 1730–65, named for the king who reigned from 1723 to 1774. The character of the period is usually designated as Rococo.

Louis XVI style (LOO-ee-SEZ) The design style of 1765 to 1790 in France, named for Louis XVI who reigned from 1774 to 1792. The period is characterized by Neoclassical restraint.

maksura (mahk-SOOR-uh) Sanctuary area of an early mosque with wood or stone perforated enclosure.

Mannerism A term applied to architecture and design in Italy toward the end of the Renaissance, in which there was an effort to escape the strict classicism of the High Renaissance. The term is also used to identify work in northern Europe in the 16th and 17th centuries. The term has been applied to modern work which attempts to replace the domination of Modernism.

mansard roof A roof with steeply sloping surfaces as developed in the French Renaissance.

Mansardic style American Victorian architectural style using a mansard roof.

marquetry (MAHR-kuh-tree) Elaborate surface decoration using *inlay* in wood veneering.

megaron (MEG-uh-RAHN) The large central hall space of early Greek palaces.

metope (MET-uh-pee) In ancient Greek architecture, the square panel which alternates with *triglyphs* in the frieze of a classical Doric entablature.

mews A narrow alley used for service behind rows of larger houses.

mezzanine (MEZ-uh-NEEN, MEZ-uh-NEEN) An intermediate partial floor above a principal level of a building.

mihrab (MEE-ruhb) Niche in a mosque oriented toward Mecca.

Minimalism Design using little or no decorative detail.

Mission style 19th-century American design suggesting the design of the California missions. Often used as synonymous with Craftsman or Golden Oak design.

miter A joint between two pieces, with each cut at an angle to fit at a corner of the (usually right-angle) intersection.

Moderne (moh-DERN) French language term for modern or modernistic design.

Modernism 20th-century architectural and design styles based on function and structure.

Modernistic 20th-century decorative design using elements suggestive of the modern world.

module A single geometric unit in a series of repeated units making up a modular design.

modulor A system of dimensioning and proportion developed by Le Corbusier.

monopodia (MAHN-uh-POH-dee-uh) Decorative carving of furniture leg using grotesque head and body tapered to a single foot.

Moorish arch Semicircular or pointed arch raised by vertical stilts which may curve outward.

Morris chair 19th-century armchair with adjustable back.

mortise and tenon (MAWR-tis; TEN-uhn) A wood joint in which a projecting tongue (tenon) is inserted into a fitted opening (mortise).

mosaic Small squares of colored stone or tile fitted together to form patterns or images.

mud brick Masonry block made by impacting and drying mud in a mold.

mudéjar (moo-DHAY-hahr) Spanish decorative style developed under Islamic influence in the 13th to 17th centuries.

mullion (MUHL-yuhn) A vertical member dividing the panels or panes of a window or door.

narthex (NAHR-theks) A porch or vestibule at the front of the nave of a church.

nave The main central space of a cathedral or church.

Neoclassical A style of architecture and design derived from ancient Greek and Roman architecture.

Norman The English Romanesque style of the 11th and 12th centuries.

oculus (AHK-yuh-luhs) A circular opening or window at the top of a dome.

oecus (EE-kuhs) The main room of an ancient Greek house.

order (of architecture) One of the systems of design used in ancient Greek and Roman architecture based on column and entablature. The three important orders are Doric, Ionic, and Corinthian.

ormolu (AWR-muh-LOO) Gilded bronze used as decorative detail on furniture of the Neoclassical period.

palazzo (puh-LAHT-soh) Italian word for palace.

Palladian (puh-LAY-dee-uhn) Design based on style of Andrea Palladio.

panel A surface enclosed by framing. Paneling is a form of wall treatment using wood surface panels.

parquet (pahr-KAY) Flooring of strips of wood often forming patterns.

pediment Triangular form created by the end of a gable. The pediments of classical Greek and Roman architecture are often used as ornamental detail in interiors and furniture.

pegged lap joint Wood joint in which two pieces are overlapped and held together with a peg or pin passing through both pieces.

pendentive A triangular area of masonry used to connect the base of a dome to a square space below.

peristyle A sequence of columns surrounding a building or interior court.

perpendicular A line at right angles to another (usually horizontal) line. Also, the 15th- and 16th-century style of English Gothic architecture.

piano nobile (PYAH-noh NAW-bee-lay) Italian term for the principal (usually second) floor of a building.

pilaster (pi-LAS-tuhr) A flattened form of a column set against a wall surface.

pillar and scroll style American 19th-century style developed by Duncan Phyfe using carved classical column and scroll elements.

piloti (pi-LAHT-ee) Massive pylon-like support column used to elevate building mass above ground-floor level.

Plateresco (PLAT-uh-RES-koh) Spanish design style of the first half of the 16th century, characterized by fine detail suggesting the work of a silversmith.

polychromy (PAHL-ee-KROH-mee) Ornamental surface design using several colors.

portico A colonnade supporting a roof to form a porch, usually at the entrance to a building.

post and lintel A basic system of construction using vertical elements (posts) to support horizontal members (beams or lintels).

post-modernism 20th-century architectural and interior design succeeding modernist work, characterized by historicism and use of decorative elements.

prairie house Term used by Frank Lloyd Wight to describe his mid-western houses designed with horizontal emphasis.

provincial Design of historic periods of vernacular or informal character. French and Italian provincial style of the 17th and 18th century are often admired and imitated.

pueblo (PWEB-loh) Flat-roofed adobe house or group of houses as built by native American communities in the southwest states of Arizona and New Mexico.

pylon (PIGH-lahn) A massive masonry element as used on either side of the entrance front of ancient Egyptian temples.

pyramid A building, usually a tomb of pyramidal form as built in ancient Egypt.

quadratura (KWAH-drah-TOOR-ah) Illusionistic painting in perspective on walls or ceilings.

quadripartite vaulting (KWAH-druh-PAHR-tight) Vaulting in which each vault is divided by ribs or intersection lines into four parts.

quadro riportato (KWAH-droh-REE-pawr-TAH-toh) Paintings on panels set into a vault or paintings simulating this pattern.

quatrefoil (KA-truh-foil, KAT-uhr-) An ornamental element of four lobes.

Queen Anne English design style of the early 18th century, named for the English queen (reigned 1702–14). The style was revived in the second half of the 19th century, marking a return to Neoclassicism.

quoin (koin, kwoin) A projecting stone at the corner of a building forming a decorative corner band.

radial symmetry Symmetry across several axes in a circular pattern.

rayonnant (RAY-oh-NAH^n) A 13th-century phase of French Gothic architecture characterized by rich and complex tracery.

reeding Parallel thin semicircular moldings used decoratively.

refinements In ancient Greek architecture, small modifications in seemingly straight lines and geometric relationships intended to correct for optical distortions and improve aesthetic qualities.

Régence (ray-ZHAH^{n}S) A French design style of the early 18th century (1715–1723), a period falling between the reigns of Louis XIV and Louis XV.

Regency An English period in architecture and design of the early 19th century, corresponding in date to the regency of Prince George before he became George IV (1811–20).

reinforced concrete A system of construction in which steel reinforcing rods are embedded in concrete to absorb tensile stresses.

reja (RAY-hah) An elaborate iron grille in Renaissance Spanish church interiors.

reliquary (REL-i-KWER-ee) Chest or other container for the relic of a revered saint or other personage.

Renaissance The period beginning around 1400 in Italy and continuing in European design until about 1800 in which a revival of classical design concepts was dominant.

reredos (RER-uh-DAHS, REER-dahs) A screen behind the altar of a church usually sculptured or decorated.

Restoration period The era of Charles II of England.

Rococo (ruh-KOH-koh, ROH-kuh-KOH) A style of architecture and decoration of the 18th century following the Baroque period, which made use of simpler forms and more delicate decoration.

rolltop desk Desk with a top cover that could be rolled away.

Roman arch An arch of semicircular form as used in ancient Roman architecture.

Romanesque (ROH-muh-NESK) The architectural style of the early Middle Ages in Europe characterized by use of Roman arch forms. The term Norman is applied to Romanesque work in England.

Romanticism Interest in romantic concepts such as medieval and Gothic periods as developed in the late 18th and early 19th century.

rondel (RAHN-dl, rahn-DEL) A round element of surface decoration, often containing a sculptural element.

rose window The large round window, usually in the facade of a Gothic cathedral or church.

rotunda (roh-TUHN-duh) Round, domed interior space.

row house A house built into a continuous row of adjacent houses.

rustication Stonework treated with projecting stones and recessed joints to form a strong surface pattern.

sacristy (SAK-ruh-stee) Room of a church intended for the robing of clergy.

sail vault Vault of flattened curvature forming ceiling of an interior space.

salt-box A house form in which a gable roof extends much lower at the rear of the building than at the front, a form suggesting a commonplace kitchen salt container.

Savonarola chair (SAV-uh-nuh-ROH-luh) Italian Renaissance folding chair said to be used by Savonarola.

Savonnerie carpet (SAV-uhn-REE) French carpet of the 18th century produced by factory at Savonnerie.

screens Room adjacent to the hall of a medieval manor house acting as a vestibule or

pantry.

scroll saw Mechanical powered saw capable of cutting complex curves.

Secession A movement in Vienna at the end of the 19th century in which architects and designers (and other artists) withdrew from academic exhibitions in order to create a non-traditional style.

Second Empire French Louis XVI revival style of 1850s and 1860s.

secretary desk Desk with bookcase above and writing desk below as developed in 17th- and 18th-century England and America.

sedia (SED-yah) Italian Renaissance chair.

set-back In tall buildings, a reduction of size from one upper level to another as required by zoning laws.

sexpartite (seks-PAHR-tight) A type of medieval vaulting in which the vault surface was made up of six parts.

sgabello (skah-BEL-oh, zgah-) A small, easily portable chair developed in the Italian Renaissance.

Shaker style Reserved and simple style as developed by the American Shaker religious society.

shingle A thin slice of wood used to form external covering of buildings.

Shingle style Architectural style of the late Victorian era in America with building exteriors covered by shingles.

soffit (SAHF-it) The underside of any element.

space planning 20th-century office and other interior planning.

split lath Thin sheets of wood partially split to form a base for plaster which forms keys as it is pressed into the splits.

spool and knob Decorative detail using alternate cylindrical and spherical elements.

stave church Early medieval church in Finland using massive vertical structural members.

stereotomy (STER-ee-AHT-uh-mee, STEER-) Art of stone cutting to form elements of complex vaulted structure.

stoa (STOH-uh) Covered loggia at one side of the open marketplace (agora) in ancient Greek cities.

strapwork Carved or plaster decorative detail suggesting bands cut from leather.

stripped classicism Design of the 1920s and 1930s based on classicism but with classical detail simplified or omitted.

stylobate (STIGH-luh-BAYT) The step forming the base of a classic colonnade.

swag Decoration in the form of a hanging garland.

symmetrical balance Balance achieved with matching elements on either side of a center line.

tablinum (ta-BLIGH-nuhm) A small room or alcove in an ancient Roman house at the end of the atrium where family records and portraits were kept.

tambour door (TAM-boor) Flexible sliding door formed of parallel thin strips glued to a canvas back.

tamped earth Earth pounded to form a firm service to serve as a floor.

temple house House built in the form of a Greek temple.

tepee American native portable house formed of poles supporting skin or blanket external surfaces.

tepidarium (TEP-i-DER-ee-uhm) Room of ancient Roman bath providing moderate heat.

terrazzo (tuh-RAHT-soh, -RAZ-oh) Small chips of marble imbedded in cement and polished to form a smooth surface suitable for flooring.

textile block Concrete block developed in the 1920s by Frank Lloyd Wright with patterned surface to provide a textile-like surface pattern.

thrust The outward force exercised by arches, vaults, and domes, requiring

restraint from solid masonry or from buttressing.

tongue and groove Wood joint using projecting tongue fitting into matching groove.

torchere (tawr-SHER) A candle or lamp stand.

torchier (tawr-CHEER) Stand or fixture holding torches or candles to provide lighting.

tower house Medieval castle type in which a vertical stack of rooms creates a defensible tower.

trabeated (TRAY-bee-AY-tid) A form of construction also known as *post and lintel*.

tracery Gothic ornamental carved detail in thin, complex patterns.

traditionalism Design limited to elements borrowed from historic precedents.

transept Outward projecting arm on either side of a cathedral or church forming a cross-shaped (cruciform) plan.

transparente (TRAHNS-pah-REN-tay) An elaborately sculptured backing for an altar in a Spanish cathedral, permitting observation of the sacrament from the chancel and from the ambulatory behind.

trefoil (TREE-foil, TREF-oil) A carved decorative element having three leaf forms.

triclinium (trigh-KLIN-ee-uhm) The dining room of an ancient Roman house using three reclining platforms arranged to form an open square.

triforium (trigh-FAWR-ee-uhm) The gallery above the main nave arcade and below the clerestory of a Gothic cathedral or church.

triglyph (TRIGH-glif) A panel carved in three vertical strips used in alternation with the metopes that ornamented the frieze of a Greek Doric entablature.

triptych (TRIP-tik) A three-panel painting in which the side panels are hinged to form doors to cover the center panel.

trompe-l'oeil (trawmp-LOI)

Realistic painting technique creating an illusion of reality (literally, "fools the eye").

trulli (TROO-lee) Simple dome-topped buildings typical of Apulia in southern Italy.

truss Structural element of wood or steel spanning open spaces through use of triangulation.

Tudor The style of early Renaissance architecture of England in the reigns of the Tudor monarchs from 1485 to 1558.

turkey-work Embroidery imitative of oriental textiles used for upholstery in Renaissance England.

Tuscan Ancient Roman simplified Doric order.

tympanum (TIM-puh-nuhm) The triangular panel formed within a pediment.

unité d'habitation (ue-nee-TAY-dah-bee-tah-SYAW^n) Term given to large apartment dwellings as

developed in the 20th century by Le Corbusier.

Usonian (yoo-SOH-nee-uhn) Term coined by Frank Lloyd Wright to describe his American (U.S.) design.

vargueño (vahr-GAYN-yoh) A form of drop-fronted desk developed in the Spanish Renaissance.

vault A masonry construction in which one or more arch forms are used to cover an open space.

vernacular Design produced through common practice without assistance from trained or professional aid.

Victorian The design period in England and America corresponding to the reign of Queen Victoria (1837–1901).

villa An Italian country house, usually of considerable luxury. The term has come into more general use for any large country house.

volute (vuh-LOOT) A spiral decorative form used as the

major element in the capital of a column of the Ionic order of architecture.

voussoir (voo-SWAHR) A stone of an arch, wedge-shaped to retain its place in the completed arch structure.

wainscot (WAYN-skaht, -skuht) A lining for the lower part of an interior wall.

Werkbund (VERK-bunt) A German, and later an Austrian, organization dedicated to the promotion of better design.

Werkstatte (VERK-shte-tuh) Austrian organization promoting the work of Vienna Secession design through workshops, shops, and displays.

westwork Frontal structure of German medieval churches.

what-not Victorian shelf unit intended to hold decorative ornaments.

wheelback chair Victorian chair using a circular wheel form as a back.

wigwam A hut of grass and thatch as built by native American tribes in the eastern American continent.

William and Mary The English style of the 17th century during the reigns of **William III and Mary** (1689–1702). The design of the period is Baroque in character.

Windsor (chair) A chair with a simple saddle seat using many thin wood turnings to support a bent back rim.

wing-back chair Chair with a high back with forward projecting upholstered elements.

WPA style Architectural design of the 1930s projects of the American governmental agency using stripped classical forms.

yurt (yoort) A movable round hut used by migratory Mongolian tribes.

Bibliography

General

Ball, Virginia Kloss, *Architecture and Interior Design*, 2 vols. New York: J. Wiley & Sons, 1980

Battersby, Martin, *The Decorative Thirties*. New York: Walker & Company, 1969

Blakemore, Robie G., *History of Interior Design and Furniture from Ancient Egypt to Nineteenth Century Europe*. New York: Van Nostrand Reinhold, 1997

Bogen, Louise Ade, *The Complete Guide to Furniture Styles* (rev. edn.). Prospect Heights, IN: Waveland Press, 1997

Boyce, Charles, *Dictionary of Furniture*. New York: Facts on File, 1985

Copplestone, Trewin, ed., *World Architecture*. London: Hamlyn, 1963

Dorfles, Grillo, *Kitsch*. New York: Universe Books, 1969

Edwards, Ralph and Ramsey, L.G.G., eds., *The Connoisseur's Complete Interior Guides*. New York: Bonanza Books, 1968

Fairbanks, Jonathan L. and Bates, Elizabeth Bidwell. *American Furniture, 1620 to the Present*. New York: Richard Markek Publishers, 1981

Fletcher, Banister (Musgrove, J.,

ed.), *A History of Architecture*. (rev. 19th edn.). London: Butterworths, 1987

Framton, Kenneth, *Modern Architecture: A Critical History*. New York: Oxford University Press, 1980

Giedion, Sigfried, *The Eternal Present: The Beginnings of Architecture*. New York: Pantheon, 1964

——, *Space, Time and Architecture*. Cambridge, MA: Harvard University Press, 1941

——, *Architecture and the Phenomena of Transition*. Cambridge, MA: Harvard University Press, 1971

Harris, Jennifer, ed., *Textiles*,

5000 Years. New York: Harry N. Abrams, 1993

Hine, Thomas, *Populuxe*. New York: Alfred A. Knopf, 1986

Jervis, Simon, *Dictionary of Design and Designers*. Harmondsworth, England: Penguin Books, Ltd., 1984

Kostof, Spiro, *A History of Architecture* (2nd edn.), New York: Oxford University Press, 1995

Lucie-Smith, Edward, *Furniture: A Concise History*. New York: Thames and Hudson, 1950

McCorquodale, Charles, *A History of Interior Decoration*. New York: Vendome Press, 1983

Oliver, Paul (ed.), *Shelter and*

Society. New York: Frederick A. Praeger, 1969

Oman, Charles C. and Hamilton, Jean, *Wallpapers: An International History and Illustrated Survey from the Victoria and Albert Museum*. New York: Harry N. Abrams, 1982

Pevsner, Nikolaus, *Outline of European Architecture*. New York: Penguin Books, 1943

——, *Pioneers of Modern Design from William Morris to Walter Gropius* (rev. edn.). Harmondsworth, England: Penguin Books, 1966

——, *The Sources of Modern Architecture and Design*. New York: Praeger, 1968

Pile, John, *Furniture, Modern and Post Modern*. New York: John Wiley & Sons, 1990

Praz, Mario, *An Illustrated History of Furnishing*. New York: George Braziller, 1964

Rappoport, Amos, *House: Form and Culture*. Englewood Cliffs, NJ: Prentice-Hall, 1969

Thornton, Peter, *Authentic Decor: The Domestic Interior, 1620–1920*. London: Weidenfeld & Nicolson, 1984

Trachtenberg, Myron and Hyman, Isabelle, *Architecture from Prehistory to Post-Modernism/The Western Tradition*. New York: Harry N. Abrams, 1986

Venturi, Robert, *Complexity and Contradiction in Architecture* (rev. edn.). New York: Museum of Modern Art, 1977

Wanscher, Ole, *The Art of Furniture*. New York: Reinhold Publishing Corp., 1967

Whiton, Sherrill, *Interior Design and Decoration* (4th edn.). Philadelphia: J.P. Lippencott, 1974

Wiffen, Marcus and Koeper, Frederick, *American Architecture, 1607–1976*, 2 vols. Cambridge, MA: MIT Press, 1981

Ancient Egypt, Greece, Rome

Badawi, A., *Architecture in Ancient Egypt and the Near East*. Cambridge, MA: MIT Press, 1966

Brown, F., *Roman Architecture*. New York: Braziller, 1965

Edwards, I.E.S., *The Pyramids of Egypt*. Harmondsworth, England: Penguin Books, 1947 rev. 1961

Lawrence, A.W., *Greek Architecture*. Harmondsworth, England and Baltimore: Penguin, 1973

Scully, Vincent, *The Earth, the Temple and the Gods*. New Haven, CN: Yale University Press, 1962

Smith, W.S., *The Art and Architecture of Ancient Egypt*. Harmondsworth, England and Baltimore: Penguin, 1958

Stern, P.V.D., *Prehistoric Europe from Stone Age Man to the Early Greeks*. New York: Norton, 1969

Stuart, James and Revett, Nicholas, *The Antiquities of Athens*, 3 vols. London: John Haberkorn, 1762; repr. New York: Benjamin Blom, 1968

Vitruvius, *De Architectura, Libri X*, trans. M.H. Morgan. New York: Dover Publications, 1960

Early Christian, Byzantine, Romanesque

Conant, K.J., *Carolingian and Romanesque Architecture: 800–1200*. New York: Pelican Books Ltd., 1959

MacDonald, W., *Early Christian and Byzantine Architecture*. New York: Braziller, 1962

Oursel, R., *Living Architecture: Romanesque*, trans. K.M. Leake. London: Oldbourne, 1967

Gothic

Branner, R., *Gothic Architecture*. New York: Braziller, 1961

Fitchen, John, *The Construction of the Gothic Cathedrals*. London: Oxford University

Press, 1961

Jantzen, Hans, *Kunst der Gotik*. Hamburg: Rowphalt Taschenbuch Verlag, 1957; repr. New York: Minerva Press, 1962

Italian Renaissance

Ackerman, James S., *The Architecture of Michelangelo*. Harmondsworth, England and Baltimore: Penguin, 1970

——, *Palladio*. Harmondsworth, England and Baltimore: Penguin, 1966

Borsi, Franco, *Leon Battista Alberti*. New York: Harper & Row, 1977

Lowry, B., *Renaissance Architecture*. New York: Braziller, 1962

Masson, G., *Italian Villas and Palaces*. London: Thames and Hudson, 1966

Murray, Peter, *The Architecture of the Italian Renaissance*. New York: Schocken Books, 1966

Palladio, Andrea (intro. Adolph K. Placzek), *The Four Books of Architecture*. Venice: 1570; London: Isaac Ware, 1738; repr. New York: Dover Publications, 1965

Thornton, Peter, *Seventeenth Century Interior Decoration in England, France and Holland*. New Haven: Yale University Press, 1978

——, *The Italian Renaissance Interior, 1400–1600*. New York: Harry N. Abrams, 1991

Wundram, Manfried, Pape, Thomas and Martin, Paolo, *Palladio*. Köln: Taschen, n.d.

Baroque and Rococo

Blunt, Anthony, *Baroque and Rococo Architecture and Decoration*. New York: Harper & Row, 1978

Furst, Viktor, *The Architecture of Sir Christopher Wren*. London: Lund Humphries, 1956

Hitchcock, Henry-Russell, *Rococo Architecture in

Southern Germany*. London: Phaidon, 1969

Millon, Henry A., *Baroque and Rococo Architecture*. New York: Braziller, 1961

Portoghesi, Paolo, *The Rome of Borromini*. New York: Braziller, 1968

French and English Renaissance

Blunt, Anthony, *Art and Architecture in France, 1500–1700*. Harmondsworth, England: Penguin, 1957

Summerson, John, *Inigo Jones*. Harmondsworth, England: Penguin, 1966

——, *Sir Christopher Wren*. Hamden, Connecticut: Archin Books, 1965

Eighteenth Century

Adam, Robert and Adam, James, *Works in Architecture*, 3 vols. London, 1773, 1778–1822; (excerpts) London: Alec Tiranti, 1959

Campbell, Colen, *Vitruvius Britannicus*. 2 vols. London, 1727

Chippendale, Thomas, *The Gentleman & Cabinet-Makers Directory*, 3rd edn. London, 1762; repr. New York: Dover Publications, 1966

Hepplewhite, George, *The Cabinet-Maker and Upholsterer's Guide*. London, 1786; 3rd edn. London: I. & J. Taylor, 1794; repr. New York: Dover Publications, 1969

Sheraton, Thomas, *The Cabinet-Maker and Upholsterer's Drawing Book*. London, 1793; repr., New York: Dover Publications, 1972

Yarwood, Doreen, *Robert Adam*. New York: Scribner's Sons, 1970

American Colonial and Revival

Hamlin, Talbot, *Greek Revival Architecture in America*. New York: Oxford University Press, 1944

Isham, Norman M. and Brown, Albert F., *Early Connecticut Homes*. New York: Dover Publications, 1965

Kelly, J. Frederick, *Early Domestic Architecture of Connecticut*. New Haven: Yale University Press, 1924; repr. New York: Dover Publications, 1963

Kettell, Russell Hawkes, *Pine Furniture of Early New England*. New York: Doubleday Doran, 1929; repr. New York: Dover Publications, 1929

Victorian

Church, Ella Rodman, *How to Furnish a Home*. New York: D. Appleton & Co., 1881

Kassay, John, *Book of Shaker Furniture*. Amherst, MA: University of Massachusetts Press, 1980

Ochsner, Jeffrey Karl, *H.H. Richardson: Complete Architectural Works*. Cambridge, MA: MIT Press, 1982

Pevsner, Nikolaus, *High Victorian Design*. London: Architectural Press, 1951

Schaefer, Herwin, *Nineteenth Century Modern*. New York: Praeger Publishers, 1970

Scully, Vincent, Jr., *The Shingle Style*, rev. edn. New Haven: Yale University Press, 1971

Sprigg, June, *Shaker Design*. New York: Whitney Museum of American Art and W.W. Norton, 1986

Wilk, Christopher, *Thonet: 150 Years of Furniture*. Woodbury, NY: Barron's, 1980

Arts and Crafts

Briggs, Asa, ed., *William Morris, Selected Writings and Designs*. Baltimore: Penguin Books, 1962

Cathers, David M., *Furniture of the American Arts and Crafts Movement*. New York: New American Library, 1981

Clark, Fiona, *William Morris Wallpapers and Chintzes*. New York and London: St. Martin's Press, Academy Editions, 1973

Day, Lewis F., *Decorative Art of William Morris and his Work*. London: H. Virtre and Co., 1899

Eastlake, Sir Charles Lock, *Hints on Household Taste in Furniture*, 3rd edn. London: Longmans Green & Co., 1872

Gere, Charlotte, *Nineteenth-Century Decoration: The Art of the Interior*. New York: Harry N. Abrams, 1989

Massobrio, C. and Portoghesi, P., *La Seggiola di Vienna*. Turin: Martano Editore, n.d.

Parry, Linda, *William Morris Textiles*. New York: Viking Press, 1983

Smith, Bruce, *Greene and Greene Masterworks*. San Francisco: Chronicle Books, 1998

Volpe, Tod M. and Cathers, Beth, *Treasures of the American Arts and Crafts Movement, 1890–1920*. New York: Harry N. Abrams, 1988

Watkinson, Ray, *William Morris as Designer*. New York: Van Nostrand Reinhold, 1967

Art Nouveau; Vienna Secession

Amaya, Mario, *Art Nouveau*. London: Dutton/Studio Vista, 1960

Basrilli, Renato, *Art Nouveau*. London: Hamlyn, 1966

Barnes, H. Jefferson, *Some Examples of Furniture by Charles Rennie Mackintosh in the Glasgow School of Art Collection*. Glasgow: Glasgow School of Art, 1969

Brunhammer, Yvonne, *et al.*, *Art Nouveau Belgium/France*. Houston TX: Institute for the Arts, Rice University, 1976

Burkhardt, Lucius, ed., *The Werkbund*. Venice: La Biennale di Venezia, 1977

Graham, F. Lanier, *Hector Guimard*. New York: Museum of Modern Art, 1970

Howorth, Thomas, *Charles Rennie Mackintosh and the Modern Movement*. New York: Wittenborn, 1953

Macleod, Robert, *Charles Rennie Mackintosh*. London: Hamlyn, 1968

Madsen, S. Tschudi, *Art Nouveau*. New York: McGraw Hill, 1967

Osthaus, Karl Ernst, *Van de Velde*. Hagen: Folkwang-Verlag, 1920

Rheims, Maurice, *The Flowering of Art Nouveau*. New York: Harry N. Abrams, n.d.

Ruckschio, Burkhardt and Schachel, Roland, *Adolf Loos*. Salzburg and Vienna: Residenz Verlag, 1982

Schmutzler, R., *Art Nouveau*. London, 1962; New York: Harry N. Abrams, 1964

Sekler, Eduard F., *Josef Hoffmann: The Architectural Work*. Princeton, NJ: Princeton University Press, 1985

Selz, Peter and Constantine, Mildred, eds., *Art Nouveau*. New York: Museum of Modern Art, 1960

Spencer, Robin, *The Aesthetic Movement*. London: Dutton/Studio Vista, 1972

Eclecticism

The American Revolution, 1876–1917. New York: Brooklyn Museum, 1979

Drexler, Arthur, ed., *The Architecture of the Ecole des Beaux Arts*. New York: Museum of Modern Art, 1977

De Stijl; Bauhaus

Herzogenrath, Wulf, ed., *50 Years Bauhaus*. Toronto: Art Gallery of Ontario, 1968

Hochman, Elaine S., *Bauhaus: Crucible of Modernism*. New York: Fromm International, 1997

Jaffe, Hans L.C., *De Stijl*. New York: Harry N. Abrams, 1967

Naylor, Gillian, *The Bauhaus*. London: Dutton/Studio Vista, 1968

——, *The Bauhaus Revisited*. New York: Dutton, 1985

Overy, Paul, *De Stijl*. London: Dutton/Studio Vista, 1968

Scheidig, Walter, *Crafts of the Weimar Bauhaus*. New York: Van Nostrand Reinhold, 1967

Whitford, Frank, ed., *The Bauhaus: Masters and Students by Themselves*. London: Conran Octopus, 1992

Wingler, Hans, *The Bauhaus*. Cambridge, MA: MIT Press, 1969

Art Deco; Industrial Design

Buddensieg, Tilmann and Rogge, Henning, *Cultura Industria: Peter Behrens e la AEG, 1907–1914*. Milan: Electa Editrice, 1979

Bush, Donald J., *The Streamlined Decade*. New York: George Braziller, 1975

Hennessey, William, *Russel Wright, American Designer*. Cambridge, MA: MIT Press, 1983

Heskett, John, *Industrial Design*. London: Thames and Hudson, 1980

Hillier, Bevis, *Art Deco*. Minneapolis: Minneapolis Institute of the Arts, 1971

Meikle, Jeffrey L., *Twentieth Century Limited*. Philadelphia: Temple University Press, 1979

Schoenberger, Angela, ed., *Raymond Loewy: Pioneer of American Industrial Design*. Munich: Prestel-Verlag, 1990

Sembach, Klaus-Jurgen, *Style 1930*. New York: Universe Books, 1971

Windsor, Alan, *Peter Behrens, Architect and Designer, 1868–1940*. New York: Whitney Library of Design, 1981

Modernism

Ambasz, Emilio, ed., *Italy: the New Domestic Landscape*. New York: Museum of Modern Art, 1972

Banham, Reyner, *Theory and Design in the First Machine Age*. New York: Praeger, 1960

Bayley, Stephen, ed., *Conran Dictionary of Design*. London: Conran Octopus Ltd., 1985

Blake, Peter, *The Master Builders*. New York: Knopf, 1964

Clark, Robert Judson, *Design in America: The Cranbrook Vision, 1925–1950*. New York: Harry N. Abrams, 1983

Frankl, Paul T., *Form and Re-Form*. New York: Harper & Bros., 1930

Garner, Philippe, *Contemporary Decorative Arts*. New York: Facts on File, 1980

——, *Twentieth Century Furniture*. New York: Van Nostrand Reinhold, 1980

Giedion, Sigfried, *Mechanization Takes Command*. New York: Oxford University Press, 1948

Hiesinger, Kathryn B. and Marcus, George, eds., *Design Since 1945*. Philadelphia: Philadelphia Museum of Art, 1983

——, *Landmarks of Twentieth Century Design: An Illustrated Handbook*. New York: Abbeville Press, 1993

Hine, Thomas, *Populuxe*. New York: Alfred A. Knopf, 1986

Hitchcock, Henry Russell, *Architecture: Nineteenth and Twentieth Centuries*. Harmondsworth, England and Baltimore: Penguin, 1968

—— and Philip Johnson, *The International Style: Architecture since 1922*. New York: W.W. Norton. 1932, 2nd edn. 1966

Larrabee, Eric and Vignelli, Massimo, *Knoll Design*. New York: Harry N. Abrams, 1981

Mang, Karl, *History of Modern Furniture*. New York: Harry N. Abrams, 1979

McFadden, David, *Scandinavian Modern Design*. New York: Harry N. Abrams, 1982

Morgan, Ann Lee and Naylor, Colin, eds., *Contemporary Architects*. Chicago/London: St. James Press, 1987

——, ed., *Contemporary Designers*. Detroit: Gale Research Co., 1984

Myerson, Jeremy, *New Public Architecture*. London: Laurence King, 1996

Phillips, Lisa, *et al.*, *High Styles: Twentieth Century American Design*. New York: Whitney Museum of American Art/Summit Books, 1985

Pile, John, *Open Office Planning*. New York: Whitney Library of Design, 1978

Pulos, Arthur, *The American Design Adventure*. Cambridge, MA: MIT Press, 1988

Sembach, Klaus-Jurgen, *Contemporary Furniture*. New York: Architectural Book Publishing Co., 1982

Smith, C. Ray, *Interior Design in 20th Century America: A History*. New York: Harper & Row, 1987

Walker Art Center, *Nelson, Eames, Girard, Propst: The Design Process at Herman Miller* (Design Quarterly 98–99). Minneapolis: Walker Art Center, 1975

Wilson, Richard Guy, Pilgrim, Dianne H. and Tashjian, Dickman, *The Machine Age in America 1918–1941*. New York: Harry N. Abrams, 1986

Alvar Aalto

Fleig, K., ed., *Alvar Aalto*, 3 vols. Zürich: Verlag für Architectur Artemis, 1963

Gutheim, Frederick, *Alvar Aalto*. New York: Braziller, 1960

Schildt, Goran, *Alvar Aalto: The Early Years*. New York: Rizzoli, 1984

——, *Alvar Aalto: The Decisive Years*. New York: Rizzoli, 1986

Marcel Breuer

Wilk, Christopher, *Marcel Breuer, Furniture and Interiors*. New York/London: Museum of Modern Art/Architectural Press, Ltd., 1981

Le Corbusier

Blake, Peter, *Le Corbusier*. Baltimore: Penguin Books, 1964

De Fusco, Renato, *Le Corbusier, Designer: Furniture 1929*. Woodbury, NY: Barron's, 1977

Le Corbusier: Oeuvres Complètes, 7 vols. Zürich: Girsberger, 1937–67

Le Corbusier, *Creation is a Patient Search*. New York: Praeger, 1965

——, *The Modulor I and II*. Cambridge, MA: Harvard University Press, 1980

——, *1929 Sitzmobel*. Zürich: Galerie Heidi Weber, 1959

——, *Towards a New Architecture*, trans. F. Etchell. London: The Architectural Press, 1927; New York: Praeger, 1970; New York: Dover Publications, 1986

Charles and Ray Eames

Drexler, Arthur, *Charles Eames Furniture from the Design Collection*. New York: Museum of Modern Art, 1973

Library of Congress and Vitra Design Museum, *The Work of Charles and Ray Eames*. New York: Harry N. Abrams, 1997

Neuhart, John, Neuhart, Marilyn and Eames, Ray, *Eames Design*. New York: Harry N. Abrams, 1989

Eileen Gray

Adam, Peter, *Eileen Gray: Architect, Designer*. New York: Harry N. Abrams, 1987

Walter Gropius

Fitch, James Marston, *Walter Gropius*. New York: Braziller, 1960

Giedion, Sigfried, *Walter Gropius*. New York: Reinhold, 1954

Louis I. Kahn

Brownlee, D.B. and DeLong, D.E., *Louis I. Kahn: In the Realm of Architecture*. New York: Rizzoli, 1991

Scully, Vincent, Jr., *Louis I. Kahn*. New York: Braziller, 1962

Mies van der Rohe

Blaser, Werner, *Mies van der Rohe: Furniture and Interiors*. London: Academy Editions, 1982

Drexler, Arthur, *Mies van der Rohe*. New York: Braziller, 1960

Glaeser, Ludwig, *Ludwig Mies van der Rohe: Furniture and Furniture Drawings*. New York: Museum of Modern Art, 1977

Johnson, Philip C., *Mies van der Rohe*. New York: Museum of Modern Art, 1947

Tegethoff, Wolf, *Mies van der Rohe: The Villas and Country Houses*. New York: Museum of Modern Art/Cambridge, MA: MIT Press, 1986

Richard Neutra

McCoy, Esther, *Richard Neutra*. New York: Braziller, 1960

Eero Saarinen

Temko, Allen, *Eero Saarinen*. New York: Braziller, 1962

Skidmore, Owings and Merrill

Danz, Ernst, *Architecture of Skidmore, Owings and Merrill, 1950–1962*. New York: Praeger, 1963

Louis Sullivan

Morrison, Hugh, *Louis Sullivan,*

Prophet of Modern Architecture. New York: W.W. Norton, 1935
Sullivan, Louis H., *The Autobiography of an Idea.* New York: Dover Publications, 1956

Frank Lloyd Wright
Gill, Brendan, *Many Masks: A Life of Frank Lloyd Wright.* New York: Putnam's Sons, 1987
Hitchcock, Henry Russell, *In the Nature of Materials.* New

York: Sloan and Pearce, 1942
Kaufmann, Edgar, Jr. and Raeburn, Ben, *Frank Lloyd Wright, Writings and Buildings.* New York: Meridian, 1960
Wright, Frank Lloyd, *An Autobiography.* London/New York: Longmans Green and Co., 1932

Post-modernism and Deconstructivism
Jencks, Charles and Chaitkin, William, *Architecture Today.*

New York: Harry N. Abrams, 1982
Jencks, Charles, *Modern Movements in Architecture.* Garden City, NY: Anchor Press, 1973
——, *The Language of Post-Modern Architecture.* New York: Rizzoli, 1978, rev. edn., 1981.
Johnson, Philip and Wigley, Mark, *Deconstructivist Architecture.* New York: Museum of Modern Art, 1988

Klotz, Heinrich, *The History of Postmodern Architecture.* Cambridge, MA: MIT Press, 1988
Kron, Joan and Slesin, Suzanne, *High Tech.* New York: Clarkson N. Potter, 1978
Papadakis, Andreas C., ed., *Post-Modernism on Trial.* London: Academy Editions, 1990
Riewoldt, Otto, *Intelligent Spaces: Architecture for the Information Age.* London: Laurence King, 1997

Picture Credits

Index